Introductory Sociology

Introductory Sociology

Third Edition

Tony Bilton, Kevin Bonnett, Pip Jones, David Skinner, Michelle Stanworth and Andrew Webster

MACMILLAN

First edition 1981
Reprinted 1982 (twice, with corrections), 1983 (twice), 1984, 1985, 1986, 1987
Second edition 1987
Reprinted 1988 (twice), 1989, 1990, 1991, 1992, 1993, 1994, 1995
Third edition 1996
Reprinted 1997

Published by
MACMILLAN PRESS LTD
Houndmills, Basingstoke, Hampshire RG21 6XS and London
Companies and representatives throughout the world

ISBN 0–333–66510–4 hardcover
ISBN 0–333–66511–2 paperback

A catalogue record for this book is available from the British Library.

10 9 8 7 6 5 4 3 2
05 04 03 02 01 00 99 98 97

Typeset by Footnote Graphics, Warminster, Wilts

Printed in Hong Kong

Contents

PART 3

Preface to the Third Edition

Many authors describe new editions of their books as 'revised and updated'. Though sometimes such revisions are quite substantial and the book *is* relatively new, equally often they represent only small improvements. This third edition of *Introductory Sociology*, however, is not just revised. While a few echoes of our past attempts remain, it is for the most part, entirely new. Sociology has changed a great deal over the past decade or so, and in our professional lives as lecturers and researchers we have tried to keep up to date. Because of our knowledge of the extent of these changes we felt that tinkering, however substantially, with the existing edition of the book would be more difficult than starting again. So we have revised our focus, in order to concentrate on the debates which, over recent years, have redefined the discipline. This has required not only starting the book afresh but also restructuring the way we introduce the reader to the principal areas of inquiry.

Three elements of contemporary sociology, in our view, should underpin an up-to-date introduction to the subject. These are:

- debates about the nature of **modernity** and its future;
- debates about the impact of the **globalisation** of social relations and institutions on modern human lives:
- debates about the relationship between these features and personal **identity**.

Indeed, these issues preoccupy not only sociologists: they are concerns common to a number of other academic disciplines, such as philosophy, history and politics, as the twenty-first century approaches.

Because the outcomes of such debates are by their very nature uncertain, we know we have set ourselves a daunting task. Some of what we have to say is both difficult to express and, inevitably, to understand, but we believe it is a project worth undertaking. These sorts of issues consume the efforts of most of the leading figures in contemporary sociology, yet because they tend to write principally for those also at the cutting edge of the discipline much of what they have to say is difficult for the uninitiated to engage with. Quite understandably, this has resulted in many introductory texts shying away from confronting such problematic areas. Nevertheless, we think it is time to address these issues in a readable and accessible way, and this is what we have tried to achieve. In short, we think this book is about sociology *today*, and we hope it is a book you will find both understandable and stimulating.

Structure of the Text

The book consists of four separate sections. Part 1 introduces the reader to the essential principles of the sociological approach. From everyday experience to wider social structures and processes, sociology provides new insights into the dynamics of social life. These dynamics are today shaped by modernity and globalisation, both of which influence our lives and sense of personal identity. Chapters on each of these establish them as key issues in contemporary society which we return to throughout the text in the more substantive chapters of Parts 2 and 3. The remaining chapters in this section introduce the concepts, theories and methods used in sociology, thus providing the reader with a vocabulary with which to use the rest of the book.

Part 2 examines the structures of inequality associated with class, race, gender and politics, and while each of these is dealt with as a discrete topic in a separate chapter links between them are made throughout this section of the book.

Part 3 explores other dimensions of social existence – such as education, work, crime, knowledge and belief, family and health, illness and medicine – that are of central importance in contemporary society.

Part 4 provides a full explanation and discussion of sociological theory and attempts to show the direction it is taking today.

Glossary

For the first time we have included a glossary of terms and concepts. The glossed items are highlighted in **bold** type in the text and defined, where space allows, in the margin; the complete list of definitions can be found at the end of the book.

Acknowledgements

We would like to thank a number of people who have helped us during the writing of this book. Our long-suffering publisher at Macmillan, Frances Arnold, has been supportive and encouraging throughout, deftly employing both stick and carrot to ensure that noses and grindstones were kept in reasonable proximity. Others whose efforts were indispensable in enabling the book to be produced on the right side of the millennium were Oonagh Jones, who dealt with the daunting task of compiling the glossary with exceptional diligence, ability and good humour; Susan Clarke, who was exemplary in producing a large part of the typescript more quickly than we had any right to expect; and Keith Povey, whose calm professionalism meant that the post-writing production process was managed with the minimum of fuss. The help of a number of fellow sociologists in reading early drafts of the manuscript was also much appreciated, and the comments of Bob Burgess, Steve Fenton, Tony Giddens, Peter Langley, Tony Lawson, Chris Middleton, Rob Moore, John Scott, Frank Vanclay and Alan Warde were particularly helpful. Our thanks, too, must go to our colleagues in the Division of Sociology and Politics at Anglia for their forbearance in coping with the moods and vicissitudes associated with protracted authorship: Sally Bienias and Gina Marshall suffered the brunt of these, with Tom Ling, Janet McKenzie and Jennifer Rubin not far behind. Finally, to our students, who put up with our ideas being tried out on them (usually without complaint), our gratitude.

Anglia Polytechnic University
Cambridge

Tony Bilton, Kevin Bonnett
Pip Jones, David Skinner
Michelle Stanworth, Andrew Webster

Further Information

The publisher, Macmillan, offers readers support services for queries, reviews, inspection copies and information requests via the Internet at the World Wide Web Site: http://www.macmillan-press.co.uk. Further details about the text and the authors can be obtained via the authors' home page on the Internet at http://www.anglia.ac.uk/hae/soc-pol/.

Acknowledgements

The authors and publishers wish to thank the following for permission to use copyright material:

BSA Publications Ltd, for extracts from J. Finch and L. Hayes, 'Inheritance, Death and the Concept of Home', *Sociology*, 28, 2, (1994); and D. Layder *et al.*, 'The Empirical Correlates of Action and Structure: The Transition from School to Work', *Sociology*, 25, 3 (1991).

Cambridge University Press, for an extract from Ernest Gellner, *Legitimation of Belief* (1974) pp. 191–207.

The Guardian, for extracts from 'Rats of the Rubbish Society Fight Back', *The Guardian* (9 September 1995); Will Hutton, 'The Polarisation of Work', *The Guardian* (28 October 1994); Amitai Etzioni, 'The Parental Deficit', *The Guardian*. Copyright © *The Guardian*.

HarperCollins Publishers, for extracts from Pip Jones, *Studying Society: Sociological Theories and Research Practices* (1993).

The Controller of Her Majesty's Stationery Office, for Crown Copyright material.

Newspaper Publishing PLC, for extracts from Polly Toynbee, 'Happy Families: a game of charades?', *The Independent* (22 February 1995); and 'Hard times in Moscow', *Independent on Sunday* (29 November 1993).

The Observer, for an extract from Melanie Phillips, 'The Social Conservative Critique of Individual Liberationism', *The Observer* (26 February 1995) Copyright © *The Observer*.

Routledge for extracts from M. Hamilton, *The Sociology of Religion: Theoretical and Comparative Perspectives* (1995), pp. 24–6; A. D. King, *Global Cities* (1991), pp. 142–5; and T. A. Dijk, *Racism and the Press* (1993), p. 54.

Every effort has been made to trace all the copyright holders but if any have been inadvertently overlooked the publishers will be pleased to make the necessary arrangement at the first opportunity.

PART 1

Introduction: Studying Modern Society

1

Introduction

Aims of the Chapter

This chapter provides a basic introduction to the way in which sociology explores and makes sense of our behaviour and our society. It challenges those accounts of social behaviour that explain it in terms of simply biological, psychological or merely individual predispositions. We try to show how our sense of who we are is constructed through interaction with others yet also constrained by society. We also introduce some key themes which figure in sociological analysis today: modernity and globalisation, identity and postmodernity. These are explored more fully in subsequent chapters.

Introduction

In the summer of 1995, the Indonesian government introduced legislation to cut traffic pollution: cars carrying fewer than three passengers would be banned. In Jakarta now, street children are hired out at the edge of the town by drivers to make up the numbers. So the police have to check cars to see whether the people inside are really 'related'.

Similar stories could, no doubt, be recounted elsewhere, and the events this particular one describes are not really dramatic or surprising. Yet it is sociologically very interesting. Not only does it show 'human ingenuity' in the way drivers get around government legislation, but a little reflection also reveals some fairly complex social processes going on here. First, it shows how street children use a whole range of livelihood strategies to cope with their precarious situation, though would we want to say whether this particular strategy could be defined as 'work'? It also shows how social action – here government legislation – can have unforeseen or unintended effects; and it would be intriguing to hear drivers telling police about the street kids in the back and to know whether the kids are tutored in a potted family history in order to sound more convincing: what would such a history include?

This simple story of hiring street kids illustrates – even by just scratching the surface – how social action and the circumstances in which it is expressed are multilayered in meaning and significance. This is one basic way in which we can understand the whole of the discipline of sociology. Sociology lifts the lid on the ordinary and extraordinary, digs around in the hidden meanings and contexts of our lives, and shows that what we take for granted rests on complex and dynamic social processes. These processes can also be shown to have a long history, just as the events in Indonesia today can only be explained in terms of a legacy of social, economic and political factors that have shaped that particular society over many years.

So sociology tries to give us an insight into much that we take for granted, and in doing understands people as social beings. Its approach is, therefore, quite distinct from many other disciplines. We can show this by looking more closely at the development of human society.

Human History, Human Societies and Human Beings

Human history and the development of human beings has been, in part at least, a tale of the progressive harnessing and exploitation of natural and personal resources and the organisation and co-ordination of their behaviour. Some one million years ago, the variety of early ancestors of modern human beings began to develop tools, to use fire, and to co-ordinate their behaviour and organise themselves into social groupings. Around one hundred and twenty thousand years ago, our direct descendant, homo sapiens, expanded out of Africa and, triumphing over homo erectus and homo neanderthalis, settled in virtually every part of the planet. Today, members of that same species live their lives within highly complex national and international social, political and economic arrangements, able to transport themselves and material objects and to communicate with each other both physically and symbolically over vast geographical distances in short spaces of time, and to reach out beyond the confines of the planet to the rest of the universe. At the same time, they have significantly changed – and continue to do so relentlessly – the physical face of the planet; they are in the process of consuming its natural resources and of eliminating its other animal inhabitants at an alarming rate; they have created the capacity to destroy the planet and all its life-forms many times over; and while a small minority of them live and consume resources in unparalleled luxurious comfort, a majority barely subsist from day to day.

The grand sweep of human history, then, is a remarkable – and sobering – story, and, though not the central focus of this book or of the discipline of sociology, is nevertheless a significant backdrop for both of them. This is because a – if not the – distinctive feature of human life, the lives of human individuals, has been their inclination to organise themselves into *social groupings* – that is, into collectivities engaging in bounded patterns of interaction, whether in the form of hunter-gatherer bands, clans, tribes, nation-states, empires or whatever.

That basic fact has been the essential starting point and the stimulus for sociology, a discipline primarily concerned with the systematic study of the development, organisation and operation of human societies of whatever type – in short, with *what social life is all about and how it can be explained.* But that simple definition makes no direct or explicit reference to the central participants in social life – human individuals, those agents in the discovery of fire, in the exodus from Africa, in the building of the pyramids of Egypt and the Great Wall of China, in the development of the internal combustion engine, in the generation of nuclear energy, in the creation of the information superhighway.

Human beings are simultaneously both ordinary and extraordinary creatures when compared individually with each other and in comparison with other animal species. Each of us comprises about 60 per cent water, we each have a brain weighing about 1.5 kilos, and we each produce about 1.5 litres of urine daily. Observation of customers at any large supermarket reveals only modest variations in height, though more distinctive differences in shape and bulk! More strikingly, however, no two of our supermarket visitors are exactly alike facially, no two have identical DNA structures, no two have the same fingerprints. In short, each of us is unique.

In the animal kingdom, we are the only four-limbed creatures who walk permanently upright on two limbs. But our short-term running speed and long-term endurance, our senses of smell, hearing and vision are grossly inferior to those of many other animals on the planet. Yet we are the species which dominates the earth, which has constructed magnificent churches and temples, elaborate technologies and media of communication, complex systems of economic production and distribution, intricate systems of belief and philosophies, and so on. In short, we are a creative species.

Thus, a discipline aiming to understand social life, to explain patterns of social organisation, or whatever, also has to concern itself centrally with the encounter between the unique, creative individual – with the *subject*, the active being – and society. It has to examine and evaluate the significance of *biographical, objective influences* on human lives and our *subjective* capacities for *autobiography*, and the connections between them. As we shall see later in this first part of the book, various approaches within sociology have addressed this issue differently: they have recognised commonly that human lives are stories but have disagreed about *how* those stories are written and by *whom.*

Society and the Subject: The Biographical Constitution of Identity

Non-social influences on human life

We have already implied that human beings and social life are, of course, not untouched or unconstrained by influences of nature, by their biological make-up and the physical environments surrounding them. Hunger, thirst, physical fatigue, the gradual but inexorable degeneration of the human body, and so on, all constrain the nature of human life and social experiences, shaping what we can do and can be. For instance, however much they may wish it otherwise, vigorous physical exercise is simply beyond the capacities of virtually all 70-year-olds. Similarly, in the realm of sexual reproduction, the stimulus to sexual activity between male and female is not dependent, unlike in many species, on the trigger of the female coming 'on heat', and despite the fact that the average male ejaculates many millions of sperms in every millilitre of semen, the possibility of conception is still restricted to only a few days in each month.

Social patterns and individual experiences are inhibited by ecological conditions, too: we may be able to deploy increasingly sophisticated bodies of knowledge and technologies and to harness resources imaginatively in order to win some control over them, but we are still subject to and constrained by them. Thus, the harsh extremes of climate in polar and desert regions have precluded such areas as the typical sites of human existence, and, as media images of physical destruction and widespread deaths all too frequently remind us, humans and their communities, no matter how 'developed' or 'advanced', are largely powerless in the face of the elemental forces of earthquakes, hurricanes, and the like.

We can also acknowledge that individuals have particular *psychological* characteristics or traits which influence their behaviour and capacities, in the form of specific skills and aptitudes and/or psychological dispositions and temperaments. For instance, we are not all and cannot all be as equally adept on the tennis court as Monica Seles or Pete Sampras, and nor are we all as emotionally controlled as Steffi Graf or as temperamentally explosive as John McEnroe when questionable umpiring decisions go against us.

However, while biological, physical, environmental and psychological influences on human life are clearly important (and, to lay persons, often highly persuasive forms of 'explanation' of human beings and their behaviour), for sociologists they are not and cannot be the sole or even the most significant basis for understanding human lives.

Social influences on human life

Other distinct and complex elements are intimately involved in shaping human experience and behaviour too. In the same way that we do not exist in an unbounded physical world, so we do not live in shapeless social environments or an undefined social world that we can ignore, adjust or amend simply according to our wishes and desires. Societies, sociologists have traditionally argued, do have distinctive social, economic and political patterns and processes, There are multiple social frameworks and social locations – structured social environments characterised by regularities – in which individuals develop from childhood into adulthood and through into old age.

Now it is easy to underestimate and be naive about the ways in which our behaviour and elements of our selves are embedded in these wider social environments and processes. This is partly because in everyday life we do not usually define ourselves, our experiences, and events in these terms but in more 'personal', individual ways. Many of us live in societies which embrace a deeply held commitment to philosophies and ideals of **individualism**, with a strong emphasis on human beings as unique individuals each with their own special qualities and idiosyncrasies and responsible for their own actions, and with success, happiness, and fulfilment defined in terms of individual achievement. For sociologists, moreover, the predominance of such individualistic perspectives in everyday thinking is not difficult to understand, since those perspectives have not simply come from nowhere. Rather, the birth and development of modern *capitalist* societies in Europe was accompanied by a philosophy of individualism and by beliefs that human beings were free to choose their rulers, their employers and their religions.

individualism
Doctrines or ways of thinking that focus on the autonomous individual, rather than on the attributes of the group.

Stressing the powerful impact of social influences on individuals does not commit us to a simple **deterministic** position: we do not need to see these social influences as something independent of human minds and wills or as necessarily determining individuals and their identities in any simple mechanical or automatic fashion. It does, however, alert us to the fact that they do form distinct frameworks and **structures** which shape individuals' identities and socially regulate their behaviour and which are not clearly manipulable at will. That is, many of the things we experience as individuals are beyond our control but are products of society as a whole, its historical development and its current patterns of organisation.

determinism
A simple causal, reductionist explanation (*see* biological determinism).

structures
Refers generally to constructed frameworks and patterns of organisation which, in some way, constrain or direct human behaviour.

One banal but nevertheless basic fact is important here: that our own society and its social institutions, arrangements and conventions predate us. It was there before we were born, so that our arrival in it sets us off on associations with both the living and the dead, in a **socially constructed** world made in part by previous and present generations. Thus, our selves and identities develop within more or less clearly defined and experienced social contexts, significantly shaped by the complex interplay of influence of intimate and anonymous predecessors and contemporaries, from our loved ones, family and kin through to the bureaucratic **State** and the giant transnational corporation.

social construction
The process whereby 'natural', instinctive, forms of behaviour become mediated by social processes. Sociologists would argue that most forms of human behaviour are socially constructed.

Gender roles and ethnic group membership

We can illustrate the argument here by considering the impact of **gender** roles and the importance of *ethnic group* membership. While neither being masculine or feminine, nor being white or Afro-Caribbean, Native American, or indigenous Australian imposes any simple social strait-jacket, such group memberships carry with them specific and distinct formative influences.

nation-state
A form of political authority unique to modernity comprising various institutions such as the legislature, judiciary, police, armed forces, and central and local administration. It claims a monopoly of power and legitimacy within a bounded territory.

gender
See p. 660.

As sociologists have emphasised for many years, while men and women differ biologically from each other in a number of respects, many of the differences in behaviour patterns between them, both within and across different societies, are *social constructions* – that is, they are the outcomes of social definitions and expectations which have been built up around them and modified over decades and centuries. Thus, even allowing for changes in patterns of paid employment, the impact of feminist movements and the rise of the phenomenon of '*new men*', in most Western societies, the predominant responsibility for child-rearing and domestic tasks is still expected to lie with women, and there is still greater social licence extended to both adolescent and adult males in expressing their sexuality than there is to their female peers.

Clearly, men and women can (and do) resist such prescriptions about their behaviour and definitions of their identity. But those prescriptions and definitions are frequently buttressed and **ideologically** reinforced by powerful and strategically located **institutional** sources, such as the mass media, politicians, religious bodies, moralists, professional experts and social commentators, as well as by everyday experiences in the home, in the workplace, or in the street, so that they are not easily ignored or set aside.

ideology
A perception of reality or way of thinking. Its usage is associated with Marx, where the term implies a mistaken sense of reality or false consciousness.

institutions
Social practices that are regularly and continuously repeated, legitimised and maintained by social norms.

Similarly, membership of an ethnic group – whether that be black Afro-Caribbean in Britain, Native American in the United States, indigenous

Australian, or whatever – may locate individuals in a social group with a sense of collective identification based around often very distinctive historical and contemporary experiences and cultural traditions, customs and practices. Thus, there may be more or less rigidly prescribed social obligations surrounding dress, diet, choice of marriage partner, observance of religious rituals and practices, and so on which individuals are expected to meet.

subculture
The set of values, behaviour, and attitudes of a particular group of people who are distinct from, but related to, the dominant culture in society.

ethnicity
See page 238.

Again, there is no suggestion here that those individuals blindly or unquestioningly conform to those obligations (as, for example, many first-generation immigrant groups in Britain and elsewhere have found with their children). Nor, indeed, does it suggest that **subcultural** patterns in **ethnic groups** remain stable and unchanged. But they do impact upon individuals, often serving as vital sources of social support and collective belonging for members of ethnic groups, particularly where they are marginalised minorities experiencing disadvantage, discrimination and outright hostility.

Normative sources of constraint

Living in a social world, then, is an action-constraining experience: we do encounter the social world around us as limiting and constraining, even if we all do not do so equally. Those constraints may range from the naked physical coercion of, say, forced or slave labour to the much more subtle mechanisms of generating compliance which operate in societies and in social groups within them. The point is that, irrespective of the level of sophistication or development involved, social living places both 'external' constraints on individuals, and 'internal' constraints too, as they take on board an awareness of the social world around them.

norms
Socially accepted 'correct' or 'proper' forms of behaviour. Norms either prescribe given types of behaviour or forbid them.

values
Associated with Parsons, whose concept of shared values refers to a consensus of morals, principles and standards of behaviour.

This is because the behaviour in which human beings are engaged is underpinned by beliefs, values, ideas, purposes and goals. Societies are characterised, as we have suggested, by complex, more or less definite (though, of course, not unchanging) networks of relationships, institutions, organisations, groups and practices, but there are also important shared cultural **norms** and **values** and symbols interwoven into those social arrangements and into the consciousness of individual members. Thus, people work out their lives individually and collectively by drawing on shared ideas about what is desirable and undesirable, appropriate and inappropriate, good and bad, right and wrong.

Indeed, we cannot and should not ignore the strength and shaping capacity of societal norms and values for individuals' behaviour and their own sense of self. A whole series of everyday ordinary social practices in which we engage and which we may regard as making up our *identities* are outcomes of our interactions and relationships with others and are rooted in socially generated norms and values.

The most obvious illustration of this is laws – systematically codified legal rules with formal social sanctions attached to them in the form of graded punishments and retributions, and with designated agencies responsible for their construction, interpretation and enforcement. There is, then, a 'reality' to laws and the legal system – lawbreaking and the subsequent apprehension of lawbreakers by the authorities can produce very definite consequences. But, as any casual reading of newspapers confirms, laws clearly do not have anything like a completely binding capacity. In 1994, for instance, there were over 5 million recorded notifiable offences in England and Wales, to say nothing of the many more which did not come to the attention of the police (estimated by research, such as the British Crime Surveys, to be at least three times the known figure). Yet one might also argue, especially given the low detection rates for many crimes, that what is remarkable is not how many times laws are broken but how few times that is so.

Of course, most social rules which we follow in our lives are not legally enforced, they do not have laws backing them up, but they do operate with persuasive power nevertheless. Customs, conventions, fashions and so on exercise constraint on individuals, even though their violation is subject to no formal sanctions and may evoke no great informal ones either. For example, there is no law preventing men wearing dresses, yet few, if any, choose to do so; there is no law requiring us to use cutlery in a restaurant, yet few, if any, of us risk incurring the hardly fatal or even mildly scarring sanctions from our fellow diners of disapproving glances, whispers, or mocking laughter.

Habituation, pragmatic acceptance and practical constraints

Norms and values, too, then, are in a sense 'real' even though they are not straightforwardly visible. They may not be a part of the material world, but their existence influences individuals and their actions just as the physical world does – there is constraint from a world of *ideas*. As we have suggested, these ideas, norms and values are essentially *inter-subjective* elements in social relations – that is, they are dependent upon and sustained (or changed) through shared experiences among social actors. But if and when they are profoundly absorbed and internalised and become powerfully ingrained in actors' consciousnesses, they may take on an *objective* reality for us as individuals and for our societies – so much so that they become part of our lives, our identities and our mental wallpaper, so that we may not even recognise them as constraints. That is, normatively shaped behaviour often becomes habitual and routine.

Indeed, habitual action figures prominently in our day-to-day social activities. Much social life involving face-to-face interaction with others does depend to a great extent on routine, on shared but unstated cultural assumptions about what is done or said and why. We take for granted, in ourselves and in others, certain competences, abilities and shared responses, so that our behaviour and theirs becomes reasonably understandable and predictable. Such habitual and routinised behaviour gives shape and form, and hence stability and meaningfulness, to our existence, providing what Giddens (1984) calls a sense of **'ontological security'**.

ontological security
A stable mental state derived from a sense of continuity and order in events.

normative
An approach which sees social behaviour as the result of conformity to norms (*see* norms).

However, compliance with social rules, values and expectations may not always be habitual, or based on **normative** acceptance, but upon *pragmatic* acceptance – that is, they may not be fully internalised but may evoke a more qualified, unenthusiastic and by no means uncritical conformity in individuals. They conform without being convinced of any absolute or unconditional moral rightness of certain norms and values and social arrangements based on them, merely accepting things as they are as everyday 'facts of life' which cannot 'realistically' involve alternatives.

The most obvious circumstances in which this occurs are those where social actors are materially and/or socially powerless – that is, where very definite practical constraints limit their room for manoeuvre. Many people wake on Monday mornings, rise and head off to their employment not because they are convinced of the moral rightness and intrinsic spiritual benefit of the system of wage labour, but because they (more or less grudgingly) accept that, for them, there is no realistic alternative – there is food to be provided, children to clothe, bills to be paid, so that being 'gentlemen or gentlewomen of leisure' is not an 'identity option' available to them.

Choices made by social actors, then, are limited by the resources practically available to them, and those enjoying material privilege and political power are substantially relieved of many such practical constraints on action. The well-known exhortation to 'choose your parents carefully' is clearly pertinent to the biographical constitution of individuals and their identities, since the business of becoming who they are and their material quality of life – their *life chances* in health, education, employment etc. – is intimately related to their parents' occupations, income and wealth.

The Subject and Society: The Autobiographical Construction of Identity

Recalling our earlier notion of human lives as stories, our account so far has highlighted the ways in which those stories are significantly scripted by objective biographical influences. But to terminate our account at that point would be to leave the analysis fundamentally flawed and incomplete. That is because human behaviour may indeed be moulded within distinct social arrangements and social relationships, and individuals may come to be what they are and to develop a sense of self and identity in part as a result of social influences operating on them – in short, as a result of being persons in social contexts.

But that is only a part of the story, and our earlier discussion of the significance of normative sources provides a useful link to advance the account further.

Conscious actors, creativity and agency

Human behaviour is distinctive in being informed by what Max Weber called 'an orientation to values' – that is, it is guided by ideas, beliefs, principles, and so on, and not simply by automatic programmed responses. But this is, of course, dependent upon human beings' special ability for reasoning, reflecting upon themselves, their behaviour, their experiences, and their environments – in short, their capacity for *conscious and self-conscious thinking* and *creativity*. Social life, then, is characterised by humans, both collectively and individually, investing events, actions and experiences with conscious *meaning*, *purpose* and *interpretation*, at whatever level of significance, whether that be in their food production, their childrearing practices, their leisure activities, their disposal of the dead, or whatever.

agency
Purposeful action. This term implies that actors have the freedom to create, change and influence events.

To use the sociological jargon, human beings are characterised by **agency**, the potential capacity for influencing events and for behaving independently of the defining constraints of society. They are what Giddens (1984) has called (more or less) 'knowledgeable agents' who construct perceptions of the social world in which they are located, know a great deal about the circumstances and consequences of what they do in their day-to-day lives, and can articulate what they do and their reasons for doing it. Being aware of their circumstances and influences upon them, they can meaningfully entertain the possibility of exercising choice.

Box 1.1: Human 'Knowledgeability'

'To be a human being is to be a purposive agent who both has reasons for his or her activities and is able, if asked, to elaborate discursively upon those reasons … Awareness of social rules, expressed first and foremost in practical consciousness, is the very core of that "knowledgeability" which specifically characterises human agents. As social actors, all human beings are highly "learned" in respect of knowledge which they possess, and apply, in the production and reproduction of day-to-day social encounters.'

Source: Giddens, (1984) *Constitution of Society*, pp. 3, 21–2.

Social subjects, then, are active beings with an active role in negotiating their way through social arrangements and social relationships in which they find themselves, and they are creatively involved in negotiating their own social roles, self-images and identities. As we shall see later, the American sociologist Erving Goffman (1969) suggests that human beings are very adept at 'the presentation of the self' – that is, at adjusting the image of themselves which they wish to portray, depending upon the company and the circumstances and contexts in which they find themselves.

Identity, the self and interaction

Everyday behaviour, then, is not simply a matter of following clear-cut social scripts but, both potentially and actually, of creating, improvising, adjusting and negotiating. Social actors work out their lives with what have variously been called 'shared meanings', 'shared understandings', 'mental knowledge', and so on, and in doing so, they make sense of what they and others are doing in their social lives. They produce, reproduce and amend these meanings, understandings and knowledge by applying them and/or subtly refining and reformulating them in practical circumstances and contexts: norms and values, rather than being absolutely substantial things from which social order is unambiguously constructed, are better regarded as negotiable ideas.

But reference to '*shared* meanings' and to 'negotiation' should clearly signal that these conscious, creative, knowledgeable human agents are not doing any of this in splendid isolation but in *processes of interaction* with others. Thus, in particular, identity formation and individuals' perceptions of themselves are not and cannot be totally unbounded – the views, opinions and reactions of others are clearly significant in contributing to and influencing the conceptions we have of ourselves. But as conscious agents, we endeavour to deal with varied and frequently conflicting responses from others so as to develop a coherent sense of self or identity. Thus, those responses are not simply absorbed or imposed – they are filtered, evaluated, accommodated, cunningly manipulated, or even ignored. For instance, we do not simply or invariably take on board the views or evaluations of *any* other social actors with whom we interact: we are, often consciously, selective in according importance and legitimacy to some while granting little or none to others. Hence, for generations of teenagers, it did not matter if their teachers or moralists did not appreciate the Rolling Stones in the 1960s, the Clash in the 1970s, Madonna in the 1980s, or Take That in the 1990s, if their age peers – their '**significant others**' – shared their adulation of them.

significant others
Those particular individuals whose views, opinions and reactions contribute to and influence, the conception we have of ourselves.

Marrying Constraint and Creativity: The Duality of Structure and Agency

So far we have attempted to explore, on the one hand, biographical objective influences on human lives and identities and, on the other, our subjective capacities for autobiography. We have suggested that it is difficult to deny that individuals are in no small measure products of their biographies, that they are who they are in part because of social influences, and that what they can do and actually do is limited to some extent by their location in society and their social and material resources. But we have also suggested that we do not have to see social actors and their identities as pre-programmed, as passively swept along by and reducible to social forces, but as conscious agents who (attempt to) act autonomously, to take action they regard as most appropriate to their interests, and who are (potentially) able to create and re-create the social world. But it does not follow that we should therefore perceive these conscious agents as exercising some simple 'free will' and society as 'the plastic creation of human subjects' (Giddens, 1984: *Constitution of Society*, p. 26).

This is because it is much too simple to separate or *dichotomise* 'societies' or 'systems of social institutions' on the one hand and 'individuals' on the other. 'Structure' and 'agency', 'constraint' and 'creativity', are not contrasting and independent polar opposites: rather, there is a complex process of *interplay* between the constraints of structures and agents' autonomy – a 'double involvement' or interdependence in which *human beings create society and are at the same time created by it*. This is sometimes referred to by sociologists as a *dialectical* relationship, where two apparently contrasting elements work upon each other to produce a synthesis.

Box 1.2: Social structure and human creativity

Changes have occurred in the past century or so in the experiences of women in a number of realms of social life, such as education and employment. Certain changes in the economy and in the occupational structure have been influential in bringing about and shaping these different experiences. These include the growth of white-collar clerical, administrative and social service and welfare occupations, such as secretarial jobs, nursing and school teaching, and the decline of 'heavy industry' manual work and its replacement by 'lighter' mechanised and automated systems of production.

But those experiences *and* the structural changes themselves have also been affected in turn and at the same time by the conscious actions, ideas and attitudes of women themselves, most notably, though not exclusively, in their efforts to gain more equal recognition and consideration. Women, then, have been affected by structural changes *and* have themselves been instrumental in shaping the course and detail of those structural changes through their individual, interpersonal and collective actions and ideas.

In this view, social structure and human creativity interact with each other and change each other in simultaneous and mutually influencing processes: human beings, their behaviour and their identities are located in a two-way process of being shaped by structures of society and contexts of social constraints and of creatively impacting upon them and maybe helping to alter them through their behaviour. Thus, for example, history both forms human beings and is made by them through their practices and their active involvement in their societies. As the American sociologist C.Wright Mills observed in *The Sociological Imagination*:

Every individual lives, from one generation to the next, in some society ... he (sic) lives out a biography, and ... he lives it out within some historical sequence. By the fact of his living he contributes, however minutely, to the shaping of his society and to the course of its history, even as he is made by society and by its historical push and shove.

[Mills, 1970, p. 12]

Social life as enabling and constraining

One major implication of this argument is that it is possible to conceive of social structures and the patterns and features of our social lives as both (simultaneously) *enabling* and *constraining*. That is, the impact of society and systems of interaction on individuals is not simply and inevitably one of limitation and constraint, but they may also provide opportunities for the growth of individuals and their selves and their identities. For example, many (valued) personal experiences and emotions depend on and are made meaningful through *collective* activity: religious celebration and the enjoyment of watching sport, for instance, are enhanced and made more meaningful individual experiences by being conducted in collective association with others.

We can illustrate the point here with another example. Although not all schools of sociological thought would agree (as we shall see later), it is possible to argue that *language* is both enabling and constraining. It is enabling in that its acquisition can enrich our lives and our understanding of the world: it greatly expands our cognitive and practical capacities, and as a symbolic system shared by a community it provides us with the means of communicating with others and of articulating our own perceptions, experiences, emotions, etc. It is also the central vehicle for the transmission of a historically constructed package of cultural values, meanings and practices.

Language, then, gives us capabilities, but it also can be said to shape and confine us. At the most simple level, we do not get to choose our native language, and learning that particular language may constrain thought and action because it may fashion and set certain limits to cognition and perception. Thus, it is argued that the vocabulary, grammar, structures and categories embodied in a language affect how its speakers 'see' reality: if, for example, one's language embraces various words for 'snow', then one's perception of weather and one's physical environment will be subtly, if not qualitatively, different from those who know only 'snow' or 'sleet'.

The enabling and constraining capacities of language can be further demonstrated in the case of children. While, on the one hand, children's language acquisition and the sharing of a common communication system with adults means that the latter can (attempt to) control and regulate them via linguistic messages, children themselves can also use language for their own purposes to 'resist' or to negotiate and bargain with adults. Generations of parents have often come to see their children's growing language facility as a mixed blessing, as the gleam in their offspring's eyes grows ever brighter with the realisation that merely being able to ask the questions 'Why should I?' or 'Why can't I?' is a vital weapon in the family battle for a negotiated order.

The Challenge for Sociology: Modernity and Globalisation, Postmodernity and Identity

This chapter so far has been concerned primarily with social processes, individuals and their identities, and, as we have shown, none of these is simple and unchanging. Indeed, we can suggest that understanding the social world and the individuals in it has become an increasingly complex and problematic business which poses new challenges to sociology.

modernity
A term designed to encapsulate the distinctiveness, complexity and dynamism of social processes unleashed during the eighteenth and nineteenth centuries, which mark a distinct break from traditional ways of living.

project of modernity
A belief in the possibilities opened up by modernity involving a commitment to social progress through a rational and reasoned engagement with the world (*see* modernity).

the Great Transformation
The name given by Karl Polanyi to the historical moment, characterised by massive social, political, technological, economic, and intellectual change, which marks the onset of modernity (*see* modernity).

As following chapters demonstrate, sociology emerged and flourished in the late nineteenth and early twentieth centuries – the era of '**modernity**' – and, as a '**modernist project**', it was committed to the idea that it is possible to produce reliable, verifiable knowledge about society which human beings could use to shape their futures for the better. In everyday language 'modern' often means 'up to date' or 'contemporary'. Sociologists use it in a different sense – modern societies have a long history! Modern societies emerged out of a period sometimes referred to as **The Great Transformation** (Polanyi, 1973); this phrase suggests the magnitude of the changes that took place during this time. The Great Transformation involved complex social, economic, political and cultural processes which together contributed to the development of strikingly new forms of social life. The all-encompassing nature of the changes make these processes hard to date exactly or explain fully. What we can say is that, although they were to gain a worldwide influence, initially, they centred on Western Europe. Also, while their origins can be traced back hundreds of years, it is really in the nineteenth century that recognisably modern societies appeared. The formation of modernity involved a number of interrelated processes, contemporary aspects of which are examined in more detail in many of the succeeding chapters in this book. Here we can identify some of the main features.

- First, a rapid, continuing growth in productive capacities was made possible by *new kinds of economic activity and new ways of working*. Crucial factors in the emergence of modern societies were, firstly, the development and application of more efficient forms of food production, and, later, the replacement of agriculture as the dominant form of productive activity by industrial manufacture. Manufacturing had occurred for many hundreds of years: what was new was the scale of the undertaking and how it took place. The

Industrial Revolution was primarily about new ways of organising and controlling production: the factory system, for example, established greater control over workers and allowed the segmentation of tasks into sophisticated divisions of labour.

- Secondly, a precursor of industrialisation was the development of *a new, dynamic form of economic activity – capitalism* – which was initially applied to agriculture and trade but, by the nineteenth century, became the driving force behind the growth of industrial manufacturing. Capitalism involved new attitudes and institutions: entrepreneurs engaged in the sustained, systematic pursuit of profit; the market acted as the key mechanism of productive life; and goods, services and labour became commodities whose use was determined by rational calculation.
- Thirdly, there were significant changes in *population growth and movement*. As birth rates rose and death rates fell, the estimated number of people in Europe grew rapidly from 120 million in 1750 to 468 million in 1913 (Kumar, 1978). This period witnessed mass movements from the countryside to the city in a process of urbanisation. Also significant was the extent of forced and voluntary migration around the world: a striking example of this was the way in which North and South America were rapidly peopled by European migrants and African slaves.
- Fourthly, we saw the development of *new forms of government*. The nation-state, claiming absolute control over a bounded territory, became the key unit of power. This era saw the establishment of highly developed political apparatuses: bureaucratic organisation allowed the State to play a greater role in the lives of ordinary people. This was accompanied by the development of new political ideas such as nationalism, citizenship, democracy, liberalism, socialism and conservatism. The development of new philosophies of government was part of a wider change in the intellectual and cultural landscape. *The Enlightenment* of the eighteenth century was a crucial moment in the emergence of new ways of understanding the natural and social worlds. It heralded an era of great medical, scientific and technological innovation. Religious institutions and doctrines declined in influence, a process called *secularisation*, and for an emerging secular intelligentsia, science, truth and progress were the new faith.
- Finally, *Western expansion around the world* was a crucial, but often neglected, factor in the formation of modern societies. As early as the fifteenth century, Europeans began to travel the globe. In the years that followed, contacts between The West and the Rest (Hall, 1992) meant trade, plunder and, eventually, *colonisation*. This expansion

provided wealth, raw materials and, later, markets, which drove European economic development. In other regions it led to the destruction of existing social forms in the face of Western power.

That sociology emerged as an academic discipline during the nineteenth century is no coincidence. It was a response to a prolonged period of unprecedented social change when it seemed that the old order, the old certainties, the old ways of life were disappearing. So rapid and far-reaching were the social changes experienced by the early sociologists that the impression that they were witnessing the birth of a different kind of society was overwhelming. Social theorists of the nineteenth and early twentieth centuries saw their task as being to make sense of the Great Transformation and understand the new societies coming into being.

Contemporary theorists have kept faith with the key assumption of the founders of sociology that a fundamental break existed between the social forms emerging in the nineteenth century and any that had preceded them. Today's vision of modernity, however, differs in emphasis from earlier analyses in three important respects:

- There is a heightened sensitivity to the complexities of the processes involved so that, for example, contemporary theorists are unlikely to attempt to identify a single, central factor shaping modern societies.
- There is a greater awareness that modernity is a double-edged phenomenon, offering new opportunities for human development but also generating great suffering.
- Growing interest in the meaning of modernity is itself part of the debate about whether current social changes amount to another Great Transformation, this time into '**postmodernity**'.

postmodernity
For its supporters, the further transformation in social, cultural, economic and political arrangements which takes a society beyond modernity.

It is these three issues that pose new questions and present new challenges to contemporary sociology.

Given this sketch of modernity, it was, perhaps, not surprising that early theorists tended to assume that, as the most important forces at work, the dynamics of modernity would shape and structure all societies in a similar – positive – way. Societies were understood in terms of national boundaries, or particular forms of society (for example, capitalism), and individual societies could be seen as more or less conforming to the form and content of 'a modern society'. Modernity provided a sort of template for social development.

Today, the dynamics of modernity are no longer seen in terms of templates or models of a single 'modern society'to which all are destined. It is true that most societies in the world are industrialised, urbanised nation-states, yet their industries, their cities and their governments are shaped by *global* processes that cut across states and societies. The worldwide spread of electronic media and communications networks has, for example, been accompanied by and has facilitated the growth of transnational business corporations, globally integrated financial systems and systems for the production and distribution of material and cultural goods, and the development of transnational political and military institutions, such that 'It is increasingly difficult to understand local and national destinies without reference to global forces' (McGrew, in Hall *et al.*, 1992, p. 63). As we shall see in Chapter 3, the driver behind these global processes is modernity itself that cannot be, as it were, hemmed in by national boundaries. Thus, individual societies do not set their own socio-economic or political agendas: transnational companies, for example, driven by the modernist demands for global integration and control, may well pull out of a particular country even though its plants seem to be flourishing, precisely because of a global strategy to redeploy investment elsewhere. Sociology must then acknowledge the uneven and unequal global effects of modernity. Moreover, the problems that society needs to address today and in the future are *supranational*, such as the survival of the planet, the conservation of resources and the massive imbalances of material comfort, wealth and opportunity enjoyed by some and not others.

These parallel processes of a growing integration and convergence and a growing division and divergence means that modernity does not have the same 'pay-off' wherever it is felt. Nor is it experienced in the same way. This suggests, as we noted earlier, that the notion of a modern 'identity' which members of modern societies come to share looks much less secure. The scale, scope and availability of globally produced material and cultural goods, whether burgers, jeans or television programmes such as *Neighbours*, does, it is true, depend on people recognising and sharing in the same **symbolic world**. Yet the speed at which cultural and material goods are produced and consumed means that we begin to lose the sense of what is important, what is significant for our own personal identities in our own society. The overarching values and direction provided by modernity now look unstable, uncertain: some sociologists suggest that we are now living in an increasingly postmodern world where stable identities can no longer be assumed.

symbolic world
The world of thought; a conception of reality based upon mental perceptions.

According to this viewpoint, the stable, clear, and distinct identities of modernity and the clear categories of taste and style – such as high and low art – are swept away (which may cause some uncertainty in the gallery!). So too are the social hierarchies (of class and status) associated with them. Identities are still constructed, it is suggested, but more

Source: *Spectactor*

'Yes I know he's the gallery curator but is he art?'

through what we consume than, say, through our work, our family background, our sense of place. It is precisely for this reason that sociologists have, as Chapter 2 shows, recognised the central place that consumption has in contemporary society.

What would this mean at the level of the everyday? At its most extreme, it would mean that 'postmodern' individuals are no longer 'unified subjects', they no longer possess fixed, stable, permanent or coherent identities but are increasingly composed of fragmented, multiple and sometimes contradictory identities. Earlier in the chapter we argued that an individual's personal identity is to a great extent dependent on the routines of everyday life and the norms and expectations they carry. We also argued that as creative social actors we could nevertheless negotiate our identities through interaction with others. However, we said too that we sought to control our interaction such that we can develop a coherent sense of self.

Clearly, the challenge that postmodernism presents to sociology is that postmodern social actors may either not wish to or – looked at in more negative terms – are denied the opportunity to develop a 'coherent sense of self'. Is this conceivable at both the level of the individual and the wider societal level? And if it is, how should sociology respond, since postmodernism would also appear to deny any stable identity to the discipline itself, its boundaries and focal concerns lost in a blur of meanings? We shall leave such a weighty question until the close of the book in the final chapter.

What is clear is that the interplay of *modernity* and its *global* dynamics, and *postmodernity* and *identity* have become of central interest to sociologists. These four issues are addressed in various ways throughout this book and help to structure the debates which characterise the discipline today. We try to show in both the substantive and the more conceptual chapters how contemporary sociologists are developing new ways of exploring and making sense of society today. As an introductory text, there will be much that is left unsaid which the reader will need to follow up. What we can do, however, is describe in more detail what modernity means, since this is an important lens through which we can view some of the central concerns of the subject. This we shall now do in Chapter 2.

Summary of the Chapter

- Social life can be understood in terms of objective, biographical and subjective, autobiographical terms.
- Social behaviour and social identity are embedded in wider social environments and processes: in this way sociology challenges simplistic notions of individualism.
- The social world constrains us through norms and values shared and reproduced through intersubjective social relations: they are often unconsciously expressed in the habit and ritual of everyday life.
- Social structures – especially in their material form – disadvantage some and advantage others.
- Social actors are creative agents who construct their sense of personal social identity and who can challenge existing social constraints and social structures.
- Social structure and social agency are interdependent, mutually influencing processes.
- Social structures are both enabling and constraining.
- Sociology has its roots in understanding the dynamics of 'modernity'. Today, processes associated with 'globalisation'and 'postmodernity' pose new challenges that a traditionally modernist sociology must address.

References

Giddens, A. (1984) *The Constitution of Society*, Cambridge, Polity Press.

Goffman, E. (1969) *The Presentation of Self in Everyday Life*, Harmondsworth, Penguin.

Hall, S. (1992) 'The West and the Rest', in S. Hall and B. Gieben (eds), *Formations of Modernity*, Cambridge, Polity Press in association with The Open University Press.

Kumar, K. (1978) *Prophecy and Progress: The Sociology of Industrial and post-Industrial Life*, Harmondsworth, Penguin.

McGrew, A. (1992) 'A Global Society?', in S. Hall *et al.* (eds), *Modernity and its Futures*, Cambridge, Polity Press in association with The Open University Press.

Mills, C. W. (1970) *The Sociological Imagination*, Harmondsworth, Penguin.

Polanyi, K. (1973) *The Great Transformation*, New York, Octagon Books.

2 Living in Modernity

Aims of the Chapter

This chapter aims to further understanding of the meaning and significance of the concept of modernity by exploring the distinctiveness of life in modern societies. It will highlight the many ways in which structural changes, often of global proportion, have altered and continue to alter our everyday experience. In particular, the chapter will consider the impact of four key processes of modernity: the development of industrial capitalism; the growth of rational forms of thought and organisation; the rise of the nation-state; and the separation of social life into 'public' and 'private' realms.

Introduction

modernity
A term designed to encapsulate the distinctiveness, complexity and dynamism of social processes unleashed during the eighteenth and nineteenth centuries, which mark a distinct break from traditional ways of living.

the Great Transformation
The name given by Karl Polanyi to the historical moment, characterised by massive social, political, technological, economic, and intellectual change, which marks the onset of modernity (*see* modernity).

The last chapter introduced the term '**modernity**' as an attempt to encapsulate the continuing worldwide impact of the processes unleashed during **the Great Transformation**. This chapter explores this important but nebulous concept in more detail and, in doing so, introduces some of the central concerns of sociologists past and present. Modernity involves changes of global proportion but, in this chapter, particular emphasis will be placed on the ways in which large-scale developments have impacted on everyday experience: in other words, this chapter will consider what is distinctive about living in modernity. In doing so it returns to Chapter 1's theme of social constraint and social agency by telling a story not only of people caught up in and shaped by structural changes but also of how these same people have actively engaged with those changes and made themselves at home in them.

Becoming Modern: Transformations of Time and Space

Major changes in the use of both time and space were central to the formation of modernity (Berman, 1982; Harvey, 1990; Giddens, 1990). Advanced transport systems and other forms of communication, for instance, facilitated contacts across distance and required the synchronisation of activity using clocks and calenders. Thus, as Anthony Giddens (1990) argues, the railway timetable epitomises the modern era – 'a time-space ordering device' which 'permits the complex coordination of trains and their passengers over time and space'. Similarly, money 'provides the enactment of transactions between agents widely separated in time and space'.

Giddens and others discuss spatial and temporal change in order to demonstrate the uniqueness of the institutions which emerged during the Great Transformation. If, however, we consider the impact of modernisation on the lives of ordinary people, then this too involves an altered experience of these two fundamental categories. As the case studies that follow will illustrate, becoming modern meant transformations of time and space.

Living as a slave

One marker of the onset of modernity was a shift in eating habits. The staple diet of people of all classes in eighteenth-century England, for example, included the daily intake of produce from around the world:

> **Tea from China, sugar and coffee from the West Indies, tobacco from Virginia, chocolate from Africa and America, rum from the Caribbean: all were consumed on an increasingly large scale.**
>
> [Walvin, 1992, p. 4]

At first glance this may appear a trivial development but it is actually a measure of the rapid growth of global communication and commerce at that time. This was as much about movements of people as it was movements of produce; American tobacco and the Caribbean sugar which sweetened tea and coffee were harvested by European colonists using slaves transported across the Atlantic from Africa. Wealth generated in the colonies helped to finance commerce and manufacturing in Europe: the country who profited most from the slave trade, Britain, was to become the pioneer of industrial capitalism.

Enslavement is a graphic example of how people could be caught up in the development of modernity against their will. The institution of slavery declined in the 1800s but, in some ways, it highlights the dark side of the modern experience. Between the seventeenth and nineteenth centuries an estimated 24 million Africans were enslaved (11 million of whom survived the journey to the Americas) in one of a number of great movements of population that feature in modern history. They were plucked from their existing homes and cultures, transported around the world in appalling conditions, and put to work in the service of capitalism. For the slave owner, the labour power of the slave was a commodity to be traded and exploited as efficiently as possible. Although chiefly on rural plantations, slaves' work had many proto-industrial characteristics. Much thought and attention was devoted to the management of slave labour in order to maximise productivity and profit.

Living by the clock

Another indicator of the emergence of modern societies was the new significance of clock-time as a basis of social organisation. A crucial aspect of this was the way in which, in the eighteenth and nineteenth centuries, the tempo of agricultural and manufacturing labour increasingly came to be set by the clock and the calender in a way very different from pre-modern forms of work. Historian E.P. Thompson (1967) argues that, prior to the development of industrial capitalism, work-rhythms were set by factors such as the period of daylight, the breaks between tasks and the constraints of deadlines or other social duties. Industrial life, in contrast, was regulated by the clock. Factory production implied the synchronisation of labour – it began punctually, had a steady pace and took place for set hours and on particular days of the week. In addition, the clock injected a new urgency to work. For both employer and employee 'time is now currency: it is not passed but spent.'

The tyranny of the clock is one important example of the way in which the experience of work altered as ordinary people, although nominally free, became subject to the surveillance, discipline and regulation of industrial capitalism. Employers in the early modern era actively set out to destroy the pre-modern practices of their employees and introduce new attitudes towards work. The pace of this change was, however, uneven: Thompson writes that throughout the nineteenth century in Britain it was still common for trades and craftspeople to work irregular hours, often taking unofficial holidays on 'Saint Monday'.

Living in the city

The city, writes Michel De Certeau, 'is simultaneously the machinery and hero of modernity' (quoted in Harvey, 1990). Urbanisation was a key dimension of the making of modern societies. During the early modern era large numbers of Europeans moved from the countryside to urban centres: in Britain, for example, in 1810, 20 per cent of the population lived in towns and cities; one hundred years later the figure had risen to 80 per cent (Kumar, 1978). Cities changed qualitatively as well as quantitatively and their unprecedented scale and complexity required new levels of planning and organisation. The urban experience was, however, not of order and rationality:

> **“Of this enormous Babel of a place I can give you no account in writing: it is like the heart of all the universe; and the flood of human effort rolls out of it and into it with a violence which almost appals one's very sense.”**
>
> **[Thomas Carlyle on London, 1824, quoted in Jennings, 1985]**

Thomas Carlyle was not alone in viewing the novelty of the early modern city as lying in its chaos and energy. A crucial element of this was the rate at which the buildings of the city were growing and spreading. Many commentators in the nineteenth and early twentieth centuries suggested, however, that urbanisation produced a new kind of social as well as physical environment: they identified a sea-change in personalities, attitudes and relationships emerging out of city life.

The idea that the city provided a distinctive social experience is a recurring theme of modern literature. An early example comes from the writings of Parisian poet and essayist Charles Baudelaire (1821–1867). He highlighted the distinctiveness of the urban life by describing a new character type, the *flâneur*, who wandered Paris observing its many sights and enjoying the anonymity of the crowd. Baudelaire's writings are often quoted because they capture both the estrangement and the wonderment experienced by new city dwellers.

An issue which preoccupied commentators of early modernity was the break-up of older, stable forms of community in the move from countryside to city. Sociologists of this period suggested that the city presented people with new problems of social integration: Ferdinand Tonnies, for example, argued that urbanisation transformed the basis and character of social contacts. He charted a shift from *gemeinshaft* – intimate, sentimental and stable relationships between friends and neighbours, based on a clear understanding of social position – to *gesellschaft* – impersonal relationships of organisation and association. Many of the same themes are evident in the writings of Georg Simmel who described the emergence of a distinctive urban personality. He argued that the pace, complexity and segmentation of modern life increased the number of non-intimate, standard relationships such as ones based on legal rules or the exchange of money. They also fostered a more calculating and self-conscious state of mind, with city dwellers often adopting a blasé attitude to the multiplicity of sights and people they encountered. In other words, city life produced a greater sense of individuality and detachment.

Global Processes, Local Experiences

Writing about urbanisation can be seen as an attempt to define a distinctively modern outlook and way of life: the big city becomes a metaphor for modernity as a whole (Donald, 1992). The move from the countryside to town was, however, only one aspect of modernisation. The three figures introduced in the last section – the slave, the clock-watcher and the city-dweller – illustrate only a few of the many ways in which the formation of modernity involved the reworking of social worlds and individual biographies. Each example raises questions about living in modernity but any claim to offer a definitive account of what it means to be modern is hampered by two fundamental characteristics of modernity itself – its dynamism and its complexity.

An adequate description of modernity must rest not only on the uniqueness of its institutions but also on the continuing pace and scope of social development. Sociologists like to talk of 'structures' as a way of conceptualising the social forces which shape or constrain action but, unlike other structures such as buildings, modern social structures are in a permanent state of change. The capacity of modern social forms to remake themselves was recognised by some of the earliest interpreters of the Great Transformation:

Constant revolutionising of production, uninterrupted disturbance of all social conditions, everlasting uncertainty and agitation distinguish the bourgeois epoch from all others. All fixed fast-frozen relations ... are swept away, all new-formed ones become antiquated before they can ossify. All that is solid melts into air, all that is holy is profaned, and man is at last compelled to face with sober senses, his real conditions of life, and his relations with his kind.

[Karl Marx and Frederick Engels, 1967]

One way to illustrate this potential for ongoing development is to return to the case studies of the last section. Transportation and slavery was only the first stage of a continuing history of migration, exploitation and disadvantage experienced by the descendants of slaves (Gilroy, 1993). Similarly, both the urban environment and conditions of work have altered frequently since the Great Transformation. These examples of change are part of a wider phenomenon:

Modernity ... not only entails a ruthless break with any or all preceding historical conditions, but is characterized by a never-ending process of internal ruptures and fragmentations within itself.

[Harvey, 1990, p. 62]

The social forms of modernity have, therefore, altered greatly over time. One important distinction that should be drawn is between the process of becoming modern (the contours of which are described in Chapter 1) and the condition of actually being modern. During the first half of the twentieth century the influence of modernity spread and modern institutions achieved a new dominance and sophistication.

These developments had a major impact on habits, outlooks and aspirations.

Box 2.1: The development of modern societies in the twentieth century

- *New forms of capitalism and industrial production*. Western economies came to be dominated by relatively few, large, often transnational, corporations. These established a close relationship with governments in a system of '*organized capitalism*'. (Urry and Lash, 1987).

Manufacturing increased in scale, accompanied by the growth of sectors of the economy dedicated to the circulation of commodities and the provision of services. This era sees the development of new, advanced techniques of *mass production*, such as the moving assembly line, and of *mass marketing*, such as advertising and consumer credit. These innovations are often referred to by the catch-all term **Fordism** which refers to the car-maker Henry Ford who pioneered many of them. The systematic application of science and technology to production, distribution and marketing was a crucial feature of this period. Many of the new industries of the twentieth century, such as electricity, chemicals, cars, power, consumer electrical goods, were science-based.

Fordism
A form of industrial economy based on mass production and mass marketing prevalent in the post-war period. These techniques and processes were pioneered by Henry Ford in the manufacture and sale of Ford motor cars.

New forms of production depended on new techniques for the management and control of labour. Specialisation increased and the occupational structure altered to include growing numbers of professional, managerial, administrative and technical workers.

- *Population growth slowed* in the West but *urbanisation continued*, making this the era of the great industrial cities.
- *Nations and nationalism spread around the world* so that, by the middle of the twentieth century, almost the entire globe was divided into bounded territories.

The twentieth century **State**, in both its totalitarian and democratic forms, was *unprecedented in its scope and influence*. In different ways both Communist and Capitalist governments oversaw economic life. Through, for example, systems of education and welfare, the State increasingly intervened directly in people's everyday lives. This period witnessed the extension of bureaucratic forms of administration. Like industry, government utilised new technologies of communication to mobilise and control their citizens.

nation-state
A form of political authority unique to modernity comprising various institutions such as the legislature, judiciary, police, armed forces, and central and local administration. It claims a monopoly of power and legitimacy within a bounded territory.

A striking manifestation of the power and reach of the modern State was the *increased scale and ferocity of warfare*, as governments mobilised whole populations in the pursuit of cross-national conflicts, sometimes on a global scale.

globalisation
The process whereby political, social, economic and cultural relations increasingly take on a global scale, and which has profound consequences for individuals' local experiences and everyday lives.

- *Intellectual and cultural change*. This period witnessed the development of a mass society in which the consumption of goods and media messages took on a new importance.

Science and technology became increasingly powerful, commanding massive resources and playing a key role in industrial production, warfare and other aspects of modern life.

- **Globalisation.** As Chapter 3 will explain, although direct colonial rule declined, a world economic and political system based on Western economic and military power was consolidated.

Of course, by remarking that to be modern is to live with social change, we are actually highlighting an important, common experience of modernity. The endless remaking of our social and physical worlds generates both excitement and disorientation (Berman, 1982). It also promotes the questioning and reappraisal of existing social conventions (Giddens, 1991).

If the pace and scope of change is one complication to any attempt to define what it is to be modern, then a second, related, issue is the diversity of experiences of and responses to modernity. Geographical variations are an important aspect of this. Chapter 3 will describe how the formation of modernity had global ramifications but that these were very different in regions beyond the West. This variation used often to be understood in evolutionary terms – the world was divided into different societies at different stages in a single process of modernisation. Most social scientists now reject this approach and recognise the varied consequences of the spread of modern social forms. Some critics of evolutionary theories of modernisation suggest that **underdevelopment** and poverty in other parts of the world have been integral to the story of Western development: in the words of the anti-colonialist Franz Fanon (1967), Europe is the creation of the Third World. Fanon pointed out that most accounts of modernity exclude those he dubbed 'the wretched of the earth' – the voiceless, faceless poor who populate the countryside and shanty towns of the Third World.

underdevelopment
A term coined by Andre Gunder Frank to describe the economic and social conditions of those Third World countries whose markets, labour and resources have been exploited by the development of Western capitalism (*see* dependency theory *and* Third World).

The inequalities of modernity do not only exist across space but are evident in particular shared social contexts – consider the slave and master on a colonial plantation, employer and employee in a factory, and rich and poor walking the same city street. Age, gender, class and race differences have generated contrasting experiences of modernity. This does not simply reflect existing divisions – modernity itself generates diversity and inequality. As the chapters in Part 2 will show, the very categories of class, race and gender as we now understand them are products of the modern era.

To sum up, although there are common features of life in modern societies, the global processes of modernity have generated diverse, changing, local experiences. It is important to bear this in mind as we go on to discuss four key developments – the rise of industrial capitalism, the growth of rationality, the dominance of the nation-state, and the separation of public and private spheres.

Living with Industrial Capitalism

Living as a worker

The impact of industrialisation on both the social and natural world was profound. The industrial revolution unleashed violent, elemental forces. The following describes England's Black Country in the 1830s:

> **The earth seems to have been turned inside out. ... The coal ... is blazing on the surface ... by day and by night the country is flowing with fire, and the smoke of the ironworks hangs over it. There is a rumbling and clanking of iron forges and rolling mills. Workmen covered in smut, and with fierce white eyes, are seen moving amongst the glowing iron and dull thud of the forge-hammers.**
>
> **[quoted in Jennings, 1985, p. 165)**

As the discussion of clock time has already indicated, the development of capitalism and industrial production had major consequences for the mass of ordinary people: this is usually illustrated by referring to the ways in which the factory provided a strikingly new working environment. Just as significant, in the countryside and the city, was the new supremacy of the wage as a source of livelihood. In premodern societies financial remuneration was only one of a repertoire of strategies for achieving well-being: much production was for subsistence or to fulfil non-monetary obligations. Under the new conditions of industrial capitalism, a regular wage became crucial for the survival of the mass of the population. The wage depersonalised relations between employer and employee, turning the worker into abstract labour to be exploited as efficiently as possible in the pursuit of profit.

By the twentieth century a conventional view of work was established which was very different from a hundred years before: it was waged; it took place outside the home; and it was performed predominantly by men. The household lost much of the role, which it enjoyed in premodern times, as a key arena of economic activity. This development contributed to the marginalisation of women from production. Chapter 12 will explain how, as industrial capitalism took hold, men's lives became much more clearly compartmentalised into periods of paid work, leisure and unemployment.

Premodern societies were characterised by significant social differences and inequalities but the economic conditions of industrial capitalism generated new kinds of social division. The separation of home and work helped to sharpen gender differences inside and outside the home: women were squeezed out of economic activity and left with a more clearly defined domestic role. Age divisions were heightened as children and the elderly were excluded from production and segregated socially. The fluid, impersonal relationships of capitalism also generated the modern class structure.

Capitalism proved itself organisationally and technologically dynamic, generating new experiences of work and encouraging the development of ever more sophisticated techniques for the management and control of labour. Employers increasingly engaged in the observation, organisation and regulation of their workers. One consequence of this was that employees often lost control over their work as tasks were divided into complex divisions of labour. In the twentieth century this was epitomised by the development of large-scale mass production – pioneered by motor manufacturer Henry Ford who used a moving assembly line to manufacture low-cost products for a mass market.

alienation
Originally utilised by Marx to describe feelings of estrangement experienced by workers under industrial capitalism. Now more generally employed to describe people's feelings of isolation, powerlessness, and self-estrangement.

The new conditions of work increased output (Ford could make a car for a tenth of the cost of old-style craft production) but they also prompted considerable dissatisfaction and conflict. A recurring theme of nineteenth and twentieth-century thought has been that a contradiction exists between the development of mechanical and human potentials under industrial capitalism. A wide range of critics have argued that modern work conditions are dehumanising (Meakin, 1976). The **alienation** and exploitation of industrial labour were not accepted passively: workers reacted both informally via sabotage, absenteeism, pilfering, day-dreaming and sheer bloody-mindedness and also in a more organised fashion through trade unionism and other forms of political activity. This resistance has, in turn, contributed to changing conditions of work.

Box 2.2: Working for Ford

What is it like to work on an assembly line? Huw Beynon (1973) studied the lives of shopfloor workers at the Ford plant at Halewood on Merseyside in the late 1960s. The following quote from one of his interviews gives an indication of the monotony and estrangement experienced.

'You don't achieve anything here. A robot could do it. The line here is made for morons. It doesn't need any thought. They tell you that. "We don't pay you for thinking" they say. Everyone comes to realise that they are not doing a worthwhile job. They're just on the line. For the money. Nobody likes to think that they're a failure. It's bad when you know that you're just a little cog. You just look at your pay packet – you look at what it does for your wife and kids. That's the only answer.'

Beynon describes how workers survived or resisted these conditions through union militancy and individual acts of rebellion, sabotage or 'having a laugh'. He describes one notable incident:

'They started by peeling the foreman's orange, carefully, removing the fruit and filling the skin with bostic [glue]. The new remoulded orange was returned to the supervisor's bag. And they watched him try to peel it. Bostic bombs were manufactured and hurled into the steel dumper rubbish containers. Explosions ... flames twenty feet high. Someone could have been killed.'

Living as a consumer

Capitalism generated a consumer revolution as well as an industrial one: the dominance of the wage and the rise of large-scale production drew the mass of people into a world of commodities. The range of goods available grew rapidly. By the turn of the twentieth century an infrastructure of mass consumption was in place involving, for example, national and international distribution of products and the establishment of trademarks and brandnames. Department stores, mail order catalogues, billboards and public exhibitions all promoted consumption. This era also witnessed the birth of occupations, such as design, marketing and advertising, devoted to selling goods.

consumerism
A culture centred on the promotion, sale and acquisition of consumer goods.

The emergence of '**consumerism**' was not only about institutional change; it also involved shifts in attitudes and behaviour (Ewen and Ewen, 1982). One example of this is the way in which the practice of following changing fashions in clothing, previously confined to elite groups, now become commonplace. Increasingly, clothing needs were satisfied via the market as people made purchases from an ever-changing array of mass-produced goods. Choices in clothes, hair style and even body shape came to be seen as expressions of self. As this example suggests, a crucial change in outlook was a growing interest in novelty – a willingness to reject existing goods and practices in favour of new ones (Campbell, 1992).

Some have argued that the developments outlined above amount to the invention of the consumer. Certainly during the twentieth century powerful forces have sought to influence and shape consumer needs and desires. In the early modern period producers consciously set out to create markets and audiences for their products, socialising consumers into new values and giving them the knowledge and competence to distinguish between goods. Later producers and retailers developed advanced techniques, such as market research, for observing consumer behaviour and utilised the new science of psychology to sell goods more effectively (Bowlby, 1993).

In retrospect, the 1950s and 1960s seem the golden era of mass consumption in the already industrialised countries of the West. Across the developed world sustained rises in real income contributed to the growth of leisure industries and to the spread of consumer goods such as cars, televisions and washing machines. The emergence of a 'consumer society' was, for some social critics, a disturbing development which could only be explained in terms of the manipulation and exploitation of consumers. They viewed the growing preoccupation with the acquisition of goods as a threat to individuality and independent thought:

> **People recognise themselves in their commodities; they find their soul in their automobile, hi-fi set, split level home, kitchen equipment.**
>
> **[Marcuse, 1964, p. 9]**

Such arguments may, however, exaggerate the coherence and influence of the messages of advertisers and marketers. Also, by portraying consumers merely as dupes or hedonists they ignore the key role that consumer goods came to play in modern social life. Goods such as cars, washing machines and refrigerators have been part of major changes in the running of households and in their relationship with the wider economy (Gershuny, 1983). Consumer goods are cultural as well as material resources, mediating relationships and embodying meaning. Our conventions about clothing, for example, add up to a system of classification which involves differences of gender, age and class, recognises times of the day, week and year and marks spaces and occasions. Clothes and other goods establish and reflect distinctions between social groups (Bourdieu, 1984).

As the discussion of clothing implies, consumer goods have become the raw materials of life in modernity, implicated in a whole range of social activities. While viewing consumption simply as the result of manipulation is simplistic, the growing involvement of industrial capitalism in these everyday practices is highly significant.

Box 2.3: Consumption as opposition?

The term consumption is often associated with passivity. This can, however, blind us to the creativity of consumers. The varied ways in which we utilize goods often challenges the intentions of producers. In some cases, far from demonstrating conformity, they can express resistance to dominant structures and values. Youth subcultures, for example, have appropriated everything from the motor scooter to the safety pin to establish oppositional identities. Such is the dynamism of capitalism, however, that it is able, in turn, to reappropriate and sell this rebellion back to us as commodities.

Living with Rationality

The Enlightenment
An eighteenth century philosophical movement based on notions of progress through the application of reason and rationality. Enlightenment philosophers foresaw a world free from religious dogma, within human control, and leading ultimately to emancipation for all humankind.

secular
Not concerned with religion.

With hindsight, the intellectual revolution of the eighteenth-century **Enlightenment** was a crucial element of the Great Transformation. It instigated what has been dubbed 'the project of modernity' (Habermas, 1987) by challenging religion, myth and tradition and trumpeting a new faith in progress through knowledge and reason. How this change in the world of ideas altered the outlook and behaviour of ordinary people is open to question; Chapter 16 will describe how religious beliefs and institutions – albeit in distinctively modern forms – continue in the contemporary world. Nevertheless, in contrast to any that preceded them, modern societies are **secular** societies characterised by a belief in the power of rational thought.

For proponents of the modern project, reason, particularly as manifested in science and technology, promised mastery of nature and society. Thinkers of the early modern era were convinced that progress in knowledge promised the solution to all social ills:

> **The Golden Age of the human race is not behind us but before us; it lies in the perfection of the social order.**
>
> [Henri Saint-Simon quoted in Kumar, 1978, p. 13]

rationality
A preoccupation with calculating the most efficient means to achieve one's goals.

This approach to political problems indicates a shift in outlook often referred to as the growth of **rationality**. The concept of rationality is hard to define (partly because it has become so entrenched in the modern mind-set) but it involves the systematic pursuit of goals – finding the optimum means to a specified end. It is impersonal and is preoccupied with technique, calculation and control. Sociologist Max Weber (see Chapters 4 and 17) broke new ground when he argued, in the early years of the twentieth century, that key developments of the Great Transformation were, at heart, all manifestations of the growth of rationality: the rise of science and academia signalled the dominance of rational thought; industrial manufacture involved the rationalisation of production; capitalism was about the calculating, systematic pursuit of profit; codified law was the rational organisation of justice, and so on. Living in modernity, therefore, meant being subject to these rational forms of thought and social organisation. This is best illustrated by referring to an example of rationality which particularly preoccupied Weber – bureaucracy.

Bureaucracies are quintessentially modern forms of organisation – think of the complex hierarchies of government civil services, transnational corporations or even educational establishments. They are large impersonal organisations in which power lies with the institutional structure rather than with the individuals who people it. Bureaucracies involve the specialisation of tasks with clear demarcations of authority and formal rules and regulations. In the modern world we are subject to the discipline of bureaucracies as employees who have clear sets of duties and responsibilities and we are expected to subsume our own feelings and interests to that of the organisation. We also have to deal with impersonal bureaucratic structures as citizens and consumers. These systems of rational thought and organisation can be inhuman or dehumanising and, ironically, in some circumstances can be irrational and inefficient – as anyone who has been tangled in red tape will testify.

Box 2.4: The McDonaldisation of society?

Max Weber viewed bureaucracy as the ultimate manifestation of rationality in social organisation. American sociologist George Ritzer (1993) has recently argued that in the contemporary world the fast-food restaurant is a more appropriate model for the influence of rationalisation. In 1991 it was estimated that the leading one hundred restaurant chains operated 110,000 outlets in the USA alone – that is, one per 2,250 Americans. According to Ritzer, the success of these chains is based on the four key elements of 'McDonaldisation':

- *Efficiency* – economies of scale, assembly-line production of food and limited menus cut costs and facilitate the fast processing of customers.
- *Calculability* – every aspect of the food production and consumption process is measured and evaluated on the basis of rational calculation.

- *Predictability* – according to Ritzer, 'in a rational society people prefer to know what to expect in all settings at all times'. McDonald's epitomise the drive towards 'a world that offers no surprises'. Enter a McDonald's anywhere in the world and not only will the menu be the same but you can guarantee that the french fries will be 9/32s of an inch thick and the hamburgers 3 and 3/4 inches in diameter.
- *Control* – McDonald's exercises rigid control over its employees, taking skills and autonomy away from individual workers and investing it in the organisation of production, so that, instead of a chef, there is a food production line. Technology plays an important part in this: people serving drinks, for example, have no discretion about how much they pour – this is determined by automatic dispensers. Control is exercised over the customers as well as employees: hard seats, bright lights, and, in some cases, security guards ensure that they do not linger too long when consuming their food.

Critics of McDonald's would argue that its success also illustrates the irrationality of supposedly rational systems. Rational organisation has succeeded in producing and promoting food of poor quality and devaluing the experience of having a meal.

A new faith? Living with science and technology

Rational forms of thought and organisation may be defining features of modernity but our relationships with them are far from straightforward. This is apparent if we consider people's experiences of an area of modern social life often said to epitomise the triumph of reason and rationality – science and technology.

During the twentieth century, science has become a huge undertaking and technologies have grown rapidly in pervasiveness, scale and power. Scientific knowledge and technological systems have played a pivotal role in transforming the natural world into a created environment subject to human co-ordination and control. The size and complexity of these systems means, however, that our ability, as individuals, to shape or even understand them is compromised. It is an inevitable consequence of modern life that people use technologies – such as electricity, medicines and computers – without really understanding how they work. We **trust** the claims of scientific knowledge and take the advice of technical experts: a striking illustration of this is the way we hand our bodies over to doctors – medicine, as a profession and a form of knowledge, claims to understand our own health better than we ever could ourselves. So large and complex are contemporary medical, sci-

trust
Modern life requires people to rely on large-scale, abstract systems of knowledge, expertise and social organisation beyond their full understanding or control (*see* risk *and* reflexivity).

entific and technical systems that even the experts are in the position of taking science and technology on trust when addressing issues beyond their own narrow specialisms.

Conventional accounts of modernisation portray the pre-eminence of science and technology as evidence of the triumph of reason over religion and superstition. As the discussion of trust above suggests, however, there are limits to how rational we can be in our dealings with scientists and their machines. It is legitimate to ask whether religion has merely been replaced by a newer form of faith, this time in science and technology. Certainly, supposedly rational technologies can often be a source of wonder – who prior to the modern era would have believed that technologies would allow us to light darkness, talk across distance, fly through the air or see inside a living human body? Lack of knowledge and influence can make technologies appear immaculate, costless and beyond human agency. New technologies have frequently been ascribed magical qualities, particularly when they have done what was previously thought impossible (Corn, 1986).

Box 2.5: Technological futures: fact and fiction

A way of considering the role that faith plays in our contact with the technical is to note technology's ability to engender powerful hopes and fears for the future. The Internet is the latest of a long line of developments to prompt utopian and anti-utopian visions of a world transformed by technology. Technical advances have often been portrayed as routes to heaven or hell – a source of deliverance or damnation.

The popularity of science fiction is another indicator of the mythical power which technology can have in the modern world. The links between science fiction and science fact are interesting. For example, before he was employed by the US space programme German scientist Werner Von Braun designed fictional rockets for the film industry. Walt Disney's 'Man in Space' – featuring a Braun-designed rocket – promoted the concept of sending humans into space among the American public and politicians. More recently, a million people petitioned NASA to name the first space shuttle after Star Trek's 'Enterprise'. The blurring of the lines between fantasy and reality suggest that hopes and fears for the future are an important driving force behind technological and scientific innovation.

Questions concerning our understanding of science and technology have been given a new urgency in recent years. Increasingly, the most pressing threats to modern life, such as nuclear war, global warming

Source: *Private Eye*

'Well, this certainly buggers our plan to conquer the universe.'

and large-scale pollution, are science and technology related; awareness of such problems has contributed to a heightened sense of **risk** (Beck, 1992). In the premodern world there were many sources of danger, but most, such as plagues or natural disasters, were seen as beyond human control. Now we feel responsible for assessing and preventing risks; this is true at a personal as well as a global level – we must decide what is a healthy diet, whether using a VDU is harmful during pregnancy, balance the potential benefits or harm of inoculating our children, and so on. Often we lack the knowledge or power to resolve such problems. We are also frustrated by the inability of experts to give us definitive answers or solutions. Here lies a paradox of contemporary life: we are at once more and more dependent on science and technology and, at the same time, increasingly aware of their limitations.

risk
A term encapsulating the distinctiveness of people's experiences of danger in late modernity. Increasingly, the threats we face are of global proportion and are side-effects of social development. Awareness of risk can undermine our confidence in abstract systems of knowledge, expertise and social organisation (*see* late modernity, trust *and* reflexivity).

Living and Dying with the State

During the Great Transformation people in the West became subject to a new form of authority invested in the nation-state. National government was not only a product but also a carrier of modernisation. The nation-state took a variety of forms – totalitarian and democratic – but in every case claimed ultimate control over a bounded geographical territory. In doing so it established an unprecedented position of power and influence over its population.

During the nineteenth and twentieth centuries the state played an increasingly important part in ordinary people's lives. For example:

- Through codified systems of civil and criminal law it claimed the ultimate right to judge and punish wrong-doing and to mediate in disputes between individuals. The state disciplined people through incarceration in new prisons and asylums and, in some cases, was prepared to kill those who transgressed its laws. It sought to regulate not only public conduct but also 'private' behaviour by, for example, policing sexual activity and childrearing.

- Government also established a key role in economic life either by taking control of production out of the hands of capitalists or by establishing a close relationship with them. One consequence of this was that the state became the largest employer in modern societies.
- National systems of education and welfare meant that, for example, all children were required to attend school and that people in poverty could expect some aid from the state.

As this list suggests, the nation-state developed a role which was at once coercive and supportive of its people. Sometimes both elements coexist within the same function: welfare systems, for example, by starting from the assumption that all of a nation's population have the right to a minimum level standard of living, enshrine the idea of social citizenship, but welfare systems have another side which is about maintaining the work ethic and disciplining 'the undeserving poor' (Morris, 1994).

The development of the modern state was an element of the rationalisation story: the reach and power of modern government rested on new, impersonal, bureaucratic forms of organisation. The state's authority was maintained through a mixture of force and consent. It exercised a monopoly of coercive power within its borders, engaging in the surveillance of and, if necessary, violence against its people. Through control of both material resources and information it sought influence over their thoughts and actions. Highly significant was the way in which subjects of the state were reconstituted as 'citizens' sharing a common destiny. Nationalism – loyalty to the nation-state – became a potent source of identity and a justification for behaviour of great brutality. An aspect of this was summed up by George Orwell writing in Britain in 1941:

As I write, highly civilized beings are flying overhead, trying to kill me. They do not feel any enmity to me as an individual, nor I against them. They are only 'doing their duty', as the saying goes. Most of them, I have no doubt, are kind-hearted law-abiding men who would never dream of committing murder in private life. On the other hand, if one of them succeeds in blowing me to pieces with a well-placed bomb, he will never sleep the worse for it. He is serving his country, which has the power to absolve him for evil.

[ORWELL, quoted in BAUMAN, 1989, p. ii]

As this example suggests, a striking illustration of the authority of the state is the way it mobilised its citizens for war. Thanks chiefly to other developments already discussed, in industrial production, rational organisation and science and technology, warfare in the modern era was of a scale and ferocity previously unknown. It is estimated that as many as 187 million people – civilians as well as soldiers – have been killed in wars during the twentieth century (Hobsbawm, 1994). Even in times of peace, nation-states have demonstrated a huge commitment to armies and arms. At times of war they have organised all human and economic resources at their disposal in order to fight other states.

Box 2.6: Modernity and the Holocaust

There is no greater testimony to the potential power and destructiveness of the modern state than the millions who have died at the hands of totalitarian governments during the twentieth century. The Holocaust – the attempt during the Second World War by the Nazi-controlled German state to destroy the Jewish population of Europe – is an horrific example of this. Between five and six million Jews were killed by the Nazis as part of a wider programme of genocide against Slavs, Gypsies, the mentally ill, the disabled, homosexuals and political opponents.

The origins of the Holocaust lie in Anti-Semitism which has a history stretching back to the Middle Ages. 'The Final Solution' (the Nazi euphemism for genocide against the Jews) was, however, a phenomenon of modernity. It was made possible by developments already discussed in this chapter. A historian of the death camps writes:

'[Auschwitz] was … a mundane extension of the modern factory system. Rather than producing goods, the raw material was human beings and the end-product was death, so many units per day marked carefully on the manager's production charts. The chimneys, the very symbol of the modern factory system, poured forth acrid smoke produced by burning human flesh. The brilliantly organized railroad grid of modern Europe carried a new kind of raw material to the factories. It did so in the same manner as with other cargo. In the gas chambers the victims inhaled noxious gas generated by prussic acid pellets, which were produced by the advanced chemical industry of Germany. Engineers designed the crematoria; managers designed the system of bureaucracy that worked with zest and efficiency more backward nations would envy. Even the overall plan itself was a reflection of the modern scientific spirit gone awry. What we witnessed was nothing less than a massive scheme of social engineering …' (Feingold quoted in Bauman, 1989, p. 8).

As this quotation vividly suggests, the Holocaust was rationally planned and carried out by a bureaucratic organisation which worked ceaselessly to become more efficient at genocide. Initially, killing was carried out by death squads who shot their victims by the thousand and buried them in mass graves. Within a few years far more sophisticated techniques were applied in Extermination Camps. These camps processed large numbers of people quickly and cheaply: the Final Solution was financed by selling the labour of some camp inmates, seizing their possessions and recycling the by-products of death such as victim's hair.

Of all the experiences of modernity it is hard to imagine any more terrible than those of the children, women and men who were the 'raw material' of genocide. The Holocaust, in the words of sociologist Zygmunt Bauman (1989), is a 'test of the hidden possibilities of modern society'. Bauman sees the Final Solution as a telling illustration of the way institutions of modernity distance people from moral responsibility for their actions. It demonstrates the ethical blindness of rational bureaucracies whose members can argue that 'I was only following orders.' One of the reasons why the gas chamber replaced the gun as the means of genocide was that new technology depersonalised the killing. The Holocaust also shows the terrible potential for harm which lies in the state's claim to be able to do anything it wishes within its sovereign territory and it highlights the potential for evil that lies behind blind loyalty or obedience to nation.

Living in Public and Private

The section on urbanisation earlier in this chapter described how sociologists of the late nineteenth and early twentieth centuries associated the modern city with new kinds of personality, perspective and social contact. Such commentators have been accused of romanticising premodern communities but, nevertheless, they did identify potentially significant trends. At the end of the twentieth century it is clear that living in modernity has meant major shifts in the experience of public and private worlds, in the conduct of social relationships and in people's sense of self.

Living in public

Highlighting the scale and impersonal character of the city encapsulates much of the distinctiveness of the environment in which modern life is conducted. Urbanisation was, however, only one of a number of factors which contributed to the evolution of a new kind of public sphere. Just as significant was the development of forms of mass communication such as newspapers, books, advertising billboards, theatre, cinema and, later, radio and television: these addressed people as members of publics or audiences.

If some developments of modernity grouped people together in anonymous masses, then other pressures contributed to a heightened feeling of individuality and self-consciousness. The complexity and flux of the modern social environment presented people with new problems and opportunities as they attempted to do two fundamental things – interact with others and maintain an identity. Relationships in premodern times took place in comparatively small-scale and stable contexts and rested on clear notions of social position, grounded, for example, in kinship or feudal hierarchies. The following trends have all contributed to a transformation in the ways in which people are sociable:

- The dynamic character of modernity has undermined custom and tradition as a grounding of social relationships, forcing us to reflect on and re-evaluate our contacts with others. An element of this is that there is now less emphasis on ascribed or inherited status when defining who people are and more emphasis on actively selected or achieved social positions.
- Many social practices in premodern societies rested on the relative similarity of background and outlook of all participants. Modern societies are far more diverse – living in modernity, therefore, requires us to deal with people who are different from ourselves.
- In comparison with earlier social forms, there is a greater level of complexity and specialisation in modern societies. The range of social roles has grown rapidly.
- In premodern societies 'others' could be clearly categorised either as familiar or as strangers. Living in modernity requires a more subtle range of stances towards the many people we come across. Even when, for example, we choose not to engage with those we meet in passing on the street, in a bar or at college, we must manage that non-contact by maintaining a stance of 'civil indifference' (Goffman, 1969).
- Modern life is characterised by a great number of impersonal relationships, particularly those governed by formal rules where contact is not really with an individual but with their bureaucratic rank or professional status. A whole variety of social interactions come into this category, such as those between lecturer and student, bus driver and passenger, doctor and patient, and so on.

The fluid, large-scale and often impersonal character of modern societies makes impression management – how we present ourselves to others – a highly significant but problematic endeavour. Difficulties arise out of 'the pluralisation of lifeworlds' – a diversification of both the contexts of social interaction and the types of encounter that can take place (Berger, 1974). This puts strain on our skills of what Erving Goffman calls 'self-presentation'. Goffman argues that acting is an appropriate metaphor for the conduct of modern life since this requires that we play a variety of roles each with a different stage and script. Goffman highlights some of the problems of identity we face in the modern world. In the kind of social environment described above, people are forced to reflect constantly on who they are and how they fit into the world around them.

Box 2.7: Public and private worlds: the impact of mass media

The development of mass media, notably books, newspapers, cinema and broadcasting, contributed to a new kind of public sphere. It was a major factor, for example, in establishing nations as 'imagined communities' (Anderson, 1983). Mass media allowed people to participate in events and communities over long distances. One has only to think of modern democratic elections, World Cup soccer, national lotteries or royal weddings to realise the intensity with which we can share in these electronically mediated events.

Interestingly, the most powerful contemporary media span the public and the private. Television, radio and newspapers bring the outside world into our homes. The times of programmes also help set the routine of life within the home and their content provides us with something to talk about around the dinner table – that is if we are not eating in front of the TV!

Being private

Early analysts of the Great Transformation viewed developments such as urbanisation, industrialisation and the growth of bureaucracy as signalling the rise of a society of impersonal relationships. This was, however, only part of the story: intimacy and familiarity did not disappear but instead became compartmentalised in a new private sphere. In fact, an important element of modernity has been a far sharper distinction between public and private worlds. Nowhere is this more apparent than in attitudes towards home, family and marriage.

In some respects, developments of modernity limited the role of the household. Industrial capitalism robbed it of much of its productive function, separating resting-place and workplace. Other changes, such as the establishment of formal education systems, took away some of the household's responsibility for socialising the young. Far from withering away, however, the household was given a new significance as 'home', thanks largely to a domestic ideal which portrayed the family as a crucial site of intimacy (Crow and Allan, 1980). In the words of one of its supporters, the modern family came to be viewed as 'a haven in a heartless world' – a source of support and security in an often impersonal and threatening social environment (Lasch, 1979). As Chapter 15 will explain further, however, there is a variety of interpretations of these development available. Some critics argue that the modern preoccupation with the intimate family is itself 'anti-social', sucking life out of the world that lies beyond the boundaries of home: 'As a bastion against a bleak society it has made that society bleak' (Barrett and McIntosh, 1982).

Home life often fails to live up to the aspirations of the domestic ideal. Feminists have shown how notions of privacy have masked violence and exploitation. They point out that the modern household has run on the unending labour of women which, thanks to ideologies of domesticity and motherhood, has not been fully acknowledged or rewarded.

Box 2.8: Private rituals, public pressures

The modern home may have been screened from the outside world by ideas of privacy but this does not mean that it was unaffected by public pressures. Accounts of domesticity among working-class people in Britain in the first half of the twentieth century, for example, recount a highly rountinised and ritualised way of life (Martin, 1981). This was shaped by both the powerful desire to show a 'respectable' face to other members of local communities and also by the need to survive on limited financial resources: the housewife, in particular, saw order and discipline as crucial to keeping her family's heads above water. This helps to explain the importance often attached to rules and rituals of housework such as those described by playwright Alan Bennett (1994):

'My mother maintained an intricate hierarchy of cloths, buckets and dusters, to the Byzantine differentiations of which she alone was privy. Some cloths were dish cloths but not sink cloths; some were for the sink and not for the floor. There were dirty buckets and clean buckets, brushes for indoors and brushes for the flags. One mop had a universal application while another had a unique and terrible purpose and had to be kept outside, hung on the wall. And however rinsed and clean these utensils were they remained tainted by their awful function. ... Latterly, disposable cloths and kitchen rolls tended to blur these ancient distinctions but the basic structure remained, perhaps the firmest part of the framework of her world. When she was ill with depression the order broke down: the house became dirty. Spotless though Dad kept it she saw it as "upside down", dust an unstemmable tide and the house's (imagined) squalor a talking point for the neighbours.'

As this quote indicates, ideals of domesticity gave housework a symbolic meaning and personal investment which distinguished it from most other forms of labour.

Living in Postmodernity?

This chapter has focused on the ongoing development of modern social forms and their impact on everyday experience. The global processes of modernity have reworked all aspects of social life: they have even, as the last section suggested, transformed how we see ourselves and our relationships with others. Defining characteristics of the modern experience are diversity and dynamism. This can be seen if we consider some of the themes highlighted in boxed discussions during the chapter. McDonald's and the Internet are relatively recent developments while other experiences which, a few years ago, would have been seen as quintessentially modern now appear rather dated: assembly-line manufacturing is a dwindling part of economic activity in the West; the era of mass consumption has gone to be replaced by a multiplicity of consumer 'lifestyles'; and the disciplined working-class home has given way to a more diverse range of family forms and new values of intimacy. Once again, all that is solid appears to be melting into air.

Since the 1970s new social trends have prompted some commentators to suggest that another Great Transformation is under way – talk is of the imminent arrival of '**postmodernity**' (Lyotard, 1984; Bauman, 1989). The following is a, necessarily, tentative summary of some of the recent changes which have provoked debate about the future of modernity:

postmodernity
For its supporters, the further transformation in social, cultural, economic and political arrangements which takes a society beyond modernity.

- Intellectual life is dominated by *a crisis of faith in the big modern ideas* of science, progress and reason.
- *Changes in production and the economy*: the worldwide development of capitalism undermines the power of national governments or corporations to regulate economic life. A new international division of labour means that *manufacturing takes place on a global scale* with much industrial production outside of the West. In Europe and the USA service-sector employment continues to grow and there are fears about long-term mass unemployment.

From Fordism to Post Fordism: the size of productive units shrinks; mass production is replaced by more flexible systems which allow a greater range and faster turnover of goods; mass marketing is replaced by 'niche marketing'.

- *Rapid population growth and urbanisation* is taking place in the Third World while, in the First World, cities are in decline.
- *Transnational economic, cultural and political activity* threatens the influence of the nation-state. This is accompanied by crises within many of the political ideologies of modernity, notably Marxism.
- A growing emphasis on consumerism and a proliferation of media generates *cultural fragmentation*.
- Many of the changes outlined above are aspects of a process of *globalisation*. Recent years have also seen regional shifts in wealth and power from Europe to Asia and from the Atlantic to the Pacific.

Chapters that follow will return to these developments and assess their significance. It is worth noting here, however, that talk of the onset of postmodernity is further evidence that life in the contemporary world is as fast-changing, exciting, threatening and disorientating as it has ever been. Many of the old certainties are going, forcing us to (re)evaluate social developments and our own place in them. This means we require the skills and insights of sociology more than ever.

Summary of the Chapter

- The onset of modernity unleashed processes of global proportion – notably the development of industrial capitalism, the dominance of rational forms of thought and organisation, the extended reach of the nation-state, and major changes in social relationships and in people's sense of self – which had and continue to have profound impacts on the conduct of everyday life.
- A defining characteristic of modernity has been the continuing pace and scope of social change.
- The global processes of modernity have generated diverse, local experiences.

References

Anderson, B. (1983) *Imagined Communities*, London, Verso.
Barrett, M. and M. McIntosh (1982) *The Anti-social Family*, London, Verso.
Bauman, Z. (1989) *Modernity and the Holocaust*, Cambridge, Polity.
Beck, U. (1992) *Risk Society*, London, Sage.

Bennett, A. (1994) *Writing Home*, London, Faber & Faber.

Berger, P. (1974) *The Homeless Mind*, Harmondsworth, Penguin.

Berman, M. (1982) *All That is Solid Melts Into Air*, London, Verso.

Beynon, H. (1973) *Working For Ford*, Harmondsworth, Allen Lane.

Bourdieu, P. (1984) *Distinction*, London, Routledge & Kegan Paul.

Bowlby, R. (1993) *Shopping With Freud*, London, Routledge.

Campbell, C. (1992) 'The desire for the new' in R. Silverstone and E. Hirsch (eds), *Consuming Technologies*, London, Routledge.

Corn, J. (ed.) (1986) *Imagining Tomorrow*, London, MIT Press.

Crow, G. and G. Allan (1990) 'Constructing the domestic sphere: the emergence of the modern home in post-war Britain', in H. Corr and L. Jamieson (eds), *The Politics of Everyday Life*, London, Macmillan.

Donald, J. (1992) 'Metropolis: the city as text', in R. Bocock and K. Thompson (eds), *Social and Cultural Forms of Modernity*, Cambridge, Polity.

Ewen, E. and E. Ewen (1982) *Channels of Desire*, New York, McGraw-Hill.

Fanon, F. (1967) *The Wretched of the Earth*, Harmondsworth, Penguin.

Gershuny, J. (1983) *Social Innovation and the Division of Labour*, Oxford, OUP.

Giddens, A. (1985) *The Nation-State and Violence*, Cambridge, Polity.

Giddens, A. (1990) *The Consequences of Modernity*, Cambridge, Polity.

Gilroy, P. (1993) *The Black Atlantic*, London, Verso.

Goffman, E. (1969) *The Presentation of Self in Everyday Life*, Harmondsworth, Penguin.

Habermas, J. (1987) *The Philosophical Discourse of Modernity*, Cambridge, Polity.

Harvey, D. (1990) *The Condition of Postmodernity*, Oxford, Blackwell.

Hebdige, D. (1979) *Subculture: The Meaning of Style*, London, Routledge.

Hobsbawm, E. (1994) *Age of Extremes*, London, Michael Joseph.

Jennings, H. (1985) *Pandaemonium*, London, Andre Deutsch.

Kumar, K. (1978) *Prophecy and Progress*, Harmondsworth, Penguin.

Lasch, C. (1979) *Haven in a Heartless World*, New York, Basic Books.

Lyotard, J. F. (1984) *The Postmodern Condition: A Report Knowledge*, Manchester, Manchester University Press.

Marcuse, H. (1964) *One-Dimensional Man*, London, Routledge & Kegan Paul.

Martin, B. (1981) *A Sociology of Contemporary Cultural Change*, Oxford, Basil Blackwell.

Marx, K. and F. Engels (1967) *The Communist Manifesto*, Harmondsworth, Penguin.

Meakin, D. (1976) *Man and Work*, London, Methuen.

Morris, L. (1994) *Dangerous Classes*, London, Routledge.

Ritzer, G. (1993) *The McDonaldization of Society*, Thousand Oaks, Pine Forge Press.

Thompson, E. P. (1967) 'Time, work discipline and industrial capitalism', *Past and Present*, vol. 38.

Urry, J. and S. Lash (1987) *The End of Organised Capitalism*, Cambridge, Polity.

Walvin, J. (1992) *Black Ivory: A History of British Slavery*, London, Harper-Collins.

3 Globalisation and Modernity

Aims of the Chapter

This chapter discusses the concept of 'globalisation' and its roots in modernity. The concept raises new issues for sociologists who are shown to handle it in different ways. You should understand the tensions between the global and the local as they relate to economic, cultural and political processes.

Introduction

modernity
A term designed to encapsulate the distinctiveness, complexity and dynamism of social processes unleashed during the eighteenth and nineteenth centuries, which mark a distinct break from traditional ways of living.

capitalism
An economic system in which the means of production are privately owned and organised to accumulate profits within a market framework, in which labour is provided by waged workers.

We saw in earlier chapters the way in which sociology has been especially concerned with understanding the development of modern society and the impact of **modernity**. This has created a core set of interests that has informed the conceptual and applied work of sociologists for over a century. Modernity has been associated with the onset of industrialisation, the growth of **capitalism** (its inequalities and forms of conflict), and the appearance of an increasingly complex and differentiated institutional culture. The classical contributions of Marx, Weber and Durkheim were, in their differing ways, devoted to improving our understanding of all these aspects of modernity. Engaged with its time, sociology could do no other than this. The great body of material that now makes up the sociological discipline has grown rich through addressing the issues set by the agenda of modernity.

We can, however, see an additional item emerging on the sociological agenda today which, as we suggested in Chapter 1, poses new challenges for sociology. This too is tied into aspects of modernity, but reflects changes in the contemporary temporal and spatial dimensions of the social, of the boundaries of 'society'. If sociology were to be created anew today, it is unlikely it would begin with the same set of issues that have dominated it since its nineteenth-century origins. While undoubtedly exploring processes of industrialisation, gender and family relations, the emergence and maintenance of a legitimate nation-state, cultural dimensions of class, ethnicity, community and so on, most if not all of these would have to be located in a new context, a *global* context.

The dimensions of modernity can only be mapped out properly today in global terms. The conventional assumption that these features can be understood within the spatial and socio-cultural boundaries of a nation, like Britain, Germany and Japan, will no longer do. The dynamics of modernity have made the world grow small, increasingly interlinked. Time and space, and so our sense of the local and the distant, the traditional and the strange have taken on new meaning in a context notable for its electronic

transnational corporations (TNCs)
Large corporations, emanating principally from the US, Japan and Europe, whose activities are aimed at global markets.

globalisation
The process whereby political, social, economic and cultural relations increasingly take on a global scale, and which has profound consequences for individuals' local experiences and everyday lives.

and satellite communication, **transnational corporations** and international, even global, political authorities (such as the European Union or the United Nations). The key term for this is the **globalisation** of modernity.

This contrast between the conventional and a newly emergent sociological agenda is summarised in Box 3.1. The first list of concerns points up some – though not all – of the issues which have been central to sociological debate. Note the key themes of industrialism, capitalism, class and nation-state. Note too that each of these (and other) features has often been equated with and understood in terms of the social boundaries defined by nations: 'society' was British society, Dutch society, or whatever. The second list presupposes a global context for industrialisation, capitalism and culture, and patterns of linkage that are not contained by, and so perhaps threaten, the conventional national boundaries of 'society'. Note too the attendance to new non-class forms of social protest and change (such as radical ecology), indicative of new socio-political dynamics at work in society today.

Of course, the second of these two lists has not fallen from the sky: the agenda it sets out and the concerns this creates arise from our interrogation of the traditional sociological agenda and an awareness that this needs to be modified. For example, it is only because so much importance has been given to the role of the nation-state in the past that we can understand the challenge that the globalisation of modernity poses to the legitimacy and autonomy of the state today.

Box 3.1: Changing sociological agendas

Some key concerns of classical sociology

- the growth and impact of industrialisation
- the development of capitalism and class conflict
- the emergence and legitimacy of the nation-state
- the growing complexity and differentiation of social institutions
- the congruence between 'society' and 'nation'
- the importance of class-based sources of protest and change

Some key concerns of contemporary sociology

- the emergence of global industrialisation
- capitalism as a world economy
- the growth of transnational economic and political structures
- the compression of time and space
- the legitimacy and role of nation-bound political institutions
- the origins and impact of (non-class) social movements

This chapter provides a summary of the recent sociological debate on the global dynamics of modernity. This debate may seem to be about abstract and remote processes that have little bearing on our lives at the local level. Nothing could be further from the truth since it is in the very dynamic of globalisation that its dimensions operate at *both* the global and the local level *at the same time*. Those who work for large transnational corporations find that despite achieving high levels of productivity they are to be made redundant as part of a world-wide 'restructuring' of the firm; our TV programmes are sponsored by foreign companies whose products are available in the high street; the fallout from the Chernobyl power station registers in our fields 1,500 as well as 15 miles away; peace initiatives at world level destabilise our local communities in Central and Eastern Europe; our homes cost more as interest rates rise because of international currency speculation via the electronic financial exchanges. These are just some illustrations of the effect of global dynamics at the local level: they will shape a society's labour market and its pattern of inequality, its consumption, its health, its political stability and legitimacy and the life chances of its households and families.

Sociology is now exploring such global/local processes and developing new concepts and new research questions that bring them to life: why has modernity led to the globalisation of social life? In what sense is this process unique to the modern era? Is it caused by one or many factors? How do people in different nations respond to global processes? Is globalisation uniform or uneven in its effect? How can nation-states sustain their power as socio-political systems when supra-national and trans-national organisations and agencies threaten to undermine them? Are people at the local level threatened by globalisation? Does this explain the growing attractiveness of regionalism, ethnicity, the 'community' and tradition as protection against a culturally 'homeless' global society? Finally, and most important, in what sense are these global processes not merely *international* but truly *global*? The term 'international' implies a pattern or set of relationships between discrete nations or countries. 'Global' implies a system of relations that cannot be reduced to or explained in terms of the interests or activities of particular nations. To say that there are global structures and processes is to imply that there are new global phenomena which supersede and so shape international and national levels of social behaviour.

Modernity and Globalisation

In the previous chapter we saw that modernity was, and for many still is, equated with progress. Moreover, such progress has often been identified with Western ideas and political culture. That is, when we think of modernity, we should think of Western modernity. The collapse and formal dissolution of the Soviet Union and the apparent demise of socialism throughout Europe was seen by some as the inevitable result of the historical triumph of free-market capitalism and liberal democracy on a world scale. A few commentators even spoke of this as heralding 'the end of history' (Fukuyama, 1989) in the sense that history thus far had been some sort of trial of strength between liberal capitalism and all else. However, the trials and tribulations of world capitalism since late 1989 – growing protectionism, currency crises, the decline of once strong economies – makes triumphalist declarations of history's end look a little premature.

Sociologists have however recognised that modernity does have certain global characteristics, even if these do not necessarily add up to some liberal capitalist new world age. Giddens (1990) has developed one of the more detailed discussions of the dynamics of modernity that together produce a *globalised modernity*. That is to say, from this point of view, the globalisation of social life is unique to modernity and an expression of it. We saw in Chapter 2 some of the ways in which people experience modernity and sociologists theorise about it. Giddens has shown how the spread of the features of modernity on a global scale is *made possible* by the play of three processes unique to modernity: these are

- the separation of time and space
- the disembedding of social systems
- the reflexive ordering of social relations

Each of these processes involves, in different ways, a going beyond of the here-and-now, beyond the physical and temporal constraints of immediate social relations. Each encourages a spreading, an opening, a diffusion of relationships. In this way modernity carries within itself the basis for its own diffusion and installation at a global level.

Let us look briefly at each of these three features in turn.

The separation of time and space

In pre-modern society, the time of day or season of the year was directly related to a particular space or locale within which time could

Source: *New Statesman and Society*, 22 September 1995 (Ian Baker)

'We've been on the information superhighway for three hours. Let's pull over for a coffee.'

be marked out: this was often based on the rhythm of agricultural life where the time of day was marked through the tasks that has to be completed. There was neither the need nor the technology – the mechanical clock – to refer to time in any other way. Standard clock-time and its universal application based on Greenwich allowed time to be separated from any specific locale. This was followed by the universal standardisation of calendar years and dates. Birthday cards, international newspapers, currency deals, and international travel timetables all presuppose this global time frame. Global space has its own framework through world maps whose grid of lines of longitude and latitude privilege no particular locale. As a result of these processes, time and space are no longer jointly tied to place, to tradition, to face-to-face interaction. Global communications via computer networks are devoid of both face-to-face interaction and locale: some see the emergence of 'electronic tribes' operating in cyberspace requiring the development of a whole new type of social anthropology that can understand the electronic 'community'.

The disembedding of social systems

This second dimension of modernity, which encourages its globalisation, follows directly from the first, Giddens describes this as the 'lifting out of social relations from local contexts of interaction'. In advanced modern society the social relations that allow us, for example, to exchange money are not tied to any particular instance of exchange or transaction: it is the disembedded invisible institutional relations that lie behind money – whatever particular form it takes – that make it acceptable. It is the liquidity of the banks, the assumption that credit cards are 'credit-worthy', that cheques will be cleared, and so on, that sustain the billions of face-to-face and remote transactions made every day. Again, another important form of social relation that is routine in our daily lives is expertise, that of a doctor's, a mechanic's, a plumber's, even a sociologist's! While we call on experts to assist in specific situations, the knowledge they have and the trust we put in it mean that we do not need to *know* the expert: authoritative knowledge is trusted precisely because it is distant, disembedded from the immediacy of interpersonal ties. Money and expertise are two examples of forms of social relationship that we find only in modern social systems.

The reflexive ordering of social relations

reflexivity

A process of examining, questioning and monitoring the behaviour of the self and others promoted by the social conditions and experiences of late modernity.

Finally, the modern social actor is a reflexive person, monitoring and questioning her own behaviour and that of others, recognising both social constraint and the possibilities of social change open to them. This **reflexivity** is enhanced by and in turn helps to reinforce the two dimensions of modernity sketched out above. The security and parochialism of traditional life are replaced by the options and uncertainties of a modern culture whose reference point is both global and local.

One can see how these three dynamics of modernity facilitate and help create the globalised context within which and through which we experience the world. The reflexive tourists sitting on their beaches in Montego Bay, Provence, Vancouver or Sydney worry about contracting skin cancer through the growth of the ozone hole, calculate the price of the hotel bill yet again as international currency rates change, devour the latest poolside 'blockbuster' whose mass readership depends on globally recognized themes, detail and storyline, and read with a sense of foreboding the latest tour-company collapse and wonder whether they will ever make it 'home'.

Giddens's account of the globalising processes of modernity is completed by his argument that there are four broad components that make up the world system, and which give it its basic institutional 'shape'. Thus the global system is one which

- is made up of *nation-states*
- operates in a *world capitalist economy*

- creates an *international division of labour*
- is dominated by a *world military order*

While Giddens has given a clear picture of the dynamics and dimensions of globalisation in broad terms, there are those who argue for a more historically based explanation for how globalisation has appeared. Robertson (1992), for example, has set out the various 'phases' marking out its development, from a situation in the fifteenth century of a very low degree of 'global density' to one that in the late twentieth century is both very high and complex. He describes the phases as follows:

- Phase 1: *The Germinal Phase* (1400–1750) – characterised by the growth of new national communities, the widespread influence of Catholicism, new conceptions of the individual, and the birth of modern geography and the calendar.
- Phase 2: *The Incipient Phase* (1750–1802) – characterised (especially in Europe) by the emergent nation-states, international trade, regulation and legislation, and the dominance of 'the West'.
- Phase 3: *The Take-off Phase* (1870s–1920s) – characterised by a strong notion of the modern ideal towards which all societies should aspire, the emergence of global communication, the establishing of a world time and almost global acceptance of the Gregorian calendar, the organisation of international events (such as the Olympic Games), and the onset of global warfare (First *World* War).
- Phase 4: *The Struggle-for-Hegemony Phase* (1920–1960s) – characterised by conflict between states for power and leadership in the world; attempts to control conflict through the development of the United Nations; the emergence of two superpower blocs and the Cold War, the nuclear age and the growing poverty of the Third World.
- Phase 5: *The Uncertainty Phase* (1960s–1990) – characterised by a new awareness of global concerns for environment and a challenge to materialist values; the end of the Cold War and of the twin power blocs of US and Soviet Union; the strengthening local nationalism correlated with increasing global cultural patterns and communication processes, post-socialism and the emergence of renewed traditional beliefs such as Islam.

Although Robertson and Giddens approach globalisation in different ways, they both share, as do most sociologists writing today, the view that the dynamics of contemporary globalisation are not reducible to what goes on at the level of the nation-state. In other words, the global whole is greater than the sum of its parts and now has a dynamic that will continue to shape and create social, economic and political problems as well as opportunities for individual countries in the world today. There are then truly global social 'actors' that are only found at the global level, such as transnational corporations (Ford, Siemens, Exxon, or Hoffman La Roche for example). As Harvey (1990) notes, these massive corporations that operate globally are not indifferent to where they locate their research, development and production activities; in fact, *precisely because* they have the technical capacity to orchestrate their affairs globally (through electronic and related communication systems) they can target much more effectively where in the global space they decide to set up plants to take advantage of local factors (such as cheap labour).

In the rest of this chapter we shall examine three aspects of the global system – the economic, the cultural and the political – from a sociological perspective. This is a system, as we stressed above, which is unequal and uneven in its effects. It is one in which the promise of 'modernity', of health, wealth and happiness for all, now looks hopelessly optimistic. Yet in the 1950s and 1960s many social scientists believed that the globalisation of modernity would inevitably mean the modernisation and industrialisation of all societies just as had been achieved by those in 'the West'.

Modernisation Theory and the Misreading of Global Modernity

Modernisation theory grew out of the work of American sociologists such as Parsons (1967) and Smelser (1969) whose exploration of the growing institutional complexity of society had provided a powerful model of what was distinctive of modern industrial society and the role (or function) played by its component parts. The defining feature of modern society was said to be a system of norms and values that were conducive to an open, democratic, entrepreneurial and participatory society. In contrast, non-modern traditional societies lacked such features, being tied to tradition for its own sake. Modernisation theorists could, and did, apply this broad framework to explain the different developmental stages achieved by countries around the world, and could prescribe the normative changes that were needed for less developed countries to join the modern world. While in theory there was no specific country to be emulated, 'the West' and more notably the United States were in practice held out as the embodiment of 'modern-isation'.

Although there are major differences between traditional and modern societies – compare an East African nomadic life with that of the New Yorker – modernisation theory made the mistake of assuming that the

dynamics of *modernity* were, once set to work, likely to lead to growing social and economic similarity in the world which would include of course a growing equality and improved standard of living for all countries. The simplistic thesis that a process of value-change that would usher in economic growth for all reduced modernity to a process of benign modernisation; it fails to recognise that modernity, both within and across societies, can produce chronic inequalities and disadvantage, not as a pathological, unfortunate side effect of development, but as a likely outcome of the institutional structures of modernity that were sketched out above.

One can see how modernisation theory assigned a positive value to modernity in its treatment of Western expansionism. The cultural and economic influence of countries like Britain, France and other Western states could only be understood as positive or benign, introducing from outside – or exogenously – the values of democracy and the free market. The colonial empire of Britain, for example, did, of course, introduce a range of modernising features – some technological, such as the railways, others economic, such as new currencies and financial systems. But the historical record also shows how the bulk of these colonial initiatives were principally directed towards the interests of the colonial power rather than being oriented towards the needs of the colony. Often, colonies were little more than administrative conveniences inasmuch as their geographical and cultural boundaries made little sense as far as the local peoples were concerned. Many years later, this was to lead to some of the most bloody civil wars after formal independence had been granted, such as in Nigeria. In short, while the trappings of modernity were brought to many overseas territories in this way, the institutional structures of the world capitalist economy within which they were given expression meant that they had at least as damaging as they had positive impacts on what we now call the Third World.

underdevelopment
A term coined by Andre Gunder Frank to describe the economic and social conditions of those Third World countries whose markets, labour and resources have been exploited by the development of Western capitalism (*see* dependency theory *and* Third World).

dependency theory
A theory most commonly associated with the work of Andre Gunder Frank. It challenges modernisation theory by arguing that underdevelopment is not an early stage in a country's evolutionary process, but a condition resulting from their exploitation by modern first world countries and regions (see underdevelopment *and* First World).

It took a good two decades or so – through the 1960s and 70s – for the sociology of development to come to terms with the prevailing and even growing poverty of the less developed countries. Only by recognising the persistence of unequal social structures that prevail at the global level were more acceptable explanations of chronic **underdevelopment** – rather than merely the lack of development – provided. One of these was (and remains) the account of **dependency theory** which was initially associated with the work of Andre Gunder Frank (1971) but which is now one of the principal world system theories adopted by many, though not all, social scientists.

Frank's analysis of the underdevelopment of Third World countries rests on the central proposition that development and underdevelopment should not be seen, as the modernisation theorists believed, as simply the later and earlier stages of an evolutionary process through which all societies pass. Instead, dependency theory argues that the development of western capitalism from the sixteenth century onwards *created* the underdevelopment of what we now call the Third World, through exploiting labour, resources and markets of pre-colonial, colonial and post-colonial territories. Frank had noted that Latin America grew most rapidly this century when it was relatively isolated from First World (especially US) capitalism, which led him to his belief that much of the time the exploitation of the Third World through unequal trade and exchange keeps them in a permanent state of socio-economic dependency on dominant capitalist states, or the 'metropolitan' countries of the world. Dependent states are merely satellites whose surplus is extracted, especially by powerful transnational corporations. While the elites of poorer countries depend themselves on sustaining their ties with overseas capital little will change.

Dependency has occupied a key place in development theory and has gained much of its strength from its global focus. Yet it has had its critics, not least because of its tendency to condemn all of the Third World to chronic underdevelopment when many countries, especially in South East Asia, have experienced real growth over the past decade. Critics, too, pointed to the need for a more sophisticated understanding of the character of transnational firms in the world economy, an issue we will now discuss more fully.

The Globalisation of Production: Transnational Corporations

A central feature of the contemporary world is the globalisation of production, a process of industrial globalisation that has grown at an astonishing pace over the past decade. A simple indicator of this is the growth of foreign direct investment by First World transnational corporations (TNCs): this has grown four times faster than the gross national product of their countries over the period 1980–90. TNCs from the three strongest regions in the world, the US, Japan and Europe, now operate on a global stage. The greater the globalisation of their activities the more we have to recognise TNCs as placeless, less associated with any one country. Governments throughout these three areas find it more difficult to rely on TNCs to act in the national interest and invest locally. This leads to situations in some countries such as Britain where a disproportionate amount of manufacturing investment during the last years of the 1980s came from Japanese, not British, companies, while British companies invested overseas.

We should not underestimate the power and scale of TNCs today: they form what Sklair (1991) has called a new 'transnational capitalist class' operating within the world capitalist economy. They have three priorities:

- to keep production costs as low as possible
- to target production to rapidly changing markets
- to stay innovative through the latest science and technology

This last point means that all TNCs develop new products that are increasingly science-based and related to new areas of research associated with bio-technology, new materials science and electronics. Acting globally requires TNCs to give their subsidiaries more freedom to respond quickly and flexibly to changing conditions and markets. The goal is to achieve what has been called 'lean production', a flexible, global capacity which relies on fast computer-based communication and management information systems.

One result of this, of course, is that work and the way it is experienced by workers becomes very different: the workforce tends to become divided into those who might be regarded as members of the 'primary' labour market – those in relatively highly skilled, secure, well-paid, typically male-dominated jobs which have good career prospects – and those who make up the secondary labour market in lower-paid, insecure, low-skilled and low-mobility jobs, often occupied by women, working-class youth or ethnic minorities. The relationship between the firm they work for and the local community in which they live can become increasingly meaningless as TNC investment and employment policies operate according to its global rather than local agenda.

Sociologists have explored the impact of this new globalised system of production in various ways. Some – especially those working in political economy (e.g. Froebel *et al.*, 1980; Sanderson, 1985) – have focused on the changes in the way in which labour has been reorganised globally, such that today we see a *new international division of labour* in which TNCs take advantage of low wage labour in less developed countries by establishing 'world market factories' free from union involvement, often employing cheap female labour. This account can be regarded as a version of dependency theory discussed above.

Fordism

A form of industrial economy based on mass production and mass marketing prevalent in the post-war period. These techniques and processes were pioneered by Henry Ford in the manufacture and sale of Ford motor cars.

A second approach has focused on the way in which a so-called Fordist system of production has been superseded by a post-Fordist one in the modern world. In general, **Fordism** refers to a system of mass production inspired by the Ford Car Company's assembly-line process which

Box 3.2: From Fordism to global Post-Fordism

Fordism:

- mass production of standardised products
- strong centralised control over labour
- assembly-line system
- mass production for mass consumption
- oriented to First World markets

Post-Fordism

- rapid modification of products for new markets
- identification of specific target groups for products
- specialisation in specific product area
- flexibility of assembly-type production system
- global orientation

manufactured identical cars for a mass market. Generalised across a wide range of industrial sectors, such 'Fordism' was commonplace during the post-war period in First World economies.

post-Fordism
Computer controlled and sophisticated production systems which emerged during the 1970s. Their key emphasis is on flexibility and the production of specialised, tailored goods to meet the demands of a competitive world economy.

just-in-time production
A finely balanced and controlled manufacturing production system designed to produce goods to meet demand as and when required.

Post-Fordism, it is argued, emerged during the 1970s in response to a growing competitiveness in the world economy, especially associated with Japanese and South East Asian enterprise. The more traditional, longer established TNCs found themselves having to change the way they were organised in order to meet the competition from these new centres of capitalism. The era of 'flexible specialisation' arrived wherein companies turned over new products more quickly, shed large numbers of long-serving blue-collar workers and moved into smart, high-tech production for a global market with considerably varied consumers. Automated, computer-controlled and networked manufacturing systems, fed with continual flow of information provided by Research and Development labs, market intelligence and sales personnel can fine-tune manufacturing to meet needs as they appear, the so-called **'just-in-time' production system**.

Implications

At least three implications follow from what has been presented so far. The power, global orientation and exploitative potential and practice of TNCs today means that they have a major impact on national and international patterns and experiences of employment and the

development of new technologies. Moreover, their 'placelessness' can create serious problems for national governments who can find it exceptionally difficult to rein-in and control firms on behalf of 'the national interest'. Where controls are imposed – by declining First World or disadvantaged Third World countries – TNCs can simply avoid them by moving part or all of their activities to another site within their global arena.

Finally, this last point is particularly of relevance when one considers controls over the environmental impact of TNC production: 'green' companies in Germany, the United States, Britain or elsewhere can be very dirty overseas, or simply relocate banned activities to less stringent regulatory contexts (often poorer countries). Yet at the 1992 Rio 'Earth Summit' in Brazil, the role of and control over TNCs was an issue almost completely neglected by the elite politicians during their week-long debate.

The Globalisation of Culture

The global spread of capitalism entails the spread of commodities that, while fine-tuned to local markets, carry messages and advertising slogans that deliberately reach out to as wide a market as possible. One only has to see the global familiarity of Mickey Mouse, Levi jeans, Coca Cola or Madonna's latest hit single/video to realise how successful global marketing has become. Does this spread of global commodities imply a globalisation of culture – especially a Western, US-dominated one? When we buy a Coke in Amsterdam, Berlin, Accra or Rio we are all sharing in a common transnational form of consumption: but do we all really think 'it's the real thing'?

Cultural imperialism

One answer to this question is provided by neo-Marxist sociologists, such as Tunstall (1977) and Becker *et al.* (1987), who argue that the strength of world capitalism is directly related to its ability to sell not merely goods but ideas, and more generally ideologies, which sustain our levels of consumption. **Consumerism** and the consumer culture it reflects has a powerful grip on societies throughout the world, including the less developed and post-socialist countries of Eastern and Central Europe. One of the first 'Western' stores in post-socialist states is the boutique selling Nike and Reebok sport/fashion shoes: highly profitable, easy to import and a very visible statement about 'being modern', which here means of course 'being Western'.

consumerism
A culture centred on the promotion, sale and acquisition of consumer goods.

The growth of consumerism has been heavily reliant on the growth of a transnational mass media dominated by firms such as SONY, Sky TV, CBS and so on. These try to reproduce at the global level what they have succeeded in establishing at the national: a large, hungry market for their goods, especially in the leisure and service sectors. As a result, the mass media have become hugely expanded both in terms of the *scope* of the audiences they reach and in terms of the *range* of the media available to those audiences.

Exposure to and consumption of media products has become an integral part of the everyday lives of most members of contemporary society, and for those in 'the West' the media occupies a considerable proportion of their leisure time, providing them to a considerable extent with their picture of the wider world. Television, for example, represents the major and most pervasive mass medium of today, and is of course a vehicle through which a range of satellite and terrestrial media products can be delivered. Television is the principal leisure activity of most adults and children, the 'organiser' of their entertainment and social life, missed when unavailable, and a source of information and ideas widely regarded – as in TV news – as authoritative and trustworthy.

socialisation
An on-going process whereby individuals learn to conform to society's prevailing norms and values (*see* norms *and* values).

Given these high levels of exposure, the media constitute important agencies for **socialisation**. They represent an institutionalised channel for the distribution of social knowledge and hence a potentially powerful instrument of social control (as well as social critique) sustaining or challenging the status quo. Much of our knowledge of the world we gain indirectly through the media, especially about people, places, events and how to make sense of the world more generally – how to interpret the current state of the economy, why the police should or shouldn't be armed, what is happening in Central Europe and so on. At school, work, university or in the pub, last night's 'tele' makes for lively and easy conversation, a conversation in which, usually, a broad consensus forms about what went on, or what the meaning of the story was. The globalised media allow us to travel virtually without moving from our chair, and if we do travel extensively by plane, to receive our 'home' programmes on satellite TV or the Internet. Although media products are no doubt entertaining, they also help to construct and reproduce a broad range of social norms and values. One of the most detailed series of studies that has documented this is that undertaken on TV news by the Glasgow University Media Group.

A key feature of the globalisation of the media is, of course, that it requires the existence of globalised media corporations. Indeed, we can see a concentration of media ownership with major corporations

including Time Warner, News Corporation Ltd and Reuters. While these TNCs might make us more informed about the world, they also structure and package 'the world' they present to us in certain ways, and most obviously in such a way that we are likely to go out and buy something – whether merchandising attached to a programme, or other consumption goods more generally.

Box 3.3: Media empires

Time Warner, formed by a merger of Time Inc. and Warner Communications, is the world's biggest media corporation, with assets greater than many developing countries. Apart from films, books and magazines (including *Time, Fortune* and *Sports illustrated*), it has a major stake in the world's rapidly growing cable market.

News Corporation Ltd, owned by Rupert Murdoch, has the widest newspaper readership in the world, and the largest satellite TV system in Europe, opening a new market in Asia and the Pacific Rim. In the US, Murdoch acquired Fox TV and 20th Century Fox movie studios.

Reuters is a British-based news agency which has the largest stake in foreign newslines, especially covering developing countries. Many newspapers will use Reuters information rather than employing overseas correspondents. Reuters also owns part of the UK's ITN and Worldwide Television News.

Source: Based on *New Internationalist*, June 1994.

These massive firms depend on new informations systems and communications technologies (such a fibre-optic cable) to condense, pack, transmit and unpack information around the world. While the infrastructural costs of building these media technologies is very great and so only met by the most powerful firms, some believe that the growing public access to new communications technologies, such as the Internet, will empower 'ordinary' users to set their own agenda, to construct their own audiences and constituencies through the 'virtual communities' that 'the net' has spawned in recent years. It is clear that this has happened and indeed is something which the major corporations are keen to control, typically through gearing up the cost of use. More generally, attempts by developing countries to develop their own media agencies make little headway against corporations, like News Corp, that benefit from the renewal of the General Agreement on Tariffs and Trade (GATT) in 1994/5 which allows media giants to flood local markets.

cultural imperialism
The aggressive promotion of Western culture based on the assumption that its value system is superior and preferable to those of non-Western cultures.

The strength of the globalised media firms is clearly central to any arguments about **cultural imperialism**, since these firms can be seen to swamp localised media forms and messages, and so construct a set of values and meanings about what should be regarded as good, stylish, right, or wrong, just as they have long done in 'the West'. According to this view, the vitality of local cultures is undermined. One key vehicle through which this occurs is the way the global firms tend to use English as a 'world language' (see Table 3.1).

Table 3.1 World use of the English language

Official language	*Population (in billions)*
English	1.4
Chinese	1.1
Hindi	0.7
Spanish	0.28
Russian	0.27
French	0.22

In historical terms, the ubiquity of English is relatively recent: it has much to do, first, with the impact of British colonialism – on whose land 'the sun never set'. But second, and more important, has been massive, post-1945, influence of the United States: the country which possesses the largest commercial market in the world has been the single most important reason for the spread of (American) English, as well as 'burgers'. In addition, the communications technology upon which global interconnectedness so heavily relies uses English for the bulk of its data information storage and exchange. The leisure industry is similarly tied into English, especially via the English-language based music industry: Madonna is unlikely ever to have to go to language school to sell her records!

In short, Becker and similar theorists believe that this dominance of western cultural products ensures the long-term survival of capitalist world markets for TNCs, now focusing more and more attention on **post-socialist states**.

post-socialist states
The former Soviet states of central and Eastern European countries who, since the 1980s, have abandoned or adapted socialist practices and principles in favour of capitalist ones.

While the thesis of cultural imperialism highlights the power of TNCs and the ideological baggage they bring with them and impose on others, it has been criticised for failing to recognise that countries subject to TNC influence do not necessarily absorb this like some sort of cultural sponge. Sklair (1991) has argued that local cultures not only reinterpret or mediate transnational messages in ways which give them modified meaning, but can also counteract these messages with those of their own. The work of Sreberny-Mohammadi, for example, has shown how local culture mixes with and redefines 'global' culture; she shows how local culture can prevail in the face of overseas ideologies, partly because the two are kept distinct by people at the local level: 'the trans-cultural mix of symbols is apparent when one young [Egyptian] girl organises a traditional religious feast yet defiantly wearing a denim skirt and earrings' (1991).

Smith (1992), from a slightly different perspective, has challenged the very possibility of a cultural imperialism that can create a homogeneous, uniform 'global culture'. The notion of a global culture is a contradiction in terms, he suggests, since any culture must be rooted in a sense of community, history and heritage. He accepts that while the dynamics of a transnational consumerism may prevail, sustaining a world capitalist economy, the notion that it will engender a common Western-centric culture is untenable. A 'global culture' would, by definition, be universal and so lack any specific roots, would be timeless since it would have no shared history and would be merely 'technical' having no capacity for inspiring a sense of emotional commitment or loyalty to it from anyone. He, like many other sociologists, argues instead that globalisation has led people in different countries to renew their loyalties to the local, to tradition, ethnicity and nationalist culture. So, for example, the re-emergence of a (re-traditionalised) Islamic culture in the Middle East is presented as an alternative to both capitalism and **socialism** and is one which is now growing in strength in southern central Europe.

socialism

An economic theory or system in which the means of production, distribution and exchange are owned collectively, usually through the state.

These criticisms of the cultural imperialism thesis show how we must expect to see a reawakening of local culture and local politics at national and regional levels in part *as a response to* the globalising pressures we all experience in our own immediate context. As Robins (1994) has said, 'It is the escalating logic of globalisation – paradoxically it seems – that is the force behind the resurgence and revaluation of local economic and cultural activity. What seems to be emerging is the centrality of a new global–local nexus' (p. 197). This is expressed in a variety of ways: for example, Robertson (1992) has pointed out the 'strong move across the world towards indigenous, communal medicine', but, note, 'much of it encouraged by the World Health Organisation' (p. 171) a well-known transnational agency. Thus, 'in various parts of the world – Africa, Latin America, Asia and in various Islamic countries – while the drive towards the indigenisation of health care has taken the form of demands for local autonomy, there also appears to be a desire for local medicine to make a definite contribution to "world health"' (ibid).

Here we see that the globalisation of modernity must not be understood to mean a globalisation of sameness or uniformity: on the contrary, the dynamics of globalisation, especially in its cultural dimensions, creates greater pressures towards local variety while at the same time incorporating communities into an uneven and unequal world economic system. That this system is first and foremost a capitalist one seems to have been further reinforced by the collapse of socialism in the Second World of Central and Eastern Europe. It is to this question of a changing global politics that we now turn.

Globalisation and Political Change

> **“The seismic changes which have transformed Europe as a whole in the past few years cannot be understood purely in terms of development within Europe. The fact that political union is even on the European agenda reflects deep-seated global economic and political trends as well as internal factors. At the heart of these changes has been the decline of the bi-polar system dominated by the two super-powers – the United States and the former Soviet Union.”**
>
> **[PALMER, 1992, p. 143**

Palmer draws attention here to the key socio-political shifts that have occurred in the world over the past decade, especially since 1989 when the dismantling of the Berlin Wall led to a dismantling of central and Eastern European socialism and the eventual end of the Soviet Union itself. The Soviet leader, Gorbachev, had opened up a moribund socialist state to new internal debate and self-critique via *glasnost* but failed to secure a restructuring of the polity and economy via *perestroika* which could have secured a renewed Socialist future. The changes that took place were rapid and in many ways revolutionary in that fundamental social change and a removal of the existing political elites went hand in hand. Yet the models that have since been adopted by most *post-socialist* states are very close to those of western liberal democratic capitalist countries rather than providing an alternative to either/both capitalism or an over-centralised state socialism.

The most important strategic implication of these dramatic changes was the end of the Cold War and the confirmation of the United States as the sole superpower: its orchestration of the 1991 Persian Gulf War against Iraq bore witness to its dominance, or hegemony, in setting the political and military agenda for other countries to follow. The American President, George Bush, declared the arrival of a 'New World Order' of peace and prosperity for all: a few years on and the civil wars in Europe and chronic recession world-wide suggest otherwise.

Nevertheless, the geo-politics of the world have experienced momentous changes over the recent past. While the specific story of the demise of Soviet socialism is of central importance, there are broader political changes which result from the process of globalisation. Most important of all, the globalisation of capitalism, the growth of international agencies and the strengthening of new political and economic unions, such as the European Union, have posed a major challenge to the sovereignty and autonomy of all nation-states.

All nation-states hope to have control over the social, economic and political activities within their borders, though, clearly, this is not always secured. From a modernist perspective, control must, to be effective in the long term, be legitimated via some form of democratic accountability to the people. Although mature liberal democracies, such as The Netherlands, Britain, and France, remain sovereign states led by representative governments, they, as others, have found it increasingly difficult to control the movement of capital, whether finance capital (as in currency speculation) or productive capital such as factory investment. As we saw earlier, TNCs' investment strategies can often disregard the national interests of their 'mother country' and ship investment overseas to cheap labour sources. Moreover, international laws, such as those regulating pollution at sea or in the air, require national governments' observation. In these circumstances, the growing sense of loss of control by the nation-state of the economic and political direction of the country can pose severe legitimation problems for government: this can feed as many calls for reactionary nationalism to reinstate cherished values as it does demands for new democratic mechanisms through which people's voices can be heard at local and international levels (Held, 1991). Power is leaking upwards and outwards from the nation-state or larger transnational political authorities as it is leaking downwards to regional, even local and ethnic, communities. Ironically, then, the political dynamics of modernity at the global level challenge the institutional roots and structures of the nation-state which modernity helped to foster in the first place.

To summarise, we are seeing two different but related processes at work in the world today: on the one hand, the growing economic incorporation of countries within an unequal and unevenly successful capitalism; on the other, a tendency towards political break-up at local and regional levels often fuelled by nationalist rivalries. This, of course, confirms the two dynamics of the global–local nexus mentioned above. A satirical comment on how things might end up is provided by Rowson's cartoon.

Source: *Guardian*, 3 October 1992

A new world order?

The collapse of the Soviet Union and the end of the Cold War means that the world now has one superpower instead of two. But the stability many believed this would bring has been elusive. There are, for example, still massive numbers of nuclear weapons in a widening variety of hands whose strategic interests are no longer dictated by their respective Soviet or US sponsors. The boundaries separating one state from another have in some areas become sustainable, as new ethnic loyalties give rise to territorial conflicts no longer policed by the old power blocs. The United Nations, never designed for the circumstances of today, finds it difficult to decide whether it is to be peace-maker or merely peace-keeper. Chinese socialism remains politically intact even though it has experienced its own recent turmoil (after the violence of Tiananmen Square in June 1989). The end of the Cold War also has industrial, technological and strategic implications which sociologists are only beginning to explore.

(a) Industrial and technological implications

In most advanced capitalist countries, the defence sector has relied on a steady demand for the research, development and production of new weapons systems. This has been particularly true of Britain and the United States where almost half of all government expenditure on all forms of research went to the defence establishment. Over the past decade, however, the defence sector has been experiencing major structural and organisational problems, including:

- a dramatic growth in the costs of weapons systems
- a need to shift from mechanical to electronic-based technology
- a cut in state expenditure on defence
- an opening of all defence contracts to civil competition
- a collapse of the old certainties about 'the enemy' and thus the equipment needed to fight wars

In these circumstances, the defence sector finds itself on the defensive! We have seen a call for the end of massively expensive, open-ended contracts on huge overly sophisticated weaponry, such as the US Stealth Fighter and, in late 1992, the European fighter aircraft. State funding is projected to decline rapidly, so much so that a large discrete defence sector may no longer be a reality (Gummett, 1991).

structural unemployment
Chronic, long-term unemployment due to changes in the structure of the economy.

As a result of this, weapons companies are trying to secure new markets overseas, are moving into non-defence activities, and shedding substantial numbers of workers. For many in the defence industry, the new world order has meant a growth in long-term **structural unemployment**. Similar problems are found in East and Central Europe (Kaldor, 1991). In many ways, Soviet bloc countries were even more geared towards military expenditure than Nato countries: for example, until very recently, over one-third of Moscow manufacturing capacity was geared towards armament production. Re-orienting production to civilian, consumer goods associated with the nurturing of a new capitalist market-economy might be regarded as a 'victory' for modernity but at the same price we have long paid in the West: growing unemployment. As the ranks of the poor grow, so they become susceptible to the charms of the extreme right, whose racist scapegoating of other disadvantaged groups (in east Germany and ex-Yugoslavia for example) echoes the 1930s.

(b) Strategic implications

The end of the Cold War reduces the importance of centre of influence in the Third World which the two superpowers had established for strategic reasons. The powerful states today are likely to see poorer

Third World countries less as strategic assets in any geo-political chess-game and more as burdensome commitments best reduced as quickly as possible. This withdrawal of superpower support has in fact helped to quicken the end of local conflicts in some countries – especially in Africa – while allowing other countries to begin to shape their own political direction free of overseas agendas.

At the same time we are unlikely to see the United States reducing its interventionist, policing role where it sees fit to assert the broader interests of the 'West' (sometimes 'the free world'). Geo-politically, the United States (and other core countries) is concerned about the spread of nuclear weapons and (a legal and illegal) arms trade (especially since most conventional weapons have their nuclear version). But as Kaldor (1991) notes, the private arms trade with Third World countries is likely to grow as it provides employment and foreign earnings for First World states: the 'militarisation of the periphery' is set to grow.

(c) Ideological implications

The most important ideological outcome of the 1989 revolutions and the end of the Cold War is the demise of socialism as a powerful and credible alternative to capitalism. Some commentators believe European socialism is dead and buried. Even the diluted form of parliamentary social democracy that gets called 'socialism' in the British Labour Party seems 'out of time', discredited and unelectable. Communist parties in West and East have given themselves new names and distance themselves from the heavy-handed, state communism of the past.

However, we must remember that socialism emerged in response to and as a challenge to the inequalities of capitalism: since capitalism – now globalised – prevails, there is always a potential for this challenge to re-emerge, but perhaps via a different sort of language and organisation, perhaps based on ecology, gender, anti-consumerist movements, and so on. Certainly for many in the newly expanded capitalist world, life under the 'free market' has not meant any improvement in their quality of life.

Box 3.4: Hard times in Moscow

'Russia was always a country of disturbing contrasts. But these days, as economic freedom enriches the few and hyper-inflation impoverishes the many, it can seem like a madhouse . . . An enormous class of people get by without starving but they are worn down by the daily grind and have little hope for the future. They work at two or three jobs to make ends meet, return home to an evening meal of macaroni or boiled potatoes, and sit watching *Lotto Million* on television in the hope their number will win them the jackpot . . . Inflation for the whole of this year is expected to reach 2,200 per cent. Prices seem to rise every day . . . Marina regrets that *perestroika* happened. She is grateful to Mikhail Gorbachev for ending the Cold War. "When I was a child, we used to have bomb-shelter training at school, and I was scared of dying in a nuclear war." But that nightmare has been replaced by fear of crime. "I go home on the Metro late at night, then walk through dark alleys and worry that I will be attacked. It is not even safe in broad daylight now. There is no guarantee you will reach your flat alive." '

Source: The Independent on Sunday, 29 November 1992, p.17.

Possible Futures

The profound changes in the social, the economic and the political that have been associated with globalisation have been sketched out in this chapter. As we saw, transnational corporations operate an increasingly sophisticated global market that turns us into consumers of global products. As a result, traditional customs and patterns of consumption and distribution associated with them can be undermined, whether this be the traditional family farms of East Africa or the socialist commune of Russia. Other transnational agencies, such as the United Nations, the EC, or the World Bank construct broader political and economic agendas for regional or international security. The global media compress time and space into the briefcase that carries the portable satellite dish.

Those who see in these changes the inevitable progress of the march of modernity and liberal capitalism fail to see the uneven and unequal impact that globalised modernity has. Moreover, we have stressed that global dynamics generate at the same time a countervailing localisation of culture: hence the weakness of the culture imperialism thesis.

How then to chart the future? Change, whether locally, nationally or globally, reflects the different interests and capacities of individuals, groups and national and international agencies. McGrew (1992) has suggested, in the light of this analysis, five different possible futures for the world:

- 'the world transformed': a newly integrated global society and polity
- 'the primacy of continuity': a competitive conflict-ridden world will prevail

- 'the world in crisis': impending population, ecological and economic crises threaten the eventual collapse of any potential global security
- 'the bifurcated world': a world split between on the one hand, competing nation-states, and on the other hand, transnational agencies
- 'global politics in transition': dramatic global change means we have entered a period of transition to a new global context but whose character remains uncertain.

Sociological analysis of the impact of modernity, with which we began this chapter, and the changing sociological agenda that a globalised modernity requires, will need to explore what and how one or other of these futures unfolds in the twenty-first century.

For our purposes now, however, we need to delve more deeply into the core concepts of sociological analysis, key ideas which have shaped the theoretical development of the discipline over the last century and a half. It is to these that we now turn in Chapter 4.

Summary of the Chapter

- Globalisation is rooted in the dynamics of modernity, but opens up new questions for sociology to address.
- Globalisation encourages a growing integration and convergence of social and economic relations, yet, at the local level, diversity and unevenness
- Giddens's three key dimensions of modernity and his four-fold characterisation of the world system help explain the momentum behind the globalisation process.
- Modernisation theory neglects the negative effects of modernity, especially in former colonies and the contemporary Third World whose circumstances are characterised very differently by dependent theory.
- Key agents of globalisation are TNCs, cultural and media agencies which are new political institutions that go beyond the nation-state.
- The future of the world is not predictable simply because of the emergence of globalisation: there are many possible futures.

References

Becker, D. *et al.* (1987) *Post Imperialism*, Boulder, Lynne Rienner.

Frank, A. G. (1971) 'The sociology of development and the underdevelopment of sociology', in A. G. Frank, *Capitalism and Underdevelopment in Latin America*, New York, Monthly Review Press.

Froebel, F. *et al.* (1980) *The New International Division of Labour*, Cambridge, Cambridge University Press.

Fukuyama, F. (1989) 'Forget Iraq – history is dead', *The Guardian*, September 7, p. 15.

Giddens, A. (1990) *The Consequences of Modernity*, Cambridge, Polity Press.

Gummett, P. (1991) *Future Relations Between Defence and Civil Science and Technology*, (SPSG Review Paper No. 2), London, SPSG.

Harvey, D. (1990) *The Condition of Postmodernity*, Oxford, Blackwell.

Held, D. (1991) 'Democracy, the nation-state and the global system', in D. Held (ed.), *Political Theory Today*, Cambridge, Polity Press.

Kaldor, M. (1991) *Europe From Below*, London, Verso.

McGrew, A. (1992) 'A global society?', in S. Hall *et al.* (eds), *Modernity and its Futures*, Cambridge, Polity Press.

Palmer, S. (1992) *Beyond the Cold War*, Cambridge, Cambridge University Press.

Parsons, T. (1967) *Sociological Theory and Modern Society*, New York, Free Press.

Robertson, R. (1992) *Globalisation, Social Theory and Global Culture*, London, Sage.

Robins, K. (1994) 'Global local times', in J. Anderson and M. Ricci, (eds) *Society and Social Science: A Reader*, Milton Keynes, Open University Press.

Sanderson, S. (1985) *The Americas in the New International Division of Labour*, New York, Holmes & Meier.

Sklair, L. (1991) *The Sociology of the Global System*, Brighton, Harvester Wheatsheaf.

Smelser, N. (1969) 'Mechanisms of and adjustment to change', in T. Burns (ed.), *Industrial Man*, Harmondsworth, Penguin.

Smith, A. D. (1992) 'European unity', *International Affairs*, vol. 68, no. 1, pp. 55–76.

Sreberny-Mohammadi, A. (1991) 'The global and the local in international communications', in J. Curran and M. Gurevitch (eds), *Mass Media and Society*, London, Edward Arnold.

Tunstall, J. (1977) *The Media are American*, New York, Columbia University Press.

4 Varieties of Social Theories: A Brief Introduction

Aims of the Chapter

This chapter explores the ideas of the classic sociological theorists of the nineteenth and early twentieth centuries – Emile Durkheim, Karl Marx and Max Weber – and then examines twentieth-century developments in sociological theorising. The aim is to provide a brief history of sociological thought and to introduce the reader to the core concepts of the discipline which will be encountered in the other chapters in the book.

Box 4.1: The Enlightenment and social theorising

Summarising the effects of the Enlightenment, Badham (1986) says:

'It was during this period that faith in divine revelation, and the authority of the Church as interpreter of God's will, were increasingly undermined by this new confidence in the ability of human reason to provide an understanding of the world and a guide for human conduct. Similarly, the understanding of history as the chronicle of the fall of man from God's grace, with spiritual salvation only attainable in the next world, was largely replaced by a belief in human perfectibility and the increasing faith in man's power and ability to use his new-found knowledge to improve mankind's state. The importance of these two assumptions should not be underestimated. Without the faith in reason, social theory could not be regarded as playing any important role in society. Without the belief in the possibility of progress, whatever reason's ability to understand the nature of society, social theory would not be able to fulfil any positive role in improving upon man's fate.'

Source: Badham, *Theories of Industrial Society*, 1986.

Introduction

The three great early sociological theorists were Frenchman *Emile Durkheim* (1858–1917) and two Germans, *Karl Marx* (1818–1883) and *Max Weber* (1864–1920). Though the last part of the book examines their work in detail, a brief look at their ideas here allows us to see fundamental differences between them, not just about the defining features of modern societies but about what the central concerns of sociology should be and how its investigations should be conducted. In their work, the contrast between an interest in social *structure* as opposed to an interest in social *action* or *agency* is apparent. The debate between the sociologies of structure and action was to become the principal feature of sociological theorising for much of the twentieth century.

Their work also draws attention to another, related, debate which was to become cacophonous in the twentieth century – between those who believe in the possibility and desirability of using *science* and its methods to explain social behaviour and those who insist on its *in*appropriateness for producing sociological knowledge.

Nineteenth- and early twentieth-century sociological theorising

Emile Durkheim

At the heart of Durkheim's work is a belief in the importance of creating well-organised, ordered and harmonious societies in order for individuals to flourish and live out their lives productively and contentedly together. He conceives of the individual subject as above all in need of control and regulation; without some means of constraining and *structuring* the individual's ideas and desires, personal misery and social disorder are all too probable.

According to Durkheim ... order flows from consensus – from the existence of shared norms and values. For him, the key causes of social and individual ill-health stem from *anomie* – a lack of regulating norms. Anomie is the result of *the* potential scourge of modern competitive society – the promotion of unrestricted desires; without norms constraining behaviour, 'humans develop insatiable appetites, limitless desires and general feelings of irritation and dissatisfaction'. Durkheim (1974) went on to say that a strong, ordered society and individual liberation are only guaranteed where beliefs and behaviour are properly regulated by socialisation:

'The individual submits to society and this submission is the condition of his liberation. For man freedom consists in the deliverance from blind, unthinking physical forces; this he achieves by opposing against them the great and intelligent force which is society.'

[Jones, 1993, p.27] ”

socialisation
An on-going process whereby individuals learn to conform to society's prevailing norms and values (*see* norms *and* values).

Both order and harmony *and* individual fulfilment then, are dependent upon proper **socialisation**. We must learn how to behave appropriately in different circumstances – we must acquire properly a knowledge of the collective culture which binds us together, like a kind of social cement, as members of the same society. The beauty of efficient socialisation is that though we *think* we are acting independently and autonomously, as active agents writing our own life-stories, in fact our journeys through life are biographically structured, by norms and values which existed before us and which will continue to exist after we have left the stage.

> **When I fulfil my obligations as brother, husband or citizen, I perform duties which are defined, externally to myself and my acts, in law and custom. Even if they conform to my own sentiments, and I feel their reality subjectively, such reality is still objective, for I did not create them; I merely inherited them through my education ... the church member finds the beliefs and practices of his religious life ready made at birth; their existence prior to him implies this existence outside himself.**
>
> [DURKHEIM, 1938, pp.1–2]

objective
Factual.

structural
Pertaining to the organisation and form of society or institutions.

Durkheim is emphasising the **objective** character of norms and values – their existence outside of and independent of us as individual subjects. This is a fine example of a **structural** sociology – a sociology which emphasises how our lives are structured by social forces outside our control. Other sciences take an interest in different sorts of structural forces. Geography and geology, for example, try to explain how the physical world has come to be as it is and how we have to take account of these natural facts when we live our lives. We have to structure our lives around the facts that nights are dark, that wood is inflammable, that snow and ice can be treacherous and so on. Biology and zoology tell us about other facts – of human and animal existence – that we are stuck with and can do nothing about and which we have to take account of. For instance, human lives are crucially structured around biological processes which force us to eat, to sleep, to defecate, to keep warm or cool and so on, in order to remain healthy.

Durkheim insists that we treat the social – collective – rules and prescriptions which govern our lives as facts of just the same kind. 'Treat social facts as things' he demands. Though we cannot see social structures of norms and values in the same way as we can see the physical or biological facts which structure our lives, they are just as real and as objective a set of conditions of our existence; we can do as little about their influence on our lives as we can those features explained by other sciences.

However, Durkheim then goes further, arguing that a human society is not just made up of social facts, but that it works, as *a social system*, just like a biological system of biological facts does: this theory is called **functionalism**.

functionalism
A theoretical perspective, associated with Durkheim and Parsons, based on an analogy between social systems and organic systems. It claims that the character of a society's various institutions must be understood in terms of the function each performs in enabling the smooth running of society as a whole.

Since this is so, we should use exactly the same scientific techniques to explain these facts as other sciences do to explain the facts in which they are interested. For Durkheim, this means that sociology should embrace **positivism**.

positivism
A doctrine which claims that social life should be understood and analysed in the same way that scientists study the 'natural world'. Underpinning this philosophy is the notion that phenomena exist in causal relationships and these can be empirically observed, tested and measured.

Durkheim and functionalism

The health of an organisation depends on all the organs that make up the system working properly together, each organ performing a necessary *function* for the organism's health. In the human body, for instance, the heart is needed to pump the blood around the body, the liver is needed to purify the blood, etc. Furthermore, the performance of each organ depends upon the others performing *their* functions properly. The performance of the brain depends upon the efficient functioning of the lungs which depends upon the performance of the heart and so on. An organic system, that is, is an *integrated* system of interdependent functioning parts.

Durkheim draws an explicit analogy between an organic system and a social system. Ways of living or thinking which are firmly established in a culture are referred to in sociology as *institutionalised* behaviour and belief. Functionalism explains the existence of any institutionalised aspect of a society in the same way as a biologist explains the presence of an organ in the body – in terms of the function it performs in keeping the system in a stable state. Thus, the *integration*, *solidarity* or *equilibrium* of a society, typical functionalist terms, is equivalent to the health of an organism and is maintained by its institutions – such as its form of family, its political arrangements, its educational system – each performing their functions properly and interdependently.

This conception of a social system ties in precisely with Durkheim's emphasis on the externality of social facts. Just as humans do not *decide* to have a liver, or kidneys, or a spleen or whatever, so the existence of institutions in a social system is explained in terms of the function they each perform in maintaining the whole. In fact, functionalist sociology is above all characterised by a lack of interest in explanations given by *actors* for their ways of living and thinking. Whatever members of a society may think about its cultural features – their *manifest* functions, functionalists call these – the important reasons are those only identifiable by the perceptive functionalist observer, who is able to recognise their *latent* functions. Nothing could be further from the world of action sociology, for which, as we shall shortly see, *the* subject-matter of the discipline must be precisely these actors' theories that functionalists ignore as irrelevant.

Durkheim and positivism

As we said earlier, the Enlightenment is the name given to that period of time during the rise of modernity when thinkers began to stop relying on religion to provide them with knowledge of the world and to start to use *reason*, to think *rationally*, instead. Many writers on the history of knowledge (e.g. see the account of Gellner's views in Chapter 16) identify the Enlightenment-sponsored emergence of rationalism, the trigger that enabled *science* to explode on to the scene, as the defining moment in human intellectual history, the time when a *Great Divide* opened up between premodern thought, typified by faith in religious doctrines, and modern thinking. For many, it is the rise of rationalism, and thereby scientific knowledge, that was the real motor behind modernity, the springboard from which many of its key factors – notably the Industrial Revolution and the rise of Capitalism – were launched.

Durkheim's enthusiasm for a scientific sociology has to be understood in this context. If nature could be explained rationally by using scientific methods, then surely society could be too? We have to realise that Durkheim's account of the similarity in character between natural facts and social facts derives directly from his desire that his budding discipline blossom into a mature science to equal the other sciences. Unless he defined social life as similar in kind (*ontologically* similar) then this project would have been doomed.

Positivism is the name given to the set of ideas about reality which underpins most scientific work; Durkheim's definition of sociology's subject-matter as being social structures of social facts stems directly from his determination that sociology be positivist. What is positivism?

As a philosophy, positivism has three distinct features:

- Reality is made up of cause-and-effect relationships: things are as they are because they have been *caused* by other things.
- These are *facts* – *objective* features – which, whatever our *subjective* feelings about them, are things we are stuck with and can do nothing about. Whether we like or dislike a factual state of affairs is irrelevant; our judgements about reality must be ignored when revealing its factual character.
- We can only *prove* the existence of cause-and-effect relationships by demonstrating their existence *empirically*, by collecting evidence identifiable by the senses of others.

Thus, scientists assume that to explain a medical condition like cirrhosis of the liver, something equally natural must be causing it. The knowledge that alcohol is a major contributory factor was discovered by testing various hunches (*hypotheses*) about the causes of the disease empirically, by *experiment*, to *observe* and *measure* the extent to which liver tissue is damaged by alcohol. This factual state of affairs is something none of us can change, however much we'd like to; however much we love pouring pints of lager or bottles of red wine down our throats and wish this did not jeopardise our livers, the *facts* are that it does.

How does Durkheim make this philosophy suit the character and investigation of social life? Just as frogs do not *choose* to have bulging eyes and croak a lot, just as people don't *choose* to have bladders that need periodic evacuation, so modern humans don't *choose* to live in nuclear families or go out to work for a wage. They *think* they do of course, but the reality is that they do so because of the social facts of their world which constrain and structure their lives – they *learn* to live as they do. Sociology's job is to collect empirical evidence of the extent to which normative structural forces determine social lives; as the next chapter demonstrates, this involves *measuring* the degree to which membership of different social groups produces patterns of behaviour and belief. Thus, Durkheim is able to claim:

> **The laws of societies are no different from those governing the rest of nature and the method by which they are discovered is identical with that of the other sciences.**
>
> [DURKHEIM, 1938]

Durkheim's own study of *suicide* is generally regarded as the pioneering piece of positivist sociology. However, as we shall see shortly in our discussions of the action theories of Weber, interactionism and ethnomethodology, once the subject-matter of sociology is defined differently, as human consciousness, interpretation and creative, purposive action, the possibility and desirability of a positivist sociology is wholly rejected.

Karl Marx

At first glance Marxism is like Functionalism, a straightforward structural approach to social life, with the facts of class membership structuring the lives of individuals. For Marxists, in all societies other than Communist ones the crucial fact is that the production of goods is structured in such a way as to produce great benefits for a minority – a *dominant* class – at the expense of an *exploited* majority – a *subordinate* class. Modern capitalist society differs from historical non-Communist productive systems not in the fact that it produces its goods by one class exploiting another but simply because the classes involved have changed. In Ancient times, masters exploited the labour-power of the slaves they owned; in Feudal times, landlords were able to exploit the productive labour of serfs because they owned the land on which the serfs scratched out a living; in capitalism, a working-class – called the **proletariat** by Marx – produce goods for the benefit of a dominant class of owners of capital – a **bourgeoisie**. This capitalist class exploits the labour of its employees by paying them wages of a lesser value than the market value of the goods they produce. This is not because of any gratuitous desire to be evil on the part of wicked capitalists, however; as a productive system, capitalism can only work if wage-earners earn less than the value of the goods they produce, for without the *profit* generated by this relationship, enabling further investment, the system simply could not function.

proletariat
A Marxist term for wage-earners, the propertyless class within capitalism.

bourgeoisie
A Marxist term used to describe the property-owning capitalist class.

Marxism is not simply a theory of systems of production, though – it is also a theory of systems of ideas. Because class-based production involves an exploitation which generates gross inequality between the classes, the system is inherently fragile. Capitalism, for example, can only survive so long as the wage-earners who are disadvantaged by it put up with this. According to Marxists, of as much interest as the **base** or **infrastructure** of a class society – the exploitative way it produces its goods – is its **superstructure** – its non-economic institutions and systems of belief.

base/infrastructure
A Marxist term for the economy (*see* economic base *and* superstructure).

superstructure
A Marxist term, which refers to social forms other than the economy, e.g. politics and culture, that are determined by the economic base (*see* economic base).

As the terms suggest, Marxists see non-economic life in a class society as nonetheless intimately bound up with the system of production: the latter is the base upon which the former is built. Thus, as we shall see in later chapters, typical Marxist accounts of modern family life, education, the mass media and so on all seek to demonstrate the benefits for the capitalist **mode of production** of these ways of living, even though at first glance they may have little connection with the economy. The same is true of ways of thinking. Thus, Marxists are not only interested in identifying features of the social structure which have direct pay-offs for capitalist commodity production but also in the kinds of methods used to encourage people to live in this economically beneficial way. The most important of these methods in modern societies is socialisation. A crucial part of the superstructural support for capitalism is that people in such societies are encouraged to hold *ideas* which prop up the system: such ideas are called **ideologies** by Marxists.

mode of production
A Marxist concept which refers to the structured relationship between the means of production (raw materials, land, labour and tools) and the relations of production (the ways humans are involved in production).

ideology
A perception of reality or way of thinking. Its usage is associated with Marx, where the term implies a mistaken sense of reality or false consciousness.

So far so structural. Like functionalists, Marxists seem to focus exclusively on social forces external to the individual subject – class membership, ideological indoctrination – in order to explain social behaviour. It is the theory of the system that matters: the ideas about their world held by actors are almost certainly likely to be wrong, because of the powerful ideologies. Thus, a rejection of Marxist analysis by the working class – the very people the theory is designed to liberate – can be, and usually is, simply put down by Marxists to ignorance and mystification wrought by dominant beliefs: Marxists call this condition **false consciousness**.

false consciousness
Ways of thinking about the world or apprehending reality that are defective and which obscure the truth. Associated, though not exclusively, with Marx.

But, unlike Functionalism, as a theory of *social change*, Marxism depends upon agency – creative action – being introduced into the equation. Whereas functionalists normally explain social change, as with change in species and organisms, as the evolutionary adaptation of the system to new conditions (or something similar), most Marxists see change as subject-inspired – as the product of meaningful intent by knowledgeable agents. Their position is a sort of halfway house between implacable structuralism and action theorising. Capitalism has within it the seeds of its own destruction. The more it evolves as a system – the more capitalists (as they must) seek ever-more efficient ways of remaining profitable and avoid going bust – the more they are creating the conditions under which their workers will start to see the truth about their lives.

Contradictions within capitalism

Capitalist production depends upon capital accumulation. Capitalists accumulate capital by increasing the return from the sale of their goods while at the same time lowering the cost of their production. One major way of lowering costs is to cut labour by constantly mechanising – decreasing the labour force. This has two effects. First, smaller capitalists, lacking the capital to invest in new machinery, are unable to compete successfully. They go to the wall, and join the proletariat class. Second, unemployment increases among the proletariat. Since wage-earners are also consumers, an increase in the impoverishment of some of them reduces demand for goods. Faced with this loss in demand capitalists have to cut costs still further in order to retain profit levels and remain solvent. This is done by either decreasing their labour forces still further or by reducing wage levels. This can be done in two ways. Wages can be *actually* reduced. (The 1926 General Strike took place when miners' wages were reduced.) More topically, they can be 'increased' at a slower rate than the rate of inflation. As a result of either of these methods, demand decreases still further and this further affects supply.

As this process continues, the gap in reward between the contracting bourgeoisie and the ever-growing proletariat increases. As the proletariat become increasingly impoverished in this way, the

conditions emerge for the development of a fully-fledged class consciousness among them. The proletariat is thus transformed from merely an *objective class* – a class in fact – to being a subjective class – a class in their thoughts – as well. It changes from being just a class *in* itself to being a class *for* itself.
When this class consciousness reaches its fullest extent, the proletariat rise up and overthrow capitalism, taking over the means of production and the state apparatus as the capitalists did before them. ”

[Jones, 1993, pp. 55–6)

For Marxists this is one of the internal contradictions of capitalism. The process of its development as a system locked into the ceaseless pursuit of profit *at one and the same time* produces so much cumulative disadvantage for those wage-earners whose preparedness to accept their lot (whether through impotence, passive acquiescence or normative commitment to ideologies) is crucial to its survival, that the system is placed in terminal jeopardy. Faced with the stark facts of their world which no ideology can any longer obscure, the exploited class abandon their previously internalised false ideas and start to become conscious of themselves as a class. Armed with this new insight, they take action to overturn the system which they now see has always oppressed them.

class consciousness
Though originally a Marxist term used to describe a situation when the proletariat becomes aware of its subjugated position in relation to the bourgeoisie, it now encompasses a broader definition which includes any collective sense of identity among members of a social class.

The replacement of false consciousness by **class consciousness** then can *only* come about because of changes taking place within the system, at a structural level; but, once this happens, political action to overthrow the system is *creative* action. As Marx and Engels put it (1976): 'Men make their own history, but not under circumstances of their own choosing.'

For those of us living in the last years of the twentieth century, Marx's crystal ball-gazing doesn't seem too hot. We have seen some dramatic changes in recent years which have starkly contradicted Marx's predictions – the collapse of Communism, a rampant capitalism surging through much of the former Soviet bloc and the re-emergence of a cruel nationalism as a political force and a source of identity in Eastern Europe. As a sociological perspective, however, Marxist analysis might still be judged to provide us with the best conceptual tools with which to make sense of our times. The questions are:

- Is a focus on the *production of goods* the best way to analyse society?
- Is it the *capitalist* character of modern societies that is their defining feature?
- Is *class* membership the most important fact of our lives?
- Are ideas inextricably bound up with *economic* forces and processes?

It is against such views that Marx's nineteenth-century contemporary, Max Weber, offered an alternative account of modern society and of the task of sociological analysis.

Max Weber

According to Weber, individuals are creative actors, agents whose actions determine both the structure of society and the road down which history travels. Existing structural circumstances are constraints within which actors have to choose how to act, but it is their *perception* of these constraints that matters. It is the unique ability of human beings to interpret the world around them and to choose to act in the light of these theories that sociology has to concern itself with. Rather than being blown this way and that by structural forces outside our control, we have the capacity to chart our own progress through the waters of life. Because consciousness is the key feature of human life, sociology should not be in the business of constructing expert theories of social systems but of understanding the theories of actors themselves.

verstehen

A German term usually translated as 'understanding'. Employed by Weber to define his approach to the study of social life, namely the interpretative understanding of human agents and the meaning they themselves attach to their actions.

The method by which this is done – called **verstehen** by Weber – exploits the humanity and socialness of the sociologist. Because we are social actors too we can put ourselves in the place of those we seek to understand and come to appreciate the reasons for their actions. This is what makes sociology different from the other sciences: since leaves do not *decide* to be green, since stars do not *decide* to shine, and since teeth do not *decide* to ache, scientists interested in such facts do not have to *be* leaves or stars or teeth to do so. Sociologists do have to be like *their* subject-matter, however, for human actions are based on choice. It is for this reason that theorists of social action or agency, interested in subjects' theories and interpretations, reject the Durkheimian kind of claim that sociology should be a positivistic science like the natural sciences.

As we shall see shortly, the standard-bearers of the action tradition in twentieth-century sociology – symbolic interactionism and ethnomethodology – have typically focused on small-scale interaction in order to tease out the interpretive methods used by subjects to fashion their own identities and to establish order in the specific social occasions in which they are involved. Weber, however, like his late-nineteenth-century peers, was too preoccupied with the nature of modernity to eschew an interest in the broad sweep of history and social change and in the general character of modern society. But his focus is on *action* in modernity: the question for him is not 'how do modern social *systems* work?' but 'what are the kinds of *action* which typify modern social life?'

He classifies social action into four different types, each distinguished by particular motivations, or goals, of actors: different societies at different times in history are characterised by different forms of action.

- *Traditional* action occurs when actors choose to do things because they've always done so;
- *Affective* action occurs when actors cannot help but do something or other for emotional reasons;
- *Value-oriented* action occurs when one principle or purpose overrides all others;
- *Rational* action occurs when actors weigh up, or *calculate*, the most *efficient* ways of achieving specific ends – when they say 'I'll do this because I want that', 'I'll do *this* because I want *that*' but 'I'll do *this* because I reckon it's the most efficient way of getting *that*'.

According to Weber, modernity is about the triumph of rationality over all other forms of action. (This explanation for the rise of capitalism focuses on the nurturing role of Protestantism in fostering rational behaviour. See Chapters 16 and 17.) It is only in modern capitalist society that we see a world in which efficiency by calculation becomes the overriding motive – more important than tradition, or emotion, or principle. Capitalism, for example, above all involves the relentless pursuit of efficiency so as to increase profitability. 'Running things in a business-like fashion' – a modern capitalist notion – implies the subordination of goals thought more important in other times and places in favour of efficiency. No room for sentiment, or principle, or tradition here. Indeed, science itself is harnessed to such a project, used to construct mechanisms – such as new technologies of production – designed to 'eradicate waste' and promote efficiency – whatever the human and social costs. *Bureaucratisation* is the exemplar of rationalisation: 'not my job, mate'; 'you'll have to go to another department'; and 'sorry, more than my job's worth'. The *marketisation* of what used to be the principled provision of public services in Britain in the 1980s and 1990s is another; a world in which schoolkids or students or patients are 'consumers' – 'units' to be 'throughputted' the 'production process' and in which accountants rule the roost. Management 'theory' determines action, with 'down-sizing', 're-structuring' and so on being the buzz-words.

It is the hegemony of this sort of 'value-orientation' that Weber feared when he wrote so pessimistically about the modern world being created around him. He despaired of a world in which humans become locked in 'an iron cage of bureaucracy'; for him this is a world of spiritual barrenness – a world lacking mystery and imagination and awe, in which 'enchantment' is lost; a world with its inhabitants condemned to the 'polar night of icy darkness' created by the never-ending and ruthless rational pursuit of efficiency.

Unlike Durkheim and Marx, then, Weber does not see the sociological diagnosis of the ills of modernity leading to a prescription for their cure. For Durkheim, anomie is prevented or eradicated by the application of sturdy regulation through socialisation – by a society's commitment to maintaining a strong collective culture properly passed on through time to its members. (You might think this sounds much like the rhetoric of contemporary political leaders one hundred years later.) For Marx, a Utopia in which the diseases of class exploitation and alienation are wiped out beckons, so long as the correct medication – Marxist theory – is prescribed and taken. For Weber, however, there is no cure for the plague of modern social life – rampant rationalisation:

Weber tells us that the rise of this form of society means it is now wholly illusory to build the sort of Utopia which the birth of modernity promised for so many thinkers ... For Weber, the triumph of capitalism as a form of life signals the end of the line for progress; the train bearing the hopes for humanity's spiritual welfare has run into the buffers of terminal rationality.

[Jones, 1993, p. 73]

Twentieth-Century Sociological Thinking

As we said earlier, two of the debates apparent in the work of these three classic nineteenth-century sociologists have reverberated through the discipline for much of the twentieth century: structure versus action at the level of theory; positivism versus anti-positivism at the level of method. The next chapter, among other things, explores more of the detail of the debate concerning the possibility and desirability of a science of society; in this section, we will concentrate on twentieth-century developments in the action critique of structural theory.

Talcott Parsons and American Functionalism

Once sociology took root in the twentieth century and grew into a formidable discipline, a theoretical orthodoxy held sway. Though adapting some ideas from Weber too, the American Talcott Parsons developed Durkheimian ideas into a grand theory of the social system which became so powerful that it consigned its Marxist and action critics, in the West at least, to small outposts of impotent resistance. From the

1920s to the 1950s, 'standard American sociology' (Cheal, 1991), featuring functionalism and positivism, dominated the subject. In Britain during this time, sociology lacked any real theoretical focus, with its few practitioners concentrating mainly on collecting survey-based empirical material on aspects of British life; the principal British social science during the years of the reign of Parsons – the study of tribal societies by social anthropology – used conceptual tools which were also heavily functionalist. The action flag fluttered only in a few American universities, notably Chicago, where an action school of thought called *Symbolic Interactionism* became established.

By the 1950s and early 1960s, however, the dominance of Parsonsian functionalism came under increasing attack. Marxists, incensed by the functionalist emphasis on the benefits of consensus, harmony and integration, insisted that only by focusing on capitalism and its inherent inequalities could sociology be relevant for the times: in a world riven by class conflict and relations of power and subordination, they argued, the one-eyed functionalist preoccupation with the benefits for the social system of properly socialised individuals culpably ignored the massive *dis*benefits experienced by most of these individuals enduring life under capitalist systems.

At this time too, *Feminist* theorising began to take off. Aimed principally at exposing the inadequacies of existing 'malestream' theories for explaining the peculiar disadvantages experienced by a previously ignored constituency of half the world's population, this was at that time a focus on the structural sources of **patriarchy** (the dominance of men over women) and the relationship between capitalism and women's oppression.

patriarchy
Traditionally means 'rule of the father' and used to describe a type of household organisation in which the older man dominates the whole household. It is now more generally used to describe the dominance of men over women.

Action theorists attacked the structural-functionalist view of individuals as passive, robotic recipients of socially prescribed guidelines, demanding that sociology take up Weber's standard and properly explore the true relationship between social collectivities and the creative agents who both make them up and make them what they are. Contemporary theorists – notably Anthony Giddens and his theory of **structuration** now usually see the action camp's response to structural sociology in the 1960s and 1970s as just as one-eyed an approach as they accused their opponents' of being. However, some sort of synthesis of structural and action approaches, which to us today seems the obvious way forward, only really became possible because of the vehemence of the action attack and the stark division in sociological theorising it brought about. Sometimes, even in intellectual life, it is only all-out war, and its consequences, that bring home properly to the protagonists the need for reconciliation.

structuration theory
The emergence and transformation of structural patterning in social life. For Giddens, the theory that links structure and agency as simultaneous dimensions of social life (*see* structure *and* agency).

Symbolic Interactionism

The focus of SI is, as its name suggests, on the way human interaction works by the use of symbols of meaning. Far from social order being imposed on individuals by socialisation into an external collective culture, SI argues that things work the other way round: social order is *negotiated* by actors together, *inter-subjectively* working out what we call culture in innumerable social occasions of interaction. Inspired by the early twentieth-century work of interactionists such as George Herbert Mead, Charles Cooley and Herbert Blumer, American interactionists such as Howard Becker and, most notably, *Erving Goffman,* used ethnographic research techniques – particularly **participant observation** (see Chapter 5) – to detail the strategies and rituals typically involved in individual social encounters.

participant observation

A research method based on observation of a group where the researcher takes part in the group or community being studied.

Though rather a simplification, we can summarise the bare bones of the interests of interactionists like Goffman as follows:

- Uniquely among living things, humans are interpretive beings, able to attach meaning to the world around them and choose how to act in the light of these interpretations.
- Humans are also social beings, and whether we like it or not, most of what we choose to do takes place in the company of other, also meaning-attributing, human beings.
- Inevitably, then, being human involves attaching meaning to each other's actions: anything we parade in public (social) interaction can be interpreted as saying something about us.
- Language is the most important source of symbolic meaning in human social life, though other symbols – like dress, demeanour, expression, even smell – are important too. Social encounters, whatever their ostensible purpose, necessarily involve the analysis, using Verstehen, by others of what we are 'like'; anything we disclose in social occasions can, and usually will, be used by others to confer identities on us.
- Since this is so, we soon learn to attempt to sculpture, or manipulate, others' interpretations of us. We learn to become actors on the stage of life, but we write our own lines, using whatever props we can find in a metaphorical wardrobe-mistress's cupboard to assist us.

Goffman uses this explicit theatrical metaphor to illuminate the detail of local, small-scale encounters – to identify the usual and the unusual in the everyday rituals involved in being social. He calls our attempts to organise others' interpretations of us *impression management* and the *presentation of the self,* while the whole process he characterises as *dramaturgy*. Essentially he is describing '*everyday life*' or the '*social world*' (favourite SI terms) as places where countless little dramas take place – some serious, some not – in which the humans involved are, quite literally, actors.

For SI, then, our identity, our sense of *self*, depends a great deal upon the management and outcome of the innumerable social encounters in which we are implicated during our lives. We come to think of ourselves in the ways we do because we have this self-image confirmed or altered by those who comprise our audience. Clearly, some members of this audience occupy their seats in the stalls night after night – our parents, siblings, partners, peers, teachers, friends and so on – while, at the other extreme, others witness only one of our performances. That is, some of our audience are *'significant others'* in our lives, while other 'others' are hardly significant at all. Clearly, too, *general* cultural expectations, of the kinds concentrated on by functionalists, operate as constraints which we have to take account of when we walk on stage – a sort of *'generalised other'* setting limits to our creativity. But this is no story of biographical forces outside our control: this is the triumph of autobiography – creative actors writing their own life-stories – with the only real limits set by the desire to hear the applause of an appreciative audience.

Ethnomethodology

Whereas SI focuses on the *importance* of Verstehen – both in everyday life and in social research trying to understand the dynamics of this life – EM attempts to show how Verstehen *works*. Arguing that since human understanding of any aspect of reality can never be *objectively* correct, but only correct for the individual subject doing the interpreting, EM claims that this must be true for *sociological* accounts too. All knowledge of the world is bound to be *subject-centred* – *relative* to the subjects involved – whether they be sociologists or not. So, 'expert' sociological accounts of how things 'really' are are not achievable by humans, hamstrung as they are by their incapacity to see anything except from their personal, Verstehen-generated, point of view. The accounts of other sociologies, SI included, are thus dismissed as subjectivity masquerading as objectivity and EM argues instead that the discipline should concentrate on the one thing it *can* be objective about – *how* humans, sociologists or not, *use* Verstehen. For EM, then, Verstehen becomes the *topic*: it is not the painting the artist paints that can be objectively understood, only how the materials and brushes are used to compose it.

Imagine an empty classroom. All that fills it are desks, chairs, some tables maybe, a blackboard and so on. Now picture this room filled with students and a teacher. How is order possible on such an occasion? In principle, *anything* could happen during the 50 minutes or so the class exists as a social event. But, almost always, the lesson is an ordered occasion. Why? How? Structural explanations would point to role-playing, norms, constraint, sanctions and so on. But EM argues a different case. If structural forces were the real explanation, most occurrences in the lesson would be predictable and repeated week after week. But, as we all know from our own experiences in education, this never happens. Each class is a unique event. Once the *'members'* (the EM term for actors) of the occasion gather, the room is filled with communication and interpretation – language, laughter, gestures, actions, looks, signals and so on – the content of which will never reoccur, or make sense if it did, on any other occasion, anywhere else, ever again! In effect, what is said or done can only make sense on the occasion, and at the time, when it made sense to say or do it. Action then, is *contingent* or *context-bound*, the EM term for which is that it is *indexical*. The next time the class gathers, the only thing that will be repeated will be its physical presence: everything social will be constructed anew. Thus, EM stresses that, above all, each separate social occasion requires non-stop *work* on the part of its members to make it work – even though these members will not realise they're working at all!

Furthermore, if each member of the class was asked, at the conclusion of one of the lessons, to describe 'what happened in there', how similar would the various accounts be? This is what makes EM suspicious of claims to objective authenticity by sociological accounts, even SI ones also exclusively interested in action. How *can* anyone know how others see the world? How can *one* account be judged superior to others? The only thing we can be *sure* of, says EM, is how members arrive at their personal, subjective views, since all humans must make use of the same method – Verstehen – to do so. Aside from that, all human accounts are of equal validity – or invalidity: they are inevitably *relativist* – in this case relative to the subjects involved. In sum, the content of the communication and interpretation in an occasion is indexical and any understanding of it is subject-centred.

Clearly this is a far cry from the project of modernity – the construction of rational, verifiable and objective accounts of social life so that this proven knowledge can be harnessed to achieve progress for the human condition. Chapter 16 examines the debate between rationality and relativism in more detail; for now we will conclude this chapter by looking at a relatively recent theoretical appearance on the sociology scene, for whom also *relative* knowledge is the only possible form available to human beings.

Language and Social Life: Post-Structuralism

The influential figures in this tradition are French – for example Roland Barthes, a semiologist, the literary analyst and critic Jacques Derrida and, most significantly for sociology, the historian and philosopher *Michel Foucault*. The influence of such writers is not confined peculiarly to one academic discipline, but straddles all those disciplines – like philosophy, English, history and sociology – that deal with the role of *language* in human life.

The conventional view of language is that it is a means of communicating ideas – the most sophisticated resource humans use to express themselves to each other in symbolic form. For example, the sounds we utter and the words we write are *symbolic representations of meaning* which can be understood by others who speak and read the language concerned. For action sociology, the existence of language is the main reason for the triumph of the subject and for the possibility of meaningful social interaction – it is the key means by which we can communicate to others what we wish them to know.

Post-structuralism turns this notion of the relationship between language and knowledge on its head, arguing that far from language symbolising original *creative* thought, it actually *dictates* the thoughts we have; languages do not *represent* our meanings so much as *construct* them for us.

To understand this approach, two of its principal features need to be appreciated.

- 'Experience' and 'knowledge' are different things. Though we all *experience* the world through our senses we don't *know* what these experiences *mean* until we learn a language. Though we *feel* pain, elation, sorrow, tiredness, etc. as soon as our senses begin to work, we don't know what to *call* these experiences until we possess a language to give us their meanings. That is, languages dictate, demand or *solicit* certain meanings and interpretations from us; words and sounds *create* our ideas about reality.
- Languages – systems of meanings which construct our thoughts – are not just systems like English, Spanish, Italian or whatever. The term applies to any system of meanings which provokes particular understandings when we encounter and use them. It therefore applies to scientific representations, such as mathematical or chemical symbols, painting, sculpture – even architecture. A good way to appreciate this is to recognise that the written word is actually a picture – a line drawing. Thus, to use print to draw this picture – 'sad' – and to use it to draw this picture – ☹ – involves the

pictorial production of symbols designed to provoke similar meanings for those who see them.

Post-structuralists use the term 'text' to refer to any use of symbols which organises meanings; texts construct and direct our knowledge of our world. Without a physical manifestation to tell us, we can't know what our experiences mean; however, once we use a text, it ends up controlling what we think. We all know this is true about art – music, literature, paintings, sculpture, video, film and so on; we approach 'works of art' expecting to have our thoughts pushed in one direction or another. However, post-structuralists argue that it is the *text* that directs these thoughts – not the author who employs it to convey his or her meanings. Post-structuralists claim their insights have resulted in the 'death of the author': noone who uses language to construct a text has any control over the meaning each of us reads into the symbols. In effect we are *all* authors of texts when we encounter them – yet we are not the creators of our authorship since we cannot think *anything* we like. The language used instructs us, 'telling' us what to think – *soliciting* from us certain responses rather than others, even though these may not be the responses intended by the authors of the text themselves.

Furthermore, since who we 'are' – our *identities* – can be defined as our thoughts, meanings and interpretations, and since these are linguistic constructions, then post-structuralists insist that the possibility of an autonomous subject creating a self or identity for himself or herself is a nonsense. The idea of the 'subject' should be dead and buried, too, then. We are subject to the power which forms of knowledge exercise over us; or, to use post-structuralist jargon, our identities – who we are and what we know – are *constituted* by languages. We are helpless in the face of the power of language; we are obliged to think in directions it pushes us.

Box 4.2: The historical relativity of the meaning of language

In medieval Europe, large human bodies were considered to be beautiful, while slight, slim ones were not. A glance at any of the figures in paintings by Reubens demonstrates this clearly. This is still true of some African tribes, who use 'fattening sheds' to build up the figures of girls so that their beauty can be admired at the initiation ceremonies that mark their entry into womanhood. In our times, however, the reverse is true. Today, to be 'fat' is to be 'overweight' or 'gross' and this is sufficiently alarming and disfiguring, especially if you are female, to have spawned a whole dieting industry as well as the modern illnesses of anorexia and bulimia.

However grotesque we may believe such a definition of body image to be, it is nonetheless difficult for us to escape the modern connection between 'fat' and 'ugly' since it is a form of knowledge which has taken deep root in western culture. Seeing the words 'fat woman' drawn on a page makes it difficult to resist feelings of disapproval or pity, at least at first glance; yet the conjunction of these same words demanded the opposite response a few hundred years ago, when words like 'slim' or 'thin' would have had us turning up our noses in disapproval.

Post-structuralists therefore want to put languages, texts, or as Foucault calls such forms of knowledge, *'discourses'* (see a number of later chapters), at the top of sociology's agenda. For them, any discipline dealing with the nature of identity and the reasons why cultures are as they are must focus principally on the representations of meaning which provide the knowledge of the world for their users. This means, finally, that as in the case of EM, post-structuralists claim forms of knowledge can never be deemed to be *objectively* correct – they are just different; it can never be a matter of history ushering in new eras of 'progress' and 'improvement' as modernism suggests. History simply tells the tale of the rise and fall of different discourses, all defining normality and deviance, all 'true' for their time, and all 'untrue' for different times and places.

relativism
An approach which denies the existence of absolute truth, but maintains that beliefs, values and theories are relative to time and place. Accordingly, traditions and ways of life can only be judged in the context of the age or society that has produced them.

postmodernism
Often perceived as a cultural and aesthetic phenomenon associated with contemporary literature and the arts, it often combines apparently opposed elements to subvert meaning and fragment totality. It is characterised by a pastiche of cultural styles and elements, but implies a deeper scepticism about order and progress. Instead diversity and fragmentation are celebrated.

Here again, then, is a *relativist* sociology, denying the possibility of humans possessing objectively-true knowledge, except that in this case it is not *subject*-centred relativism, but *language*-centred **relativism**. Indeed, as we shall see throughout much of the rest of the book, some of the most enthusiastic supporters of the idea of **postmodernism** are post-structuralists who, by showing how contemporary life is diffused with a large variety of forms of knowledge, often electronically communicated from around the globe, insist that the 'project of modernity', the search for *the truth*, for *the* answers to the problem of human existence, should be abandoned. Instead, all we can do is recognise, and tolerate, different accounts of reality, since there is no human way of judging their validity. We will show how this debate about post modernism has influenced the practice of sociology in different areas later in the book; for now we turn to examine contemporary issues surrounding the practice of social research.

Summary of the Chapter

- The theories of Durkheim, Marx and Weber were all attempts to diagnose the problems of modern society and to propose solutions.

- Durkheim believed social order to be directly connected to the existence of strong social structures of norms and values and that sociology should be a science of society.
- Marx believed capitalist production to be the root of modern society's ills and that the eradication of classes was the only route to freedom.
- Weber believed that rationalisation was the defining feature of modernity and that nothing could halt its inexorable progress.
- Parsons developed a twentieth-century theory of the social system and of the importance of positivism in social investigation.
- Action theories like Symbolic Interactionism and Ethnomethodology, focusing on human subjects as creative agents, became influential as disillusion grew with structural theories.
- In recent years, the post-structuralist interest in the constituting power of language in constructing knowledge and identity has become influential.

References

Badham, R. (1986) *Theories of Industrial Society*, London, Croom Helm.

Cheal, D. (1991) *Family and the State of Theory*, Hemel Hempstead, Harvester Wheatsheaf.

Durkheim, E. (1938) *The Rules of Sociological Method*, Chicago, University of Chicago Press.

Jones, P. (1993) *Studying Society*, London, Harper Collins.

Marx, K. and F. Engels (1976) *Collected Works*, London, Lawrence & Wishart.

5 Principles of Sociological Research

Aims of the Chapter

This chapter introduces the reader to some of the basic principles of doing sociological research and discusses the key concepts and concerns that have shaped sociological inquiry. After reading this chapter, you should understand the relationship between and assumptions lying behind methodologies and methods. You should recognise how conventional research approaches in the discipline are challenged by feminism and postmodernism, though perhaps not fatally so.

Introduction

The discipline of sociology is precisely that: a *disciplined* understanding of society and the social processes which both reproduce and change it. As members of society we experience and understand these processes in one way or another but rarely, as we suggested in Chapter 1, do we reflect on why or how they occur: instead we make sense of our world, paradoxically, by ignoring much of it, or by taking much of it for granted – not only our own behaviour but also that of others. Sociology challenges assumptions, opens up new questions and never takes behaviour for granted.

This chapter provides an introduction to the major methods of research which are used by sociologists, and shows how they relate to wider methodological principles. It describes the basic features of research design and discusses the strengths and weaknesses of different research approaches. It concludes with a discussion of feminism and postmodernism which, in their different ways, have challenged the conventional assumptions of sociological research which, as we suggest below, arise from sociology's link to modernity.

Sociological Questions

To be a disciplined sociological *researcher* of social behaviour one must confront a range of theoretical and methodological issues before, during and after the research itself: it is these which this chapter explores. This is not to imply that what follows is to be seen as a 'rule-book' which all members of the profession typically follow. Instead, sociologists adopt various research techniques, often using different ones simultaneously, in order to explore and explain some particular area of social life. This can lead to considerable debate about the appropriate choice of research methods, conceptual frameworks and the like, as we will see in the substantive chapters that follow in Parts 2 and 3: you will discover, for example, a range of approaches used to understand and explore crime in Chapter 14.

What counts as a sociological research 'problem' can often surprise those new to the field. It might be expected that the subject would examine aspects of contemporary society such as family, education and ethnicity, and indeed, considerable research *is* conducted on these topics. But many other areas come within the sociological 'gaze', 'problems' that few outside the subject would have even thought of, and questions which few would think of as being problematic.

Many of the initial questions that shaped the origins of sociology were, as the earlier chapters have in their different ways shown, concerned with the 'Great Transformation' associated with the development of modernity. The pace and scope of change in social structures encouraged the first social theorists to ask very broad questions: how would social order and integration be maintained (Durkheim)?; how would the new dynamics of **capitalism** affect production relations (Marx)?; and how would the dynamics of **rationality** spread throughout social institutions (Weber)? All of these, and other, early analyses did not have the benefit of a sociological research methods manual to hand and research methods were yet to develop as formalised tools for social inquiry. Often work was quite speculative and theoretical with limited empirical investigation, though this did not stop some impressive grand theorising, such as Herbert Spencer's (1820–1903) theory of cosmic and social evolution. There were some exceptions, of course, such as Charles Booth's study of the poor in London in the last decade of the nineteenth century.

capitalism

An economic system in which the means of production are privately owned and organised to accumulate profits within a market framework, in which labour is provided by waged workers.

rationality

A preoccupation with calculating the most efficient means to achieve one's goals.

These broad historical and comparative analyses of social change provided the basis for much of the more focused empirical research that twentieth-century sociologists were later to conduct: some of the key concepts – such as culture, class, rationality and power – have been reworked and redefined through the many thousands of empirical studies that have now been completed. The absence of formalised rules of sociological inquiry in the nineteenth century prompted many of the founding sociologists to develop series of principles for conducting research, or at least principles that would help to identify and explore a specifically sociological – as opposed to, say, a philosophical, biological or historical – problem. Durkheim constructed his 'Rules for Sociological Method' while Weber developed and applied his notion of the '**ideal type**' which he used to construct more robust and useful

ideal type

For Weber, a model, a set of exaggerated characteristics defining the essence of certain types of behaviour or institutions observable in the real world. 'Ideal' signifies 'pure' or 'abstract' rather than desirable.

concepts of social behaviour and organisational structure, such as a 'bureaucracy'.

These, and other, attempts to provide a more rigorous basis to social analysis reflect the impact of modernity on sociology itself for they were driven by a belief that the new discipline must be objective and scientific. As sociological research methods have developed so the demands of **objectivity** and reliability in research have grown and become more refined. So, much of the discussion that follows reflects the sense in which sociology is a child of modernity. However, as we shall see towards the end of the chapter, some theorists now believe that modernity has been displaced by **postmodernity**. This has major implications for the sort of methodological approach that could be taken towards social inquiry. But this is for later. Here we need to begin with some basic principles that have shaped the inquiry thus far.

objectivity
An approach to knowledge acquisition that claims to be unbiased, impersonal and free from prejudice. Commonly associated with positivism (*see* positivism).

postmodernity
For its supporters, the further transformation in social, cultural, economic and political arrangements which takes a society beyond modernity.

One way of ordering the range of issues which are subject to the contemporary sociological gaze is through reference to Greer's (1969) classification. He divides research into three main areas:

- a sociology devoted to the analysis (and perhaps resolution) of *policy* problems – such as studies on poverty, crime and urban degradation
- a sociology which examines the broad *dynamics of society* and social change, where 'problems' reflect the sociologist's social and historical philosophy – such as debates over social stratification, the political sociology of the State and so on
- a sociology which asks questions about its own *prior stock of knowledge*, to refine our understanding, open new questions and challenge the assumptions of previous researchers: here questions are generated as much by the discipline itself as by developments external to it.

In practice, these three types of sociological problem often overlap in a major piece of research: Townsend's (1979) major study of poverty located the problem within the broader aspects of contemporary capitalism, challenged prior notions of poverty that had been developed by previous research and recommended a range of policies for the measurement and alleviation of poverty.

Another way of seeing the range of issues that sociologists address is to leaf through any current sociological journal, noting what the articles are trying to explore and what methods they are using to achieve this. Table 5.1, for example, is a sample listing of this sort, drawn at random from three sociological journals published between 1993 and 1994, cited by first author only.

Table 5.1 *Listing of recent research issues and methods (1993–94)*

Payne	Unemployment and the underclass	Statistical analysis of secondary data	Soc
Roberts	Youth entry to work in UK and Germany	Postal questionnaire/interview	Soc
Gregson	Domestic division of labour	In-depth unstructured interview	Soc
Webster	Commercialisation of university science	Case study interviews	Soc
Cooper	Power and gender	Feminist methodology	Soc
Brewer	Police in Northern Ireland	Ethnography	Soc
Emitboyer	Network analysis in sociology	Modelling theory	AJS
Hodson	Ethnic conflict/tolerance: Central Europe	Structured questionnaire given to 13,422 adults	AJS
Massey	Mexican migration to USA	Random sample of 19 communities/in-depth interview	AJS
Montgomery	Employment and social ties	Mathematical measures of interaction	AJS
Chrimbos	Criminal homicides in Greece	Examination of press reports on crime	IJCS
Chandler	Suicide in Japan and the West	Bivariate correlation and regression analysis	IJCS
Savells	Cajun subculture in Louisiana	Ethnography of 13 communities	IJCS

Key: Soc: *Sociology;* AJS: *American Journal of Sociology*; IJCS: *International Journal of Comparative Sociology*

secondary data
Data, normally in the form of official statistics or documentary sources, that have not been generated by the researcher.

ethnography
A research technique based on direct observation of the activity of members of a particular social group or given culture.

Such a listing of recent research illustrates some – but by no means all – of the issues and data collection techniques typical of contemporary sociology. But we should not make the mistake of thinking that the topic under investigation inevitably led to the research method listed here. For example, it is perfectly possible to conceive of a number of sociologists exploring the first topic – unemployment and the underclass – from a range of perspectives and using distinct techniques, from using official statistics on unemployment as a **secondary data** source in order to try to produce statistical measures of the phenomenon, to more qualitative techniques – such as an **ethnography** – to try to understand the experience of unemployment for those most disadvantaged and marginalised in society. Both techniques have their strengths and weaknesses, and this is precisely why, in the judgement and preferences of the researcher, one rather than another is selected. This tells us that researchers are looking for different types of data to answer different types of problem, an issue to which we return below.

Often sociological research can be most revealing when it opens up taken-for-granted aspects of everyday life. For example, taken-for-granted notions of 'the home' have certain implications for who has rights to that home, and most importantly who has inheritance rights to it and whether 'the home' can withstand the social process of inheritance.

Box 5.1: Inheritance and the idea of 'the home'

'The home is the embodiment of the modern domestic ideal, a suitable place to be occupied by 'a family'. It is a place of security, privacy and comfort. The home is conceived of as something which is actively constructed through a process which turns the raw materials of a house plus possessions into a home. It offers significant opportunities for its occupants to express their individuality and their taste, through the way in which they organise and furnish it. It is therefore, in a meaningful sense, a personal creation, and probably the most significant material thing which many people ever create and certainly the most valuable. ...

Within this imagery the home belongs to the couple, both materially and symbolically. Though their children may also 'belong' there when they are young, this is a temporary arrangement. They have not created the home, they do not have the same rights of ownership over it, and in a very real sense do not 'belong' there once they have reached adult life...

Looking at inheritance [then], some interesting questions emerge. If the home is an intensely personal creation, which powerfully expresses individuality, what happens when its creator dies ... Does the house then cease to be a 'home' and simply become 'property'? Does the home die, along with the person who created it? Or is there a sense in which a home is – or can be – passed on as a home for someone else to occupy as their own'?

Source: Finch and Hayes, *Sociology*, May 1994, pp. 417–18.

Whatever the particular substantive focus of the sociologist, each of the projects listed in Table 5.1 would have involved a number of research steps that raise methodological and practical issues which would have to be resolved. These are:

- *What is the principal research question* – what am I trying to find out, how can I describe this in a clear and unambiguous way such that I know precisely what I am looking for? If I cannot do this, am I looking for something that is not there? Or do I need to adopt exploratory research techniques to test out my basic beliefs and ideas?
- *What theoretical and conceptual framework should be adopted* which makes sense of the research question in relation to other, prior work, and through which my analysis might be best conducted later on?

- *What methods should be chosen to collect data* and how reliable and valid will these be as investigative tools for my particular project?
- *How should the data be analysed* in order to produce coherent conclusions that other researchers will be able to evaluate and perhaps use?

There are other questions too – such as does the research carry any ethical implications which need addressing? how will the findings be disseminated? who will be the users and beneficiaries of the research? and so on – but these first four listed above will be uppermost in researchers' minds.

Answers to these questions clearly vary – as Table 5.1 shows, where different data-collection techniques were chosen, even to address similar research problems. This suggests that there is no one preferred method to be used in sociological fieldwork even if there is a broad consensus over the steps to be taken, sketched out above, for good *research design*. The importance of producing research results which can be regarded by others as reliable has long prevailed. Today, as the volume of sociological data grows – both quantitative and qualitative – and becomes more readily accessible and exchanged through electronic data bases (see Table 5.2), so the importance of producing reliable and possibly compatible information is even greater. Yet measures of reliability and validity are tied up with debates about theoretical and methodological approaches in sociological research, as we shall see in a moment. Before this, however, it is important to clarify what is meant in general terms by the concepts of *reliability* and *validity*.

Table 5.2: On-line social science databases: some examples

Name of database	*e-mail address*
BIDS (Bath Information and Data Services)	*bidshelp@uk.ac.bath* Indexes over 7,000 journals
SOS-DATA (US-based list on social science data)	*listserv@uncvm1.oit.unc.edu* Information on current research
RAPID (Economic and Social Research Council)	*rapid@uk.ac.edinburgh* Indexes Council's research and publications activities
CORDIS (European Commission, Brussels)	*telnet info.niss.ac.uk login:cordis* Indexes European-funded research

Reliability refers to the replicability of the research: that is, a reliable research project will produce results which are not affected by the process of collection, the *research instrument* – say a survey, an ethnography, or an interview – and which if repeated on the same set of respondents would produce similar results. There are a number of ways of building reliability into data collection, such as 'test-retest' in which one collects data on two separate occasions using the same instrument. The problem of course is that the subject(s) of the research may have changed and so the second 'test' cannot be seen as a reliability check on the first. This is clearly a problem for all research – even in the natural sciences (see Collins, 1985) – but it is especially problematic where the focus of the investigation relates to ideas, attitudes and beliefs, all, of course, liable to change over time.

Validity refers to the quality of the data that you secure: you need to ensure that the data collection techniques that you use actually capture the data you *need, what you intend to measure and not something else.* Sometimes – often, in fact – the researcher is unsure what is the precise question that is being explored, and will use an exploratory pilot study conducted before the main research itself, to clarify matters. Even if one is clear from the start about what is needed it may be less evident how to obtain it, and thus secure valid data on 'it'. One may have to be very flexible during fieldwork to secure valid data that can be regarded as relating precisely to the topic of interest: as Whyte (1984) comments about his own research experience:

In one interview with a union leader, for example, my opening question about a problem situation elicited a response of about 500 words. No doubt the informant considered this a full response, as indeed it was, by ordinary conversational standards. However, I was dealing with a problem of some technical complexity as well as one of specifying people and process. It took me eighteen questions or statements before I felt I had the problem adequately covered. Even then, upon reviewing the transcription later, I found important elements I had overlooked.

[Whyte, 1984]

It is perhaps not surprising that some sociologists prefer to undertake research that does *not* rely upon the uncertainties associated with collecting and interpreting respondents' own views on the subject. For example, Inkeles' (1993) study of the impact of industrialisation and modernisation on the 'quality of life' explicitly avoids what he regards as 'subjective measures' , preferring 'objective indicators' 'which can be ascertained and rated by an outside observer *without* reference to the inner states of the persons presumably affected by the conditions observed' (p. 3). Such measures would include items such as 'how many square feet of housing each person enjoys', what access to food and medicine they have, and so on: he says quite bluntly, such measures do not 'involve asking people how they feel about an issue'. Clearly, not all sociologists would agree with this view, suggesting that it is precisely data on the way people feel that will give a more genuine picture of their quality of life. This issue is perhaps where the major difference lies in research approaches in sociology, a difference that is based on very distinct methodological approaches: let us consider these here.

Theoretical Approaches and Research Methodologies

There are two broad traditions that have shaped the research agendas of sociologists, though it is important to say that, today, the fault-line that used to separate the two now has many bridges joining the two, as researchers recognise that each can pay a valuable role in exploring society. The first tradition is based on the belief – and even imperative – that sociology provides scientific and objective analysis of social phenomena. This tradition has its roots in the modernist **positivism** which we introduced in broad terms in Chapter 4 when we looked at some of the key foundations of social inquiry. According to this perspective, social phenomena can be explained by showing the **causal relationship** between different phenomena which are regarded as distinct *variables*. There is the particular phenomenon one is trying to explain – the **dependent variable** – and that which one wants to test out as its likely cause – the **independent variable**. For example, if young women smoke more than others there is something about being a young women that causes this since it is evident that smoking does not produce young women! The phenomenon of a higher incidence of smoking among young women compared with men of the same age has then to be explored and any hypothesis about it corroborated through careful data collection. Evidence about both variables needs to be collected in a rigorous and reliable manner.

As we shall see in more detail later, this often involves the use of surveys that produce statistical measures of the variables and their correlation across a *sample population*, a sample so constructed that it is *representative* of a more general population. This would allow the researcher to generalise across a range of other similar cases: the relationships and regularities found in a specific study – say the attitudes of a sample of school leavers in a particular region towards the labour market – can then be said, very probably, to apply to all school-leavers in similar circumstances elsewhere.

positivism
A doctrine which claims that social life should be understood and analysed in the same way that scientists study the 'natural world'. Underpinning this philosophy is the notion that phenomena exist in causal relationships and these can be empirically observed, tested and measured.

causal relationship
A relationship where one phenomenon has a direct effect on another.

dependent variable
A technical term used in empirical research to denote a phenomenon that is caused by or explained by something else (*see* independent variable).

independent variable
A technical term used in empirical research to denote a phenomenon whose existence causes or explains the presence of another variable (*see* dependent variable).

The second major approach derives from a rather different tradition within sociology and in many ways is rooted in the ethnographic traditions of social anthropology. This approach relies first and foremost on an in-depth understanding of the cultural meanings, subjective perceptions and intersubjective dynamics of social behaviour in order to make sense of it. The broader theoretical tradition within which this approach is located is discussed in full in Chapter 18 which examines 'social action theories'. It does not seek to reconstruct these meanings into some statistical version nor try to 'correct' the subjective meanings of respondents. Instead it seeks to explain behaviour through observing it in its fullest and richest expression: through careful, close observation it is thought then possible that the meaning of the behaviour will not only be more validly understood but more accessible to others. This approach is not surprisingly heavily dependent on qualitative data collection techniques – such as **participant observation** – which allow the sociologist to share in the very culture under examination. Goffman's (1968) study of the St Elizabeth State Mental Hospital in Washington DC is a classic example of the use of this technique, as he spent over a year at the hospital, immersing himself in the everyday life of the wards, gradually building a full picture of the interaction between staff and patients. This second tradition is clearly very distinct from that inspired by a positivist approach, and has, indeed, been termed 'anti-positivist', or more appropriately 'interpretivist'. Hughes (1976) has provided a clear statement of the interpretivist position:

participant observation
A research method based on observation where the researcher of a group takes part in the group or community being studied.

Human beings are not things to be studied in the way one studies rats, plants or rocks, but are valuing, meaning-attributing beings to be understood as subjects and known as subjects. Sociology ... deals with meaningful action, and the understanding, explanation, analysis, or whatever, must be made with consideration of those meanings. ... To impose positivistic meaning upon the realm of social phenomenon is to distort the fundamental nature of human existence. (p. 25)

[Hughes, 1976, p. 25]

Table 5.3 provides a brief summary that contrasts the two broad approaches to society and thereby what each would regard as the most appropriate way of studying it.

Researchers acknowledge that *all* data relies for its meaning on the interpretive inferences of the sociologist: no data 'speaks for itself', even that which the more positivist-inclined collect. As Jones (1985) has said, 'the analysis of data about the social world can never be "merely" a matter of discovering and describing what is there. The very process

Table 5.3 *The broad methodological differences between positivism and anti-positivism*

	Positivist	*Interpretivist*
Basic view of society	Society is a system of social phenomena that are causally linked together	Society only exists as a result of meaningful social interaction
Who best defines it	The external observer (as expert sociologist)	The social actors themselves
How best to validate claims about it	Test hypotheses through rigorous collection of quantitative data	Work towards an empathy with the actor through the sensitive collection of qualitative data
Likely method	Survey	Observation

of deciding "what is", and what is relevant and significant in "what is", involves selective interpretation and conceptualisation' (p. 57). Moreover, this is complicated further since, whatever one's methodological orientation, some concepts which describe forms of social behaviour may have no *directly* observable or measurable indicators through which to register them, such as the concept of 'modernity' itself. Such a concept has to be translated into other concepts which have a more observable status. This might include features of modern society, such as the 'privatisation' of societal behaviour, which is the shift away from a more public, communal form of social intercourse to one that is more individuated and privately expressed. Of course, one may then have to refine this indicator of modernity even further before collecting appropriate and valid data. It is here that the positivist/interpretivist divide can become more plainly apparent between two sociologists. One might undertake a **quantitative** survey that tests a number of **hypotheses** about the onset of privatisation – such as, *if* privatisation is occurring *then* we would expect people to be less likely to have a strong sense of belonging to a wider community or group beyond those with whom they immediately identify. The same notion which underlines this hypothesis – a shift in people's perceived reference and membership groups – could also be explored through an in-depth qualitative study of a village, family, or whatever by the researcher who believes that privatisation can only be understood properly and accurately (i.e. validly) through immersing oneself in the respondents' lives.

quantitative
Used to describe a form of data or data analysis that is based on precise measurement.

hypothesis
A set of ideas or a speculative theory about a given state of affairs that is proposed for empirical testing.

While this methodological fault-line has been the principal divide within sociological theory and research, and while it still prevails in the great debates about the construction and direction of sociological theory, it appears to be increasingly less significant for many engaged in sociological research. So, for example, we find more and more sociologists

qualitative
Information that is not easily quantified.

using a mix of quantitative and **qualitative** methods for collecting data and explaining social behaviour. Indeed, there has been an honourable tradition for many years of the more quantitative-minded using qualitative research at an early stage of fieldwork in order to pilot surveys for later delivery, to sharpen up concepts and refine empirical indicators. But today it is also common to find sociologists using a range of methods in tandem throughout a research project, to provide different types of data which can – it is hoped – be mutually supportive, the qualitative providing the detail and depth of observation, while the quantitative provides a greater sense of representativeness and reliability.

This tactic of combining the two approaches is, however, never straightforward since the variables that one is measuring quantitatively may have no obvious and unequivocal expression in the rich qualitative data one collects through in-depth interview. Considerable inference across two such sets of data would need to be made by the sociologist. These difficulties have been experienced by many sociologists: this can be seen, for example, in Anne Oakley and Linda Rajan's (1991) study of the way women from different social classes secure support from kin, neighbours and friends during pregnancy. Quantifiable measures of social support networks needed to be blended with interpretive analysis of the women's experiences of the networks: the women's accounts of these experiences were sought in order to 'provide a description of "the meaning behind" associations between quantitative variables' (p. 37). In a sense, what was regarded as significant statistically could also have a qualitative 'significance', while at the same time qualitative 'checks' could be made on quantitative findings.

Blending different research techniques in this way is, to be sure, a demanding and often problematic task since the quantitative measures depend on the researcher defining what is to be measured *in advance* of the fieldwork, while qualitative 'measures' derive from interaction with the respondents. Strictly speaking therefore, the two strategies are not measuring the *same* thing merely via different techniques: it is *not*, for example, the same as measuring a piece of wood in centimetres and then in inches, since the wood itself remains constant whatever the scale one uses. Instead, the different techniques actually measure different aspects of the general phenomenon under investigation which depend on differing judgements about what counts as a 'good measure'. We cannot 'add' these different measures together to produce a more sophisticated mathematical measurement. Nevertheless, more and more sociologists are mixing their research techniques in this way for the rewards from blending methods in a careful and rigorous way can be very great indeed. Let us now turn to consider some of the main data collection methods used by sociologists, illustrating how they have been used in different studies.

The survey

Surveys are an important source of local, national and international information for many different agencies and organisations in Europe, the USA, Latin America, the 'Pacific Rim' countries and elsewhere. They cover a wide range of social, political and economic issues which are of concern to government, professions, academics, and others who need to have reliable and representative information on a particular issue. In the US and the UK, for example, there are regular national surveys of social trends covering occupational changes, household and family patterns, income differentials, educational achievement and so on. In the UK, the *General Household Survey* (based on a sample of 12,000 households) has been conducted annually since 1971, so providing a rich source of statistical data through which trends can be mapped. In the US a similar annual survey is the *General Social Survey*, again initiated in 1971. The longest-running survey is the British national Census which has been carried out every ten years (apart from 1941) since 1801. The data from these national and international surveys (such as the International Social Survey Programme) are typically available through electronically accessible databases. In the UK, the principal academic database is held at the University of Essex as the Economic and Social Research Council's Data Archive.

Box 5.2: Some useful statistical databases

Social Trends An annual review of social trends in the UK, published by the Central Statistical Office. It provides a summary of and commentary on data derived from a large number of independently produced surveys: it covers population changes, household and family structure, education, employment, income and wealth, expenditure, health, housing supply, environment, leisure, religion, crime and transport.

General Household Survey Published in the UK since 1971 and based on a sample of about 12,000 members of the general population resident in private households. It is particularly valuable as a source of detailed statistical data and is often used as secondary data for further analysis by sociologists.

Eurostat Annual publication of the European Union (since 1970) which records data from member states covering demography, the labour force, economic activity and agriculture.

Note: All such sources use criteria for defining categories of data, such as definitions of poverty. These criteria may differ from one survey to another. For example, the concept of the 'unemployed' is defined by *Social Trends* to mean 'people claiming benefit at Employment Service local offices...[and who] satisfy the conditions for claiming benefit'. The definition used by Eurostat is much broader to include 'those who have no job, who are looking for a job...and are immediately available for work'. Differences between the two definitions meant that in 1990, for example, 400,000 were excluded from the unemployment count in the UK.

Social surveys have a long history in academic sociological research, going back to the early statistical studies of families and poverty by Booth in London (1889–1902). Many surveys – particularly those sponsored by national government – are information-gathering, that is *descriptive* surveys, while those conducted by sociologists would gather information in an *analytical* way to explore a set of concepts, hypotheses, models and so on. Some classic examples of such surveys include British studies: Townsend's *Poverty in the United Kingdom*, Goldthorpe *et al.*'s *Affluent Worker* studies, and Douglas's *The Home and the School*; while from the US, Hirschi's *Causes of Delinquency* and Elder's *Children of the Great Depression*. More recent studies include those on social class (Marshall *et al.*, 1988), on food and consumption (Fine, 1994) and racism and ethnicity (Saggar, 1992).

All surveys must, as with any research, address the four questions outlined earlier which shape proper research design. The first question is perhaps the most important – just what is it that is to be investigated, how can the topic be clearly and unequivocally defined? One of the first difficulties in doing any research is the need to focus down precisely on what it is one wants to explore. Not only is this necessary to distinguish new work from what already exists – crucial if the research requires funding – it is also necessary to translate broad abstract issues under investigation into more concrete issues that can be explored through interview and questionnaire. There is a need in other words for a *progressive focusing down* of broad research topics into more targeted, researchable questions. For example, if one wanted to conduct a survey that sought to measure the degree to which social class is still important today, one might translate the broad notion of 'the demise of social class' into more focused issues such as the 'privatisation' of class culture, and patterns of association among different occupations, or a sense of class loyalties and behaviour in the workplace and a sense of *difference* from other social groups, and so on. These sub-topics can be translated into a range of fairly specific questions to be included in a survey.

Surveys are normally planned as a series of sequential steps:

- identification of the *'problem'* which the survey addresses (the research question, its relation to prior work and the principal proposition or hypotheses to be tested)
- identification of the *population* of respondents to be surveyed
- selection of a *sample* of respondents that represent the total population
- pilot of *interview schedule* to refine questions and topics
- preparation and despatch of final *questionnaire*
- follow-up *interviews*
- *analysis of data* collected
- results and *dissemination* of findings

In establishing the research question, it is important to determine how previous work might contribute to the new survey. Prior survey data, for example, will no doubt be of use – even its shortcomings will help to clarify what needs to be covered. Using previously collected data – or *secondary data* – in this way is a valuable and time-saving technique in developing one's own research agenda. However, such data must be used carefully, since it was produced in different circumstances, by someone else for perhaps different theoretical or empirical purposes. This is particularly true of *official statistics* produced for government. Secondary statistical data can pose particular problems here since they may be based on different measures of the phenomenon under investigation. In other words, it is important to recognise that an existing database never 'speaks for itself'. Chapter 6, for example, discusses an ongoing controversy between two main groups of sociologists over how to read data on social class and social mobility in contemporary Britain: different theoretical assumptions and different ways of interpreting the empirical data on class mean that choosing one source of secondary information rather than another is not easy. Bias in secondary information, in other words, is not simply a result of the technical quality of previous work but also a reflection of the theoretical assumptions that underlie it.

Box 5.3: Official statistics as a secondary data source

Sociologists in all countries are likely at one time or another to consult and draw on official statistics in their research. They are called 'official' as they are collected initially by government offices or departments for a range of reasons: in the UK the main office is the Central Statistical Office and the Office of Population and Surveys, one of whose more interesting and user-friendly publications is *Social Trends* (see above, Box 5.2). Similar annual publications are produced throughout Europe and the US: in the US, for example, the National Opinion Research Centre publishes the annual General Social Survey.

Official statistics are used for a number of reasons, including:

- They are frequently the only available source of data in a particular area (say, for example, data on hospital waiting lists).
- They are readily available (unless subject to some government embargo!) so researchers do not have to spend their own time and money collecting the information on which they are based.
- They allow an examination of trends over time – or time series data – on a range of areas, such as income differentials, divorce, educational achievement and so on.
- They allow before and after studies to be made – e.g. examining the effect that changes in legislation have on divorce rates.

Despite these advantages they do have a number of drawbacks:

- They have been collected for a particular purpose which has influenced how, when and from whom they were collected.
- They 'count' phenomena using a set of assumptions which might differ from those adopted by the sociologist – for example, social class membership used in the US and UK censuses depends on a specific definition of class through occupational categories which some sociologists would question (see Chapter 6).
- A series of data collected over a number of years may register changes in the way counts are made because of alterations to the criteria that are used, so it will be crucial to know if and how such modifications have been introduced.
- Finally, the status of official statistics – or, for that matter, *any* statistics – as 'facts' looks shaky when one acknowledges that who or what ends up as included in the figures reflects a long, prior process of data collection: who, for example, is to count as a criminal in crime statistics depends on the law and its implementation, local policing policy, the capacity to defend oneself from criminal accusation and prosecution, and so on. In this sense the statistics – on crime or whatever – are not 'objective' figures telling the 'real' story, but the end result of a complex process of social interaction. Sociologists who are especially critical of statistics see them therefore as merely social *constructs* that need deconstructing and demystifying.

The *sample* of the population to be surveyed needs to be selected in such a way that it is representative of the entire population. For example, if the population to be surveyed carries a specific gender balance this should be reflected in the sample that is constructed. Similarly, features of the population that relate to age and class need to be properly reflected in the sample. In order that the sample be *reliable*, sociologists will use (or build if there is not one available) a **sampling frame** from which respondents are selected using a randomising technique which ensures each has the *same chance* of being included in the sample. One of the most frequently used existing sample frames is a country's Electoral Roll or Register from which names and addresses can be drawn. Clearly, it is important to ensure that the final selection carries the representative features we know are true of the entire population: to do this, the sample is normally *stratified* (built up) to reflect the particular features under consideration before random sampling is undertaken. So if a general population was made up of 50 per cent men and 50 per cent women we would want to ensure that the specific sample taken reflected this distribution between the chosen respondents. A *stratified random sample* is normally regarded, then, as a reliable basis for representing the wider population.

sampling frame

Used in sociological research, it is an accurate list of the subjects of a total population, for example an electoral roll. Research subjects are subsequently randomly selected from such a list.

Another sampling technique is *quota*, or *judgement*, sampling. This is a quicker and more convenient way of getting at a sample than other methods but is arguably the least reliable. Typically, before interviewing takes place, the main features of the population are defined – such as sex, age, occupation, religion and so on. Interviewers are then given a *quota* of respondents from each of these categories to contact, the size of the quota being determined by what the research manager believes is the relative proportion of individuals in each category in the population as a whole. Sometimes, a clearly defined sampling frame is not easily available, for in some research – such as deviance – there is no predefined listing of 'deviants' that can be surveyed! In such situations one strategy might be to engage in *snowball sampling*, where one begins with one or a few contacts who then help you to find others and so on. While this is clearly an uncertain and contingent process and so less reliable than other sampling techniques, there may be some situations – such as trying to map out friendship patterns – where it is particularly appropriate.

In a UK-based study of young adults leaving school and entering work, the authors describe how they chose their sample population to represent the features they believed characterised the total population and the way they gathered their randomised sample from local neighbourhoods.

'The sample consisted of 1,786 18–24-year-olds interviewed in four local labour markets during the period October 1982–October 1983. The local labour markets were chosen to represent contrasting local labour market conditions but when aggregated also provided a socio-economic distribution which approximated the total population of 18–24-year-olds. Sunderland was representative of areas with a declining manufacturing base and high levels of unemployment, St Albans typified the more affluent South East with high-technology manufacturing industry, a strong service sector and a low level of unemployment. Leicester was chosen for its diverse industrial base and a level of unemployment close to the national average, while Stafford was selected for its average level of unemployment and high proportions of non-manual workers, to compensate for the above-average proportion of manual workers in Leicester ... Within each of the localities interviewing was confined to certain electoral wards, chosen to provide a representative sample of the area in terms of the socio-economic characteristics of the population. The interviewer enquired at every fifth-house or flat [apartment] in the area to identify the respondents. If respondents were identified but not available, arrangements were made to call back ... The questionnaire took between 45 and 90 minutes to administer.

[LAYDER *et al.*, (1991) p. 454]

The last comment notes the time it took to administer a questionnaire. Surveys can be based on face-to-face interviews of this sort, purely postal questionnaires, or – as is often the case – a mix of the two, the interviews typically following postal data gathering. Postal questionnaires can be a relatively quick and inexpensive method for collecting data from a large number of respondents, of whom a smaller number may be selected for a (more expensive and time-consuming) follow-up interview.

However, there are many problems with postal surveys: the response rate is often quite low (a very good return would average 30–40 per cent), respondents may misinterpret or completely ignore some questions, overly-long questionnaires will simply discourage respondents from even beginning to reply, questions themselves must be kept quite simple, and as such they may provide clues to the answers being sought, and, finally, there is no guarantee that the person completing it is actually the one who was supposed to do so! Nevertheless, if the sample is representative and the return rate is around the 30 per cent figure, valuable information can be derived from postal questionnaires especially when handling large data-sets (such as the 12,000 respondents of the General Household Survey).

Surveys that use face-to-face interviews can provide a richer data-base for subsequent analysis precisely because the researcher can try to cover all the questions, can clarify their meaning, can probe for additional information on an unexpected issue that emerges during interview, and can ensure that all the dimensions of the research question are properly covered by a much larger proportion of the initial sampling frame – perhaps as much as 80–90 per cent. It is important that the interview schedule that is used is common to all interviews in order that a consistent research instrument – the questionnaire – is used to collect data.

Interviewing does however create its own problems. These are of two kinds: (i) those concerned with the *design* of the interview schedule, and (ii) those concerned with the interview situation itself. With regard to the first, the interview must be designed such that the questions seem both sensible to the respondent and flow in a logical sequence. Moreover, because respondents often need to be 'warmed up', first questions should be broad, background points – such as their job, marital status, age, etc. – rather than anything that is likely to be particularly awkward or embarrassing , such as intimate details of their sex-life! The interview situation is problematic since it is self-evidently a form of *social interaction* and as such the data it produces reflects the circumstances in which the interview occurred – where it occurs, what the gender interaction was, whether it was being taped and so on. One must try to keep these contingencies down to the minimum in order to prevent the research instrument – the interview itself – affecting the research data. This is why those who are most positivistically inclined would prefer to avoid any interactive contact with respondents, restricting the survey to the collection of precoded questionnaire material, where **closed-ended questions** prepared by the researcher permit only one of a possible range of responses. These can then be translated to a computer programme – such as the *Statistical Package for Social Science* (SPSS) – for quantitative analysis. Responses to **open-ended questions** are more difficult to code in terms of tying them in to the specific conceptual issues of interest: one has to make many more interpretive moves to do this.

closed-ended question
The most commonly used form of question asked in questionnaires, the answers to which fall within a predicted range and thus can be pre-coded (*see* open-ended question).

open-ended question
A type of question used in questionnaires to elicit narrative information from the respondent, the answer to which cannot be pre-coded.

While surveys can handle large volumes of data, it is important to treat the data they produce with care. One cannot assume that what people report – about their attitudes, expectations, behaviour patterns or whatever – is accurate. Hughes (1976) has shown, for example, how respondents have been found to give inaccurate replies with regard to whether they had voted or not, relied on social welfare, used birth control techniques and so on. In addition, respondents may reply in ways they think are 'socially desirable', or may tend to respond in the affirmative, or simply get tired completing the schedule and complete it less carefully than they might. It is because of this that sociologists might want to add to survey data with more detailed observation of actual behaviour, or developing alternative *observational instruments* to secure what they regard as more valid and reliable evidence. We shall look at these in the next section. Table 5.4 summarises the basic strengths and weakness of surveys as methods for data collection.

Table 5.4: *Advantages and disadvantages of surveys*

Advantages	*Disadvantages*
Can handle large number of respondents	May have poor response rate
Based on reliable sampling	Can be expensive if large-scale
Standardisation of instrument allows others to replicate the research	Cannot control for the impact of the external environment on respondents
Allows rapid statistical analysis of large data-bases	No guarantee that respondents act and think the way they say they do

Those surveys that now enjoy the status of 'classics' in the sociological research archive have gained such a reputation not only for what they discovered but also *how* they went about it. And often it is the researcher's ability to recognise both the strengths and the limitations of the survey method that makes these classics especially valuable and convincing. One of these is the British survey of Young and Willmott of the movement of families from an East London suburb, Bethnal Green, to a new housing estate during the early 1950s. The survey explored the changes in kinship networks and contacts that resulted from the move. Such has been the long-standing interest in the results of this survey that forty years on there are now plans by a new team of sociologists to revisit Bethnal Green to find out what is happening there now.

Box 5.4: Surveying family life in East London

'We obviously could not see all the people in these districts. In fact we saw not more than 1,000. But these were chosen rather carefully. We wanted, as far as we safely could, to talk about all the local people although we were seeing only some of them. This object was achieved by following the usual practice of sociologists and selecting 'samples' of people for interview. In Bethnal Green, for instance, we picked from the electoral register every thirty-sixth name appearing on it. We then called on each of the people whose name had come up in this way and asked if he or she would be willing to talk to us. Most of them were. These people were in what we call the *general sample*; in addition we interviewed a second or third time, and much more intensively, a smaller *marriage sample* of couples with young children....

Both of us worked either in the borough or on the estate throughout the three years in which the research was done. One of us also lived in the borough with his own 'family of marriage' for most of the time, and both his wife and his children, who attended local schools, provided further sidelights on the place. ... As a result of this close connection with the district, we came to know well a number of local residents who gave us full accounts of their family relationships which helped us understand and assess the information given to us in the formal interviews. We also did what we could to check what people told us verbally by personal observation in homes, churches, clubs, schools, parks, public houses [bars], and street markets. But we should say, what is as obvious as it is important, that for the most part we can only report what people say they do, which is not necessarily the same as what they actually do.'

Source: Michael Young and Peter Willmott, *Family and Kinship in East London* (1957) pp. 13–14.

Observation

We saw earlier that anti-positivists would argue that the more sociological research can immerse itself in the subject of investigation the more likely will it produce a valid account of the meaning it has for the social actors involved. Not surprisingly, therefore, close observation of social action and even full participation within it are seen as the preferred methods of social research. *Ethnography* is perhaps the best term to describe the art of detailed sociological observation – literally, the description of a people – which, not surprisingly, has its roots in early social anthropological studies of marginal or isolated cultures during the heyday of European colonialism. Indeed, the tradition of ethnography has been to explore unusual or unknown cultures or social groups, and in this sense it is very much an exploratory technique which might be followed up by more formalised methods of data collection – such as survey interviewing. As Fielding (1993) has said, 'as a means of gaining a first insight into a culture or social process, as a source of hypotheses for detailed investigation using other methods, it is unparalleled' (p. 155). As with surveys, however, in-depth observational methods have both strengths and weaknesses, and a number of initial methodological and practical problems must be confronted.

The first problem is that researchers need to be able to observe in such a way that as rich a body of data as is possible is secured without their disturbing the scene by being present. In short, *how* is the researcher to join in and observe the actors under study? What is the best method of *participant observation*? There is no simple answer, for much depends on the situation being studied and the questions being asked. Participant observation can be either *overt* – known to the actors under investigation – or *covert* – hidden or disguised in some way. Covert observation is said to be less likely to disrupt or disturb the situation being observed since the researcher would merely appear as another member of the group. On the other hand, if a researcher's cover is inadvertently blown, it might be difficult, if not impossible, to keep the research project going – resentment and possible anger from those under observation may lead to the researcher being ejected from the group. In some areas of research, notably crime and deviance, being a covert observer may well drag one into activities which may be legally and ethically compromising. More generally, all covert research raises the broader ethical issue of conducting fieldwork without the informed consent of those under scrutiny. How can sociologists be accountable to their respondents in these circumstances, and how can the results of the work be controlled such that they do not adversely affect those who had been observed?

Clearly, much depends on the situation. Humphreys' (1970) US-based study of homosexual behaviour in men's 'tea rooms' (rest rooms or public toilets) though both ethically and legally problematic for him as researcher, nevertheless used a covert form of participant observation. He argues as follows:

From the beginning, my decision was to continue the practice of the field study in passing as deviant ... [T]here are good reasons for following this method of participant observation.

In the first place, I am convinced that there is only *one* way to watch highly discreditable behaviour and that is to pretend to be in the same boat with those engaging in it. To wear a button that says 'I am a watchbird, watching you' into a tea room would instantly eliminate all action except the flushing of toilets and the exiting of all

present.... The second reason is to prevent distortion. Hypothetically, let us assume that a few men could be found to continue their sexual activity while under observation. How 'normal' could that activity be? How could the researcher separate the 'show' and the 'cover' from standard procedures of measurement?

[Humphreys, 1970, p. 25]

Whether overt or covert, it is clear that observation is the research method most suited to situations in which there is no evident sample population, and where the behaviour in question is hidden or deviant. It is obvious that Humphreys would have made very little if any progress with his research had he tried to collect data on the 'tea rooms' via a clipboard and closed-ended questionnaire! But it is also true that observation is useful for all situations and not only the unusual. For example, Fox (1990) reports his use of participant observation of a fairly unremarkable situation, a group of business executives taking a course at one of the UK's major business schools:

My research was an ethnographic investigation of the experience of executives studying on the school's part-time Executive Masters programme. I was a participant observer with one cohort of these students, a group of about twenty people most of whom were men...While they were busy taking notes on and seeking to learn about finance, statistics, marketing, corporate strategy, public sector management and more I was taking notes on and seeking to learn about them.

[Fox, 1990, p. 435]

It would, of course, have been possible to survey the executives to discover what they thought about the course and its value to them. Yet Fox's participation in the class gave him an insight into the group culture and behaviour which would have been missed by a survey:

while ethnography, of the sort I was engaged in, is by its nature limited to the study of one case, it had the benefit of allowing the researcher access to a level of interactional minutiae...which other methods cannot attain.

[Ibid, p. 436]

For example,

although the managers were on the masters programme to learn about management from the faculty, in many cases they had much more managerial 'street credibility' than their teachers. This produced a degree of tension, for the students were in a sense paying customers with considerable experience and knowledge about that

which they were paying to learn. If coffee arrived late or handouts were poorly organised, the students would jokingly question whether they could trust what the business school was teaching if it could not even manage to produce coffee on time. The ability or inability of the business school to practice what it preached became a theme which much of the part-timers' banter and joking worked upon.

[Ibid, p. 435]

The ethnographic technique is clearly the preferred choice where one is studying people who do not share in the dominant (English-speaking) language-base which typifies most surveys and structured questionnaires. Ethnic minorities, for example, in inner-city areas not only share in a specific sub-culture but use a privatised language which would be inaccessible to any survey. This can apply even when subjects are using the English language but not actually speaking 'English' as conventionally understood, as in the following exchange between a Principal of a Pittsburgh inner-city school and a black teenage pupil:

Principal: Why are you stretched so thin by joy? Are you flying backwards?
Pupil: My special pinetop is smoking and wants to eyeball you fast.
Principal: I'm stalled. What is this all about?
Pupil: I wasted one of the studs for capping me. Teach blasted at me and told me to fade away to the hub and fetch you.
Principal: Don't put your head in the bowl and pull the chain.

[Cited in Deutscher, 1970, p. 19]

Observation and reliability

Wherever and whenever observation is used as a research technique, the researcher has to make a large number of inferences about the meaning 'behind' the phenomena under scrutiny. Are these inferences and accounts of behaviour reliable interpretations about what has been observed? Would two observers 'see' the activity in the same way? If not, would one be better than another, or are both equally useful though differing stories revealing distinct aspects of the observed? Could two different accounts be equally useful?

This takes us to the heart of the methodological problem of observation. It is a selective process of interpretation, and, moreover, one dependent on the role and position the observer adopts while observing. Those who adopt a participant strategy can 'overplay' their role in the group. As a result, they may not only affect the group's behaviour (and so distort matters) but also their own by 'going native', becoming less an 'observer' and more a full member of the groups being studied – the observer being captured by his or her subject-matter. The benefits of an easy familiarity with respondents can turn into the disadvantage of becoming over-familiar with them in the sense of developing more than a research relationship with them: this weakens any sense of being 'objective' as an observer.

On the other hand, validity for non-positivist observation means producing accounts of what is going on that *the observed would themselves recognise* as accurate stories of their lives. Unlike Inkeles' distancing from anything that smacks of 'subjective indicators' in his study of the quality of life, here qualitative observation and analysis tries to get as close to a sense of such indicators as possible. In fact, this may call for checking out one's interpretations of events and behaviour with those under observation, a common technique used to try to ensure that the research is a valid reconstruction of the subjective meanings of social actors. Hessler (1992) calls this technique 'touching base', a frequent checking out with respondents the interpretation one has made.

Box 5.5: 'Touching base' – validating interpretive observation

'When I was observing the development of a comprehensive health centre for the poor in a Chicano and Mexican-Indian community in a large southwestern city, I was fortunate to have met a very influential Chicano leader who must have seen some utility in taking me under his wing. I worked a bit at his candle factory, did some editing for him, and gave him one of my tape recorders. I lived for a brief time in his house along with his five children, wife, grandchild, daughter-in-law, and mother-in-law. The cultural nuances were very difficult for me to observe and record because I was a complete stranger to the community and because the Spanish spoken was a different dialect than the Spanish I had grown up with in Los Angeles. Touching base involved me getting some field notes together, making copies of them at the university across town, and blocking out names. I would sit with my informant and go over my more general recordings with him. Then I would ask him if I had observed the particular event or confrontation between a neighbourhood resident and the medical director correctly. I even checked my interpretations, which I had bracketed in the field notes. After several sessions, my informant began to get the hang of what I was trying to do with my study, and I began to get a feel for the quality and accuracy of my observations.'

Source: Hessler (1992) p. 223.

The attempt to produce valid interpretation is an important requirement for good observational sociology. However, it can *never* be entirely free of some distorting or biasing effects since the observer is clearly *not* the observed. As Stanley (1990a, p. 624) has said with regard to ethnographic observation, '...the project which drives the writing of ethnography is different from that which drives the doing of social life. Ethnographic description is actually not, and cannot be, literal description'. Rather than hide or gloss over this, some researchers turn this into a topic for discussion and debate itself, reflexively observing their own participation and observation in the social activity (see Phillips, 1971). This argument has been taken further: Gilbert and Mulkay (1984), for example, argue that there never can be a single interpretation of social action that is better than any others, whatever method is used to record or observe it. This is because they claim that all social action has multiple possible meanings each created by and dependent on the interactive context in which they are constructed. The sociologist's version of events is no more – nor any less – 'valid' than anyone else's, it merely describes particular features which that particular sociologist regarded as important to him or her. This position has encouraged more and more sociologists to explore the way *accounts* of social events and activity are constructed through the discourse and language that actors use. It is this which has led to the growth of the technique of *conversation analysis* that has been closely tied to the ethnomethodological school in social theory (see Chapters 4 and 18).

Observational methods are clearly crucial if we are to build – even if 'only' reflexively, as Gilbert and Mulkay would argue – cogent accounts of the interactive and subjective meanings of social actors. This is where their strength lies, as is evident in the vast number of qualitative ethnographies and observer studies that have already contributed to the sociological research base. The basic strengths and weaknesses of these methods are summarised in Table 5.5. In many ways, it is apparent that comparing this table with Table 5.4, observational and survey methods

Table 5.5 *Strengths and weakness of observational methods*

Advantages	*Disadvantages*
Provides in-depth data on social actors' meaning and behaviour	Problems with representativeness and reliability
Can access hidden, deviant or non-conventional subcultures	Restricted in scale of research population that can be observed
Avoids using an artificial research instrument to collect data	Problems with observer role and 'going native'

have strengths and weaknesses which are the converse of each other. This is perhaps why sociologists are, as noted earlier, keen to combine the two approaches (where appropriate) in such a way as to maximise the benefits of each.

The case study

Before we complete this discussion of the principal research tools used by sociologists it is worth considering in brief the 'case study' as a particular research *design* which might include both survey and observational methods as part of its data-collection strategy. Case studies have a continuing appeal to sociologists despite their often hostile treatment by some research methods texts because of doubts over their reliability and representativeness.

Case studies involve the detailed exploration of one or number of specific cases which might be an individual, a group, community, organisation or event, which are thought to reflect or embody some phenomenon or set of processes which in turn will throw light on a wider concern that the discipline has. They are often used to explore new areas of inquiry, to raise new issues for the sociological research agenda. Not surprisingly, therefore, they often use a qualitative approach to explore the case in as rich a detail as possible, such as participant observation or ethnography. A useful definition of the case study has been provided by Yin:

> **A case study is an empirical enquiry that: investigates a contemporary phenomenon within its real-life context; when the boundaries between the phenomenon and the context are not clearly evident; and in which multiple sources of evidence are used.**
>
> [YIN, 1989, p. 23]

Getting close to one's subject matter is crucial if one is to claim that the story one tells has integrity, or a sense of the experiences of the social actors under investigation. Where more than one case study is undertaken as multiple cases, this can only be regarded as replication not *sampling*. Platt (1988) has provided a typology of case studies which move from the specific to the more general in focus:

- ideographic case studies – in this research a case has been chosen because of its intrinsic interest and not because it necessarily points to a wider, more general phenomenon
- indicative case studies – these are case studies which show that something within them can be taken to have implications for other situations which will need to be taken into account when conducting similar case studies

- representative case studies – here the researcher selects a case on the basis of rigorous criteria which would then allow the case to claim to be 'representative' of all other cases

Platt suggests that most case studies are towards the ideographic end of the research spectrum. Their role as exploratory vehicles she likens – in an incisive phrase – to a 'social barium meal – whose progress through the [social] system illuminates it' (p. 10). Peter Townsend, for example, used case studies on individual family histories in his survey on poverty; through the details of the families' interaction with welfare agencies he could show how the wider benefit system worked.

Clearly, the interpretive and qualitative approach of case studies has meant that they can be criticised for being less reliable than other research designs. However, John Brewer (1994) has recently argued that ethnographically-based case studies can respond to the attack that they lack rigour, reliability and representativeness if they conform to a number of research design principles in advance: that is, case studies should:

- establish the wider relevance of the setting and topic – its sense of being representative of other cases
- identify what they are focusing on and what is being left out and why, with what implications
- identify the theoretical framework the study uses
- establish the authority of the findings by discussing problems that merged during research, clarifying on what grounds the data were classified into certain types rather than any other, and being open to discussion of rival interpretations
- show negative cases, if any, and how they impact on positive ones
- stress the contextual nature of respondents' accounts

Brewer's suggestions for improving what might be called the research accountability of the case study design are welcome and show how case studies *can* be a basis for generalisation and a contribution to wider social theory.

Feminist Methodology and the Critique of 'Malestream' Research

Ethnographic research design has been frequently used by feminist sociologists. This is because ethnography starts with the premise that the meanings and ideas of the observed are of paramount importance: they should not be stripped away or reduced to some statistical rendering of attitudinal scales. Letting the actor speak for him or herself is a central principle guiding research. As such, ethnography is an inherently collaborative and democratic form of research that does not seek to impose the observer's ideas on the observed, even though clearly, as was argued earlier, like all research, ethonography will seek to construct an interpretation of social actors' accounts. In a similar fashion, feminist analysis claims to be collaborative and non-impositional. It is highly critical of mainstream (malestream) knowledge which is said to be expert-based, hierarchical and, it is argued, fundamentally patriarchical. As Dale Spender, the Australian sociologist, has put it:

> **[A]t the core of feminist ideas is the crucial insight that there is no one truth, no one authority, no one objective method which leads to the production of pure knowledge. This insight is as applicable to feminist knowledge as it is to patriarchal knowledge, but there is a significant difference between the two: feminist knowledge is based on the premise that the experience of all human beings is valid and must not be excluded from our understandings, whereas patriarchal knowledge is based on the premise that the experience of only half the human population needs to be taken into account and the resulting version can be imposed on the other half.**
>
> **[Spender, 1985, p.5]**

A *methodology* based on this position does not, therefore, want to reproduce the distinction between 'objective' versus 'subjective' indicators of social action, the key difference, as we saw earlier between positivist and anti-positivist methodologies. Rather than seeing science and rationality as privileged forms of knowledge counterposed to the 'soft' and 'unreliable' discourse of subjectivity and experience, feminist methodology demands that personal experience(s) be the foundation for all research. Women's experience in particular has been ignored by male-dominated social research reflecting the more general marginalisation and subordination of women in society.

Hammersley (1992) has provided a summary of the main features of feminist methodology which he says can be seen in terms of four main themes:

- Gender divisions and the subordination of women run through all areas of social life – they are not restricted to one particular arena of interaction – such as the domestic household, or the workplace – but are a chronic feature of *all* interaction. Any research must therefore recognise and address this from the start.
- Rather than being unreliable, subjectivity and personal experience are the source of a sensitive and profoundly insightful form of

knowledge about the social world, a form of knowledge which women themselves are most able to understand and express.

- The research process must avoid creating any hierarchical division between the researcher and the researched, and instead invite the latter to help shape the interpretation of data: those who are oppressed should be given the tools to help themselves understand and liberate themselves from this oppression.
- Finally, the overall goal of feminist research is the emancipation of women, which itself provides the only basis for what is to be regarded as valid research. Feminist research is successful when it raises consciousness, when it is transformative of existing gendered relations.

These four themes clearly create a very different research agenda from that of the more traditional approaches we have discussed so far. Hammersley himself acknowledges the importance of the challenge of feminist methodology to conventional research techniques, and recognises the value of the work that it has produced. It places gender at the centre of research and by doing so poses new questions which need answering. However, he believes that though these questions do need addressing, the claim that a distinct feminist methodology is needed or can be constructed should be rejected.

In response, feminist methodologists such as Ramazanoglu (1992) have asked why Hammersley can accept the basic research findings of feminist method yet reject the very means through which these have been generated. Moreover, they reassert their belief in the need to dismiss the division between science and emotion, rationality and experience that has dominated Western thought since the Enlightenment and which has produced 'views on which western scholarship, science and universities have long relied [which] are blatantly sexist and racist, and privilege middle class males' (Ramazanoglu, 1992, p. 208). Against such a tradition, feminist methodology seeks neither to impose itself on others nor to claim some privileged position or methodology for accessing the truths of subjective experiences. As Reinharz (1992) declares, 'there is no single "feminist way" to do research. There is little "methodological elitism" or definition of "methodological correctness" in feminist research. Rather there is a lot of individual creativity and variety ... Feminist research is amoeba-like; it goes everywhere, in every direction ... The amoeba is fed by the women's movement. The women's movement, in turn, is fed by women's outrage and hope' (p. 243).

This specifically feminist call to multiple and creative research techniques might, perhaps, be regarded as having a more general appeal today among researchers who have even yet to engage with the feminists' challenge. That is, the long-standing dispute between distinct theoretical traditions of positivism and anti-positivism seems to have been superseded by a willingness to use new combinations of method allied to new theoretical approaches towards understanding social action and interaction. For example, Giddens's notion of structuration (see Chapter 19) requires entirely new methodological strategies that dissolve the conventional distinctions between structural and interpretive analysis, distinctions that created much of the positivist/anti-positivist dispute of the past. There will, therefore, be continued debate about the utility of different research methods in the future, but, perhaps, a greater preparedness to be open to a much wider range than before.

Postmodernity and Research Methodology

One of the objectives of this text is to discuss the debates not only about modernity but also *post*modernity. As we have suggested in earlier chapters, there is now a strong school of thought in sociology (and parallel schools in art, literature and philosophy) that claims that we live in a postmodern age. According to this view, the certainty of forms of knowledge – including sociological knowledge – that characterised modernity has evaporated. Instead of accounts of society and culture that are built from rational and objective inquiry, there are no privileged, expert accounts of the world. The postmodernist shatters not only certainty but traditional disciplinary and methodological conventions and replaces them with no convention, simply a limitless range of possible interpretations of the world around us. Feminism offered a different, critical approach to mainstream sociological research but has sought, for the most part, to offer its own alternative methodology. Postmodernism is certainly an alternative but one which in principle pulls the rug from under the feet of *all* methodologies.

One of the main reasons for this is that sociological inquiry is based on a core belief that it is possible to examine and explain the structure and meaning of social action. This in turn rests on an assumption that there *is* a 'subject' of social action, who – with other subjects (social actors) – gives meaning to social action. Weber himself argued that one of the first priorities of sociology was to understand 'subjective meaning'. By understanding the intended and unintended effects of social action sociologists would be able to map out and explain, through a disciplined inquiry, 'the social', the specific patterns and dynamics of society. Postmodernism challenges this core assumption of modernist sociology by deconstructing the idea of 'the subject' or 'the self'. There is no stable meaning to 'the subject'; the 'self' is uncertain, and 'the social' which sociologists believe they discover through research is simply the creation of a sociological discourse – a particular type of knowledge with no special privileged position among all other **discourses**.

Thus, from both a theoretical and methodological position, **postmodernism** challenges all of the modernist assumptions which are presumed in much of the material discussed in this chapter. But this need not be regarded as necessarily unproductive or negative, for just as feminist methodology has required sociology to be self-critical, reflexive and to acknowledge new ways of engaging with and understanding culture and society, so postmodernism has sparked an interest in new approaches to social analysis. Much of this work is highly abstract and often philosophically dense in meaning and beyond the ambit of this introductory text, though we return to it in much more detail in the final chapter of the book.

One recent methodological development we can discuss here, however, and which we can say is inspired by *both* feminism and postmodernism, is the interest in *autobiographical* forms of sociological inquiry. This interest in part reflects the wider concern in sociology with identity and a desire by many feminists to document and describe the lives of women from within their own perspective. As we saw in Chapter 1, our 'selves' are not single, stable identities but multiple, changing in context and over time, and our memories and images of our past shifting and unfixed. A growing number of sociologists have seen the value in opening their analysis to the rich social vein that runs through the biographical and autobiographical accounts of social actors. (Bell and Yalom, 1990; Benstock, 1988). Research sources become the diary, the memoir, letters and film, video and other forms of visual representation that help construct the meaning of personal lives and the contexts in which they are lived.

But what about the postmodern rug-puller we mentioned a moment ago? Surely, a strong postmodern position would argue that autobiographical techniques of social inquiry cannot provide some new foundation for the discipline; they are merely another way sociologists will try to construct a particular version of reality when in fact there is no 'reality' to be discovered. Against this strong **relativist** position, many sociologists would argue that sociology can acknowledge the ambivalence and uncertainties of our present postmodern condition but, instead of collapsing in a methodological heap of uncertainty, can do so in order to reveal and help explain the ambivalence and ambiguities of

discourse

A body of ideas, concepts and beliefs which become established as knowledge or as an accepted world-view. These ideas become a powerful framework for understanding and action in social life. For example, Foucault studied the discourse of madness, highlighting its changes over the centuries and its interplay with other discourses such as religious and medical discourses, and illustrated how these shifts affect how madness is perceived and reacted to by others.

postmodernism

Often perceived as a cultural and aesthetic phenomenon associated with contemporary literature and the arts, it often combines apparently opposed elements to subvert meaning and fragment totality. It is characterised by a pastiche of cultural styles and elements, but implies a deeper scepticism about order and progress. Instead diversity and fragmentation are celebrated.

relativism

An approach which denies the existence of absolute truth, but maintains that beliefs, values and theories are relative to time and place. Accordingly, traditions and ways of life can only be judged in the context of the age or society that has produced them.

our lives today. If this were not possible, neither the grounding of a sociological discipline nor its *critical* edge would be possible. We return to this issue in our final chapter. But at this point we move on to consider in much more detail the substantive concerns and analyses of sociology, which provide the focus for Parts 2 and 3.

Summary of the Chapter

- Sociological research explores a wide range of questions often related to the dynamics of social change, matters of social policy and broader theoretical issues associated with the development of the discipline itself.
- Researchers must determine what their principal research question is, to what conceptual framework it relates, what methods are most appropriate to collect data, and how these data can be rigorously analysed.
- Researchers should try to ensure their research is both reliable and valid and, where appropriate, be based on some form of representative sampling.
- Positivist and interpretivist methodologies have shaped the theory and practice of research, though today the opposition between the two is being gradually displaced by a more reflexive and pluralistic approach to social inquiry.
- Typical research instruments are the survey (using questionnaires and/or interviews), observational techniques (such as ethnography and participant observation), and case studies.
- Both feminism and postmodernism pose major challenges to the modernist assumptions underlying traditional sociological research.

References

Bell, S. G. and M. Yalom (eds.) (1990) *Revealing Lives: Autobiography, Biography and Gender*, Albany, State University of New York Press.

Benstock, S. (ed.) (1988) *The Private Self: Theory and Practice of Woman's Autobiography*, London, Routledge.

Brewer, J. (1994) 'The ethnographic critique of ethnography: sectarianism in the RUC'. *Sociology*, vol. 28, no. 1, pp. 231–44.

Collins, H. (1985) *Changing Order: Replication and Induction in Scientific Practice*, London, Sage.

Deutscher, I. (1970) 'What we say what we do', *Sociological Focus*, vol. 3, pp. 19–30.

Douglas, J. W. B. (1967) *The Home and the School*, London, Panther.

Elder, G. H. Jr (1974) *Children of the Great Depression*, Chicago, University of

Chicago Press.

Fielding, N. (1993) 'Qualitative Interviewing', in G. N. Gilbert (ed.), *Researching Social Life*, London, Sage.

Finch, J. and L. Hayes (1994) 'Inheritance, death and the concept of the home', *Sociology*, vol. 28, no. 2, pp. 417–34.

Fine, B. (1994) 'What we eat and why: a socio-economic study of standard items in food consumption'. Economic and Social Research Council Research Programme, *The Nation's Diet*, Swindon.

Fox, S. (1990) 'The ethnography of humour and the problem of social reality', *Sociology*, vol. 24, no. 3, pp. 431–46.

Gilbert, G. N. and M. J. Mulkay (1984) *Opening Pandora's Box*, Cambridge, Cambridge University Press.

Goffman, E. (1968) *Asylums*, Harmondsworth, Penguin.

Goldthorpe, J. *et al.* (1968) *Affluent Worker*, Cambridge, Cambridge University Press.

Greer, S. (1969) *The Logic of Social Inquiry*, Chicago, Aldine.

Hammersley, M. (1992) 'On feminist methodology', *Sociology*, vol. 26, no. 2, pp. 187–206.

Hessler, R. M. (1992) *Social Research Methods*, St Pauls, West Publishing Co.

Hirschi, T. (1969) *The Causes of Delinquency*, Berkeley, University of California Press.

Hughes, J. (1976) *Sociological Analysis: Methods of Discovery*, London, Nelson.

Humphreys, L. (1970) *The Tea Room Trade*, London, Duckworth.

Inkeles, A. (1993) 'Industrialisation, modernisation and the quality of life', *International Journal of Comparative Sociology*, vol. 34, no. 1, pp. 1–23

Jones, S. (1985) 'Depth interviewing', in R. Walker (ed.), *Applied Qualitative Research*, Aldershot, Gower.

Layder, D. *et al.* (1991) 'The empirical correlates of action and structure: the transition from school to work', *Sociology*, vol. 25, pp. 447–64.

Marshall, G. *et al.* (1988) *Social Class in Modern Britain*, London, Hutchinson.

Oakley, A. and L. Rajan (1991) 'Social class and social support: the same or different?', *Sociology*, vol. 25, pp. 31–60.

Phillips, D. (1971) *Knowledge From What?*, Chicago, Rand McNally.

Platt, J. (1988) 'What can case studies do?', in R. G. Burgess, *Studies in Qualitative Methodology*, London, JAI Press Ltd.

Ramazanoglu, C. (1992) 'On feminist methodology: male reason versus female empowerment', *Sociology*, vol. 26. no. 2, pp. 207–12.

Reinharz, S. (1992) *Feminist Methods in Social Research*, Oxford, Oxford University Press.

Saggar, S. (1992) *Race and Politics in Britain*, London, Harvester Wheatsheaf.

Spender, D. (1985) *For the Record: The Meaning and Making of Feminist Knowledge*, London, Women's Press.

Stanley, L. (1990a) 'Doing ethnography, writing ethnography', *Sociology*, vol. 24, no. 4, pp. 617–27.

Stanley, L. (1990b) *Feminist Praxis: Research, Theory and Epistemology in Feminist Sociology*, London, Routledge.

Townsend, P. (1979) *Poverty in the United Kingdom*, Harmondsworth, Penguin.

Whyte, W. F. (1984) *Learning From the Field: A Guide From Experience*, London, Sage.

Yin, R. K. (1989) *Case Study Research: Design and Methods*, 2nd edn, Sage, London.

Young, M. and P. Willmott (1957) *Family and Kinship in East London*, Harmondsworth, Penguin.

PART 2

Social Division and Power

CHAPTER 6

Understanding Social Stratification: Social Class

Aims of the Chapter

After introducing the importance of stratification to sociological analysis, this chapter explores the concept of social class, and asks whether class is still a significant feature of contemporary society. You should gain a sense of the different approaches to social class, and how these build on but go beyond the classical Marxist and Weberian perspectives. You should also be able to understand the substantive issues that surround the debates over wealth and poverty in industrialised societies.

Introduction

'What do Essex Men have in common with the bulk of the Japanese population and at least eight sociology professors? The answer is that all of them deny the importance of class divisions in modern society.'

[LEE, 1994]

The analysis of social and economic inequality has been a central concern of sociology since its inception. One reason for this, not surprisingly, was that modernity itself created new patterns of social inequality that needed to be understood. At the same time, these inequalities between social groups threw up new problems for social order as well as new capacities for social change, both of which again needed to be addressed by the emergent discipline. As we shall see, much of the subsequent analyses focused on the unequal social structures created by capitalism, and here considerable attention has been devoted to an understanding of social classes within capitalist society.

social stratification
The division of a population into unequal layers or strata based on income, wealth, gender, ethnicity, power, status, age, religion or some other characteristic.

class
A term widely used in sociology to differentiate the population on grounds of economic considerations, such as inequality in terms of wealth or income.

Social stratification is a term that refers to all forms of inequality, not merely that of **class**. Inequalities based on gender, ethnicity, age, and political power are also crucial dimensions of social stratification which sociologists have explored just as fully as class. These forms of social inequality are also often closely related, such that, for example, ethnic minorities are more likely to be found among the poor.

Most of the time, we do not experience the world as members of a particular 'class', 'ethnic minority' or any other category of social stratification. We tend to see ourselves as individuals with particular jobs, as members of families, as students who will make it – or not – and so on. And even though we might experience our 'gender' in a more immediate, everyday sense through our interaction as men and women with others, we may not see that interaction as carrying any sort of patterned inequality. It's 'only natural' that men and women behave in certain ways, and want different things. A man gets his reward at work, a woman in the home.

Our individual lives inevitably build for us personal life histories that tell us why we are where we are in society. These stories tend to speak of inequality and our positon in highly individualistic terms: we write CVs listing our biographical details, achievements and current position; we 'know' we're strong at some things but not at others, and that only by our efforts will we make anything of ourselves. In other words, inequality is not something to be explained or experienced *collectively*, for it only exists, if at all, as the advantages or disadvantages individuals have created for themselves.

Occasionally, of course, a very different story of inequality is told, one that has not an individual but a collective narrator – a trades union defending its member's pay, a civil rights march demanding votes for blacks, a women's caucus declaring equal rights for their sisters around the world, a gay and lesbian rally against discrimination on grounds of sexuality. At times like these, people regard themselves as occupying a shared position, and construct a powerful sense of a collective identity as members of a single economic class, or ethnic group, gender or sexual minority. When we see such events we should ask ourselves at least two things: what sort of response do those involved get from authority and why; and secondly, could people generate such powerful collectivities on the strength of a persuasive but nevertheless *merely* constructed sense of 'inequality'? Perhaps their stories are based on more fundamental, half-glimpsed inequalities that are masked by the concerns of everyday life.

Sociologists are interested in exploring both the experience and the realities of social inequality. Does it exist, and if so on what basis? If it exists, how do people respond to it? Are the patterns of inequality related to each other? Are some more important than others in some situations? How are inequalities mediated by everyday life? Are there major forms of inequality that can be linked to different types of society? These, and other, questions have been posed by sociologists for more than a century.

Not surprisingly, as society has changed so have the answers. Indeed, this chapter will show how two of the main traditions in the analysis of social stratification – the Marxist and the Weberian – have adapted to changing social circumstances. This is a chapter that focuses on social class. But we must note here that the economic inequalities of class tend to confirm and parallel inequalities of ethnicity and gender. This and the next chapter tell only one story about inequality, a story about

gender
Distinct from 'sex', this concept often refers to the socially constructed categories of masculine and feminine that are differently defined in various cultures. Many contemporary theorists use a broader definition to refer to the variable sets of beliefs and practices about male and female (or other genders), that not only feed into individual identities, but are fundamental to social institutions and symbolic systems.

ethnicity
To be distinguished from 'race', which emphasises biological differences based on skin colour, ethnicity denotes a sense of belonging to a particular community whose members share common cultural traditions.

class. The following two chapters show how significant **gender** and **ethnicity** are as determinants of social inequality today.

Social Class

All industrialised societies today have structures of inequality that reflect unequal economic positions. Crompton (1993) has argued that economic class is a defining feature of modern society in contrast to the ascribed status differences that typically characterise non-modern traditional social orders. The latter might include 'age-set' stratification where one's position in a social hierarchy is directly related to the changing status one receives simply by virtue of the age one reaches. The very different class structures of today reflect the onset of 'modernity' through which complex social economic and political institutions regulate and secure the interests of different social classes. The ensuing tension and conflict between classes has been a key factor for social change. As Crompton notes, 'in the modern world class-based organisations – that is organisations claiming to represent classes and class interests – have been the dynamic source of many of the changes and transformations which have characterised the modern era' (p. 4).

Social classes existed before industrial society of course but the economic hierarchies they expressed were as much to do with political, religious or hereditary forms of domination as they were an individual's relationship to the system of production – the sort of job they had, the resources under their control, the reward they received for work, and so on. Social classes in the feudal period, for example, were, by and large, closed: access to the nobility or the peasantry was determined by birth, though occasionally peasants could escape from feudal bondage to the towns, and rich merchants were sometimes able to purchase titles and estates.

The merchants (or burgesses) constituted a growing challenge to the social relations of feudalism precisely because they weakened the hereditary basis to social position, and helped open up a new (urban-based) labour market for landless workers thrown off rural estates by the commercialisation and enclosure of farmland. Labour increasingly became 'free wage labour', a commodity to be sold in an expanding **labour market**, available to private capitalists for hire. Herein lie the origins of the modern social classes of contemporary industrial capitalism.

labour market
The supply and availability of people who are willing and able to work.

Britain, often regarded as the historical reference point for this passage of events, is perhaps not surprisingly tagged as 'class-ridden', a society in which the inequalities of social class are pronounced (in both senses of the word!), from the established upper class – both landed 'gentry' and the new 'super-rich' – down to the traditional working class. However, this image and the different life-styles it evokes – often recreated through film and TV 'costume dramas' – is said by others to be out of date. The social 'revolution' of Thatcherism during the 1980s sought the dismantling of the established class hierarchy, while the Major government of the mid-1990s declared its intention to create a 'classless society': hence the quote that heads this chapter.

However, both the image of the unchanging class society and the notion of a shift towards a classless society fail to capture the reality of the underlying changes to the system of social stratification that have marked the past two decades in Britain. We have seen long periods of recession, high levels of unemployment, a credit-led consumer boom at the end of the 1980s, the restructuring of large and small firms, and a massive growth in part-time, low-wage casualised service-based jobs in retailing, leisure, and office work. At the same time, the traditions of working-class communities seemed to have been swept away by the redevelopment of older areas for privatised and more wealthy housing – such as 'the Docklands' in East London, or the sale of 'council housing' throughout Britain – while remnants of inner-city community collapse under the weight of growing levels of crime and social dislocation brought about by lack of work, homelessness or poorly paid jobs which command neither commitment nor respect from those forced to take them on. Add to this the privatisation and massive shrinkage of primary industries which were archetypically working class in terms of the social and political values they espoused – such as coal-mining and ship-building – and the magnitude of the change is even more apparent. The older established upper class whose wealth has relied on the value of property and shareholding has also been shaken by the rise and rapid fall in real value of both, while the stability of finance as a safe investment has been undermined by the collapsing value of the pound, massive insurance losses (such as at Lloyds of London) and banking scandals and mergers. Nevertheless, the wealthy, as we shall see, like the poor, are still very much with us, thanks to a massive reduction in the real level of tax they have to pay. However, their collective identity and cohesion as members of a socially privileged *British* upper class is less secure today than in the past.

In short, the last two decades have weakened the traditional social and economic bases on which the conventional model of social class has long stood. A number of changes can be mentioned here to illustrate the point, changes which are common to most Western European states. First, we have seen a growing *polarisation* of standards of living between the wealthy and the growing ranks of the poor: in 1979, according to figures for the UK, just over 5 million people were in households that fell below the income poverty line; by 1991 their number had risen to 13.5 million (DSS, 1993). In addition, a *culture of individualism* has become more prevalent and has been given added weight by government moves to encourage the private individually-based purchase of previously state-provided benefits, such as personal health insurance and pension schemes (see Chapter 13). Finally, the labour market has become more strongly *segregated* as the nature of available work has changed and so movement between occupational classes has declined: this has particularly disadvantageous effects for working-class youth entering the labour market, even though in the past their levels of occupational mobility were always relatively low anyway. We return to this issue in Chapter 7. What we need to ask, then, is whether these changes sketched out above herald a *decline* in the importance of class as a determinant of social position and reward or a *restructuring* of the terms on which a person's class position is based. In this chapter, therefore, we want to examine the contemporary evidence for and explanations of class inequality, its persistence as well as its changes, and explore the degree to which class, as both an economic status and subjective experience, is still a significant form of social stratification. To do this we must begin by discussing the traditional theories of class inequality.

Traditional Theories of Class: Marxist and Weberian Approaches

Marx's theory of property relations

For many sociologists, modern society is distinguished from earlier society by its essentially *industrial* character. Marx recognised the importance of industrialisation as a modernising process, but for him this was only properly understood as a *capitalist* and not merely industrial one. Thus, although industry produced wealth, it had done so in a highly unequal way, with one class, the bourgeoisie, monopolising the profits and value of industrial production while the mass of the working people who worked in the new factories and elsewhere were made poorer, not richer, by the social and technical advances of industrial development.

bourgeoisie
A Marxist term used to describe the property-owning capitalist class.

proletariat
A Marxist term for wage-earners, the propertyless class within capitalism.

For Marx the key classes in the capitalist mode of production are the **bourgeoisie** and the **proletariat**, or capitalists and landless wage workers. These classes are in conflict with each other as exploiter and

productive wealth
Wealth which generates additional income, such as capital invested in property or stocks and shares.

surplus value
A term coined by Marx to describe the difference between the value of the labour and the value of the product of that labour.

exploited. The bourgeoisie derive their class position from the fact that they own **productive wealth**: it is not their high income that makes them capitalists, but the fact that they own the means of production (i.e. inputs necessary for industrial manufacture – factories, machines, etc).

There is a general tendency, Marx claimed, for wages to stick at a generally exploitative level except when some skills are temporarily scarce. In addition, the capitalist owns the product and will pocket the difference between the value of the labour and the value of the product – '**surplus value**' as Marx called it – purely and simply by virtue of being owner. Property rights also allow capitalists control – through their managers – of the process of production. Workers have to sell their labour-power in order to survive and so their labour becomes a 'commodity' for sale by them on the labour-market. Thus, the crucial division between the two main classes lies in their very different relationship to the ownership of the means of production.

In his major work, *Capital*, Marx explores the emergent strains and tensions that arise between the two main classes. He argues that class conflict is not only inherent but inevitable within capitalism: the logic of capitalism is to exploit workers to realise profit, while workers' exploitation leads them eventually to challenge the system. The working class then becomes a revolutionary class ushering in first a socialist regime and finally the Communist Utopia, 'where society inscribes on its banners: "From each according to his ability, to each according to his needs!"'

It is clear that there are serious problems with Marx's account. Where socialist revolution has occurred it has done so in societies on the threshold of entering capitalism – such as Russia in 1917 – or via a nationalist populism – such as China in 1949 – rather that in mature capitalist states ripe for change. Secondly, in real terms the working class has in Western states enjoyed an increase in its wages while the development of the welfare state has ameliorated the worse effects of unemployment. Thirdly, state socialism in Europe collapsed like a house of cards between 1989 and 1992 and the ensuing scramble for capitalism in Central and Eastern Europe has, among other things, brought BMWs, McDonald's, and Marlboro' cigarettes to the streets of Bucharest, Budapest and Moscow.

Marx's ideas seemed to have been disproved by these late twentieth-century developments that will no doubt continue through into the twenty-first century. This has led to a gradual distancing from Marxist theory in general and Marxian analysis in sociology itself as the newer theories of consumption, post-modernism and post-socialism take root (see Chapters 2 and 19). Yet there is much to be said for Marx's basic assumption that class should be defined not in terms of categories such as occupation, most commonly used, but in terms of a deeper understanding of property relations, control and ownership, for herein lies much of the source of social power, even if we must accept that this does not adequately account for *all* forms of contemporary power and inequality. In addition, Marx's account envisages the expansion of capitalism on a global scale as capital seeks to exploit markets and labour overseas: to this extent, his analysis anticipates the global concentration of capital that we discussed in Chapter 3.

political consciousness
Awareness of politics or political ideas.

neo-Marxism
Contemporary schools of thought based on a development of Marxist philosophy.

neo-Weberian
A theoretical approach based on a revision of Weber's work.

What we can say in criticism, however, is that Marx's emphasis on the ownership of productive wealth and the structure of power associated with it leaves us unable to explain all the differences in rewards and **political consciousness** within the mass of the population who are not capitalists. Indeed, it is this which has led many sociologists to look elsewhere for insight into the complexity of social inequality. It is to the basic ideas of Max Weber (1864–1920) that many turn for a more nuanced analysis of patterns of inequality. Yet the Marxist insight should not be lost and still has much to offer. Indeed, today, there is ongoing debate between those who define class in revised, **neo-Marxian**, terms with those who define it in **neo-Weberian** terms. Before exploring some of the key issues of this ongoing debate, we need to turn to Weber's own examination of social stratification.

Weber's theory of market relations

Weber argued that social inequality needed to be understood in terms of a number of distinct categories which are not reducible merely to economic property relations: the ownership of land, factories, and so on *is* accepted as an important determinant of social position but it is only one factor shaping social stratification. He proposed that inequality should be understood through the three-fold categories of '*class*', '*status*' and '*power*'. Some social positions were much more to do with one of these rather than the other two: caste in India, for example, is more based on **status** differences associated with a religious ranking of ritual purity than it is to do with anything else. Weber argued that those who were advantaged in any one of these categories could use that as a basis for accruing privilege and reward more commonly associated with either of the other two: someone who enjoys high status may use this as a form of leverage to secure an improved economic or political position; alternatively powerful politicians can use their position to

status
Associated with Weber, it denotes the relative prestige of a person's social standing.

mobilise their party for economic gain. This may, sometimes, be pursued in such a way as to eventually end in mass corruption and clientelism, as was the case, for example, in Italy during the 1980s where political office at all levels of society was used in an illegitimate way to secure economic benefit.

For Weber, therefore, these different forms of inequality – class, status, and (political) power – were independent of each other. Unlike Marx, he would not have argued that social class is the principal determinant of inequality. Nevertheless, Weber did agree with Marx that in capitalist industrial society economic relations do play a particularly crucial role in shaping inequalities between individuals and groups. Unlike Marx, however, Weber wanted to stress inequalities associated with the *market* rather than with the ownership of *property*. Inequalities in **market capacity** determine the position people occupy in the social hierarchy: the capacities people have in terms of the skills they bring to the labour market as employees explains the rewards they will receive. Where people have a good market capacity – such as accountants and medics – they will have very good *life chances*: these chances include income perks and pensions together with less tangible benefits such as security of job, pleasant working conditions and considerable autonomy at work. Different groups with different occupational market capacities, and, therefore, unequal life chances, can be regarded as different social classes. Inevitably, this definition leads to a much larger number of 'social classes' than Marx's basic division between the owner and non-owner of the 'means of production'.

market capacity
The level of reward secured by individuals from the sale of their skills in the labour market.

Weber's work has been picked up by contemporary sociologists, such as Marshall *et al.* (1988) who see it as a valuable explanation for the very broad differences in occupational reward and position of manual and non-manual workers, as well as allowing gradations of social position within each class grouping – for example between senior managerial staff and routine clerical workers in the non-manual sector. Similarly, manual classes' market capacities vary as one moves down the social hierarchy from skilled, semi-skilled to unskilled manual jobs.

It is possible to acknowledge the merits of *both* the Marxist and Weberian accounts of social stratification, since they provide valuable insights into different aspects of the contemporary capitalist system. A combination of these two traditions would produce a three-fold distinction between a propertied 'upper-class' a large white-collar middle or service class, and a working class of manual workers whose life chances over their working life are much worse. Beneath these are 'the poor' – a fourth group who have the worst life chances because of being excluded from,

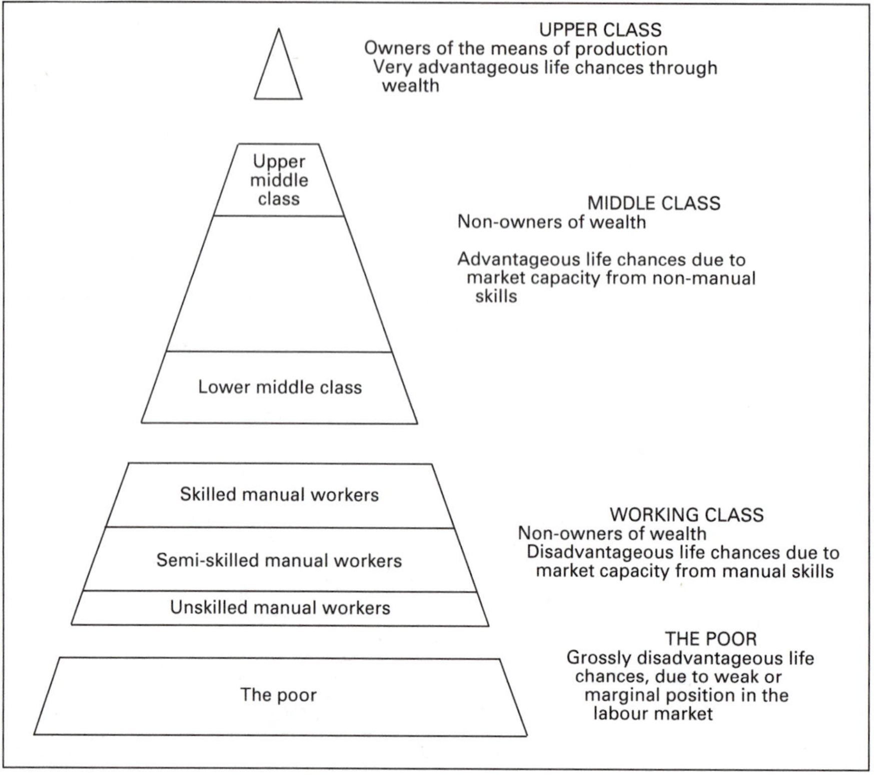

Fig 6.1 Social class stratification by income and wealth

or marginalised in the labour market – the infirm, the disabled, the aged, lone-parent families, and so on. Figure 6.1 depicts a combined Marxian/Weberian model of stratification.

Contemporary Neo-Marxian/Neo-Weberian Debate

Much of the present approach to social stratification, as we have said, combines the insights derived from the Marxist focus on *property* with those based on a Weberian concern with the *occupational labour* market. However, changes in both property ownership and the labour market have called for a more complex analysis than even Marx or Weber at their most sophisticated could have conceived. This is precisely because the national and global processes shaping current social inequality simply did not prevail at the time that either were writing.

There are changes to the pattern of propertied and occupational inequality that reflect changes at national and international – or more properly global – levels. National changes can be said to have occurred over the past thirty to forty years while the global changes reflect much more recent processes at work. With regard to the first, a propertied upper class is still apparent in all mature capitalist countries but can be seen to have experienced two key changes.

First, at the *national* level, the wealth-holding of the rich has been, to a limited extent, redistributed downwards towards the next 5–10 per cent of wealth holders while the management of private capital – whether this be of landed property or corporations – is in the hands of a powerful senior manager or service class. This means that there has been a separation of ownership from control of capital though this does *not* necessarily mean that the managers of capital are likely to work against the interests of owners and dominant shareholders: indeed, most senior management are of course major shareholders in the very companies they manage.

Secondly, at a *global* level, the stability and reproduction of a specifically *national* upper class, in Britain, Canada, France, Italy or elsewhere, is being increasingly eclipsed today by the emergence of a *transnational capitalist class,* particularly associated with the ownership and management of finance capital – the wealth associated with international banks, major currency dealers, insurance conglomerates and the like. It is important to remember that the capitalist upper class holds wealth in three different forms: in landed property, in the ownership of productive manufacturing firms, and in finance. Today, it is the last of these which is the most important form of global wealth and which is shaping the fortunes of both rich and poor in all capitalist countries. Andreff (1984) has shown the importance of what he calls 'transnational finance capital' and Carrol and Lewis (1991) the way in which international capitalists 'operate within ... transnational circuits of [capital and they thereby] can be expected to manifest less and less of a connection to 'national' priorities" (p. 507). This second process feeds back on the first inasmuch as many of the new recruits to senior management have been in banking and insurance companies operating at a global level.

Taken together these two processes have led to what Scott (1987; 1991) has called the 'depersonalisation' of capital, the gradual dissociation of the holding of major wealth from specific individuals and their families. The rich are still with us, of course – there are now over 200 billionaires in the world (60 in the US alone) – and in the UK the 200 richest people are together worth over £50 billion. But increasingly, the basis on which they will continue to enjoy and increase such fortunes depends on the dynamics of global capital investment and the profitability of money markets. As Lee (1994) notes: 'Today, impersonal capitalisation and ownership means huge international movements of money funds made at the behest of multinational corporations and wealthy governments, as they respond speculatively to the ebb and flow of money markets' (p. 410).

With regard to *occupational labour markets,* again we can see two related changes that have taken place at national and global levels, the first over the past few decades, the second of more recent origin. First, at the *national* level, there has been an erosion over the past twenty to thirty years of the traditional distinction between manual and non-manual jobs, partly as a result of the expansion of white-collar, service-sector work. Today, white-collar jobs in offices, retailing, repairs and servicing, for example, are so poorly paid and routinised that they are little different in terms of status and reward from much traditional manual, or 'blue-collar', work. This is especially true of those white-collar jobs which have become highly feminised in the sense of employing a disproportionate number of female staff. In addition, the number of working-class jobs has itself declined rapidly as the UK, along with many other European countries, has cut its level of investment in local manufacturing. The compensatory expansion of service-sector jobs has meant that many working-class members have been recruited to fill these posts. Those that fail to secure work and who remain chronically unemployed slip quickly into the most deprived '**underclass**', our 'poor', as shown in Figure 6.1.

underclass
A concept used to describe a group at the bottom of the social hierarchy who are economically, politically and socially marginalised from the rest of society.

Fordism
A form of industrial economy based on mass production and mass marketing prevalent in the post-war period. These techniques and processes were pioneered by Henry Ford in the manufacture and sale of Ford motor cars.

post-Fordism
Computer controlled and sophisticated production systems which emerged during the 1970s. Their key emphasis is on flexibility and the production of specialised, tailored goods to meet the demands of a competitive world economy.

Secondly, at the *global* level, jobs in the UK, as elsewhere, are affected by internationally-shaped patterns of global investment and employment. We saw, for example, in Chapter 3, that there has been a shift away from the older '**Fordist**' pattern of employment at national levels to a **post-Fordist** pattern in which global investment decisions to relocate work elsewhere, to move to flexible employee contracts and to establish global 'chains' or networks of production and distribution have all meant that traditional, nationally-based employment structures – such as those associated with raw materials and primary manufacturing – play a less important role. As depressed areas of Britain – once the heartlands of British industry – are hit by Fordist unemployment and a limited ability to cash in on newer jobs because of inappropriate or missing skills, so we see a growing regional and structural *polarisation of* social inequality and a growth in real levels of poverty. (We return to the issue of poverty shortly.) The labour market today simply does not provide as many of those traditional jobs for the 'lads' that Paul Willis (1977) described in his studies of working-class boys about to leave secondary school (see Chapter 11).

We can see the effects of the global dynamics of capital investment on the propertied and employed classes in Britain by looking at King's (1991) study of London as the financial centre of the world. King's account shows the dramatic changes that have taken place in terms of wealth holding, the impact on this of finance capital, and the way the latter has shaped London's social and economic structure. King encapsulates some of the key changes in London's international role, from the early part of this century as a city closely tied to the interests of empire to the present day when it acts as a 'global control centre', a world city, for international finance capital.

Box 6.1: Wealth and work in London: the changing context

'In the first half of the twentieth century, London's role in the old international division of labour was still largely that of imperial city. It was the control centre of a colonial mode of production and, as such, its largely indigenous population was characterised by a social and class composition principally influenced by this role. This social composition also included a significant working-class element based on a substantial amount of manufacturing: it was also both spatially as well as physically expressed in the built environment.

With the disintegration of the colonial mode of production and old international division of labour from the 1950s, the transition from the role of imperial to world city was well under way ... Since the 1960s, the increasing specialisation of London as world city, with its specific functions in the world-economy ... has had various important effects on the social, ethnic, and spatial composition of its population. At the lower end of the social hierarchy, the collapse of industry has left the country- and culture-specific Black and Asian migrant labour, drawn from the poorest countries in the world, largely trapped in the run-down parts of the inner city...

At the top end of the social hierarchy, however, London's enhanced role in the international division of labour as world banking, financial trading, as well as "global control" centre, has had an equally important impact on its social composition.

The first effect is the concentration of a highly paid elite principally (though not entirely) indigenous. The second effect results from the banking, financial, and trading function. As London is the principal financial centre in the capitalist world-economy, it requires the presence of representatives of the world's richest nations, most specifically, Japan and the United States ... Both the rich at the top and the poor at the bottom have significant effects on the institutions and culture of the city, as also on the extent and expression of economic and social polarization and the potential for social, racial, ethnic and political conflict (and also, co-operation) …

The effect of the world city, therefore, is to bring representatives of the richest and poorest countries in the world into the ambit of each other. It is ambit, rather than contact, because the historical economic, class, spatial and built-environment divisions, between the West End and the East End, which divide rich and poor in the Imperial City, continue to keep both groups apart...

[T]he world city becomes...an international enclave whose space, social relations, and politics increasingly depend on decisions made outside national boundaries.'

Source: A. D. King, *Global Cities*, 1991, pp. 142–5.

The class structure as depicted in Figure 6.1 is a very static model of the broad differences between social classes that does not in itself say anything in detail about the changing dynamics – national and global – which the preceding section has sketched out. However, the model is nevertheless sufficient to provide a basic understanding of the differences between (propertied) wealth and occupational differences through which social strata can be classified. It has to be regarded as a map which seeks to combine Marxian and Weberian notions of class.

There is, it must be acknowledged, an ongoing debate between Marxist and Weberian scholars today about the best way of categorising different occupational groups, about the total number of classes, about the range of middle-class positions and the class position of senior management in relation to the owners of capital, and, most importantly, how and where to locate women in the class structure to allow for the specific disadvantages associated with gender. One of the principal disputes has been between the neo-Marxist Erik Wright and the neo-Weberian John Goldthorpe: they and their respective followers have entered into protracted debate about where best to draw the line between the capitalist class and the middle classes, or where to draw that separating true working-class (or 'proletarian') jobs from lower-level middle (or 'service') class occupations (see, for example, Marshall and Rose, 1990). Much of the analysis depends on very detailed statistical analysis of income, political alignment and work-place autonomy. Both camps have been strongly criticised for neglecting (as in Wright) or dismissing (as in Goldthorpe) the significance and problem of women's position within the class structure.

Here we would argue that it is important *to combine* the theoretical insights of the two main traditions in order to make sense of class stratification. One of the more useful recent contributions that does this in order to explore the contemporary class structure in Britain, in terms of wealth and occupational advantages and the differences between them, has been provided by Runciman (1990) whose studies on stratification and the experience of inequality go back to the 1960s. Runciman argues that a proper theoretical understanding of class stratification should be based on the concept of *economic power* and the way this is attached to different roles and positions in the social hierarchy. He argues that economic power has three distinct dimensions:

- *ownership* which refers to legal title to some part of the means of production (e.g. via shareholding, trust holding, partnership, etc.);
- *control* which refers to a 'contractual right' to direct or manage some aspect of the productive process whether this be managing labour or fixed (capital) assets or both; and
- *marketability* which refers to a recognised skill or capacity which is deemed to have a particular value within the labour market.

This set of criteria allows Runciman to explore the broad similarities and differences in terms of possession of 'economic power' that people in ostensibly very different types of job have. These criteria can be used to allocate people in relatively well-paid but very different types of employment status to a similar middle-class position.

Box 6.2: Identifying a similar class location

'[C]onsider the hypothetical example of three similarly qualified adult male professional engineers aged, say, forty-five years. Mr A. works as an employee with a large cornpany on a salary of £40,000 gross (£25,000 net) per annum with a good pension scheme and a subsidized home-loan. Mr B. is the proprietor of a small engineering business which he has been enabled to acquire by remortgaging his personal assets to his bank and thereby leaving himself, after paying the bank interest, an incorne of £10,000 a year net of tax. Mr C. is a free-lance engineering consultant whose only employee is his secretary (who is also his wife) and whose income, depending on the unpredictable requirement for his services, can vary from £10,000 net of tax in a particularly bad year to £40,000 net of tax in a particularly good one. Despite the differences between them in both income and employment status, they share a common class position; and they do so because each exemplifies a different, but functionally equivalent, criterion of economic power – *control* in the first case, *ownership* in the second, and *marketability* in the third...[E]ach is equally well-established in the occupancy of a role to which there attaches similar economic power.'

Source: Runciman, 1990, p. 380.

Similarly, one can identify members of the upper class in terms of those who are most advantaged in one or more of the criteria. Runciman says: 'That there is a distinguishable "upper class" is sufficiently demonstrated by the examples of, say, the Dukes of Northumberland and Westminster (by the criterion of ownership [of land]), the chief executives of Shell and BP (by the criterion of control) and the senior partners of the biggest firms of City accountants and solicitors (by the criterion of marketability [of their expertise])' (p. 383). For their part, the working class are those 'who lack ownership of any property other than minimal personal possessions, [who] lack control over anything other than their own persons and who lack marketability of anything other than their labour to which there attaches no premium of any kind' (p. 381). Runciman suggests that the current British class structure can be seen to be made up of four broad class groupings (with subdivisions in the middle and working classes) similar to those we mapped out in Figure 6.1.

Clearly, going beyond Runciman's account and recalling our earlier argument, we need to recognise that the process through which 'economic power' is distributed across social strata is as much to do with transnational as it is national socio-economic factors. Thus, from what was argued above about the growing importance of transnational financial capital, those who occupy senior positions within this occupational and propertied sector are especially likely to be *most* advantaged within the upper class itself.

We have so far only hinted at the different material advantages conferred on different classes via wealth and occupation. It is time to explore in a little more detail the substantive differences between these two key dimensions of class stratification.

Wealth

Wealth seems to mean the same as 'property', but 'property' is a term commonly used to refer to anything from Arundel Castle to the clothes you are wearing. But this general notion of property conceals a crucial distinction between different *forms* of property. We must distinguish between *consumption property and productive property.* Property for personal consumption includes consumer durables (e.g. CD-players, clothes, cars) and family homes which are owner-occupied. Productive property is significantly different, for this includes factories, farms or building land, and stocks and shares. This kind of property is *capital* and yields income through profit on the productive use of property. Privately owned property of this sort provides massive *unearned* income through,

- rent on buildings or land
- dividends paid from profit of firms to shareholders;
- interest on money investments, such as deposit accounts or government bonds.

Moreover, the right to buy and sell property provides *capital gains,* the basis for property speculation that fuelled much of the 'boom' in the UK and Western Europe during the 1980s.

Such unearned income generates wealth, and wealth-holding tends to produce more wealth through reinvestment of unearned income. International property speculation produced rapid rises in the market value of commercial and residential properties in London during the mid-1980s, much of this fuelled by Saudi, Middle-Eastern and American wealth holders. For example, as King (1991) reports, ' The Dorchester Hotel, sold in 1976 for £9 million by its British owners, McAlpines, was bought and sold four times over before being purchased by the Sultan of Brunei for £43 million in 1985. Shortly after, it was bought by the American group, Regent International Hotels, for £45 million.' To find the wealthy multi-millionaires in more residential London settings one has only to visit Bishop's Avenue, Hampstead, Avenue Road, St John's Wood, and Kensington Palace Gardens.

The persistence of massive inequalities in the distribution of wealth is one of the most important features of the capitalist class structure: as Crompton (1993) has commented, 'If for no other reason, this *de facto* concentration of wealth and power in capitalist industrial societies should be sufficient to clinch the argument that these are still "class societies"' (p. 192). Table 6.1 summarises the distribution of personal marketable wealth between 1976 and 1991 for the UK.

The table shows that the distribution of wealth has in fact become *more* unequal over the past twenty years, as the holding of the top 5 per cent has increased when domestic households are excluded from the calculation as in the second half of the table. This reflects not only the massive gains in the value of property-based unearned income but also a reduction in real terms of the burden of tax falling on the wealthy, a

Table 6.1: *Distribution of wealth[1] in the UK, 1976–91 (percentages and £billion)*

	1976	*1981*	*1986*	*1991*
Marketable wealth				
Percentage of wealth owned by[2]				
Most wealthy 1%	21	18	18	18
Most wealthy 5%	38	36	36	37
Most wealthy 10%	50	50	50	50
Most wealthy 25%	71	73	73	71
Most wealthy 50%	92	92	90	92
Total marketable wealth (£ billion)	280	565	955	1694
Marketable wealth less value of dwellings				
Percentage of wealth owned by[2]				
Most wealthy 1%	29	26	25	28
Most wealthy 5%	47	45	46	50
Most wealthy 10%	57	56	58	63
Most wealthy 25%	73	74	75	79
Most wealthy 50%	88	87	89	92

[1] Estimates for 1976, 1981 and 1986 are based on the estates of persons dying in those years. Estimates for 1991 are based on estates notified for probate in 1991–92. Estimates are not strictly comparable between 1991 and earlier years.

[2] Percentages and total marketable wealth are of population aged 18 and over.

Source: Inland Revenue.

reduction initiated during the Thatcher administrations and continued since. Many of the 'new wealthy' are those paid high salaries with lighter tax burdens who can clearly afford to save and invest and so accumulate wealth and thereby join an upper class of corporate stock holders, financiers, landowners or inheritors of wealth. The economic and social position of this upper class is determined, in Runciman's terms, by their ownership and control of productive wealth. The vast majority of the population, even if they do own some consumption property, certainly have little access to income from productive assets.

Scott (1993; 1994) has recently argued that there is a key distinction to be made between the *deprivation* of the poor and the *privilege* of the wealthy: 'If deprivation is the condition of life of the poor, privilege is the condition of the life of the wealthy. Deprivation and privilege should be seen as complementary terms, as two contrasting departures from the normal life style of the citizen. From this point of view, deprivation and privilege are polarised conditions of life, reflecting the polarisation of wealth and poverty ... [T]he causes of poverty cannot be separated from the causes of wealth' (1993, p. 20). And, just as the poor are excluded from full participation in the social, economic and cultural rights normally enjoyed by the citizen so the wealthy are able to enjoy privileges which enable them to 'establish "private" life styles and modes of consumption from which others are excluded' (ibid, p. 25). The privileges of the rich, once seen as being kept in check by taxation, the welfare state and a common belief in appropriate levels of redistribution, are, says Scott, increasingly regarded as legitimate: 'In the climate created by the erosion of the welfare state and the establishment of an "enterprise culture", the rich have become less defensive about their privileges and less likely to feel any obligations towards the poor' (p. 28). If Scott is right, it is an important political question to ask whether this indifference of the rich towards the poor and their luxuriating in their wealth is regarded as legitimate across all sections of society.

The Distribution of Life Chances via Occupation

In the preceding section we discussed the substantive inequalities associated with wealth that mark out the boundaries of the upper class on our Figure 6.1. In this section we discuss the other *occupational strata* in our model, the middle and working classes. Rather than the result of differential access to productive property *per se,* the inequality between these two broad classes can be explained in terms of a more Weberian emphasis on their different *market capacities,* akin to Runciman's notion of the *marketability* of skills that the individual brings to the labour market. Different labour market capacities bring in turn different levels of reward which then produce inequalities in all areas of life: conditions at work, health, housing, education, mortality and justice.

However, given our earlier discussion about changes in the national and transnational economy and the impact these have on the class structure and the experience of class membership, it is important to recognise that the nature of the labour market has itself changed. Many workers in all social classes are more vulnerable to the exigencies of national and international investment decisions and government policies which encourage more 'flexible' forms of employment. Before we look at the material inequalities of the occupational strata it is crucial to see these in the context of these broader labour market changes that have occurred over the past fifteen years, and which reflect a major shift in business and state policy.

Camiller (1989) has provided a summary of the changes in the nature of capitalist investment and the state policies associated with this from the Second World War to the present day. Table 6.2 summarises his basic argument. It is clear that there has been a dramatic change in the direction and priorities of state and private capital over this fifty-year period, indeed that the current policies of both government and private sector are directly opposite to the high-wage full-employment strategies of the past.

Table 6.2 Changes in pattern of capitalist investment and state policy

Post war period	*1980s–90s*
Mass-production of standardised goods in country	Decentralisation and flexible global production process
High-wage, high-productivity, full-employment labour market for mass consumption goods	Segmentation of the labour market and high levels of structural unemployment
State ownership of infrastructure and basic industry	Privatisation and deregulation of state enterprise
Redistribution (via tax/benefits) of income on more equal basis	Rapid removal of redistributive tax policy
Public provision of universal systems of health, education, etc.	Tendency towards privatisation, reduction of welfare-state services

It should be clear that in the current situation the switch away from a policy of full employment coupled with the pressure on individual wage earners and households to secure their own means of private provision (of health care and pensions, for example) mean that occupational inequalities in terms of income and job security can play an even more significant role in determining an individual's life chances than before. In part, this explains why many households can only remain viable units where there are two earners. But as the polarisation of the labour market continues to bite, some have commented on the emergence of what have been called 'work-rich' in contrast to 'work-poor' households. In the former, we see the emergence of dual-career homes, where partners are working long hours for relatively high but never fully secure levels of pay in the white-collar professional and managerial sectors. In the latter, jobs are more difficult to find, are poor in terms of pay, typically part-time with variable hours from one working day to the next.

Broad income differences between the social classes are one measure of the different levels of reward and advantage accruing to different occupational strata. A simple and striking way of seeing these differences is in terms of a parade of income holders, from giants with most income to dwarfs with very little. Will Hutton (1993) has provided one of the more recent versions of this bed-time story: 'Suppose the British could parade through Hyde Park for an hour, their height corresponding to the average income. It is only after 37 minutes that we would see the first average-height person, with the first quarter of an hour taken up by dwarfs below three feet tall. We would have to wait three minutes before the end before we see the first over 11 feet. In the last seconds we see the real giants with one or two of the tallest over 100-yards high' (*The Guardian,* 28 December 1993, p. 9). Clearly, this indicates not only the extent of the *range* of income inequality but also the sense in which many people earn considerably less than the average income, which in 1994 stood at £18,500. The richest 1 per cent of income earners enjoy salaries at least four to five times this figure with a small minority earning in excess of £200,000. Table 6.3 provides details of the proportionate distribution of income across 'quintile groups', that is from the bottom fifth to the top fifth of income earners. It is clear that those households with the lowest disposable income are likely to be headed

Table 6.3 Composition of quintile groups of household income in the UK: by occupational group of head of household, 1991 (percentages)

	Quintile groups of households ranked by equivalised disposable income[1]					
	Bottom fifth	*Next fifth*	*Middle fifth*	*Next fifth*	*Top fifth*	*All households*
Occupational group of head of household						
Professional	–	1	4	7	14	5
Employers and managers	3	4	9	17	34	13
Intermediate and junior non-manual	3	7	14	21	22	13
Skilled manual	10	17	27	26	15	19
Semi-skilled manual	6	10	12	9	2	8
Unskilled manual	3	3	3	2	–	2
Retired	49	44	22	12	7	27
Unoccupied	25	15	9	6	4	12
Other[2]	–	–	1	1	1	1
All occupational groups	100	100	100	100	100	100

[1] Equivalised disposable income has been used for ranking the households into quintile groups.
[2] Mainly armed forces.
Source: Central Statistical Office, from the Family Expenditure Survey.

by those who are retired or unemployed (here 'unoccupied'): 75 per cent of the poorest households (the bottom fifth) could be found here. In contrast, almost 50 per cent of the highest income households (the top fifth) are headed by people in professional, employer or manager occupations.

While individual income differences by job are apparent, there is still a broad distinction between manual and non-manual work, and it is important to remember that manual workers' wages are heavily dependent on overtime work. In real terms, although the 'standard working week' has been reduced for most manual workers since the war, the reliance on overtime hours means that the working week for many of them is very similar. At the same time, many middle-class non-manual jobs require increasingly long hours per week – especially in the professional sectors, such as education, medicine, accountancy and law – which may go unrewarded in an *immediate* financial sense but which are 'expected' as part of the 'career' path of new recruits, whose **life-cycle of earnings** will eventually bring them to and beyond the average salary of the working population. That is, it is important to look at the pattern of earnings over the span of employees' working lives, and where overtime plays an important role for manual workers both its availability and the ageing worker's capacity to do it mean that the additional income it brings is never secure nor long-term. Moreover, the erosion of the redistributive effects of taxation during the past fifteen years has meant that the proportion of total income of the richer households has increased at the expense of the poorer: in 1994, the top 20 per cent of households received 50 per cent of total household income, while the poorer 40 per cent took less than 6 per cent – from giants to dwarfs indeed.

life-cycle of earnings
The pattern of earnings over the length of an employee's working life.

These differences in income, patterns of work and life-cycle of earnings mean that there are very different *life chances* between the more affluent middle and less well-off working classes. As Chapter 13 shows, differences in life chances are not merely differences in job prospects, security in old age, ability to raise a mortgage and so on, they are also have a literal meaning in the sense that data from the *General Household Survey* indicate higher levels of morbidity and mortality for the adult working class compared with middle classes. Specific occupational hazards, along with diet, poor housing and home environment, personal habits such as smoking, mental stress and lower use of the health service result in a higher rate of illness and death for manual workers, and increasingly so for female manual workers.

The Poor and the 'Underclass'

This discussion of occupational differences in life chances has provided some benchmarks against which one can measure class inequality, such as the simple measure of average income. Indeed it is this same measure which many countries use as a yardstick for estimating those 'in poverty'. If we were to use incomes of people in households that were below 'half' the average income as a measure of those 'in poverty' it is possible to see how patterns change over time. Though the UK government itself has never adopted an official definition of those in poverty using this basis, if it is taken as our measure we can see from Table 6.4 that the number of persons in poorer households has increased over the past decade. Clearly, such figures need to be treated with care since it is also true that the overall level of 'average' income has increased. Nevertheless, it is also true that since 1979 the share of total income for all lower income groups has fallen.

Table 6.4 Persons in households below half average income

1979	5.0 million	9%
1981	6.2 million	11%
1987	10.5 million	19%
1989	12.0 million	22%
1991	13.5 million	24%

Source: Households Below Average Income, DSS 1993.

There are other indicators of those in poverty which are also used today, such as those whose income is at or below the level of 'income support' when state benefit is payable (1990 = 11.5 million) or those in 'severe poverty' unable to afford basic essentials such as heating, warm clothes, hot-meals, etc. (1990 = 3.5 million).

Who is most likely to suffer from deprivation at this level? In fact while one might at first think it would be those out of work – and indeed these are among the more vulnerable – it is the *low-paid* in insecure work that constitute the bulk of those below the income poverty line. A second group is the *elderly*. Because life expectancy has increased and earlier retirement become more common, as state pensions are reduced in real terms, so the elderly have come to comprise an ever larger section of the poor. Unequal life chances continue through to old age: Dilnot and Johnson (1992) have shown that those who had been able to contribute to private pension schemes during their working life enjoy a level of pension income almost five times higher than those on state benefit alone. Over 33 per cent of pensioners in the UK were in poverty in 1991.

A third group likely to experience poverty are *lone-parent families* whether the result of choice, death, desertion or divorce: they make up a growing percentage of the poor. *Large families* too, though less common today, are vulnerable to poverty, while those who are *sick* or *disabled* typically experience chronic deprivation and isolation.

Millar (1993) has explained the growth in the numbers in poverty as the result of three related factors:

- continuing high levels of unemployment
- a rising incidence of low-paid work (in 1991 there were almost 10 million on low pay)
- the growth in 'precarious' or 'flexible' employment (in 1986 almost 8 million people were in part-time, casualised or seasonal work).

Millar puts flesh on the statistics: 'It is women who make up the vast majority of part-time and low-paid workers. It is men in unskilled and low-paid jobs who are most vulnerable to unemployment. Young people cannot get a secure hold on the labour market and instead move between unemployment, low-paid work, and low-paid training schemes, while older workers cannot get back into paid work if they lose their jobs. Black people are more vulnerable on all counts: more prone to unemployment, more likely to be low-paid, more likely to be in insecure employment' (ibid, p. 15).

Some have argued that the poor can be regarded as an 'underclass'. What does it mean to say that the poor constitute an 'underclass'? This notion, which has its roots in both UK and US sociology of the 1970s, suggests that those who are most poor suffer a growing exclusion from 'normal' society and social intercourse and constitute an increasingly homogenous class locked into a cycle of socio-economic and cultural deprivation. They are likely to be in appalling housing conditions on inner-city estates, out of work and in receipt (or not) of state benefits, unable to escape the poverty into which they (often as single-parent households) are trapped. As the policies of the 1980s have come into play – as Table 6.2 describes – so those with least 'market capacity' have poorer chances of forming a viable household.

According to this argument, these poor are not simply at the bottom of the stratification hierarchy but are in a sense *outside* it, outside the boundaries and the dynamics of that hierarchy – hence the term 'underclass'; they are 'under' the class structure. Although formed by it they are in a sense excluded from it. Ethnic minorities and immigrant workers are especially likely to be found here. For these especially, the idea of participating as members of a competitive labour market seems far removed from their daily experience. Crompton (1993) argues that the underclass has been a permanent, rather than recent, phenomenon of capitalist social structures throughout the world: she dismisses the view that the underclass is peculiar to late capitalism. Clearly, whether recent or permanent, there are a large number of people who are distinct from those who at certain crucial periods of their life (e.g. the old, families with young children) may temporarily lapse into poverty. Those who experience what Townsend (1979) has called '**relative deprivation**' at the extreme and for chronic periods are unable to participate in what he calls 'the activities ... living conditions, and amenities which are customary' (p. 31) to society. Scott (1994) believes that in such circumstances the fundamental deprivation is that of being deprived of a genuine sense of social 'citizenship'. In this sense, the class-derived deprivations of poverty produce a disadvantageous social and political *status*.

relative deprivation
Developed by Townsend in the late 1970s to conceptualise the condition of deprivation in terms of living standards when compared to the vast majority of the population.

Challenging the Significance of Social Class

What we need to ask, then, is whether these changes sketched out above herald a *decline* in the importance of class itself as a determinant of social position and reward, or a *restructuring* of the terms on which a person's class position is based.

There is a range of views on this. Some sociologists such as Abercrombie and Urry (1983) have argued that there has been a decline in the traditional sense of social class in all industrial societies, as working-class trades unionism loses its importance (reflected in declining numbers), as a spectrum of new middle classes appear, and as the property-owning industrial capitalist class is replaced by a highly qualified managerial class acting as part of a new 'service class' for contemporary business. Certainly there is a hierarchy and there are still social actors who occupy powerful positions in society but, it is argued, inequality is better measured in terms of the credentials one holds, the political influence one wields, and the consumption one can engage in. Saunders (1990) argues that the latter is the defining feature of all contemporary capitalist societies: it is not so much individuals' class position in the *production* process that determines their location and reward in the social hierarchy but instead their status as *consumers* and the style and range of consumption in which they engage. Where there is a dividing line it is between those who rely on state benefit for their consumption needs and those who have sufficiently well-paid jobs to meet the bulk of their material requirements. We return to explore Saunders's argument more fully a little later.

In related fashion, Offe (1985) has argued that *work itself* no longer has as important a meaning for a large number of people either individually or collectively – either because they are effectively excluded from the workforce by chronic unemployment (for example, in 1994 one in four adult males was unemployed), and/or because the welfare state will provide benefit to meet their basic needs, or because a collective work ethic no longer can be sustained in the growing ranks of casualised, part-time workers. As he says, 'not only has work been objectively displaced from its status as a central and self-evident fact of life ... [it] is also forfeiting its subjective role as the central motivating force in the activity of workers' (p. 148).

Perhaps it is not surprising, then, to find others arguing that class (and work-based) identities have lost their meaning for most people: that new social movements – such as the environmental movement, alternative medicines and technologies, peace movements and feminism – have all replaced the allegiances and respect that the labour movement once commanded. The close relationship between the British Labour Party, trades unions and the working class has been deliberately downplayed by the party leadership in order to appeal to this wider and changing constituency (see Chapter 10). The shift from national collective to local plant bargaining and subsequently, for many white-collar workers, to individual contracts, has further weakened trades unionism.

class decomposition
The breaking down of traditional class structures and identity.

Against this view of the **decomposition** or demise of class, two arguments can be made. First that the degree to which traditional class distinctions and inequalities have heen eroded has been exaggerated – the basic class structure is still alive and well. Secondly, that where there are significant changes they are primarily a result of the growing impact of global economic processes that are forcing a restructuring of class at national levels throughout the capitalist industrialised world (see Chapter 3).

The first of these views has been advanced by sociologists such as Bottomore and Brym(1989) and Crompton (1993). As the latter says, 'capitalist industrial societies are still stratified, and theories of social class still provide us with essential insights into the manner in which established inequalities in wealth and power associated with production and markets, access to educational and organisational resources and so on have systematically served to perpetuate these inequalities over time' (p. 206). Bottomore and Brym show from their comparative study of capitalist classes in different countries that this class still enjoys privileged access to the networks of power (in governmental, administrative and judicial circles) that have in broad terms defended the wealth on which the reproduction of this class depends: they note that up to the mid-1960s there was a 'gradual diminution of inequality' in most countries, but that since the late 1970s we can see 'an increasing inequality of income and almost certainly of wealth' such that in most countries the capitalist class has been 'remarkably successful in defending its wealth' (p. 13). In Germany and Japan, for example, they point to the very strong ties between the state, the major banks and principal firms to secure and sustain the profitability of local capitalism and the wealth on which it relies.

At the same time, the maintenance of private capitalist wealth at a national level, be it in the US, Germany, Britain, Japan or elsewhere, is increasingly subject to the *trans*national interests of private capital, which, like capital at the local national level, has its own, transnational governmental agencies and institutions acting broadly on its behalf, such as the World Bank, international commodity and currency exchanges, international banks and the International Monetary Fund (IMF). It is crucial to remember that the transnational interests of the global capitalist system may at times challenge the national interests of local capitalism. The World Bank, IMF and the exchanges act to police and regulate the wider system on its behalf, which may mean local pressures on national (say British) capital, currency holders and workers across a range of occupations. So factories in Britain, the US or elsewhere close, even when they are making a profit locally; new jobs appear because of comparatively cheaper labour elsewhere; an interest rate rise in one country forces others to defend their currencies by pushing up their own base rates so hitting their own national private capital holders; and so on.

At the head of this chapter, reference was made to a number of 'sociology professors' who believe that the traditional notion of a closed social class structure is no longer relevant, and that the analysis of social stratification which has informed much of the preceding discussion in this chapter is, at worst, completely wrong and, at best, misleading. One of the more developed critiques of class analysis is that provided by one of these 'professors', Peter Saunders (1990). In fact, Saunders, critical of what he calls a 'socialist-feminist orthodoxy' rooted in a Marxist approach to class, argues that class analysis has been too long wedded to the old notion of structured social inequalities generated by the property-relations of capitalism, as though (a) the benefits of private ownership within capitalism do not 'trickle-down' to all eventually; (b) the individual can do little to improve his or her position in the social hierarchy through upwards social mobility; and (c) there is still a dominant capitalist class today. Against this, he argues that stratification is best understood through the application of a neo-*Weberian* model of class which stresses differential occupational market capacity and embodies a neo-liberal individualism which believes that individuals can overcome the disadvantages that confront them. Moreover, it offers a better account of the growth of an increasingly complex and more fragmented social structure, in particular the rise of the new middle classes.

Saunders stresses that through the widespread diffusion of share-ownership (especially via the big privatisations of state enterprise in recent years) 'the capitalist class... has fragmented into millions of tiny pieces' – the millions of shareholders, including many workers, who buy into private enterprise. As such, 'the capitalist class has all but disappeared as a distinct stratum'.

Saunders claims that his analysis is based on a more objective analysis of class inasmuch as it is based on an open-minded approach to the empirical evidence. Unfortunately, there is a considerable body of empirical evidence that he does ignore – Scott's (1991) highly detailed and up-to-date data on the upper class, for example, which we have already discussed above, as well as the equivalent study by Zeitlin (1989) for the US. More importantly, it is, of course, naive to say that data 'speaks for itself', for the significance of evidence depends on what assumptions one makes in reading it in the first place.

Thus, rather than seeing the growth of shareownership as signalling the demise of the capitalist class, we have suggested in the earlier part of this chapter that we need to locate the capitalist class in two arenas, the national and the transnational. It is clear that a dominant class representing the interests of transnational finance capital shapes the fortunes of all those small shareholders Saunders is keen to point to. Moreover, Saunders's claim that it is increasingly hard to find a distinct group of private capitalists sharing a tight social network need not mean that the specific interests of private capital and this class have been somehow dissipated: indeed, Scott acknowledges the depersonalisation and institutionalisation of the ownership of capital, and thereby 'a change in the structure of the capitalist class': 'Instead of being organised around an upper circle of status superiors, the capitalist class became organised around an inner circle of finance capitalists.' These we saw have both national – in the City of London (and the equivalent finance centres of

New York, Tokyo or Paris) – and transnational networks whose members play a crucial role in shaping national and international (such as European Union) state and business policies.

We have, in fact, argued in this chapter – along the lines of Runciman's recent work – that we would do best to combine the insights of both Marxist (property) and Weberian (occupational market) approaches to the study of stratification. Both have their weaknesses, but their strengths too. One notable strength of Weber, is his additional focus on *status and power* as forms of social stratification and *social differentiation* analytically quite separate from, but in practice often tied to, class inequalities. We commented on these dimensions when describing Weber's basic approach to inequality earlier in the chapter. Marx's focus on the abiding inequalities associated with the unequal distribution of productive (and not merely consumption) property, and the globalising dynamics of capitalism, are two important insights his analysis has provided.

In other chapters in this part of the book (Chapters 8 and 9) we explore the dynamics of ethnic and gender subordination in contemporary society, so we will not discuss them here. But they are obviously two of the most important forms of social differentiation and inequality along with class. The relationship between them and social class is, however, problematic, as the later chapters suggest. We can give a sense of this here by discussing briefly some of the feminist criticisms that have been made of class theory in general, for feminism – like Saunders – has posed a serious challenge to conventional approaches to class inequality.

There are three basic criticisms that have been made of the research on social class, and all three have been most strongly directed against the work of John Goldthorpe and David Lockwood (see, for example, Abbott and Sapsford, 1987). First, conventional approaches classify households' class position as family units headed by a male breadwinner: this clearly ignores the class position of women in households, who are in paid work and who may be – and in poorer families often are – the principal or sole 'breadwinner'. Secondly, it assumes that the female partner can be regarded as sharing the same class position as the man and enjoying the same access to resources that the family breadwinner brings in: yet there is considerable evidence to the contrary. Women do not share in household resources on equal terms with men, they have less power in the home and may be physically and violently abused by male partners (Dobash and Dobash, 1980). Thirdly, there is the assumption that class takes precedence over gender as the more important determinant of social inequality.

There have been a number of responses to these attacks on class theory. Maynard (1990) has usefully described these responses as coming from 'the detractors', 'the revisionists' and 'the radicals'. The detractors – Goldthorpe, Lockwood and others who have developed the conventional approach – defend the existing practice of allocating married women to their husband's class position, both because they believe that the evidence still favours this strategy and because, methodologically, they believe that treating women separately from men could require the development of separate stratificatory schemes for each gender which would be regarded as practically problematic.

Revisionists have, however, responded more sympathetically to the feminist critique and have tried to revise the classification of women and men in households by examining more fully the jobs that women do and the resources they bring to the family unit. This has led to the notion of 'cross-class' families in which the partners have different class positions: in such cases the household as a unit would be allocated a different class position to one in which *both* partners were regarded as sharing the *same* class position.

The radical response has come from a number of feminists themselves (e.g. Delphy, 1984), who argue that we need to reconsider the whole basis on which we view social class, to move away from seeing class in terms of an economic category primarily associated with occupation and to see it instead as expressing a *more fundamental* gender division in society: that is, the first class conflict was and is a conflict between men and women. It is in the home where this conflict is rooted and reproduced, a place where the man exploits the woman as she provides both sexual and domestic services for him.

Maynard offers a number of observations on this feminist critique, particular the radical perspective, noting, for example, how there would be severe methodological difficulties in operationalising the notion of gendered classes in the context of developing empirical research on the contemporary class structure. Nevertheless, the challenge to the conventional approach to class provided by the feminist critique does open up important questions which require further debate within class theory.

Conclusion

The approach to social class we have adopted here is one in which we have sought to combine the Marxian and Weberian accounts in what we hope is a reasonably coherent fashion. Contemporary analyses of social class, we have argued, need to broaden their focus to address the impact of transnational aspects of global capitalism on national capitalist interests and the experience and cohesion of social classes within a country. While much of our empirical material has the UK in mind, the argument developed here applies to all mature industrial capitalist societies. We have also noted at various points in this chapter how the traditional dynamics of social class are being increasingly shaped by wider global forces. The globalising processes we discussed in general in Chapter 3 have important implications for the reproduction of social classes at the national level: it is to this issue that we now turn in Chapter 7.

Summary of the Chapter

- Social stratification refers to different forms of social inequality, and especially to those relating to economic, ethnic and gendered inequalities.
- Social classes in industrial society can be examined via Marxist concepts of property relations and capitalist production and Weberian concepts of market relations and occupation.
- Runciman's analysis of class in terms of economic power combines elements of neo-Marxist and neo-Weberian analysis.
- Wealth is unearned income and is highly unevenly distributed and concentrated in a relatively small minority throughout all capitalist societies. Income, also unevenly distributed, relates to occupational classes which enjoy different 'life chances'.
- Poverty has been explained in both cultural and structural terms, the latter leading to arguments for the existence of an 'underclass'.
- The traditional occupational class structure has been divided along manual/non-manual lines. While still pertinent, changes in the national and global labour markets and investment patterns have disturbed the stability of the old class structure. Moreover, class identity has been said to be eroded through the new importance of 'consumption'.
- Feminist sociology challenges the methodological assumptions of conventional class analysis for failing to treat women as a distinct socio-economic group with specific disadvantages and life chances.

References

Abbott, P. and R. Sapsford (1987) *Women and Social Class*, London, Tavistock.

Abercrombie, N. and J. Urry (1983) *Capital, Labour and the Middle Classes*, London, Allen & Unwin.

Andreff, W. (1984) 'The internationalisation of capital and the reordering of world capitalism', *Capital and Class*, vol. 22, pp. 58–80.

Bottomore, T. and R. J. Brym (1989) *The Capitalist Class: An International Study*, London, Harvester Wheatsheaf.

Camiller, P. (1989) 'Beyond 1992: The Left and Europe', *New Left Review*, vol. 175, pp. 5–17.

Carrol, W. K. and S. Lewis (1991) 'Restructuring finance capital: changes in the Canadian corporate network 1976–1986', *Sociology*, vol. 25, no. 3, pp. 491–510.

Crompton, R. (1993) *Class and Stratification*, Cambridge, Polity Press.

Delphy, C. (1984) *Close to Home*, London, Hutchinson.

Department of Social Security (1993) *Households Below Average Income, 1979–1990/91*, London, HMSO.

Dilnot, A. and P. Johnson (1992) 'What pension should the state provide?', *Fiscal Studies*, vol. 13, no. 4, pp. 1–20.

Dobash, R. and R. Dobash (1980) *Violence Against Wives*, London, Open Books.

Hutton, W. (1993) 'Snow-white ideology and the thirty million dwarfs', *The Guardian*, 28 December, p. 9.

King, A. D. (1991) *Global Cities*, London, Routledge.

Lee, D. (1994) 'Class as a social fact', *Sociology*, vol. 28, no. 2, pp. 397–416.

Marshall, G. *et al.* (1988) *Social Class in Modern Britain*, London, Hutchinson.

Marshall, G. and D. Rose (1990) 'Outclassed by our critics?', *Sociology*, vol. 24, no. 2, pp. 255–68.

Maynard, M. (1990) 'The reshaping of sociology?: trends in the study of gender', *Sociology*, vol. 24, no. 2, pp. 269–90.

Millar, J. (1993) 'The continuing trends in rising poverty', in A. Sinfield (ed.), *Poverty, Inequality and Justice*, Edinburgh, University of Edinburgh.

Offe, C. (1985) *Disorganised Capitalism*, Cambridge, Polity Press.

Runciman, W. G. (1990) 'How many classes are there in contemporary British society?', *Sociology*, vol. 24, no. 3, pp. 377–96.

Saunders, P. (1988) 'The sociology of consumption', in P. Otnes (ed.), *The Sociology of Consumption*, New Jersey, Humanities Press.

Saunders, P. (1990) *Social Class and Stratification*, London, Unwin Hyman.

Scott, J. (1987) *Corporations, Classes and Stratification*, 2nd edn, London, Hutchinson.

Scott, J. (1991) *Who Rules Britain?*, Cambridge, Polity Press.

Scott, J. (1993) 'Wealth and privilege', in A. Sinfield (ed.), *Poverty, Inequality and Justice*, Edinburgh, University of Edinburgh.

Scott, J. (1994) *Citizenship, Deprivation and Privilege: Poverty and Wealth in Britain*, Harlow, Longman.

Townsend, P. (1979) *Poverty in the United Kingdom*, Harmondsworth, Penguin.

Willis, P. (1977) *Learning to Labour*, Farnborough, Saxon House.

Zeitlin, M. (1989) *The Large Corporation and Contemporary Classes*, Cambridge, Polity Press.

7 The New Dynamics of Class

Aims of the Chapter

This chapter examines the ways in which occupational classes (the middle and working classes) have been reproduced over generations, and the ways in which this has depended on a stable, nationally determined labour market. It goes on to suggest how this reproduction is weakened through the impact of global processes at the national level. The implications these changes have for established jobs, new recruits to the labour market and social mobility are discussed, as are the effect these changes have on class identities.

Introduction

In the previous chapter we described the broad features of class inequality common to all capitalist industrialised societies. We noted early in the chapter that class was one of a number of forms of **stratification** – that include gender and ethnicity – that are not only interrelated but are also being shaped by the impact of globalisation, a process which has (as we saw in Chapter 3) both economic and cultural dimensions. Globalisation is creating important changes in the way in which class culture, identity and positions are reproduced at the national level.

social stratification
The division of a population into unequal layers or strata based on any of the following: income, wealth, gender, ethnicity, power, status, age, religion or some other characteristic.

class reproduction
The process by which class inequalities reproduce themselves.

social closure
Employed by Weber to describe the efforts made by social groups to deny entry and thereby benefit to those outside the group in order to maximise their own advantage.

social reproduction
The concept that over time groups of people, notably social classes, reproduce their social structures and patterns.

In this chapter we discuss **class reproduction** more fully and how globalisation effects it. First we provide an account of the two processes through which social classes are normally sustained, the processes of **social closure** and **social reproduction.** Then we apply these concepts to the two classes whose position in the social hierarchy is determined by their position in the *occupational labour market,* the middle and working classes. We then go on to consider how this labour market has changed in recent years in most industrialised countries, especially in light of changes in the capitalist world economy. We will argue that these two classes, which together account for the majority of the population of industrialised states, are less able to reproduce themselves at a national level because of a number of factors – some global – which are destabilising traditional labour markets in general. This suggests that classes as stable occupational groups are being fragmented both culturally and economically.

This has major implications for anyone competing for work in, say, the United States, Britain, France or Australia, especially those *newcomers* to the labour market, the young generation looking for their first job. The traditional routes through which jobs and careers have been secured are now much less likely to be available. Occupational communities in towns and cities are being broken up, new 'flexible' work patterns are appearing, and more individual mobility across a more volatile labour market is required.

In these circumstances many may think that they have little or no sense of class position or class identity, and that survival depends much more on personal enterprise and being 'entrepreneurial'. Indeed, the 1980s and 90s have seen the emergence of an **enterprise culture** through which it is said that anyone can, given initiative, skills and a bit of luck, 'get on' and 'do well'.

enterprise culture
An environment which acclaims and rewards those who take initiative by setting up businesses and creating wealth.

Is this true? What has happened to the traditional forms of class identity and class-based jobs? In what ways did occupational groups reproduce themselves in the past? Are similar patterns in evidence today? Let us try to answer these questions by looking first at the way in which boundaries between classes as occupational groups have traditionally been constructed.

Social Closure and Social Reproduction

Social classes survive from one generation to the next: they do this through both social closure and social reproduction. *Social closure* quite simply refers to the extent to which a social class is 'closed off' from any other(s). A class 'acts' in this way in order to secure its interests against other social classes, for example, by making upward social mobility into its ranks difficult for members of subordinate social groups. In practice, of course, we cannot see social classes 'acting' en masse building boundaries between them and all others. What we do see are occupational groups who enjoy certain class-related advantages – such as high levels of income, educational advantage, and so on – using their class 'resources' to sustain their relatively privileged position, and to exclude others from it. The more capacity that occupational classes have to close themselves off in this way the more that the broad class position they occupy is likely to be socially and culturally cohesive, and vice versa.

Reproduction tells us *how* social classes reproduce themselves over time, from one generation to the next. So while closure is a measure of the boundaries of different class-based occupational strata, reproduction points to the economic and cultural *resources* that classes use to sustain themselves. As we shall see, this might include educational privilege and advantage – the ability to pay the fees for a private education, for example – that can be secured by families on behalf of the children born into this class.

In general, these two terms can be used to establish the sense of class difference, and so broad class boundaries – such as those we saw in Chapter 6 relating to the manual and non-manual strata – that characterise a society. They tell us about the dynamics through which class structures are experienced and sustained as lived realities and not merely as the abstract conceptions of theories of social stratification.

We saw in the previous chapter how we could explain the broad processes that produce the class structure characteristic of most industrial societies. We noted there too that these structures were beginning to change: this was not only because of local changes in work and occupational structures, but also because of global processes which have altered the context within which class reproduction occurs. One of the principal factors for change has been the decline of manufacturing industry and the appearance of more and more factories established as subsidiaries of overseas capital investment: BMW's takeover of Rover Cars in the UK is one recent example. We saw in Chapter 3 how national economies have to be understood in terms of the dynamic of international, 'globalised' processes, notably the actions of large **transnational corporations** (TNCs) that act on behalf of what Sklair (1991) has called the emergent *transnational* capitalist class. The British government was keen to sell Britain to this transnational class as a low wage economy that had not signed up to the **social chapter** of the European Union's Maastricht Treaty. So firms will not expect to meet minimum wage costs, make provision for social welfare and rights of workers, or conform to a series of regulations – such as the protection of child labour – to which other European Union countries have agreed. This is even true, by virtue of a special clause in the terms of the Treaty, for TNCs that operate through their subsidiaries in Britain. Trades unions, weakened during the 1980s, are in no position to counter these developments, and would find it difficult to persuade members to question the character of this new form of inward investment in areas of high unemployment and doubtful job security. Countries with high labour costs, such as Germany, have seen their own trades unions prepared to take pay cuts (via cuts in hours worked) rather than lose out completely under the threat of jobs being exported elsewhere.

transnational corporations (TNCs)
Large corporations, emanating principally from the US, Japan and Europe, whose activities are aimed at global markets.

social chapter
A set of EU guidelines and recommendations which offers protection, such as a minimum wage guarantee, to workers.

So local class structures within a nation and the relative advantages and disadvantages they have enjoyed over the years are increasingly being shaped by wider external forces operating at a transnational level. Where TNCs are particularly powerful, notably in the **Third World,** the tension between domestic and global interests is most in evidence: as Sklair (1991) says, 'the transnational capitalist class, fractions of the labour force, and other support strata that the TNCs have created, will all increasingly identify their own interests with those of the capitalist global system and, if necessary, against the interests of their "own" societies as the transnational practices of the system penetrate ever deeper into the areas that most heavily impact on their daily lives' (p. 68). Before this convergence of a transnational interest, however, there is likely to be a prolonged period of casino capitalism at the global level as financial speculators move money around the world to cash in on differential rates of currency, interest, and profitability (Strange, 1990).

Third World
Developing countries not aligned politically with the large power blocs.

Given these factors at work at a global level, we should be prepared to recognise that the dynamics of class reproduction might be changing at the local level too. Before we explore this, we will first look at the way social closure and reproduction have characterised the occupational groups of middle and working classes up until relatively recently. We are not looking here at the upper class precisely because in this chapter we want to focus, as noted above, on inequalities associated with *occupational* groups, groups or classes whose material resources derive primarily through the *work* they do rather than the wealth they own or inherit.

The Middle Class

We saw in the previous chapter through the work of Runciman that though people may have different occupational situations reflecting the sort of **economic power** they possess, it is possible to place them firmly within *one* class group. This is especially true – as indeed Runciman's illustration of four engineers shows – of those who belong to the middle class. Such is the diversity – in terms of range of income, occupational authority, employment status and so on – of those belonging to the middle class that, slightly confusingly, some sociologists prefer to talk of the middle class*es*. While this is in some ways understandable, it is perhaps better to try to establish the broad boundaries of the middle class itself – in the way Runciman tries, for example – in order that its distinguishing features can be identified.

economic power
A measurement of the ability to control events by virtue of material advantage (*see* material advantage).

In this regard we can say that there are broadly speaking two key features which have characterised a middle-class position, and which have provided a boundary between the middle and working classes. First, middle-class occupations enjoy significant **material advantages**

material advantage
The possession of money and other material goods which offer people a greater chance of success in life than they would otherwise have.

over working-class jobs: not only are levels of pay much higher, they are more secure over the working life of the employee, enabling the middle class to plan to cover future medical, schooling and housing costs. Such jobs are typically less dangerous to health, and involve more autonomy and responsibility than blue-collar work. The work life-cycle of the working class is in contrast normally careerless and often disjointed, reflecting vulnerability in the labour market.

cultural advantage
Life-styles, religious beliefs, values, or other practices which give people a greater chance of obtaining economic success or social status.

Secondly, the middle class has enjoyed a **cultural advantage** derived from significantly higher levels of education and training, especially among the professions, and administrative and managerial groups. Although the expansion of educational provision has benefited all social classes since the Second World War, the sons and daughters of the middle class have enjoyed much higher levels of achievement and advancement than other social groups.

The middle classes can be divided into two forms – the 'established' and the 'new'. The former refers to those members of white-collar occupations whose jobs were associated with the emergence, from the late eighteenth century through the nineteenth century and beyond, of what we now regard as the established professions – law, accountancy, and medicine, for example – and with the civil service needed for the growing administrative demands of the nation-states of Western Europe and, later, North America. Subsequently, the ranks of the established middle class were swollen by the growth during the later nineteenth century and early twentieth century of managerial positions within private industry.

However, there were not enough children from the older middle class to fill these positions. One reason for this was, of course, the demographic impact of the First World War: the war decimated a whole generation of middle-class offspring serving as officers at the front. As a result, after the war we saw the consolidation and expansion of a 'new middle class', that is new professional, salaried groups working in administration, banking or business, recruited in part from an increasingly educated and mobile *working class*. The post-1945 growth in both private and public sector white-collar work gave further impetus to the growth of the new middle class. They were accompanied by more junior ranks of white-collar office workers – a lower middle class – often also drawn from working class ranks.

Reproduction of the middle class

While these older and newer wings of the middle class still enjoy considerable advantages over working-class groups, their reproduction and degree of closure is never fully secure. Why?

Though the growth of education and the expansion of non-manual jobs have favoured middle-class offspring, the fact is that training and non-manual job opportunities have grown at a much faster rate than the supply of children from the established middle class. It is true that the traditional professions, such as doctors, draw new members from solid middle-class backgrounds, and indeed from families who sustain networks and links – via training, hospital mentorship and placement, for example – which allow considerable closure to continue. However, elsewhere the story is rather different: the massive growth in managerial and office staffs has required recruitment from a much wider pool, including members from working-class backgrounds: many of these recruits do not have the **cultural capital** – say Oxbridge, Harvard, or Sorbonne backgrounds – of their more established peers.

cultural capital

Refers to the extent to which individuals have absorbed the dominant culture. Associated with Pierre Bourdieu, who claimed that the greater degree of cultural capital individuals possessed (the more absorbed they were in the dominant culture), the more successful they would be in the educational system.

These processes effect the cohesiveness of the middle class in two ways. First, since educational success is an important (though never sufficient) means of delivering middle-class jobs, middle-class children who do not succeed here are clearly vulnerable to losing solid middle-class status as they look for work: indeed, they may experience *downward* **social mobility** and find themselves working in low-paid white-collar work or blue-collar working-class jobs. Secondly, educational success can provide a route for *upward* social mobility of the children from traditional working-class backgrounds: where this happens the social mix of those occupying positions within the middle classes increases, so making the cultural boundary marking off the middle-class occupational groups much less clear.

social mobility

The movement of individuals, within a stratified society, from one position within the social hierarchy to another. Usually refers to positions of broad occupation or social class.

While life for older-generation middle class people has been generally good – higher pay and perks have allowed all the usual trappings of middle-class respectability, such as the well-appointed suburban home, the cleaning woman, the child-minder, two cars, and so on – concern has been growing among middle-class parents about their children's future. They can see the labour market change and some of the older, well-trodden paths to respectability – such as well-paid public sector jobs in education, health and even the military – becoming more difficult to negotiate as cutbacks in State expenditure, **privatisation**, and a decline in the number of career-long working positions in industry and elsewhere threaten middle-class occupational positions. The loss of career-long jobs is especially threatening since it means that the effort spent on securing educational credentials might come to nought. Without the prospect of a steady career, training seems less worthwhile: as Grey (1994) observes in connection with accountancy, 'Career provides a meaning and rationale for the otherwise disillusioning grind of accountancy training' (p. 494).

privatisation

The process of transfer of state assets from public to private ownership.

Moreover, as the capacity for social closure declines, we find a growing number of people who occupy an intermediate position between the two broad middle and working-class occupational groups which has some of the features of middle-class status – white-collar, office or technician-based work reliant on educational qualifications – yet in terms of material reward – wages, pension rights, job security and so on – is closer to the job insecurity and low pay typical of working-class positions. Sociologists debate whether the once-respectable, secure and relatively well-paid clerical work has now been downgraded: have routine non-manual workers such as clerks and secretarial staff become **proletarianised**? Part of the changes here relates simply to the more widely available clerical skills on offer in the labour market: in the UK, for example, in 1851 there were about 60,000 clerks, all male, working in small-scale 'professional' settings such as banks. Since then, the growth of this 'tertiary' or service sector has meant that there are over 14 million working in office, administrative, retail and 'personal service' jobs who cannot command high pay levels, whose jobs are much less secure than in the past and whose work is so tedious and routine that it is little different from the pleasures of working an assembly line in a factory. Thus, for some sociologists the work seems little different from that of the traditional ('proletarian') working class.

proletarianisation

A process whereby some parts of the middle class become absorbed into the working class.

Others, however, such as Goldthorpe (1987) argue that despite having low pay – sometimes even lower than blue-collar workers – office (and related) staffs have (i) high job security, (ii) enjoy 'staff' status and (iii) are 'functionally' associated with, though marginal to, the established middle (or 'service') class. Goldthorpe says that this group forms an important part of a new intermediate class, a 'white collar labour force'. They are unlikely to have a strong sense of collective identity precisely because there is considerable horizontal movement of workers between similar status jobs and so less possibility of a strong work-based culture developing, while many, especially women workers, take up part-time appointments, again limiting the sense in which a shared class culture might develop.

Much depends, however, on the importance given to the material conditions and rewards of this sort of work. If we believe that low levels of pay, job insecurity, and poor working conditions are of overriding significance in determining the class position of a particular occupational group, we might want to agree with Heath and Britten (1984) that there are many *women* workers in routine non-manual jobs – in offices, hotels and catering, for example – who cannot be differentiated from women in *manual* work, and so have to be seen as occupying a 'fundamentally proletarian **market position**'. Indeed, the crucial fac-

market position/situation

A term relating to the relative skills one has to sell in the labour market relative to others.

tor of *gender subordination* within work applies across the full range of occupational classes: even those women in higher status non-manual jobs – such as hotel management – find that **patriarchal** discrimination works against them as well to exclude them from more senior, better paid jobs: instead they tend to be restricted to areas such as housekeeping management (Bagguley, 1990). Determining the relationship between occupational class and gender is, therefore, of great methodological importance for studies of social stratification.

patriarchal
A system that perpetuates the dominance of senior men over women and junior men (*see* patriarchy).

The Working Class

The working class have perhaps one of the most strongly developed class cultures and have been at the centre of sociological research on stratification for many years, in both Europe and the USA. One reason for this is that the traditional working class of mining, steel-making, ship-building and so on lives and works together, which makes their communities relatively easy to study. A strong sense of community encourages a strong sense of identity. Insiders can be clearly distinguished from 'outsiders', especially those who represent officialdom, employers, authorities or 'the better off'. The working class are brought together by their common experience of adversity and subordination yet their disadvantage limits their chances for improving their position.

Thus, the reproduction of the working class has two dimensions. First, the class is located in the labour market such that its disadvantage within capitalism must be seen as structural and thereby difficult to overcome. Yet, second, precisely because of this, the ongoing experience of subordination produces a range of cultural frameworks for interpreting and *drawing on* the experiences of working-class life in order to 'get by', 'make out', or adjust to the situation. This might be expressed in working-class pride and 'respectability', or in the masculinity and toughness of the school and shop-floor.

There are many studies of this traditional working class which focus on the mutual support – often kin-based – among members of mining (Dennis *et al.*, 1956), textile (Wild, 1979) and steel (Beynon *et al.*, 1991) communities. These studies, often rich in observational detail, tell the story of the working class, a story which at best is insightful and credible, but at worst is overly romanticised. There is too a tendency to extrapolate these community studies to the working class as a whole, to assume that this is a story which holds true for all manual workers. However, this notion of a homogeneous traditional working class has been challenged, not least by Penn(1985) who has shown in his studies of the *skilled* working class that these constitute a distinct group between the middle and the (less skilled) working classes. Indeed, it is the division between occupational strata among the working classes that explains why some occupational groups will use the social resources they have available to close off their occupation from others. Mining communities have, for example, exercised this form of social closure to construct strong boundaries between the mineworkers and sub-contracted, non-unionised workers brought into the coal industry, as has happened in the US, UK and Germany.

During the 1960s some US and European social scientists claimed that the skilled stratum of the working class, found in the new automotive and electronic industries whose products came to dominate the consumer markets of the post-war era, were experiencing a wholesale shift in their class culture and broad social position in the social hierarchy: their better pay and conditions, their specialist skills, their **individualistic** (rather than collective trades-union) orientation towards other workers and employers – all these suggested a new stratum of affluent workers experiencing a process of '**embourgeoisement**' whereby they took on a middle-class status. Indeed, in the US this view was accompanied by wider claims declaring the disappearance of the unequal class structure *per se*, as more and more of the older jobs with their low pay and poor working conditions were replaced by well-rewarded skills-based work.

individualism

Doctrines or ways of thinking that focus on the autonomous individual, rather than on the attributes of the group.

embourgeoisement thesis

An explanation for declining working-class solidarity which claims that, through increasing affluence, the working class tend to adopt middle class values and thus become absorbed into the middle class.

However, the evidence for this, even in the US, was patchy and British studies which looked in detail at the so-called 'affluent' workers (Goldthorpe *et al.*, 1968) cast doubt on the impact of better pay and new forms of work on the real position these workers had. Rather than a collective upward mobility into the ranks of the middle class, Goldthorpe *et al.* showed that the most significant change among affluent workers was that they led more privatised, and home-centred lives rather than ones where the company of kin, neighbours and friends was part of the daily routine. New homes in new towns meant mortgages which had to be paid for: workers were more **instrumental** in their work, earning as much as they could even if this meant putting in long hours of overtime in tedious and noisy assembly-line work. These two factors, privatisation and instrumentalism, encourage 'a more individualistic outlook' among the manual workers, with a simultaneous weakening of communal and kin orientations. But this did not lead to any strong desire to attain and identify with a middle-class life-style and values, more typical of white-collar work.

instrumentalism

An approach by workers to work which seeks to derive satisfaction not so much in the task or job itself, but from benefits such as good rates of pay or secure employment.

Reproduction of the working class

We saw in Chapter 6 that there are major material inequalities between the social classes in contemporary industrial societies. We saw that the occupational strata among the working class experience some of the worst life chances in terms of levels of pay, job security and life-cycle of earnings. These poor life chances relate in Weberian terms to their poor market-situation, itself a direct result of the low 'cultural capital' of the working class: as we saw in our discussion of the middle class, qualifications are increasingly important credentials in society. So educational disadvantage and poor job prospects are linked.

It is this link which is crucial to the reproduction of the working class. It results from both the under-resourcing of schools in inner-city areas as well as the favouring of middle-class children in schools more generally: for the latter, as Chapter 11 describes, schooling is often an extension of pre-school family experience, culture and tuition. While it is not impossible, of course, for working-class children to overcome these constraints (Halsey *et al.*, 1980), the experience of disadvantage and discouragement at school – especially among working-class racial minorities – can push children to leave school at the first (statutorily permitted) opportunity, in the UK at 16, in the US at 15. The traditional 'pull' of the local labour market and its 'adult' status will draw young boys and girls into jobs which have little or no prospect of security or good levels of pay (Ashton *et al.*, 1990). Escaping the constraints of school as soon as possible, young working-class members run into the constraints of their subordinate position in the labour market (Willis, 1977).

de-industrialisation
A concept used to describe economic changes due to the decline of industrial manufacturing and the increase of output and employment growth in the service sector of the economy.

deskilling
Developed by Braverman to describe what he believed to be strategies of employers to reduce the skills required of their labour force, which often occurs alongside the introduction of new technological processes into the work place.

There is, however, a crucial condition that must hold for any reproduction and closure of the working class to occur at all: there must be a reasonably stable labour market for them. Thus any wider changes in the structure of capitalism that threaten local labour markets threaten the availability of paid jobs: if these decline in number one can expect an increase in the absolute numbers of those in poverty, those comprising the so-called 'underclass', discussed in Chapter 6.

Changes in the Labour Market

There were two important trends during the 1970s and 1980s which characterised the labour markets of all industrialised states: these were **de-industrialisation** and **deskilling**, both most closely associated with traditional industrial sectors (such as raw materials and manufacturing) and, therefore, both of greatest significance for the traditional working class. *De-industrialisation* typically refers to the process through which the number of jobs in these sectors declines in absolute terms and also, compared with the volume of service-sector work in the economy, in relative terms too. During this period, many jobs were lost due to cuts in, and the privatisation of, state-sponsored employment as well as to competition from cheaper labour markets abroad to which many jobs were exported. *Deskilling* is associated with a process through which firms respond to the threat of de-industrialisation and competition by introducing more machine-based technologies which can replace the skill and tacit knowledge of human labour – for example, the use of robotics on car assembly line work. In addition, labour itself is reduced to the smallest of possible tasks. As Chapter 12 describes in more detail, the deskilling thesis has been most strongly argued by Braverman (1974) and a number of European sociologists (Wood, 1982; Gorz, 1982). The British car industry during the 1970s and early 1980s exemplified both de-industrialisation and deskilling, with a result that during the same period the numbers experiencing structural unemployment – the loss of a certain type of work for good – as well as long-term unemployment grew steadily. Thus, the decline in traditional working-class jobs created major problems for the cultural and economic reproduction of the working class: substantial sectors of the old working class were no longer *working*.

Yet the story about the relationship between classes, specific occupations and the labour market is even more complex than relayed so far. In many ways, in some of the older industrial states of Europe, such as France and Britain, the process of deindustrialisation and deskilling had been going on for some time: Andrew Gamble (1985) has argued that British industrial decline can be traced back to much earlier failures – from the 1920s onwards especially – of British capitalists to invest in new infrastructural technologies as they became available. In many ways, Britain was living on borrowed time, borrowed to a significant degree from the wealth derived from the old colonial empire.

So it is not surprising, then, that the OPEC-created oil crisis of the 1970s, which hit Britain and France particularly hard, should have triggered a rapid rise in unemployment, especially among the working class, as **growth rates** fell to below zero. During the past decade, however, unemployment has continued to rise throughout most industrialised countries – throughout the whole of the EC for example – while average growth rates have been positive. In other words the traditional connection between economic growth and job creation seems to have come unstuck.

growth rates
Levels of economic expansion.

Recent evidence from the Commission of the European Communities (CEC) shows that growth rates need to be above 2 per cent to create any jobs, and that lower than this and jobs are actually destroyed. Extrapolating from this data, a recent report (Hingel, 1993) notes that CEC economies would have to 'increase by 68% in order to absorb the present 10.6% [rate] of unemployment': this average would in fact vary by country. Thus, 'the equivalent domestic figures are situated between 198% of necessary economic growth in the case of Britain and 49% in the case of Germany' (p. 7). These differences reflect the different capacities – in terms of technological and institutional infrastructures (such as science and education and regional development agencies) – available in different countries. But even allowing for this the growth required in the strongest European country – Germany – to soak up unemployment is still high at nearly 50 per cent. Clearly, this is not going to be achieved, not least because of the additional economic costs that German reunification has meant.

What is going on here? Why has the simple relation between economic growth of the economy as a whole and an expanding job market been altered? There are three main reasons which have been advanced: these relate to

- *the restructuring* of the economy
- *the polarisation* of the labour market
- *the globalisation* of production

As we shall see, the impact of these three factors has altered the nature of the labour market such that the traditional patterns of the occupational structure, recruitment to jobs, mobility within the labour market and, more generally, the reproduction of social classes, have all changed significantly too. This is true for *all* occupational groups, both middle and working classes. In many ways, the traditional labour market has *failed to keep pace with* the wider changes associated with these three processes.

Box 7.1: Inertia in labour markets

'The past two decades have exposed an alarming gap between the speed at which different markets, cultures and institutions respond to change. Financial capital moves vast distances in seconds. Its productivity is measured in minutes. The microelectronics revolution has radically reduced the useful life of physical capital, machines and computers. Consumer goods markets are in constant flux, subject to rapid shifts in demand, from product proliferation in periods of boom to basic value-for-money products in recession ...

In contrast, the labour market – which includes the way we prepare people for work, generate skills, set pay rates and retrain the unemployed – has moved only slowly. Schools have not produced enough employable school leavers, government has not done enough to match the unemployed to potential jobs, and the market has not found a way to link the huge array of unmet needs with a vast potential labour force.

The distinction between these markets is not purely economic. It reflects a cultural and political imbalance. The financial markets are awash with information and analysis, measuring minute movements in financial assets. Consumers have a plethora of information and advice on what to buy....In contrast the labour market is malnourished. There are more television programmes and magazines devoted to food and drink than there are to work and jobs. For most people there is little easily available information about the quality of employers, about training and education or likely career opportunities in five or ten years time. We are well abreast of the latest developments in the currency markets, fashions for clothes and cars, but often quite clueless about the technologies which will soon revolutionise – and perhaps abolish – our jobs.'

Source: *Demos*, vol. 2, 1994, p. 8.

Let us look at these three processes in turn, exploring the impact they have on both middle and working classes.

The restructuring of the economy

During the late 1970s and throughout the 1980s, Western European industrialised economies saw a rapid drop in the relative contribution to total economy activity of manufacturing and related industrial sectors. Much of the older post-war infrastructure was insufficiently technologically competitive, while employment structures in manufacturing lacked the flexibility and skills to move into the new markets being captured by countries such as Japan and South Korea. There was a large restructuring of the labour market towards more service sector work. Domestic consumer markets were depressed through prolonged recession in the earlier part of the period, only resolved by a massive expansion of credit and an accompanying property boom, which in itself did little to secure new investment in the basic *industrial* infrastructure. Instead many imports flooded into countries such as Britain, the Netherlands and France. The slump of the late 1980s and early 1990s – as the credit-bubble burst – was therefore inevitable.

lean production
A highly competitive, streamlined, flexible manufacturing process which operates with a minimum of excess or waste (*see* just-in-time production).

Pacific rim
Those south-east Asian countries with fast developing economies that border the Pacific Ocean, such as Taiwan, Hong Kong, Malaysia and South Korea.

During the latter part of the 1980s, however, larger corporations had sought to *restructure* their production to be more flexible, to engage in **lean production** techniques to compete more effectively with the countries of the Far East and so-called **Pacific Rim**. For some commentators this was confirmation of a final shift away from the Fordist, mass production approach which had dominated industrial strategy from the 1950s onwards, to a post-Fordist approach, of targeting products to more specialised markets and of producing such products 'just-in-time' rather than carrying large stockpiles of goods and commodities as in the past.

These changes in the character of production inevitably have had a massive impact on the labour market itself. For some (for example, Leadbeater, 1987; Atkinson and Gregory, 1986), this has led to the *segmentation of the labour market* into three parts: a *core* of securely employed workers (typically in knowledge-based work enjoying above average levels of pay), a *periphery* of casualised workers – the self-employed, part-time staff and so on – who have few if any occupational rights or benefits (such as guaranteed sick-pay), and finally a growing number of *structurally unemployed* who are likely to remain out of work for good.

According to this view, therefore, this restructuring of work has meant that the older manufacturing jobs have gone for good, that new skills are needed to enter the *post*-industrial labour market – typically more knowledge-based, specialist skills, but ones which can be adapted to new needs and opportunities that arise. Restructuring has, therefore, opened up a *skills-gap in a whole generation of workers* who, – now 45 or 50+ years old, are unlikely to find secure work again. While a depressing thesis, some commentators (notably in the US) believe that given proper training and education a new generation of skilled, flexible working – and middle – classes will emerge which will be more attuned to the restructured labour market: the job losses among workers, and long-term structural unemployment that brings poverty and deprivation to many, is temporary and most likely to be felt by the present post-40s generation, and will be relieved once a supply of newly skilled workers is available. The new jobs, will, however, be very different from the old, reflecting the shift in the occupational structure from manual towards non-manual work, and especially the growing importance of knowledge-based jobs, requiring ever more sophisticated, but flexible skills: in fact, according to the Canadian sociologist Stehr (1994), we can characterise contemporary society as a 'knowledge society'.

The 1980s also brought significant changes in the provisions of social security, health and the general welfare provided by the State. Reductions in real levels of benefit, the creeping privatisation of health care and insurance cover, and an erosion of occupational rights and union power, have all meant that *the capacity to survive depends more and more on one's position in the labour market,* since unemployment becomes increasingly difficult to cope with as the holes in the security net widen. Thus those in weak or vulnerable positions in the restructured labour market are more than ever threatened by poverty and poor life chances. It is this which leads many commentators to point out that the recent restructuring of the labour market has not merely changed the *sort* of jobs on offer, but has brought an increasing **polarisation** between those in secure, non-manual work and the growing army of low-paid, often casual workers. This takes us to the second trend we need to discuss.

polarisation of the labour market
A labour market divided between jobs which are well paid and secure and those which are not.

The polarisation of the labour market

Those who believe that the labour market has become 'polarised' (Sassen, 1988; Pahl, 1991; Morris *et al.*, 1994) claim that the restructuring of the economy has tended to divide labour into two: well-paid and secure jobs for the middle and upper-middle classes on the one hand, and insecure, low-paid work for the sons and daughters of the older working classes or those experiencing downward social mobility from the middle class. Those in this second position are unlikely to be able to improve their life chances through education and training, since the labour market itself does not generate an expanding number of skilled jobs. Instead we see the growth of large numbers of low-skill, low-wage jobs, and this will become a permanent, not transitional, feature of the labour market. Most of the people in this sort of work will become members of the so-called **underclass** discussed in Chapter 6 (see pp. 159–61).

underclass
A concept used to describe a group at the bottom of the social hierarchy who are economically, politically and socially marginalised from the rest of society.

Box 7.2: The polarisation of work

'[T]he trends are unmistakable. If you are unemployed your chances of moving to a full-time job are negligible – your best chance is to find part-time or casualised employment. Nor, when you hold such a job, is it very likely that you will move from that into full-time employment. ... It is hard to sustain the argument that people actively prefer the kind of work that is now on offer. ... Zero-hour contracts, for example, in which firms agree no guarantee of work, pay no social overheads, offer no holiday, pension or sickness entitlements but simply require the holder to work as many hours of work as there are available, have hardly arisen because such work is actively preferred. ... [These] changes are going to the very marrow of our society.

One Harvard economist, Robert Lane, shows that in the new insecure labour market it is hard to sustain friendships; you need stability and continuity for that. And long-term commitments (marriage, children, and mortgages) are almost impossible when nothing is secure. The 40-hour week and full-time employment were never "burdens" on business as the hard right Department of Employment insists; they were the cement which bound society together.'

Source: Will Hutton, *The Guardian*, October 28 1994, p. 2.

The polarisation of the labour market, by definition, divides work into secure, better-paid and insecure, poorly paid types. However, there are differences in the way this polarisation is experienced by gender and ethnicity. As Morris *et al.* (1994) show in their study of the US labour market over the past twenty years, for some of the time some groups gravitate towards the better-paid jobs but then subsequently suffer a gradual drop towards more insecure work: this has been particularly true, for example, of black men and white women. Again, as noted before, gender and ethnic status mediate class in important ways.

One of the more developed sociological analyses of this process of polarisation of the labour market has been provided by Castells (1989). He argues that over the past two decades the most important feature of capitalist corporations is their increasing reliance on science and technology and more general forms of knowledge and information as the basis of their competitiveness. Knowledge and information are the principal factors of production today. For example, access to and control over information technology (IT) is crucial if corporations – even those outside the electronics sector itself – are to orchestrate their research, development, production and distribution of new products effectively. Moreover, new science-based technologies such as biotechnology have had a major impact not only in bioscience areas, such as pharmaceuticals, but also in energy, food, and other sectors. Production is, therefore, dependent on information – a term used in its broadest sense.

This transformation within industry has had a major impact on the labour market: knowledge-based occupations for professionals and highly educated middle classes become richly rewarded but require constant effort on the part of those who occupy them to stay in the race. Long hours of stressed work which requires constant monitoring and filtering of the informational sea surrounding them puts considerable pressure on individuals. For those without these knowledge-based skills, work is insecure, low-paid and always in danger of being replaced by automation. The 'informational mode of development' , as Castells describes this situation, confirms the break-up and fragmentation of the traditional class structures and the basis of their reproduction.

So the middle classes are under increasing pressure 'to deliver' professional expertise quickly and correctly if their employers are to remain in business, and while often well-rewarded for this, are vulnerable to a much greater competitive pressure than in the past. In part, this also reflects companies' interest in reducing their core of professional expertise to the minimum while subcontracting out less central needs to other agencies: hence the massive rise of consultancy firms surviving on short-term contracts from larger firms. Many of those working for such consultancies would, twenty years ago, have been more secure members of the established middle class.

jobless growth
Economic growth which fails to produce rising levels of employment.

The working class is increasingly squeezed by the onset of the informational mode of development, not only through automation which has created **jobless growth**, but also by the professionalisation and fragmentation of the labour market: as a result the working class becomes increasingly casualised and disorganised, both structurally and politcally. The fragmentation of the once large working-class occupational structure and the parallel decline of unionism undermine the social and cultural basis on which working-class identity has relied. The cultural reproduction of the working-class today looks very different from that secured in the past. An interesting illustration of this is provided by Warwick and Littlejohn's (1992) study of four mining communities in the UK, *Coal, Capital and Culture*, which provides a stark contrast with a much earlier study by Dennis *et al.* (1956) *Coal is Our Life*: whereas the Dennis study describes the strong community ties of a trad-itional (male-dominated) Yorkshire mining town, Warwick shows how such 'occupational communities' have changed dramatically over the past decade as the core of their community – their mines and the support structures on which they depend – have been closed or privatised. In these circumstances the cultural reproduction of the working class is threatened, and strategies of occupational closure less and less possible.

The globalisation of production

While the restructuring of the economy has brought major changes in the sort of work available on the labour market, and the polarisation of this work has produced a highly segmented labour market, the *globalisation* of production has meant that significant sections of the labour market are shaped by transnational organisations – notably multinational corporations – whose location, investment and relocation strategies are determined globally not locally. Sadler (1992) discusses the arrival of Japanese car-assembly plants in the North East of England, once famous for coal and steel production, but, by the 1980s, suffering severe decline. Attracted by regional development aid and other incentives provided by the British State, the car firms could impose their own version of workplace flexibility and labour market needs simply by hanging the threat of relocation over the workers' – and the government's – heads.

As we saw in Chapter 3, transnational corporations – such as the global car corporations, Nissan, Honda and Ford – are establishing globalised systems for research design and production to cover all their plants and research centres. To do this requires the development of computer-based management control systems whose purpose – unlikely ever to be fully achieved for a variety of local, contingent reasons – is to integrate, monitor and control the manufacturing process. Moreover, these same corporations – through their control over the productive sector – **outsource** some of their needs to 'preferred suppliers' who must meet their detailed design or other product and component specifications.

outsourcing
The process of sub-contracting work, i.e. securing certain research and development needs from external contractors, that were previously met inside the firm.

First World
Modern industrial capitalist societies, such as those of Europe, North America and Japan.

This change in the organisational structure of workplaces associated with the globalisation process has an important impact on the nature of the local labour market, and thereby on the formation of occupational class and class identity. In the past – what some commentators would claim to be 'Fordist' periods of mass production for primarily large domestic markets in **First World** states – local labour markets were associated with and generated substantial numbers of manufacturing (and service-based) jobs. These were in important ways also generators of localised communities and identities. As both the segmentation of work (as described above) and the globalisation of the production process have occurred, the previously established labour market – both in terms of what is being supplied to the labour market in the form of specific skills, and in terms of what is demanded from that market by employers – is being destabilised and indeed broken up. This means that *within* First World states such as the US or Britain, local regions can carry pockets of well-paid work associated with globalised production as well as cheap, casualised, low-skilled work which may in various ways serve global interests but through an intermediary subcontractor firm or agency.

Class reproduction?

The three processes described above have had an important impact on the structure and stability of traditional manual and non-manual labour markets in most industrialised states today. In many ways they suggest that the traditional occupational class model which we sketched out in Chapter 6 is undergoing important changes. One change we can see is that the boundaries between classes – while still marked – are being redefined by processes such as **segmentation**. In addition, the **gendering** of occupational structures – the gendering of the division of labour – is similarly shaped by these processes: the global corporation's desire for a flexible labour force, for outsourcing some of its production requirements to cheaper subcontracted labour, have meant greater numbers of women entering (but not progressing within) the labour market.

segmentation
The restructuring of social class boundaries associated with the polarisation and fragmentation of occupational groups.

gendering
The process by which division occurs according to gender. For example, the gendering of the labour market refers to the labour division where women are concentrated in certain job areas, usually low paid, part-time, often casual ones and men are concentrated in others.

For the middle class, secure white-collar work is still available and an 'elite' of knowledge-based (predominantly male) professionals and managers can be easily found working in finance, manufacturing, service, or other sectors. Yet, many of the cultural and material resources on which they once relied – schooling, contacts, good pay – no longer guarantee life-long security. Life-long careers themselves, as noted above, are becoming less the norm: in Britain, for example, fewer than one-third of jobs are full-time, 'tenured' career posts. The middle classes now find that they must be more prepared for sudden changes in their job security, perhaps through global firms making strategic changes in investment and market policies. In response, according to Scase (1992), the middle classes have had to become more '**entrepreneurial**' to survive on their well-paid but less secure perch in the labour market. This is especially so for managerial staffs who have found their organisational position (within firms or large public sector agencies) more vulnerable to contracting-out, to global investment switches and to mergers and privatisation. Many in these circumstances have fallen back on what property assets they have and sought to maintain their middle class position through self-employed, often consultancy-type, work. Being 'entrepreneurial' in this way is one way of surviving in this more volatile labour market, but clearly the terms on which middle class 'reproduction' is sustained are rather different from the past.

entrepreneurial
Activity in business or economic development based on the promotion of new innovative ideas and decision making.

intragenerational mobility
The movement of individuals, within one generation, from one social position within the hierarchy to another. Usually refers to positions of broad occupation or social class.

intergenerational mobility
The movement of individuals, between different generations, from one social position within the hierarchy to another. Usually refers to positions of broad occupation or social class.

Implications for social mobility

These changes in the occupational labour market and so in the boundaries of broad occupational class positions have important implications for patterns of *social mobility*, the movement of people up or down the social hierarchy, either within one generation (**intragenerational mobility**) or between generations (**intergenerational**

mobility). Typically, sociologists identify three main factors that affect the general level of social mobility in modern industrial societies:

- the changing number of positions (such as types of occupation) to be filled
- the methods of access and entry to these positions
- the number of suitable offspring available to fill the positions.

With regard to the first of these, over the past two decades there has been a marked decline in the number of manufacturing jobs as the economies of such societies have shifted towards service-sector work especially of the intermediate non-manual type. Women have been the most likely recruits to these positions.

More broadly, and in regard to the second point, entry to positions in the labour market has increasingly depended on the qualifications and skills one has. Thus education and 'credentials' grow ever-important. Where working-class children manage to secure good qualifications, they are therefore in a good position to experience upward social mobility relative to their class at birth. However, analyses of statistical data (Goldthorpe, 1980; Heath, 1981; Gallie, 1988) indicate that the chances for entering secure, well-paid middle-class jobs are much higher for the sons (and to a lesser extent the daughters) of middle-class parents than for the children of working-class origin, even when qualifications are held constant. Greater overall levels of mobility, therefore, do not therefore necessarily mean increasing equality of opportunity for children of all social classes. And, if we look at the children from disadvantaged ethnic backgrounds, or the disabled, then we see higher barriers to social mobility within or between generations.

With regard to the third factor noted above, the expansion of middle-class white-collar work, at both intermediate and solid middle-class levels, has meant that there has been an 'inadequate' number of middle-class children to fill these new posts. As a result, working-class children – with the necessary qualifications – have been able to move upwards into the new professional posts: therefore, when we examine the background of professional and managerial staffs in Britain, almost 25 per cent were drawn from the working class in 1991. Again, though, data on female mobility (Heath, 1981) show that women from all social classes are systematically excluded from top managerial and professional jobs, as well as from skilled manual work. As a result, women are concentrated in routine non-manual work, in lower professions – such as nursing and teaching – and in low-paid manual jobs. Thus, while over 50 per cent of the daughters of professional and managerial households enter non-manual jobs, these are at the routine, intermediate level with little or no chance of work-life upward mobility. There is, in other words, strong evidence for the so-called '**glass ceiling**' for many non-manual women workers.

glass ceiling
A metaphorical concept used to explain how women are prevented from attaining top (managerial and professional) jobs.

Traditionally, mobility has been lowest for the sons and daughters of the working class: put another way, children tend to recruit to jobs similar to those of their parents. The stronger this pattern the stronger the sense of a stable class identity through occupational membership over time, and in this sense the stronger the social closure of class. Higher levels of social mobility into the lower ranks of the middle class simply reinforces the blurring of class boundaries around that intermediate level, so weakening any strong sense of class identity.

Changes in mobility patterns

Given the impact on the occupational labour market of restructuring, polarisation and globalisation, does this in any way affect the patterns of social mobility just described? If, for example, the labour market is now segmented into two broad polarised sectors – the core of secure work and the periphery of casualised low-paid jobs – we might expect that entry into core work is increasingly difficult, for both sons and daughters of working-class households for whom securing the credentials for such work is especially problematic. We might also find – as Savage *et al.* (1992) argue – that staying in middle-class jobs and avoiding downward intragenerational mobility can become more difficult for professional white-collar workers. As we shall see in more detail in Chapter 12, Charles Handy (1991) argues that the future for the established middle-class worker will be very different from the expectations of the past. For many, these new circumstances will lead to a broad downward mobility into lower-class positions.

Box 7.3: The future of professional work

'The next generation of full-time core workers, be they professionals, managers, technicians or skilled workers, can expect to start their full-time careers later – and to leave them earlier. This is the crucial point. The core worker will have a harder but shorter job, with more people leaving full-time employment in their later forties or early fifties, partly because they no longer want the pressure that such jobs will increasingly entail, but mainly because there will be younger more qualified and more energetic people available for these core jobs. ... Work will not stop for people after 50 but it will not be the same sort of work; it will not be a *job* as they have known it.'

Source: Charles Handy, *The Age of Unreason*, pp. 36–7.

blue-collar worker
A term used to describe manual workers.

white-collar worker
Non-manual employees, such as office or administration staff.

The growth of a large part-time casualised job sector has meant a large increase in the number of women – especially married women – entering the labour market, while the decline in traditional **blue-collar** work has meant that many men have been ejected from the labour market into long-term unemployment, early retirement or chronic sickness rather than securing new jobs in the intermediate or more senior **white-collar** service sector. The scale of this severe downward mobility into the ranks of the poor or, as some would argue, underclass, has varied by region and, within regions, by gender. In the study by Bagguley (1990), of socio-economic change in the north-west region of the UK, specifically that area around Lancaster, the drift in downward mobility for *men* of *all* social classes as a result of restructuring of the economy has been twice the national average, while *women* in the area had *better* chances of surviving in the service class or entering the intermediate white-collar strata: relative to national averages for *female* workers, women's upward mobility rates are better in this area. This reflected the expansion of health service jobs, hotels, catering and casual clerical work. Nevertheless, *relative* to male workers, of course, such women were still disadvantaged in terms of pay and conditions.

For the secure middle classes, the erosion – but not entire removal – of their secure, life-long position in well-paid white-collar work, means that the possibility of downard mobility *during* their working life increases, though a full-scale survey of this phenomenon has yet to be conducted. We can see, however, as Scase's (1992) notion of entrepreneurialism suggests, the emergence of greater numbers of self-employed consultants among the ranks of the middle class: technically, this denotes a small degree of upwards mobility. In the UK, for example, it involves a move up one rank in the national Census's classification of 'socio-economic groups' – from SEG 4 (professional workers – employees) to SEG 3 (professional workers – self-employed). While the rewards for work of this kind can be very great, they can also be intermittent and more immediately dependent on the state of the economy than are the jobs of professionals employed in large organisations where job losses may take longer to work their way through. Thus, the security of middle-class self-employed work is never very high, and households where this is found will be likely to rely on other earnings from other household members to buffer any short-term loss of income. Moreover, these professionals are, more than any other class group, likely to avoid downward mobility by being able and willing to travel considerable distances for work, either as long-distance commuters to their regular place of work, or as mobile consultants prepared to travel extensively to access possible client markets.

As one can see from the above, mobility patterns are dependent on the changing structure of the labour market, changes which affect both inter- and intragenerational mobility. One group we should give close attention to here are the new recruits to the labour market, those making the transition from school to work. How do the new dynamics of class affect them?

Youth entry to the labour market

Traditionally, most sons and daughters of the working and middle classes have secured work within the same class location as their parents. This is still true today, but just as the wider changes in the national and global labour markets are changing the terms on which intergenerational class reproduction is occurring, so, logically, we should expect to see these changes having an important impact on the work-chances and occupational class position of the young. The transition from school to work is affected by a number of factors, including,

- the class position of the family household, and the resources it can use to secure better employment for its young members
- the gender of the new job-seeker
- the locality within which work is sought
- the educational skills the young possess and bring to the labour market
- the policies of the state which relate to youth training and employment.

Much depends, too, on the *first* job that the young worker secures after leaving school, for this can initiate an employment pattern which, in today's segmented labour market, is likely to mean either secure or insecure work in the future.

Box 7.4: First jobs and future life chances

'The transition from school represents a crucial point of intersection between major life domains, namely the educational system and the labour market. It is at this point that most young people are at considerable risk in their attempts (and frequently that of their parents) to ensure continuity in their life course. Apart from those people for whom the first job is a temporary expedient or fill-in job, such as students or young people waiting to enter jobs, such as nursing, with age requirements for entry, the level at which they enter the labour force is crucial in influencing their future life chances. It plays a large part in influencing the amount of income they will receive, their chances of obtaining occupational security and their chances of increasing their income and status in later life.'

Source: Layder *et al.*, 1991, p. 453.

There are two broad, very different, arguments made about the current state of the labour market and its impact on youth employment in the industrialised countries of Europe, the US and the Pacific Rim. On the one hand, there are those (such as Ashton and Maguire, 1986; Casey and McRae, 1990; Allmendinger, 1989) who argue that the segmented structure of today's labour market coupled with the decline of apprenticed-based work in manufacturing industries closes off many of the former employment opportunities once enjoyed by the young. Furthermore, according to this view, the problems for the new job seeker have been exacerbated by the global changes in employment which have 'exported' many jobs to cheaper labour markets overseas (though much of this is in the form of sweatshop labour of course).

On the other hand there are others (e.g. Raffe, 1987) who believe that youth employment is not structured in this way but is 'cyclical', reflecting the general state of the economy. Thus, during recession – which all industrialised countries experienced during the 1980s to a greater or lesser degree – the young are first to suffer, either because they are easier to dispose of if they have a job or because no one wants to take on new labour. However, when the economy improves, the young are first to benefit from the availability of new jobs, especially in urban areas where the demand for service sector work, such as in retailing, can grow quickly.

Perhaps, as Lee (1991) has suggested, both arguments have some value since it is clearly possible that as a restructuring of labour has occurred this has produced a two-tier labour market, which, as economies come out of recession, provides many new jobs, whose longevity is uncertain. As Lee says, in many countries 'large firms cut back their training places and labour overheads during the recession of the early eighties. Insecure, low skill work simultaneously became more widespread, because hiring young workers and "trainees" on low wages offered a means by which more marginal (mostly smaller) firms might survive' (p. 89).

What is apparent from the segmented labour market perspective is that throughout the European Community there are a number of industries where one finds a disproportionately large number of young people employed, and where wage rates are low and the chances of intra-generational mobility poor. However, it is important to recognise the way the various factors noted above – relating to household resources and so on – influence the specific chances of young individuals seeking work. Locality, for example, is an important factor inasmuch as where young people live determines the sort of work they can pursue since their geographical mobility is likely to be less than other job seekers. As a result, some studies have shown that in certain rural areas middle-class youth take up jobs which have worse life chances than do those of some working-class youth in urban regions, where the range of jobs is better.

State policies towards youth training are also important (see Chapter 12). Lee (1991) compares (the then) West German and British policies on this and found that Germany has institutionalised stronger training programmes and cultivated stronger links (and continuity) between vocational and academic study, apprenticeships, and firms than has been the case in Britain. For example, in the former West Germany 90 per cent of school-leavers moved from school into an apprenticeship scheme of one form or another. In Britain, there has been a switch in policy in schools and colleges towards a New Vocationalism but this has typically been underfunded, poorly managed, and, most importantly, regarded with lower status than the traditional academic training most undertake. In reality, therefore, Britain has tended to create a 'cheap, "surrogate" labour force of trainees' which have made it even 'more attractive to profit-making firms to work young people hard rather than to train them' (Lee, 1991, p. 102).

There are, therefore, important regional and national differences in the life chances of working and middle-class youth seeking to move into the labour market. At the same time, the broad dynamics shaping the labour market as a whole – segmentation, polarisation and globalisation – will mean that the changes now being experienced by adult workers – a growing vulnerability, high pay accompanied by ever higher job pressures, casualised insecure work, and so on – will have to be confronted by the new workers too.

The New Dynamics of Class and Class Identity

We saw in the first half of this chapter how the social reproduction and social closure of the middle and working classes depended on a number of conditions: differential access to cultural credentials, differential access to work and a broad structure of occupational roles which had provided for long-term non-manual and manual employment, albeit unequally rewarded (in ways we discussed in more detail in Chapter 6). The social reproduction of class is central to its shared sense of social identity: so occupationally-based cultures have been very important for all classes, particularly so when they are related to residential communities, as was true of mining.

The changes sketched out above suggest that the capacity for social reproduction of both classes has been reduced, as uncertainties over work life chances for both those in work and those new to the labour market increase. The promise of modernity as we move into the globalised world of **late modernity** now looks less secure. Growth without work – as we saw in the recent EC studies – becomes the norm. The developmental payoff of industrialisation in terms of a gradual overall improvement in standards of living, life chances and personal security seems less, rather than more, likely for many people today. Gorz (1989) has argued that the polarisation processes mapped out above will produce extreme divisions between a privileged, relatively small professional class and a new, mass 'servile' class.

late modernity

A term which implies change within modernity, characterised by increased reflexivity and globalisation, but without a qualitative shift to postmodernity. Similar phrases are high modernity and radicalised modernity (*see* reflexivity *and* globalisation).

Whatever vision of the (not-so-distant) future is offered, it may well be the case that the changes we describe will mean that class identities become more difficult to reproduce over generations. As Brown and Scase (1991) suggest, 'The restructuring of class relationships has increased material inequalities but reduced the subjective awareness of them. Inequalities, privileges and disadvantages are now more likely to be viewed as the outcome of *individual* actions rather than of structurally-determined economic and political forces. A strongly nurtured dominant ideology of individualism has reinforced a prevailing culture of *indifference* which serves to sustain both the privileges and deprivations experienced by different groups in society' (pp. 21–2).

It is this which some would argue points towards a new – **postmodern** – era, in which class identity has become less central in people's lives precisely because we have moved into a post-modern *consumption*-oriented society. That is, identity is derived more by what we consume than by the work we do (or do not do). Identities in the postmodern world are less stable, more subject to the changing consumption styles and desires we have (Featherstone, 1991; Bauman, 1992). As we saw in Chapter 2, this may well be the case for many, whatever occupational position they have. But clearly, the dynamics of segmentation, polarisation and globalisation will ensure that the *chance* of being a consumer will ultimately depend on one's chance of securing income, which, for many, still relates to the job they do.

postmodernity

For its supporters, the further transformation in social, cultural, economic and political arrangements which takes a society beyond modernity.

Summary of the Chapter

- This chapter focuses on classes as occupational groups, divided in broad terms into the middle and working classes.
- Occupational groups are sustained over time via process of social reproduction and social closure.

- The stability of both classes is being threatened by important changes in the occupational labour market at the national level, often, though not always, a reflection of global processes in the world economy.
- Stable class identities are weakened as a result of these changes.
- The enterprise culture associated with the new labour market masks the uncertainty and fragmentation that characterises contemporary work.

References

Allmendinger, J. (1989) 'Educational systems and laour market outcomes', *European Sociological Review*, vol. 5, no. 3, pp. 231–50.

Ashton, D. and M. J. Maguire (1986) 'Young adults in the labour market', *Research Paper*, 55, Department of Employment, HMSO, London.

Ashton, D. *et al.* (1990) *Restructuring the Labour Market: The Implications for Youth*, London, Macmillan.

Atkinson, J. and D. Gregory (1986) 'A flexible future: Britain's dual labour force', *Marxism Today*, April, pp. 12–17.

Bagguley, P. (1990) *Restructuring: Place, Class and Gender*, London, Sage.

Bauman, Z. (1992) *Intimations of Postmodernity*, London, Routledge.

Beynon, H. *et al.* (1991) *A Tale of Two Industries*, Milton Keynes, Open University Press.

Braverman, H. (1974) *Labour and Monopoly Capital*, New York, Monthly Review Press.

Brown, P. and R. Scase (eds) (1991) *Poor Work: Disadvantage and the Division of Work*, Buckingham, Open University Press.

Casey, B. and S. McRae (1990). 'A more polarised labour market', *Policy Studies*, vol. 11, pp. 31–9.

Castells, M. (1989) *The Informational City*, Oxford, Basil Blackwell.

Dennis, N. *et al.* (1956) *Coal is Our Life*, London, Eyre & Spottiswoode.

Featherstone, M. (1991) 'The body in consumer culture', in M. Featherstone *et al.* (eds), *The Body: Social Process and Cultural Theory*, London, Sage.

Gallie, D. (ed.) (1988) *Employment in Britain*, Oxford, Blackwell.

Gamble, A. (1985) *Britain in Decline*, London, Macmillan.

Goldthorpe, J. H. (1980) *Social Mobility and Class Structure in Modern Britain*, 1st edn, Oxford, Clarendon Press.

Goldthorpe, J. H. (1987) *Social Mobility and Class Structure in Modern Britain*, 2nd edn, Oxford, Clarendon Press.

Goldthorpe, J. H. *et al.* (1968) *The Affluent Worker: Industrial Attitudes and Behaviour*, Harmondsworth, Penguin.

Gorz, A. (1982) *Farewell to the Working Class*, London, Pluto Press.

Gorz, A. (1989) *Critique of Economic Reason*, London, Verso.

Grey, C. (1994) 'Career as a project of the self and labour process discipline', *Sociology*, vol. 28, no. 2, pp. 479–98.

Halsey, A. *et al.* (1980) *Origins and Destinations*, Oxford, Clarendon Press.

Handy, C. (1991) *The Age of Unreason*, London, Century.

Heath, A. (1981) *Social Mobility*, Glasgow, Fontana.

Heath, A. and N. Britten (1984) 'Women's jobs do make a difference', *Sociology*, vol. 18, no. 4.

Hingel, A. J. (1993) 'A new model of European development: innovation, technological development and network-led integration', *FAST* Programme, CEC, Brussels.

Layder, D. *et al.* (1991) 'The empirical correlates of action and structure', *Sociology*, vol. 25, no. 3, pp. 447–64.

Leadbeater, C. (1987) 'In the land of the dispossessed', *Marxism Today*, April, pp. 18–25.

Leadbeater, C. and G. Mulgan (1994) 'The end of unemployment: bringing work to life', *Demos*, vol. 2.

Lee, D. (1991) 'Poor work and poor institutions: training and the youth labour market', in P. Brown and R. Scase (eds.), *Poor Work: Disadvantage and the Division of Work*, Buckingham, Open University Press.

Morris, M. *et al.* (1994) 'Economic inequality: new methods for new trends?', *American Sociological Review*, vol. 59, p. 205–19.

Pahl, R. (1991) 'Debating social class', *The International Journal of Urban and Regional Research*, vol. 15, pp. 107–29.

Penn, R. (1985) *Skilled Workers in the Class Structure*, Cambridge, Cambridge University Press.

Raffe, D. (1987) 'Youth unemployment in the United Kingdom', in P. Brown and D. N. Ashton (eds), *Education, Unemployment and the Labour Market*, Lewes, Falmer.

Sadler, D. (1972) *The Global Region*, Oxford, Pergamon.

Sassen, S. (1988) *The Mobility of Labour and Capital: A Study in International Investment and Labour Flow*, New York, Cambridge University Press.

Savage, M. *et al.* (1992). *Property, Bureaucracy and Culture*, London, Routledge.

Scase, R. (1992) *Class*, Milton Keynes, Open University Press.

Sklair, L. (1991) *Sociology of the Global System*, London, Harvester Wheatsheaf.

Stehr, N. (1994) *Knowledge Societies*, New York, Sage.

Strange, P. (1990) *Rival States, Rival Firms*, Cambridge, Cambridge University Press.

Warwick, D. and G. Littlejohn (1992) *Coal, Capital and Culture*, London, Routledge.

Wild, P. (1979) 'Recreation in Rochdale, 1900–49', in J. Clarke *et al.* (eds), *Working Class Culture*, London, Hutchinson.

Willis, P. (1977) *Learning to Labour*, Farnborough, Saxon House.

Wood, S. (1982) *The Degradation of Work? Skill, Deskilling and the Labour Process*, London, Hutchinson.

Gender Relations

Aims of the Chapter

This chapter provides an overview of some of the social processes that shape gender relations in contemporary societies. It emphasises that there are many forms of masculinity and femininity. It describes and assesses two major accounts of the individual acquisition of gendered identity, and argues for the necessity of viewing gender as a property of social institutions and of culture as much as of individuals. Therefore, the chapter examines in some detail the way that key institutional areas – divisions of labour, the social organisation of childbirth and childcare, sexuality and popular culture and the media – have been permeated by gender, and considers some of the implications of this for contemporary gender relations.

In thinking about gender, even more than other areas of social life, people frequently have recourse to explanations in terms of 'naturalness', and so our discussions of childbirth and childcare, of sexuality, and indeed of gender difference itself begin by contrasting biological explanations with social ones. But we also question in this chapter whether biological and social phenomena can be so neatly separated. Even the **bodies** *of men and women, it is suggested here, are constituted partly by social processes.*

Introduction

In late August 1995, some 25,000 women from all over the world gathered in China. Their intention was to press their agendas upon the government delegations from 185 nations who had been invited by the United Nations to debate a programme of action for women for the coming decade. There was anything but consensus in the early days: marching with their mouths bandaged, Tibetan women bore silent witness to the Chinese occupation of their country – and were harrassed by Chinese police; a 'conservative' nine-delegation alliance (including the Vatican, Iran and the Sudan) vigorously opposed proposals for sexual and reproductive freedoms; all delegates applauded the recognition by the UN that women's rights are human rights, and yet many argued that the emphasis on *rights* detracted from the way in which, especially in poorer countries, lack of resources spelled disaster for women.

The reporting of the conference in the media often focused upon disagreements among delegates, highlighting the fact that an identity as women does not generate a uniform consciousness or a uniform set of priorities and interests; other circumstances, and other identities –

national, ethnic, religious, class – may be crucial. But the conference also illustrates the widespread recognition of, and challenge to, patterns of inequality that generate gender disadvantage. Not only did Benazir Bhutto's eloquent call for an end to **female infanticide** win widespread acclaim, but there was also remarkable commitment – from diverse groups – to seek measures that might improve the health, educational standing and economic power of women across the world.

female infanticide
The murder of female babies and infants.

biological determinism
A simple causal, reductionist approach that explains human behaviour in terms of biological or genetic characteristics.

social construction
The process whereby 'natural', instinctive, forms of behaviour become mediated by social processes. Sociologists would argue that most forms of human behaviour are socially constructed.

cathexis
Originally employed by Freud to describe a psychic charge or the formation of an emotional attraction towards another person. More generally associated with the social and psychological patterning of desire and the construction of emotionally charged relationships

masculinities
Various socially constructed collections of assumptions, expectations and ways of behaving that serve as standards for forms of male behaviour.

femininities
Various socially constructed collections of assumptions, expectations and ways of behaving that serve as standards for female behaviour.

Men, Women and Gender Difference

What is gender difference, and where does it come from? Why, for example, in Western societies, are men more sparing with their smiles? Why are they less likely to coo over other people's babies, or to abandon careers to care for their own?

Answers to such questions can be placed along a continuum, according to the importance they attach to biology in explaining gender difference. At one end of the continuum, **biological determinists** highlight similarities in male behaviour across different environments. They argue that male traits (whether a preference for competitive sport, or a lack of 'maternal' feeling) have their roots in chromosomal differences (e.g. XYY chromosomes) or in hormonal differences (e.g. testosterone) or in some other natural characteristic that distinguishes men from women.

At the other end of the continuum, **social constructionists** contend instead that gender differences derive from social and cultural processes. These processes create systems of ideas and practices about gender that vary across time and space. They also create gender divisions of labour, allocating women and men to different activities and responsibilities. Individuals raised within such a framework will come to have appropriately gendered identities and desires. For example, Connell (1987) argues that every society has a gender order, composed of a historically-specific division of labour, a structure of **cathexis** or desire, and a structure of power. The gender order generates a variety of **masculinities** (some dominant, some not) and of **femininities**. The gender order acts as a framework within which gender differences emerge and are reproduced or challenged.

Assembling evidence on the issue of gender difference is more difficult than is sometimes suggested. To support a biological determinist case, we would need, first, to establish that a substantial and universal difference exists: that men across societies are characterised by more or less identical behaviours (and that the same is true of women). Second, we would need to show that this difference is caused by biology – and not, for example, by similarities in the upbringing of boys, or in the responsibilities they have as adults. The more segregated the worlds that women and men inhabit, the harder it is to demonstrate that nature, rather than nurture, accounts for gender difference.

Sociological, historical and anthropological research shows that femininity and masculinity vary dramatically across cultures. The definition of womanhood among bourgeois women in Victorian Britain, for example, involved physical delicacy, exclusion from paid work and lack of sexual feeling; womanhood in many rural parts of Africa today is synonymous with physical robustness, breadwinning and sexual confidence. In the face of such diversity, it is difficult to sustain a claim that there is a necessary connection between female bodies (or male bodies) and particular gender traits.

'Femininity' and 'masculinity' are subject to change not only across cultures, but also over time. Masculinity in the 1940s and 1950s, in the United States of America, had breadwinning at its core; it was imaged in popular culture by the sober-suited, domestically incompetent, hard-working family man played in films by actors like James Stewart. Ehrenreich (1983) argues that this form of masculinity became, over time, less prominent. The publication of *Playboy* magazine (promoting an exploitative bachelor style), the writings of the beat poets (who scoffed at conventional morality), the trumpeting of the dangers of workaholism – these and other cultural influences helped to articulate new masculinities and contributed, Ehrenreich argues, to the erosion of a breadwinner ethic.

If masculinity changes over time, so too men – even at a single point in time – are likely to be diverse. 'Men' are no more homogeneous than are 'human beings' or 'Germans' or 'the young'. Even within a single society, different social and cultural contexts – linked to race or ethnicity, to age or physical capacities, to sexual orientation or social class – alter the meaning of male or female bodies, and of gender difference, often in quite dramatic ways. The delicate bourgeois lady of Victorian England co-existed with the sturdy hard-working housemaid. Indeed, without the robust housemaid, the fragility of the lady would have been unthinkable.

essentialism

An approach which assumes some universal essence, homogeneity and unity in the phenomena under study. Such approaches to gender, for example, identify traits and behaviour common to all men and women.

This recognition of diversity puts paid to **essentialist** views of gender – to views that claim to identify some natural feature (or essence) that all women (or all men) share in common. As Brown and Jordanova (1982, p. 390) conclude: 'there is no such thing as woman or man in asocial terms; women and men, or rather femininity and masculinity, are constituted in specific cultural settings according to class, age, marital status and so on'.

Box 8.1: Ain't I a woman?

Because gender varies so dramatically across time and space, sociologists have to be careful to challenge the universal validity of models developed in particular contexts. Often descriptions of femininity (or masculinity) are presented as standard that really only fit Western white middle-class heterosexuals. Such models of femininity (or masculinity) render invisible – or make 'deviant' – the experience of other groups of women (or men). They make diversity invisible.

In nineteenth-century America, for example, the dominant femininity emphasised women's delicacy, and their need for male protection. This description may have seemed 'real' to some people, but of course it did not correspond to the experience of a great many women. The definition was challenged forcefully by Sojourner Truth, a feminist activist.

Truth was a former slave. She campaigned vigorously for extension of suffrage to black men and to all women. At a convention in Ohio in 1852, women's rights campaigners were jeered at by hostile men who insisted that women needed protection, not the vote. Sojourner Truth strode to the platform to repudiate these claims. She declared:

'That man over there says women need to be helped into carriages, and lifted over ditches, and to have the best place everywhere. Nobody ever helps me into carriages, or over mud-puddles, or gives me any best place! And ain't I a woman? Look at me! Look at my arm! I have ploughed, and planted and gathered into barns, and no man could head me! And ain't I a woman? I could work as much and eat as much as a man – when I could get it – and bear the lash as well! And ain't I a woman? I have borne thirteen children, and seen most all sold off to slavery, and when I cried out with my mother's grief, none but Jesus heard me! And ain't I a woman?' (in hooks, 1982, p. 160).

Collins (1990, pp. 14–15) comments that although Truth had never learned to read, she demonstrated in her speech that an idea of 'woman' that appeared to reflect bodily reality was in fact a cultural construct, and relevant only to certain sections of the female population.

Gender and the body

If gender difference is socially constructed, what remains of the relationship between gender and the body? Does the fact that males and females are anatomically different have nothing to do with gender?

gender
Distinct from 'sex', this concept often refers to the socially constructed categories of masculine and feminine that are differently defined in various cultures. Many contemporary theorists use a broader definition to refer to the variable sets of beliefs and practices about male and female (or other genders), that not only feed into individual identities, but are fundamental to social institutions and symbolic systems.

sex
The division of human beings into male and female on the basis of chromosomal and reproductive differences; it has been defined as a biological category, in contrast to the social category of gender (*see* gender).

berdache
A practice among the native people of North America to allocate male gender roles on the basis of cultural preference rather than on the assumption of a biological predisposition (*see* gender).

One answer, influential in the 1970s and early 1980s, is that **gender** is the 'cultural' gloss put on a 'natural' foundation of **sex**. 'Sex' refers to universal differences in male and female bodies – in chromosomes, genitals and reproductive capacities. Sex is rooted in nature; it distinguishes males from females. 'Gender', on the other hand, refers to the socially constructed and infinitely variable categories of masculine and feminine. As Anne Oakley explained in her influential book *Sex, Gender and Society*, bodies are the trigger for the assignment of gender difference; femininity of some sort will be elaborated for anatomical females, and masculinity of some sort for males. 'The chief importance of biological sex,' argued Oakley (1972, p. 156), 'is in providing a universal and obvious division around which other distinctions can be organised.'

Examination of other cultures throws doubt on the claim that 'male' and 'female' are universal categories based on natural anatomical differences. Before the twentieth century, among many of the native peoples of North America – for example, the Cheyenne and the Ojibwa, the Navajo and the Iroquois – anatomy was not the only criterion for deciding whether a person would rank as a man or a woman. Following a practice called **berdache**, anatomical males who strongly preferred basket-weaving or burden-carrying – women's work – to hunting with the bow or going to battle, could move in female circles, dress as women did, and even take husbands. Although they retained their male genitals, they ceased to be males. Activities were as significant as anatomy in determining sex (Whitehead, 1981).

In contemporary Europe and North America, the usual approach to sex is rather different. We assume – indeed, we believe it to be objectively true – that men can readily be distinguished from women. This assumption is part of what Garfinkel terms our 'natural attitude' towards sex (see Box 8.2). Kessler and McKenna (1985) argue that although we may perceive the Western view of sex to be objectively correct, it is as much a constructed reality as that of the societies that practised berdache. When we come across a 'man' who wears stilettos and speaks of giving birth, instead of accepting the evidence of our senses – that not everyone fits neatly into male or female – we search for further evidence (facial hair, name, jewellery). We conduct ourselves, in everyday life, so as to confirm the view that sex is clear-cut, and in so doing we shore up the belief that a male/female distinction is 'universal and obvious'.

This type of evidence from other cultures and from our own suggests that the simple division into male and female sex – only recently regarded as an obvious and universal distinction based upon bodies – is itself a social construction. In Western societies, it is our gender ideas (not bodies themselves) that make us insist that people are unambiguously male or female. The process of gender attribution – whereby we classify people as male or female – is a social process, that varies from one social setting to another.

Box 8 .2: Male and female: a universal and obvious distinction?

Garfinkel (1967, pp. 122–8) describes the 'natural attitude' of modern Western societies towards sex:

- There are two, and only two, sexes – female and male.
- Every individual is either male or female. There are no exceptions.
- A person's sex is invariant. Once a male, always a male.
- Genitals are the key to sex. A male has a penis. A female has a vagina.
- The male/female dichotomy is natural and objectively given. It exists independently of social criteria for being male or female.

Professionals play a large part in sustaining the natural attitude. Where the anatomical sex of a baby is ambiguous, consultants authorise treatment to reconstruct it as either male or female. Adult **transsexuals** are people whose anatomical sex is out of synch with their gender identity. Where an anatomical man claims he is a woman, he may be referred for psychiatric and medical treatment including surgery to remove the penis, and create a vagina and breasts. Transsexuals are often keen to have such surgery. What is interesting is that in Western societies it has been perceived as less problematic to want to have a surgical reconstruction of the genitals, than it is to be a woman with a penis. Transsexualism, Kessler and McKenna claim (1985, p. 120), 'is a category contructed to alleviate ambiguity – to avoid the kinds of combinations (e.g., male genitals–female gender identity) that make people uncomfortable because they violate the basic rules about gender'.

transsexuals
People whose gender identity is at odds with the gender indicated by their body and who take steps to change their body to match their perceived identity

Ideas about masculinity and femininity mould male and female bodies in more concrete ways, too. There are a range of social practices – from body-building to cosmetic surgery, from hormonal treatment to nutrition, from sport to styles of dress to forms of work – that contribute to bodily difference. In Western societies, women are on average smaller than men, and slimness is a strong element in definitions of femininity. If, as some commentators suggest, a high proportion of girls spend their teenage years on weight-reducing diets, is this not a powerful example of the ways in which gender 'produces' sexual difference?

As Ruth Hubbard (1990, p. 69) argues,

> **If a society puts half its children into short skirts and warns them not to move in ways that reveal their panties, while putting the other half into jeans and overalls and encouraging them to climb trees, play ball, and participate in other vigorous outdoor games; if later, during adolescence, the children who have been wearing trousers are urged to eat like growing boys, while the children in skirts are warned to watch their weight and not get fat; if the half in jeans runs around in sneakers or boots, while the half in skirts totters about on spike heels, then these two groups of people will be biologically as well as socially different.**
>
> **[Hubbard, 1990, p. 69]**

Our male and female bodies are, in short, the product of the interaction of nature and of social processes – including those of gender. This recognition challenges the opposition between biological determinism and social construction with which the chapter began; the search for 'biological' differences between the sexes, unadulterated by culture – or, for that matter, for 'cultural' differences that have not had an impact on our bodies – may in fact be misguided.

Gender identity

By the time children in Western societies reach their second birthday, many will have acquired a firm sense of themselves as male or female, a gender identity that remains throughout life. In addition, many pre-schoolers have a firm awareness of gender stereotypes, insisting that certain activities or items of clothing are not for girls and others not for boys. Yet – as a consideration of transsexuals makes clear – gender identity does not automatically follow from biological sex. Money and Ehrhardt (1972, cited in Oakley, 1981, p. 53) report a case in which a seven-month-old boy lost his penis through an accident. A few months later, the boy's genitals were surgically reconstructed as female. He was assigned a girlish name, girlish clothing, a girlish hairdo. According to the researchers, he developed 'normally', as a very feminine girl.

socialisation
An on-going process whereby individuals learn to conform to society's prevailing norms and values (*see* norms *and* values).

Socialisation theory offers a straightforward account of the acquisition of gendered identities. Infants are seen, from this perspective, as blank slates, waiting to be written on by their environment. Through their interactions with people close to them, and through exposure to the values of their society, infants learn what sex has been attributed to them (male? or female?) and what is expected of them as little girls or boys. Reinforcement (praise and other rewards for gender-appropriate behaviour, punishment for deviation) brings the message home. A process of modelling (imitating parents or older siblings or teachers of the same sex) may also occur, until eventually children internalise – i.e., incorporate as part of their sense of self – the gender prescriptions of their society. And the more polarised the culture around gender, the greater will be the gender difference in the identities of girls and boys.

In spite of public interest in gender equality in the past two decades in Europe and America, it is undeniably the case that children receive frequent reminders of difference between the sexes. The division of labour in most families will point to different responsibilities for women and men. Boys' clothing differs from girls' clothing in crucial details (*Star Trek* pyjamas v. *Forever Friends* nightgowns, or joggers v. leggings), and on the occasions when children dress up, the differences are even sharper. Even bedrooms are gendered: floral designs and ruffles or pleats for girls, military or animal designs for boys.

Parents, whatever their intentions, tend to treat girls and boys differently in ways that influence their development. Parents are far more likely to engage their infant sons in rough physical play – tossing them up in the air, or wrestling with them – than they are their daughters (McDonald and Parke, 1986) and it has been argued that long-term consequences (in this case, a head start for little boys in the development of physical confidence, aggressiveness and motor skills) may follow. Adults respond differently to the communicative efforts of girls and boys. In a study by Fagot and her colleagues (1985) of infants aged thirteen months, when boys demanded attention – behaving aggressively, or crying, whining or screaming – they tended to get it. By contrast, adults tended to respond to girls only when they used language or gestures or gentle touches; girls who tried attention-grabbing techniques were likely to be ignored. There was little difference in the communicative patterns of girls and boys at the start of the study, but by the age of two, the girls had become more talkative, and the boys more assertive, in their communicative styles. There is a possibility that, through patterns of reinforcement, adults helped to create these gender differences, as socialisation theory predicts.

But although socialisation theory may explain certain aspects of gendered behaviour, it cannot stand as a complete explanation for gendered identity and gendered desires. For one thing, socialisation theory makes children the passive receivers of gendered messages from their environment. But this assumption is incompatible with research that shows that even very young children often make gender-stereotyped choices for themselves. A study of pre-school children in North Carolina (Robinson and Morris, 1986) found that their Christmas presents tended to be heavily gender-stereotyped (e.g., military toys for boys, dolls and domestic items for girls) . But these gifts, it turned out, had been purchased largely at the insistence of the children themselves. The toys that had been selected for them by grown-ups tended to be (like art supplies, games, musical instruments) sex-neutral. Children's early 'spontaneous' gender commitments cannot readily be explained by socialisation theory.

Moreover, socialisation theory may be insufficiently subtle to account for the complexity of gender identity and gendered desires. The attachment of adult men and women to elements of masculinity or femininity which they would like to slough off (something experienced by many women in the women's movements and men in men's movements), the depths of emotion surrounding gendered desires (excitement or passion or shame), and the conflicts that continue to trouble 'fully socialised' women and men – all these suggest that socialisation theory operates too much at the level of conscious processes, and pays too little attention to the underlying psychic processes by which gender may be embedded.

psychoanalytic
Pertaining to the unconscious processes of the mind. A psychoanalytic approach would attempt to explain human behaviour by uncovering some of these processes.

One of the most influential of the **psychoanalytic** theories of gender identity – those that take account of unconscious processes – is the perspective developed in Chodorow's (1978) book *The Reproduction of Mothering*. Nancy Chodorow traces the implications for emotional development of the fact that mothers generally care for infants in their early years, while fathers are more emotionally distant. The formation of the self involves separating from the mother with whom the infant is initially psychically merged. But this process operates differently for girls and boys. Girls can separate gradually, maintaining a continuous sense of relationship with the mother who is, after all, experienced as like. For boys, on the other hand, separating from the mother, who is experienced as different, involves repressing the feminine aspects of themselves, and rejecting much of the tenderness that was central to that early relationship. Boys' sense of maleness is, Chodorow suggests, achieved at great emotional cost.

As a result of these processes, adult men are likely to have a more autonomous sense of self, and to be more independent, more instrumental and more competitive in their dealings with others; they are also likely to have difficulty expressing emotions and to be anxious about intimacy. Women, on the other hand, have more need and more ability to sustain relationships with others; they have greater empathy with others; they have difficulty, however, in maintaining the boundaries of an independent and autonomous self.

Thus, assymmetrical mothering helps to explain, in Chodorow's view, the reproduction of divisions of labour around childcare. 'Because women are themselves mothered by women, they grow up with the relational capacities and needs, and psychological definition of self-in-relationship, which commits them to mothering. Men, because they are mothered by women, do not' (Chodorow, 1978, p. 209).

In Chodorow's view, however, these patterns are not inevitable. Changes in the social arrangements for care of children – changes such as dual parenting, that would involve fathers in emotional intimacy with their children and in close physical care – could break the cycle, developing in both women and men the parts of their psyches that are currently stunted and raising a generation of children who might be very different.

Chodorow's theory of the reproduction of mothering has been influential within sociology. Many writers on masculinity, in particular, have found her analysis helpful in understanding the problems some men experience in relating to others.

We can, however, question the scope of the theory, the range of situations to which it might apply. We might ask, on the one hand, how many societies are characterised by full-time mothers and emotionally distant fathers? Can the idea that women are psychologically driven to mother be squared with the evidence of variations in mothering at different times and in different places – with, for example, communal patterns of mothering in some African communities, or with the strong tendency of wealthy mothers in eighteenth-century France to send their babies away to be wet-nursed? We can challenge, on the other hand, the idea of a single femininity (a self attuned to relationship, lacking autonomy) and a single masculinity (instrumental and uncomfortable with emotion). It is not clear whether Chodorow's account would apply, for instance, to the black London schoolgirls in Riley's (1988) study who expected to be economically independent ('doesn't everybody?') and to enter emotional relationships on their own terms.

Moreover, the proposed solution of dual parenting has been rejected by some critics, who point out that it rests upon a particular model of family life – not all children have a reliable father who could be more closely involved in their care – and upon a faulty logic. If men are as lacking in the *capacity* to mother as Chodorow suggests (and not simply the will), if they are unable to empathise with or to relate to others, then how could they possibly be entrusted with the intimate care of children?

Limitations of theories of gender identity

More important than the specific limitations of Chodorow's theory , or of socialisation theory, is the need to recognise that all such theories, however well-crafted, are limited in what they can explain.

These theories tend to be deterministic, underestimating the fluidity of gendered behaviour and the capacity of women and men to change. In her retrospective study of a sample of white American women, Gerson (1985) found that the orientations they held in adolescence towards domesticity or careers provided a poor guide to their later behaviour; changes in circumstance (e.g., divorce) or in opportunity (e.g., promotion) marked for many women the first stage in constructing completely new identities. Identity may, in short, be more malleable than accounts of the acquisition of gender identity often imply. A little girl can wear frilly pyjamas and still grow up to be a tough union negotiator; and a little boy who plays at warfare can become nevertheless a gentle and caring father.

Theories of gender identity may contribute also to an unhelpful view of gender as a watertight compartment of identity that co-exists with, but evolves independently from, other aspects of identity. Such theories may give the impression that while women are differentiated by race, ethnicity, sexuality and class, the meanings that 'womanhood' holds for them will be, nonetheless, common to all. But earlier in this chapter, it was emphasised that the meaning of femininity (or of masculinity) often differs dramatically for people in different social positions, even within the same society. As one anthropologist puts it (Moore, 1994, p. 25), 'class, race, sexuality and religion completely alter the experience of a "lived anatomy", of what it is that sex, gender and sexual difference signify'. Or in the snappier words of a poet: 'The juice from tomatoes is not called merely *juice*. It is always called TOMATO juice' (Gwendolyn Brooks, cited by Spelman, 1990, p. 186). There may be no such thing as 'gender identities' that are not also constituted as identities of race, ethnicity, sexuality, and class; this is an issue we return to at the conclusion of Chapter 9.

Moreover, gender is not primarily a property of individuals, but a property of societies, of social institutions, and of culture. Theories of gender acquisition may help us to understand why individuals accept their positions in a gendered world, or even why individuals sometimes feel compelled to resist. But such theories cannot explain how the social world came to be gendered. To account for inequalities in earnings; to explain why, in parts of the USA, childcare workers earn less than parking lot attendants; to account for the concentration of power among men rather than women in the Church, in the Labour Party, in the medical profession; to understand why rape in marriage was legal in Britain until 1991 – in short, to understand gender relations, gender disadvantage and their links to the distribution of power – we have to look beyond psychological processes to social patterns and societal arrangements. Indeed, thinking of Chodorow's analysis, we might wonder whether a gendered society – a society, for example, in which women's average pay is only three-quarters that of men – has any part to play in ensuring that it is women, rather than men, who mother. Could it be that structures outside the family influence the parenting commitments of women and men, and not the other way around?

The rest of this chapter will be concerned with key aspects of the social processes that construct our gendered world. The implications of changes in divisions of labour, in the social organisation of childbirth and childcare, in popular culture and the media, and in sexuality will be explored.

Divisions of Labour

discourse
A body of ideas, concepts and beliefs which become established as knowledge or as an accepted world-view. These ideas become a powerful framework for understanding and action in social life. For example, Foucault studied the discourse of madness, highlighting its changes over the centuries and its interplay with other discourses such as religious and medical discourses, and illustrated how these shifts affect how madness is perceived and reacted to by others.

In pre-industrial Britain, prior to 1780, economic activity – the production of agricultural goods, craft production and so forth – was organised through households. Household members, male or female, young or old, contributed to the family's livelihood. Although women might do some jobs and men others, depending upon region and class, a distinction between men as breadwinners and women as housewives did not characterise pre-industrial divisions of labour.

Industrialisation re-located much productive activity to factories, shops and offices. This separation of 'work' from 'home' signalled a profound shift in gender relations and gender **discourse**. The 'home' came to be understood not as the site of a family enterprise, but as a refuge from the world of work. Women were defined as the keepers of the home, whose nature it was to create harmony and virtue rather than services and goods.

This ideology of domesticity, and the associated notion of separate spheres for women and men, originated in the middle classes but affected all women in different ways. For the wives of wealthy men, it spelled a life of enforced idleness. For the daughters of the lower-middle class, it meant a desperate search for a husband; debarred from higher education and many forms of employment, an unmarried 'lady' risked impoverishment and degradation. For working-class women, the ideology of domesticity brought not relief from labour, but exclusion from skilled occupations, even lower earnings and sharper segregation from men in daily life. The notion that masculinity required a wife who 'didn't have to work' inspired the trade union movement to set its sights on securing for male workers a 'family' wage. As a result, much of the work (paid and unpaid) that working-class women did to sustain their families became invisible, while single or separated or widowed working-class women could expect to live and die in poverty. Although the ideology of domesticity has been dealt a severe blow in the post-war period by changing patterns of employment, its legacy lives on in four important ways.

First, the ideology of domesticity lives on in contemporary divisions of labour – in the association of (dominant forms of) masculinity with rational calculation, productive work and the exercise of authority and of femininity with emotionality, domestic work and the provision of care. It is no accident that, of the six million adults found to be involved in Britain in what is called the **community care** of the elderly and disabled, the majority are women (Green, 1988). Nor is it an accident that although people of both sexes tend to value family and intimate relationships, men in Western societies express this commitment primarily in terms of financial maintenance, while as well as earning women tend to shoulder responsibility for day-to-day physical and emotional care and for the running of the home. The gender division of labour, in its broadest sense, encapsulates these differences.

care in the community

A range of informal and professional care of the elderly, disabled and sick undertaken in the community, rather than in institutional settings, typically by female relatives.

Second, the ideology of domesticity renders invisible important forms of work, with consequences that are practical as well as theoretical. For much of the twentieth century, only paid employment (preferably that done by men, in large-scale enterprises, on full-time 'permanent' contracts) has been given full recognition as work. This narrow definition obscures those forms of work (e.g., labour-sharing between households) that are characteristic of the **informal economy** and that may become, Pahl (1988) argues, more important in the future. The narrow definition excludes domestic work (done mainly by women), which is a crucial factor in maintaining quality of life; with the work done by the 'average' housewife in Britain valued at £369 per week (*Daily Express*, 3 February 1993), few families could afford to replace this unpaid work with services bought in. Last but not least, the narrow definition excludes the important subsistence work done (mainly by women) which provides the basic necessities for much of the rural population of

informal economy

Includes unwaged work such as housework or labour-sharing between households.

countries in the south; Beneria (1982) made a cogent case that the failure of economic statistics to take account of subsistence work perpetuates development policies that increase Gross National Product but endanger lives.

Third, the ideology of domesticity contributes to the continuing tendency to see the work women do as a natural by-product of femininity – of pliability, say, or 'caring' – rather than skill. The skills involved in housework, for example, often go unnoticed – except perhaps by housewives themselves, struggling to measure up for curtains or to stretch housekeeping money from one week to the next. In Britain, as Beechey and Perkins (1987) demonstrate, jobs of part-time women workers in the social services, often involving complex competencies, tend to be classified and paid as 'unskilled caring work'. Further afield, multinational companies, shifting some of their production of computer parts, toys, clothing and pharmaceuticals to new factories in countries in the south, often justify recruitment patterns by reference to the naturally nimble fingers of young women; as Elson and Pearson (1981) pointed out, the 'natural' dexterity of these women in fact reflects their earlier training in sewing and darning techniques that parallel the assembly process. Thus, in global as well as national divisions of labour, the definition of skill is underpinned by discourses of gender. Phillips and Taylor (1980, p. 79) explain: 'Far from being an objective economic fact, skill is often an ideological category imposed on certain types of work by virtue of the sex and power of the workers who perform it.'

Fourth, the ideology of domesticity has contributed to practices that have produced and reproduced gender segregation within employment. Over the past 150 years, for example, ideas about the protection of women have often been deployed to secure their exclusion from certain types of work – from night work in factories, say, or from heavy work in the printing trades. Although such arguments have often been hypocritical – restrictions on night work for women factory workers were seldom extended to hospitals or to cleaning jobs – they have been, nevertheless, effective.

Feminisation of the labour force

While gender segregation in employment has deep roots in the nineteenth century, events in the second half of the twentieth century have posed a challenge. The economic growth of the 1950s and 1960s created expansion in employment, an expansion met in Britain first by seeking commonwealth workers and then by recruiting indigenous women. From 1960 onwards, the service sector began to overtake

Source: Jacky Fleming

manufacturing. During the 1970s and 1980s, as described in detail in Chapter 7, **de-industrialisation** and **deskilling** generated massive unemployment in all industrialised states, and radically altered the nature of employment.

de-industrialisation
A concept used to describe economic changes due to the decline of industrial manufacturing and the increase of output and employment growth in the service sector of the economy.

deskilling
Developed by Braverman to describe what he believed to be strategies of employers to reduce the skills required of their labour force, which often occurs alongside the introduction of new technological processes into the work place.

A consequence of these changes has been – in countries such as the USA and Canada, in Sweden, Italy, Germany or Britain – a massive influx of women into the paid labour force, and an increasing tendency for them to stay longer in employment and to take shorter career breaks when children are young. In Britain, almost 90 per cent of the new jobs that have been created since 1970 have gone to women (Cohen and Borrill, 1993).

Thus we have witnessed in recent decades feminisation of the labour forces of many industrialised countries. The extent of change has been documented by McDowell (1992). Using statistics for Britain, she shows that between 1971 and 1988 the number of British women of working age who were in (or seeking) employment rose by 1.7m, while the number of males in employment fell by a similar amount. Women constituted 38 per cent of the labour force in 1971, but almost half in 1988. The 'flexibility' for which women workers were notorious in the earlier part of the twentieth century appears now in a 'post-Fordist' era to be part of their appeal to employers. Hagen and Jenson (1988, p. 11) remark that 'It is not without irony that women, who have always been at the margin of the labour force, now might even replace men as the "model worker".'

Table 8.1 Changes in employment patterns: Britain, 1971–88

1971	*1988*
% of women aged 15–59 who were in or seeking employment: 56%	% of women aged 15–59 who were in or seeking employment: 70%
No. of males in employment 13,424,000	No. of males in employment 11,978,000 (= loss of 1.8m)
No. of females in employment 8,224,000	No. of females in employment 10,096,000 (= gain of 1.7m)
Women as a % of total labour force: 38.0%	Women as a % of total labour force: 45.7%
% of female workers who are part-timers: 33.5%	% of female workers who are part-timers: 42.8%
	% of workers in each category who are service employees: 56% of men 81% of women 91% of female part-timers
Ratio of hourly earnings of female to male, full-time workers only: 63.3%	Ratio of hourly earnings of female to male, full-time workers only 76.0%

Source: Adapted from McDowell (1992) pp. 183–4.

However, feminisation does not mean that gender segregation has now been eradicated, nor that women have come out on top in employment terms. On the contrary, restructuring has been accompanied by the reproduction of gender segregation and the creation of new forms of inequality between – and among – women and men.

In the first place, female workers tend to be concentrated in a remarkably narrow range of occupations. Although eighteen occupational orders are listed in the New Earnings Survey 1985, over 70 per cent of full-time women workers are contained in only three groups: clerical work; professional and similar occupations in education, welfare and health; and personal services. At finer levels of analysis, the segregation is sharper: 'personal service workers', for example, turn out to be mainly domestic staff and school helpers (98.1 per cent are women), counter-hands and kitchen assistants (92.5 per cent female), or cleaners, road sweepers and caretakers (74.4 per cent are women). **Horizontal gender segregation** – the tendency for men and women to be separated into qualitatively different types of jobs – is a persistent feature of employment patterns in Britain.

horizontal gender segregation

The separation of men and women into qualitatively different types of jobs.

vertical gender segregation
The separation of men and women to higher or lower levels of the occupational hierarchy within the same occupation.

Second, **vertical segregation** is also marked, with women concentrated at the lower levels of the occupational hierarchy in terms of wages or salary, status and authority. Among full-time workers, in 1991, a far smaller proportion of women than men (10 per cent v. 26 per cent) are in the top stratum of professionals, managers and employers; fully 33 per cent of women (as compared with 19 per cent of men) are classified as semi-skilled or unskilled workers in manual or personal services (OPCS, 1991, table 5.6, p. 91) – and again, finer levels of analysis would reveal sharper segregation.

In spite of the popular image of women storming the citadels of male employment, then, the feminisation of the labour force has not resulted in a fundamental challenge to demarcations or divisions of reward between men's and women's work. Bakker (1988, p. 31) refers to 'the paradox of, on the one hand, an enormous growth in female labor force activity and, on the other hand, an intensified segregation of women into secondary, low-wage jobs'. The paradox can be accounted for, in part, by the nature of restructuring itself. 'Women as a group have more work,' Bakker explains, 'but it is often poorly-paid, unprotected and part-time, because restructuring has brought fewer good jobs in its wake.'

Another explanation invokes wider divisions of labour, arguing that childcare responsibilities force women into part-time work and jobs at the bottom of hierarchy. But while part-time work may disadvantage some women, it cannot explain the employment position of all. In Britain, Bruegel (1994) points out, black women workers and especially Afro-Caribbean women are likely to work full-time regardless of their childcare responsibilities, and they are, nevertheless, concentrated in less-rewarded jobs.

Comparative data offers an even more serious challenge to explanations that focus on women's responsiblities for childcare. In Britain, 43 per cent of women workers are part-time and the move into part-time work often follows a career break for the care of children. In France, by contrast – where women tend to leave the labour market only if they have three or more children, or are made redundant – only one woman worker in five is part-time. If women's disadvantaged employment position were due to the relationship between family responsibilities, interrupted work histories and part-time work, Beechey (1992) argues, we would expect job equality for French women, whose work profile resembles that of men. But, in fact, though French women have had more success than British in moving into lower-level managerial positions, the degree of horizontal and vertical segregation in the two countries is not dissimilar.

What this analysis points to is the importance of understanding how women – and especially mothers – become constructed as 'inferior' workers. One factor is discourses that blame working mothers for social problems; in Britain, over a long period of time, 'being a mother and being a paid worker have been constructed as contradictory' (Beechey, 1992, p. 163). Another is educational and training programmes. Another is the role of the state in structuring the labour market, by, for example, drafting employment laws that create temporary contracts without maternity and other protections, and hence encourage the development of a two-tiered labour force.

And finally, explanations would have to consider how gender has been embedded in organisational processes. Several studies (e.g., Astrachan, 1986) have shown that men are rather more prepared to accept equal partnerships with women in their personal relationships than they are equality with female colleagues in the sphere of work. This reluctance may be reflected from time to time in outright resistance to equality for women workers. Crompton and Jones (1984) looked at three large white-collar bureaucracies, and found only one that practised overt discrimination. They did find, however, that the organisational culture of all three establishments perpetuated horizontal and vertical segregation and offered deterrents to women's promotion.

Consequences of gender-segregated employment

The first consequence of gender segregation in employment is marked gender differences in earnings (see Table 8.2). Among full-time non-manual employees in Britain in April 1994, women earned on average £150 less per week than men. For manual workers, the male advantage was £99; male manual workers were paid, on average, marginally more than women in non-manual jobs.

Men boost their take-home pay by working overtime to a greater extent than women do. This does not, however, account for the male earnings advantage; non-manual women earned £150 per week less than their male colleagues, even though their working week had only 1.9 fewer hours. Even with the effects of overtime excluded, there is a male earnings advantage of £1.69 per hour for manual workers, and £3.51 for those in non-manual jobs.

These data are for full-time workers only. Part-time workers – predominantly women – have poorer prospects, greater insecurity and lower hourly rates, than full-time colleagues; during the 1980s, the hourly pay of part-time women workers fell from 81 per cent to only 75 per

Table 8.2 *Earnings and hours worked by women and men, April 1994: adults in full time work, whose pay was not affected by absence*

	All women	All men	Manual Women	Manual Men	Non-Manual Women	Non-Manual Men
Average gross weekly earnings (before tax or other deductions) (£)	262	362	182	281	278	428
Proportion whose gross weekly earnings were:						
less than £170 (%)	23	8	53	11	17	5
less than £300 (%)	71	46	94	65	66	31
Average hours worked per week (hours)	37.6	41.6	40.1	44.7	37.0	38.9
of which overtime hours are:	0.9	3.3	2.1	5.6	0.6	1.4
Average gross hourly earnings (excluding overtime pay and overtime hours) (pence)	688	865	445	614	742	1093

Source: Department of Employment (1994) *New Earnings Survey 1994*, London, HMSO, Part D (tables D86, D87, D92, D93).

cent of that of their full-time counterparts (McDowell, 1992), thus placing them at an even greater disadvantage compared to men.

Secondly, gender segregation in employment contributes to women's vulnerability to poverty. In 1994, well over half of full-time women manual workers, but only 11 per cent of their male counterparts, earned less than £170 per week, placing women disproportionately among the low-paid. The earnings advantage enjoyed by men in employment is likely to be carried over into old age, since women's occupational pension entitlements are generally less than those of men. The gendered concentration of poverty is not a new phenomenon, as Lewis and Piachaud (1987) point out; but now, as at the turn of the century, women make up the majority of the poor.

The third consequence of employment patterns relates to the impact of the economic recession and of restructuring. While women in general lag behind men in earnings, the last two decades have seen a widening of inequalities within each sex. McDowell (1992), for example, emphasises that full-time women at the top and at the bottom of the earnings hierarchy have closed some of the earnings gap between themselves and their male counterparts; on average, during the 1980s, the hourly earnings of full-time women workers rose from 72 per cent of men's to 76 per cent. At the same time, within each sex, there was a widening of differentials; the rich got richer and the poor got poorer. According to Bruegel's (1994) analysis of London living standards during a similar time period, the distance between winners and losers among women has been greater than that among men. Direct racial discrimination, and the vulnerability to unemployment that comes from a concentration in manual work, she finds, have combined to place the majority of black women firmly among the losers.

Childbirth and Childcare

The conception, bearing and raising of children is an area of human activity that may appear to be driven by biology: humans, like other animals, reproduce; and women, like other mammals, bear the growing infant. But in the case of human beings, all behaviour surrounding reproduction – from the decision to have intercourse, to contraceptive knowledge, from the taboos and obligations surrounding pregnancy, to the manner and place of birth – is meaningful in social (rather than biological) terms.

In all societies it is women who give birth to children, but the implications can and do vary dramatically. During the eighteenth and nineteenth centuries in Europe, as changes in economy and society re-shaped the lives of women and men, the identity of 'women' and of 'mothers' came substantially to overlap. By contrast, in some tribal societies – where fertility is the responsibility of everyone, and where men are thought to play an important part in life-creation – the notion of motherhood is a more peripheral part of women's identity (Moore, 1994).

The social conditions surrounding childbirth and childcare have changed dramatically in Western societies in the past century, in ways that are important for gender relations. Among the most significant changes are, first, the availability of more effective means for preventing or terminating unwanted pregnancies; better fertility control, combined with a shrinking ideal family size, mean that the proportion of women's lives typically devoted to pregnancy and early infant care has been dramatically reduced.

Second, while women today spend less time in pregnancy and breastfeeding, the care of children has come to be defined in a far more rigorous way; mothering involves responsibility not only for the physical maintenance of children, but for detailed attention to their psychological, social and intellectual development. One illustration of this is the concern that emerged in the 1980s with what is called 'pre-conceptual care'; young women are urged to behave, to eat, to exercise, to cultivate their minds and their bodies as if they were already mothers months – or even years – before they conceive. While fatherhood is high on the public agenda in Western societies today – and while the prevailing view of the 1950s, that fathers should hold themselves at a distance from the messy world of childhood, has greatly reduced appeal – it is still mothers, nevertheless, who take the greatest responsibility for childcare. Motherhood is seen, in a way it was not in the past, as a full-time occupation as well as a lifelong identity; and mothers may be expected to lavish as much 'care' on two children as they might have provided for six in pre-modern times.

Third, the most dramatic increases in the 'workload' of mothers have occurred during the same period that women's paid work load has accelerated. A demanding form of motherhood sits uneasily with the feminisation of the labour force. Some Western countries have accommodated this, to an extent, by extensive programmes of nursery provision, afterschool programmes, and schemes for parental leave; others have not. In England and Wales, in 1988, day-nursery places were available for only 2 per cent of children under the age of five, and most mothers in paid work had to rely on informal arrangements with family members, neighbours or friends. In the absence of adequate childcare arrangements, guilt and exhaustion are often the concomitants of the conflicting demands placed on women as mothers and workers.

medicalisation
A process of increased medical intervention and control in areas that hitherto would have been outside the medical domain.

Fourth, in Western societies in the course of this century, pregnancy and childbirth have become increasingly **medicalised**. There has been a dramatic increase in the proportion of babies born in hospital (from 15 per cent in 1927, to over 99 per cent in 1990), and a proliferation of reproductive technologies for monitoring pregnancy, for intervening in childbirth and for care of newborn infants. In some respects, medicalisation has made childbearing safer for women and their babies (though medicalisation has also brought new dangers in its wake – Oakley, in Stanworth, 1987). But it also provides a prime example of the ways in which women's lives and bodily processes have become more closely regulated by professionals, the majority of whom are men.

Fifth, and finally, although most children are born to married women in their twenties and thirties, the past decades in some countries have seen a marked increase in births to single women; in the UK, in 1990, live births outside marriage represented 28 per cent of all births but 80 per cent of births to women under twenty years of age. Many of these

autonomous motherhood
Single parents who, either by choice or circumstance, have taken on independent responsibility for caring for their children.

women are in a continuing relationship with the father of the child; others are not, and will bring up the baby alone. A much larger category are the growing numbers of formerly-married women who, following divorce or separation, are caring for children on their own. There has been an increase in '**autonomous motherhood**', involving women who – by choice or circumstance – have assumed independent responsibility for bringing up a family.

Box 8.3: Making babies

In modern societies, medical science provides the dominant cultural categories through which pregnancy and childbirth is understood. Emily Martin (1989) argues that the terms used in obstetrical discourse are reminiscent of Fordist production. Indeed, she suggests that childbirth, like factory labour, is subjected to time-and-motion study – so many minutes allowed for this stage of labour, so many minutes for that. One consequence is that mothers' active involvement in childbirth tends to be devalued and that of the obstetrician, glorified. Barbara Katz Rothman contends (1987, p. 161) that in spite of campaigns and movements to reclaim some control for women over birthgiving, 'the pattern in hospitals remains the same. Doctors deliver babies from the bodies of women. The women may be more or less awake, more or less aware, more or less prepared, and more or less humanely or kindly treated, but within the medical model the baby is the product of the doctor's services.'

The trend towards autonomous motherhood reflects the increasing capacity of women (and men) to leave marriages where they are unhappy, to have a sex life outside marriage, and to bring up their 'illegitimate' children. On the other hand, in the context of lower earnings and lower occupational opportunities for women, and cutbacks in public provision, autonomous motherhood often also means an increase in poverty and hardship. The rise in the number of lone mothers, and the meagreness of the support many receive from fathers or from the state, has contributed most in the postwar period to the '**feminisation of poverty**' (McLanahan *et al.*, 1989). Women not only bear the children, but they carry a disproportionate share of the cost of bringing up the next generation.

feminisation of poverty
A pattern of increasing concentration of poverty among the female population.

Popular Culture and the Mass Media

Ever since the second-wave women's movement in the 1970s triggered off a new interest in the analysis of gender, the mass media and popular culture have been a focus for this research.

content analysis
The analysis of the content of communication; usually refers to documentary or visual material.

Content analyses measured the frequency of portrayals of women and men in particular roles or situations. They often produced alarming evidence of the cultural invisibility of girls and women, especially in the public sphere. One American study (Grauerholz and Pescosolido, 1989) examined all the titles for young readers in the catalogue of children's library books. Over the period from 1900 to 1984, there were three male characters for every one character who was female; this gender imbalance was particularly marked in the 1940s, 1950s and 1960s. The bias toward males in children's literature was most pronounced among adult and animal characters; within these categories, male characters continued to become more prominent right into the 1980s.

Studies of magazines have raised questions about the place of popular culture in shaping conceptions of masculinity or femininity. Women's magazines – even those as different as *Woman's Own* and *Cosmopolitan* – display a strong concern with personal relationships (especially with men), and with physical appearance and the cultivation of beauty and style. This is apparent not only in feature articles but also in their advertisements and their advice columns. Men's magazines, on the other hand, tend to represent specialised interests. They tend to be concerned with sports and hobbies (computers, fishing, cars, and the like) or with business and finance, or with sex. Even the general men's magazines such as *Esquire* have few articles on interpersonal relationships. In the magazines, it seems, femininity is defined by appearance and relationships with men, masculinity by a single-minded pursuit of projects (including sex) and an indifference to relationship (Renzetti and Curran, 1989, pp. 114–17).

According to Ferguson (1983), who looked at women's magazines in Britain between 1949 and 1980, such magazines promote a cult of femininity that locks women into subordination. Ferguson's argument is all the more interesting, of course, because women's magazines are one of the few areas of popular culture in which women are often (as editors and managers) in controlling positions.

More recent approaches to popular culture, however, have taken issue with the kind of analysis represented above. Content analyses may often obscure the complex processes by which meaning is produced. They obscure, for example, the heterogeneity of the audience; different groups of readers and watchers find different meanings in the 'same' magazine or television programme. They deny the range of pleasures available from popular culture. In an alternative to Ferguson, Winship (1987) points to the pleasures that women get from their magazines, and insists that women (or men) may still produce oppositional readings of the forms of popular culture they enjoy. Research based around content analyses fails, finally, to recognise that meaning comes in part from the social context of its reception: the controversy surrounding a television programme like *Murphy Brown* will influence the possibilities that people see in it, while the reading of romance novels provides a basis for community and conversation for women readers, rather as football does for a great many men. In short, the impact of popular culture and the media is now recognised to be more complex, more differentiated, and more ambiguous than simple content analyses might suggest. Gender may be a part of virtually all media productions, but they are subject to a variety of readings or interpretations.

And often the meaning of these images is far from obvious. Is Steven Spielberg's film of *The Colour Purple* a film invocation of racist stereotypes of abusing black men, a betrayal of the lesbian sexuality that was so central to Alice Walker's book, or a celebration of the solidarity and endurance of black women? Do action films with macho heroes attempt to mould men into one narrow form of masculinity? Do they, instead, help men to come to terms with levels of male interpersonal violence? Or could the appeal of action films be that they allow a display of tenderness between men in acceptable (heterosexual) form? Should we see 'slasher films' primarily in terms of their portrayal of women as the ultimate victims of violence – for the way they make terror 'sexy' – or should we see them, as Clover (1992) suggests, in terms of the emerging tendency for the hero (the person who vanquishes the monster, like the film characters Ripley in *Aliens* or Jamie Lee Curtis in *Halloween*) to be gendered female? Should we think of popular romances as books that sell women the illusion that they can be happy by losing themselves in love, or instead as Modleski (1982) argues, as providing women with psychological relief from their fears of men and a fantasy of revenge for ill-treatment? These competing interpretations demonstrate that the analysis of popular culture raises as many questions as it answers.

However, as the example of prime-time television suggests, in the midst of flux and change there are certain continuities that are worthy of remark. On the one hand, there is the appearance of new themes – including issues of gender equality; the prominence on British television of women like Kate Adie (chief reporter for the BBC), or Zeinab Badawi (major news anchor on Channel 4); the presence of Oprah Winfrey as the monarch of US chat shows or of comediennes like Ruby Wax: all these features indicate that, to a degree, television has responded to the challenge posed by changes in gender relations in recent decades.

On the other hand, a survey of American prime-time television covering the decades from 1955 to 1985, demonstrated that women throughout this period continued to be the second sex (WIFP, 1986). Two-thirds of the characters in the 20,000 television programmes surveyed were male, and over three decades there was little sign of change. Moreover, throughout the post-war period, female characters were more restricted than male characters in appearance and age. Few female characters made it on to screen other than the physically attractive, and women were much more likely than men to be thin (Silverstein *et al.*, 1986). Twice as high a proportion of female characters as of male were under 25 years of age; four-fifths of female characters, compared with a half of males, were under 35.

Nor is British television different in this respect. The Broadcasting Standards Council monitored all evening television programmes for one week in September 1993. On the four terrestrial channels, they found only 30 per cent of the speaking roles were taken by women; the more 'serious' the programme, the fewer women there were. In news broadcasts, 64 per cent of the major appearances, and 88 per cent of the minor ones, were taken by men. Not only were most of the regular reporters men; overwhelmingly, men were chosen as interviewees, experts and studio guests (Holland, 1994).

symbolic annihilation

A term used to signify how, as a result of under-representation in the media, women have been dismissed and ignored in the public domain.

When it comes to the presence and representation of women in the mass media, the phrase '**symbolic annihilation**' – used by Gayle Tuchman and her colleagues in 1978 to signify low visibility of women – still has currency today.

Sexuality

From an essentialist perspective (and such a perspective colours much commonsense thinking) a man and woman who are attracted to one another and who become sexually involved are 'doing what comes naturally'. Sexuality appears here as a universal phenomenon that reflects deep-seated sexual drives.

Sociologists insist instead that sexual beliefs, practices, relationships and identities follow social patterns rather than natural ones. Sexuality is socially constructed – and, as a consequence, almost infinitely variable. Even sexual pleasures and desires are as much a matter of culture and history as they are of bodily potential. Kissing may be the order of the day among the teenagers of *Heartbreak High*, the Australian television series, but the adolescents of the Trobriand Islands find far more pleasure in biting off the eyelashes of the beloved (Malinowski, 1932).

Box 8.4: Sexual scripts

sexual script
Culturally defined set of guidelines prescribing appropriate forms of sexual behaviour and ways of managing sexual encounters.

The concept of a **sexual script** was developed by Gagnon and Simon (1973) as one way of understanding the social construction of sexuality. A sexual script provides a kind of blueprint for sexual desire and sexual practice. Through socialisation, individuals internalise the sexual script, learning not only how to behave towards sexual partners, but also to desire particular things in particular circumstances, and to pursue gratification in particular ways.

But for the concept of sexual scripts to be useful, the gendered nature of scripts needs to be acknowledged. Rose and Frieze (1989) invited undergraduates at a college in midwestern America to describe in detail actions on a hypothetical first date. The respondents produced a script for men that was much more detailed than the one for women. Both male and female daters, undergraduates agreed, would worry about appearance, try to impress their partner, and laugh, joke and talk. Men were expected also to take responsibility: for deciding what to do, for picking up the date, for paying, for initiating physical contact, and for promising to be in touch. Men, the authors conclude, were the planners, the economic providers, and the sexual initiators. Women, on the other hand, were expected to be 'sexual objects and emotional facilitators'; they had to find ways to keep the conversation going, and it was their responsibility, above all, to set limits to sexual demands.

The belief that it is men's place to initiate sex, and women's responsibility to act as the gatekeepers who say how far a sexual encounter will go, is one plank in what is commonly called the double standard of sexual morality.

Gagnon and Simon's concept of the sexual script offers an insight into the ways in which sexual practice may differ across time and place, and between women and men. This approach has also been criticised: for being a-historical; for failing to consider where sexual scripts and sexual meanings come from; and for failing to consider how the sexual behaviour of women and men reflects not only the learning of cultural scripts but also the effects of differential social power.

The claim that commonsense thinking treats sexuality as universal and natural should, more accurately, be restricted to heterosexuality.

There are many forms of sexuality; in contemporary Western societies, heterosexuality is in a dominant or hegemonic position. Although many heterosexuals insist that they come by their preference 'naturally', it is noticeable that a great deal of effort is expended in reinforcing heterosexuality. States play a crucial part: by, for example, denying citizenship to known homosexuals or lesbians; by refusing to recognise the marriages of same-sex partners; by discriminating against arts projects that show non-heterosexual families in a positive light; by maintaining a higher age of consent for homosexual practice. By these and other means, Western states help to ensure the dominance of heterosexual identities and the relative invisibility of alternative sexualities.

Sexual identities are constructed, too, in more routine settings. Many workplaces, for example, allude to heterosexuality constantly in the way people look and dress, in practices of sexual harassment, in 'secret' affairs, in jokes and gossip. The sexual 'normality' of daily life in the office is, as Pringle points out (1989, p. 94), 'relentlessly heterosexual', creating difficulties for homosexual men or lesbian women who want to fit in. Rich (1984) coined the term '**compulsory heterosexuality**' to draw attention to the possibility that desire for the other sex is not merely a preference, but something that has to be 'imposed, managed, organized, propagandized, and maintained by force'.

compulsory hetero-sexuality

Associated with Adrienne Rich, this concept implies that heterosexuality is not so much the natural form of sexual preference but is imposed upon individuals by social constraints.

The suppression of alternatives to heterosexuality is of broad significance for an understanding of gender difference, gender relations and gender inequality. The culturally constructed fear of homosexuality and lesbianism – **homophobia** – functions to police the behaviour of all men and women, whatever their sexual preference. The question 'What are you, a fag?' is not reserved exclusively for erotic display between men: it may be directed at boys or men who allow themselves to enjoy 'womanly' things, who display tenderness, whose clothes or interests or occupations do not fit a macho mould. As Kinsman (1987, p. 105) argues, 'queer baiting' and the social taboo against pleasure, sex and love between men serves to keep all men in line, defining what proper masculinity is.

homophobia

Fear of homosexuality and lesbianism.

If heterosexuality as an institution shapes the behaviour of all individuals, its impact is different on women and men. In Western societies, heterosexuality incorporates a **double standard of sexual morality**. Sexual activity, even promiscuity, is seen as tolerable or admirable in boys, while – except in the context of love and domesticity – an active sexuality brings girls into disrepute. As Willis (1977) said of the behaviour of a group of working-class 'lads', 'Girls are pursued, sometimes roughly, for their sexual favours, often dropped and labelled 'loose' when they are given' (p. 146). The lads expect to be promiscuous, but promiscuous girls are despised.

double standard of sexual morality

The assumption that promiscuous or sexually assertive behaviours are to be expected or admired in men, but that the same forms of behaviour are deviant and innappropriate in women. For example, there is no male equivalent of the term 'slag'.

Since Willis wrote about 'the lads' in 1977, it is likely that more girls are prepared to assert their right to sexuality. But the double standard has by no means evaporated. From interviews in three London comprehensives, Lees (1986) documents the significance of sexual reputation in the experience of adolescent girls. To be branded as a 'slag' has severe consequences, and girls are wary about behaving, dressing or speaking in a manner that might attract this dangerous label. But the way that the term 'slag' is used suggests that it is about a girl's relationship to men rather than about sexual activity *per se*; a young woman who is unattached (sexually active or not) is more likely to be called a 'slag' than one who sleeps with a regular boyfriend. The term slag functions, Lees suggests, to steer girls into the 'safety' of steady heterosexual relationships.

Box 8.5: Sex and violence in the courtroom: the impact of the sexual double standard

Fictional accounts of rape and sensational reports in the media often give disproportionate attention to that small minority of rapists who attract the label 'psychopaths'. The image of rape they produce is at odds with analyses of actual rape cases in Western societies, which indicate that few rapists are seriously disturbed, that many plan their crimes carefully, and that many are friends, relatives, acquaintances or workmates of the victim.

When rape is analysed in terms of its relationship to the social construction of sexuality and to the power relations between women and men – rather than being viewed as an idiosyncratic act by disturbed individuals – then we can begin to understand its incidence and its social implications.

The incidence of rape is related to the sexual double standard through cultural expectations about male initiative – taking in sexual encounters and female compliance. Pressures on men to 'prove themselves' by establishing sexual dominance may, in turn, be reinforced by the representation of women, not as complex human beings, but as objects to be admired and 'consumed'.

But the double standard has its most pernicious impact in courtrooms. The fact that a victim of rape is a woman who is or who has been sexually active is often introduced in court, by the defendant's lawyers, to discredit her – the implication often being that women who are sexually active in one circumstance have no right to refuse in another; they are seen to have placed themselves, in some sense, beyond the protection of the law.

The belief that it is up to women to set limits on sexual encounters often translates into the idea that if men go too far, it is women (and not men) who should be blamed. As Matoesian's detailed (1993) analysis of courtroom cross-examination demonstrates, qualities that serve a woman

patriarchal
A system that perpetuates the dominance of senior men over women and junior men (*see* patriarchy).

well in everyday life are likely, in rape trials, to be deployed against her. Evidence that a rape victim is independent and clear-headed, that she is friendly and open in her dealings with men – e.g., that she 'calmly enters a man's car' – tends to discredit her testimony. Matoesian (1993, p. 223) concludes: '**Patriarchal** ideology functions as a dominational resource for interpreting the sexual reality of the incident: a resource powering and concealing the sense of what happened. If a woman dates a man, if she goes off with him to an apartment, if she kisses him and so on ... then, according to the legal system, she has consented to sexual intercourse.'

The double standard constitutes a crucial part of the explanation why the proportion of convictions from arrest to judgement is lower for rape than for other serious crimes such as murder, burglary, other sexual offences or aggravated assault. The double standard – permitting promiscuous sexuality to men and forbidding it to women – has, as Connell (1987, p. 113) says, 'nothing to do with greater desire on the part of men; it has everything to do with greater power'.

The double standard of sexual morality, then, both reflects and reinforces gender inequality. Men are encouraged to show they are 'real men' by dominating and objectifying women. Women are encouraged to demonstrate their love and to enhance their attractiveness to men by curtailing their own independence. Girls and women who do not dress primarily to please males, who go their own way, who do not defer to male authority, who value the company of other women – and above all, women who publicly side with other women, whether they call themselves feminists or not – run the risk of being dismissed as 'dykes' or 'man-haters'. The supression of lesbianism functions, in effect, to put a brake upon female autonomy; through heterosexuality, Rich (1984) argues, women are persuaded to turn aside from other women, and to place men at the centre of their lives.

Rich's analysis of compulsory heterosexuality sits oddly, of course, with commonsense thinking about the impact of sexual liberalisation in the 1960s and 1970s, when changes in legislation regarding divorce, homosexuality, and abortion, and changes in sexual mores, ushered in a new 'more permissive' sexual climate. In many Western societies, the years since the 1960s have seen a greater tolerance of premarital sex, a widespread recognition of women's capacity for sexual pleasure; and more explicit public discussion of sexuality.

Many feminist writers have pointed out, however, that sexual practice continues to be structured by sexism. Consider, for example, the continued importance (in spite of the promotion of 'safer sex') of definitions of the sexual act centring on the penis and on intercourse; sensuality and alternative forms of touching tend to be seen merely as foreplay, the prelude to 'the real thing'. Or the way in which dominance and submission are often presented as 'sexy', so that inequality is eroticised and, therefore, reinforced. Or the fact – as the study of tourist operations in Britain by Adkins (1992) demonstrates – that getting and holding a good job often depends for women on being sexually pleasing to men; women's sexuality is often commodified, becoming something they provide for others, not something they do for themselves. The working-class wives studied by Rubin (1976) in San Francisco in the 1970s, often complained that sexual liberation had created another set of demands – at the end of the day, after working for pay, caring for the children and looking after the house, they were now expected to have orgasms too!

Some writers have argued that the term 'sexual liberation' is relevant only to men. But in spite of the ways that sexism and the double standard – and the greater social power of men – continue to structure sexuality, a verdict of 'no change' for women will not do. On the contrary, although full sexual equality would certainly depend upon equality in other spheres, sexual liberalisation has been important for women. As Segal (1994) points out, it was women who were penalised in earlier decades most severely for sexual activity – being, for example, the ones who were 'blamed' for pregnancy, and the ones who died from back-street abortions. By reducing the dangers associated with sexuality, sexual liberalisation may arguably have had a greater positive impact on women's lives than on men's.

Moreover, recent work on sexuality has challenged the notion of male sexual confidence. Hall's (1991) study of advice literature for men in the first half of the twentieth century vividly exposes male anxieties about sexuality. The tendency to define men as healthy and women as pathological worked against a sympathetic resolution of male sexual problems. She raises the possibility that insecurity about sexuality may be one of the motivations that drives some men to seek power over women in other respects (Hall, 1991, p. 173). Her work suggests that the popular image of men as sexually in control, and as insistent on their own gratification at the expense of their partner, may mistake a patriarchal discourse of masculine potency for the real thing.

The discussion of sexual liberalisation and debates over how to read the sexual history of the past three decades illustrates again that sexuality is historically constructed. Earlier in the twentieth century, in Western societies, legitimate sexual activity seemed to be firmly established

hegemony
Commonly used to describe the domination of one class, nation, or group of people over others. It was extended by Gramsci to denote a more general and intellectual dominance, especially when hegemonic ideas influence people's political and cultural perceptions.

within the family; in recent decades, sexual relationships – whether one-night stands, or those involving deeper commitment – take place before marriage, alongside marriage, after marriage, without marriage, and fewer people blink an eye. Partly because the connection between family and acceptable sexuality has been effectively challenged, sexuality has become more open to commercial exploitation – as any glance at magazines and film will testify – and less significant as a means of binding people together in long-term relationships. In addition, **hegemonic** heterosexuality, though hotly defended by, among others, fundamentalist religious groups, has lost some of its taken-for-granted authority. All of these things suggest alterations in the social organisation of sexuality that might eventually lead to deeper changes in the gender order.

Summary of the Chapter

- Answers to questions about the origin of gender difference range from those that emphasise biological sources to those that stress the social, cultural and historical construction of women and men.
- The diversity of masculinities and femininities in different times and places, and among different social groups, works against the idea that there is some fixed essence or nature that all women or men have in common. The simple division into male and female sex can itself be seen as a social process, varying from one social setting to another.
- Bodies are moulded into male and female patterns by social processes that are linked to our ideas about gender. A neat division between bodies as natural and personalities as social cannot be sustained. And the boundary between what is social and what is biological is itself shifting and ambiguous.
- Gender identities are shaped by the processes, conscious and unconscious, that are set in train by contemporary patterns of childrearing. However, gender is not primarily a property of individuals, but rather of societies, of social institutions and of cultures.
- The early period of industrialisation gave rise to an ideology of domesticity that lives on in contemporary divisions of labour – by, for example, rendering invisible some important forms of work.
- In recent decades, in industrialised countries, there has been a feminisation of the labour force, but this has intensified some forms of gender disadvantage and has been accompanied by a widening of differentials within each sex. Horizontal and vertical gender segregation in employment contributes to marked gender differences in income, and to the greater

vulnerability of women to poverty.

- Childbearing is an activity that carries different meanings in different times and places. For example, the social conditions surrounding childbirth and childcare have changed dramatically in Western societies over the past century, in ways that are important for gender relations.
- The impact of popular culture on gender relations is complex and differentiated, and the meaning of texts and visual images is often ambiguous. In spite of changes in the media that acknowledge the greater prominence of women and girls in public life today, women and girls are still less visible in the popular media and more stereotyped than are men.
- Sexual beliefs, practices, relationships and desires follow social patterns rather than natural ones. In contemporary Western societies, heterosexuality is a dominant or hegemonic form of sexuality, reinforced by the state and by many routine practices. The restrictions on same-sex sexuality serve to enforce particular expressions of masculinity and femininity, albeit in a manner that is contested.

References

Acker, J. (1990) 'Hierarchies, jobs, bodies: a theory of gendered organizations', *Gender and Society*, vol. 4, no. 2, pp. 139–58.

Adkins, L. (1992) 'Sexual work and the employment of women in the service industries', in M. Savage and A. Witz (eds), *Gender and Bureaucracy*, Oxford, Blackwell.

Astrachan, A. (1986) *How Men Feel: Their Responses to Women's Demands for Equality and Power*, New York, Doubleday.

Bakker, I. (1988) 'Women's employment in comparative perspective', in Jenson, Hagen and Reddy (eds) (1988).

Beechey, V. (1992) 'Women's employment in France and Britain: some problems of comparison', in L. McDowell and R. Pringle (eds), *Defining Women*, Cambridge, Polity Press.

Beechey, Veronica and Tessa Perkins (1987) *A Matter of Hours*, Cambridge, Polity Press.

Beneria, L. (1982) 'Accounting for women's work', in L. Beneria (ed.), *Women and Development: the Sexual Division of Labour in Rural Societies*, New York, Praeger.

Brown, P. and L. Jordanova (1982) 'Oppressive dichotomies: the nature/culture debate', in E. Whitelegg *et al.* (eds) *The Changing Experience of Women*, Oxford, Martin Robertson.

Bruegel, I. (1994) 'Sex and race in the labour market', in M. Evans (ed.), *The Woman Question*, 2nd edn, London, Sage.

Chodorow, N. (1978) *The Reproduction of Mothering*, Berkeley and London, University of California Press.

Clover, C. (1992) *Men, Women and Chainsaws*, London, BFI.

Cohen, Nick and Rachel Borrill (1993) 'The new proletariat', *Independent on Sunday*, 16 May.

Collins, P. H. (1990) *Black Feminist Thought*, London, Unwin Hyman.

Connell, R. W. (1987) *Gender and Power*, Cambridge, Polity Press.

Crompton, Rosemary and Gareth Jones (1984) *White-Collar Proletariat*, London, Macmillan.

Ehrenreich, B. (1983) *The Hearts of Men*, London, Pluto Press.

Elson, D. and R. Pearson (1981) ' "Nimble fingers make cheap workers": an analysis of women's employment in third world export manufacturing', *Feminist Review*, no. 7 (Spring) pp. 87–107.

Fagot, B. I. *et al.* (1985) 'Differential reactions to assertive and communicative acts by toddler boys and girls', *Child Development*, vol. 56, pp. 1499–505.

Ferguson, M. (1983) *Forever Feminine*, London, Heinemann.

Gagnon, J. and W. Simon (1973) *Sexual Conduct*, London, Hutchinson.

Garfinkel, Harold (1967) *Studies in Ethnomethodology*, Englewood Cliffs, N.J., Prentice-Hall.

Gerson, Kathleen (1985) *Hard Choices: How Women Decide about Work, Motherhood and Career*, Berkeley, University of California Press.

Grauerholz, E. and B. Pescosolido (1989) 'Gender representation in children's literature', *Gender and Society*, March, pp. 113–25.

Green, H. (1988) *Informal Carers* (General Household Survey 1985, Supplement) London, HMSO.

Hagen, E and J. Jenson (1988) 'Paradoxes and promises: work and politics in the postwar years', Jenson, Hagen and Reddy (eds) (1988).

Hall, L. (1991) *Hidden Anxieties: Male Sexuality, 1900-1950*, Cambridge, Polity Press.

Holland, P. (1994) 'Girls on film', *Everywoman*, August, pp. 24–25.

Hooks, B. (1982) *Ain't I a Woman?*, London, Pluto Press.

Hubbard, Ruth (1990) 'The political nature of "human nature"' in D. Rhode (ed.), *Theoretical Perspectives on Sexual Difference*, New Haven and London, Yale University Press.

Hulbert, K and D. Schuster (eds) (1993) *Women's Lives Through Time. Educated American Women of the Twentieth Century*, San Francisco, Jossey-Bass.

Jenson, J., E. Hagen and C. Reddy (eds) (1988) *Feminization of the Labour Force: Paradoxes and Promises*, Cambridge, Polity Press.

Kessler, Suzanne J. and Wendy McKenna (1985) *Gender: An Ethnomethodological Approach*, Chicago and London, University of Chicago Press.

Kinsman, Gary (1987) 'Men loving men', in Michael Kaufman (ed.), *Beyond Patriarchy*, Oxford, Oxford University Press.

Lees, Sue (1986) *Losing Out: Sexuality and Adolescent Girls*, London, Hutchinson.

Lewis, J. and D. Piachaud (1987) 'Invisible women, invisible poverty', in J. Millar and C. Glendinning (eds), *Women and Poverty in Britain*, Brighton, Wheatsheaf.

Malinowski, B. (1932) *The Sexual Life of Savages in North-Western Melanesia*, London, Routledge & Kegan Paul.

Martin, E. (1989) *The Woman in the Body: A Cultural Analysis of Reproduction*, Milton Keynes, Open University Press.

Matoesian, Gregory (1993) *Reproducing Rape: Domination through Talk in the Courtroom*, Cambridge, Polity.

McDonald, K. and R. D. Parke (1986) 'Parent–child physical play', *Sex Roles*, vol. 15, pp. 367–78.

McDowell, L. (1992) 'Gender divisions in a post-Fordist era: new contradictions or the same old story?', in L. McDowell and R. Pringle (eds), *Defining Women*, Cambridge, Polity Press.

McLanahan, S, A. Sorensen and D. Watson (1989) 'Sex differences in poverty, 1950–1980', *Signs*, vol. 15, no. 1 (Autumn) pp. 102–22.

Modleski, T. (1982) *Loving with a Vengeance: Mass-Produced Fantasies for Women*, London, Routledge.

Money, J. and A. E. Ehrhardt (1972) *Man and Woman, Boy and Girl*, Baltimore, Johns Hopkins Press.

Moore, H. (1994) *A Passion for Difference*, Cambridge, Polity Press.

Oakley, A. (1972) *Sex, Gender and Society*, London, Temple Smith.

Oakley, A. (1981) *Subject Women*, Oxford, Martin Robertson.

Oakley, A. (1987) 'From walking wombs to test-tube babies', in M. Stanworth (ed.), *Reproductive Technologies*, Cambridge, Polity Press.

OPCS (Office of Population Censuses and Statistics) Social Survey Division (1991) *General Household Survey 1991*, London, HMSO.

Pahl, R. E. (1988) *On Work: Historical, Comparative and Theoretical Approaches*, Oxford, Basil Blackwell.

Phillips, Ann and Barbara Taylor (1980) 'Sex and skill: notes towards a feminist economics', *Feminist Review*, no. 6.

Pringle, R. (1989) *Secretaries Talk: Sexuality, Power and Work*, London, Verso.

Renzetti, C. and D. Curran, (1989) *Women, Men and Society*, Needham Heights, MA., Allyn and Bacon.

Rich, A. (1984) 'Compulsory heterosexuality and lesbian existence', in A. Snitow *et al.* (eds), *Desire: The Politics of Sexuality*, London, Virago.

Riley, K. (1988) 'Black girls speak for themselves', in M. Woodhead and A. McGrath (eds), *Family, School and Society*, London, Hodder & Stoughton.

Robinson, C. C. and J. T. Morris (1986) 'The gender-stereotyped nature of Christmas toys', *Sex Roles*, vol. 15, no. 1/2, pp. 21–32.

Rose, S. and I. Frieze (1989) 'Young singles' scripts for a first date', *Gender and Society*, vol. 3, no. 2 (June) pp. 258–68.

Rothman, B. K. (1987) 'Reproduction' in B. Hess and M. Ferree (eds), *Analyzing Gender*, London and Beverley Hills, Sage.

Rubin, L. (1976) *Worlds of Pain: Life in the Working Class Family*, New York, Basic Books.

Segal, L. (1994) *Straight Sex*, London, Virago.

Silverstein, B. L. *et al.* (1986) 'The role of the mass media in promoting a thin standard of bodily attractiveness for women', *Sex Roles*, vol. 14, pp. 519–32.

Smart, C. and S. Sevenhuijsen (eds) (1989) *Child Custody and the Politics of Gender*, London, Routledge.

Spelman, Elizabeth (1990) *Inessential Woman*, London, The Women's Press.

Stanworth, Michelle (ed.) (1987) *Reproductive Technologies: Gender, Motherhood and Medicine*, Cambridge, Polity Press.

Tuchman, G. *et al.* (eds) (1978) *Hearth and Home: Images of Women in the Mass Media*, Oxford, Oxford University Press.

Whitehead, Harriet (1981) 'The bow and the burden strap: institutionalized homosexuality in native North America', in Sherry Ortner and Harriet Whitehead (eds), *Sexual Meanings*, Cambridge, Cambridge University Press.

WIFP/Women's Institute for Freedom of the Press (1986) *Media Report to Women*, November–December, p. 7.

Willis, Paul (1977) *Learning to Labour*, Farnborough, Saxon House.

Winship, J. (1987) *Inside Women's Magazines*, London, Pandora.

CHAPTER 9

Race and Ethnicity: Inequalities and Identities

Aims of the Chapter

This chapter introduces the sociological analysis of racial and ethnic divisions. It explores their continued significance as bases for both social inequalities and social identities. The chapter concludes by linking discussion of race and ethnicity to consideration of other dimensions of stratification covered in detail in Chapters 6, 7 and 8.

Introduction

The meaning and significance of the term 'race' has altered markedly during the modern era. The idea that the world's population could be divided into distinct groups developed during the early stages of globalisation: as Europeans expanded their geographical influence they came into greater contact with 'others'. Chapter 3 has already described how contacts between what Stuart Hall (1992a) terms 'the West and the Rest' were unequal and exploitative; Europeans enslaved others and colonised their lands. It was in this context that powerful notions developed of the superiority of the North European 'race' over all others. The attitudes of the colonial era are summed up at the start of Rudyard Kipling's poem 'The White Man's Burden' written in 1899:

> Take up the White Man's burden –
>   Send forth the best ye breed –
> Go bind your sons to exile
>   To serve your captives' need;
> To wait in heavy harness
>   On fluttered folk and wild -
> Your new-caught sullen peoples,
>   Half devil and half child.

As this quote suggests, beliefs about the different capacities of distinct 'races' offered an explanation and justification for the sharp inequalities in colonial societies; the colonisers' racial characteristics were purported to equip them to rule over their 'child-like' subjects and they believed it their duty to control and civilise the innate savagery and deviousness of the 'half devil' natives.

In the nineteenth century, Western science played a key role in developing the concept of 'race'. Peoples of the world – within and beyond Europe – were classified and ranked into superior and inferior races

Source: Photographed by Corinne Day

each with inherent capacities and characteristics. These groups were often talked of by scientists as separate species at higher or lower points on the evolutionary scale. There are clear parallels here with the way in which science of this period justified gender and class inequalities as rooted in innate biological differences (Gould, 1984).

Box 9.1: 'Race' and science

Two examples, cited by geneticist Steve Jones in the 1991 Reith Lectures, illustrate how entrenched scientific racism was in the early modern era.

When Victorian John Langdon Down identified the chromosomal disorder in children we now know of as Downs Syndrome he chose to call it Mongolism. Down believed that a superficial resemblance to people from central Asia (the Mongols) indicated that the children he studied were throw-backs to an earlier phase in human evolution. Thus disability was equated with membership of a lower ranked race.

In 1906 the Bronx Zoo in New York opened a new exhibit – an African Pygmy called Ota Benga was placed in the same cage as a chimpanzee. The aim was to popularize theories of evolution by demonstrating that apes and humans were related. Ota Benga was eventually released, partly because of his habit of shooting arrows at the visitors to the zoo who mocked him, but killed himself a few years later (Jones, 1995).

eugenics
A nineteenth and early twentieth century scientific and political movement directed towards the genetic improvement of the human species.

Although disputed, scientific ideas about racial difference continued to have a significant impact in the twentieth century. Arguments by **eugenicists** led, for example, in the 1920s, to introduction of immigration restrictions to the USA designed to prevent members of the 'Nordic' race being swamped by inferior genetic material from Eastern and Southern Europe. Most horrifically, in the 1940s, ideas of maintaining 'racial hygiene' had a direct influence on the Nazis' Final Solution which set out to destroy systematically 'inferior' races (discussed briefly in Chapter 2).

In the aftermath of the Nazi Holocaust scientists were keen to debunk not only racial hierarchies but also racial classifications as they were conventionally understood (Kohn, 1995). Advances in genetics, in particular, undermined the notion of 'pure' races and showed that variations within groups were as significant as those between them. More fundamentally, scientists challenged the links between biology and behaviour which had underpinned earlier beliefs. The impact of this sea-change in scientific opinion on everyday understandings has, however, been complex. Beliefs do not have to be coherent to be powerful and remnants of the old scientific account are still 'common sense' to many – part of the unquestioned, often contradictory, assumptions by which people conduct their lives and understand the world. In particular, the belief that that superficial variations in appearance between peoples are markers of more profound differences in capacities and outlook and that these 'racial' categories are natural and obvious has proved remarkably resilient.

Introducing a recent collection of writing on race and racism, James Donald and Ali Rattansi (1992) highlight what they see as a paradox: while genetic or physical characteristics that might distinguish 'races' are hard to define and appear trivial, notions of racial difference continue to be highly influential. This chapter will examine this influence under two broad headings:

- Race appears to have a major impact on life chances. There are numerous examples of *inequalities* of wealth, status and power along lines of race.
- Race remains a potent basis for *identity*; our sense of sameness and difference.

reify
To treat a social phenomenon as if it is an independent thing, with its own qualities.

ethnicity
To be distinguished from 'race', which emphasises biological differences based on skin colour, ethnicity denotes a sense of belonging to a particular community whose members share common cultural traditions.

Donald and Rattansi's paradox presents sociologists with a problem: how to explore the importance of the 'race' concept without **reifying** it? Some social scientists attempt to do this by dropping all talk of race in favour of **ethnicity**. Ethnic differences are deemed cultural rather than physical, based on shared traditions, experiences and ways of life. This approach has the merit of highlighting questions of identity but there are issues left unresolved if race is ignored:

- In discussions of ethnicity the emphasis is on the active choice of identity. In some circumstances attribution by others is a more significant factor: someone can, for example, be the victim of racism whatever his or her own sense of ethnicity.
- As the first point suggests, by focusing almost exclusively on cultural difference, some analysts of ethnicity have down-played key issues of power and inequality. A crucial question is why some cultural differences come to be 'racialised' (Miles, 1989) – that is, seen as markers of race divisions. This is important since those ethnic differences given a racial dimension usually have a clearer relationship to disadvantage.
- Accounts of ethnicity often utilise an understanding of cultures, adapted from anthropological studies of tribal societies, as stable, exclusive ways of life. As the third part of this chapter will argue, this is an inappropriate way to understand complexities of identity and difference in contemporary life. Ironically, some wrongly ascribe similar qualities to ethnic groups that used to be applied to races and in doing so continue old discussions of fixed, obvious differences in another, coded, form.

reflexive
Normally employed to indicate a process of self-reflection, which may modify beliefs and action (see reflexivity).

Rather than avoid all talk of race, this chapter will utilise an alternative means of dealing with Donald and Rattansi's paradox; to be **reflexive** in the use of 'race' *and* 'ethnicity'. This means seeing racial inequalities and racial identities as social rather than natural phenomena. It also involves asking questions about how social divisions come to be racialised – how and why are racial classifications used to label, constitute and exclude social groups?

Box 9.2: Problems of terminology

Everyday and academic 'racial' classifications are full of ambiguities: at times groups are defined by skin colour, country of origin, descent or even by religious affiliation. Labels can appear contradictory so that, for example, the majority of 'West Indians' in Britain were actually British born. Another complication is that racial terms and classifications alter over time and are the subject of controversy and struggle. An example of this is the term 'black'. Previously seen as pejorative, it was claimed as a source of pride by African American radicals in the 1960s who rejected the classification 'coloured' then in common usage. Recently in Britain, 'black' is again the centre of dispute as Asian academics and political activists have argued over its validity as a blanket term for all non white groups (Modood, 1994).

Disputes about the meaning and usage of words can be off-putting. It is important to ask, however, why they occur so frequently in discussions of race. That the language is uncertain, changing and, above all, political shows that, far from being natural and fixed, as they are often presented, racial and ethnic divisions are socially constructed.

Inequalities of Race: The British Example

We can find inequalities with a racial or ethnic dimension around the world. There are, however, great variations in the nature and significance of such inequalities. In Europe, racial divisions have emerged out of a colonial past and a recent history of inward labour migration. It would be simplistic to argue that these are in some way equivalent to the situation in South Africa where, until the early 1990s, races were defined and segregated by law. Equally, patterns of racial and ethnic disadvantage have very different flavours in the 'melting-pot' societies of the USA and Australia. If these varied divisions are not the natural and inevitable product of something called 'race' but instead socially constructed it follows that they can only be understood in their particular historical and political contexts. This argument will be developed through a discussion of race inequalities in one such context – contemporary Britain.

Post-war migration: global and local contexts

Discussions of race in Britain since the 1950s have focused on the consequences of the mass migration of people from the New Commonwealth (India, Pakistan and the West Indies). This migration was not a novel event; British history is full of inward and outward movements of population. Although it has been and continues to be a net exporter of people, Britain has experienced other sizeable influxes of migrants. During the 1800s, for example, large numbers of people from Ireland settled in Britain. Similarly, between 1870 and 1914 many Eastern European Jews crossed the Channel fleeing religious persecution. Significantly, both these groups were initially treated as racially distinct from the British in a way which would appear incongruous today (Miles, 1989).

New Commonwealth migration to Britain was part of a worldwide process. In the period following the Second World War around thirty million people entered Western Europe in one of the great migratory movements of history (Castles *et al.* 1984). The long boom this area enjoyed during the 1950s and 1960s was threatened by labour shortages in key sectors of the economy. Governments and businesses actively recruited foreign workers in an attempt to solve this problem. If this was the 'pull' for people to uproot themselves and move into Western Europe then the 'push' was the underdevelopment which beset other parts of the world. In particular, newly decolonised countries suffered from over-population, economic crisis and political instability. Thus the movement of people into Western Europe was an important aspect of the development of the global system as outlined in Chapter 3: it was at once a story of nation-states, the world capitalist economy and the international division of labour.

Patterns of migration may have been shaped by the economic and political inequalities of the World System but there were important local factors specific to Britain. People of Caribbean, Indian and African origin have lived in Britain for hundreds of years (Fryer, 1984). One of the main reasons for this long and rich history is Britain's Imperial past. Post-war migrants were drawn from ex-colonies and citizenship of the Commonwealth gave migrants the right of permanent settlement. This was in marked contrast to some other European countries such as Germany and Switzerland which attempted to operate a 'guest-worker' system whereby migrants could be forced to return to their place of origin at the end of their employment contracts.

People arriving from the West Indies, India and Pakistan in the 1950s and 1960s found Britain to be, in many ways, an inhospitable place. Open racial discrimination was lawful; job or room advertisements would often state 'No Coloureds'. While work was available, there was an acute housing shortage and migrants ended up in the areas and accommodation which whites did not wish to occupy. Whatever skills or ambitions migrants brought with them, most were slotted into the lower echelons of the labour market. This West Indian woman's experience is typical:

I remember getting up every morning to go to the Labour Exchange to see if there were any jobs. I was actually looking for nursing work but they wouldn't have me. Somebody told me that they would take me on as an auxiliary nurse and that later I could train. But when I got to the hospital, the woman there offered me a cleaning job. ”

[quoted in BRYAN *et al.*, 1985, pp. 22–3]

Migrant labour was seen as a way of filling the jobs which others did not want. Employers, white employees and their trade unions (Miles and Phizacklea, 1992) channelled migrants into those jobs which were low paid, had poor conditions and involved shift work.

Almost from its inception, New Commonwealth migration into Britain prompted rigorous public debate about its desirability. A range of analysts (see Miles, 1993; Saggar, 1992; Layton-Henry, 1992; Solomos, 1993) have described how race became an increasingly high-profile political issue during the 1950s and 1960s. Successive Immigration Acts passed in 1962, 1968 and 1971 by both Conservative and Labour governments restricted primary migration from the New Commonwealth. Although the legislation did not mention race explicitly, examination of the intentions of its promoters and its subsequent impact, leaves no doubt that it was designed to prevent black immigration. No equivalent concern was expressed about migration from Ireland or from the Old Commonwealth (Canada, Australia and New Zealand).

Hand-in-hand with the restriction of immigration, and in the face of mounting evidence of disadvantage faced by migrants, came a series of Race Relations Acts in 1962, 1966 and 1976 which attempted to outlaw discrimination on grounds of race. The thinking behind this dual strategy was summed up by Roy Hattersley, a junior minister in the government which introduced the first Act: 'Integration without control is impossible but control without integration is indefensible.' This reasoning has been challenged by some commentators: 'Hattersley's clever syllogism was really arguing that in order to eliminate racism within Britain, it is necessary to practise it at the point of entry into Britain' (Miles and Phizacklea, 1984, p. 57).

Arguably, this remains a contradiction in government policy and highlights the difficult position the migrants, their children and grandchildren have occupied within the British social formation.

Patterns of inequality

With few exceptions, since the 1970s only dependants of existing settlers from the New Commonwealth could enter Britain. Despite this, the non-white population has continued to grow, primarily because the lower than average age migrants have generated higher than average birth rates. Estimates of the growing size of Britain's non-white population are summarised in Table 9.2 (p. 242).

If present trends continue, by the turn of the century this figure should stabilise at around 6 per cent. By this time the majority of black

Table 9.1 *Percentage of British population drawn from ethnic minorities*

1951	0.4%	
1961	1%	
1971	2.3%	
1981	3.9%	
1991	5.5%	(estimates are drawn from a variety of sources)

people will be British born and most of the others will be residents of long-standing. Although a black presence in Britain is now well established, it is striking how many continuities exist between the problems faced by members of minorities today and those which confronted migrants who arrived in the 1950s and 1960s.

If we examine the position of Britain's racialised minorities since the 1960s we can see that the Race Relations Acts have had a limited impact. Major studies conducted by an independent research organisation, Political and Economic Planning (later the Policy Studies Institute) in 1966/67, 1974/75 and 1982 (Daniel, 1968; Smith, 1977; Brown, 1984) revealed a continuing pattern of disadvantage. A striking illustration of this is the way that it was possible to identify a distinctive black experience of employment and unemployment. Into the 1980s minority workers were:

- Concentrated in particular sectors of the economy. Asians, especially Pakistanis predominated in manufacturing while there are high numbers of West Indians in transport and services.
- Found mainly in occupations at the lower end of the occupational scale.
- On average, even in comparison with white workers in the same socio-economic group, lower paid.
- Working longer hours, more likely to do shifts and less likely to be given supervisory responsibility than white workers in the same occupational category.

From the 1950s until the 1970s, minority unemployment was 'hyper-cyclical' – that is it expanded and contracted faster than that for the majority population. When mass unemployment took hold in the late 1970s, however, a different picture emerged in which minorities were at higher risk of unemployment and, on average, unemployed for longer. This pattern continues so that, for example, figures from the national Labour Force Survey for the period 1989–91 indicate that black unemployment rates are approximately double those for whites (Jones, 1993). They also show that qualifications do not afford minorities the same protection against joblessness that they give others.

Box 9.3: Dimensions of racial disadvantage

The labour market is only one of many spheres of social life where there is evidence of 'racial disadvantage':

- Amin and Oppenheim (1992) highlight the high levels of poverty among minorities.
- Although there has been improvement since the 1960s, people from minorities still, on average, live in markedly lower-quality and lower-value housing. They are more likely to suffer from overcrowding and lack of basic amenities (*Social Trends*, 1993).
- A contributory factor to inferior housing has been poor treatment by local state agencies. This is evident in other areas such as social services where research indicates that black people 'are under-represented as clients receiving the preventative and supportive elements of social services provision, but over-represented in those aspects of social services activity which involve social control functions and/or institutionalisation' (Skellington with Morris, 1992).
- Black people more likely to be compulsorily admitted to psychiatric hospitals and once there are more likely to receive physical treatments such as drugs and ECT. Disparities are most striking in the diagnosis and treatment of schizophrenia, perhaps the most stigmatising of all mental illness (Littlewood and Lipsedge, 1982).
- In 1989 the Prison Reform Trust reported that if all groups were imprisoned at the same rate as black people the prison population would be 300,000 instead of 50,000. A range of studies have pointed to unequal treatment of black people by the police and courts (see Hood, 1992; Skellington with Morris, 1992). This issue will be explored in more detail in Chapter 14.
- Chapter 11 will examine evidence of educational underachievement by minority children.

Signs of change?

While the story from the 1960s to the early 1980s was one of continuity in patterns of disadvantage experienced by minorities, recent studies suggest that significant changes are under way. A Policy Studies Institute report examining the situation at the start of the 1990s (Jones, 1993) points to some shifts in patterns of minority employment.

A key change during the 1980s has been that men from the minorities have started to enter professional and managerial jobs in larger numbers than before. As Table 9.2 illustrates, some groups, notably African

Table 9.2 *Job levels of male employees by ethnic group 1988–90 (percentages) (Reproduced Jones, 1993)*

	All origins	*White*	*Total ethnic minority*	*Afro-Caribbean*	*African Asian*	*Indian*	*Pakistani*	*Bangla-deshi*	*Chinese*	*African*	*Other Mixed*
Prof/Manager/Employer	27	27	21	12	27	25	12	12	30	21	30
Employees & Managers – large establishments	13	13	7	5	6	9	4	1	7	9	11
Employees & Managers – small establishments	7	7	5	3	10	5	4	5	10	3	7
Professional workers – employees	7	7	8	4	11	10	4	6	14	9	12
Other non-manual	20	20	22	19	30	18	16	14	19	34	31
Skilled manual & Foremen	32	33	28	39	26	29	34	5	10	20	18
Semi-skilled manual	15	15	23	23	13	24	31	65	36	18	16
Unskilled manual	4	4	5	5	3	4	6	5	4	4	2
Armed Services/inadequately described/not stated	1	1	1	1	0	0	1	0	1	3	3

Source: 1988, 1989, 1990 Labour Force Surveys (GB).

Asians and Indians have come to enjoy labour market positions that are different but comparable to the majority population, while others, notably Pakistanis and Bangladeshis, continue to occupy a much weaker position.

Care must be taken when we interpret these developments. Rather than a march towards equality for all minorities they point to greater differences within and between groups. This must be understood in the context of wider changes in the British labour market – discussed in more detail in Chapter 7 – which have taken place in recent years: like the rest of the population, minority workers have been caught up in a major economic restructuring taking place on a national and, indeed, international, scale. As with so many other aspects of this process, the outcome is greater polarisation of experience. On the one hand, the growth of the number of professional and managerial positions and labour shortages in some occupations and regions has created opportunities for highly qualified members of the minorities. On the other hand, mass unemployment, the decline of manufacturing, the flight of jobs from the inner cities where minorities are concentrated, and restructuring in the public sector have worsened the prospects of those at the lower end of the socio-economic scale. One major reason why the percentage of minority workers higher up the scale is increasing is that some of those who would previously have been counted as manual workers are now jobless and hence missing from the statistics.

Some commentators on the Right (Honeyford, 1993) have claimed that recent labour market data indicates that racism no longer has a serious impact on the life chances of minorities. As we have seen, however,

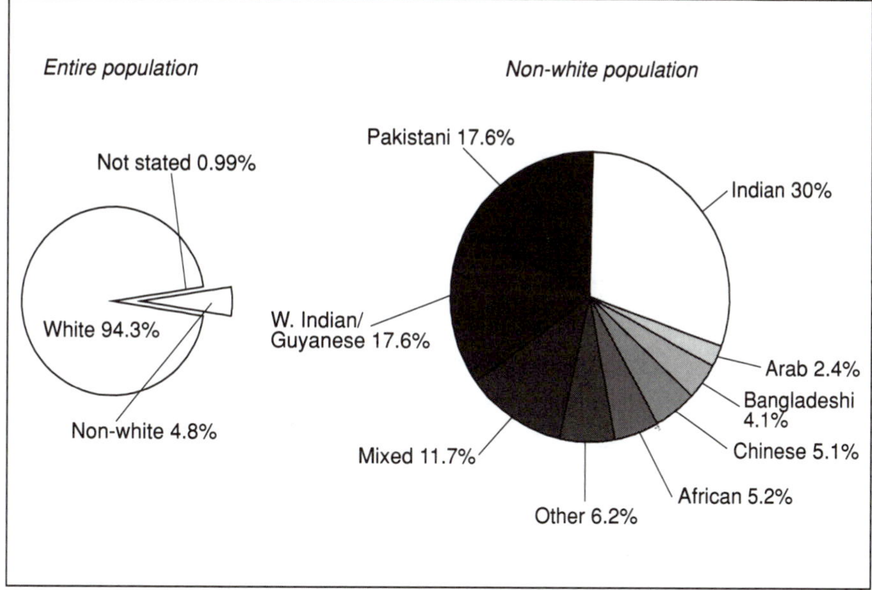

Source: *Population Trends*, vol. 67 (1992), Office of Population, Censuses and Surveys, HMSO. Reproduced from Skellington with Morris, 1992.

Figure 9.1 Britain's minority populations: population by ethnic group in Great Britain, 1990.

disadvantages persist. It should also be noted that apparently positive patterns of employment have also been influenced by actual or potential discrimination. This helps to explain why, for example, when we consider different categories of 'Professional and Managerial' employment, minorities have entered self-employment in far larger numbers than they have joined the middle management of medium or large firms (Ram, 1992). Similarly, the professions may be attractive to members of minorities because they hope that educational credentials provide some protection against racism in recruitment.

Box 9.4: The limits of 'racial dualism'

Britain's black population is drawn from many different regional and ethnic groups (see Figure 9.1). These groups each have their own histories of migration and have brought distinct cultural traditions, expectations and skills (Hiro, 1991). As the recent labour market data illustrates, differences in circumstances within and between groups are growing.

According to Tariq Modood (1992(b)) many analysts are guilty of '*racial dualism*', seeing racism as the only factor shaping the life chances and expectations of non-white Britons and largely ignoring the significance of ethnic differences . Madood challenges these assumptions by examining the experiences and aspirations of various Asian groups. He identifies a major divide between, on the one hand, the many Hindus and Sikhs from

India who are gaining entry into the professions, building successful businesses and achieving educational success and, on the other hand, the Sunni Muslims from Pakistan and Bangladesh who are suffering acute disadvantage. While Modood's account of Indian success is simplistic, he raises important questions concerning, firstly, whether it is legitimate to discuss a single 'black' experience in Britain and, secondly, the links between discrimination and disadvantage.

Explaining Inequalities: Practices and Structures of Exclusion

The last few pages have outlined some of the patterns of inequality experienced by racialised minorities in one particular context – Britain since the 1950s. How can the persistence of such disadvantage be explained?

immigrant–host model

An approach to racial inequality in Britain in the post-war period which saw assimilation as the solution to racial disadvantage, based on the view that the problems experienced by immigrants arose from their situation as new arrivals.

Early discussions of 'race' in post-war British sociology focused on the social processes and consequences of immigration. The assumptions which informed this work have been summarised as the '**immigrant–host model**' (Richardson and Lambert, 1985). Immigrants were seen as strangers whose different cultural traditions were an impediment to acceptance by the majority and to economic success. The racism of Hosts (that is the indigenous population) was viewed as a product of ignorance and confusion in response to strangers. It was assumed that the normal consensus and stability of British society which had been temporarily disrupted by the migrants' arrival, would be restored through their 'assimilation' into mainstream culture. From the late 1970s onwards, however, these assumptions, and the sociology of 'race relations' and ethnic difference which they spawned, looked increasingly beleaguered (Solomos and Back, 1994) In the light of the experiences of migrants' children, predictions of gradual assimilation and decline in disadvantage rang hollow. Some radical critics (for example, CCCS, 1982) went as far as to argue that the Immigrant-Host approach reflected and reinforced racist assumptions by defining migrants and their cultures as social problems and largely ignoring the role of structured inequalities in shaping their experience.

Critics of the 'race relations problematic' shifted the focus of sociological analysis on to the ways in which social practices and structures generate and reproduce racial disadvantage and, in particular, on to the problem of racism and its role in generating inequality. This theme is developed in the pages that follow.

The impact of racism

Although legislation was passed in Britain in the 1960s and 1970s outlawing discrimination on grounds of race, racism continues to blight the lives of Britain's minorities. Most blatantly this takes the form of violence and harassment from some members of the white majority. This is part of a Europe-wide phenomenon with a long and inglorious history (Holmes, 1991; Bjorgo and Witte, 1993). The extent of the problem is hard to measure but in July 1993 Peter Lloyd, Minister of State, told the Parliamentary Home Affairs Select Committee that the number of racial attacks taking place in Britain could be as high as 140,000 a year. While this estimate is contentious, other studies confirm that in some areas the threat or reality of harassment has a major impact on the quality of life of minorities (Gordon, 1990).

Violence and abuse may be the most blatant manifestations of racism in Britain but other, more insidious, practices have equally significant consequences for members of minorities. Studies have revealed the existence of open racial discrimination in such key areas as the police force and business management (Jenkins, 1986; Smith, 1985). Since, however, racial discrimination is illegal we would expect it to be usually, in some way, disguised. This raises a methodological problem for researchers attempting to explain inequalities of race: how does one measure the extent and impact of attitudes and practices which are rarely made explicit in public arenas?

Box 9.5: Evidence of discrimination

The persistence of disadvantage in the labour market suggests that racial discrimination is a significant factor limiting employment opportunities. But how do we detect and measure this since it is hard to prove in its subtler forms? A ground-breaking study (Smith, 1977) used interesting methods. As part of the research actors giving similar bogus job histories applied for a series of manual jobs. 'British' applicants were significantly more likely to be invited for interview and to be offered jobs than those from minorities. Similarly, when letters of application were sent for a range of white-collar posts those with a 'West Indian' or 'Asian' name attached were 30 per cent less likely to be invited for interview than comparable applications from 'Britons'. Interestingly, there was no comparable discrimination against 'Greek' applicants, suggesting that discrimination was against racial difference rather than simply foreign-ness. Repeats of these applications trials in the mid-1980s generated the same kind of results (Brown and Gay, 1983).

A recent study (Esmail and Everington, 1993) used a similar approach to show that racial discrimination is prevalent in the medical profession. The researchers composed curriculum vitae for six fictional doctors of similar age and experience, three with 'Asian' names and three 'British'. When these were sent, in pairs, as applications for appropriate NHS hospital posts, 'British' candidates were twice as likely to be short-listed for interview as 'Asians'. Esmail and Everington's research was stopped before completion and they were threatened with prosecution for making fraudulent applications. Themselves doctors, the two researchers were also sanctioned by the General Medical Council – clearly they had touched a raw nerve! It would be surprising if the problem of discrimination was confined to medicine – a sphere with relatively large numbers of minority workers. Similar findings emerged from a study looking at speculative employment enquiries made to one hundred of the largest companies in Britain (Noon, 1993): 48 per cent of companies responded better to letters from fictional MBA students signed 'Evans' than they did 'Patel'.

These studies reveal something of the influence of everyday discrimination in employment. They only, however, consider *one* phase of the recruitment process. They tell us nothing about what takes place during interviews or once people enter employment. They also reveal little about the ways in which minorities may limit their applications in the expectation of experiencing discrimination.

In addition to problems of methodology, analysts face a related dilemma – how to define and operationalise the concept of racism. In everyday discussions it is common for people to understand racist beliefs as the irrational prejudices of a few abnormal individuals and racist practices narrowly as acts of open and intentional discrimination. Social scientists have challenged both these assumptions on a number of different grounds:

- Racist beliefs are shared, cultural phenomena not simply aberrations of deviant individuals – this theme is developed later in the chapter.
- By seeing racism as irrational, we may miss the ways in which it can be a 'rational' or useful way of justifying and preserving inequalities in access to resources in employment, housing or other areas of social life (Cashmore, 1987).
- As Braham, Rattansi and Skellington (1992) point out, in addition to 'direct discrimination', 'knowingly and deliberately applied' it is important to consider 'discrimination in its covert, indirect and unintentional forms'. This broader approach to racism is highly significant since, if it is accepted, attention moves from motives to outcomes. Supporters of the shift would argue that it is possible to participate in racist practices without *necessarily* holding racist beliefs. Those employed to

execute Britain's immigration law, for example, could be said to be implementing racist rules whatever their personal beliefs.

- Policies or practices not directly constructed in relation to race may have a the side-effect of disadvantaging minorities. Elite schools whose entry requirements include evidence of regular church attendence, for example, automatically exclude the children of non-Christian minorities.

institutional racism
A theory of racism which draws attention to the ways institutions reproduce racial disadvantage.

In different ways, these points all beg one question: can social organisations and structures rather than individuals can be dubbed racist? Some political activists and sociologists believe so and have adopted the term **institutional racism** – originally applied to the US context – to refer to all processes which generate or reproduce racial inequalities (Carmichael and Hamilton, 1968; Sivanandan, 1982). The concept of institutional racism has the great merit of highlighting the systemic processes which reproduce disadvantage – suggesting that racism can be rooted within society's organisational structures. The concept of institutional racism has, however, been the subject of controversy: Robert Miles (1989), for example, argues that it stretches the use of the word 'racism' to breaking point and maintains that the term should only be applied to forms of belief. There is, however, a danger of getting bogged down in abstract debates about the meaning of words. A more significant pitfall of the concept is a potential lack of rigour. Although they may be of polemical value as a call for fundamental change, blanket descriptions of institutions or even societies as racist may actually stand in the way of effective study and reform of the mechanisms of inequality. As the debate about definitions itself suggests, racism is a multi-faceted phenomenon with many causes and manifestations (Cohen, 1992) Analytically, therefore, distinctions between state, institutional or individual racism and between beliefs and behaviour are crucial.

Box 9.6: Dimensions of racism: the example of housing

Any satisfactory explanation of the relationship between racism and disadvantage must develop an analysis on a number of different levels. In a review of the factors which generate racial inequalities in housing, Norman Ginsberg (1992) attempts to do this by identifying three distinct phenomena:

- *Subjective (or individual) racism* – This is evident in overt prejudice and discrimination by individual house-sellers, landlords, estate agents and council officials against minorities. A related subjective issue is the way the fear or reality of harassment limits the housing choices of minorities.
- *Institutional racism* – Ginsberg cites a number of studies which suggest that, in both private and public sectors, a range of institutional practices

(some now reformed) have, intentionally or unintentionally, disadvantaged minorities. An often-quoted example from the public sector has been the operation of rules for housing allocation utilising criteria such as length of residency or family connections with the area. This is by no means the only practice which reproduces inequalities. Studies show how, under pressure to fill housing quickly, council officials offer poor accommodation to minorities in the expectation that they will take it. Also significant is the way officers avoid conflict with white residents by not allocating minorities to certain accommodation. In the private sector, Building Societies, by refusing loans on properties in particular areas or below a particular value have, indirectly, discriminated against minorities.

- *Structural (or State) racism* – Ginsberg argues that there is a danger in focusing on local factors to the exclusion of wider structural influences and, in particular, the role of the State. For example, the government policy of selling off council housing stock has heightened racial disadvantage because better properties are creamed off by existing white tenants while blacks are over-represented among the growing numbers of homeless on council waiting lists.

Thus to explain or tackle disadvantage, in housing or any other area, we must be clear about the impact of quite different processes. Although, Ginsberg argues, it is important to distinguish between these factors (which may vary in importance from context to context) he acknowledges that they usually operate together:

'To confront institutional racism effectively is often to take on an entrenched power structure, which has been legitimated by common sense racism and sustained by structural racism.'

Many of the problems analysts of racism and disadvantage face have their roots in the ambiguity and power of the concept of 'race' highlighted at the start of the chapter. The significance of racial inequalities is great but these are social not natural phenomena. This means that the structured inequalities of race are capable of social intervention. It also means, however, that this intervention must not exaggerate the obviousness or coherence of racial divisions. As Donald and Rattansi (1992) write: '"Race" can produce simplified interpretations of complex social, economic and cultural relations for antiracists as well as racists.'

Race, Culture and Identity

The introduction to this chapter argued that the significance of race in the contemporary world could be organised under two broad headings – inequalities and identities. So far, we have considered inequalities of race in some detail. It is now time to shift focus on to questions of cultural identity – how people understand themselves and others. Of course, issues of inequality and identity are intimately related: cultural exchanges take place in an unequal setting. Beliefs about race are themselves powerful – manifestations of or even ways of maintaining social divisions. This is illustrated by the Kipling poem quoted at the start of the chapter: his account of racial similarities and differences reflected and justified the inequalities and exploitation of colonialism.

To write in terms of identity is not to imply that understandings of race are simply a matter of personal choice or prejudice. Identities are shaped by wider societal influences. This is why many contemporary sociologists understand notions of race in terms of either **ideology** (Miles, 1989) or **discourse** (Goldberg, 1993). Discourses are ways of knowing and talking about the world which constrain thought, action and representation; constitute identities; and structure social relationships. Thinking in this way directs enquiry towards how systems of meaning are produced, how they work and in whose interest; these are all issue pertinent to the study of race.

ideology

A perception of reality or way of thinking. Its usage is associated with Marx, where the term implies a mistaken sense of reality or false consciousness.

The changing character of racialised discourse

As the discussion at the start of the chapter indicated, although race may have been an influential concept for hundreds of years, the form and object of racialised discourse has altered over time and varied from context to context. Discussions of racial differences today are, for example, of a very different kind from those which took place in colonial societies. Similarly, a century ago in Britain, groups such as the Irish and Southern Europeans were discussed as distinct races in a way which would appear strange today.

Although the term 'race' has a long history, the term 'racism' only entered common usage following the Second World War as a response to the horrors of the Nazi Holocaust. Because of the pseudo-scientific justifications utilised by the Nazis, analysts such as Ruth Benedict (1983, first published 1942) defined racism as bad science: unfounded beliefs about the superiority of one race over another based on inherited biological characteristics. Fifty years on, however, this definition is increasingly irrelevant. Arguments which explicitly talk of races as biological categories or openly claim the superiority of one group over another are comparatively rare, confined to the political and intellectual margins.

discourse

A body of ideas, concepts and beliefs which become established as knowledge or as an accepted world-view. These ideas become a powerful framework for understanding and action in social life. For example, Foucault studied the discourse of madness, highlighting its changes over the centuries and its interplay with other discourses such as religious and medical discourses, and illustrated how these shifts affect how madness is perceived and reacted to by others.

The decline of old-style scientific racism has provoked a variety of responses within sociology. Michael Banton (1988), one of the key figures in the British sociology of race relations, has argued that the only legitimate definition of racism is one based around biologically grounded claims of racial superiority. Exasperated by the changing and variable use of the term, Banton, in his later work, has dropped it, preferring to talk only of the continued use of 'racial typologies'.

In contrast to Banton, Martin Barker (1981) argues that racism has not disappeared but taken different forms. He describes the emergence of a '**new racism**' which:

new racism
Forms of racism which are based on ideas of cultural difference rather than claims to biological superiority.

- Claims that the significance of racism in contemporary societies is exaggerated.
- Defines groups not as biological types but as cultural communities.
- Denies that hostility towards other groups is necesarily racist and instead talks of the incompatibility of cultures and argues it is 'natural' for people to wish to be with their 'own'.
- Bases its arguments on notions of difference rather than superiority.

Barker's definition has some limitations. There is a danger of exaggerating the coherence of racist ideas: popular beliefs about race are neither coherent or consistent but a ragbag of 'facts' and allusions. Remnants of older racisms which use biology or colonial history are still evident even if it is not always considered appropriate to express them publicly. Despite these reservations, Barker has highlighted two of the key characteristics of contemporary discussions of race: firstly, that the definition and extent of racism is contested and, secondly, that statements about race are often coded as claims of cultural difference. The implication of his work is that, rather than operate with a definition of racism based on a fixed content or object, we should talk of racism*s* manifested in plural forms.

Box 9.7: Making the headlines: racism and the press

One area of social life where there is a vigorous debate about the extent of racism is news coverage. A study by van Dijk (1991) supports those who claim that the British press, in common with those from other countries, portray minorities in a negative and stereotypical fashion. One way he justifies this argument is through a systematic anlysis of the headlines of 'race' stories in five papers – *The Times*, *Guardian*, *Daily Telegraph*, *Daily Mail* and *Sun*. Table 9.4 summarises his findings for a six-month period in the mid-1980s during which there were a series of highly publicised episodes of urban unrest involving both white and black youths. Measuring headline content in this way puts the hostility of much press coverage in stark relief; incidents of inner-city unrest are defined as race riots and, more generally, there is a strong association of race with violence, conflict, crime and social problems. Van Dijk points out that even the non-violent actions of minorities are often described using aggressive metaphors.

Table 9.3 *Most frequently used words in the headlines of race stories in five British newspapers, August 1985–January 1986*

388	police	40	mob	27	Tory
320	riot	39	day	27	Tottenham
244	black	39	murder	26	family
200	race	39	woman	26	plea
88	city	38	fear	26	section
85	row	38	teacher	26	time
84	attack	36	communicate	26	world
81	Asian	36	hate	25	group
77	Hurd	35	ban	25	immigrant
67	racist	35	victim/ize	25	protest
66	MP	34	immigration	25	raid
66	school	34	white	25	win
65	head	33	death	24	kill/er
65	Honeyford	33	London	24	Kinnock
63	Handsworth	32	claim	24	power
61	report	32	plan	23	children
60	council	32	union	23	hit
55	Britain	31	racism	23	threat
54	inquiry	30	leader	22	youth
53	job	30	minister	21	parents
48	fight	30	shoot	21	speak/speech
48	law	30	work/er	21	strike
47	Brixton	29	Grant	21	terror/terrify
47	charge	29	racial	21	Thatcher
46	face	29	rule	22	talk
45	chief	29	warn(ing)	21	comment
45	man	29	blame	20	deal/er
44	Labour	28	order	20	fail/ure
41	call	27	end	20	peace
41	court	27	Jarrett	20	Powell
41	home	27	left	20	told
41	violence	27	street(s)	20	urge(nt)

Source: Van Dijk, 1991.

Race and national identity

For supporters of the concept, a prime example of the New Racism is the way that the politics of race in Britain has become dominated by a debate about national identity and national belonging.

Nation-states are not only the primary administrative forms of modernity, they are also 'imagined communities' (Anderson, 1983). The rhetorics of patriotism and national identity are some of the most emotive cultural forms of the modern era. These concepts are very powerful but they are also nebulous and contested. Although, for example, there is much talk of 'Britishness' or an 'English way of life' quite what these are is open to question. How do these phrases fit with the claims of cultural distinctiveness made for Scotland, Wales or the various English regions? Do all Britons share a single way of life despite differences of class or gender? Is Britishness a fixed quality or one which alters over time? Such ambiguities have not prevented the concept of national identity playing an important role in contemporary discussions of race.

One of the most effective strategies followed by those hostile to a black presence in Britain has been to argue that blackness and Britishness are mutually exclusive categories. Growing ethnic diversity is portrayed as a threat to the order and cohesiveness of the British way of life. Analysis of political debates about race reveal that this argument has taken a variety of forms (Solomos, 1993):

- In the 1960s and 1970s black immigration was portrayed as a threat to national identity. For example, in 1978, prior to her election as Prime Minister, Margaret Thatcher talked of 'the British people's fear' of 'being swamped' by 'alien cultures'. While migrants were alien, a few years later, Thatcher felt no difficulty in describing the Falkland Islanders, living 8,000 miles away, as belonging to the nation:

'Their way of life is British; their allegiance is to the Crown' (quoted in Miles, 1993).

- In the 1970s and 1980s emphasis shifted on to the threat minorities posed to the order of British society. A striking example of this was the way black youths were constructed as a social control problem requiring special policing.
- In the 1990s the argument that minorities are in Britain but not British is less likely to focus on black criminality than the problems of a 'multi-cultural society'. Calls for separate Muslim schools, campaigns to ban Salman Rushdie's novel *The Satanic Verses* and,

indeed, attempts to develop policies of 'anti-racism' are portrayed as un-British and evidence of the incompatibility of cultures and the unwillingness or inability of migrants to become British.

Cultural change and ethnic absolutism

The vision of an ethnically pure nation sharing a common way of life has always been a myth – albeit a potent one. The great migrations of the post-war period have, however, openly challenged notions of unified, shared national cultures not only in Britain but across the Western world (Hall, 1992(b)). There is a growing multiplicity of religions, languages and ways of life within and across national boarders. This is a striking illustration of the trends outlined in Chapter 3: globalising pressures are accompanied by the reawakening or reinvention of local identities.

multi-culturalism
An approach which acknowledges and accommodates a variety of different cultural practices and traditions.

An influential way to express the growing cultural diversity of Western societies is to talk the language of **multi-culturalism** – dividing up societies neatly into homogeneous traditions or communities. This approach has serious limitations, not least because it shares many assumptions with the New Racism about fixed, immutable differences between ethnicities.

> **Culture is conceived along ethnically absolute lines, not as something intrinsically fluid changing and unstable, and dynamic, but as a fixed property of social groups rather than a relational field in which they encounter one another and live out social, historical relationships.**
>
> **[Gilroy, 1993b, p. 24]**

ethnic absolutism
An understanding of ethnic divisions which views them as fixed and absolute, resting on unchanging cultural traditions.

The realities of contemporary life are more interesting than proponents of '**ethnic absolutism**' contend; what is striking are the variety of subjectivities and the complex patterns of cultural change currently emerging.

Box 9.8: A dilemma of identity? Mixed descent

A visible challenge to ethnic absolutism are the growing numbers of relationships taking place between members of different ethnic groups. In the USA there are an estimated one million children and adolescents of mixed descent. In Britain this is the fastest growing of all population categories. The prevalence of mixed relationships calls into question the vision of societies divided into hermetically sealed 'communities'. In addition, the experiences of those of mixed descent challenge popular assumptions about ethnic identity.

Until recently it was commonly considered that being of mixed descent presented children with problems of social integration and identity construction. This belief has, for example, become an orthodoxy among social workers involved in adoption and fostering, many of whom argue that the only way to deal with these difficulties is to place mixed race children with black parents. A study by Barbara Tizard and Ann Phoenix (1993) challenges these assumptions. Interviewing a British sample of mixed race teenagers they found the majority had a positive self-image. The young people utilised a variety of successful strategies of identity construction and did not necessarily have to feel 'black' to feel good about themselves.

diaspora

Migration or dispersal of people or communities. Originally associated with the Jewish experience, this now more generally refers to the ways in which ethnic groups, although dispersed throughout the world, nevertheless share elements of a common culture or heritage.

The term '**diaspora**' refers to the forcible or voluntary geographical dispersal of a people. It was first used to conceptualise the Jewish experience but has, more recently, been used to understand how groups whose origins are in India or Africa can, although spread throughout the world, share elements of a common experience and culture. It would be a mistake, however, to see Diaspora as the transportation of ways of life unchanged from location to location. In Britain, for example, studies of migrants and their children have long charted the emergence of minority cultures which are distinct from both those of their 'home' and those of the majority population (Watson, 1977).

An important consequence of global Diasporas is the way that movements of people, meetings of ways of life and, indeed, the globalisation of media, have generated novel expressions of culture. Striking examples of this relate to the influence of what Paul Gilroy (1993a) terms 'The Black Atlantic' – a cultural network spanning Africa, the Americas, the Caribbean and Britain which has proved a source of strength and continuity to people of African descent wherever they are in the world. This is not, however, simply about the maintenance of cultural traditions: the development of white youth subcultures in Britain since the 1950s can, for example, also be understood as a dialogue with the music, dance, dress and aspirations of the Black Atlantic (Hebdige, 1991). It would be simplistic to view this only as the appropriation of black culture by whites; we can also see the creation and sharing of new hybrid cultural forms. This process is most pronounced in inner-city areas with mixed populations where black styles, musics, and language have had a profound influence. Roger Hewitt's (1986) study *White Talk Black Talk*, for example, highlights the impact of Jamaican creole on the speech of young white Londoners. Similarly, Simon Jones (1988) describes how, in parts of Birmingham, the sensibilities of white,

Afro-Caribbean and Asian youths fuse around a shared interest in reggae music.

Box 9.9: The limits of hybridity

The appeal of black expressive forms to young whites and the emergence of hybrid cultures has prompted optimism about the decline of racism. Care must be taken about how these developments are interpreted. An ethnographic study of a racially mixed London council estate by Les Back (1993) shows that it is possible for hybridity and racial violence to exist side-by-side. Back found that, in contrast to their parents, the young white and black people he studied shared a colour-blind world of inter-racial friendships, bound together by a strong sense of shared neighbourhood. This was, however, only one of a number of factors which influenced white youngsters' wider outlook on racial difference: family and the media also had a formative role. Equally, while black and white youths lived in peace, Vietnamese residents of the estate were perceived as outsiders and were frequently harassed and attacked.

Examples of cultural change and hybridity are important because they illustrate the ways that identities are actively constituted and negotiated. This is not to say, however, that ethnicity is declining in significance – far from it. As Chapter 3 has already argued, a common response to the globalising character of late modernity has been the revival (perhaps redefinition would be a better word) of local identities and ethnic differences.

In the British context, the 'ethnic revival' can, in part, be understood as a defensive response on the part of migrants in the face of discrimination and disadvantage. The history of West Indian migrants is a case in point. People arriving from the Caribbean in the 1950s and 1960s saw Britain as the 'Mother Country' and fully expected to participate in the mainstream of British life. The dashing of these hopes heightened their own perception of cultural distinctiveness. In the face of hostility from the established churches, for example, many West Indians established their own congregations and took solace in Pentecostalism – a religion promising salvation in the next life (Hiro, 1991; Pryce, 1979). In the 1970s many of the younger generation, victims of racism and with limited opportunities, were drawn to Rastafarianism – a religion with a black messiah (Ethiopian Emperor Haile Selassie) which prophesied the fall of Babylon (the West) and a return to Africa (Cashmore, 1983).

Paradoxically therefore, the ethnic revival is itself a symptom of the greater awareness of difference which springs from increased contact

reflexivity
A process of examining, questioning and monitoring the behaviour of the self and others promoted by the social conditions and experiences of late modernity.

between ways of life and the growing pace of cultural change. These processes inevitably promote greater reflection (or **reflexivity**) about identity (Giddens, 1991). Hybridity is one response to these developments but just as significant are the ways people attempt to deal with problems of identity by proclaiming absolute, fixed ethnicities. The aggressive assertion of 'Englishness' is an example of this phenomena – a claim of ethnic absolutism in the face of cultural uncertainty. Similar processes are at work within minorities. We can see the growing appeal of religious orthodoxy among some of Western Europe's six million Muslims. Campaigns around issues such as the banning of *The Satanic Verses,* the right of girls to wear head-dresses to school and the state funding of Islamic schools suggest that, for many Muslims, the free expression of ethnic difference may be a more significant political goal than economic equality (Modood, 1992(a)).

Box 9.10: Who are the fundamentalists?

cultural relativism
An approach that denies that any one way of living is superior to others: all cultures are equal.

The theme of Salman Rushdie's long, difficult novel *The Satanic Verses* (1988) is the shifting identity of the migrant and the **cultural relativism** engendered by the experience of migration. Rushdie is himself of Muslim origin, born in India, raised in Pakistan and now living in Britain. Soon after its publication in 1988, Muslim organisations around the world called for *The Satanic Verses* to be withdrawn. Bans were imposed in many countries including India, Pakistan, Bangladesh, Saudia Arabia, Eygpt, Somalia, Malaysia, Indonesia and South Africa. I Khomenai, the then spiritual and political leader of Iran, proclaimed a Fatwah (a religious death sentence) against Rushdie and the author has been forced to live in hiding under armed protection.

Supporters of Rushdie portray him as a martyr to the cause of free expression, a victim of intolerant fanatics, but what lies behind the controversy over *The Satanic Verses?* (Appignanesi and Maitland, 1989). Rushdie's followers have focused on the injustice of the Fatwah, which has its origins outside Europe, rather than tackle the deep offence felt by many of Britain's one million Muslims who see the campaign to ban *The Satanic Verses* as symbolic of their struggle to achieve recognition of their cultural distinctiveness. They claim that the book, by mixing the sacred and the profane, the holy and the obscene, challenges two key tenets of Islam – that the Koran is the word of God and that Mohammed was a perfect person.

Opponents of *The Satanic Verses* who argue that the offence caused is so great that the book should not be generally available, are characterised as 'fundamentalists', but are the book's supporters equally 'fundamentalist' in their portrayal of a ban as a threat to the key values of liberal humanism? They could be accused of treating literature as sacred in much the same way as Muslims treat the Koran. They also choose to ignore that, in Britain, free speech has always been conditional: there are many examples of self and state censorship, including laws preventing obscenity, blasphemy against Christianity and incitement to racial hatred. (Parakh, 1989; Madood, 1992*a*) One might also ask why more outrage has been heaped on symbolic burnings of *The Satanic Verses* than towards other problems of a multi-cultural society such as racial violence.

Muslim fundamentalism

A contentious, often pejorative, term used to describe a political and religious movement which adopts a fundamental interpretation of Islamic religious law.

Although it represents itself as the maintenance of tradition, so-called '**Muslim fundamentalism**' is very much about the here and now – a reaction to the uncertainties of globalisation and the political, economic and cultural marginalisation suffered by many Muslim migrants in Western Europe. Rather than a simple expression of an essential ethnic identity, militant Islam is a created and selected identity, part of a bid by religious leaders to construct and lead an imagined community. This becomes clearer when we consider why this identity has more appeal to some Muslims than to others: it is a more powerful idea for the young than the old, for working class rather than middle class, for Pakistani rather than Bangladeshi and so on (Samad, 1992). To remark on this is in no way to explain away the demands of the Islamic militants: it simply places their claims in the wider story of Diaspora. Nothing sums up the ironies and complexities of ethnicity at the end of the twentieth century better than the resurgence of Islam in Western Europe – an identity whose raison d'etre appears the continuation of an ancient way of life and protection of eternal truths has been actively chosen – even ethnic absolutists have been reflexive in their rejection of reflexivity.

Postscript: Dynamics of Inequality and Identity: Race, Class and Gender

Race and ethnic differences are not the only bases for inequality and identity in modernity: Chapters 6, 7 and 8 have described the divisions of class and gender which structure modern societies. Although social relationships of race, class and gender are often considered in isolation from each other, in reality they operate together to generate structures of power and inequality. Similarly, gender, class and race are all potential (and sometimes competing) sources of identity and collective action. The need to understand the interplay of these distinct but related forms of difference is made more presssing by the recent economic and cultural changes analysed in earlier parts of the book. Chapter 7, for example, discussed the significance of growing polarisation of labour markets; this is not only a class issue – labour markets are gendered and racialised (Brah, 1993). Earlier chapters have also discussed the uncertainty and fragmentation of contemporary cultural life; an important aspect of this is the way in which identities of race, class and gender mix and clash.

Theorising inequalities of race and class

Although there is a strong link between racialised differences and disadvantage, as we have already seen, members of minorities can be found at all levels of the class structure; there is, for example, a small but growing black middle class in Britain (Jones, 1993; Cashmore, 1991). How, then, do we theorise race and class inequality?

At one time, discussions in this area could be characterised as a debate between Marxist and Weberian positions. Put very broadly, Marxists argued for the primacy of class relations, maintaining that racial divisions were illusory or ideological, reinforcing the interests of Capital (Westergaard and Resler, 1976). Weberians' multi-dimensional model of stratification meant that they were prepared to assign more explanatory power to race and racism; races, in some circumstances, could be treated as analytical categories – status groupings competing for scarce resources and/or power (Rex and Moore, 1967). As Chapter 6 has already argued, however, analysis of class is today much harder to divide into two clearly defined camps, Marxist and Weberian. That this holds true for discussions of race and class is illustrated by two recent developments.

Race and the underclass

underclass

A concept used to describe a group at the bottom of the social hierarchy who are economically, politically and socially marginalised from the rest of society.

The concept of an **underclass**, originated in the USA to describe groups permanently trapped in poverty, now regularly crops up in discussions of racial disadvantage. Despite its popularity, the term is a nebulous and contested one, applied to issues of class and gender as well as race (Morris, 1994; Chapters 6 and 7 in this book). Usage of the term underclass has taken two forms: it is understood primarily as either a culturally or a structurally distinct grouping. Proponents of the structural account pose important questions about the position of minorities. Their argument is that, due to discrimination and their marginal status of migrant workers, minorities are over-represented among the socially and economically disenfranchised and may even, en masse, constitute an underclass. Such claims are often linked to a discussion of the special problems of the inner cities where minority populations are concentrated.

The notion of a racialised underclass has been expounded in a variety of forms. John Rex and Sally Tomlinson (1979) argue that the position of many black people in Britain can be understood in terms of an underclass occupying a systematically disadvantaged position in comparison with the bulk of the white working class in relation to employment, housing, education and political influence. Rex and Tomlinson start from a neo-Weberian perspective but, interestingly, a similar argument has been used by some neo-Marxists who maintain that black people constitute a '**sub-proletariat**' (Sivanandan, 1982; Castles and Kosak, 1985).

sub-proletariat
Used by some neo-Marxists to describe a socio-economic group that is a sub-division of the area lower than working class (*see also* underclass).

Challenging the primacy of class

A growing awareness of the significance of racism in shaping life chances and forming identities has led to a vigorous debate amongst neo-Marxists about race and class. Most now recognise that it is not enough to portray 'race' and racism as capitalist ideology masking the unitary interests of the working class. There are, however, serious disagreements about whether it is legitimate to treat racial groupings as analytical categories .

Some neo-Marxists, notably Robert Miles (1989), argue that, while racism is a significant social phenomenon, it is the class relations of capitalism which are the fundamental organising principle of society. To discuss race rather than racism is to confuse the appearance of capitalist societies with their 'essential relations' of class. In other words, the social structure is capitalist and class divided but racism and the use of migrant labour plays an important part in determining positions within that structure.

Others, for example Stuart Hall, John Solomos and Paul Gilroy, claim Miles's argument makes little sense given the crisis Marxism currently faces as a political and intellectual project (Solomos and Back, 1994). Analysis of race (and indeed gender) in the contemporary world points to new issues of inequality and power not adequately addressed by classical Marxism. The significance of racial divisions challenges the myth of a unified working class emerging out of objective economic conditions. Although this form of analysis has the stamp of Marxism in its discussion of capitalist development and its emphasis on struggle, cynical Weberians might well argue that it is groping towards a multi-dimensional account of class, status and power divisions! Like the Weberian perspective, it sees danger in a search for '**underlying structures**' which dismisses

underlying structures
Associated with realism, this concept refers to organisational features of society which, though not observable, nevertheless affect human behaviour.

the ways in which social divisions are defined in ethnic terms. Racial inequalities and identities are very real to those who live them. One crucial illustration of this is that, for both minority and majority populations, race often proves a more meaningful basis of political action than class.

Race and gender divisions

double burden
A term used to refer to the double oppression of sexism and racism experienced by black women.

Black women suffer both racism and sexism (Bryan *et al.* 1985). Highlighting this '**double burden**' tells only part of the story, however, since race and gender divisions work together to produce quite diverse patterns of inequality. When we consider the British context we see that:

- The relationship between gender and race disadvantage varies between contexts and between minorities – for example, Afro-Caribbean girls perform better than boys in the education system, while for other groups, notably Pakistanis and Bangladeshis, boys do markedly better than girls (Jones, 1993).
- Although there are differences in earning, conditions and status between minority and majority women workers (Lewis, 1993), these are less pronounced than those experienced by men. Some commentators have drawn parallels between the employment position of women and minorities, arguing that they both form reserve armies of labour or operate in secondary labour markets.

There are major gaps in our knowledge of gender and racial disadvantage: many studies have ignored minority women. This is a considerable absence since they have a distinctive social position which cannot be understood simply by combining the experiences of black men and white women. Gender-blind research has also generated inadequate analyses of the significance of race. Both these points are made by Heidi Safia Mirza (1992) in *Young, Female and Black,* a study of young Afro-Caribbean women. Mirza argues that discussions of race and education have focused almost exclusively on boys and this has led to a distorted picture of race and educational performance, contributing to a spurious analysis of educational 'under-achievement'. In particular, explanations of boys' low exam passes based on family structure or cultural deficits ring hollow once girls' relatively good performance is taken into account. The young black women Mirza interviewed had aspirations and experiences which were distinctive from both those of young black men and young white women. Their prospects were limited by factors which had little to do with their background: the girls suffered from poor schooling and low teacher expectations and, when they left education, had to operate in a racially and sexually segregated labour market.

Box 9.11: Unpacking the fashion industry

Race, class and gender can intersect to distribute people into different occupations or different levels of employment hierarchies within occupations. One example of this is provided by Annie Phizacklea's (1990) analysis of the gendered and racialised division of labour in the British fashion industry. This sector of the economy has developed in a very specific way. Unlike their counterparts on mainland Europe who farm production out to other parts of the globe, large clothing suppliers and retailers utilise a **dual sector model** – subcontracting manufacturing to small firms forced to operate very tight profit margins. Often, in the face of redundancy and few alternatives, men from minorities, who had originally worked for large manufacturers, have become subcontractors. These small employers exploit family and cultural ties to recruit female workers who have few other work options available. The survival of the firms is dependent on the poor conditions and low pay experienced by these women.

dual sector model
A model of work which suggests there are both primary and secondary labour markets (*see* polarisation of the labour market).

Phizacklea's study is not intended as a general model of the labour market but as one example of how dynamics of race, gender and class can be articulated.

As with class, discussions of race inequalities and differences raise difficult questions for the analysis of gender. This is illustrated by the academic and political debate that has taken place amongst feminists about race inequalities. Second-wave feminism as it developed in the 1960s and 1970s was based around notions of a common experience and common interests of all women. This fundamental tenet of sisterhood was challenged by black women within the Women's Movement (Davis, 1981). In the 1980s black radicals in Britain argued that the experiences of Asian, African and Afro-Caribbean women challenged feminist orthodoxy (Hazel Carby, 1982; Valerie Amos and Pratibha Parmar, 1984). They argued that women from different ethnic backgrounds had distinct traditions and concerns which were not reflected in the priorities of the Women's Movement. White feminists are accused of '**cultural imperialism**' in the judgements they make about minority lifestyles and of failing to address racism both outside and within the Women's Movement.

cultural imperialism
The aggressive promotion of Western culture based on the assumption that its value system is superior and preferable to those of non-Western cultures.

What might appear at first sight a parochial dispute amongst feminists actually highlights a fundamental debate about power and inequality (Ramazanoglu, 1989). Black critics asked difficult questions of gender theory. Can all women be said to share a common experience of

patriarchal
A system that perpetuates the dominance of senior men over women and junior men (*see* patriarchy).

oppression? What is the relative status of racism and sexism? Do black men share the same positions of **patriarchal** power as white men? This not to say, however, that all these questions have been answered adequately: a new wave of analysts have, for example, challenged black feminists' claims to speak for all minority women, pointing to the diversity of their traditions, experiences and social locations (Brah, 1992).

Complex identities: racism, gender and sexuality

The phenomenon of 'ethnic absolutism' discussed earlier in this chapter can be seen as an attempt to impose order on to a changing and fragmented cultural landscape. It recognises the significance of ethnic divisions while denying the many ambiguities of identity evident in the contemporary world. These ambiguities do not only relate to 'ethnicity' itself but also to the ways race intersects with other potential sources of identity such as gender, sexuality and class. It is to this intersection which we now turn.

Historically, ideas about gender and sexuality have been inseparable from racist beliefs and practices (Ware, 1992). Racial stereotypes are, for example, usually about gender and sexuality as well as race: consider the portrayal of Afro-Caribbean men which focuses on uncontrolled sexual potency and their potential for violence and criminality, or the image of Asian women as sexually exotic, passive and unambitious – the docile victims of a traditional culture. The power of such stereotypes highlights the role notions of masculinity and femininity can play in maintaining racial and cultural differences. These connections can be traced back to the era of slavery and colonialism when the protection of white femininity against defilement by blacks justified acts of great barbarity. In the post-slavery American South, for example, (black men) accused of sexual interest in white women were often lynched. The policing of white femininity went hand in hand with the sexual exploitation of black women by white men: rape was a routine aspect of plantation slavery while prostitution was institutionalised in colonial societies. Perhaps it is the legacy of this era that despite the number of cross-racial sexual relationships entered into in contemporary societies, these are still considered transgressive and/or exotic by many.

identity politics
A form of political agenda based around issues of shared experiences and forms of self-expression (*see* personal is the political).

Race, class, gender and sexuality can all be bases of community and action – the dilemmas this can throw up are illustrated by the problems of '**identity politics**'. This chapter has already discussed the difficulties racial difference has posed for the Women's Movement. Similarly, political currents which seek to mobilise people around shared racial identity in struggles against racism and racial disadvantage or for the free expression of ethnicity have found it difficult to deal with gender difference. It is worth citing two examples of this.

The USA in the 1960s saw the growth of black political consciousness expressed through the Civil Rights Movement and more militant forms of Black Nationalism. In the late 1960s and 1970s some of the assumptions and practices of this black politics were questioned by women within these movements. For example, Michele Wallace in *Black Macho and the Myth of Superwoman* (1991, originally published in 1978) argued that it had a male bias and marginalised black women. Wallace maintained that the militants understood liberation in masculine terms – emphasising qualities of sexuality, physical prowess and aggression. In this world-view black freedom meant asserting male power and establishing a subservient feminine role for black women. This analysis has been met with hostility from men and some women within the black community in the US. Concern with women's issues was seen as a distraction from the main issue of racial disadvantage or, in some cases, feminism and gay rights were seen as white issues. Michele Wallace was attacked for breaking the taboo of criticising other blacks in front of whites. In a similar way, Alice Walker's novel *The Color Purple* was criticised for discussing physical and sexual abuse in black families (Walker, 1988). When the film of the book was nominated for an Oscar some political groups picketed the ceremony.

In 1989 a major demonstration was held in London calling for the banning of *The Satanic Verses*. There was also a counter-demonstration by Far Right groups. Sections of the marchers united with the fascists to attack a small third group – Asian women from the organisation Women Against Fundamentalism who had come to proclaim their support for Rushdie. Once again, to understand this hostility, we have to consider the challenge that groups like Women Against Fundamentalism offer to the construction of a united Islamic Community in Britain (Yuval-Davis and Sehgal, 1992).

By revealing variations in black experiences and aspirations, these examples highlight the contested, changing and sometimes contradictory character of identities of race, gender and sexuality (Hall, 1992(b)). These complexities of identity thrown up by analysis of race bring into stark relief a wider problem: the pace and global character of social change force us to be more reflexive about who we are and how we fit into our social environment (Giddens, 1991; Bauman, 1992).

Rethinking race, class and gender

Taking race seriously involves challenging conventional approaches to understanding both class and gender. Debates about the Underclass and the future of Marxism are, for example, far from resolved but that they are taking place suggests that it is not enough to integrate divisions of race into existing models of the class structure. Instead, discussion of race and racism must be an important part of a rethinking of the nature and significance of social class. Similarly greater awareness of racial disadvantage has prompted challenges to '**essentialism**' in gender theory. Elizabeth Spelman in *Inessential Woman* (1990) argues that feminist analysis has wrongly attempted to isolate gender from other sources of identity and isolate sexism from other sources of oppression: 'Though all women are women no woman is only a woman.'

essentialism/ totalism

An approach which assumes some universal essence, homogeneity and unity in the phenomena under study. Such approaches to gender, for example, identify traits and behaviour common to all men and women.

Equally no working-class person is only working class and no black person is only black, and, therefore, while it may sometimes be legitimate for sociologists to discuss race, class or gender separately, to understand fully the dynamic and complex nature of inequalities and identities in late modernity we must consider how divisions of race, class and gender intersect to produce specific effects.

Summary of the Chapter

- Racial and ethnic divisions are highly significant bases for both inequality and identity in the contemporary world.
- Although racial and ethnic differences are often represented and understood as obvious, fixed and physically based, they are social constructions which change over time.
- The experience of racialised minorities in Britain must be understood in the context of the colonial legacy, patterns of post-war migration, changing labour markets, recent economic restructuring and the different histories and traditions of various ethnic groupings.
- Racism has played a crucial role in limiting the life chances of minorities in Britain. To understand this fully we must consider not only the impact of individual prejudice but also the extent to which racism is rooted in institutional structures and shared beliefs.
- The globalising tendencies of late modernity destabilise traditions and bring people into greater contact with cultural difference. The meeting of ethnicities generates new hybrid cultural forms but, paradoxically, can also lend an urgency to the reassertion of 'absolute', unchanging ethnic identities.

- Although divisions of race, class and gender are often discussed in isolation from each other, in reality they operate together to generate complex patterns of both inequality and identity.

References

Amin, K. with C. Oppenheim (1992) *Poverty in Black and White*, London, CPAG.

Amos, V. and P. Parmar (1984) 'Challenging imperial feminism', *Feminist Review*, vol. 17.

Anderson, B. (1983) *Imagined Communities*, London, Verso.

Appignanesi, L. and S. Maitland (eds) (1989) *The Rushdie File*, London, Forth Estate.

Back, L. (1993) 'Race, identity and nation within an adolescent community in south London', *New Community*, vol. 19, no. 2 (January).

Banton, M. (1988) *Racial Consciousness*, Longman.

Barker, M. (1981) *The New Racism*, London, Junction Books.

Bauman, Z. (1992) *Intimations of Postmodernity*, London, Routledge.

Benedict, R. (1983) *Race and Racism*, London, Routledge & Kegan Paul (first published 1942).

Bjorgo, T. and R. Witte (1993) *Racist Violence in Europe*, London, Macmillan.

Brah, A. (1992a) 'Difference, diversity and differentiation', in J. Donald and A. Rattansi (eds), *'Race', Culture and Difference*, London, Sage.

Brah, A. (1992b) 'Women of South Asian origin in Britain', in P. Braham, A. Rattansi and R. Skellington (eds), *Racism and Antiracism: Inequalities, Opportunities and Policies*, London, Sage.

Brah, A. (1993a) '"Race" and "culture" in the gendering of labour markets: South Asian young women and the labour market', *New Community*, April.

Braham, P., A. Rattansi and R. Skellington (eds) (1992) *Racism and Anti-racism: Inequalities, Opportunities and Policies*, London, Sage.

Brown, C. (1984) *Black and White Britain*, London, PSI, Gower.

Brown, C. (1992) 'Same difference: the persistence of racial disadvantage in the British employment market', in P. Braham, A. Rattansi and R. Skellington (eds), *Racism and Antiracism: Inequalities, Opportunities and Policies*, London, Sage.

Brown, C. and Gay, P. (1983) *Racial Discrimination: 17 Years After the Act*, London, PSI.

Bryan, B., S. Dadzie and S. Scafe (1985) *The Heart of the Race: Black Women's Lives in Britain*, London, Virago.

Carby, H. (1982) 'White woman listen: black feminism and the boundaries of sisterhood', in Centre for Contemporary Cultural Studies Race and Politics Group, *The Empire Strikes Back: Race and Racism in 70s Britain*, London, Hutchinson.

Carmichael, S. and Hamilton, C. V. (1968) *Black Power: The Politics of liberation in America*, London, Jonathan Cape.

Cashmore, Ellis E. (1983) *Rastaman*, London, Allen & Unwin.

Cashmore, Ellis E. (1987) *The Logic of Racism*, London, Allen & Unwin.

Cashmore, Ellis E. (1991) 'Flying business class: Britain's new ethnic elite', *New Community*, April.

Castles, S. and G. Kosack(1985) *Immigrant Workers and Class Structure in Western Europe*, London, Oxford University Press.

Castles S., H. Booth and T. Wallace (1984) *Here for Good: Western Europe's New Ethnic Minorities*, London, Pluto Press.

Centre for Contemporary Cultural Studies (CCCS) Race and Politics Group (1982) *The Empire Strikes Back: Race and Racism in 70s Britain*, London, Hutchinson.

Cohen, P. (1992) '"It's racism what dunnit": hidden narratives in theories of racism', in J. Donald and A. Rattansi (eds), 'Race', Culture and Difference, London, Sage.

Daniel, W. W. (1968) *Racial Discrimination in England*, Harmondsworth, Penguin.

Davis, A. (1981) *Women, Race and Class*, London, Women's Press.

Donald, J. and A. Rattansi (eds) (1992) *'Race', Culture and Difference*, London, Sage.

Esmail, A. and S. Everington (1993) 'Racial discrimination against doctors from ethnic minorities', *British Medical Journal*, 306, March.

Fryer, P. (1984) *Staying Power: The History of Black People in Britain*, London, Pluto.

Giddens, A. (1990) *The Consequences of Modernity*, Cambridge, Polity.

Giddens, A. (1991) *Modernity and Self-Identity: Self and Society in the Late Modern Age*, Cambridge, Polity.

Gilroy, P. (1987) *There Ain't No Black in the Union Jack*, London, Hutchinson.

Gilroy, P. (1993a) *The Black Atlantic*, London, Verso.

Gilroy, P. (1993b) *Small Acts*, London, Serpent's Tail.

Ginsburg, N. (1992) 'Racism and housing: concepts and reality', in P. Braham, A. Rattansi and R. Skellington (eds), *Racism and Antiracism: Inequalities, Opportunities and Policies*, London, Sage.

Goldberg, D. T. (1993) *Racist Culture*, Oxford, Blackwell.

Gordon, P. (1990) *Racial Violence and Harassment*, London, Runnymede Trust.

Gould, S. J. (1984) *The Mismeasure of Man*, Harmondsworth, Pelican.

Hall, S. (1992a) 'The West and the rest: discourse and power', in S. Hall and B. Gieben (eds), *Formations of Modernity*, Cambridge, Polity.

Hall, S. (1992b) 'The question of cultural identity', in S. Hall, D. Held and T. McGrew (eds), *Modernity and Its Futures*, Cambridge, Polity.

Hall, S., C. Critcher, T. Jefferson, J. Clarke and B. Roberts (1978) *Policing the Crisis: Mugging, the State and Law and Order*, London, Macmillan.

Hebdige, D. (1991) *Subculture: the Meaning of Style*, London, Routledge.

Hewitt, R. (1986) *White Talk, Black Talk: Inter-racial Friendship and Communication Amongst Adolescents*, Cambridge, Cambridge University Press.

Hiro, D. (1991) *Black British, White British: A History of Race Relations in Britain*, London, Grafton.

HMSO (1993, 1994, 1995) *Social Trends*, HMSO.

Holmes, C. (1991) *A Tolerant Country? Immigrants, Refugees and Minorities in Britain*, London, Faber & Faber.

Honeyford, R. (1993) 'Why are we still fed the myth that Britain is a racist society', *Daily Mail*, 14 April.

Hood, R. (1992) *Race and Sentencing*, Oxford, Clarendon Press.

Jenkins, R. (1986) *Racism and Recruitment*, Cambridge, Cambridge University Press.

Jones, S. (1988) *Black Culture, White Youth*, London, Macmillan.

Jones, S. (1994) *The Language of Genes*, London, Flamingo.

Jones, T. (1993) *Britain's Ethnic Minorities*, London, PSI.

Knowles, C. and S. Mercer (1992) 'Feminism and antiracism', in J. Donald and A. Rattansi (eds), *'Race', Culture and Difference*, London, Sage.

Kohn, M. (1995) *The Race Gallery*, London, Jonathan Cape.

Layton-Henry, Z. (1992) *The Politics of Immigration*, Oxford, Blackwell.

Lewis, G. (1993) 'Black women's employment and the British economy', in W. James and C. Harris (eds), *Inside Babylon*, London, Verso.

Littlewood, R. and M. Lipsedge (1982) *Aliens and Alienists: Ethnic Minorities and Psychiatry*, Harmondsworth, Penguin.

Miles, R. (1989) *Racism*, London, Routledge.

Miles, R. (1993) *Racism After 'Race Relations'*, London, Routledge.

Miles, R. and A. Phizacklea (1984) *White Man's Country: Racism in British Politics*, London, Pluto Press.

Miles, R. and A. Phizacklea (1992) 'The British trade union movement and racism', in P. Braham, A. Rattansi and R. Skellington (eds), *Racism and Antiracism: Inequalities, Opportunities and Policies*, London, Sage.

Mirza, Safia H. (1992) *Young, Female and Black*, London, Routledge.

Modood, T. (1992a) 'British Asian muslims and the Rushdie affair', in J. Donald and A. Rattansi (eds), *'Race', Culture and Difference*, London, Sage.

Modood, T. (1992b) *Not Easy Being British: Colour, Culture and Citizenship*, Stoke-on-Trent, Trentham.

Modood, T. (1994) 'Political blackness and British Asians', *Sociology*, November.

Morris, L. (1994) *Dangerous Classes*, London, Routledge.

Noon, M. (1993) 'Racial discrimination in speculative applications: evidence from the UK's top one hundred firms', *Human Resources Management Journal*, vol. 3, no. 4.

Parekh, B. (1989) 'Between holy text and moral void', *New Statesman and Society*, 24 March, pp. 29–33.

Phizacklea, A. (1990) *Unpacking the Fashion Industry: Gender, Race and Class in Production*, London, Routledge.

Pryce, K. (1979) *Endless Pressure*, Harmondsworth, Penguin.

Ram, M. (1992) 'Coping with racism: Asian employers in the inner city', *Work, Employment and Society*, vol. 6, no. 4.

Ramazanoglu, C. (1989) *Feminism and the Contradictions of Oppression*, London, Routledge.

Rex, J. and R. Moore (1967) *Race, Community and Conflict*, London, Oxford University Press.

Rex, J. and S. Tomlinson (1979) *Colonial Immigrants in a British City: A Class Analysis*, London, Routledge & Kegan Paul.

Richardson, J. and J. Lambert (1985) *The Sociology of Race*, Ormskirk, Causeway.

Rushdie, S. (1988) *Satanic Verses*, Viking.

Rutherford, J. (ed.) (1990) *Identity: Community, Culture, Difference*, Edinburgh, Lawrence & Wishart.

Saggar, S. (1992) *Race and Politics in Britain*, London, Harvester Wheatsheaf.

Samad, Y. (1992) 'Book burning and race relations: political mobilization of Bradford muslims', *New Community*, July.

Sivanandan, A. (1982) *A Different Hunger: Writings on Black Resistance*, London, Pluto Press.

Skellington, R. with P. Morris (1992) *Race in Britain Today*, London, Sage.

Smith, D. J. (1977) *Racial Disadvantage in Britain: The PEP Report*, Harmondsworth, Penguin.

Solomos, J. (1988) *Black Youth, Racism and the State*, Cambridge, Cambridge University Press.

Solomos, J. (1993) *Race and Racism in Contemporary Britain*, London, Macmillan.

Solomos, J. and L. Back (1994) 'Conceptualizing racisms: social theory, politics and research', *Sociology*, February.

Spelman, E. (1990) *Inessential Woman*, London, Women's Press.

Tizard, B. and A. Phoenix (1993) *Black, White or Mixed Race*, London, Routledge.

Van Dijk, T. A. (1991) *Racism and the Press*, London, Routledge.

Walker, A. (1988) *Living By the Word: Selected Writings 1973–1987*, Women's Press.

Wallace, M. (1990) *Black Macho and the Myth of Superwoman*, London, Verso.

Ware, V. (1992) *Beyond the Pale: White Women, Racism and History*, London, Verso.

Watson, J. L. (ed.) (1977) *Between Two Cultures: Migrants and Minorities in Britain*, Oxford, Basil Blackwell.

Westergaard, J. and H. Resler (1976) *Class in a Capitalist Society*, Harmondsworth, Penguin.

Yuval-Davis, N. and G. Sehgal (eds) (1992), *Refusing Holy Orders: Women and Fundamentalism in Britain*, London, Virago.

10 Power, Politics and the State

Aims of the Chapter

In this chapter we show how political sociology focuses on power in society and on the relationship between state power and social groups. We outline the nature of the state and examine models of the distribution of power before using the example of Britain's Thatcher governments to show how political change may be analysed. We go on to see how different forms of social division, not only class, can be mobilised politically and we look at the impact of globalization on power and democracy.

Introduction

Power in the state and power in social life: this is the terrain of political sociology. In this chapter we shall explore changing dimensions of power and politics, but we will not attempt to provide a general introduction to government and politics, constitutions, or state institutions. Instead we will focus on the central concerns of political sociologists: the relationship between state and society, and the distribution of power in society. Not surprisingly, sociology has often tended to adopt a *society-centred approach* to politics, focusing on the interests of social groups and the ways in which they mobilise power to defend or promote these interests. Increasingly, though, sociologists have also paid attention to the state and its organisation, studying the pre-modern state and drawing lessons about the importance of nationalism, warfare and administrative organisation (Mann, 1986; Giddens, 1985). Sociologists are today concerned to analyse the diverse nature of power and the complexities of the relationship between state and society.

Politics is often assumed to be 'what politicians do'. At worst this means just the back-biting competition of political contests and intrigues. More generously, politics can refer to the challenging task of governing, making policies and attempting to implement them. In their efforts to govern, politicians work within particular state institutions and use the agencies of the state such as administrative bureaucracies or police forces. Sociologists have often distanced themselves from this focus on government and institutions, leaving that to political scientists.

Instead, the sociological analysis of politics has been seen as the study of political behaviour within a *social* context, exploring the relation of politics to the entire social structure in which it is embedded. But more than this, sociology has analysed power and domination in many different areas of society from the workplace to the family. Political sociology certainly does study behaviour that is 'political' in a direct sense – such as voting or forming pressure groups. In this chapter, much of our focus will be on directly political action, as well as on the relationship between the state and power in society. However, sociologists recognise that the study of power must range much wider than this: we acknowledge that 'politics' is potentially present in all social relationships, because politics essentially involves the exercise of power. As Worsley (1964, pp. 16–17) says: 'We can be said to act politically when we exercise constraint on others to behave as we want them to ... the exercise of constraint in any relationship is political.'

So, political behaviour is essentially 'power behaviour', not by any means confined to particular governmental institutions or forms, but present in any social situation. Thus, political decisions are being made, and hence power is being exercised, not only when taxation laws are changed by parliaments or when Nazis herd people into concentration camps, but also when parents forbid their daughter to attend an all-night party or when an individual worker is sacked. In this sense, since all areas of social life involve elements of power, politics cannot be seen as involving merely 'what politicians do'. Instead *any process involving the exercise of control, constraint and coercion in society* is potentially political. Any unequal relationship has political dimensions, and since unequal relationships exist throughout social life, any search for patterns in social life must also involve a search for patterns in the distribution of power. A sociological approach to politics always involves analysis of the operation of power in social contexts and relationships, and investigation of the consequences of power for social conflict and stability.

This is not to say, however, that we should neglect the more conventional conception of politics as what politicians do, in government and through state institutions. Sociologists have always been deeply concerned with the relationship between power in society and politics in the state. Sociology explores both the social influences on government and the unequal consequences of government policies for different social groups.

Rethinking the relationship between state and society

Marxist political theory is perhaps the most famous example of an approach which explains state power by the structure of power in the wider society. Here the underlying economic structure of society consists of a set of social relations between classes. These class relations have exploitation and domination in their very nature – so politics and the potential for conflict are built into the heart of any class society. It follows that the state and government are (directly or indirectly) a reflection of these underlying class relations in society. In a later section of this chapter we explain this perspective in more detail, seeing how modern Marxist theorists have modified it extensively (Jessop, 1982). Even so, they have come under increasing attack – especially now that European communist regimes have been consigned to the dustbin of history.

This current drive to go beyond Marxist approaches can be seen in the work of sociologists such as Michael Mann and Anthony Giddens. For them, we cannot understand the nature of power or the roots of change in society today unless we move away from assuming that economic power and economic class are the primary root of politics. This is not just a critique of Marx: these theorists claim that there are many dimensions of power with different *institutional bases*. These approaches are grounded in historical evidence from non-capitalist societies, and they put state and state power at the centre of analysis. This implies a partial move away from society-centred analysis toward a greater emphasis on state power and the changing relationship between state and society in different times and places. This trend towards taking the state more seriously as a partly independent source of power and change was powerfully stated in the work of Skocpol and others (Evans *et al.*, 1985) as they told us to 'bring the state back in'. Political sociologists today pay much more attention to the complex ways in which power in society and power in the state relate to one another. We therefore open the chapter with a discussion of the modern state and democracy, to provide the context for other sections which explore the ways in which power is distributed in modern society, and the ways in which political change in contemporary society can be understood.

The Modern State

We often assume that politics can take place in isolation within one country through its own autonomous government. We can then link this national government with the structure of power and inequality in that one society. However, these convenient assumptions may be too simple, and certainly out of date today.

The idea that the world should be entirely divided up into autonomous nation-states is a peculiarly modern notion, and such a world has only come to exist in the last few decades. The key concept is the modern sovereign **nation-state**, which has sole legal jurisdiction and (as Weber emphasised) a monopoly of legitimate violence in a specific, bounded

nation-state

A form of political authority unique to modernity comprising various institutions such as the legislature, judiciary, police, armed forces, and central and local administration. It claims a monopoly of power and legitimacy within a bounded territory.

territory. We tend to assume that every people that considers itself a nation has a right to self-determination by means of a separate political nation-state; so when 'peoples' or societies and states do not fit, there is a potential problem. Even within the United Kingdom, the 'unity' is severely stretched by this aspiration for self-determination among various national groups within the legal UK state. The boundaries of the nation-state, and the 'monopoly of force' within it, have been challenged over the years by nationalist movements, most notably in Ireland.

It is only in the twentieth century that the whole world has been divided into separate nation-states. After all, Germany and Italy did not manage to consolidate all their component regions and provinces into fairly unified nation states until late in the nineteenth century. Our world of autonomous *sovereign* nation-states (i.e. claiming legal independence and jurisdiction within a boundary) is even more recent – since the break-up of colonial empires in this century.

Even this straightforward concept of sovereignty is decidedly problematic. The modern state claims legal authority, shared with no other, within the territory. For example, no Church organisation can override the state's laws, and no privileged group can claim to be above the law. Thus a principle of *legal equality* for citizens underpins the modern state, and this *legal citizenship* is normally also extended to political citizenship, in as much as the state (or at least the government in charge of it) claims to be accountable to citizens, and to rule with their consent. The right to challenge policies and laws is fundamental to citizenship, but it is accompanied by the duty to accept the resulting decision and obey it. However, it is obvious that few modern states actually maintain practical autonomy from powerful outside bodies. Many states voluntarily 'pool' some of their sovereignty in order to act in concert with other states, and diminish some autonomy through this co-operation. The European Union is the most obvious example, but others include NATO (North Atlantic Treaty Organisation) and the International Monetary Fund, with both the latter dominated by the United States. Other powers beyond the state have no such formal status; the power of the international money markets in forcing sterling out of Europe's Exchange Rate Mechanism in 1993 is one obvious example. In the realities of global power today, it is not clear that simple notions of either sovereignty or citizenship are sustainable. As we discuss in the final section of this chapter, national states must co-operate to find any power to resist the global pressures which impact on any one country. However, this raises the problem of how citizenship and accountability can have meaning in globalised politics.

A further source of strain concerns *nationhood* and national self-determination. The break-up of empires and protected territories has created a world of nominally autonomous sovereign states, where previously rule was divided or exercised by an external power. Within any political unit there may be different social groups who possess, or gain, the identity of 'a people'. Often language or ethnic distinctions can form the basis; if the 'peoples' have separate cultural traditions then the divisions are established. It is a new and modern step, however, to suggest that every people should regard themselves as a nation (for example, Moslem Bosnians) and that every nation should have its own nation-state. This 'principle' may be bloodily promoted in the most modern states, as in the former Yugoslavia, as new small states are established. It is a powerful force for fragmentation in the contemporary world which exists simultaneously with the other forces demanding co-operation and the pooling of sovereignty.

The making of the modern state

The rise of capitalism in Western Europe is associated with the rise of centralised, specialised state institutions employing increasingly complex and sophisticated techniques of administration and social control. Paradoxically, however, this complex modern state has developed out of a **feudal** political structure which was rather simple in comparison with ancient centralised states such as Egypt or that of the Incas.

feudalism
A social and political power structure prevalent in parts of Europe during the twelfth and thirteenth centuries, where power was fragmented and overlapping among authorities including church, monarchy and local lords.

The *feudalism* of medieval Europe was characterised by an extreme fragmentation of political power and production. Feudalism was based on the countryside, dependent upon agrarian production, with a dominant class of feudal lords monopolising economic and political control over localised areas. Whilst there was, theoretically, a hierarchy of allegiance from lower to higher lords and ultimately to the king, this was a fluid system of military alliances which allowed no stable centre of political power to exist. Ultimately based on conquest, the power of the local lord depended on his ability to obtain surplus labour or produce from his serfs, and on his ability to defend his area of land. Thus, larger states were only conglomerates of these local areas of domination, and the great empires of Eastern and Central Europe were little more than loose federations of principalities. Only with the pacification of large areas by dominant lords could wider trade and larger markets emerge. The decline of feudal arrangements was strongly associated with the rise of militarily successful monarchs supported by lords sufficiently powerful to claim dominance over large areas, and with the rise of towns as trading centres, which led to the development in importance of merchants and manufacturers. The independence of the town introduced an economic dynamism which undermined the rural base of feudalism, and paved the way for the emergence of new, economically powerful classes and a landless class of wage labourers.

Thus, by the sixteenth century in Britain and the seventeenth century in Europe, a far more centralised form of political domination emerged with the development of absolutist monarchies, which imposed laws and taxes over their territory and enforced them by the central monopolisation of the use of force. Clearly, this emergent central administration needed functionaries to run it, and initially these were powerful men, trusted as allies of the monarch. Gradually, they were replaced by administrators whose power depended only upon their official position and not upon their personal military power or wealth. Professional lawyers became more important as codifiers and modifiers of a recorded body of law, replacing arbitrary rule by nobles or local customary laws.

These features show the trend towards a *centralisation of power* and a *rationalisation* of politics. The state comes to be the only legitimate authority in a territory, and its administration increasingly operates on set principles and procedures. The trend to rational administration by officials culminates in bureaucracy and in the constitutional nation-state. As Poggi defines it:

> **there is a unity of the State's territory, which comes to be grounded as much as possible by a continuous geographical frontier that is militarily defensible. There is a single currency and a unified fiscal system. Generally there is a single 'national' language ... Finally there is a unified legal system that allows alternative juridical traditions to maintain validity only in peripheral areas and for limited purposes.**
>
> **[Poggi, 1978, p. 93]**

However, this *constitutional nation-state* need *not* be democratic: European states became 'fully' democratic – that is, with votes for all citizens and free political association – only in the twentieth or the late nineteenth century. This development followed earlier struggles for representation within these states by the new economic groups, above all the *bourgeoisie*: the merchants, traders and manufacturers. However, such struggles came at different times with varying degrees of success. In all cases, the constitutional nation-state still aided the rise of capitalism because it maintained peace, protected property rights and contracts, protected foreign trade, and often regulated money as a means of exchange, all of which aided trade and the development of markets.

At the same time, the growing bourgeoisie could be threatened by this centralised state if it was not represented in it, and if the monarch tried to tax or regulate trade for his own purposes. In much of Europe, this led to struggles by the bourgeoisie (in alliance with other dissatisfied social groups) to gain political representation or to reverse a slide back to personal absolutism by the monarch. The seventeenth-century struggles in England are often seen as establishing the conditions for capitalist expansion through the winning of dominance for Parliament and the constitutional regulation of the monarchy. In France, the developments came later but perhaps went further with the French Revolution and the construction of a republic and the new constitution.

The contrast between English and German roads to capitalist development is highly significant. The English road gradually established the principles of representative liberal democracy, as first the commercialised land-owners, then the industrialists, and finally the working class gradually won access to state power and slowly established notions of individual citizenship and rights of political expression. This 'evolution' was punctuated by struggle and conflict, but there is still a marked contrast with the German route, where the political failure of the bourgeoisie led to a continuing 'bureaucratic absolutism' lasting until the end of the First World War. The central state made concessions to the growing working class and organised the growth of industrialised capitalism, but democratic institutions and principles were weak and had extremely shallow roots. Thus, in Germany and elsewhere in Europe, one road to capitalist development and expansion in the twentieth century was authoritarian and undemocratic, gaining its ultimate expression in **Fascism**. In Germany, full liberal democracy has only been stabilised in its Western portion since the Second World War; and this form of state could only be established in Portugal and Spain after the downfall of fascistic regimes in the 1970s. There is no natural and inevitable link between liberal democracy and capitalism, even though it is now the dominant form of regime in Western Europe. Elsewhere in the world, the establishment of capitalism has gone together with very different kinds of state.

Fascism
An authoritarian and undemocratic system of government in the twentieth century, characterised by extreme nationalism, militarism, anti-communism and restrictions on individual freedom. The will of the people was held to be embodied in the leader (e.g. Mussolini in Italy).

Democracy and the representation of interests

Having been established in late-twentieth-century Western societies and beyond, democracy – some form of government answerable to the people – is the most widely lauded political form. There is an apparently universal agreement about the desirability of democracy: it is promoted as self-evidently the most appropriate form of government for modern societies, so nearly all regimes claim a democratic justification for their rule. Indeed, towards the end of the 1980s, commentators such as Fukuyama (1989) heralded 'the universalisation of Western liberal democracy as the final form of human government'. We were witnessing 'the end of history', moving beyond ideological conflict at the culmination of social and political evolution. This evolution towards liberal democracy, partly fashioned by the defeat of Fascism, was now completed by the collapse and death of communism in the Soviet Union and Eastern Europe. For Fukuyama, the West had won, and Western liberal democracy and free-market capitalism were now being confirmed as the only viable and desirable political and economic systems.

But, as we have suggested, this widespread dominance of democratic forms of government is relatively recent in origin, even in European countries, where Fascist dictatorships ruled in opposition to democracy, liberalism and socialism in the 1920s and 1930s and beyond. The notion that there is a natural and unstoppable historical tide towards democracy looks plausible today, but this complacent model ignores the bitter struggles through which democracy has been won, and neglects the political revolutions and the wars that have been fought to secure it. Furthermore, we should be wary of any model that links the fight for democracy to any one class. It has often been claimed that the 'natural' proponents of liberal democracy are the individualistic capitalists who wished to benefit from political and economic freedom. But the freedoms associated with Liberalism (such as removing restraints on free market capitalism) have often been valued more highly than democracy itself; when the working class have seemed to be a threat, bourgeois classes have often been only too happy to support authoritarian regimes (as with the rise of Hitler). There is a long history of struggle for more equal or socialistic democracy by poorer groups. From the English Levellers of the seventeenth century to the working-class volunteers who went to Spain to fight Franco's fascists in the 1930s, there is a rich history of struggles for a democracy linked to equality, not to liberal capitalism. The extension of democracy in Western European countries is a mixed result of pressures: bourgeois Liberalism and popular struggles combined with the decisions of conservatives to make democratic concessions to avoid anything worse, such as revolution (Rueschemeyer *et al.*, 1992; Moore, 1967).

Democracy as both a practice and an ideal had its roots in the city-states of Ancient Greece. Ancient Athenian democracy was direct participatory democracy: it was literally rule by the people, with many important political positions allocated by rota and by lottery. All citizens had the opportunity for daily participation in government, with a direct public voice in law-making and policy. This, however, was an isolated and exceptional case; for centuries after, democracy was generally perceived (at least by the powerful) as undesirable and dangerous, with popular rule likely to produce disorder and corruption. Even among the Greeks, Plato saw non-aristocratic people as too unreliable to exercise power prudently and responsibly, and Aristotle saw democracy as a perverted form of rule. Their negative view of democracy echoed through the centuries: political philosophers and theorists and rulers continued to regard democracy with grave suspicion and outright distaste because it would give political power to the selfish, the self-interested and the ignorant, who would be vulnerable to manipulative leaders – in short, it would be rule by the mob.

Successful pressure for democracy came only slowly. There were isolated demands for democracy in seventeenth-century America and in Britain (such as the Levellers), but it was only with the revolutions of the late eighteenth century (above all, in America and France) that democracy became a prime focus of political debate and struggle. Non-revolutionary philosophies also began to make democracy more central: for example, Utilitarianism (a significant inspiration behind late-nineteenth and early-twentieth-century Liberalism) advocated the greatest happiness of the greatest number as its abiding principle and regarded this as best achievable by democratic government.

Important social groups wanted democratic rights for themselves to control governments and prevent authoritarian rule. It was a much more radical demand to claim that every adult person should have democratic citizen rights, as Tom Paine and the French revolutionaries did. Revolutionary democracy brought again the widespread fear of what Tocqueville called 'the tyranny of the majority'.

Even when government was extended through the nineteenth century, political citizenship was limited, excluding particular social groups such as non-property owners, women, foreigners and (in the case of the USA) slaves as not sufficiently reliable and responsible persons to have voting rights. Comprehensive, universal democracy – participation of all adult members of society in the political process – was not put into practice in its full form until well into the twentieth century (Therborn, 1976). The industrial male working class won the right to vote through their own organised collective efforts, often backed by enlightened middle-class support or by an upper class that felt it advisable to make concessions. It took longer for other groups to gain voting rights: it was not until 1928 that women could exercise the right to vote in Britain, for example. In some states of the USA, it needed the civil rights movements of the 1960s for black people to win real political citizenship .

This extension of democratic rights meant, at least formally, that political power could be grasped by ordinary people. In principle, elections could be used to gain power and bring about social reform or even radical change. In Western Europe (if not in the USA), this process of inclusion crystallised new lines of political cleavage around divisions between those with property and those without, and an alignment of political parties and organised groups defending the capitalist status quo against those attempting to transform it. Today, political alignments and party programmes are changing further, with new regional parties (such as the Scottish Nationalists) or issue-parties (such as the Greens) taking many votes, even in systems where class parties have been dominant.

Power in Society: Society-Centred Approaches

As we saw in the introduction, political sociology's focus on power looks beyond the workings of governments and parliaments and professional politicians. Instead, politics is embedded within particular social structures and processes: it takes place in societies with distinct social and economic arrangements. Power in society directly affects power in the state, but the impact of politics also changes the distribution of power in society. It is a two-way relationship.

Since political sociology has developed in the context of modern Western societies, sociologists have always been faced with the potential tension between two distinct institutional systems – the liberal democratic constitutional state and the capitalist economy. Liberal democracy proclaims equal rights for citizens: each vote is worth the same, and each of us should be equal before the law. However, equal rights do not necessarily bring equal amounts of power. If the capitalist economic system produces systematic inequalities in economic power and benefit, will these produce great inequalities in political power? Liberals and socialists have often been deeply divided over this question.

For the Liberal theorist, economic advantage is not the key to political advantage. The political system gives rights and protections to all, and in any case, there is more to politics than economic interests. The democratic process should reflect all the diverse political demands and interests in society. What is more, in the classic Liberal account, the class most likely to win individual democratic rights was the bourgeoisie.

This middle class wanted political and economic freedoms and rejected aristocratic rule. When political citizenship is extended (to women or to poor people) this is a logical extension of universal Liberal principles on individual rights. *Socialist* critics of 'bourgeois rights' (Marx, for example) have argued that economic freedom for the capitalist must bring them economic and political privilege. The formal equality of rights hides and justifies the practical reality of inequality; people cannot exercise their rights if the economic system denies them power, resources or influence.

Thus, debates have revolved around questions of the distribution of power, especially the relationship between economic power and political power. This disagreement can be seen sharply in the competing models of the distribution of power provided by *Pluralist* and *Marxist* analyses. For the Pluralists, liberal democratic institutions genuinely confer substantial political rights, opportunities and benefits on citizens, preventing any concentration of power in any one social group. Even if only a small elite actively decides policy and governs, the elite is influenced by social pressure and answerable to all citizens. In the Marxist critique, liberal democratic political arrangements are largely spurious, cosmetic illusions hiding the reality of concentrated power in the hands of a small economically powerful class in society.

Pluralist accounts of the distribution of power

Pluralist accounts of the distribution of power reject the assertion that class interests are the key to politics. Instead, there are many social divisions and all manner of political needs and preferences among the citizens. Instead of perceiving huge social rifts in the social structure, Pluralists see multiple, overlapping social groups with varied and cross-cutting political interests. Instead of class conflict, Pluralists envisage a fluid and indeterminate power structure, in which power and influence over decision-making are dispersed among a variety of social groups. So long as politicians are open to multiple influences, and so long as people have the means to give voice to all their diverse demands, then it is possible to achieve a genuine pluralist democracy or '**polyarchy**' (Dahl, 1989).

polyarchy

A pluralistic view of the distribution of power which rejects the notion of class division. It sees power emerging through the interplay of various social groups with multiple cross-cutting political interests.

People have gained this voice, according to Pluralists, through the extension of citizenship rights and through democratic rights to organise collective representation via political parties (such as mass socialist parties) and via social and industrial organisations (such as consumer groups, trade unions, and so on). Pluralism is thus not purely about individual rights, because the driving force behind liberal democratic politics is the political activity of organised groups. The social structure of Western societies is seen as one in which a plurality of social groups exists, each pursuing their own interests and goals. Modern twentieth-century politics is distinctive because of the variety of social groups and sectional interests to which individuals belong, such as social classes, occupational groups, gender groups, ethnic groups, religious groups, and so on. So a key element in the pattern of the distribution of power is the increased *social complexity* and *social differentiation* of modern industrial societies which engenders a diversification of group interests. Society is an arena of diverse and contending interests, but, according to Pluralists, it is not one fundamentally riven by social divisions: rather, there is an underlying common interest in maintaining a framework in which different groups can compete and pursue their interests without destroying the basic foundations of society. This means that political actions which step outside of the boundaries of liberal democracy are violating the commonly-shared 'rules of the game'. Violent or radical politics can be defined as a threat which undermines the mutual tolerance and limited political competition built into the system. Neo-Nazis, Black Power movements, student radicals and striking workers have all been seen as 'enemies within' at various times, breaking the fundamental consensus that underpins democratic pluralism.

For pluralism to work, there have to be opportunities and mechanisms available for groups to articulate their interests precisely and effectively. Democratic politics involves a process of competition among organised interest groups to win the ear of government, and political decisions are the outcome of complex processes of accommodation, bargaining and compromise between the demands of various groups attempting to exert influence over formal political decision-makers in government.

Although Pluralist theorists see government as playing a crucial role in the resolution of diverse group interests, it is essentially a society-centred, not state-centred, approach. This is because government stands apart from group interests as a largely neutral mechanism or referee, mediating and arbitrating between competing groups and interests, and one which is effectively autonomous from control by one group or from serving the interests of one group. All legitimate interests have some claim to be heard and to be taken into account in policy formation: no one group or major interest is either decisively or systematically favoured or disregarded. Democracy, then, involves competition to influence decision-making among a multiplicity of interest groups, and no single social group prevails on all issues and is consistently dominant, though some may be more influential in some spheres and on some issues than others. Thus, no single group is consistently dominant in monopolising power. The power structure is fluid and complex, not unitary and monolithic.

Specifically, Pluralists reject any simple equation of economic power with political power, precluding the possibility that a dominant economic class holds the reins of power. According to Pluralist theory, significant changes to traditional capitalism and private ownership mean that this ruling class can no longer exist:

- capital has had to accommodate the countervailing power of organised labour in the workplace;
- the economy is increasingly politically regulated, as the state plays a more interventionist role, planning economic development and directly controlling some of its key sectors through nationalisation;
- owners of capital have become a much more fragmented category with the rise of joint stock companies and large corporations, with increasingly diversified shareholding rather than traditional concentrated ownership;
- the increased scale and size of economic enterprises has required the expansion of managerial direction and control of companies;
- since the functions of controlling capitalism are no longer in the hands of a few, so economic power can no longer be concentrated in a dominant class.

Neo-pluralism: criticisms and the pluralist response

These arguments against a classic ruling class do not in themselves demonstrate that the structure of power is as the Pluralists describe it. Many critics have pointed out the highly optimistic assumptions behind their models. Key criticisms focus on the actual distribution of influence and the boundaries of legitimate politics:

- Different groups have markedly different resources. The amount of influence they bring to bear will depend crucially on the economic resources they can mobilise, or the negative consequences which they can bring about by some action. For example, trade unions can mobilise collective resources and impose costs on employers through strikes, but individual workers in small firms can do neither;
- The Pluralist focus on explicit political influence and open political competition neglects other 'faces ' of power. Bachrach and Baratz (1963) showed how issues could be actively kept off the political agenda and social groups denied a voice. An example of this 'second face of power' was the silence in British politics concerning political and social discrimination against Catholics in Northern Ireland until the civil rights protests of the 1960s put the issue on the agenda. Even then, the lack of any resolution of the issue drove the conflict outside the boundaries of peaceful liberal democratic politics;

- A 'third face of power' (Lukes, 1974) may be found when politics systematically serve the interests of one social group rather than others, even when no explicit political conflict or decision can be seen. Here, we ask the question 'who benefits?', bearing in mind that the power to retain privilege may be most potent if is never questioned or challenged. One example here could be the taken-for-granted maintenance of male dominance in social institutions, until it is questioned and challenged;
- Political groups or movements which seek radical change in society are often seen as illegitimate. If their demands to change the system question the fairness of current political arrangements and break its rules, they can be marginalised and suppressed. Pluralist democracy only works on the assumption that we all stay within liberal democratic rules and laws and do not mobilise direct and forcible means to power. Violent protests, for example by animal rights campaigners, raise this problem about the boundaries of political conduct for groups who feel powerless or without a voice. Hence the criticism is that pluralism has to assume a degree of moderation and basic conformity to the system which is not really present.

In responding to these criticisms, Pluralist theorists have revised their positions. Many have conceded that the formal political equality of liberal democracies does not in reality square with some of the socio-economic inequalities of contemporary society. These neo-Pluralists (Dahl and Lindblom, 1976) recognise that particular interest groups like big business, or institutions like multinational corporations, occupy positions of particular importance and influence and so they exercise greater political muscle than other interests (such as consumer groups) in influencing government policy-making.

Thus, while they maintain that governments are genuinely controlled by electoral competition, lobbying and influence by interest groups, they acknowledge that business interests do have great influence on public policy – a polyarchy exists, but it is a *deformed polyarchy* (Dahl, 1989). Despite this, neo-Pluralists still see a significant number of diverse interest groups as influencing the political process so that it is misleading to ascribe a single purpose – such as serving the interests of capital – to the government.

As we shall see later in this chapter, it is not only the Pluralists who emphasise the diversity of groups and interests in society. Power is mobilised by many different social groups and political movements which focus on social issues which may have no direct link to class division (environmental pressure groups such as Greenpeace, for example).

Clearly, participation in these different political groupings can cut across other lines of social division, and their concerns are not in any simple sense reducible to economic interests. But none of these considerations need persuade us that the model of Pluralist politics is adequate. The image of a fluid, open power structure with neutral state institutions open to influence by all may be an attractive ideal. But it is not a picture of power today that would be recognised by many active political citizens in Western societies.

Marxist models of the distribution of power

Society-centred models of power need not be based on class. There are many social divisions that can form the basis for politics: region, gender and ethnicity are obvious examples. However, Marxism certainly does base its model of power on economic classes, and has been enormously influential in doing so. The fundamental reason for this is the power of Marxism's claims that:

- the most important structural feature of modernity is capitalism;
- capitalism rests on economic class relations which necessarily involve exploitation and domination;
- there is thus a fundamental class conflict at the root of capitalist societies;
- furthermore, these economic relations shape the other social relations in society so that class is ultimately the most powerful and fundamental political division in society. Other divisions are conditioned by class, and will not be so decisive in determining the society's political development.

Even though Marx and Engels acknowledged that politics and social change could not simply be 'read off' from the economic level, they did regard economic factors as ultimately decisive. Furthermore, while later Marxists have tried to make their analysis more subtle, and find more room for politics and ideology, the fundamental primacy of economic structures is usually affirmed. We will explore now how these basic Marxist propositions have been developed in varying directions.

Instrumentalist Marxist models

The work of Marx and Engels sometimes suggested crude and direct models of politics where the state is an instrument of the ruling class: that is, where the economically dominant class either rules directly, or others rule at their behest. For example, in the *Communist Manifesto*, we learn that the state in capitalism is simply 'the executive committee of the whole bourgeoisie'. But elsewhere, as in Marx's analysis of French politics in *The Eighteenth Brumaire of Louis Bonapartre*, or in Engels' *Letter to Bloch* (Marx and Engels, 1968), they offer much more fine-grained accounts, acknowledging the importance of specific political and ideological influences. Even here, though, the analysis of ideas and political interests is constantly related back to economic interests.

The instrumentalist Marxist position is deeply sceptical about democracy in capitalist states: parliament and government are not the major sources of power, because real power is primarily a consequence of ownership and control of material resources and is integrally related to economic and class inequality. Democracy and real popular participation must remain severely limited, or even illusory, so long as Western societies remain capitalist societies in which a dominant economic class holds sway.

That dominant economic class enjoys preponderant economic power through its ownership and control of the means of production. It has close links with and penetrates important institutions such as the mass media, the military, the churches, and so on and is closely associated with those in key decision-making domains – the command positions – of the state. Thus, the dominant economic class is a ruling class. Even if not ruling directly, capitalists are at the heart of an exclusive unified group sharing a common social background and recognised common interests and exercising a decisive degree of power and influence over political decision-making consistently and persistently.

Given their emphasis on economic power as the crucial precondition for political power, these Marxist explanations have to demonstrate that the private ownership of capital still matters, and that the needs and goals of capital play a dominant role in shaping contemporary societies. Thus they point to persisting massive material inequalities, in which the distribution of wealth remains distinctly heavily skewed and concentrated in a few hands – an economically powerful class comprising a small minority of the population, with the vast bulk of people possessing little real wealth.

class reproduction
The process by which class inequalities reproduce themselves.

social closure
Employed by Weber to describe the action of social groups who restrict entry and exclude benefit to those outside the group in order to maximise their own advantage.

Although the dominant class has not remained unchanged in its social composition, it has remained a significantly exclusive group, socially distinctive from and relatively impenetrable by other groups in the class structure. This was achieved by various important strategies of **class reproduction** or **social closure**, such as:

- intermarriage and kinship connections;
- interconnected economic interests like interlocking directorships where individuals are directors of more than one company;

Source: I. Hislop (ed.), (1991), *30 Years of Private Eye Cartoons*, London, Private Eye/Corgi.

'Capitalist Bastard, Capitalist Bastard . . .'

- exclusive educational experience, such as the public schools and Oxford and Cambridge Universities in Britain, or the Ivy-League colleges in the USA;
- cross-sphere contacts and linkages, where individuals occupy and/or shuttle between elite positions in various spheres (such as MPs who hold company chairships or directorships; former Civil Servants or government ministers joining the boards of private companies; or high-profile business personnel who are appointed to **QUANGOS**).

QUANGOS – Quasi Non-Governmental Organisations
Nominally independent bodies whose members are funded and appointed by central government to supervise or develop activity in areas of public interest.

While acknowledging that some economic redistribution has occurred, on this view the basis for the social system is not really changed. Thus the spread of share ownership and the advent of so-called people's capitalism have made only marginal dents in patterns of wealth-holding, because, as Scott(1982) and others maintain, substantial private shareholdings, and hence the power to exert decisive control over economic enterprises and their corporate strategies, remain tightly concentrated in a few hands. It is also possible to argue that even if there were not an identifiable group of capitalists, the influence of capitalist institutions and their managers is likely to be the most powerful voice in politics.

Marxists, then, maintain that in Britain and elsewhere a capitalist class has not disappeared but has survived and persisted during the twentieth century. Their domination has been enhanced by enjoying social advantages, especially social connections and shared social backgrounds with state personnel and government administrators; by the privileged position enjoyed by its representative organisations (such as the Confederation of British Industry in Britain); by the support and influence of international capital and financial organisations (such as the International Monetary Fund, and the World Bank); and by the way that governments depend upon business confidence. This reflects a dominant value system which tacitly equates business interests with the national interest and which proclaims and defends the principles of private property and ownership, free enterprise, profit, the free market economy and all the inequalities that follow from this.

Such a strong version of the instrumentalist argument has a problem in explaining how Labour or Social Democratic governments also serve to maintain capitalism. One response to this question is to suggest that the state often has to act 'on behalf of' capital to reduce political resistance and adapt capitalism to solve some of its problems – a 'puppet' government which does what capitalists think they need might not be able to act in their longer-term interests (Miliband, 1968). Thus, in Britain, Marxists have argued that Labour governments have not significantly threatened capitalist class interests and have been just as concerned to run capitalism efficiently. They have not wanted, or been able, to make any substantial or qualitative changes to the capitalist economy and political system. Their interventions, such as public ownership programmes, have not significantly damaged or undermined private capital and have not changed the logic or the dynamic of capitalist investment and profit.

Structuralist Marxist approaches

These points about the power of capitalism as a system, and the dependence of the state upon a profitable economy, have been developed further by structuralist Marxists such as Althusser and Poulantzas. They argued that the actions of individual groups or classes are fundamentally constrained by the structures in which they are located and which exert an independent influence over social and political processes: there are inherent limitations imposed by the structure of society and particularly by the system of economic production in which social actors operate.

On this view, instrumentalist Marxism misunderstands the impersonal nature of power. This is because power is located not in particular groups of individuals but in *systems* of domination. It is not a matter of what individuals do or who occupies which elite positions: what is important are the *structural constraints* which a capitalist system places on them and their lives. Hence, the social backgrounds and networks, the values, motives and so on of those in elite and other positions are largely irrelevant to understanding power relations, since these individuals are merely 'bearers' of objective structural relations who can do little other than fall in line with and reflect in their actions the logic of the capitalist system.

For a structuralist, then, it is possible for large numbers of people from quite humble, non-capitalist backgrounds to administer the state and the economy, but it would still be a capitalist state and society run in the interests of the capitalist class. The actions of politicians, state officials and so on are simply the surface manifestations of underlying structural relations, and the structural constraints of the capitalist system mean that dominant class interests will almost inevitably prevail, because the state and its personnel are compelled to satisfy the requirements of capitalism. This position has serious problems, however. There is a danger that Marxism simply produces a new functionalism, where the reproduction of the system is inevitable and guaranteed; and there is little place for the political processes where the interests of capitalism are defined and fought out in political programmes. These considerations led Poulantzas to move away from structuralism towards a more Gramscian emphasis on political alliances and programmes, and to examine more fully how the state worked as an institution (Poulantzas, 1978).

Gramscian Marxist approaches

Marxist approaches which draw on the ideas of the Italian writer and political activist Antonio Gramsci offer a much more qualified society-centred approach. This approach generally identifies a greater element of human autonomy and it specifically acknowledges the complexities of political processes and recognises struggles in the political arena over policies and strategies. Stuart Hall, David Coates and others emphasise that both traditional and structuralist Marxist approaches are in danger of reducing the political too simply and straightforwardly to the economic, and of underplaying the reality of political divisions and struggles not only between classes but also within classes.

power bloc

An alignment of social groups, generally under the dominance of one of them, which is able to monopolise the levels of political power in a society over a sustained period.

They prefer to use the idea of *power blocs* to analyse the social basis for exercising power. A **power bloc** is 'an alignment of social groups, generally under the dominance of one of them, which is able to monopolise the levels of political power in a society over a sustained period' (Scott, 1991, p. 33). This coalition of social groups comprises classes, fractions or sections of classes, status groups and so on which may be divergent and even possibly potentially conflicting, but which effectively hold the reins of power by forming an alliance around a political programme that unifies their interests to some degree. For example, governments after 1945 in Western Europe generally adopted policies which combined state economic management with expanded welfare states. Many different groups could unite behind such a programme because it brought benefits to each of them.

The current power bloc may exclude certain groups (for example, the Thatcher governments excluded trade unions), but it may also try to co-opt and incorporate other social groups where necessary – for example, when such groups are a greater threat outside the power bloc than in it. Power blocs, then, are not necessarily constant in composition: they are often re-shaped as different groups are admitted over time, and they may experience shifts in the internal balance of power among their constituent groups as fractions emerge in leading positions within them. Such changes may be associated, for example, with shifts in the relative strengths of different fractions of capital. Thus, in Britain in the early nineteenth century, the landed and commercial classes were key elements in the power bloc as powerful economic interests and as occupants of key positions in the state; the second half of the nineteenth century saw the rise of increasingly powerful industrialists which presaged their incorporation into a new power bloc of landed, commercial and urban manufacturing capital; and the twentieth century witnessed the relative decline of the manufacturing sector and an accompanying rise in power for the **finance fraction** of the capitalist class (Coates, 1984, p. 117).

finance fraction

That part of capital, for example banking, concerned solely with financial activities rather than production.

hegemony

Commonly used to describe the domination of one class, nation, or group of people over others. It was extended by Gramsci to denote a more general and intellectual dominance, especially when hegemonic ideas influence people's political perceptions.

Ideological hegemony is the second key concept in Gramscian Marxism. Power blocs always face potential demands and challenges from below. These demands may force political concessions to accommodate them and they create a need to foster acceptance among the wider populace. Thus, it is necessary for the power bloc to attempt to create and sustain **hegemony**, where subordinate groups accept the cultural domination of particular ideas. If people interpret politics through particular taken-for-granted frameworks ('of course everybody is selfish and self-interested') then the 'natural' dominance of the current political order is more secure. This is especially true if the consent of people through the ballot-box is important.

Attempting to establish hegemony involves the power bloc in trying to build a widespread consensus around the ideas and the political programme they wish to secure. Full hegemony is achieved when subordinate groups accept the central patterns, practices and relationships of a particular social order as normal, natural and inevitable. In such circumstances, dominance is achieved by consent rather than by force, since problematic and contested definitions of social reality have given way to a single prevailing ideology through which people interpret their own interests. But sustaining hegemony is a process which has to be worked at perpetually by use of a variety of social and political institutions and strategies to mobilise and reproduce consent, whether that be using the mass media, manipulating nationalist sentiments, making welfare concessions or whatever. There may also be competing hegemonic claims, battling for dominance and competing to construct a political programme for the future.

relative autonomy
Where a link exists between two institutions, for example the State and economy, but where each institution has a degree of independence in causing outcomes.

Structuralist and Gramscian approaches come together when Marxist theorists emphasise the **relative autonomy** of the state. This concept suggests that there is a necessary separation between economic power and the formation of political programmes through the state. The interests of capital are not self-evident, and not all capitalists have the same interests. There may be significant differences in interest between manufacturers and financiers, for example. This is why the formation of power blocs and the ideological construction of political programmes are so important. Moreover, in liberal democratic systems it is necessary to secure some alliance of interests in a popular base for political programmes. All of this necessitates relative autonomy for politics. At some times, when political forces are balancing one another, and when policy programmes are in crisis, it may be possible for political leaders to seize enhanced autonomy. In doing so, they may impose programmes 'for the good of the nation' which entail direct costs for sections of capital (Jessop *et al.*, 1988). In the following section we will look in some detail at Britain's Thatcher governments as an example of this enhanced relative autonomy for politics.

Through these theoretical innovations, the Marxist tradition has renewed itself and tried to maintain its critical perspective on politics in capitalist society. Even so, many social theorists (including former Marxists) now ask themselves whether class and class politics really are the key to understanding power in contemporary society. Other sociologists still regard capitalism as the key institutional structure of modernity, and the dynamics of capitalist profit-making as the most powerful force re-shaping our lives. On this view, Marxist analysis is far from redundant.

State and Society: Analysing Political Change

Political sociology today focuses on the relationship between state and society. We cannot regard state institutions or government policies as simply reflections of the social groups and interests in society. The relationship works both ways: transformations in society affect the state, and changes in the structure of the state will affect policies and their impact on society. We have to take the structure of the state seriously, because this will limit the possibilities open to policy-makers since not every change can be implemented successfully. Equally, if interests are mobilised effectively, they will have great impact on the formation of government policies and the outcome of state actions. These interests, however, are not autonomous and automatic. Interests have to be actively defined and effectively mobilised to have any political reality. Often policies will have practical effects which change the structure and power of social groups; the practical economic and social position of people can be changed. This in turn provides a changed practical basis of social experiences which ideologies have to work with as they try to interpret and define experience. Social and political change will affect that sense of group interest that can move people to organise and act politically.

Possibilities for radicalism

These general features of the relationship between state and society give us some indications of the tasks facing any government that sets out to achieve radical change. They will have to secure certain conditions and achieve political room for movement:

- A base of support in society must be established where particular social groups back the programme; alliances must be formed which include some strong groups while excluding or marginalising others.
- Organised resistance inside the state or in society must be defeated or marginalised.
- There must be an ideological appeal to particular groups, and if necessary there must be an ideological campaign to redefine interests in ways that give a base of support, and to deny those definitions of group interests that oppose the new politics.
- There must be effective means of implementing policies so that they have practical effects – there must be powerful state agencies and practical means of putting policy into practice.
- If necessary there must be a restructuring of the state and of wider

social institutions to ensure that resistance to policy is removed or weakened.

- Radical restructuring may actually take away the social and political basis for groups to exist, organise and resist.

Even if all these conditions are achieved, there is little point unless the new regime has an effective programme to pursue which has an *overall strategic stance* (whatever policy adaptations occur in practice), and a *clear political agenda and world-view* that can form a foundation for the ideological task of establishing a *new social base of support*. This world view does not have to be coherent but it does need to offer people a new way of making sense of their experience. As Hall put it in his far-sighted article on 'The Great Moving Right Show' (1978), a radical government would have to be:

> **aiming at a new balance of forces, the emergence of new elements, the attempt to put together a new 'historic bloc', new political configurations and 'philosophies', a profound restructuring of the state and the ideological discourses which construct the crisis and represent it as it is 'lived' as a practical reality: new programmes and policies pointing to a new result, a new sort of 'settlement' – 'within certain limits'. These elements do not emerge, they have to be constructed.**
>
> **[reprinted in HALL, 1988, p. 43]**

The radical government would need to recast policies, political interests, and the structure of political support on a new basis; this, Hall argued, was what the Thatcher governments of Britain in the 1980s set out to do (Hall and Jacques, 1983), and we will apply our frameworks to this period shortly, after outlining some important keys to understanding political change.

Dimensions of political change (i): interests and policy

Political sociology has always put a strong emphasis on the interests and influence of social groups. We saw earlier that the means of voicing influence and representing interests will vary greatly – from individual voting to formal **corporatist** arrangements. Just as important, ruling groups need to be able to rely on alliances of support to underpin their power and back policy.

corporatism
A way of linking organised interests, especially economic ones, to the State, where the corporate 'partners' contribute to shaping and sometimes implementing policy.

As Figure 10.1 shows, however, influence can go the other way as well. Ruling groups will often seek to redefine interests in society through ideology – for example, denying the importance of class interests and promoting belief in self-help and individualism. Alternatively national

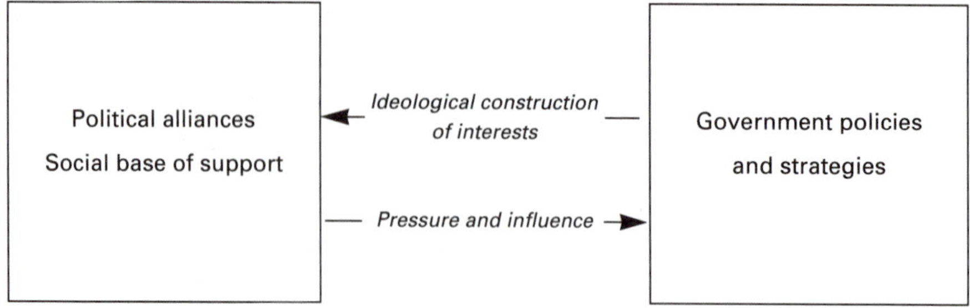

Figure 10.1 Interests and policy

or ethnic differences might be exploited against 'outsiders', submerging identities which might otherwise form a basis for resistance. Such efforts to redefine political interests and identity have sometimes been known as *hegemonic strategies* (Jessop *et al.*, 1988) because they seek to achieve what Gramsci called hegemony: a new moral and political 'common-sense' about the social world. Where others resist this attempt at hegemony, then there is a battle to provide people with believable frameworks with which to make political sense of their social position and their everday experiences.

Dimensions of political change (ii): social and political effects of policy

As Figure 10.2 suggests, this is also a two-way process.

Government policies will be influenced by organised interests, but the power of these interests will be affected by the impact of the policies on social groups. For example, in the 1980s Britain trade unions were seriously weakened as a political force. This was partly due to direct policies, such as legislative restraints on the unions, but it was also because of the wider impact of economic policies that expanded unemployment and produced dramatic changes in jobs and the workforce. If policies produce wider changes to social and economic structures, then old social groups may be broken up. New groups may be formed, or indi-

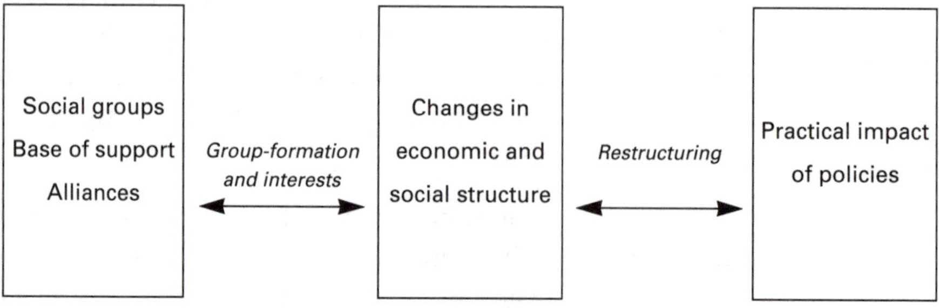

Figure 10.2 Social and political effects of policy

viduals might be left isolated from others in a similar position; either way, the potential social basis for common interests and group influence has been changed. Rapid changes in work and housing tenure (the expansion of home-ownership) during the 1980s did not in themselves create a new politics, but they did set new conditions for ideology to work with in the battle to define and represent political interests.

Dimensions of political change (iii): implementing policy

Quite apart from social backing, governments need practical means to put their policies into practice, as Figure 10.3 attempts to show. There must be a strong set of state institutions to implement policy, with practical instruments available to make changes happen in the wider society. For example, it would be foolish to promise full employment if the government had no means to influence the creation of jobs; similarly it would be a mistake to declare policies based on controlling the growth of the money supply whilst simultaneously dismantling controls on the 'creation' of money through lending and credit.

Policy changes require not only some means to implement them, but also ways of preventing, marginalising or defeating resistance. These conditions are illustrated in Mrs Thatcher's disastrous Community Charge or Poll Tax (1989–90); not only was the tax difficult and expensive to collect, but it also stimulated widespread resistance. Policy was formed in a way that failed to involve interests outside government, or anticipate their resistance; the consequence was that the policy failed and the Prime Minister was seriously weakened. In other policy areas, potential resistance can be reduced by damaging or removing one part of the state and replacing it with something more controllable.

These different dimensions of policy change can be drawn together, as in Figure 10.4; we shall now go on to employ these frameworks in a more systematic account of recent British politics.

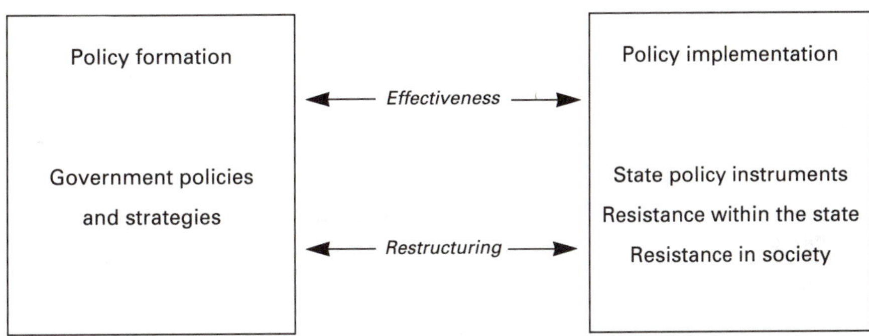

Figure 10.3 Implementing policy

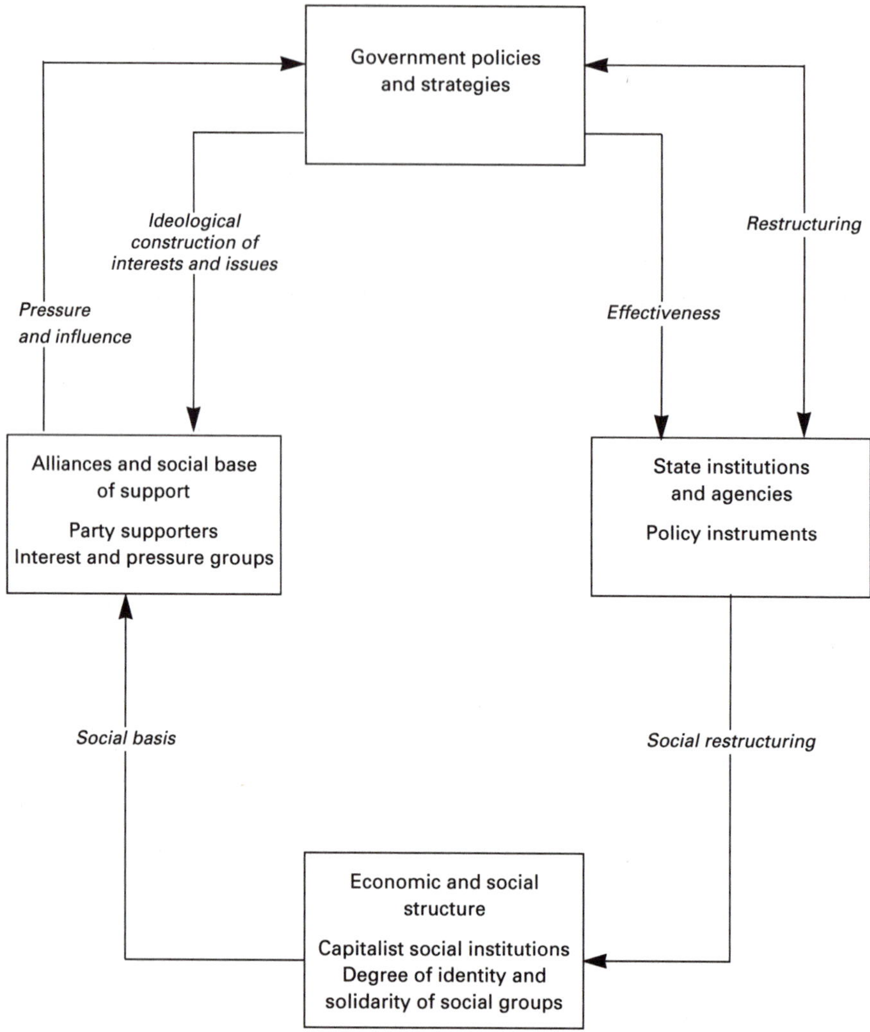

Figure 10.4 Understanding social and political change

Analysing Political Change: Thatcherism in Britain

Thatcherism
A system of political principles, beliefs, policies and practices, based on notions of economic individualism and the free market, expounded by Margaret Thatcher and her Conservative governments between 1979 and 1990 (*see* free market *and* New Right).

We can assess the usefulness of the frameworks we have just set out by analysing a practical case study. The Conservative governments in Britain when led by Margaret Thatcher (1979–90) should be seen as radical in intent and effect. Unusually, this leader gave her name to an ideology – **Thatcherism** – and that may suggest that we should focus primarily on that. However, it is just as important to analyse the practical impact of these policies on social groups and social institutions: were the radical intentions matched by radical political and social effects?

While we should not overemphasise the significance of ideology (Jessop *et al.*, 1988), there were distinctive roots to Thatcherism in **New Right** doctrines, especially those of Hayek (Levitas, 1985; Bosanquet, 1983; King, 1987). At the heart of these is a belief in economic individualism in the free market. Individuals must be free to pursue their self-interest with the minimum of interference from the state. For the New Right neo-liberals this is because free economic activity is the source of capitalist wealth-creation and also because state power is coercive – it shackles our individual freedom. More traditional Conservative themes re-enter because this free economy must be backed up by a strong state (Gamble, 1988) in order to bring law and order, defend national security, and provide a minimum level of welfare. However, any attempt to alter the outcomes of free market forces by state planning in the economy, or by egalitarian social policy to promote social justice, will only result in less wealth and less freedom. The market brings us all wealth, however unequally, and liberty is expressed in the pursuit of individual self-interest (see Chapter 15, 'Theorising Modern Family Life').

New Right
A strand of right-wing Conservatism, which is primarily concerned with the non-interference of the state into economic and business affairs and the realm of individual autonomy. Although the state is seen as coercive in limiting individual freedom, a strong element of moral conservatism often exists in New Right thinking.

This doctrine harks back to nineteenth-century **laissez-faire Liberalism** by demanding a non-interventionist state and a free market. However, because these things may not already exist it may be necessary to engage in some dramatic state intervention to reshape society into this model: to create a nation fit for enterprise. Such a radical goal demands radical policies to create far-reaching social change; it also demands a project to consolidate the political base of support for this programme.

laissez-faire Liberalism
A political and economic approach based on a general principle of non-interference by government and freedom for markets and property owners.

Thatcherism in Britain (i): interests and policy

A well-known description of Thatcherism's popular appeal was given by Stuart Hall: '**authoritarian populism**'. Hall (1978) emphasised the extent to which Thatcherism set out to build a new base of political support. By appealing to certain aspects of people's experiences and desires Mrs. Thatcher could highlight individualistic and materialistic aspirations at the expense of class identity and collective interests. This was the *populist* element, which was backed by an *authoritarian* dimension which emphasised law and order and 'Victorian values'. Thus in Thatcher's ideology the 'moral order' dimension of Conservatism co-existed in an incoherent mixture with the doctrine of 'individual freedom'. For Hall, the contradictory nature of this mixture is fundamental to its appeal. However, changing the climate of ideas and the popular mood is not enough. It is also necessary (as Gramsci emphasised) to build alliances of support and weaken forces of resistance. The trade unions were an obvious target for this process. Not only were the

authoritarian populism
A term used by Hall to describe Thatcherism's mixture of free market economics, conservative moral values, and its appeal to individualistic and authoritarian elements in popular 'common-sense' values (*see* Thatcherism).

unions organised opponents to Thatcherism, they also impeded the free market and acted as a force for collectivism rather than individualism. At the time many people feared and resented union power and they could be drawn into a popular base. The outcome could thus be a *change in the balance of political forces* as well as a new *'common sense'* which rejected class identity in favour of individual aspiration.

It is important not to overstate the power of Thatcherite ideology. Undue emphasis on authoritarian populism can lead to an overestimation of its degree of ideological success, and to a neglect of other important dimensions of Thatcherism (Jessop *et al.*, 1988). Taylor-Gooby (1986) and Edgell and Duke (1991) have done empirical work on popular acceptance of Thatcherite ideology. These studies showed substantial levels of support for welfare and state intervention, and rather limited support for the core ideas of the New Right. It may be harder to change 'common-sense' than some analysts imagined.

Even so, the Thatcher governments did command support among a range of social groups. Small business people were the most natural supporters of the grocer's daughter, but larger companies were generally supportive of this most pro-business government, despite concerns in 1980–1 over economic policy. Although different parts of capital benefited in varying degrees, none was excluded from the Conservatives' political base. Less predictably, a large proportion of manual workers, especially skilled workers, voted Conservative through the 1980s. Forms of private consumption were extended to manual workers, especially through the sale of council houses and shares in privatised companies. Cuts in income tax helped to boost economic confidence among those who stayed in employment, fostering a climate of 'popular capitalism'. This led some political analysts to predict that class identities were finally giving way to individualism or to other social cleavages (Dunleavy and Husbands, 1985). The proportion of voters who kept a strong party identification and did not shift their vote across parties constantly diminished; however, this 'de-alignment' did not signify any new stable alignment to the Conservatives (Crewe, 1992). The base of popular support for Thatcherism looked increasingly insecure over time.

Thatcherism in Britain (ii): social and political effects of policy

If the practical impact of Thatcherite policies was to bring about profound changes in the social structure, then we might expect that the social basis for political interests was changed in turn. Of course political organisations and definitions of political interests need to be built and fought for – they do not just arise naturally out of social structures. But these structures and institutions provide the direct experiences and the practical sources of power which political action and **discourse** build on.

discourse
A body of ideas, concepts and beliefs which become established as knowledge or as an accepted world-view. These ideas become a powerful framework for understanding and action in social life. For example, Foucault studied the discourse of madness, highlighting its changes over the centuries and its interplay with other discourses such as religious and medical discourses, and illustrated how these shifts affect how madness is perceived and reacted to by others.

Throughout the 1980s policies had effects which changed the underlying political terrain. Some effects were intentional, while others were part of longer-term trends which were hastened by government policies. There was a huge decline in male employment in manufacturing, while more and more women were employed in the workforce as a whole. Council housing was sold off and not replaced, with mortgage-based home ownership becoming the pattern for the majority. Trade unions were greatly weakened by unemployment, by legislation and by confrontations which the government was determined to win such as the miners' strike of 1984–5. Often when a powerful group was defeated this gave the political opportunity to impose dramatic changes from above, such as huge closures in coal mining.

In these ways a New Right government strongly opposed to state interference engaged in extensive intervention in order to create society in the free-market image. Many social institutions were reformed in the market image, whether through privatisation or by restructuring, as in health and education. This was as much about removing the power-base of opponents as about reforming society. For example, if Local Education Authorities opposed government policies, then individual schools should be freed to pursue their own self-interest by opting out from LEA control. Reforms to the National Health Service attempted to bring the logic and discipline of the market into institutions that could not be fully privatised.

These reforms may have dramatic effects. Not only do they create fragmented and competitive units (schools, health trusts, etc.) where the style and substance of management is transformed; the reforms also weaken some of the main institutional bases for collectivist politics. Public sector unions and managers were at the heart of a non-market, pro-welfare political culture which the New Right hoped to destroy. So long as these institutions remained strong, there was a strong base for opposition to the culture of competitive, materialistic individualism. Reform was therefore necessary both to create the market society and to disable resistance.

Households also provided fertile ground for Thatcherite politics in the economic conditions of the late 1980s. Borrowing money became much easier and the proportion of income saved fell greatly. The strong pound cheapened imported goods and a housing boom made home-owners feel wealthy. In these circumstances issues of tax and spending loomed very large. There was a shift from public spending (on schools, roads, etc.) to private consumption. All these factors seemed, for a time, to create the individualistic pro-market consumer that Thatcherites dreamt of.

Perhaps, in retrospect, this change in individual attitudes turned out to be a temporary phenomenon. However, given the changes in social institutions and in employment and consumption, it is hard to deny that some important foundations for collectivist, class-based politics were substantially eroded in the 1980s and early 1990s.

Thatcherism in Britain (iii): implementing policy

As we saw earlier, two key dimensions must come together to allow effective implementation: firstly, the state must possess adequate administrative means to put the policy into practice and actually change things in society, and secondly, the government must be able to defeat or at least marginalise potential sources of resistance. Without any effective means of economic intervention no government will be able to control the economy. But if particular groups (whether business, trade unions, or financial markets) have the power to resist or subvert economic policy, then policy will not be effective whatever the 'organisational capacity' (or administrative power) of the state (Marsh and Rhodes, 1992; Savage and Robins, 1990). These authors demonstrate that many Thatcherite policies which were radical in intent were far less dramatic in practice, because of the problems of implementation and resistance. A few examples may illustrate this.

Monetarism In the early 1980s, the Thatcher government claimed that inflation could be cured by controlling the rate of growth of the money supply – that is, controlling how much money and credit was created in the economy. Financial targets were set and the economy was squeezed hard in order to achieve them. However, at the same time the government deregulated financial markets and accepted that it could not directly control financial institutions as they expanded credit, leading to the late 1980s boom based on borrowing. By that time, targets for money growth were abandoned; monetarist rhetoric could not produce successful monetarist policy, even though inflation was reduced by periods of general squeeze and recession.

Local Government Policies pursued by central government in the 1980s were resisted strongly by local government. Labour-controlled metropolitan councils (such as the Greater London Council under Ken

Livingstone) were especially resistant; as a result they were abolished. Local council planning controls held back developers (e.g. in London's Docklands). Consequently their decisions were overridden by successive Environment Secretaries, and local power was side-stepped by the creation of Urban Development Corporations. These were not subject to local democratic control and hence they protected central government from resistance. By encouraging the opting-out of schools, Conservative governments in the 1990s hoped to effectively abolish Local Education Authorities. While these measures apparently devolve power down to smaller local councils or to individual opted-out schools, these small units become directly dependent upon a strengthened central state. The quest for effectiveness in securing national policies against resistance led to far-reaching changes in the local state and in the democratic accountability of social institutions.

Many other examples could be cited (see Jessop *et al.*, 1988 and Marsh and Rhodes, 1992). The general point is that the radical changes made by Conservative governments in the 1980s and 1990s had complex social and economic effects. The reforms by no means always worked as intended, but they did change social institutions in very significant ways. The political and social terrain was changed, and so was the administrative power of the central state. Even when the popular base of support was thoroughly eroded in the mid-1990s, the structural changes were embedded in ways that would prove very difficult to reverse for any incoming government with different policies, regardless of the strength of their ideology or their popular base. Thus we can see that the frameworks set out in Figures 10.1 to 10.4 can be helpful in illuminating processes of political change and in analysing their consequences – at least within stable parliamentary democracies.

Beyond Class Politics

Class identity and political action

In our earlier discussion of analyses of the distribution of power in society we observed how much political sociology rested on society-centred explanations which focused on the extent to which and the ways in which political power was concentrated narrowly in the hands of one particular social class. While we suggested that such analyses tended to underplay the independent capacity of the state and the complex interplay between state and society, they did highlight the significance which political sociology has attached to social processes and group interests for understanding politics, and more specifically the importance it has accorded to *social class* as a, if not the, key dimension of modern capitalist societies.

Both Marxist and non-Marxist political sociologists have traditionally favoured class analysis. For them, important social conflicts have a class basis and class character, and class is the main line of social division or cleavage, generating specific political interests and forming a major basis on which interests and identity are founded. In this section we will question the extent to which class position is, or ever was, the sole or major basis on which interests and identity are founded. However, there were good historical reasons for giving class a centrality in analysing the politics of modernity.

The process of transition to liberal democracy in Europe, as we suggested earlier, was not merely a matter of winning political rights of citizenship for individuals. It was intimately tied up with collective struggles to promote social and material equality in societies based on a capitalist economic system, in which material wealth and productive resources were massively skewed towards a minority and where the majority of the population had only its labour power to sell. Thus, nineteenth- and much twentieth-century politics was substantially a politics of dominant and subordinate classes, with the latter struggling to gain an equal foothold in the political process. The main vehicles through which they did so were mass socialist parties and organised labour movements, whose goals were the creation of a more equal redistribution of wealth, power and other life-chances for subordinate classes.

These working-class representative organisations achieved some success in such realms as the creation of welfare state systems, the regulation of worker/employer relations, the acquisition of employment rights and improved working conditions, and in bargaining for greater rewards. However, levels of inequality and disadvantage remained persistently high throughout the twentieth century. So, much political sociological attention has focused on the political response to those circumstances, examining the nature of working-class consciousness, the patterns and processes of working-class electoral behaviour, and the nature of the relationship between the working class and its representative political organisations.

For example, Marx's vision was of capitalism becoming increasingly polarised into two warring classes of bourgeoisie and proletariat, with the latter becoming conscious of their common interests and developing a revolutionary consciousness prior to sweeping away capitalism. However, such changes have failed to materialise, and academic work tried to explain why. Thus, some sociologists have examined the significance of *heterogeneity* among the working class and of variations in their images of society and their political consciousness associated with differences in their residential and occupational communities. Others have argued that the existence of a *dominant value system* – a prevailing set of ideas propagated by the dominant class and successfully disseminated by institutions such as the education system, the mass media and religious organisations – helped to foster, however partially and pragmatically, working-class acceptance of the status quo. Such a pragmatic acceptance of capitalism, it was argued, was reinforced by the adaptive reaction to capitalism and its inequalities by the representative organisations of the working class. The predominant style of the politics of working-class movements has been largely *reformist:* organised labour movements have been largely committed to improving the market position of workers, and left-wing political parties have been largely democratic socialist parties.

In the realm of electoral politics, too, the connections between class position and political party allegiances have been extensively explored and analysed, revealing the consistent support for socialist and social democratic parties by the majority of the working class in Western European societies. In Britain, at least for much of this century, class has constituted the single most important variable associated with voting. Roughly two-thirds of the working-class vote went regularly to the Labour Party, and this support was founded on a widespread (though by no means universal) view among those voters of the Labour Party as their 'natural' party and the guardian of working-class interests. The middle-class vote, moreover, was traditionally even more class cohesive than that of the working class, with only about 20–25 per cent at most of middle-class people deserting the 'party of their class' and voting Labour.

Class divisions, social divisions and political identity and interests

While we can recognise both historical and contemporary links between class and politics, it is important to remember that we cannot make any simple assumptions about the relationship between class position, class interests, political values and political action. It may be that people do feel some sense of class location and identity, that class position does affect their everyday lives, and that they do live in social and political environments influenced by class interests and inequalities. But what that means to them may be highly variable and subject to change and fluctuation over time.

Moreover, class position, class identity and class consciousness, whatever form they may take, are only one of a number of bases of social division on which a sense of interests and political identity may be formed. People construct social identities and consciousness out of multiple social experiences, so that there is a diversity of bases on which they may mobilise or be mobilised for political action.

Social divisions and interests other than class position may predominate at any one time or may come to assume priority over time, and these may reduce the salience of class division and class interests. Thus, for example, class divisions and class interests are frequently cut across by non-class variables such as religious affiliation, age, gender, or ethnicity. Gender and ethnic divisions, for instance, both currently and in the past, have created distinctive interests both in the workplace and outside. Many manual working-class workplace cultures have been traditionally aggressively masculine, exhibiting discrimination against and hostility towards women workers; black people have experienced racism from whites both inside and outside the workplace; and white male workers organised in trade unions have often gained at the expense of unorganised workers such as women and ethnic minorities – that is, trade unions have often appeared to be organisations defending *white working-class males'* occupational interests.

Electoral politics: beyond class alignment?

In the 1960s, certain political and academic commentators took the view that the class politics typical of nineteenth-century and pre-Second World War capitalist societies was fast becoming an anachronism, that the death of class politics was imminent, and that the 'end of ideology' was just around the corner. The blossoming of the Welfare State systems, improvements in material standards of living, and changes in working conditions were said to be eroding the formerly solid class-based political loyalties, with so-called 'affluent' manual workers allegedly no longer seeing themselves as working class nor their interests as represented by Socialist or Labour parties.

embourgeoisement thesis
An explanation for declining working-class solidarity which claims that through increasing affluence, the working class tend to adopt middle class values, and thus become absorbed into the middle class.

However, this '**embourgeoisement thesis**' oversimplified the extent of substantial change in the class structure and in the class position of manual workers, as well as overestimating the weakening of levels of electoral support for the Labour Party in Britain, as celebrated studies such as those of Goldthorpe *et al.* in Luton (1969) demonstrated. But what the thesis (and, significantly, the authors of the Luton study) did was to signal certain shifts in electoral behaviour that were to become more visible in the 1970s and 1980s. Evidence in the last two decades or so has suggested that electoral political support has become less predictable and more volatile, that party loyalty has become less stable, and that the traditional links between class and party loyalty have become more blurred and problematic and have been progressively eroded. In other words, processes of *partisan de-alignment* and *class de-alignment* have occurred.

The notion of partisan de-alignment suggests that there has occurred a general decline in the strength of people's loyalties to and identification with political parties. Thus, studies by Crewe *et al.* (1977), Butler and Kavanagh (1984) and others argued that those claiming 'strong' attachment to and identification with political parties declined during the 1970s and 1980s, at least in part as a result of growing scepticism about political parties' capacities for handling national economic decline and problems such as inflation and unemployment. One manifestation of that in Britain was the increase in third party support, and in votes for nationalist parties. In the 1970 General Election, Labour and Conservatives together gained 89.5 per cent of votes cast, but only 75 per cent in 1974, 70 per cent in 1983 (at the height of the success of the Liberal/Social Democrat Alliance), 73 per cent in 1987, and 76 per cent in 1992.

The notion of class de-alignment suggests a significant weakening of the class/voting link. The first phase of this process in Britain involved a discernible increase in support for the Labour Party among middle-class voters in the late 1960s and the 1970s. In the 1964 British General Election, for example, the Conservatives led Labour by 53 per cent among middle-class voters but by only 35 per cent in 1979, by 40 per cent in 1983, and by only 36 per cent in 1987.

But, apparently more dramatic than this, the 1970s saw a significant decline in working-class electoral support for the Labour Party. In the 1964 General Election, the Labour Party led the Conservatives by 28 per cent among working-class voters but by only 7 per cent in 1979 and by only 7.5 per cent in 1987. In the 1983 General Election, only 38 per cent of manual workers voted Labour and only 39 per cent of trade unionists did so, and in 1987 the figures were 42 per cent and 42 per cent respectively, with less than half of all manual worker unionists voting Labour. This shift was particularly visible among *skilled* manual workers: in 1974, almost twice as many skilled manual workers voted for the Labour Party as voted for the Conservatives (49 per cent to 26 per cent), but in 1979 their votes were almost equally divided between the Labour and Conservative parties (42 per cent to 40 per cent), and in 1983, 1987 and 1992, more skilled manual workers voted Conservative than voted Labour (39 per cent to 35 per cent in 1983, 40 per cent to 36 per cent in 1987, and 41 per cent to 40 per cent in 1992).

If, as the class de-alignment thesis suggests, the established links between class and political loyalties have been undermined in recent decades, it is important to identify the processes and influences which have contributed to the severing of those links and to estimate the permanence or otherwise of the disconnection. In order to do so, we need to examine processes of social change and changes in the structural and cultural experiences of people as members of social classes in contemporary societies. While this does not necessarily mean that class politics does not matter any more, it does mean that such changes have had effects on the way classes are constituted and on the nature of class location and class experiences which in turn have had significant political consequences (see Chapter 7).

Most notably, we can point to important social changes in the past four decades which have profoundly influenced the internal structure and composition of social classes. These have particularly affected the working class, by reinforcing and opening further lines of division within them, affecting their sense of class identity, thereby affecting their aspirations and priorities and impacting upon their political responses and affiliations. Especially important here have been changes in the *economy* and *occupational structure*, in *residential patterns*, and in *working-class culture* and patterns of *consumption*.

One of the most significant changes of the post-war era has been the emergence of a more complex occupational structure, in large part as a consequence of *sectoral shifts* in the economy, with the decline of certain industries and spheres of employment and the rise and restructuring of others. Traditional heavy manufacturing and extractive industries such as shipbuilding, heavy engineering, mining and metal production contracted as part of a general decline in manufacturing employment – a process accelerated by the economic policies of the Thatcher governments of the 1980s – and gave way to the development of newer advanced technologies in industries such as car-making, light engineering, chemicals, electronics, and so on which required fewer workers with different kinds of skills. Those working in such employment, moreover, have come to typify the way in which capitalist economies such as Britain are increasingly differentiated into a body of 'core workers' working in full-time, reasonably secure jobs for good wages and an increasing number who work in insecure, often part-time jobs which are much less well paid.

These changes have resulted in shifts in the shape of the class structure and in the internal composition of classes – a more complex hierarchy both between and within class boundaries. The decline of traditional manual occupations and an overall contraction in the size of the working-class base has produced a smaller, more heterogeneous and less unambiguously 'proletarian' group working in a more diverse and sectorally uneven economy than in the nineteenth century and the first half of the twentieth century.

Alongside these occupational structural changes, shifts in working-class residential patterns have impacted upon sources of class identity and solidarity and political loyalties. Increased geographical mobility and urban redevelopment programmes have relocated many working-class people from traditional urban working-class communities into suburban housing estates, new towns, and the like. Such communities and their associated industries often provided one basis for class solidarity and for political identity, so that their demise can only have weakened that solidarity and concomitant political identification with the Labour Party.

At the same time, access to mass consumption opportunities has altered many working-class people's lives. The period of relative economic prosperity enjoyed by Western capitalist societies in the two decades after the Second World War – 'the post-war boom' – transformed patterns of mass consumption, leisure and entertainment with the increased availability of consumer durable goods (such as TVs, fridges and cars), of package holidays, and home ownership. Better standards of living, plus the opportunity to define oneself through consumption, became more commonly part of working-class experience.

These changes, then, influenced working-class people's sense of class, their aspirations, and their material and political interests and loyalties, accelerating the growth of a *privatised instrumentalism* which came to dislodge older communal solidarities and political identifications. This shift was signposted originally by the 'affluent worker' studies of Goldthorpe *et al.* (1969) which, while dismissing simple notions of economic and political embourgeoisement, concluded that relative affluence was having important consequences for working-class identity and consciousness and was initiating significant changes in the boundaries and balance between these workers' private, non-work lives and their 'point of production' work lives.

They were identified as differing from their predecessors by exhibiting a greater instrumentalism in their attitudes towards their work and their politics, and a greater privatisation in their home lives. That is, they worked purely for money, de-emphasised the centrality of work and workplace identities in their lives, and instead affirmed their central life identities in their private spheres of family and leisure. They embraced a more qualified commitment to trade unionism and to the Labour Party, seeing them as a means to an end rather than as ideological expressions of working-class solidarity.

Goldthorpe (1978, 1988) and others argued that the periods of inflation and economic recession during the 1970s and 1980s *intensified* rather than diminished the orientation towards privatisation and the instrumental stance towards those traditional working-class movements. As the working class has become more 'mature', such responses have become perfectly reasonable from their point of view: they see what capitalist society has to offer, they demand their share and attempt to exploit their market power to the full. Formerly central working-class organisations become less participatory and more 'distant' institutions which are evaluated increasingly in terms of what they can do for working-class people. Hence, if they fail to 'deliver' satisfactorily, there is less 'emotional' motivation to remain loyal to them.

While the relative economic security, affluence and full employment of the 1960s were sufficient to sustain their loyalties to trade unionism and Labour voting, the more qualified and fragile commitment meant that in the changing socio-economic circumstances of the 1970s and 1980s, with inflation and then recession rearing their heads, political affiliations could be and were more easily dislodged. Moreover, as Hall (1983), Gamble (1988) and others pointed out, the absence of a deep commitment among such working-class people made them susceptible to the ideologies of the New Right Conservatism of Mrs Thatcher.

Sectoral cleavages: from class politics to consumption politics?

Despite periods of economic crisis and recession, the post-war era in Western capitalist societies such as Britain has witnessed, as we suggested earlier, improvements in material living standards in which many people, including sections of the working class, have shared. It has also been characterised by an apparently ever-growing materialist ethos, propagated systematically by media advertising, exhorting people to acquire goods and services and attempting to persuade them that consumption of those goods and services is the key to happiness and self-fulfilment. Intensified and enabled in the last two decades by the expanded availability of credit facilities and the friendly, flexible 'plastic', there are increasingly strong pressures on people to define themselves through consumption, with, some argue, distinct political effects.

Dunleavy and Husbands (1985) and others have suggested that an increasingly significant line of social division or cleavage has emerged

consumption sector cleavage
A social division based on people's relationship to consumption and their location within the private or public sectors of production and consumption.

which cuts across class lines and which may take primacy over class divisions in its effect on political attitudes and loyalties. This is a **consumption sector cleavage**, with people's involvement in the *public* or *private* sector as both employees and, especially, as consumers as its central focus.

As well as positing a division between public sector and private sector employees, these authors also identify the emergence of a growing social division between those dependent on state provision and those choosing to purchase private provision of certain basic resources and services such as housing, transport, health care, pensions and education. That consumption sector cleavage, it is argued, goes a long way towards explaining the phenomenon of class de-alignment and more specifically the respective electoral success and failure of the Conservative and Labour parties in Britain in recent decades. Thus, in Britain, those dependent on the public sector have been more likely to be loyal to the Labour Party, while those relying on the private sector have been more likely to support the Conservative Party.

In both the 1983 and 1987 General Elections, among public sector manual workers, Labour led the Conservatives by 17 per cent, while among private sector workers, Conservatives led Labour by 1 per cent. In 1992, however, while Labour led Conservatives by 12 per cent among public sector manual workers, among private sector manual workers the 1983 and 1987 position changed notably, with Labour actually leading Conservatives by 18 per cent.

In 1979, among manual workers relying on public sector housing, transport and health care, Labour led the Conservatives by 29 per cent, while among those relying on only one of these, Conservatives led Labour by 10 per cent. Similarly, in the case of housing tenure, in 1983 and 1987, Labour led the Conservatives by 21 per cent and 34 per cent respectively among council tenants, while among owner-occupiers, Conservatives led Labour by 38 per cent and 27 per cent respectively. Among manual worker council tenants in 1983, 1987 and 1992, Labour led the Conservatives by 38 per cent, 37 per cent and 42 per cent respectively, while among manual worker owner-occupiers, the Conservatives led Labour by 22 per cent and 11 per cent respectively in 1983 and 1987: but in 1992 Labout led Conservatives by 1 per cent.

Thus, according to this argument, if social class location used to play the dominant role in shaping political affiliations, consumption sector location is becoming an increasingly influential line of division, with the working class particularly divided by sectoral cleavages. The 1992 data on public and private sector manual workers and manual worker owner-occupiers may, however, require some qualification of the strength of the impact of sectoral location.

The public sector/private sector issue was, however, heavily exploited by Margaret Thatcher and the Conservative government in 1979 and after. They attributed much of Britain's national and economic decline to excessive state/public sector involvement in the economy and in people's lives generally. Thatcherism was successful (if only partially) in convincing a significant number of voters (including working-class voters) that state control and involvement were barriers hindering Britain's national and economic recovery. A return to a free market economy with less state involvement and public provision, less dependency on a **'nanny state'** and greater private initiative, enterprise and self-help was the only way forward.

'nanny state'

A pejorative term used to describe the Welfare State, which implies that the Welfare system is over-protective and does not encourage individual responsibility.

One might, of course, draw the conclusion that increased private consumption is a simple reflection of increased demand for greater personal choice and control and an increased disinclination to have services provided by the state. While there may be some truth in this, we must also recognise that this has not been entirely independent of *political agency*: government policies have actively promoted private housing consumption through the subsidised sale of the stock of public council housing to tenants, and through drastic cutbacks in state expenditure on public housebuilding programmes. Similarly, transport policy has been skewed towards roadbuilding and private transport and away from public provision.

New social cleavages, new social movements

In this section of the chapter, we have recognised that sources of social division or cleavage other than class location play an important part in the construction of social identity and hence provide a potential basis for political identity and action. We have, however, attempted to reflect the importance which political sociology has attached to social class location as a major line of social division and basis of political identity in Western capitalist societies. We have also highlighted the ways in which social changes and changes in class composition and experience have had significant ramifications for class politics, loosening and at least partially displacing political loyalties and identities.

When experiences change because social structures change, social actors are faced with the problem of what alternative frameworks are available for making sense of their social position and re-casting or constructing new political identities. The solution to that may come 'from above' in the form of ideological mobilisation by politicians and political parties. Dictators may mobilise support around the banner of national interest and destiny, as Hitler did in Germany with notions of the 'Volk' and the superiority of an Aryan master race. Thatcherism in Britain, as we have seen, attempted to build a social base around ideas of economic individualism and popular capitalism, a free economy and a strong political state emphasising 'law and order'. More recently, the Labour Party in Britain, under the leadership of Tony Blair, has been engaged in a systematic reconstruction of its political programme in attempts to shed the image of a class and trade-union-based party and to appeal to a wider social constituency.

Frameworks to make sense of experience, however, may also come 'from below', generated by social actors and social movements on the ground, and in this context, much attention has been focused on examining the significance of what have come to be called *'new social movements'* as distinct forms of political mobilisation and sources of individual and collective identity. New social movements are those which have sprung up in the latter part of the twentieth century, concerned with such matters as

- citizenship rights and personal autonomy and identity (for example, the American black civil rights movement; Feminist movements; Gay Rights movements)
- the preservation of the environment (for example, Greenpeace, Friends of the Earth)
- peace and military power (for example, the Anti-Vietnam War movement, the Campaign for Nuclear Disarmament)
- animal rights (for example, anti-vivisection movements, the Animal Liberation Front)
- national identity and self-determination (for example, ETA, the Basque separatist movement.)

Social movements have been typically features of modernity, and organised labour movements were the first modern social movements in capitalist societies, where the main focus of social conflict has typically been the workplace. Such movements, as we have suggested earlier, were concerned with contesting and transforming the distribution of material resources, opportunities and power between social classes.

For many analysts of new social movements, such as Kriesi *at al.* (1995) and others, the latter part of the twentieth century has seen the decline of 'old' social movements and the emergence of new social movements, a phenomenon which is closely linked to the gradual but fundamental transformation of the conflict structure of contemporary societies

'We need a shorter banner or another member'

Source: I. Hislop (ed.), (1991) *30 Years of Private Eye Cartoons*, London, Private Eye/Corgi.

which is marginalising older social divisions and cleavages or even rendering them irrelevant. The rise of new social movements, then, is said to reflect either a transition into a new phase of modernity or even to herald a qualitative shift beyond modernity. Green movements and peace movements, for instance, represent fundamental challenges to industrialism and militarism, two of what Giddens (1990) calls the 'institutional dimensions of modernity', which have involved the harnessing of science and technology for economic growth and the domination of nature and for developing the means of mass violence.

The distinctive feature of contemporary societies, it is argued, is that lines of social cleavage and conflicts persist, but they are no longer those of the workplace and class: social conflict has shifted away from workplace and class relations to *civil society* and non-economic, non-class forms of cleavage and identity. According to many theorists, there is a more *fragmented* character to modern societies with no single focus but a plurality of struggles and co-existing movements, none of which is prior to or more 'real' than the others.

New social movements, it is argued, reflect that fragmentation: they are at the centre of a new politics of identity which is not generated by common interests of class position or experiences of the workplace, either in the focus of their demands or in the identities to which they appeal. The target of their opposition is not capitalist society or capitalist social relations, and they appeal to bases of collective identity which either transcend class or are irreducible to it – gender identity, sexual identity, membership of the planet, or whatever.

Some new social movements fuse 'the personal' and the 'global' – that is, they embrace a politics which combines a sense of personal identity with a stress on fundamental human and global concerns, transcending not only boundaries of class but also of the nation-state. The concerns of feminist movements, for instance, are in principle addressed to all women irrespective of class or country, on the basis that all women confront problems specific to them *as* women. Similarly, gay and lesbian movements provide a basis for identity based around sexual preference, seeking to instil 'gay pride' and attempting to expose and to critically confront homophobic attitudes and beliefs among heterosexuals. Others, such as green movements and peace movements, are even more explicitly concerned with *global* forces of social transformation and the impact of globalisation processes to which we have referred frequently throughout this book.

The social composition of these movements, too, has been linked to the fragmentation of the class structure and new class cleavages. Many new social movements have successfully attracted a broader cross-section of the population, and they tend to find strong support among those in ambiguous class locations such as those in 'new' middle-class service-oriented occupations like academics, teachers and social workers, and in socially peripheral groups such as students, the unemployed and the retired.

Some take the argument further and suggest that new social movements are displacing class-based movements as the potential principal agents of social transformation and a new social order. Touraine (1971), for instance, sees new social movements as key agents in the transition from industrial to 'post-industrial' society, and Inglehart (1977) argues that Western industrial societies are undergoing a fundamental shift from a 'materialist' to a 'post-materialist' culture. According to him, where basic needs have been satisfied by material prosperity for certain sectors of society, people turn their attention to non-material goals, away from 'an overwhelming emphasis on material well-being and physical security toward a greater emphasis on the quality of life' (1977, p. 3). Thus, priority is given to such issues as personal freedom, self-realisation and identity fulfilment, concern about the costs of prosperity and the associated need for environmental protection.

In the light of these arguments, it is clearly tempting to cry 'class politics is dead, long live the politics of new social movements'. However, we should be careful not to see new social movement politics as some unambiguously inevitable and universal shape of things to come. Firstly, while we may well recognise that class-based political loyalties have significantly loosened in recent decades, it would be premature to assume that class no longer plays (nor will play) a part in shaping political identities and affiliations. Material inequality and disadvantage have become more stark in many respects in Britain and elsewhere in the past decade or so as a result of patterns of economic change and government policies, so that class politics is unlikely to disappear or recede completely into the background.

Secondly, new social movements are not all the same: they are by no means a homogeneous, unified social and political phenomenon. There is considerable diversity in their ideologies, their organisational styles and their political strategies: some employ conventional political channels (such as nationalist movements in mainland Britain), others use direct action (such as animal rights groups), while others use both parliamentary and extra-parliamentary strategies. Moreover, there are frequently divisions within new social movements over these matters – divisions between 'realists' and 'fundamentalists' run through green movements, feminist movements, and so on.

Thirdly, a significant factor is the response of the state and established political parties to new social movements and the strategies adopted towards them. While the reactions of the state and political parties to such challenges vary from society to society and from movement to movement, the *issue of incorporation* and *integration* faces all new social movements. Like trade unions and socialist movements in the past, they have to confront the issue of mainstream political parties taking on their concerns (such as developing 'green' policies, or creating a Minister for Women) or of being drawn into the conventional realms of politics and having to compromise on their goals, especially when their success depends on access to the state.

However, new social movements have impacted significantly by challenging and extending the boundaries of conventional politics,shaking up and broadening political agendas by politicising issues and cleavages previously uncontested, excluded or suppressed and thrusting them into the mainstream of politics. Social and cultural cleavages may exist in societies, but these only become political cleavages and conflicts if and when they are politicised. This is what has happened with nuclear energy, pollution, gender inequality, sexual discrimination, and so on. Green movements, for example, have made people more knowledgeable about the consequences of industrialism, about the dangers and threats to natural environments and other animal species and the need to protect them. They and other new social movements have politicised the issue of nuclear power and challenged the idea that its production and use is a technical matter to be decided upon by 'experts'.

So, while we may question the extent to which the political future will be solely based around the issue concerns of new social movements, we can also suggest that they are equally unlikely to be simply institutionalised and incorporated into the political mainstream, let alone simply go away. For one thing, the political responses from mainstream politicians frequently lag behind the expectations and aspirations of new social movements: for example, governments have not gone anything like as far in their policy measures as green movements demand because of what they see as the political costs of implementing environmental policies that would require considerable sacrifices and changes in life-styles. For another, policies which governments do adopt frequently generate further conflict and resistance and provoke counter-mobilisation by other movements: for example, the successes achieved by the efforts of feminist movements and others in America to win women the right to exercise choice over abortion has generated militant and often violent responses from 'pro-life' movements.

Our discussion in this section has attempted to highlight issues surrounding political identity and action, and we have sought to address the ways in which frameworks for the construction of political identities may be shaped and changed over time. It remains to be seen whether or not the decline of class politics proves to be terminal, and whether and how far the concerns and bases of identity of new social movements become centralised on the political agenda. It may well be that we are moving into an era characterised by an absence of any dominant frameworks of political identity.

Globalisation, Power and Democracy

Two simultaneous, and apparently contradictory, trends are at the heart of modern politics: *globalisation*, accompanied by *fragmentation* into small states and regions. These two trends bring dangers and challenges, as we saw earlier in this chapter. One danger is that these new nations turn to a warlike nationalism which can lead to the seizure of territory and the unilateral declaration of new states – as in the former Yugoslavia today. At worst, such fragmented *nationalism* is underpinned by racism, 'ethnic cleansing' and chronic territorial warfare. It offers a sobering corrective to any optimism about 'the new world order'. Despite such fragmentation, we are also confronted with the powerful links between societies and economies that override national boundaries. Many of the economic, political, military and ideological powers that shape our lives work across nations – and increasingly they operate on a *global* scale. The challenge is not only how to build an effective politics with enough global reach to gain control over these forces. It is also how to find some glimmering of accountability and democracy in this global politics.

Globalisation itself is nothing new. Empires of great territorial reach have an ancient history in the world. What is new is the scale and intensity of global links which shrink space and time through the speed and low cost of electronic communication and air travel. In the last few decades space, time and cost have rapidly ceased to be such great barriers, making it feasible to run global economic enterprises and make worldwide financial transactions, turning instant global communication into a routine phenomenon.

David Held is one of the foremost writers on the politics of globalisation. Held is committed to analysing and promoting the possibilities of a new form of politics and democracy which transcends the nation-state; globalisation is an opportunity as well as a threat. He provides (Held, 1993a, pp. 38–9 a clear summary of the features of globalisation as follows:

- political, economic and social activity is rapidly becoming global in scope;
- states and societies are linked in ways that are greatly intensified, and this is facilitated by rapid communication;
- people, ideas and cultural products move around, merge and influence each other more rapidly than ever before.
- military power and intelligence activity can operate on a truly global scale using high technology;
- economic activity can create globally integrated production and marketing, extending global economic activity far beyond trade (which has been worldwide for centuries);
- transnational political organisations such as the UN (United Nations), IMF (International Monetary Fund), the European Community (EU) or NATO (North Atlantic Treaty Organisation) go beyond the nation-state and its sovereignty;
- with the end of the Cold War following the collapse of European communism, the world is no longer divided into huge opposed superpower blocs. New alliances will be required.

Simultaneous integration and fragmentation

In considering these features of globalisation, we must always be clear that global linkage need *not* mean greater unity and uniformity. On the contrary, it may lead to a decentred fragmentation where no clear new structure is discernible. As Held puts it:

> **globalization can generate forces of both fragmentation and unification. By creating new patterns of transformation and change, globalization can weaken old political and economic structures without necessarily leading to the establishment of new systems of regulation. Further, the impact of global and regional processes is likely to vary under different international and national conditions – for instance, a nation's location in the international economy, its place in particular power blocs, its position with respect to awareness of political difference as much as an awareness of common identity; enhanced international communications can highlight conflicts of interest and ideology, and not merely remove obstacles to mutual understanding.**
>
> **[Held, 1993a, p. 38]**

The forces which create globalisation do not work to create uniformity or homogeneity at the national level, nor even at the immediate local level. The impact of global forces creates unevenness in development, greater inequality, increased division and difference. At the same time as workers are connected by being employed by the same multinational firm, they also become less able to act collectively to defend their interests against an employer who can always shift work somewhere else. Forces for change are distant and seemingly uncontrollable: can any form of resistance come to terms with globalised power?

Even if economic resistance seems harder than ever to pursue, *localism* or *small-scale nationalism* is paradoxically made much more possible by globalisation. It is no longer necessary for a small country such as Scotland, for example, to be self-supporting and capable of its own defence. In the past, small weak states had to rely on powerful neighbours and perhaps accept absorption into larger states (such as the United Kingdom). Now economic growth and military security depend on transnational, even global relationships. It is possible for Scotland or Ireland to use the European Community to by-pass the political and economic dominance of England. In the EU they have access to funds and important decisions (and an independent Scotland would have a voice as a member state).

Parts of the former USSR such the Baltic states have found it possible to proclaim independence – by virtue of links to wider economic and military networks. However, any small state which goes it alone assuming that globalisation will give it security may be in for some rude shocks. Fragmentation may simply leave them vulnerable, which implies new pressures for economic and military alliances with stronger states, thus leading to the formation of potentially antagonistic groupings. Much rests on the capacity of transnational organisations to recast themselves as providers of security and economic opportunity.

Towards a new cosmopolitan democracy?

Globalisation challenges the ways in which national states and democratic processes can work as the national state finds itself less able to resist external events and forces. New local, regional and nationalist movements challenge the nation-state from within, questioning the sovereignty over them which the state claims. Yet again we see the dual dynamic of internationalism and localism, linkage and fragmentation.

David Held has argued that dramatic changes in political institutions are needed to give any semblance of democracy in this new context where issues such as 'aspects of monetary management, environmental questions, elements of security, new forms of communication' cannot be controlled adequately by national governments (1993b). Held argues for strengthening transnational organisations such the European Community whilst making them much more democratically accountable through institutions like the European Parliament.

New cross-national institutions of this kind need to be created (e.g. in Southern Africa or Latin America), and also international organisations such as the World Bank need to be controlled more democratically. Held also advocates strong commitment to enhanced rights for citizens – civil, political economic and social rights – and these need to be written into national constitutions as well as being enforced by a strengthened body of international law.

Thus Held has a vision of a cosmopolitan global democratic order which would require 'the formation of an authoritative assembly of all democratic states and agencies – a reformed General Assembly of the United Nations, or a complement to it' (Held, 1993b, p. 15). This *world parliament* would become 'an authoritative international centre for the consideration and examination of pressing global issues, e.g. health and disease, food supply and distribution, the debt burden of the Third World, the instability of the hundreds of billions of dollars that circulate the globe daily, ozone depletion, and the reduction of the risks of nuclear war' (ibid.).

Held's vision is an inspiring one, and it shows how much control we lack when so much of the power and politics which affects our lives now operates at the global level. But to achieve this new global democratic order, states and their citizens will have to recognise that their local and national interests can only be served by acting collectively in larger groupings. The challenge is to sustain constructive forms of local and national identity at the same time as participating in larger international groupings and institutions. The alternative is to cease having any real influence over the global forces that shape our lives, and to face the danger of increasingly bitter local conflicts.

Conclusion: New Directions in Political Sociology

We have seen in this chapter that political sociology is currently being pulled in many directions. This is a reflection of two things: the flux and diversity of opinion within sociology today, and the rapid change and disorder in the contemporary world of politics. For both these reasons it is impossible for political sociology to cling to simple models of power in society and it is certainly not enough to focus on politics within any one society without considering wider power structures beyond the nation-state. If as sociologists we retain any normative commitment to a just and democratic society, then we must not only rethink our analysis of the present but also renew our ideas about possible futures. This renewal of political analysis and vision needs to operate simultaneously at two very different levels. At the macro level we must rethink our models of power structures in the context of globalisation and transnational politics, as we saw with Held's work in the previous section. At the micro level, by contrast, we must acknowledge the diversity of power relations and the constant renewal of political struggles in a multitude of forms. Vicious nationalist civil war is as much a part of contemporary politics as protests over animal rights. That does not mean that every power struggle is as strong or consequential as any other – we do not have to descend into total relativism about power structures. But sociology has to be acutely aware that in the contemporary world, as in the past, political identities must be defined, constructed and mobilised before they have any impact.

postmodernism
Often perceived as a cultural and aesthetic phenomenon associated with contemporary literature and the arts, it often combines apparently opposed elements to subvert meaning and fragment totality. It is characterised by a pastiche of cultural styles and elements, but implies a deeper scepticism about order and progress. Instead diversity and fragmentation are celebrated.

From power structures to power/knowledge?

Throughout this book we have seen how the models used to understand social structures in modernity have increasingly come into question. For some social theorists, especially those linked to **postmodernism**, the very notion of large-scale *macro* structures has come under serious attack. For example, Foucault's conception of power demands that we approach it in a *micro* way, seeing power present in all social relationships and working in specific ways in all kinds of particular institutional settings – whether the prison or the clinic (this is discussed in detail in other chapters, especially Chapter 15, 'Theorising Modern Family Life', and Chapter 18, 'Making Social Life'). For Foucault, we must explore the intimate relationship between power and knowledge, as bodies of ideas become established and put into practice as powerful discourses. It follows that notions like 'ruling class domination' simply obscure the micro-realities of power (Smart, 1983) where power has a 'net-like' structure linking all sorts of different social positions in different intersecting ways.

For example, an expectant mother has a possible dependent relationship to medical staff and a potentially dominant relationship to the child once born. But the actual nature of these power relationships will change as social discourses change concerning parenting and patient–doctor relations. Indeed, this could be a site of political pressure if women form a movement (such as the National Childbirth Trust) to challenge dominant philosophies of maternity provision. Foucault's ideas fit very well with the shift towards diverse non-economic political struggles. When feminists demonstrate that 'the personal is political' then sociologists must examine seriously power and domination in the family, as well as the 'control of bodies' through powerful discourses, whether in medicine or in advertising. These power relationships, and the struggles relating to them, do not fit into any neat hierarchical model of the power structure – hence Foucault's image of the 'net'. Whether such conceptions of power/knowledge can be made compatible with longer-established approaches to power such as Marxism is a matter for debate among political sociologists, and this debate is part of the wider disputes over modernity and postmodernism explored throughout this book.

Understanding a changing political world

Sociologists today face the challenge of understanding a highly complex and apparently fragmented political world. It never was enough to focus on social groups and their interests within one nation-state. We have to look beyond the forms of power which cut across societies and shape them from outside: whether this power is from international capitalism, military blocs, or global commercial culture (Chapter 3, 'Globalisation and Modernity' explores these issues). Even when we do look within one society to consider social groups and their politics, we find a multitude of issues and interests at stake. Many of these concerns are themselves global in scope: environmentalism, concern over nuclear weapons or poverty in less-developed economies, for example.

What we clearly cannot do is construct a simple model of the social structure within one society and deduce the interests and politics of social groups from that. The social world is much more complex than that – which makes things interesting and unpredictable, but also makes sociological explanations hard to come by. One assumption of political sociology is overdue for revision: we cannot focus solely on power within single societies, taking for granted that these societies have boundaries which coincide with the legal nation-state. As we have suggested earlier in this chapter, our world of separate nation-states is a very recent creation, and power relations certainly do not stop at national boundaries. Sociology has unforgivably neglected war and international power relations in describing societies – a remarkable failing in the face of the twentieth century's history of technologically sophisticated bloodshed. At the present time we see remarkable transformations in world politics as the Cold War divide in the West collapses along with communism, and as new nation-states struggle to establish themselves in a very disorderly new world.

Just as the great political blocs break up, we see powerful moves to greater global interdependence and dominance through economic expansion and the shrinking of barriers to travel and communication. The huge forces for global connection go together with strong tendencies to fragmentation – and both seem invulnerable to the familiar forms of politics and government with the nation-state.

Thus political sociologists face the challenge of making sense of a dramatically changed political world – both within societies, with diverse interests and struggles, and across societies with the forces of globalisation and fragmentation:

- New forms of politics within societies have redefined the issues and redefined political interests on a non-class basis. Many of these issues are global in scope, such as environmentalism, or opposition to racist regimes.
- We see a revival of forms of politics which liberals and Marxists both expected to wither away – racism, expansionist nationalism and fundamentalist religious movements.
- The global interdependence of nations is greatly increased; global economic structures (including commercialised culture) transcend national boundaries and increase the need for new transnational forms of politics.
- Globalisation brings with it forms of power – economic, political and cultural – which go beyond the effective control of national states, let alone individual citizens.

- Communist regimes have collapsed and the state-socialist model is discredited in favour of capitalism. Socialist politics based on trade unions and economic interests is seriously weakened within most capitalist societies.
- The renewed arms race of the 1980s highlighted political sociology's neglect of war and military power, especially as opposition to nuclear bombs and power stations grew massively as a social movement. However, the end of superpower rivalry after the collapse of communism has also left political sociologists wondering how to analyse a disorderly new world.

Summary

- Political sociology pays attention to power in society.
- Power is an element in all social relations, but political sociology focuses on social divisions that have been mobilised into political divisions – especially, but not only, economic classes.
- This focus on social power must also show how power in society relates to power in the state institutions through which politicians govern.
- There has been long debate between those who see power as highly concentrated (e.g. in a dominant class) and those who see power as distributed widely across many different groups and settings.
- Political interests and action are not static and given. Ideologies and structural changes play an important part in defining and re-defining political identities.
- Policies pursued by governments may have an impact on society which changes the lives and experiences of people, altering the potential social and political divisions in society.
- Political sociologists have attempted to trace and account for changes in the relationships between social class and politics and to evaluate the historical and current significance of class politics and class-based political identities.
- A distinctive feature of contemporary politics has been the emergence of new social movements, appealing to bases of identity other than class location.
- The pace of change in the contemporary world is so great that we can expect a degree of flux in politics, with new issues and interests emerging.
- Power is both local and global. We can expect to see more transnational political initiatives, but also more diverse local struggles. The future of

democracy and political accountability in this new world seems fragile and uncertain.

References

Bachrach, P. and M. Baratz (1963) 'Decisions and non-decisions', *American Political Science Review*, vol. 57.

Bosanquet, N. (1983) *After the New Right*, London, Heinemann.

Butler, D. and D. Kavanagh (1984) *The British General Election of 1983*, London, Macmillan.

Coates, D. (1984) *The Context of British Politics*, London, Hutchinson.

Crewe, I. (1992) 'The changing basis of party choice 1979–1992', *Politics Review*, September.

Crewe, I. *et al.*, (1977) 'Partisan Dealignment in Britain 1964–74', *British Journal of Political Science*, vol. 7, pp. 129–90.

Dahl. R. A. (1985) *A Preface to Economic Democracy*, Cambridge, Polity Press.

Dahl. R. A. (1989) *Democracy and its Critics*, New Haven, Yale University Press.

Dahl, R. A. and C. Lindblom (1976) *Politics, Economics and Welfare*, Chicago, Chicago University Press.

Dunleavy, P. and C. Husbands (1985) *British Democracy at the Crossroads*, London, George Allen & Unwin.

Edgell, S. and V. Duke (1991) *A Measure of Thatcherism*, London, Harper-Collins.

Evans, P. R. *et al.* (eds) (1985) *Bringing the State Back In*, Cambridge, Cambridge University Press.

Fukuyama, F. (1989) 'The end of history?', *The National Interest*, no. 16.

Gamble, A. (1988) *The Free Economy and the Strong State*, London, Macmillan.

Giddens, A. (1985) *The Nation-State and Violence*, Cambridge, Polity Press.

Giddens, A. (1990) 'Modernity and Utopia', *New Statesman and Society*, 2 November, pp. 20–2.

Goldthorpe, J. (1978) 'The Current Inflation: Towards a Sociological Account', in J. Goldthorpe and F. Hirsch (eds), *The Political Economy of Inflation*, London, Martin Robertson.

Goldthorpe, J. (1988) 'Intellectuals and the Working Class in Modern Britain', in D. Rose (ed.), *Social Stratification and Economic Change*, London, Hutchinson.

Goldthorpe, J. *et al.* (1969) *The Affluent Worker in the Class Structure*, Cambridge, Cambridge University Press.

Hall, S. (1978) 'The great moving right show', *Marxism Today*, December, reprinted in Hall (1988).

Hall, S. (1988) *The Hard Road to Renewal*, London, Verso.

Hall, S. and M. Jacques (1983) *The Politics of Thatcherism*, London, Lawrence & Wishart.

Held, D. (ed.) (1993a) *Prospects for Democracy*, Cambridge, Polity Press.

Held, D. (1993b) *Democracy and the New International Order*, London, Institute for Public Policy Research.

Inglehart, R. (1977) *The Silent Revolution: Changing Values and Political Styles among Western Publics*, Princeton, New Jersey, Princeton University Press.

Jessop, B. (1982) *The Capitalist State*, Oxford, Martin Robertson.

Jessop, B., K. Bonnett, S. Bromley and T. Ling (1988) *Thatcherism*, Cambridge, Polity Press.

King, D. (1987) *The New Right*, London, Macmillan.

Kriesi, H. *et al.* (1995) *New Social Movements in Western Europe: Comparative Perspectives*, London, University College London Press.

Levitas, R. (1985) *The Ideology of the New Right*, Cambridge, Polity Press.

Lukes, S. (1974) *Power: A Radical View*, London, Macmillan.

Mann, M. (1986) *The Sources of Social Power*, Vol. 1, Cambridge, Cambridge University Press.

Marsh, D. and R.A.W. Rhodes (1992) *Implementing Thatcherite Policies*, Buckingham, Open University Press.

Marx, K. and F. Engels (1968) *Selected Works*, London, Lawrence & Wishart.

Miliband, R. (1968) *The State in Capitalist Society*, London, Weidenfeld & Nicolson.

Moore, B. (1967) *Social Origins of Dictatorship and Democracy*, London, Allen Lane.

Poggi, G.(1978) *The Development of the Modern State*, London, Hutchinson.

Poulantzas, N. (1978) *State, Power, Socialism*, London, Verso.

Rueschemeyer, D. *et al.* (1992) *Capitalist Development and Democracy*, Cambridge, Polity Press.

Savage, S. P. and R. Robins (1990) *Public Policy Under Thatcher*, London, Macmillan.

Scott, J. (1982) *The Upper Class*, London, Macmillan.

Scott, J. (1991) *Who Rules Britain?*, Cambridge, Polity Press.

Smart, B. (1983) *Foucault, Marxism and Critique*, London, Routledge.

Taylor-Gooby, P. (1986) 'Privatisation, Public Opinion and the Welfare State', *Sociology*, vol. 20, pp. 228–46.

Therborn, G. (1976) 'The rule of capital and the rise of democracy', *New Left Review*, 103.

Touraine, A. (1971) *The Post-Industrial Society*, New York, Random House.

Worsley P. (1964) 'The distribution of power in industrial societies', in P. Halmos (ed.), *The Development of Industrial Societies*, Sociological Review monograph No. 8.

Dimensions of Contemporary Social Life

11 Education

Aims of the Chapter

This chapter explores central sociological issues in education. We consider the changing social context of education, including the major policy shifts of recent decades. We examine debates about the social nature of the curriculum, and about the relationship of education to the labour market and to social inequality. In addition, we document the ways that class, race, ethnicity and gender are reflected in educational outcomes. Finally, the chapter compares a range of sociological explanations for patterns of educational success and failure, from explanations that focus upon 'natural' differences, and those that target the schools, to accounts that explore how pupils use education in the formation of their own identities.

Introduction

When we think about 'education' in the modern world, we readily conjure up a vision of pupils waiting their turn for the big scissors, revising anxiously for a biology test or 'having a laff' with friends when teacher's back is turned. Through our shared experience of schooling in the modern world, we have a taken-for-granted picture of what education is.

And yet, features that seem integral to schooling today were hotly contested during the nineteenth century. In Leeds, for example, proposals to divide according to age provoked lively resistance; parents retorted that pupils should remain in family groupings (Frith, 1977). In Scottish fishing villages, parents agitated to keep schools closed during the fishing season so that pupils could devote themselves to bait collecting; attempts to make attendance at school compulsory were unpopular with families whose standards of living depended partly on children's labour (Paterson, 1988).

Case studies such as these are not mere historical curiosities. Rather, they tell us things of significance about schooling in the modern world. They remind us, first, that the content and process of schooling is never self-evident. It is subject always to contestation by groups with different agendas to assert and conflicting views of education's purpose. Second, these examples touch upon the key role of education in attempts by the state to consolidate economic change. And third, these case studies signal the importance of schooling not only in terms of skills and knowledge but also in the construction of identities. The proliferation in the modern world of delicately-graded age identities – with the interests of six-year-olds, say, quite sharply differentiated from those of children aged eight – owes a great deal to mass education. Moreover, while children in Scottish fishing villages in the early part of the nineteenth century saw themselves as workers *and* pupils, state-regulated schooling helped to define such children as 'deviant pupils' from 'problem families' (Paterson, 1988). Education has contributed to the construction of 'pupil' and 'worker' as incompatible identities.

Educational Policy and Educational Reform

Dominant views as to the proper purpose of education vary from one society to another: in a new and ethnically diverse nation, education could be a tool for forging a common national identity; in a society undergoing rapid economic development, education could be a vehicle for preparing people for new urban and industrial rhythms of life; in a revolutionary society, education might be directed towards winning hearts and minds to the revolutionary cause.

The period since the Second World War has been marked by two competing, though equally emphatic, perspectives on the nature and purposes of education: in the early post-war decades, 'equal opportunities' was the watchword; in the 1980s and 1990s, 'employability' moved to the fore. It is worth examining more closely these different views.

Before the Second World War, education in Britain was, on the whole, unashamedly gender-biased and class-confirming. In the words of A.H. Halsey (1977, p. 176), education was 'the stamp put on the social character of individuals whose jobs and life-styles were predetermined by social origin'.

meritocracy
A democratic system based on the allocation of position or occupation according to merit.

By contrast, the new education that was shaped in the shadow of the war was heralded as a ladder of opportunity up which working-class children could climb. Equal opportunities in education were seen as the key to a more open society – a **meritocracy**, in which people could move freely up or down the occupational heirarchy according to personal merit. In a meritocracy, the education system would ensure that individuals were allocated to a station befitting their ability; being born into a humble home would be no barrier to success, and being born into a wealthy or powerful family, no cushion against failure.

This perspective underpinned a number of policies that broadened educational access. The 1944 Education Act entitled all children for the first time to a secondary education. The expansion of educational provision through the raising of the minimum school-leaving age (to 15 years in 1947, to 16 years in 1971–72), and through the expansion of the university and polytechnic system, was dramatic enough to warrant the term 'educational explosion'. By 1970, 18 per cent of 18-year-olds were in full-time education, compared with 3 per cent in 1938.

Along with the widening of access went other changes. Arguments for equal opportunities fuelled the movement from a system of secondary education where pupils were divided on the basis of tests and references between grammar schools, secondary modern schools, and in some areas, technical schools (a bi-partite or tri-partite system) towards a comprehensive system of secondary education. Arguments for equal opportunities also played a part in shifting the curriculum of primary schools towards a child-centred model, in which the pace of learning was more closely geared to the current interests and capacities of each individual pupil.

But perhaps the dominant theme in the educational philosophy of the 1950s and 1960s was a widespread belief in the positive power of education. Education was more than a means to individual advancement: it was seen often as the solution to social problems such as delinquency or poverty, and as the key to a more civilised, more democratic and more prosperous society. Some such faith was manifest, for example, in international aid programmes, where development money was channelled into establishing education systems – in Ghana, for example – modelled on those of richer northern countries. At home, politicians were committed to more education for the nation, and many parents clamoured for better education for their offspring. In the liberal philosophy that drove the development of British education in the post-war period, education was seen as a Good Thing.

This liberal philosophy later became the subject of an energetic critique. Critics, most vociferously those from the **New Right**, claimed that British education was a failure: it was accused of being financially profligate, overly influenced by faddish educational theory, and insufficiently attentive to the wishes of parents; above all, it was said to be ineffective at preparing children for work in a competitive world economy.

New Right

A strand of right-wing Conservatism, which is primarily concerned with the non-interference of the State into economic and business affairs and the realm of individual autonomy. Although the state is seen as coercive in limiting individual freedom, a strong element of moral conservatism often exists in New Right thinking.

National Curriculum

A standardised educational course of study taught in British State schools as specified by the Department for Education.

It is with these criticisms in mind that Conservative governments began after 1979 to initiate sweeping changes. In primary and secondary schools, key elements of the reform were the specification of a **National Curriculum**, the introduction of tests of basic skills and knowledge throughout pupils' school careers, and arrangements to make the results of testing more widely known. Concern for equal opportunities gave way to anxiety about standards and assessment.

The reforms also included: the devolution of budgets, so that individual schools rather than local authorities became accountable for effective use of resources; emphasis on consumer choice for parents; incentives for private education; and provisions to ensure greater parental and business involvement in the government of schools. What these disparate elements have in common is their connection to a set of educational priorities very different from those of the 1950s and 1960s.

So, for example, several measures, such as the pressure applied to universities to obtain more of their funding from corporations, were designed to forge a closer relationship between business and education. If in the 1950s and 1960s, British education was often judged according to its success in providing equal opportunities, in the 1980s and 1990s the criteria of success has been 'employability': do the schools and colleges produce school-leavers and graduates with the type of skills that industry specifies? Do they pursue the types of knowledge that corporations desire? Moreover, during the 1980s and 1990s, schools and universities, like hospitals and primary health care centres, have been enjoined to take the operation of the free market as their model. Local management of schools, and provisions for parental choice, were intended to make schools operate more like businesses, on the assumption that competition between schools and the operation of **a free market** system within education would promote greater efficiency and wider choice for the consumer.

free market

A form of trade or business environment free from outside interference or restrictions.

But at the same time that competition and consumer choice became educational watchwords, more and more aspects of the educational curriculum were brought under the direct control of the state. From 1944 onwards, centralisation had proceeded slowly, reversing the trend of the previous eighty years. After 1979, centralisation speeded up dramatically, culminating with the 1988 Education Reform Act. This legislation not only specified the nature of the core curriculum that state schools would be required to teach but provided also a legal basis for centrally prescribed attainment targets, programmes of study and testing. It may seem contradictory that such a far-reaching programme of government intervention was instituted by Conservative governments that prided themselves on rolling back the state and encouraging individual freedom of choice. But as Kirk (1989) explains, antagonism to local government (for whom education had been the major area of responsibility), plus hostility to the teaching profession (whose constancy of purpose in the 1985–86 industrial dispute shook the government of the day) combined to make intervention attractive. But even more than that, Conservative governments, confronted with a stubborn recession and rising rates of unemployment, hoped that education and training, properly and rapidly reformed, would provide the quality of labour needed to revive the economy.

In describing the shifts in educational philosophy – from education for the sake of a fairer society, to education for the economy, from equal opportunities and child-centred learning to unequal assessments and common standards – the discontinuities in educational policy over the period since 1944 have been highlighted. This helps to demonstrate the point underlined at the beginning of the chapter, that the purpose of education is never simply self-evident. It is always open to debate.

But some commentators have been at pains to show that there are substantial continuities between the educational programmes of the early and the later post-war decades. The book *Unpopular Education*, for example, argued that the enthusiasm for equal opportunities of the 1950s and 1960s entailed a commitment to forms of selectivity and hierarchy, to educational failure for many children, and to the use of education less to inform than to select and categorise (Centre for Contemporary Cultural Studies, 1981). From this point of view, it has been suggested that the emphasis on standards and testing and selectivity that characterises the Educational Reform Act of 1988 is not such a departure from the spirit of the 1944 Education Act as it may at first glance appear (Griggs, 1989).

functionalism
A theoretical perspective, associated with Durkheim and Parsons, based on an analogy between social systems and organic systems. It claims that the character of a society's various institutions must be understood in terms of the function each performs in enabling the smooth running of society as a whole.

conflict perspective
A theoretical approach, such as Marxism, focusing on the notion that society is based on an unequal distribution of advantage and is characterised by a conflict of interests between the advantaged and the disadvantaged.

The Social Context of Education

The growth of educational provision throughout the 1950s and 1960s was paralleled by an explosion of research within the sociology of education. The bulk of this research was aimed at monitoring effects of educational expansion on equality of opportunity, and much of it was informed by a **functionalist perspective** (see Chapter 4). However, from the 1970s, many writers in the sociology of education found an alternative **conflict perspective** useful for analysing the place of education in modern society. As the discussion below suggests, these perspectives draw upon similar bodies of data concerning the relationship between education, the economy and social equality, but interpret them in radically different ways.

A structural-functionalist account

From a structural-functionalist perspective, the changes connected with industrialism give rise to specific 'functional imperatives' –

needs which must be met if any society is to survive and prosper. The education system performs three vital functions on behalf of society.

First, the education system helps to develop the human resources of an industrial nation. In pre-industrial society, the range of 'occupations' is limited, and new recruits can usually learn to do a job adequately by working alongside skilled practitioners. But industrialisation brings with it marked changes in the occupational structure. New, highly specialised occupations emerge; mechanisation reduces the number of jobs requiring sheer muscle power; new forms of technology necessitate higher levels of human judgement and expertise; and there is an increased need for white-collar, technical, professional and managerial workers. Educational expansion is seen in functionalist analysis as a direct response to the general technical requirements of industrial production – the need for a labour force in which skills and talents are developed to the full, and matched to the complexity of jobs in a modern industrialised world.

Second, the fact that industrial societies have a plurality of occupations, with varied levels of skill, necessitates a sophisticated mechanism to select individuals according to their talents and train them for the jobs they can most effectively fill. Education therefore has a vital selection or allocative function. As well as developing pupils' talents, schools and universities use grades, reports and references to evaluate their performance. Educational results are used by employers to select the most able candidates for jobs. Education determines, through its selection function, who will be allocated to humdrum occupations, and who to the more rewarding posts. The selection of individuals through the education system ensures, more or less, that those who come to occupy the more desirable jobs are those who deserve them on the basis of their greater attainments and, presumably, their greater capacity.

Third, it is argued from a functionalist perspective that schooling contributes to social cohesion, by transmitting to new generations the central values of society. A standardised curriculum exposes all pupils – whether their parents are Jamaican, Irish or Polish, whether they are working class, middle class or upper class – to their 'common cultural heritage'; in British schools, for example, British political institutions will be introduced, and 'fundamental values', such as honesty, individualism, or a respect for parliamentary democracy will be emphasised. The transmission of a common heritage through education ensures fundamental agreement on basic values despite the fact that there are dramatic differences in the circumstances of people's lives.

Although the functionalist approach dominated the analysis of education in the early post-war decades, since the 1970s it has come under attack from several quarters. The assumptions on which it is based appear to be highly problematic. First, the degree of 'fit' between the skills taught in school, and the technical requirements of efficient production, is far from clear; most pupils know only too well that much of the material on which they are examined – be it algebra or Latin, R.E. or human biology – has little direct connection with the tasks that face them when they enter employment. Educational certificates may make you eligible for certain jobs, but they do not necessarily make you proficient. Critics from the New Right have focused strongly on the charge that schools and colleges fail to prepare people for jobs.

Second, though schools do undoubtedly sort pupils into successes or failures, it is not clear whether this selection is related to the intellectual merit of the pupils themselves, or to **ascriptive characteristics** such as their ethnic or social class backgrounds, or their sex. Some would argue that rather than acting as neutral selection agents indifferent to the background of pupils, schools, in the main, confirm pupils in the status to which they were born.

ascriptive characteristics
Traits or characteristics that are inherited (e.g age, colour, sex, height), rather than being the result of personal achievement.

Third, the notion of a common cultural heritage is difficult to sustain. Would the values and ideas promoted by the schools be equally endorsed by all sectors of society? Many **content analyses** of curricular materials show racist, ethnic, social class and sexist biases; moreover, it can be argued that the values and knowledge selected for transmission within schools will be more familiar, and more beneficial, to some groups in society than to others. Within sociology, a renewed emphasis upon the curriculum in recent years has replaced the notion of 'transmission of core culture' with a series of questions: How is it that, out of all the knowledge, ideas and values that are available in a society, only certain ones are selected? What are the criteria behind the selection of partial curricula? Which groups in society benefit most from a particular selection of knowledge?

content analysis
The analysis of the content of communication; usually refers to documentary or visual material.

A conflict account: correspondence theory

Partly in response to growing dissatisfaction with functionalist theory, many analysts turned to conflict perspectives in search of a more adequate account of the relationship between education, the economy and society. One of the best-known conflict models is that proposed by Bowles and Gintis, in *Schooling in Capitalist America* (1976). Like the functionalists, they see an intimate link between schooling and the economy; but, unlike the functionalists, Bowles and Gintis claim that it is the requirements of industrial **capitalism**, rather than the general needs of industrialism, which shape the educational system.

capitalism
An economic system in which the means of production are privately owned and organised to accumulate profits within a market framework, in which labour is provided by waged workers.

The social relations of production under capitalism are characterised, Bowles and Gintis emphasise, by rigid hierarchies of authority (from directors to unskilled manual workers) and by fragmentation of tasks. Apart from a minority of professionals and executives, most workers perform mundane tasks allowing little scope for initiative, responsibility or judgement. Because of the hierarchical pattern of work, and of its fragmentation, most people have minimal control over what they do and how they do it. The explanation for this lies not in the demands of technology itself, but in the capitalist need to control workers more closely in the interest of profit.

Bowles and Gintis argue that schooling operates within the 'long shadow of work': that is, the education system reflects the organisation of production in capitalist society. For example, the fragmentation of work processes is mirrored in the breaking-up of the curriculum into packages of knowledge, each subject divorced from all others; lack of control over work is reflected in the powerlessness of pupils with regard to what they will learn in school or how they will learn it; and the necessity of doing unfulfilling jobs for pay is paralleled by the emphasis in schools on learning for grades, rather than learning for its own sake. Therefore, Bowles and Gintis claim, there is a *correspondence* between the nature of work in capitalist societies, and the nature of schooling.

While stressing those aspects of schooling that inhibit independence of mind, Bowles and Gintis (1976, p. 42) also point out that schools are not uniform: 'But schools do different things to different children. Boys and girls, blacks and whites, rich and poor are treated differently. Affluent suburban schools, working-class schools, and ghetto schools all exhibit a distinctive pattern.'

streams
Within a school, the division of cohorts into separate classes that are ranked according to perceived ability, e.g. lower stream, upper stream.

For example, in schools (or **streams**, or tracks) that cater largely for working-class children, the emphasis may be placed on obedience and rule-following; pupils may be closely supervised, and subjected to the same sort of discipline, which they will experience later in factories or shops. In schools that cater for the privileged, the emphasis will be on encouraging leadership qualities for a future elite. Thus, the emphasis in Bowles and Gintis's account is on the personality characteristics – particularly patterns of authority and control – that the schools foster and reward.

They also stress that capitalist societies are characterised by persistent inequality and by relationships of subordination and domination between social classes. Inequalities cannot be explained, they argue, by reference to the distribution of intelligence; instead, inequalities are the

means of production

A Marxist concept which refers to the raw materials, land, labour and tools required for the production of goods.

inevitable result of capitalist relations of production, in which the **means of production** are privately owned and all other people must compete in the market-place to earn a living. Thus class inequality is a necessary feature not of all societies, but of capitalist societies. Schools play an active part in reproducing inequality across generations by moulding pupils to slot into their place in a labour force that is divided along lines of social class, gender and ethnicity.

At the same time that education creates the conditions for the reproduction of inequality, it also helps to legitimate that inequality: that is, education helps to justify in people's minds a system of inequality, and to reconcile them to their own position within it. How does schooling do this? As long as most people believe that education gives everyone a fair chance to prove their worth and as long as privilege and disadvantage are widely believed to stem from fair competition in the educational arena, then inequality may appear to be justified by different levels of educational attainment. The successful ones view their privileges as a well-deserved reward for ability and effort, while subordinate groups are encouraged to personalise their failure: they are encouraged, that is, to treat poverty or powerlessness as the inevitable result of their own individual limitations – lack of intelligence, ambition or effort.

While correspondence theory contains a vivid analysis of relationships between education, the economy and social equality, many sociologists of education have been critical of this account. Three issues in particular give rise to doubts.

First, the tendency to see all aspects of the education system as oppressive will not do. Many ordinary people are keen to get an education, for its effects in broadening the mind as well as for its occupational returns; are they merely duped in their enthusiasm, or are there aspects of the curriculum and of the educational process that are liberating or fulfilling? Some aspects of education reflect reforms won through the efforts of working-class people, community groups, feminists and others. The campaigns and negotiations that led to the development of our current educational system involved compromises some of which, in the words of Apple (1988, p. 123), 'signify victory, not losses' for the majority.

Second, Bowles and Gintis concentrate on social class to the neglect of other forms of inequality. They do not consider the part played by education in structuring race and gender.

Third, it is doubtful whether the concept of 'correspondence' is adequate to describe the relationship between education and its social context. The notion that the education system reproduces economic relations and class inequalities automatically, through correspondence, is rejected by many other writers from the conflict tradition who see education's part in the reproduction of inequalities as involving challenge and negotiation, a process that is far from automatic.

A brief comparison of functionalist and correspondence theory

macro-level
A level of sociological analysis which focuses either on large collectivities and institutions or social systems and social structures (*see* structures).

The two competing perspectives that have been outlined above have, in fact, certain weaknesses in common. As structural approaches, both emphasise the **macro-level** of analysis – the relationship between education and other social institutions – and devote relatively little attention to the dynamic interactions of teachers and pupils in schools. Both approaches tend to give enormous weight to the power of education to shape pupils' minds and their lives; the functionalist vision of pupils who eagerly display their newly acquired technical skills would be as unrecognisable to many secondary teachers as Bowles and Gintis's vision of pupils who have been moulded into conformity. Both accounts concentrate more on the structure of education than on its content, and yet, as Moore (1988) points out, the education system is the principal site in our society for the generation of knowledge and of frameworks for understanding and this activity of knowledge-production may be more important than education's role in servicing the labour force. Finally, both functionalist and correspondence accounts have been criticised for positing too tight a fit between education and the economy, and for exaggerating the extent to which schools act as providers of a ready, willing and able supply of labour (Moore, 1984).

But if functionalist and correspondence approaches share certain weaknesses, they differ radically in the way they conceive of the relationship between education and inequality. As Karabel and Halsey (1977, p. 35) explain: 'where functionalists have often viewed the educational system as offering opportunities for mobility for individuals, conflict theorists have generally stressed the role of education in maintaining a system of structured social inequality'.

This review of structural-functionalist and correspondence theories suggests three themes about the social context of education that deserve closer scrutiny: education and the labour market, education and inequality, and the social nature of the curriculum.

Education, work and the labour market

In Britain in the nineteenth century, the key argument made in favour of education stressed its civilising impact – the potential of education to

Table 11.1 *Participation of 16–18-year-olds in education and training[1]: by age and type of study, international comparison, 1988*

Country (and minimum leaving age)	*16 years*	*16 to 18 years*		
	Full-time %	*Full-time* %	*Part-time* %	*All[2]* %
United Kingdom (16)[3]	53	36	33	69
Belgium (14)	92	82	4	86
Denmark (16)	90	79	–	79
France (16)	82	73	8	81
Germany, Fed. Rep. (15)	71	49	43	92
Italy (14)	54	47	18	65
Netherlands (16)	93	77	9	86
Spain (16)	68	58	–	58
Australia (15)	76	52	17	69
Canada (16/17)	100	77	–	77
Japan (15)	93	84	3	87
Sweden (16)	84	73	–	73
USA (16–18)[4]	95	80	1	81

Source: Dept for Education, *Social Trends 23*, London, HMSO, 1993, Table 3.16, p. 44.
[1] Includes apprenticeships, YT and similar schemes.
[2] Includes higher education for some 18-year-olds.
[3] Includes estimates for: those studying in the evening; for those in private-sector further and higher education.
[4] Minimum leaving age varies between states.

create committed and compliant citizens. Specific skills were sometimes encouraged – as when, for example, training in laundering and housewifery began to figure prominently in the education of working-class girls (Davin, 1987) – but, on the whole, schooling was seen less as a programme of labour force preparation and more as a vehicle for moral instruction.

Education's role in promoting economic growth and efficiency has, however, often been invoked during the twentieth century and especially during the past two decades. In 1976, the Labour Prime Minister Jim Callaghan initiated a 'Great Debate' about education, a focus of which was the alleged unpreparedness of school-leavers for employment. Since then, education has frequently been blamed for failing to provide the discipline and the technical skills which would fit young people for the labour force, and the rise of youth unemployment from the 1970s onwards appeared to lend substance to this claim.

In the context of rising youth unemployment, successive governments have trumpeted the necessity to make education a servant of the economy.

The Youth Opportunities Programme, established in the 1970s, and the Youth Training Scheme that replaced it in the 1980s, were designed ostensibly to provide the training and work experience that young people lacked. The state – by, for example, assigning responsibility for the education and training of 16–19-year-olds to the Manpower Services Commission – has taken a more direct hand in managing the transition from school to work.

Does it make sense to blame the lack of competitiveness of the British economy on the shortcomings of the schools? It is certainly true that the workforce of the United Kingdom is less well qualified than that of other industrial countries. As Table 11.1 indicates, the UK comes off badly in international comparisons. In 1988, only 36 per cent of 16 to 18-year-olds in the UK were in full-time education or training, compared with 84 per cent in Japan, 77 per cent in the Netherlands or 58 per cent in Spain.

On the other hand, there is little evidence that educational shortcomings are at the root of youth unemployment. Educational qualifications play only a small part in Britain in the recruitment of new workers. Employers often, for example, prefer older workers, hoping to capitalise on their experience, and gambling on the fact that, with homes to keep up and children to support, older workers may be more stable (Moore, 1989). Studies of the labour market suggest that the crisis of youth unemployment is due not to lack of employable skills, but to the wider collapse of the job market itself (Coffield *et al.*, 1989).

The emphasis upon training youth for work has been interpreted by many writers as an attempt to divert attention away from the deep-seated changes in the economy which generate unemployment, and for which education cannot possibly offer a remedy (Clarke and Willis, 1984; Rees and Gregory, 1981). Finn (1987) goes so far as to argue that some of these measures have been designed less to solve unemployment, than to conceal it.

In thinking about the relationship between education and the economy, the empirical question of whether or not schools successfully prepare children for the world of work is not the only one to consider. Bailey (1989) puts forward the more challenging question of whether education ought to give the highest priority to job training; what would be the implications instead of an educational system that was designed to develop people's capacity to be creative, to approach with interest and understanding the physical and social world in which they live?

Table 11.2 *Highest qualification level attained[1]: by socio-economic group of father, 1990–1, Great Britain (percentages)*

Qualification level	*Professional*	*Employers and managers*	*Intermediate and junior non-manual*	*Skilled manual and own account non-professional*	*Semi-skilled manual and and personal service*	*Unskilled manual*	*Total*
Degree	32	17	17	6	4	3	10
Higher education	19	15	18	10	7	5	11
A level	15	13	12	8	6	4	9
O level	19	24	24	21	19	15	21
CSE	4	9	7	12	12	10	10
Foreign	4	4	4	3	2	2	3
No qualification	7	19	18	40	50	60	35
Total	100	100	100	100	100	100	100

[1] Persons aged 25–59 not in full-time eucation.

Source: *Social Trends 23*, London, HMSO, 1993, table 3.26, p. 48.

Education and social inequality

As emphasised earlier, education was seen in the 1950s and 1960s as an instrument for severing outmoded links between social origins and adult success. The evidence on this issue is, however, far from reassuring. Although more and more people have had experience of extended education, educational achievement continues to be systematically linked to social background. The proportion of adults who possessed a degree at the beginning of the 1990s ranged from 32 per cent for those whose fathers were professionals, to 6 per cent or less for men and women whose fathers were in manual or personal service work.

Halsey, Heath and Ridge (1980), whose study *Origins and Destinations* reconstructed the educational careers of 8,529 men, concluded that the expansion of secondary and higher education in the 1950s and 1960s did little to iron out social class differentials; it may, in fact, have benefited middle-class people more than their working-class fellows. They found a pattern of unequal access to the more prestigious secondary schools that had remained – in spite of the educational reforms of the post-war era – 'depressingly constant over time' (Halsey, Heath and Ridge, 1980, p. 203). Class inequality grew more severe as pupils moved up the educational ladder. For example, a boy from the service class, compared with a working class boy, had:

- 4 times more chance of being in school at age 16
- 10 times more chance of being in school at age 18
- 11 times more chance of entering university.

Origins and Destinations is locked within a tradition, characteristic of social research in the first two post-war decades, that monitored progress (or not) towards equality of opportunity only in terms of social class. In recent years, the impact of race, ethnicity and gender on educational achievement has also begun to receive the attention it deserves.

Box 11.1: Meritocracy in post-war Britain?

By comparing the oldest cohort of men in their sample with the youngest and most recently educated cohort, the authors of *Origins and Destinations* refute the idea that the working class may have 'caught up' with other groups. Class differentials in educational attainment do not appear even to have narrowed, let alone equalised, over time.

During the period being analysed, the proportion of working-class boys entering university increased by 2 per cent, but that of boys from the 'intermediate class' (clerical workers, small proprietors, foremen) and from the service class increased by 6 per cent and 9 per cent respectively. The expansion of university places resulted in greater absolute gains for middle-class than for working-class men; differentials between the classes were preserved. Halsey and his colleagues (1980, p. 210) conclude: 'the 1944 Education Act brought England and Wales no nearer to the ideal of a meritocratic society...Secondary education was made free in order to enable the poor to take advantage of it, but the paradoxical consequence was to increase subsidies to the affluent.'

This conclusion is all the more persuasive because it is consistent with a range of other investigations, not only in Britain but in other countries as well. While there is, as we shall shortly see, disagreement about the *explanation* for persistent social class inequality in education, the *fact* of that inequality is not in dispute. Education's role as a promoter of social mobility for the working classes has been outstripped by its effectiveness in confirming the privileged location of children from middle-class homes.

An inquiry set up to investigate the education of children from ethnic minorities in British schools concluded: 'Whatever the reasons, and they are certainly complex, West Indian children are not doing at all well in the educational system' (Swann Report, 1985, p. 60). Among the data that impressed the Committee was a survey of pupils leaving school in five areas in 1981/82. This appeared to show the relative failure in school of pupils who originated from the West Indies. Only 6 per cent of school-leavers of West Indian origin, compared with 17 per cent of those from Asian backgrounds and 19 per cent of other leavers, got five or more higher grades at CSE or O level; only 5 per cent got one pass or more at A level, compared with 13 per cent of Asian school-leavers and 13 per cent of those from the ethnic majority; and only 2 per cent of West Indian school-leavers, compared with 9 per cent of Asians or 9 per cent of those from the ethnic majority, went on to a full-time degree course in polytechnic or university (Swann Report, 1985, ch. 3, Annexe B).

We should, however, be cautious about accepting Swann's conclusions too readily, and even more cautious about notions that ethnic minority pupils or black and Asian pupils do badly in British schools. For one thing, as Rattansi (1988) points out, the Swann Report may exaggerate the underachievement of black pupils. The examination successes of black pupils have been improving steadily, and at a rate faster than that for other groups, so that findings from the early 1980s will by now be seriously dated.

Second, different sectors of the ethnic minority population have a different relationship to the education system. So, for example, in a 1985 study of average performance in O level and CSE examinations, children from Bangladeshi, Turkish and Caribbean origins performed well below children from English, Welsh, Scottish and Irish backgrounds; but the latter were significantly outclassed by pupils whose origins were African Asian, Indian or Pakistani (Kysel, 1988).

One of the most striking changes in the social distribution of educational achievement in the past ten years has been a noticeable improvement in the performance of females relative to males (Table 11.3). For example, in 1980/81, there were substantially more men than women in the sixteen to twenty age range in full-time or part-time education; by 1990/91, participation rates were virtually identical. In 1970/71, 18 per cent of male school-leavers in the UK but only 15 per cent of female had one or more A levels or equivalents. By 1990/91, both

Table 11.3 Changing educational performance of women and men, 1970/71 to 1990/91, UK

Area of education	*1970 / 71*		*1980 / 81*		*1990 / 91*	
	Male	*Female*	*Male*	*Female*	*Male*	*Female*
% of men and women aged 16–18 in education, full-time or part-time			54	48	60	61
% of men and women aged 19–20 in education, full-time or part-time			32	23	32	32
% of school-leavers with 1 or more A-levels or SCE H-grades	18	15			22*	25*
% of school-leavers with 2 or more A-levels or 3 or more H-grades	15	13			20	22
% of school-leavers with no graded examination result	44	44			9	6
% of persons enrolled in higher education, full-time or part-time, who are male / female	67	33	63	37	55	45
% of persons gaining postgraduate qualifications who are male/female			65	35	58*	42*

* 1989/90

Sources: Department for Education, *Statistical Bulletin*, 2/93, Government Statistical Service (January 1993) para 11 and tables 4,6,7; and *Social Trends 23* (1993) table 3.11.

groups show marked improvement, but girls have overtaken boys. Between 1970/71 and 1990/91, the proportion of school-leavers with no qualifications was dramatically reduced, but they are now more heavily concentrated among males (9 per cent) than among females (6 per cent). In 1980/81, of those enrolled in full-time or part-time higher education in the UK, 37 per cent were women; ten years later, the proportion has risen to 45 per cent. In 1980/81, 35 per cent of people obtaining postgraduate qualifications were women; in 1989/90, 42 per cent.

These changes are impressive. However, women have a long way to go to catch up their historic educational disadvantage. In 1991, of people aged 16–69 outside full-time education, 11 per cent of men but only 6 per cent of women have degrees, while 40 per cent of women compared with 33 per cent of men have no educational qualifications whatsoever (*General Household Survey 1991* (1993) table 10.14, p. 218).

Moreover, the returns to education – the payoffs in terms of income and occupational success – are unequal for women and men. In Britain in 1991, the median gross weekly earnings for women with degrees in full-time employment was £300–£350, while their male counterparts averaged £400–£450. Of people in full-time employment, 49 per cent of men with degrees, but only 19 per cent of women with degrees, earn £450 or more a week (*General Household Survey (1991)* 1993, table 10.11, p. 214).

Finally, within education, subject-choice continues to be gender-differentiated. The pattern of examination results at GCSE level reflects the channelling of girls still into domestic subjects, arts and languages, and boys into technical subjects, maths and 'hard' sciences. Among 18-year-old school-leavers, the disparities in proportions of girls and boys with particular A-level passes are so marked that out of twelve central subjects, only History can reasonably be seen as a subject that is 'integrated' (Department for Education, 1993, table 13). On degree courses in the UK in 1990/91, the proportion of women students ranged from 80 per cent in Education to only 13 per cent in Engineering and technology (*Social Trends 23*, table 3.18). Forty-four per cent of men, compared with 22 per cent of women, were enrolled on courses in science, including medicine, dentistry, health, engineering and technology (Department for Education, 1993, table 7). Thus, in spite of the effectiveness of some equal opportunities programmes, gender continues to structure educational experience in powerful ways.

One last, crucial point must be made. Any attempt to explain the relationship between social differences and educational performance is

Table 11.4 *Highest qualification level of the population[1]: by ethnic origin and sex, 1988–90, Great Britain (percentages)*

Highest qualification held	*Ethnic origin*					
	White	*West Indian/ Guyanese*	*Indian*	*Pakistani/ Bangladeshi*	*Other[2]*	*All[3]*
Males						
Higher	15	—	19	8	22	15
Other	57	58	51	40	56	57
None	29	36	30	52	21	29
Females						
Higher	13	16	13	—	20	13
Other	51	52	46	28	52	51
None	36	32	41	68	28	36
All persons						
Higher	14	11	16	6	21	14
Other	54	55	49	34	54	54
None	32	34	36	60	25	32

[1] Aged 16 to retirement age (64 for males, 59 for females).
[2] Includes African, Arab, Chinese, other stated and mixed origin.
[3] Includes those who did not know or did not state their ethnic origin.
Source: *Social Trends 22*, London, HMSO, 1992, table 3.30, p. 65.

likely to be mistaken if it does not take into account the complex ways and changing ways in which gender, ethnicity and social class interact. The impact of ethnicity is not the same across genders; nor is the impact of gender the same across different ethnic groups. In the adult population of Britain, men tend to outperform women among whites, and among people of Indian, Pakistani/Bangladeshi, and 'other' origins; but among people of West Indian/Guyanese backgrounds, it is women who are more likely to have a higher qualification and less likely to be without qualifications. On the other hand, among candidates in 1990/91 for degree courses in universities and polytechnics, men from all ethnic minority groups had higher acceptance rates than women from the same groups (THES, 1992).

The social nature of the curriculum

Since the emergence in the 1970s of what was called 'the new sociology of education', associated with the work of sociologists such as M. F. D. Young, there has been enhanced attention to the part played by schools in the creation and validation of knowledge. This change of orientation has brought a deeper concern with the ways schools shape people's consciousness: what kinds of understanding, what world-views, are promoted by our schools?

Before the 1970s, the curriculum was rarely the object of sociological study, and its content tended to be taken for granted. But, as Raymond Williams (1981) points out, there is a *selective tradition* in educational knowledge. Out of the vast stock of knowledge available in a complex society – from theories of artificial intelligence to the location of the next illegal rave – only a fraction is selected for transmission in school.

What is selected, and what left out, has consequences for wider patterns of social control. Schooling may help to sustain the status quo by the images of society that it promotes. Hand's (1976) analysis, for example, identifies two themes that reverberate through the teaching of English literature: the dangers of revolutionary change (communicated through the ways that Orwell's *Nineteen Eighty-Four* and *Animal Farm,* for instance, are analysed); and (through the pessimistic accounts contained in such books as Golding's *Lord of the Flies* and Wyndham's *Day of the Triffids*), despair about the possibility of constructive social action. One of the main impacts of the English curriculum, Hand argues, is to give pupils the impression that the status quo is unchangeable – to suppress the systematic examination of possible alternative social worlds.

It is not only the teaching of English that has implications for social control. Many of the nineteenth-century promoters of science education saw this as a means to undermine dogmatic thinking and to enable ordinary people to be more critical of authority and more confident about their own understanding. However, Young argues (in Dale *et al.*, 1988) that science was eventually incorporated into the curriculum in the form of facts to be memorised rather than as a method for establishing and testing knowledge. This dulled its critical cutting edge. According to Young, school science has encouraged in pupils the development of three equally flawed relationships to science: that of pure scientists (who are not interested in the uses of science); of applied scientists (who pursue applications, but leave others to decide on goals); and that of science failures (who are helpless in the face of scientific expertise).

The nature of the curriculum has implications, too, for the creation of a particular national identity. Brown (in Dale *et al.*, 1988, p. 222) points out: 'It is no coincidence that mass schooling was invented at roughly the time when nation states had come into existence and the need arose to instil in their citizens the idea that the new entity had first claim on their loyalties.' Brown shows how history, geography and science work differently (and with different degrees of success) to foster national identity, and he suggests that this outcome may have been insufficiently emphasised in accounts of modern schooling that focus upon the economic context of education.

What are the implications for national identity of the imposition on schools of a National Curriculum by a recent Conservative government? The National Curriculum prescribed for state schools (though not for private ones) core and foundation subjects (English, mathematics, science, technology, history, geography, art, music, PE and a modern foreign language) and, for the core disciplines, attainment targets and programmes of study. By prescribing that this shall be studied intensively, and that only superficially, or not at all, the National Curriculum appears to embody the selective tradition in a particularly rigid form, allowing little room for alternative definitions of what counts as 'our' tradition. However, early research within the schools indicates that the National Curriculum may be less uniform in practice than its proponents have hoped and its detractors have feared. Different schools, the authors found, bring different resources, and different subject and **pedagogical** commitments, to the working-out of policy, and they also face different problems with, for example, staffing, plant and facilities. These differences set limits to the capacity of the state to dictate a uniform result. Bowe, Ball and Gold (1992) conclude:

pedagogy
The science and principles of teaching.

the different parts of the Education Reform Act may well be taken up differently by different LEAs, schools and departments within schools, thus producing very different outcomes that may actually work against a *National* Curriculum.

[Bowe, Ball and Gold, 1992, p. 84]

Social Difference and Educational Attainment: Extra-School Explanations

Sociologists are concerned not only to monitor the persistence of a relationship between educational attainment and social difference, but also to explain it. These explanations fall into two broad types. Intra-school explanations explore the impact of particular features of the educational regime – the impact of curriculum, of school organisation, of teacher expectations and classroom dynamics. Such explanations argue for the power of schools to influence the social distribution of achievement. The current section will be more concerned with extra-school explanations that focus upon the qualities that social groups bring with them to the school. These theories assume that the source of educational inequality lies in social differences which schools may be relatively powerless to influence.

Naturalistic explanations: who's a clever boy, then?

intelligence quotient (IQ)
A measurement of intelligence based on the ratio of a person's mental age (as measured by IQ tests) to his or her actual age.

Across the population, the existence of a substantial correlation between IQ (**intelligence quotient**) scores and educational performance may appear to lend scientific weight to the commonsense idea that social groups who succeed in school do so because they are naturally bright. But there are serious problems with the notion, on the one hand, that IQ scores reflect 'natural' abilities, and, on the other, that these scores can explain educational attainments.

First, it has to be recognised that however we choose to define 'intelligence' there is no test for its measurement that can separate natural ability from cultural influence. By the time infants can build towers of blocks, or respond to questions, environmental factors – diet, levels of attention, patterns of speech, and so forth – will have shaped their intellectual development. Attempts through the study of identical twins to measure the genetic contribution to IQ have had little success; the data from these studies is, as Kamin (1977) demonstrates, notoriously unreliable. Tests of intelligence cannot be said, therefore, to measure natural ability; at best, they measure the way that a person's intelligence has developed in interaction with a particular environment.

Second, it is clear from sociological studies that many factors besides measured intelligence enter into the social distribution of achievement. The classic longitudinal survey *The Home and the School*, which examined over 5,000 primary pupils in England and Wales, found that the educational disadvantages of working-class pupils compared with middle-class pupils persisted even when their measured intelligence was identical; of children in the above-average ability band, 51 per cent from the upper middle class, 34 per cent from the lower middle class, but only 22 per cent from the lower working class were allowed entry to grammar school (Douglas, 1967). The authors of *Origins and Destinations* estimate that each year in the post-war period, 6,000 fewer working-class boys went to selective schools than would have been expected on the basis of measured intelligence alone (Halsey *et al.*, 1980, p. 209).

Third, it is clear that cultural factors influence the performance of different social groups on the tests themselves. Lack of experience with timed tests, distrust of the tester, or fear of failure, are examples of the many variables which, experiments have shown, can lower the IQ score of a group (Kamin, 1977). Tests that necessarily draw upon people's familiarity with objects, shapes, words, and testing procedures are unlikely ever to be objective or culture-free. It is for these reasons that many sociologists and educationalists are convinced that IQ tests put a naturalistic gloss on differences between pupils that are, in fact, socially created.

Box 11.2: Race, heredity and intelligence

The issue of cultural bias in intelligence tests is at its sharpest in controversies about race and intelligence. Jensen (1969) sparked off a furious row when he claimed that the higher average IQ score of white Americans over black Americans was due largely to genetic difference, and that it justified different approaches for educating white pupils and black. In a court case in the late 1970s, it was reported that while only 10 per cent of California's school population were black, 25 per cent of pupils who had been classified by IQ tests as 'mentally retarded' were black. These pupils, the judge found, had been segregated into 'dead-end' classes and given inferior teaching, a treatment that caused them to lag further behind their schoolmates as the years go by. After hearing expert testimony, Judge Peckham concluded that the the disproportionately high number of black children in classes for the retarded was due to 'racially and culturally biased' IQ tests which discriminated against children from the black community. He deplored the assumption of some educators that black children were intellectually inferior to whites, and saw this assumption as 'all the more invidious when "legitimated" by ostensibly neutral scientific IQ tests'. He banned the use of IQ tests on minority children, a ban later extended to all children in California (*The Economist,* 8 December 1979).

Whatever the details of this particular case, the judge's decision seems to be reasonable in several respects. First, the evidence for a largely genetic basis to group differences in IQ scores is highly unsatisfactory. As Kamin (1977) has shown, most of the evidence used by Jensen and his supporters comes from studies with severe methodological faults. Second, we can question the *relevance* of Jensen's emphasis on heredity. The objective of education is clearly not the raising or equalising of IQ scores *per se*; and it is equally clear that the knowledge and skills of a group of pupils can be increased without any alteration to IQ. Could IQ scores be a red-herring that distracts us from more fundamental issues of learning? Third, we can challenge the policy *implications* of the concern with inheritance of IQ. Suggestions that a large genetic component to IQ would necessarily entail a reduction in educational support for 'low IQ' groups should be seen as political judgements and contentious ones at that. Even if it were the case that certain groups were genetically disadvantaged in terms of IQ, and that IQ represented intelligence – neither of which has been demonstrated – this could provide a powerful argument for devoting extra resources to developing the potential of these pupils to the full.

Cultural deprivation: that's the way they like it, uh huh?

Theories of cultural deprivation focus not upon the innate qualities of particular social groups, but upon their *cultural inheritance*. Children who are 'culturally deprived' may be bright enough, but held back by values and attitudes that are not conducive to educational success.

In the early post-war period, theories of cultural deprivation were often used in connection with social class. Bernstein (1971) argued that the reliance by many working-class families on a **'restricted code' of speech** made it more difficult for working-class children to undertake abstract analytical work. Other theorists targeted other aspects of working-class culture, among them an inability to defer gratification, lack of parental interest in children's education, and a lack of ambition.

restricted code of speech
A form of speech which relies on terse exposition and sometimes slang to communicate, as opposed to elaborated forms of speech.

Since the 1970s, it is black and Asian pupils who are more often said to be culturally deprived. Theorists have proposed a range of cultural obstacles to educational success, from the prevalence of 'mother-centred' families to lack of parental interest, from low self-esteem to the tensions of culture clash. Many of these suggestions have been effectively discounted; for example, Brah and Minhas (1988) refute the widespread notion that the education of Asian girls suffers from the tensions of mediating two contradictory cultures, the 'liberal' culture of the school and the 'repressive' culture of home. There is no evidence, they point out, of greater intergenerational conflict in Asian families than there is within other communities; the culture clash argument is based on misleading and ethnocentric comparisons.

But as a type of explanation, theories of cultural deprivation continue to flourish. Attempts to assess any particular theory of cultural deprivation must come to terms with two general reservations, as outlined below.

Culture and context

Cultural deprivation theories sometimes operate with a simplistic idea of culture, reducing it to an arbitrary collection of attitudes and values – a kind of lifestyle decision, like the choice between Coca-Cola or Pepsi – without recognising the links between culture and the material and social context in which people live.

Source: Alex Graham Ltd (Solo Syndication)

'Nonsense! Best years of his life!'

We should be cautious, for example, about claims that particular social groups 'lack interest' in the education of their children. Often, such claims are based on the way that parents relate to the school. In an early study, Douglas (1967, pp. 81–2) used a measure of parental interest that included teachers' comments on parents' attitudes, and records of the number of times that parents visited the school; he found that higher levels of interest from middle-class parents (and especially fathers) were a key factor governing their children's chances of entry to grammar school. But manual workers work longer hours than people in middle-class jobs, and are less likely to be allowed time off with pay; the lesser 'interest' of working-class fathers may simply reflect this fact. What we might emphasise in parents' relationship to the school, rather than cultural values, are the constraints that prevent the translation of interest and concern into practical help, or the social distribution of knowledge and power that may make it easier for middle-class parents to 'work the system': to hold their own in disagreements with teachers, to fight discrimination on behalf of their children, to know what books and equipment to buy – and to have the money to buy them. An emphasis upon 'culture' may, at its worst, produce an **ideological** cover for differences in material privilege; where it is claimed that parents

ideology
A perception of reality or way of thinking. Its usage is associated with Marx, where the term implies a mistaken sense of reality or false consciousness (*see* false consciousness).

displayed sufficient 'interest' to send their children to independent schools, we may note that, with fees running at over £7,000 a year, this kind of 'interest' is a luxury few parents could afford.

Theories of cultural deprivation, then, should not be allowed to obscure the important ways in which material circumstances impinge on educational success. These include the stringent costs associated with 'free' schooling, from the expense of sports kit to the burden of supporting young adults in the period between school-leaving age and entry to higher education.

Moreover, whatever the values of a pupil's culture, adverse living conditions mitigate against educational success. Children from low-income families are likely to have less time for schoolwork, since they are more likely to be drawn into paid work to meet basic needs (Finn, 1984); housework, too, and unpaid family labour, tends to fall more heavily on working-class than on middle-class pupils, and far more heavily on girls than on boys (Griffin, 1985).

Material circumstances are likely to be important in understanding the attainment patterns of different ethnic groups. If differences in economic circumstance were properly allowed for, Rattansi argues (1988), the gaps in attainment between whites and blacks documented by studies such as the Swann Report would be much less marked. The ethnic minority groups that perform most impressively in the educational system tend to be those where there is a well-established middle class. The groups that perform least well, such as Turkish or Bangladeshi children, are those where the adult population is most heavily concentrated in manual work. Indeed, Williams (1988) suggests that while educationalists today rarely resort to **biological determinism** to explain ethnic differences in achievement, *cultural* determinism flourishes. By 'cultural determinism', she identifies a tendency to assume that ethnic groups have a homogeneous culture, and a refusal to recognise that cultural character derives in part from the changing economic and social context in which ethnic minorities are embedded.

biological determinism

A simple causal, reductionist approach that explains human behaviour in terms of biological or genetic characteristics.

Box 11.3: Schools for the rich, schools for the poor?

In the face of cuts in government spending on education, the cost to families of 'free' schooling has become greater over the past two decades. Since well-off parents can supplement inadequate provision in state schools, or pay the fees for private schooling, the gulf between the standard of education available to the children of the rich and those of the poor, has increased. For example, spending on school books in state schools fell in 1984–5 in real terms by £5.1 million, while in the same year, in the independent sector, spending on school books doubled (Boseley, 1986). As long ago as 1982, Her Majesty's Inspectorate found that an increasing reliance by state schools upon contributions from parents was leading to 'marked disparities' in the standard of schooling between affluent areas and areas serving the poor.

Deprivation or difference?

The second reservation about cultural deprivation theories, associated with the work of critics such as Keddie (1973), takes issue with the notion of 'deprivation'. All cultures, these critics assert, represent equally valid ways of life, and there is no universal standard according to which a particular culture can be evaluated. When theorists judge working-class cultures or the cultures of ethnic minority groups to be wanting, they use as a yardstick the values of the dominant culture; children in Britain and America have been identified as 'deprived' because of 'deficiencies' in their culture, when in fact they are merely different. Critics who argue in this way tend to refer to cultural deprivation theories as 'deficit theories'.

These critics point to a number of negative consequences that follow from cultural deprivation theories. Cultural deprivation theories tend to imply, say the critics, that children are doomed to failure because of their own inadequacies – the children who are the victims of deprivation become the ones who are blamed. The very idea that black or working-class pupils are culturally unprepared to benefit from educational opportunities, may give some schools an excuse for neglecting them; some of the most stringent critics of 'deficit' theory assert that it is this neglect that explains the underperformance by some pupils from working-class and particular ethnic backgrounds.

compensatory education

An approach introduced in the 1960s and 1970s to inner city schools with high proportions of working-class children, or children from ethnic communities. It involved an allocation of extra resources and special facilities aimed at counteracting what was perceived to be educational disadvantage as a result of cultural differences.

Many programmes of **compensatory education** and educational enrichment that were introduced in the 1960s and 1970s (such as Headstart in the USA or the Educational Priority Areas in England and Wales) were denounced as misguided by some critics for institutionalising a 'deficit' view of black or working-class children.

Conclusion: deprivation in culture, society and education

In our discussion of cultural deprivation, we have argued against those theories that seem to reduce culture to a lifestyle choice, and then to 'blame' under-achieving groups for making the 'wrong' decision. A more sophisticated view recognises that values that affect educational decisions – confidence, commitment to education as a strategy for advancement, willingness to play the game – are not attitudes which can simply be dropped or acquired, but are rooted instead in the shared experiences of working and community life and, indeed, in the experiences of schooling itself.

There is not room here to consider the socio-linguistic theories of Basil Bernstein in detail, but his work on the acquisition of skills and competencies, on experience and modes of control, attempts to examine how the realities of working-class and middle-class life encourage different sorts of skills and interests. He and his colleagues find, for example, that, while many working-class mothers regard play and learning as separate activities (a view that reflects the nature of manual occupations), middle-class mothers tend to view toys and play as opportunities for enquiry; it is possible that middle-class mothers enable their children to take explicit educational advantage from play. Middle-class children, then, may arrive at school with advantages in two respects: they may indeed have learned more as a result of their **socialisation**, and their expectations may be more in line with those of the school. It is useful to conceive of the competencies and experiences that may be more prevalent in middle-class households as resources, resources that are differentially distributed throughout the class structure, and that may be of concrete advantage to children who receive them. Inheritance, it has been said, can be 'cultural' as well as financial.

socialisation
An on-going process whereby individuals learn to conform to society's prevailing norms and values (*see* norms *and* values).

However, a problem with this type of formulation – as with cultural deprivation theory – is that it tends to take for granted a single model of the educable child – primarily white and middle class. The educational failure of certain groups is then 'explained' by the degree to which they deviate from this model. But instead of asserting that children who do not conform to the model are less well prepared for school, we could as easily argue that the school is less well prepared for them – that the education system is insufficiently responsive to their gifts and their needs.

Social Difference and Educational Attainment: Intra-School Explanations

The impact of the curriculum

In an earlier section, we highlighted the social nature of the curriculum, and considered how the selection of the curriculum has implications for social control and for the creation of a national identity. But what is selected in the curriculum, and what left out, has consequences also for success and failure. Studies of the physics curriculum, for example, indicate that applications of science are often introduced only as an afterthought, examples are used (e.g., combustion in a petrol engine) that appeal to boys more than to girls, and textbooks and materials portray illustrations of four male characters for every one female (Samuel, in Whyld, 1983; Kelly, in Arnot and Weiner, 1989). This may increase the sense that physics is a masculine field, and help to explain why boys are drawn to the subject far more often than girls.

The relationship between the curriculum and the reproduction of social inequality is analysed more broadly in the writings of Pierre Bourdieu (e.g. Bourdieu and Passeron, 1990). Even when schools treat all pupils equally, Bourdieu argues, through the selective tradition in the curriculum, the school will serve to legitimate the success of pupils from particular social backgrounds and the failure of others.

habitus

Pierre Bourdieu's term for the everyday habitual practices and assumptions of a particular social environment. People are at once the product of, and the creators of, their habitus.

Each social class, according to Bourdieu, possesses its own set of meanings or cultural framework, which is internalised through socialisation within the family; henceforth this **habitus** shapes perception, thought, taste, appreciation and action. Although one culture is not intrinsically superior to another, the power of the dominant class enables them to impose their own framework of meaning on the school as if it were the only legitimate culture. Through this symbolic violence, the dominant class succeeds in defining which topics are worthy of consideration, and the appropriate relationship to those issues – in effect, the dominant class defines what counts as knowledgeable or intelligent activity.

As pupils move up the educational ladder, those from the dominated class are progressively eliminated, or shunted into less prestigious forms of education; by contrast, the habitus of children from the dominant class provides them with cultural capital which is translated into academic and eventually occupational success. The educational system acts 'neutrally', in the sense that it evaluates all pupils according to their mastery of the dominant culture. But those who have inherited a cultural capital that accords with the school will appear naturally more gifted. As Lee (1989) argues, drawing on Bourdieu, schools translate working-class culture into working-class failure and deficiency. Thus, schooling reproduces relations of inequality between the classes – and, of course, between other social categories as well. In the process, schooling validates the superiority of dominant groups, and confirms for the others their own sense of worthlessness, their distance from 'what really counts'.

Box 11.4: Cultural capital, the selective tradition and ethnicity

Bourdieu's analysis of how a particular curriculum validates the success of those in tune with it focuses upon social class, but the selective tradition may equally translate gender or ethnic or racial differences into cultural capital.

A curriculum that takes for granted white racial superiority and the cultural centrality of Europeans, for example, demands extra detachment and forbearance from black pupils who wish to succeed. In the quotation below, one of the Black Sisters – a group of girls of Asian and Afro-Caribbean origins at sixth form college in the Midlands – offers a telling critique of the selective tradition.

Judith: 'With me like I go into school and I listen to the teacher and I put down just what they want. Christopher Columbus discovered America, I'll put it down, right. Cecil Rhodes, you know that great imperialist, he was a great man, I'll put it down. We did about the Elizabethans, how great they were. More European stuff; France, equality, liberty and fraternity, we'll put it all down. At that time they had colonies, were enslaving people. I'll put it down that it was the mark of a new age, the Age of Enlightenment. It wasn't , but I'll put it down for them, so that we can tell them that black people are not stupid....I'm just saying to them, I can do it right, and shove your stereotypes up your anus' (Mac an Ghaill, 1988, p. 28).

instrumental
An approach which involves the adoption of a strategy best suited to the attainment of a particular goal, as opposed to following a course of action for its own sake.

Pupils like Judith may succeed in school by adopting an **instrumental** approach, but success is gained at the cost of cultural integrity. They do not have the luxury of treating education as a quest for truth.

The impact of school organisation

There was in the early post-war period considerable optimism about the power of education to remedy social problems, and this optimism fuelled educational reforms: programmes of pre-school education were designed to give a 'headstart' to disadvantaged pupils, and a groundswell of opinion supported a movement towards comprehensive secondary education.

Arguments for comprehensive schools stressed the damaging effects of the tripartite system on the majority of pupils who did not gain entry to grammar schools: the errors of the 11-plus examination (which resulted, according to Yates and Pidgeon (1957) in approximately 70,000 children being allocated each year to the wrong type of school); the fact that these errors tended to penalise working-class children; the concern that secondary modern schools – with their stigma of failure, their less academic curriculum and their lack of preparation for national examinations – depressed the overall performance of their pupils; and, finally, the recognition that the tri-partite system contributed to Britain's low rate of entry to higher education compared to its economic and political rivals: all these led to a groundswell of opinion in favour of comprehensive reorganisation, and by 1984, 82 per cent of state secondary pupils in England (and in Scotland and Wales, 96 per cent) were in comprehensives.

The new type of secondary system would, it was hoped by its advocates, raise overall standards of educational attainment, contribute to a narrowing of class differentials in education, and help to dismantle the social and cultural barriers between the social classes that looked so anomalous in the post-war era. Have these goals been accomplished?

One thing is clear: during the period of comprehensive reorganisation, standards, measured in terms of examination successes, have continued to rise. More pupils are succeeding in school and gaining qualifications than ever before.

On the other hand, it is less clear that comprehensive reorganisation has contributed to the narrowing of class differentials. Many comprehensive schools, concerned about comparisons with grammar schools, organised themselves so as to concentrate on the most able. The operation of streaming and banding in many comprehensives means, according to researchers like Ball (1981), that comprehensive schools merely re-create the tripartite system under one roof, with the majority of working-class pupils getting, within a nominally comprehensive framework, a less prestigious and less academic education. Heath (1989) delivers a harsh verdict:

'So we have a striking contrast. There has been constantly rising educational attainment ... during the course of the twentieth century. But class inequalities first in access to selective secondary schools, then at O and next perhaps at A-level, have shown no overall tendency to decline.... In the face of this remarkable resilience of class inequalities, educational reforms seem powerless.

[Heath, 1989, pp. 186–7]

This pessimistic view was shared by many, but it does not go unchallenged. McPherson and Willms (1989) argue that Heath over-generalises from data that came too early in the operation of the comprehensive system and too exclusively from England and Wales. Using more recent data from Scotland (where comprehensive reorganisation was more radical and allowed for less creaming), McPherson and Willms claim to have found that improvement in overall standards has been accompanied by equalisation; that is, that comprehensive reorganisation has begun to undermine class differentials by levelling up, improving everyone's educational standards while enabling working-class pupils to make up lost ground.

Thus, some researchers argue that comprehensive reorganisation hasn't made a difference to fundamental levels of class inequality in education; others, that it has. There is no prospect of settling this issue in the near future, because the trend since the 1980s has been to move from comprehensive schooling to new forms of selection. The disparagement of comprehensive schools, the encouragement given by recent Conservative governments to independent schools and the introduction of the assisted places scheme have all contributed to a rise in the proportion of pupils in fee-paying schools, from 5 per cent in 1981 to 7 per cent in 1991. The 1988 Education Reform Act hastened the return to selective systems: one consequence of opting out is to enable schools in more affluent areas, funded partly by parental contributions, to select which pupils they will take; the City Technology Colleges will offer well-financed courses to a minority of pupils, while most will have to make do with more mundane facilities and equipment. Griggs says (1989, p. 68), 'It seems that once more good schooling is to be rationed because it is too expensive to provide on a mass scale.'

Labelling theory and classroom processes

While sociologists such as Jencks (1973), Halsey *et al.*, (1980) or Macpherson and Willms (1989) deploy survey data and official statistics in order to explore the question of whether schools make a difference, sociologists working in **social action** traditions have shown that on a small-scale at least schooling makes an important contribution to the social distribution of achievement. Schools do not merely react to pupils with varying qualities in a neutral way; they play an active part in creating children who are more or less educable, more or less knowledgeable, more or less manageable.

social action
A perspective that usually concentrates on the micro-level of social life, in order to show how human interpretation, arising out of the interaction with others, gives rise to social action.

Those working in interactionist traditions stress that pupil identities (such as 'less able' or 'disruptive') are not fixed in childhood. Success or failure is the product of a career moulded over a long period, the outcome of which is never guaranteed. The relative failure of boys of Afro-Caribbean origin, or of working-class children, is not predetermined by their intelligence or their attitudes. Rather, this failure has to be created anew for each new generation of pupils, and in this act of creation the interactions of teachers and pupils plays a significant part.

Even in the most 'progressive' infant classes, there exists what Bernstein (1977) calls an 'invisible pedagogy' – hidden criteria of judgement – according to which pupils will be approved of or not. Teachers may encourage the nursery class to do 'whatever interests them'. They will not, however, look with favour on pupils who are interested in talking dirty or in setting fire to the Wendy house.

Though surveillance and evaluation are unavoidable aspects of classroom encounters, teachers, as the study *Deviance in Classrooms* makes clear, do not always react in the same way to instances of rule-breaking. Their response depends first upon how they interpret the action (is it serious? will it spread?); and, second, upon the view or typification that they have developed of the pupil concerned (Hargreaves *et al.*, 1975). Pupils become typecast on the basis of earlier impressions – a boy who has been classified as a 'skiver', for example, may be suspected of copying when he hands in an excellent piece of work. By analysing how teachers arrive at such judgements – by highlighting how teachers differentiate between the bright and the dull, the model pupil and the problem child – researchers have begun to show how teachers are implicated in the process of pupil failure. Classroom observation studies in a variety of settings testify that,on the whole, teachers tend to give more of their time to pupils whom they believe to be bright; it may be partly the case that 'bright' children learn more than their classmates because of this extra attention.

social stratification
The division of a population into unequal layers or strata based on income, wealth, gender, ethnicity, power, status, age, religion or some other characteristic.

ethnocentric
The description of the inability to understand the validity or integrity of cultures other than one's own.

In short, a process of **stratification** occurs in many classrooms, with teachers meting out different treatment to more or less favoured groups of pupils. By analysing interaction in three junior and three middle schools, Green (1985) was able to show that teachers who had highly **ethnocentric** attitudes differed sharply in their teaching behaviour between black pupils and white. Boys of European origin were particularly favoured; they were given a lot more individual teaching time than their numbers would warrant, and plenty of opportunity to introduce ideas into the flow of discussion. Girls and boys of Afro-Caribbean origin, on the other hand, received much less individual attention and considerably less praise and encouragement.

Nor is it only Afro-Caribbean pupils who are likely to suffer from negative expectations. Asian girls may be typed as 'passive' or 'docile' in ways that lead to them being overlooked and underestimated in class (Brah and Minhas, 1988). In general, teachers' expectations tend to reflect the priority given to males in our culture. Teachers in secondary schools tend to prefer teaching male pupils, and expect boys to be more critical, more forthcoming and more enthuasiastic than girls. Even in primary schools, where girls are more successful than boys, the excellence of their work may be attributed by teachers to a desire to please rather than to creativity or intellectual promise (Clarricoates, 1980). Expectations – because they involve ideas about what 'such pupils' are 'really like' – enable ideologies about ethnic groups, social classes, and genders to shape relations between pupils and teachers in the classroom.

The impact of stratification is likely to be at its sharpest where pupils are divided into different bands or streams on the basis of 'ability'. The fact of being placed in a low stream may discourage pupils and damage their self-confidence. Teachers may expect little of low-stream pupils, and attempt less with them. This may be part of the reason why ability-grouping tends to boost the performance of top-stream pupils, but depress that of pupils in lower groups. And since streaming and banding are often linked to social class – the higher a pupil's social class background, the greater the chance of being allocated to the top stream – ability grouping may well play a part in the underachievement of working-class pupils. In his study *Beachside Comprehensive*, Ball (1981) indicates, like Hargreaves (1967) and Lacey (1970) before him, that ability-grouping may also contribute to the formation of pupil subcultures with an anti-school bias. The differentiation of pupils into three broad bands of ability on entry to Beachside encouraged a polarisation between the top and middle bands. Initially, both bands were described by teachers as pliable and a pleasure to teach, but by the second year the higher record of detentions and absences among middle-band pupils, their avoidance of extra-curricular activities and the fact that nearly half of them claimed to dislike school are all signs, Ball argues, of the emergence of an oppositional culture. This **anti-school culture** can be seen partially as a group response to failure, pupils dissociating themselves from the school that devalued their efforts. But of course, the subculture contributed to further failure; disorder in middle-band classes disrupted the efforts of even those pupils who remained committed to school.

anti-school culture
A way of behaving which is dedicated to subverting school rules, typically exhibited by those pupils who see themselves as educational failures.

Wright (1988) has shown that anti-school cultures may be triggered too by a school's practices around race. In a Midlands comprehensive school where she conducted classroom observation, teachers frequently made racist comments in class. Children who refused to let these 'jokes' go unchallenged became known as troublemakers, and the disillusionment of the 'troublemakers' increased as they moved up the school. They became the core of an anti-school group that developed in the third, fourth and fifth years, composed entirely of black girls and boys, who structured themselves like a gang, used Patois to distance themselves from the school and tried to appear threatening.

Table 11.5 *Different bands, different worlds?: Comparison of top band and middle band, second year cohort at Beachside Comprehensive*

	Top band (Mrs Culliford's form)	*Middle band (Mrs Tanner's form)*
Teachers' stereotypes of each band	Academic potential, neat workers, bright, alert, enthusiastic, want to get on, rewarding	Not up to much, rowdy, lazy, cannot take part in discussions, not interested, unrewarding
% of pupils from working-class homes	36%	78%
% of teacher's class time devoted to maintaining order	1.5%	12.5%
Average number of detentions, per pupil, per year	0.4	3.8
Average number of absences in term 1, per pupil	8.1	12.6
Average number of minutes spent on homework, per pupil	47	16
% of end of year subject tests graded at 50% or higher	58%	11%
Number of extra-curricular activities or club memberships, per class	43	10
% of pupils who dislike school	13%	48%
Views held about each band by pupils in the other band	Brainy, unfriendly, stuck-up, arrogant	Thick, rough, boring, simple

Source: Compiled from Stephen Ball, *Beachside Comprehensive*, Cambridge, Cambridge University Press, 1981, ch. 2.

By showing how teachers may act (wittingly or unwittingly) as agents of differentiation, researchers working in social action traditions have helped to illuminate the impact of schooling itself on the distribution of achievement. But one problem with this approach is the tendency to see the classroom in 'splendid isolation', divorced from wider processes of social control. Hence some researchers have attempted, by combining structural and action approaches, to set classroom interaction within a broader framework. Sharp and Green (1975), for example, demonstrate that in Mapledene, an infant school where the child-centred philosophy puts a premium on allowing pupils to develop at their own pace, teachers used notions of the 'readiness' of children for intellectual advance to justify inequality of treatment. All children, teachers claimed, are equally valued as individuals, but some are more 'ready', and it was these who commanded most of the teachers' time and attention. The child-centred philosophy enabled teachers to ignore children who were falling behind, on the grounds that they were not yet ready for intellectual growth. But Sharp and Green refuse to see these patterns of interaction as an offshoot merely of the consciousness of individual teachers; instead, they argue, the constraints under which teachers operate – including not only the demands of classroom control in the face of large numbers of pupils, but also the pressures even at an early age to classify pupils in the interests of eventual ocupational placement – make it difficult for a teacher to do other than stratify, whatever her own philosophy and expectations might be.

Box 11.5: The cooling-out process

When Beachside Comprehensive (Ball, 1981) switched from banding to mixed-ability teaching, many of the behavioural problems that had previously been concentrated in the middle bands disappeared; lessons were far less often disrupted and far fewer pupils gave signs of disaffection with school. Yet even within mixed-ability classes, teachers continued to distinguish between 'bright' pupils, and those deemed 'average' or 'dull' – to sponsor some pupils for success, and to write others off as incapable. According to Ball (1981, p.278), 'the stratification of pupils produced through the bands is condensed and reproduced within each mixed-ability form-group'. This stratification of pupils even within the same classroom, Ball argues, seriously undermines the egalitarian objectives of comprehensive education.

One consequence of the switch from banding to mixed-ability teaching was that fewer pupils whom teachers regarded as 'not up to much intellectually' succeeded in retaining high ambitions; in other words, fewer pupils 'over-aspired'. This suggests that processes of stratification that are more subtle than streaming or banding may be all the more effective at diverting opposition; where pupils can be persuaded that certain courses of action are not for them – where they can be induced to lower their sights, without being allocated to lower streams or failed in an obvious way – then they may be left with the conviction that it is not 'the system' that is at fault, but themselves. This has been termed the 'cooling-out process'; pupils who are cooled out abandon their educational ambitions 'voluntarily', while believing that they have had a fair chance. Some educational practices do not serve simply to fail people, but to convince them that failure is an individual, rather than a structural problem.

Active and Passive Pupils: Pupil Identity and the Curriculum

Labelling theories and the studies of classroom interaction described above concentrate on the ways in which teachers' expectations and practices help to mould the educational careers of pupils with varying forms of difference. But though such an approach acknowledges that identities are fluid, pupils' identity-formation (as 'dim', say, or as 'troublemaker') is seen largely as a reaction to labelling by others. Pupils are not characterised as the shapers of their own identities.

Such a passive model of pupils is characteristic to an even more marked degree of perspectives we discussed earlier in the chapter; naturalistic explanations, theories of cultural deprivation, explanations which centre upon the curriculum or on school organisation, all operate to a greater or lesser extent with the model of a passive pupil whose educational career is 'determined', sometimes by extra-school factors (intelligence; values and attitudes), sometimes by processes embedded in schooling itself.

In this final section, we focus upon the efforts of pupils – conceived as actors who deploy cultural resources related to their gender, ethnicity and social class – *actively* to create their own identities. This type of explanation draws heavily upon **ethnographic** traditions of research.

ethnography

A research technique based on direct observation of the activity of members of a particular social group or given culture.

Willis (1977) in a classic study combining structural and action traditions, analysed the perspectives of a small group of working-class boys in secondary school. The 'lads' had little time for the qualifications and the good jobs to which the school claimed to hold the key. Drawing on the traditions of their working-class community, they scorned office jobs as soft and effeminate, and favoured 'real' knowledge with practical application over the abstract and 'irrelevant' book-learning of the school. In resisting the school's attempt to control them, the lads perfected techniques for 'having a laff', for evading restrictions, and for maintaining solidarity. School became for them a kind of training ground to practise ways of remaining human in the factory jobs that they eventually expected to occupy.

Willis's analysis suggests that disaffection from school is not merely a reaction to failure. Pupils come to school already equipped with class cultures; these enable (some of) them to see through the ideologies of the school, and to find a rationale for challenging the school's authority. Nor is the eventual failure of pupils like 'the lads' merely a result of economic forces beyond their control, as correspondence theory might seem to imply. Schools, Willis suggests, are partially independent of economic forces, and so are their pupils, who act creatively, often in ways that contravene expectations. Thus schools do not merely 'reproduce' the social relations of capitalism; within schools, there is resistance, rejection, innovation and change.

If working-class culture enables 'the lads' in Willis's study to re-interpret and to resist the ethos of the school, they also make use of a particular culture of masculinity. Their scorn for office jobs, for example, and for the qualifications that lead to such jobs, is a technique for affirming their masculinity as much as their class commitment. In a parallel fashion, Measor and Woods (1988) describe how a group of girls made an enormous fuss about school regulations requiring them to wear safety glasses for work in physical sciences. A certain distance from the physical sciences was as important to them for demonstrating their femininity as scorn for office jobs was for Willis's lads.

Brown (1989) identifies two approaches to pupil orientations. On the one hand, an educational differentiation approach (e.g., Bourdieu and Passeron; or Bowles and Gintis) emphasises how schools sift and sort pupils so as to cool out unrealistic aspirations. A cultural differentiation approach (e.g., Willis) implies that working-class pupils voluntarily 'fail' themselves. Both approaches, Brown argues, underestimate the range of responses of 'ordinary' working-class boys and girls. According to Brown, the most widespread strategy among ordinary kids is an alienated instrumental orientation – a limited form of compliance. Desiring modest success, including decent jobs with good rates of pay, many kids were willing to exchange limited commitment and effort at school for modest levels of attainment.

This has something in common with the limited forms of compliance displayed by some groups of working-class girls, especially those from Afro-Caribbean backgrounds. Fuller (1983) found girls in a London comprehensive to be sharply critical of many aspects of school and impatient of restrictive routines. Yet they aspired to educational qualifications as occupational stepping stones. They worked the system skilfully enough to make academic success possible, while displaying more defiance than many of their white female schoolmates: enough defiance to maintain self-respect (and, Fuller suggests, the respect of their male schoolmates) but not enough so as seriously to endanger their chance of getting qualifications. The Black Sisters, a girls' group of Afro-Caribbean origin interviewed by Mac an Ghaill (1988), walked the same fine line, to the confusion of their teachers who were accustomed to a higher level of deference from pupils who want to get on (refer back to Box 11.4).

Box 11.6: Pupil strategies and youth unemployment

If the school strategy of many ordinary kids involves conditional compliance – going through the motions in exchange for modest qualifications – then what might be the impact of continuing high rates of youth unemployment? Brown (1989) predicts two different sorts of response.

If the rewards for sustained effort are perceived no longer to be there, reasons for offering even limited compliance collapse, and more pupils, even in junior school, could become anti-school. The controls exercised by teachers may become less tolerable as the rewards diminish. This possibility is underscored by Mac an Ghaill's (1988) observation that as unemployment rates rose around Kilby, teachers came to be perceived as more authoritarian, and hostility towards them by some groups of pupils was much more pronounced.

On the other hand, the collapse of the job market also makes it more difficult to leave school with dignity. More young people are likely to become reluctant stayers-on; long-term unemployment, as Brown puts it (1989, p. 246), 'not only threatens the ordinary kids' chances of getting on, but indefinitely postpones their acquisition of the status of working-class adult'. This is reflected in increasing numbers of pupils staying in some form of education, including FE, past compulsory school-leaving age. Brown is not alone in suggesting that rising unemployment is likely to result in sharper divisions among young working-class people.

Both the scenarios described above bring home the need to consider pupil strategies in the light of a changing labour market. Eggleston *et al.* (1986) demonstrated that decisions about staying on at school by black and Asian pupils are related to their difficulty – greater than that of white pupils – in obtaining jobs. The willingness demonstrated by the Black Sisters (Mac an Ghaill, 1988), or by the girls interviewed by Fuller (1983), to use schools of which they were critical to acquire credentials, owes something to a realistic appraisal of women's chances of becoming independent without such qualifications.

As we have seen, resistance may operate in many different ways. The subtle strategies that pupils develop in order to reconcile their educational aspirations with aspects of their gender, ethnic and social class identities need not involve wholesale confrontation. Mac an Ghaill (1988) describes two working-class groups at Kilby school, eight boys of Afro-Caribbean origin (the Rasta Heads), and nine boys of Asian origin, mainly Indian (the Warriors). Both groups were fired by a powerful awareness of racism, and by a celebration of their own cultural origins. Both groups colonised space within the school, taking symbolic possession of certain areas and times. The Rasta Heads, for example, 'systematically arrived late for lessons, disturbed other students by demanding their seats at the back of the classrooms, continually interrupted teachers, tried to cause arguments, talked incessantly throughout lessons, and slept when asked to complete written work' (Mac an Ghaill, 1988, p. 99). Both groups used language as a means of resistance – the Warriors spoke in Gujerati or Punjabi, the Rasta Heads in Patois – to infuriate teachers and to demonstrate their intention to resist deculturation. Both groups saw teachers as authoritarian, and pushed liberal teachers so as to expose what they felt was the hypocrisy underlying surface reasonableness. But in spite of these similarities, the two subcultural groups had one crucial difference. The resistance of the Rasta Heads was highly visible and often took the form of open confrontation; when they had been absent, for instance, they would forthrightly refuse to bring a letter of explanation from their parents. The Warriors used more indirect, invisible forms of resistance; after absenting themselves to play pool, they often brought forged letters and so successfully avoided disciplinary action. These different strategies were both an ironic comment on, and a reinforcement of, the stereotypes held by teachers of the rebellious Afro-Caribbean youth and the passive Asian schoolboy.

Conclusion

Mass education – the provision of universal schooling, the elaboration of clear educational paths that point the way to predictable occupational futures – is rooted in **modernity**. The expansion of educational provision was stimulated by – and helped to consolidate – the creation of national cultures. The educational system helped to produce, to validate and to disseminate secular knowledge and an individualistic and materialistic culture. Moreover, mass systems of education have played an important part in the structuration of social classes and in the consolidation of distinctive patterns of racial and gender divisions, contributing to the reproduction of complex patterns of assymmetrical life chances.

modernity

A term designed to encapsulate the distinctiveness, complexity and dynamism of social processes unleashed during the eighteenth and nineteenth centuries, which mark a distinct break from traditional ways of living.

But, as this chapter has emphasised, in none of these 'activities' has education been uncontested. Different groups with different agendas have constantly challenged the nature and purposes of education. In the past two decades, this questioning has included a downscaling of belief in what education can deliver: fewer and fewer people see education as the simple instrument of progress for which it sometimes passed in the early post-war decades. Education, like the notion of progress itself, has had to accept a more tentative and less grandiose role.

And yet, some of the contemporary changes that have shaken modernity may owe something to, or be dependent upon, education. For example, education is crucial to the growth of knowledge workers within an increasingly service-oriented labour force. It is an important arena in which social pluralism and cultural complexity is expressed and created. For example, in Britain, the tri-partite system – the division of secondary schools into grammar, technical and secondary schools in the early post-war period – was premised upon and enabled a rigid set of identities. Tripartism yielded to comprehensive schools. With axes of stratification that are internal – and therefore, more fluid, more detailed, and more difficult to challenge – comprehensives provide a ground for the rehearsal of more complex identities, which the ethnography of pupil life is beginning to tap.

It remains to be seen whether the growth of more differentiated forms of educational provision – such as the provision for individual schools to opt out of local authority control, encouraged in Britain by the 1988 Education Reform Act – marks a further stage of complexity or whether instead it cloaks in *'difference'* the perpetuation of long-standing forms of inequality.

Summary of the Chapter

- Schooling is important for the skills and knowledge it conveys and develops, and for the part it plays in the construction of identities.
- The shifts in educational philosophy since the Second World War – from education for the sake of a fairer society, to education for the economy; and from equal opportunities and child-centred learning to unequal assessments and common standards – have involved both continuities and discontinuities in educational policy and practice.
- The expansion of education in the post-war years has provided some opportunities for upward mobility by working-class pupils, and has helped to confirm pupils from middle-class backgrounds in middle-class jobs.
- Girls and women have made educational gains in recent years, but have a long way to go before their historic educational disadvantage is eradicated.
- There is a great deal of variation in educational performance across ethnic and racial groups, especially when gender and social class are also taken into account.

- Explanations for patterns of educational success and failure that focus upon 'intelligence', may put a naturalistic gloss on differences between pupils that are, in fact, socially created.
- The usefulness of educational accounts that focus upon the cultural inheritance of particular groups of pupils depends upon how sophisticated is their notion of culture, how they see the relationship between culture and material circumstances, and whether they can avoid stigmatising certain children as 'culturally deficient'.
- What is taught in schools is always subject to selection and, therefore, choice. These choices will always be disputed – by educational specialists, politicians and citizens alike.
- Pupils display a wide range of different orientations to schooling, orientations that express and in turn help to create their gender, ethnic and class identities.

References

Apple, M. (1988) 'Facing the complexity of power: for a parallelist position in critical educational studies', in Cole (ed.) (1988).

Arnot, M. and G. Weiner, (eds) (1989) *Gender and the Politics of Schooling*, London, Hutchinson.

Bailey, C. (1989) 'The challenge of economic utility', in Cosin *et al.* (eds).

Ball, S. (1981) *Beachside Comprehensive*, Cambridge, Cambridge University Press.

Bates, I. *et al.* (eds) (1984) *Schooling for the Dole?*, London, Macmillan.

Bernstein, B. (1971) 'A critique of the concept of compensatory education', in *Class, Codes and Control*, vol. 1, London, Routledge & Kegan Paul.

Bernstein, B. (1977) 'Class and pedagogies: visible and invisible', in Karabel and Halsey (eds).

Boseley, Sarah (1986) 'Crisis warning on school books', *Guardian*, 31 March.

Bourdieu, P. and J. C. Passeron, (1990) *Reproduction in Education Culture and Society*, London, Sage.

Bowe, R. and S. Ball with A. Gold (1992) *Reforming Education and Changing Schools: Case Studies in Educational Sociology*, London, Routledge.

Bowles, S. and H. Gintis (1976) *Schooling in Capitalist America*, London, Routledge & Kegan Paul.

Brah, A. and R. Minhas (1988) 'Structural racism or cultural difference: schooling for Asian girls', in Woodhead and McGrath (eds).

Brown, P. (1989) 'Schooling for inequality?', in Cosin *et al.* (eds).

Centre for Contemporary Cultural Studies (1981) *Unpopular Education*, London, Hutchinson.

Clarke, J. and P. Willis (1984) 'Introduction', in Bates *et al.* (eds).

Clarricoates, K. (1980) 'The importance of being Ernest ... Emma ... Tom ... Jane', in R. Deem (ed.) *Schooling for Women's Work*, London, Routledge & Kegan Paul.

Coffield, F., C. Borrill and S. Marshall (1989) 'On the dole', in Cosin *et al.* (eds).

Cole, M. (ed.) (1988) *Bowles and Gintis*, London, Falmer Press.

Cole, M. (ed.) (1989) *The Social Contexts of Schooling*, Lewes, Falmer Press.

Cosin, B., M. Flude and M. Hales (eds) (1989) *School, Work and Equality*, London, Hodder & Stoughton with the Open University.

Dale, R., R. Ferguson and A. Robinson (eds) (1988) *Frameworks for Teaching*, Milton Keynes, Open University.

Davin, A. (1987) '"Mind that you do as you are told": reading books for Board School girls, 1870–1902', in G. Weiner and M. Arnot (eds), *Gender under Scrutiny*, London, Hutchinson/Open University Press.

Department for Education (1993) *Statistical Bulletin* 2/93, Government Statistical Service (January).

Douglas, J. W. B. (1967) *The Home and the School*, London, Panther.

Eggleston, J. *et al.* (1986) *Education for Some*, Stoke-on-Trent, Trentham Books.

Finn, D. (1984) 'Leaving school and growing up', in Bates *et al.* (eds).

Finn, D. (1987) *Training without Jobs*, London, Macmillan.

Frith, S. (1977) 'Socialization and rational schooling: elementary education in Leeds before 1870', in P. McCann (ed.), *Popular Education and Socialisation in the 19th Century*, London, Methuen.

Fuller, M. (1983) 'Qualified criticism, critical qualifications', in L. Barton and S. Walker (eds), *Race, Class and Education*, Beckenham, Croom Helm.

Green, P. (1985) 'Multi-ethnic teaching and the pupils' self-concepts', *Annexe B* in Swann Report, 1985.

Griffin, C. (1985) *Typical Girls?*, London, Routledge & Kegan Paul.

Griggs, C. (1989) 'The rise, fall and rise again of selective secondary schooling', in Cole (ed.) (1989).

Halsey, A. H. (1977) 'Towards meritocracy? the case of Britain', in Karabel and Halsey (eds).

Halsey, A. H., A Heath and J. Ridge (1980) *Origins and Destinations*, Oxford, Clarendon Press.

Hand, N. (1976) 'What is English?', in G. Whitty and M. Young (eds), *Explorations in the Politics of School Knowledge*, Driffield, Nafferton Books.

Hargreaves, D. (1967) *Social Relations in a Secondary School*, London, Routledge & Kegan Paul.

Hargreaves, D., S. Hestor and F. Mellor (1975) *Deviance in Classrooms*, London, Routledge & Kegan Paul.

Heath, A. (1989) 'Class in the classroom', in Cosin *et al.* (eds).

Jencks, C. *et al.* (1973) *Inequality*, London, Allen Lane.

Jensen, Arthur (1969) 'How much can we boost IQ and scholastic achievement?', *Harvard Educational Review*, vol. 39, pp. 2–51.

Kamin, L. (1977) *The Science and Politics of IQ*, Harmondsworth, Penguin.

Karabel, J. and A. H. Halsey (eds) (1977) *Power and Ideology in Education*, Oxford, Oxford University Press.

Keddie, N. (1973) *Tinker, Tailor*, Harmondsworth, Penguin.

Kirk, G. (1989) 'The growth of central influence on the curriculum', in Cosin *et al.* (eds).

Kysel, F. (1988) 'Ethnic background and examination results', *Educational Research*, vol. 30, no. 2 (June) pp. 83–9.

Lacey, P. (1970) *Hightown Grammar*, Manchester, Manchester University Press.

Lee, J. (1989) 'Social class and schooling', in Cole (ed.) (1988).

Mac an Ghaill, M. (1988) *Young, Gifted and Black*, Milton Keynes, Open University Press.

McPherson, A. and J. Willms (1989) 'Comprehensive schooling is better and fairer', in Cosin *et al.* (eds).

Measor, L. and P. Woods (1988) 'Initial fronts', in Woodhead and McGrath (eds).

Mirza, Heidi Safia (1992) *Young, Female and Black*, London, Routledge.

Moore, R. (1984) 'Schooling and the world of work', in Bates *et al.* (eds).

Moore, R. (1988) 'The correspondence principle and the marxist sociology of education', in Cole (ed.) (1988).

Moore, R. (1989) 'Education, employment and recruitment', in Cosin *et al.* (eds).

Paterson, F. M. S. (1988) 'Schooling the family', *Sociology*, vol. 22, no. 1 (February) pp. 65–86.

Rattansi, A. (1988) 'Race, education and British society', in Dale *et al.* (eds).

Rees, T. and D. Gregory (1981) 'Youth employment and unemployment', *Educational Analysis*, vol. 3, no. 3.

Sharp, R. and A. Green (1975) *Education and Social Control*, London, Routledge & Kegan Paul.

Swann Report (1985) *Education for All*, London, HMSO.

THES (1992) 'Ethnic women losing out to ethnic men in fight for places', *Times Higher Education Supplement*, 17 July, p. 1.

Whyld, J. (ed.) (1983) *Sexism in the Secondary Curriculum*, London, Harper & Row.

Williams, J. (1988) 'Anti-racist and anti-sexist education: why are women and black students educational problems?', in Dale *et al.* (eds).

Williams, R. (1981) *Culture*, London, Fontana.

Willis, P. (1977) *Learning to Labour*, Farnborough, Saxon House.

Woodhead, M. and A. McGrath (eds) (1988) *Family, School and Society*, London, Hodder & Stoughton.

Wright, C. (1988) 'School processes: an ethnographic study', in Woodhead and McGrath (eds).

Yates, A. and D. Pidgeon (1957) *Admission to Grammar Schools*, London, Newnes.

12 Work and Non-Work

Aims of the Chapter

Work has been of central interest to sociology for much of our social and material fabric rests on the work that we do, whether paid or not. The chapter examines the relationship between work, non-work and the variety of experience associated with both, especially as mediated by gender. The boundaries between work and non-work are growing increasingly blurred, while the importance of work as a source of personal identity declines.

Introduction

This chapter discusses work and non-work and the relationship between the two. Our idea of 'work' and 'non-work' refers to forms of social behaviour which are, in broad historical terms, relatively recent, associated with the onset of industrialisation. In the past, not only were work and non-work (and the forms of leisure accompanying this) much less easy to distinguish but they were less tied to specific times, places and **social framing** than is the case today. Today we go to work at a certain time, in a certain place and then return to relax in another time and place. It is true, of course, that not all – the unemployed, domestic labourers, the retired, some of the disabled, for example – participate in such a ritual.

social framing
To place within a particular bounded social context.

While this ritual can still be seen each day on the commuter trains of London, New York or Budapest, the pattern of work and non-work for those commuters is beginning to change. The security and stability of doing a job for which one trained is being eroded fast as the nature of the labour market changes and the sort of skills required. Former commuters now stay at home, since it is for many – not only unpaid housewives – a place of work. Leisure is defined through participation in a consumer lifestyle which can create new 'leisure pursuits' – almost on a daily basis it seems – for an individuated but mass market of people, desperately trying to 'fill' their free time. 'Work' on the fabric of the house – as in DIY – is defined as leisure. Making full use of your leisure is hard work.

The boundaries of work and non-work have always been unclear, especially if both provide similar forms of satisfaction and pleasure. These boundaries are now even more blurred, however, as time away from formalised work itself becomes something to be bought and sold as a commodity. The commercialisation of leisure increasingly means that people have to spend a considerable amount of money to enjoy their 'free' time. Today, the leisure market is one of the largest commodity markets in the economy, so a lot of people are working hard to provide the goods and services demanded by those in search of leisure.

The Place of 'Work' in Contemporary Society

If you are 'looking for work', what is it you are doing? The obvious – though not necessarily only – reply is 'trying to get a job'. We need a job to earn enough to buy all those things necessary for survival – and more. This tells us immediately that work is not merely a physical and mental activity but a social and economic activity that typically produces some good or service for others. But what of those working for pleasure, or without pay, as domestic workers such as housewives do? Is their work any less a form of work simply because it is outside the labour market? And, as a social activity, work provides a form of identity and status, so that even when we lose our job we may still define ourselves through our work – 'I am an unemployed miner', 'an out-of-work academic', and so on. Self-employed workers may regard themselves as being 'in work' all the time even when 'work is scarce', while some work – such as that of priests or artists and novelists – is regarded more as a 'calling' than 'work': to speak of an unemployed priest or novelist might be seen as rather odd. Some people may never 'work' in any of these senses, perhaps because they are very rich or desperately poor and excluded from 'normal' social and economic exchange.

All this is to illustrate the difficulty of tying down precisely and unequivocally what is meant by 'work'. Typically, of course, having a paid job is probably how most people would define the term: nevertheless, it is clearly a restricted notion and one which says nothing about the variety of work in which people engage. It also says nothing about the way work is viewed. Two workers doing the same job may respond to it in very different ways, and these may in part reflect their particular gender, home situation, age, ethnicity, educational career and so on. The meaning of work is not uniform for any group of workers. Grint (1991) stresses the heterogeneous nature of the meaning of work.

Box 12.1: Defining work

'What counts as work ... and what we take as skilled or difficult or dirty work, is inherently unstable and ambiguous. It depends on the social relations within which it is undertaken but it may also be a contested concept within those same relations. Work is more than employment but less than all forms of social activity; indeed employment is a form of work but not all work is employment. … [T]he point really is not whether this or that activity is actually work, but what such activities involve, whose interpretation of the activity carries the most weight, and why this should be the case.'

Source: Grint (1991) p. 32.

There are both positive and negative images of work which have a long history: work as drudgery, as demeaning, as merely a means to a more important end, as opposed to work as rewarding, as a route to salvation or as a source of pleasure and interest. Both images are closely associated, of course, with the emergence of industrial society – from the negative image of 'dark satanic mills' to the more positive 'heaven helps those who help themselves'. Notice how each of these contrasting images is charged with religious and moral symbolism: work is as much a moral as it is a productive activity. This is perhaps most clearly expressed in the Indian **caste system** where different castes and their trades, *jati*, are equated with different degrees of religious purity.

caste system

A system of social division and stratification, influenced by Hinduism on the Indian subcontinent, in which an individual's social position is fixed at birth.

The Emergence of the Modern Concept of Work

Historically, the notion of work as paid labour – a job – emerged as the importance of the *wage* as the main source of a person's livelihood grew. In pre-industrial agricultural societies wages were only part of a range of livelihood strategies: people might sell their labour on an occasional basis but were more likely to engage in share-cropping, subsistence agriculture, tenancy, barter arrangements and so on. Similar strategies – and more – have to be adopted by the poor in less developed states in the South today. But where industrialisation and urbanisation occurred from roughly the eighteenth century onwards, increasingly we find families and households more reliant on wage labour precisely because other forms of livelihood were denied them. As a result, households could no longer sustain themselves as productive units, relying on outside jobs to secure their means of survival. The household became a *consumption unit* instead. In the early nineteenth century, the centrality of the wage labour market was apparent from the first recognition then of a clearly defined part of the population as 'unemployed'.

As factory production developed so work regimes became more regulated by factory owners keen to ensure control over labour: time and work – whether related to 'clocking-in', 'shift-work', 'time-and-motion' studies – became of central importance. Work came to be done at certain times, days of the week and weeks of the year. More generally, 'work' came to be regarded as something done at certain periods of adult life – not during 'childhood', nor in 'retirement'. In addition, the location for 'work' became more clearly defined – the factory, the office, the mine – and separated from 'the home'. It was this last development, the separation of home from work, that heightened gender differences which prevail today, inasmuch as women, even when not confined to the domestic sphere, tend to be responsible for work within the home.

By the twentieth century the conventional view of work was very different from that of the pre-industrial period: work was now performed *outside the home, was waged, and performed predominantly by men*. Indeed, similar assumptions were held by the sociology of work during its earlier period: it studied almost exclusively male waged labour in the formal economy. In Chapter 6 we saw that the same comment can be made of some of the traditional approaches to social stratification. In recent years, however, there has been a growing awareness of the inadequacy of this approach. On the one hand, social scientists acknowledge that a task can be completed not only via the 'formal economy' (the wage labour market) but also through the household economy, the 'communal economy' and even the so-called '**black economy**'. Only the first of these would show up in any statistics on 'work'. On the other hand, feminist analysis has examined the work women undertake in the home and shown how extensive this is – in cooking, cleaning, caring for family members (especially children and the elderly), and other domestic tasks. And, as Schwartz Cowan (1983) has suggested, the improvement in domestic technologies and equipment has not eased the burden of housework, merely raised the expectations of cleanliness, food preparation and so on. Oakley (1974) calculates an average working week for a housewife at 77 hours. The wage-equivalent for such labour has recently been estimated at over £18,000. Some feminists have called for housework to be rewarded in this way. Other feminists are wary of joining in with this demand since it would confirm housework as women's work.

black economy
A form of unofficial economic activity; for example, work carried out for payment in kind or for unrecorded payments for tax avoidance purposes.

The constraints on women entering the labour market on terms equal to those enjoyed by men has meant that they are – as we saw in Chapter 8 – concentrated in specific occupations, normally ones that mirror their domestic labour responsibilities, that is, the caring, nurturing, teaching and secretarial 'pink-collar' jobs. Here it is apparent that there is a strong relationship between the arenas of work and home: though separate physically and culturally, the one feeds back on the other. Often, however, the sense of separation of the two spheres, of a strong boundary between the home and the labour market, has, for women, been much less evident: the household itself becomes a place of paid and non-paid work.

Box 12.2: Blurring the boundary between home and work – for women

'Much of women's paid work has been carried out by offering domestic services within the home, for example, child-minding, or taking in laundry, or within the homes of others as full time domestic servants. The latter was the single most numerous occupation for women until the 1930s. Taking in lodgers is an economic activity which exists on the very boundary of the public and private spheres. ... Davidoff ... has emphasised the very different connotation attaching to the word "landlord" (one who owns property and collects rent) as compared to "landlady" (one who, usually living on the premises, provides houseroom and services for cash).'

Source: Crompton and Sanderson (1990).

The establishing of a new household and formalising this through marriage is often for women the beginning of their being marginalised from or restricted within the labour market. For men, on the contrary, it is – especially for the professional middle classes – a base on which to build a respectable career. Oakley's (1974) now classic study of the 'housewife' shows how this role not merely constrains women but is 'basic to the structure of modern society and the ideology of gender roles that pervade it' (p. 24). She claimed that housework was in many ways similar to manual forms of industrial labour – repetitious, routine, tedious, and so on. Over 75 per cent of her sample of young mothers expressed resentment and dissatisfaction with their lives, even though they also viewed their work as of value to the home.

Overall, then, work patterns today should not be thought of as simply descriptions of different types of 'job' that map out modern livelihood strategies. More fundamentally, they are a description of the way the occupational labour market is structured to favour some over others, to give some more autonomy and security than others, to allow some to experience work as a career and others to experience it as a drudgery, and to reproduce gender divisions in work *and* home.

Table 12.1 *Broad types of work*

Category	*Power/status*	*Gender*	*Example*
Professional	High	Male-dominated	Accountant
Managerial	High	Male-dominated	Executive
White collar	Middle	Female-dominated	Secretary
Blue-collar	Low	Male-dominated	Car worker

Nevertheless, many sociologists will routinely divide work into types of job, often into four broad categories that carry different levels of material and cultural 'reward' in terms of levels of pay, job security, perks, skill and power. These four are summarised in Table 12.1.

Broad summaries such as this are of limited value, for they say nothing about the informal or 'black economy', domestic labour, the experience and meaning of work or the variation of work *within* these broad categories. For example, it is women who predominate in the cleaning and textile sectors of 'blue-collar' work, not men. Nevertheless, the broad pattern of *types of occupation* over time is of use in showing the changing structure to the labour market in industrial capitalist states. Some sociologists following the American Daniel Bell believe, for example, that we now live in a **post-industrial society** where the traditional dominance of manufacturing work and the older industrial classes has given way to an information and knowledge-based economy where the more important jobs are those requiring technical and professional qualifications. Table 12.2 summarises Bell's (1973) image of the shift towards a post-industrial society.

post-industrial society
A society where industrial manufacturing declines as a rapid growth in service and information sectors occurs.

As we saw in Chapter 3, the contemporary dynamics of globalisation have in some ways confirmed Bell's broad proposition of structural changes in the labour market. In other ways, however, the new flexible work patterns generate new forms of job-insecurity *for all* in a way which Bell never properly fully recognised. We shall return to this below when we look at the future of work.

Table 12.2 The coming post-industrial society

Industrial Society	move to	*Post-industrial society*
Manufacturing	———>	Dominance of service sector
Labour supply	———>	Knowledge supply
Blue-collar	———>	White-collar/technical staffs
Machine technology	———>	Information-based technology
Industrialists	———>	Technocracy/technical elite
Business firms	———>	Flexible organisational structures

The labour process

As waged-labour, work involves working for someone else, the employer. The employer may be a large or small organisation, public or private, in an industrial, service or other sector and so on. As a worker, a person experiences work as a labour process, a particular type of work carrying its own social, technical and economic requirements to be completed properly, whether this is writing a book or ploughing a field. The onset of industrialisation brought significant changes to the labour process, most importantly with regard to the worker's own control over the work done, and the reward it should receive.

Marx (1954) was the first to discuss the impact of capitalist industrial growth on the labour process and, so, on the experience of work. Briefly, he argued that the advent of machinery and automation gradually removed the workers' control over the labour process, in part by enabling their skills to be broken up between the new machines which they tended, or by the machines incorporating those very skills themselves. The knowledge and skills required for the completion of tasks thereby come under the owner and controller of that capital which buys the factory, runs the machines and employs the workforce. The same principle which breaks down work into routine and meaningless tasks means that management, by organising and co-ordinating its elements, can gain a virtual monopoly of knowledge and therefore control over the labour process. These arguments were developed in more recent years by *labour process theory* (see e.g. Braverman, 1974).

deskilling
Developed by Braverman to describe what he believed to be strategies of employers to reduce the skills required of their labour force, which often occurs alongside the introduction of new technological processes into the work place.

Braverman argues that the labour process was one characterised by **deskilling** and the degradation of work. Work tasks no longer required the application of a range of skills developed through apprenticeship and job experience but merely the completion of mindless, repetitive, and very limited tasks in pace with a machine-based manufacturing process. Braverman saw these developments as the result of the application of so-called 'scientific management' inspired through the managerial philosophy of Frederick Taylor, whose impact was first felt in the 1910–20 period. Taylor (1911) argued that management had responsibility for deciding how work tasks should be completed and to this end should specify every detail of a task and the time taken to complete it: from this was born the 'time and motion' study so often used to orchestrate labour and ensure its efficiency on the assembly-line. This approach seeks to overcome any reliance on worker skills, often tacit and variable in the way they might be applied to complete a particular job. Instead, the skill is deconstructed and reduced to a series of codified, regulated, and therefore controlled actions which any worker can complete.

Braverman's attack on the capitalist labour process was simultaneously an attack on the class inequality residing in worker–manager relations: while managers themselves may not necessarily be owners of capital they acted on behalf of capitalist interests, either those of remote shareholders or proprietors of firms. But Braverman also notes that *all* occupational groups, *including white-collar management*, are inevitably subject to the same process of deskilling and control, as capital seeks ever greater efficiencies in all aspects of the labour process, including its management. Later sociological work in the USA and Europe seemed to bear out the deskilling of office or clerical work.

neo-Marxism
Contemporary school of thought based on a development of Marxist philosophy.

Braverman's **neo-Marxist** analysis had a significant impact on the sociology of work during the mid to late 1970s. There were many who regarded his attack on the labour process within capitalism as timely and well-founded. But there have been an increasing number who have challenged his account on both theoretical and empirical grounds. A number of criticisms have been made.

First, a key criticism is that the notion of 'deskilling' depends on Braverman providing us with some clear benchmark of what 'skill' actually is, so that we can then make sense of how far or in what way it has been 'de-skilled'. Yet Braverman provides only a very limited – and in a sense non-sociological – notion of skill as 'craft mastery', of a technical competence associated with the use of tools and machinery. However, sociologists have shown that skill is much more fluid a notion than this: what a skill is and how it is to be rewarded depends on the social negotiation between workers and their employers. We can see this, for example, in the way typing skills have been redefined as 'keyboard skills' associated with word processors, and (especially when used by men) accorded a higher status than before. Professional and occupational groups, and trades unions will, then, strive to sustain and secure a definition of their 'skills' over time as the labour market changes.

bureaucracy
A type of organisation run by officials, and based on a hierarchical structure of authority best suited for the efficient pursuit of organisational goals.

Second, even if the fragmentation and deskilling of work *is* in some sense occurring in the way Braverman describes, this is only *one* of a number of strategies contemporary employers use to secure compliance from workers. Indeed, Friedman (1977) argues that rather than trying to reduce worker involvement in work tasks, many firms secure worker efficiency better through offering greater rather than less involvement. Edwards (1979) takes this further, suggesting that managers increasingly resort to a form of '**bureaucratic**' control over workers where workers' compliance and commitment is sought through the implementation of rules and regulations throughout the organisation as well as incentives schemes which act as an 'elaborate system of bribes' (p. 145). Current attempts at 'total quality management' (Webster and Robins, 1993), where all firm members are expected to conform to a range of clearly defined measures of efficiency and 'quality' of product development in return for bonuses and profit-sharing, is an extension of this strategy. One sees this, for example, in the computing and engineering and aerospace industries where the quality of a complex product design is crucial to eventual market success.

Third, others suggest that work today demands a broader range of flexible skills – technical, social and organisational – based on higher levels of training and educational achievement. Research in the US on engineers (Spenner, 1990) and on dock workers (Finlay, 1988) confirms more recent European studies (Bottrup and Clematide, 1992) on the impact of new technologies and management strategies. These show that in some contexts occupations can experience a re-skilling of work tasks in order to utilise the new technologies that are acquired by firms: crane drivers on the docks, for example, have had to develop new skills to contend with containerised cargo shipments. Similar conclusions have been drawn in recent studies of clerical workers (e.g. Crompton and Sanderson, 1990). Finally, Gallie (1991) has shown how important it is to approach the question of skill from a social class perspective. His research shows that while the majority of non-manual, 'intermediate', and skilled manual workers believe their work today demands a higher level of skill, the majority of manual workers felt that the responsibility and skill involved in their work had either remained the same or declined.

This later work shows that we need to be careful of Braverman's claim that the impact of new technologies on the workplace is always towards deskilling. Much depends too on the wider social context within which employers introduce technology into the workplace. As this context changes, so the broad impact of the technology might be very different.

Box 12.3: New technology, skill and social context

'When introducing new technology, managers face a clear choice: they can use it as an opportunity to increase the skill level in the labour force, by involving the workers in the control of technology, or they can utilise the technology to further centralise control over the production process and simplify and fragment work tasks. International comparisons suggest that whether managers choose to upskill the work force or deskill it will depend in part on the national system of vocational education and training and the structure of the firm. In Germany, where workers have a relatively high level of intermediate skills, managers tend to utilise the new systems of programmable automation to further enhance the skills of the labour force. ... In Britain, where the level of training and hence skills of the labour force are lower ... the tendency has been to use programmable automation to increase the control managers have over the production process. One consequence of that is the further deskilling of the tasks of workers.'

Source: Green and Ashton (1992) p. 288.

We get a better understanding of the impact of technologies by locating them within the contemporary labour market and globalised innovation and production system. We saw in Chapter 7 that this system has tended to produce a polarised occupational structure in industrial capitalist states where those in secure work are more likely to be competent in a range of technical skills while the growing ranks of casualised, insecure jobs may use new technologies (such as the check-out assistant in the supermarket) but in a routine and uniform way. This view is also borne out by Gallie's (1991) UK-based study mentioned above. It is also clear that recent international comparative studies of class and occupational structure show a growing variety to the way in which skill is perceived as important while confirming the trend towards polarisation of the labour market. Overall, therefore, these various studies do not suggest that the workforce as a whole is experiencing de-skilling.

worker resistance
Strategies employed by workers to subvert the labour process.

This last point has important implications with regard to one of Braverman's other arguments: that is, the homogenisation of the labour process would, he believed, encourage a greater sense of political solidarity among the working class. While **worker resistance**, as we shall see, has been in as much evidence in recent years as in the past, this has not necessarily led to a growth in solidarity. Some workers, typically white, male, technical or professional employees, are in a much better position to resist management control than others, and may, in fact because of this, be quite reluctant to carry others along with them. While the dynamics of the labour process are important factors shaping the context within which work is experienced, they do not *determine* the meaning of that experience which is highly variable, not least by gender, age and ethnicity.

The meaning of work and work satisfaction

There are, broadly speaking, two ways in which we can understand the meaning work has and the satisfaction it gives to people. On the one hand, one can say that the experience people have of work is a direct result of that work itself, boring work producing a bored worker with little or no job satisfaction. On the other hand, one could say that it is the attitudes workers *bring to* their jobs that is more important in determining work experience and what they expect of work. In this second case, workers might find their jobs 'boring' but may expect little else and in this sense be 'satisfied' with the work they do. In short, it seems sensible to try to understand *both* the nature of work and the orientation workers have towards it.

Employees' conditions of work are influenced by a wide range of factors – their level of pay, the physical nature of the job they do, the surroundings in which they work, the level of autonomy they have in their job, and, of particular importance, the sort of *technology* it involves. The term 'technology' here should be understood to refer to the socio-technical relations that characterise a manufacturing, service or other job. So, for example , in car manufacture, the Japanese **'just-in-time' (JIT) production** system is a complex system in which workers, components, the physical lay-out of plant, the **information technologies** managing the flow of materials and work patterns, and so on, are all orchestrated to ensure quality products are produced 'in-time' without excess stock having to be held, and for a well-targeted market. The spread of this type of production in Western Europe and the USA has led to the phrase the 'Japanisation' of production. Workers are subject to considerable surveillance and are used in a flexible way to meet changing production schedules and objectives. The experience of work here is then likely to be rather different from that of, say, a farm worker working in isolation on the fields.

just-in-time production

A finely balanced and controlled manufacturing production system designed to produce goods to meet demand as and when required.

information technology

Computerised, electronic, technology related to the gathering, recording and communicating of information.

The notion that the particular type of technology – or socio-technical system – that a worker is exposed to shapes their experience has been most forcefully argued in a now classic study by Blauner (1964). Blauner argued that some work was more *alienating* than other types as a result of the different technologies workers are required to use. **Alienation**, according to Blauner, has four dimensions: powerlessness, meaninglessness, isolation and self-estrangement. Individuals are powerless when they cannot control their own actions or conditions of work; work is meaningless where it gives employees little or no sense of value, worth or interest to them; work is isolating when workers cannot identify with their workplace; and self-estranging when at the subjective level the worker has no sense of involvement in the job.

alienation

Originally utilised by Marx to describe feelings of estrangement experienced by workers under industrial capitalism. Now more generally employed to describe people's feelings of isolation, powerlessness, and self-estrangement.

Blauner applied his model to four different industrial sectors using different technologies:

- printing – craft-based technology
- textiles – machine-tending technology
- car production – assembly-line technology
- chemicals – continuous process technology.

Of these four, the technology most likely to produce alienating work is assembly-line technology. The powerlessness of the work is reflected in the way the worker follows a routine set of tasks at a constant pace on the line; the job is mind-numbingly meaningless, and isolated from fellow workers and dull and monotonous. Chemical process work, on the contrary is much less alienating, as workers are more in control of a highly automated plant with considerable levels of responsibility attached to their jobs.

However, there are many problems with Blauner's claims, not least his failure to recognise that the same technology – such as an assembly plant – can be experienced in a variety of ways. Look, for example, at JIT production – typical of the car industry thirty years on from Blauner's study.

The spread of a JIT system should not lead us to expect that those workers exposed to it *all* share the *same* work experience. Studies have shown that local cultural circumstances with regard to manager/union relations, levels of hierarchical control and reward and performance appraisal policies mean that the experience of JIT work can be very different between countries and firms (Jenkins, 1994). For example, the French automobile industry has been much less inclined towards the high levels of surveillance and job control practised by US corporations. Much depends on the *social organisation* of work and the 'psychological contract' management makes with workers: in return for meeting JIT demands workers are told that they will be well rewarded with good levels of pay and career progression, *as individuals*. Indeed, work experience over recent years has been increasingly shaped by the individualisation of the job 'contract' (for those who have one!) as unions have found their negotiating power undermined by anti-union legislation. What a worker then wants out of work may be less likely to be *collectively defined* because of this shift.

This individualisation of work and the need for individual workers to be more flexible in the skills they have to respond to changing technical demands in their jobs means that Blauner's characterisation of work experience is increasingly out of date. Assembly lines still exist, of course, but no longer in the way he described. They are part of a production system which relies on information technologies to design, engineer and produce new products no longer prepared for homogeneous mass markets as was true in the 1960s.

polarisation of the labour market
A labour market divided between jobs which are well paid and secure and those which are not.

In broader terms, a worker's experience of technology is dependent on where his or her job falls in the increasingly **polarised labour market** (see above and Chapter 6). Automative technologies or computerised work systems, for example, now typically enhance workers' job satisfaction and skill deployment in the better-paid, secure public and private sector jobs; in casualised, non-skilled manual work they have merely reproduced low levels of job satisfaction, especially for the many women found in this type of work. Perhaps, for such poorly paid, vulnerable workers, it is rational *not* to look for intrinsic reward in the work they do. Here, therefore, we should – as with all jobs – be particularly interested in the attitudes people bring to their work.

Workers' Orientations to Work

Rather than presupposing, as did Blauner, that workers' experience is a direct result of the technology they confront, other sociologists stress the orientation of the worker to his or her job. Another now classic study, Goldthorpe *et al.*'s *Affluent Worker* (1968), explored the attitudes towards work of Luton-based Vauxhall car workers in the UK during the early 1960s. They suggested that although the monotony, fragmentation and deskilling of jobs on the assembly line meant that workers derived little intrinsic satisfaction from them, they were not looking for this in the first place. The job was principally a means of securing a relatively good ('affluent') wage which would enable them to enjoy the sort of life they sought *outside* the factory. Work was simply an instrument to achieve this other end: in short, the workers had an instrumental orientation to their jobs. Outside work they sought a 'privatised' home-centred family life on the new housing estates of Luton. The two terms – **instrumentalism** and **privatism** – lie at the heart of the *Affluent Worker* research.

instrumentalism
An approach by workers to work which seeks to derive satisfaction not so much in the task or job itself, but from benefits such as good rates of pay or secure employment.

privatism
A concept used to describe a focus centred on the home and family life.

The importance of this study is that it showed how worker attitudes can only be understood by looking beyond as well as within the factory (or whatever the place of work) itself. Workplaces are not closed systems but relate to and are experienced in terms of external, and especially domestic and household, structures and expectations. As well as showing this, the study had important implications for the way in which the workers' orientation had an affect on their *political* loyalties and attitudes. Instrumentalism and privatism, it was suggested, would be likely to weaken strong class identification among the workers and bring a decline in strong affiliation with trades unionism. Again, the significance of the world of work goes far beyond the factory gates.

Despite the valuable contribution the *Affluent Worker* study has made, it has been subject to a number of criticisms (see Grieco, 1987). One of the more recent criticisms has been provided by Devine (1992). She looked again at car workers in Luton, this time in the very different circumstances of the late 1980s, a period of recession and, for this area in particular, growing unemployment. Some of this downturn related to the restructuring of industry we discussed in Chapters 6 and 7.

Rather than trying to recompose the original randomised sample of workers, Devine focused on thirty couples, ranging in age from mid-20s to late-60s, a group identified via snowball sampling (see Chapter 5). Her respondents painted a rather different picture from that drawn by Goldthorpe *et al.* in the 1960s. Rather than still seeing instrumentalism and privatism, she found couples were concerned about their working conditions and had not withdrawn into home-centredness. Their main concerns were finding good housing and secure jobs rather than necessarily seeking jobs with the highest level of pay. Moreover, the pattern of links that households had with others around them depended very much on which stage of the life-cycle they were in, whether both partners were earning or just one, whether other kin used Luton-based relations to help find work, and so on.

Much of this may, of course, reflect the wider socio-economic changes experienced in the Luton housing and labour markets. But Devine believes that the *Affluent Worker* studies exaggerate the degree of instrumentalism and privatisation among the car workers. She also suggests that the workers' political inclinations still reflected a broad sense of working-class identity, even if the vehicles through which this might be expressed – such as unionism – had been dismantled by the anti-union legislation of the then Thatcher administration. Most workers saw themselves in the same boat, one likely to tip them into the growing sea of unemployment. That this did not trigger off worker radicalism or resistance does not mean that workers were prepared to acquiesce to poor working conditions, but rather that they adopted what might be called a realistic pessimism in light of the changing labour market.

Orientations to work must therefore be seen to reflect a number of factors, which the preceding discussion has touched on. These are:

- the nature of the technology to which workers are exposed
- the relationship between home and work

- the stage of life-cycle of a household
- the relation between paid work and domestic labour
- the wider labour and housing markets
- the wider political milieu.

Gender, Ethnicity, Age and Work

The attitudes towards work we have sketched out above have said little about how these are shaped by gender, ethnicity or age. Yet these are clearly significant variables influencing the experience, conditions, security and benefits of work, which we can discuss briefly here.

Gender

Chapter 8 has discussed the dynamics of gender in considerable detail and raised the question of how women's work patterns and their more general participation in the labour market differs considerably from that of men. Thus, women are disproportionately represented in work which is seen as an extension of their domestic life. In the US and UK, for example, a significant proportion of women work in secretarial, teaching, catering and retail jobs. There has been a greater number of women securing other occupational positions over the past two decades in industrial society where women now comprise around 50 per cent of the total workforce.

One key factor which is known to restrict women's opportunity in the labour market is marriage. Married women are not only less likely to work, but even when they do work they are more likely to feel the need to migrate with their husbands if these men secure new employment elsewhere, rather than staying with their job. If both partners have strong careers and intend to pursue them, the household structure and role expectations therein are likely to be very different from that of the conventional nuclear family. On the other hand, evidence from the US (Roos, 1983) suggests that declining fertility (number of children in the home) is enabling more women to return to the labour market more quickly. There is related evidence which shows that women are returning to work more quickly after the birth of a child so as not to lose their 'labour market position' (what a Weberian might call their 'market situation' – see Chapter 6). Much depends here, of course, on the employers' policies towards maternity leave and the terms on which mothers can rejoin their work (McRae, 1994).

Even though there may have been some improvement for women in the labour market, the constraints of domestic responsibility and subordination to male partners' priorities still mean that women have a much greater problem in securing that continuity and experience of work which is so important for employability. As a result, career progression upwards tends to hit the so-called '**glass ceiling**' fairly soon with an effective barrier to higher earnings. Progression is also hampered because women suffer from having fewer contacts with people who might assist them in finding better work, just as when working they receive generally less training or staff development (Wholey, 1990). In part this reflects the perspective common among male managers that women are not interested in careers, even when the evidence points to the contrary. The US is often cited as one country in which women have managed to break through the glass ceiling: however, in 1994, only 4 per cent of senior executive posts were held by women. As Grint (1991) notes, those that do break through tend to be found in the 'triple-P' departments, of purchasing, publicity and personnel.

glass ceiling
A metaphorical concept used to explain how women are prevented from attaining top managerial and professional jobs.

We saw earlier that technology has been associated with *both* deskilling and reskilling of work, but many commentators believe that the advent of new technology-based jobs work is particularly disadvantageous to women. Some feminist analysts believe that technology is itself gendered to work against women. As Frissen (1992) has put it:

> **In feminist analyses, technologies are often described as 'toys for the boys'. According to these approaches an important reason for difference in access to technology between women and men, is that the value system underlying technological practices is fundamentally masculine.**
>
> **[Frissen, 1992]**

Not all agree with this view, however, since closer examination of the relationship of *both* men and women to technologies in general and machines in particular suggests no simple masculine/**technophilic**, women/**technophobic** relation (see Packer, 1996). This does *not*, however, thereby imply that where women do feel comfortable with and skilled at using new technologies they will then be promoted in recognition of their abilities in the workplace, whether the laboratory, the office, the factory or elsewhere. Instead, in such a situation, technical skills may be given less importance as a (predominantly) male management identifies other skills as necessary for promotion. Again, we see here how the definition of 'skill', and so its reward, is socially constructed, this time around a gendered view of competence. In this situation

technophilic
An aptitude for, and willingness to engage with, technology.

technophobic
Fear of, and reluctance to engage with, technology.

women may experience considerable job dissatisfaction as their skills are under-valued and under-rewarded.

gendered division of labour
The division of work roles and tasks into those performed by men and those performed by women.

The **gendered division of labour** is one that still firmly favours men over women. Although women's participation in the labour market is increasing proportionately and the range of work they do broadening, the demands of the domestic division of labour continue to prevent any fundamental change for most women with regard to their relation to work.

Ethnicity

ethnicity
To be distinguished from 'race', which emphasises biological differences based on skin colour, ethnicity denotes a sense of belonging to a particular community whose members share common cultural traditions.

race
A contentious concept within sociology, typically associated with a group connected by common origin, typically associated with skin colour.

We saw in Chapter 9 that **ethnicity** and **race** are key determinants of social inequality. Racism in the workplace, and in recruitment within the labour market, tends to produce a situation where ethnic and racially defined minorities experience chronic disadvantage. This is despite the fact that members of these minority groups often have the same credentials as ethnic (chiefly white) majorities. As with women, we tend to find Afro-Caribbean, Indian, Pakistani and other racially defined groups in a limited range of lower-paid jobs, though typically some of these groups – notably male Indians – tend to be slightly more successful in the labour market. Not surprisingly, female black workers are among the most vulnerable to poor, low-paid work.

Disadvantages in the labour market reflect prejudice and discrimination such that there is an equivalent racist version of the glass ceiling experienced by women. Sometimes, as was true in the case of slavery and more recently apartheid, this ceiling is quite openly and formally installed by state law, as in South Africa before 1990. Certain jobs are closed to workers as is living and working in certain areas of the country. Surprisingly, perhaps, the removal of formalised racism, as in South Africa, can have a much greater impact on improving the position of black and 'coloured' people than all the anti-discriminatory legislation that has been passed over the years in liberal democracies.

Ethnic minorities in Europe and the USA have suffered from discrimination in the workplace for a variety of reasons. Some analysts stress the demand for cheap labour by private capital, others the failure of (ethnic majority) trades unions to support the minority workers' interests to the full, while others – focusing on the 'outsider' status of many ethnic workers – stress the inherent weakness of those seeking jobs as migrant labourers, such as the Turkish workers employed in Germany or the Vietnamese in the United States. For these, employment rights are often completely ignored. And, as Piore (1979) has argued, such workers are least likely to press for their rights, since they regard their job as temporary and merely a way of securing income that can be taken back home: in a sense, such migrant workers are probably a much better example of the 'instrumentalism' that Goldthorpe *et al.* claimed could be found among the Luton car-workers in the UK.

It should be noted, however, that over the past twenty years black workers, in particular in the United States, have begun to break out of the subordinate labour market ghetto they have occupied for so long. Hout (1984), for example, has shown that African-Americans occupy a much more diversified range of jobs across the social classes than was true in the 1960s, and he suggests that the growth of public sector work has been an important vehicle for social advancement. Nevertheless, compared with other ethnic, in-migrant labour such as the Irish, Koreans and Italians, black Americans are still structurally disadvantaged in the US labour market.

Insecure and low-paid work often in harsh physical environments has led to limited work satisfaction for all these ethnic minorities. Within ethnic *communities* work is much more likely to provide a greater sense of work satisfaction and autonomy where kin, extended kin and the wider ethnic group can provide a mutually supportive **micro-economy**. Asian communities in Britain, for example, are characterised by a high level of self-employed (typically male-run) small businesses tied into the local ethnic community.

micro-economy
The productive activities of any small area located within a wider, macro-economy.

Age

demographic age profile
The size and structure of the population based on age.

The **demographic age profile** of all industrialised countries is changing to reflect the growing numbers of the 'elderly', especially, of course, among the retired. But there is also an age-profile characterising the labour markets of industrial societies. That is, certain types of work are more likely to be undertaken by people at different stages of their adult life-cycle than others. For example, one finds younger members of society disproportionately represented in more physically demanding work (such as in warehouses, the police, or building work), or work such as computer programming, which depends on the acquisition of skills for handling new technologies. In some jobs, as Kaufman and Richardson (1982) have shown, there is a U-shaped distribution of young and old adult workers – jobs which are low-paid and careerless, such as gardeners, elevator-operators and cashiers.

One of the more important age-related phenomena of recent years is the widespread redundancies among middle-income, middle management who have been encouraged to take 'early retirement'. The restructuring of industry which we discussed in Chapter 7 has not only led to the polarisation of the workforce but also to substantial numbers of older workers experiencing an unexpected vulnerability in their jobs. National (as in the US) and international (as in the EU) legislation has been implemented in the past decade to counter discrimination against workers on the basis of their age; costs of paying off early retirements have also risen and been seen to be more expensive than keeping some workers on. As a result, the speed at which the older worker was being removed from the labour market has declined though not stopped. Many have sought to draw on their pre-existing contacts and networks to establish small 'consultancy' businesses, often acting on a casualised basis on behalf of their previous employer. This has been especially true of managers who once worked in the now privatised public utilities in the UK. The production of 'business cards' for the self-employed middle-aged has no doubt been one of the growth industries of this period of restructuring!

According to Scase (1992) the organisational and economic restructuring of recent years has meant that the notion of the traditional manager responsible for administering a business division is no longer regarded as vital to a company's managerial strategy: instead such responsibilities can be '**outsourced**' or subcontracted to smaller, cheaper business advisory firms. Stripping out middle management in this way has also been related to the growth of information technology (IT) which enables more control from the centre while allowing a horizontal, rather than hierarchical, management structure to emerge among those still in the firm. The combined effects of this '**downsizing**' of the labour force and 'fragmenting' (Shutt and Whittington, 1987) of large corporations into smaller, more flexible, units means that there are many thousands who, aged between 45 and 50, cannot find work, and for whom any pension is too far off in the future.

outsourcing
The process of subcontracting work, i.e. securing certain research and development needs from external contractors that were previously met inside the firm.

downsizing
Management jargon for reducing job numbers.

Government policies in Western Europe are seeking to harmonise the age at which both men and women leave the labour market. In the UK, harmonisation around the age of 65 is to be phased in during the period from 2010 to 2020. Many retirees still seek part-time work, not merely to supplement typically low levels of state or employer pension, but also to try to sustain that sense of identity work had brought them. Typically, one-third of males in Western Europe work after official retirement (CEC, 1994) even if this work has a lower status than when they were employed.

We saw in Chapter 7 how changes in the structure of the labour market will lead to a situation in which the notion of a secure long-term career will become reserved for perhaps only a third of the working population of whatever social class. The uncertainties experienced by middle management in recent years are likely to become the norm for many service-based occupational groups, and increasingly so for those engaged in manufacturing and related sectors. The future of work will no doubt be different and sociologists will need to explore the implications this will have for occupational and class identities traditionally so dependent on the job one does. Some labour market analysts such as Handy (1985) argue that society must move away from being so 'job-fixated' and instead look at the 'array of possibilities if we start to play around with the conventional notion of the 100,000 hours lifetime job' (p. 37). But first, we need to ask how workers are responding to the changing labour market, how trades unions cope with the fragmentation of work itself and the traditional places of work, and whether, as a result, new forms of industrial conflict can be expected in the future.

Industrial Conflict

The 1980s and 1990s have seen significant changes in the way in which workers have sought to protect their position in their jobs and the labour market more generally. Worker resistance to management strategies – over pay, conditions and rights, for example – has traditionally been expressed through strikes, absenteeism, sabotage, pilfering, or negotiation through official trades unions or professional association agencies. We can see from the preceding discussion that the restructuring of the labour market has created rising numbers of the unemployed, in both public and private sectors of the economy. Jobs have also been 'lost' to peripheral workers in overseas countries. State legislation has eroded worker and union rights, and traditional sources of union power, identity and leadership – such as in coal mining – have been destroyed. Industrial conflict, which clearly reflects wider socio-political conflict, has as a result experienced something of a decline if measured in terms of strike action, as workers have found it increasingly difficult to act in unison on a national basis via their trades unions. Unemployment is now – whether one takes official or hidden (i.e. including those who would like to work) levels of unemployment – at its highest historical level throughout Europe. The notion of 'full employment' once accepted by all political parties as a desirable goal, no longer receives full political support, even among members of left-of-centre parties.

We can view the current situation in a number of ways. As the fragmentation of work continues so we might expect to see a fragmentation of unions, or at least of union-power. Moreover, we can see the growth of new jobs in the part-time, casualised sector – such as retailing and catering – where unionism has been traditionally weak. Furthermore, these jobs are also highly feminised and as such have been less likely to be union-oriented. The shift away from national bargaining over conditions and pay has led to plant bargaining and – more worrying for unions – individualised contracts for members of staff. The traditionally big public sector unions find their power eroded through privatisation and, in the UK, being subject at local level to new forms of management and trustee 'ownership' designed to take the state out of negotiations over pay etc.

In short, the old 'labour movement' appears to have lost much of the momentum that it had built up over the pre- and post-Second World War period. The collectivism it once expressed – though this was always in part over-romanticised by the movement itself – is difficult to sustain as the labour market's polarisation splits workers into a core, secure, privileged stratum and a large, casualised and insecure mass of workers.

In this situation worker resistance can be either bought off quite quickly, or dismissed by simply employing other, new workers, as has happened in a number of recent disputes in the UK (at the Timex watch factory, for example). Alternatively, employers may threaten to relocate production elsewhere (as has happened in some British car plants). Given this, from both a worker's and an employer's perspective, one of the most important factors shaping the future of working conditions is the European Union which has sought to introduce minimum levels of pay, worker rights, and equality of opportunity. The British government under the Major administration of the early 1990s sought to opt out of these requirements but found that many corporations operating as multinational firms had decided to adopt the same conditions throughout Europe, including among their British-based operations. The institutional importance of the EU for the protection of worker rights is, therefore, highly significant and will help to shape the context in Europe of future industrial conflict. At the same time, the EU is not hostile towards European industry, which it is keen to see 'competitive' with that of the **Pacific Rim** and the United States. So it will continue to juggle with the interests of workers and private capital and no doubt there will be legislation on the European statute books which pulls in conflicting directions.

Pacific Rim
Those south-east Asian countries with fast developing economies that border the Pacific Ocean, such as Taiwan, Hong Kong, Malaysia and South Korea.

The Future of Work?

As work patterns change, and as the relationship between the labour market and the notion of full-time, secure work has changed, so it seems that the future of work over the next twenty-five years will change dramatically. Whether these changes are in the direction of Handy's (1985) rather utopian vision of job-sharing and, by implication, leisure-sharing across all social classes, where the distribution of income is much more even and people willingly accept this, or in the direction of increasing polarisation, growing unemployment, social deprivation and more being spent on social control and video surveillance (in and out of work), depends on society's responses to the political options sketched out in Chapter 10.

Leisure

The history of the development of paid work is paralleled by the histories of not only unemployment (where access to labour markets is denied) but also *leisure*, time free from the specific demands of paid labour. Leisure is, in fact, difficult to define, and is often seen in negative terms as non-work. Normally, it refers to activity where there is no compulsion, where there is autonomy and personal control over what one is doing. Handy calls it 'discretionary time'. Like work, leisure takes place at particular times and in particular locations, as at the cinema, the theatre, watching television, on holiday, the sports centre, and so on. Leisure has grown as a result of

- a growth in real disposable income for most workers
- a reduction in hours worked and more free time (notably, since the 1960s, the five-day week and the free weekend)
- paid holidays (from the early 1970s in Western Europe)
- the commercialisation of leisure such that more opportunities and outlets for leisure pursuits are available
- a contraction of working life as schooling gets longer and retirement years longer, as life expectancy increases and retirement is itself taken earlier, primarily by those with good occupational pensions.

This last point means that the leisure industry has two very important sectors in the population to target – the youth and young adults, and the elderly markets. The demographic shift of recent years means that in the UK there are over 9 million men and women aged 60–75, many seeking some form of leisure activity. The growth of leisure time does not mean, of course, that everyone is in a similar position to take it up: most of all, the unemployed find it particularly difficult to convert free time into leisure as they have little money, few social contacts, and a sense of lost identity, self-esteem and personal status. They also have almost *too much* time to 'enjoy' leisure. It is having paid work, then, that is central to our enjoyment of leisure. Moreover, as domestic labourers, women's leisure is often circumscribed or experienced through that of others – her partner's, her children's, and so on.

Glyptis (1989) has suggested that there are three ways in which the relationship between work and leisure has been characterised by sociology. The first, referred to as the 'extension' or 'spillover' approach, looks at the ways in which an individual's personality and attitudes are expressed in *both* work and leisure. The second, the 'oppositional' approach, sees leisure as entirely antithetical to the world of work, somewhere to forget work or at least to compensate for it. The final approach sees the two spheres as simply unconnected with each other: this is called the 'neutrality' approach.

Such broad characterisations have all found supportive evidence such that the way the two relate is clearly dependent on context, personality and opportunity. There are also very different predispositions towards leisure. Perhaps one way of showing this variation is through McGoldrick's and Carter's (1982) classification of types of leisure activity undertaken by households where the principal male breadwinner had recently retired. They describe the various leisure orientations as 'rest and relaxers', 'home and family men', 'hobbyists', 'good timers', 'committee and society men', 'volunteers', 'further education men', 'part-time jobbers' and 'new jobbers'. Such categories of leisure are useful in providing us with an array of the sort of behaviour people define as leisure. However, they say nothing about the way we should understand leisure in its wider social context. For this, we need a more theoretical argument.

There are three principal theoretical approaches to leisure: neo-Marxist, feminist and postmodern. Let us look at each one briefly.

Neo-Marxism

This approach (see e.g. Clarke and Critcher, 1985), as one might expect, ties leisure into the interests of capitalism. Leisure is appropriated by private capital, commodified and sold to a mass market which has little sense or realisation of the way their leisure is being prepacked and made ready for their consumption. Moreover, while it is geared to a mass market, contemporary capitalist leisure is highly class-based in the sense that it carries the structured inequalities of capitalist class society. The market for commercial leisure goods grows constantly, so that eventually people can only experience a sense of leisure if they have bought it – through the theme park, the health club, the holiday abroad, the latest 'leisure shirt' from the mail-order catalogue. Sport, so central to leisure, is a vehicle both for social control and sales of goods – the latest team-shirt, for example. Sports men and women become themselves commodified as sponsors of sports companies', oil companies', or tobacco companies' wares.

Against this view, some sociologists (e.g. Rojeck, 1995) have argued that leisure cannot be reduced to the interests of capital in this way. Some forms of leisure, such as tending a suburban vegetable allotment, are completely outside the circuit of capital and indeed often explicitly hostile towards it (Crouch, 1994). Others open up new opportunities for women – such as aerobics – which were denied them in a male-dominated past. Similarly, popular cultural forms of leisure, such as bingo, the working-men's club and 'rave' music nights express localised leisure activities which cannot be conceived sensibly in terms of the class interests of capital.

Despite these reservations and criticisms made against the neo-Marxist account, the commercialisation of leisure is clearly an important and defining feature of contemporary society. This notion is taken up, however, in a rather different way by those who adopt a postmodern perspective on leisure, as we shall see below.

Feminism

This second approach, as Deem (1986) observes, 'places women at the forefront of its analysis and sees them as an oppressed group with certain experiences and interests in common' (p. 11). Not only is a woman's leisure more restricted than that of a man's, but women are typically the providers of leisure *for men:*

> **women service men's leisure activities, by undertaking domestic work and childcare, so that men are free to go out to the pub or to have leisure time out of the house ... [M]any sites where leisure takes place are barred or made unattractive to women (football, rugby, working men's clubs, many pubs) by admitting them on male terms ... Men see leisure as a right; women do not and are not encouraged by men to do so.** ”
>
> **[Deem, 1986, p. 13]**

Deem herself studied female leisure activities in Milton Keynes, a new town located in the south of the UK. She studied two groups of women, one made up of those actively engaged in out-of-home leisure pursuits who belonged to various organisations and clubs, and a random sample of women, most of whom had limited or no involvement with external organisations. While noting differences between the two groups she shows how close their experience of leisure actually is.

Box 12. 4: Women and leisure

'Both groups have problems and constraints which it is necessary for them to overcome if they are to have any leisure of their own. Whilst some of those constraints and problems are of necessity individual and idiosyncratic, many of them are both structural and ideological and there is a limit to which individual women can challenge such constraints. ... Even women who are able to challenge or resist some of the constraints surrounding the possibilities of achieving leisure outside the home and inside it are limited by the extent to which male dominance permeates society. Whether it is the difficulties women face in being able to escape from the household tasks in the evenings or weekends, the places and activities with which they feel comfortable, vulnerability when travelling across a city, or the extent to which women are made to feel that sport and physical activity are unfeminine, it is male dominance, in its many forms, which stands at the roots of these constraints...Where women are active in leisure pursuits outside the home it is usually within a range of "suitable" and "gender appropriate" activities – women's organisations, caring and community activities, evening classes, keep fit and yoga groups, bingo – which are enjoyable, but are also where women feel and are perceived by men to be "safe" and "women in their place".'

Source: Deem (1986) pp. 39–40.

In her conclusions to her study, Deem identifies a number of factors which enable women to participate in leisure activities. These include:

- access to private transport
- an independent source of money
- some form of work
- a self-confident approach to life
- a sense of a legitimate right to leisure
- a social support network.

In the light of this, Deem argues that three changes need to take place if women are to enhance their experience of leisure: improving the environment for women's leisure through an integrated public policy that combines leisure provision with better public transport, childcare facilities, and support for women's organisations; increasing (non-commercial) leisure provision in general in ways which women themselves determine; and finally, changing the domestic division of labour and the relationship between work and leisure that is peculiar to women as a result.

Postmodernist leisure

postmodernity
For its supporters, the further transformation in social, cultural, economic and political arrangements which takes a society beyond modernity.

This last theoretical approach to leisure draws on the much wider perspective within sociology of **postmodernity**. As we have seen in earlier chapters, **postmodernism** claims that society today is one in which the *boundaries* between social institutions, social structures, moral and immoral codes, the right and the wrong ways of doing things – are all breaking down. Postmodern culture breaks down the tired and hierarchical traditions of modernity and opens up new opportunities for expression and new forms of self-realisation while never allowing us a stable meaning to our experience of life. As Featherstone (1991) puts it:

If we examine definitions of postmodernism we find an emphasis on the effacement of the boundary between art and everyday life, the collapse of the distinction between high art and mass/popular culture, a general stylistic promiscuity and playful mixing of codes.

[Featherstone, 1991, p. 65]

postmodernism
Often perceived as a cultural and aesthetic phenomenon associated with contemporary literature and the arts, it often combines apparently opposed elements to subvert meaning and fragment totality. It is characterised by a pastiche of cultural styles and elements, but implies a deeper scepticism about order and progress. Instead diversity and fragmentation are celebrated.

What has this to got to do with leisure? For the postmodernist, leisure cannot be conceived of as simply an activity that takes place in a certain place at a certain time, for this is to assume that we experience leisure as a sort of social package, clearly defined and bounded. Instead, the boundaries defining leisure are continually being dismantled, principally through our immersion in **consumerism** – the consumption of cultural commodities through TV, the media, fashion, sport, music, and so on. But this consumption is an active, not reactive, process, as Willis (1990) declares:

“

[S]ymbolic work and creativity mediate, and are simultaneously expanded and developed by the uses, meanings and 'effects' of cultural commodities. Cultural commodities are catalyst, not product; a stage in, not the destination of, cultural affairs. Consumerism now has to be understood as an active, not a passive process. Its play includes work.

[Willis, 1990, pp. 17–18)]

consumerism
A culture centred on the promotion, sale and acquisition of consumer goods.

Unlike the neo-Marxist position, this perspective celebrates consumerism as a vehicle for creative cultural activity rather than as a driver of capitalist profit-making. Leisure is, as Fiske (1992) would argue, now part of a '*semiotic democracy*' in which we can invest different meanings and different lifestyles, which we 'elect' or choose to buy into.

Clearly, this postmodern approach raises questions about the relationship between the production of leisure by the 'consumer industries' and the terms on which their products are consumed. There is a tension between the fact that the culture industry – such as the media, and especially TV – produces images and products geared for niche markets yet also produces others to be sold on a mass basis, such as the 'Game Boy' electronic toy. It is clearly the case that leisure and the audio-visual technologies which play a key role in shaping it have become increasingly individualised and privatised. The leisure industries have moved in to define and exploit niche markets for 'discriminating categories' of individual consumers for whom a particular form of leisure activity creates a sense of personal identity. Even when leisure caters for large numbers – such as a swimming centre – one can see how this is still geared to a range of distinct, targeted needs. In Western Europe, the leisure chain 'Centre Parcs' is a good illustration of this multi-possible leisured activity.

It is nevertheless important to explore how far we are 'free' to create our own leisured meanings of these cultural objects. Some within the culture industry itself, such as the rock singer Madonna, claim to be able to help reproduce that industry but challenge its images and ideologies at the same time. Madonna's post-feminist challenge to gender stereotypes uses the very industry which has been most responsible for constructing sexist images of women.

Seen in these postmodern terms, the Marxist and feminist notions that there are constraints on being able to enjoy real leisure because of either class or gender barriers is thrown into question. However, the wider claims of postmodernism are themselves open to challenge. This remains therefore an important arena for sociological debate which ties into wider debates over the nature of consumption and the experiences we have as consumers.

One of the grounds that has been most fully worked over is the relationship between leisure, TV and popular culture more generally. Let us consider some of the issues that have been raised here.

Popular Culture, TV and Leisure

Raymond Williams (1980) has described the effect of TV on popular culture and leisure as enabling *mobile privatisation* whereby 'the public world is made available in new and extensive ways within the private sphere of the home: we travel imaginatively and stay put simultaneously'. To achieve the success it has had, TV producers have had to construct messages and the audiences for them: in a sense audiences are told *how* to view the media. As Hartley (1987) observes:

> **Since audiences don't exist prior to or outside of television, they need constant hailing and guidance in how-to-be-an-audience – hailing and guidance that are unstintingly given within, and especially between, shows and in the meta-discourses that surround television, the most prominent among which, of course, are those publications aptly called 'television guides'. In fact, so numerous are the nightly programmes available on US TV (up to 500 options) that choosing one becomes something of a viewer's nightmare: hence all the technological peripherals that are now being developed to help you 'channel hop'.**
>
> **[Hartley, 1987, p. 121]**

As Goodwin (1994) comments:

> **TV technologies are focussing on ways of making the choices more accessible: the remote control unit, gadgets which allow easier programming of video-cassette recorders, and TV screens with additional windows which permit the viewer to preview one channel while watching another. Indeed, there is now a cable TV channel, the prevue Channel, devoted exclusively to telling the viewer what is on the other channels.**
>
> **[Goodwin, 1994, p. 134]**

Sociologists have looked at different TV genres which have created a strong 'visual text' for specific audiences, for whom such shows become an important part of their leisure. These include soap operas, game shows and children's TV.

A number of studies have been conducted of soap operas (e.g. Buckingham, 1987; Ang, 1985, 1991; and Hobson, 1982). All of these show how the producers of the programmes had assumed certain types of audience for whom the programme would be made. The programmes (such as the British soap, *EastEnders*) were all targeted at the 'privatised' upper working class: as Turner (1990) remarks, it is ironic that upper-middle-class TV producers 'should feel they know what will make a show successful even if they would never be caught dead watching one'!

All soap operas invite their audiences to identify with particular characters, to follow the ups and downs of their lives, to expect twists and turns as one cliff-hanging episode follows another. The regularity and structure of the soap opera enables (and expects) its viewers to develop an insider knowledge of what is going on where, when and with whom. In the early days of soaps, those such as the still-running British *Coronation Street* were devised to be more community-focused and more romanticised in the way plots and characters were worked through. Today's new soaps indulge in social realism; and community, rather than being revered, is problematised, a neighbourhood divided along class and family lines. Some soaps challenge stereotypes while confirming others: the US *Cosby show* provides positive images of a prosperous, professional black family yet does so by conforming to the stereotype of a highly consumer-conscious white nucleated family (Miller, 1989).

texts
Any form of symbolic representation of meanings which take on a physical form, e.g. writing, film.

The debate over the meaning and impact of soaps, game shows and the like echoes that debate we discussed earlier between those who regard the consumerism of contemporary leisure as being fed by capitalist interests, and those who believe it is important to stress how individual consumers can resist capitalist images and messages to construct their own **texts**. Smythe (1987), who adopts the first of these views, has provided a powerful analysis of the logic of TV consumerism, a logic in which TV prepares audiences as consumers for advertisers' products. The TV station 'delivers' the audiences to the corporations who advertise on the channel. Merchandising in programmes provides a less explicit but as powerful an advertising technique. Others, such as Morley (1992), argue that we need to recognise the multiple interpretations of TV messages – their *polysemic* character – such that the same programmes and surrounding adverts are 'received' in very different ways. The polysemic status of TV messages is illustrated by the very different receptions that *The Cosby Show* has had.

Box 12. 5: Interpreting *The Cosby Show*

'For many African-Americans, *Cosby* represents a bold effort to break down stereotypes and provide white and black viewers alike with an improved role model of the black American. But for many white viewers *Cosby* was used to show that racial discrimination was a thing of the past and that social equality had now been achieved. Since it can be empirically demonstrated that this was *not* the case, *Cosby* was allowing its white audiences to believe that which was wrong but nevertheless comforting, whilst at the same time, the very same episodes sent a positive message to many African-Americans. This is an important example of the multiple interpretations that are possible, especially when a mass medium is central to such a diverse and multicultural society. If television is polysemic – containing many meanings – anywhere in the world, then it will certainly be polysemic in the United States.'

Source: Goodwin, 1994, p. 149.

Morley also recognises that the meaning given to TV programmes depends on the context and circumstances in which they are viewed. He acknowledges in this regard the feminist critique of TV and its relation to women's leisure: watching TV has often been determined by what the *man* wants to see, primarily because of the patriarchal attitude that defines the home as a place of rest, recreation and leisure for men whereas it is the place of (domestic) work for women. As McGuigan (1992) comments: 'women are rarely permitted to watch [TV] with undivided attention: that is one of the reasons why the fragmented and repetitive structures of soap opera are so popular with the female audience ' (p. 136).

Debates over the message, context and specific audience(s) of TV programmes are part of a much larger debate about the media itself. As the remark by Williams (1980) cited above suggests, the media in general not only provide multiple messages but also much indirect experience of events and processes happening beyond our own social experiences. We increasingly 'know' more, through the mediated experiences of TV, films, radio, the internet, the press, books, and magazines. But, as the earlier discussion implies (and our more extended commentary on the media in Chapter 3), the mass media do not merely provide neutral information about the world, but structure and package information in such a way that we make sense of the world through media interpretation. News broadcasting can be shown to carry explicit and implicit views of events that favour one reading rather than any other.

As commercial organisations, the global media companies, such as News Corporation, develop media products and media vehicles to capture as wide a market as possible. This involves the structuring of news programmes – to be seen in the home, the cinema, on a plane or the commercial internet – to maximise sales, and thereby attract global media advertising. Not surprisingly, the message one gets – whether in your own lounge or that of the airport – is of a society broadly happy with itself, enterprising, concerned about the environment, the value of the major currencies and who is likely to win the next 'Superbowl'. We are much less likely to see programmes which adopt a consistently critical perspective on society, revealing social inequalities, offering radical solutions to them, and so on (Murdock, 1989).

The more, then, that our leisure time is literally mediated by TV and other audio-visual technologies – such as MTV in the fitness gym – the more leisure will become a conduit for powerful social conventions and ideologies. Even if people as audiences are able to interpret the meaning of the media message, and indeed to reject it (see Hall, 1993), the overall interpretive and informational flow tends to favour a constructed consensus and the status quo.

Conclusion

This chapter has examined the sociological analysis of work and non-work. It is clear that the two share similar features. First, they are not easily defined and their boundaries can appear to overlap. Second, both are centrally related to the dynamics of capitalism, through what we have seen is the labour process and what we might call 'the leisure process' – the incorporation of leisure through consumerism into the capitalist market. Third, we have also shown how the meaning of work and leisure is variable depending on context and the social position – e.g. gender status – of the social actor.

We also debated the idea that work today was subject to a deskilling process, suggesting that this was not a general phenomenon but one that again related to workers' social class, gender and ethnicity and the context within which work skills were deployed. On the other hand, some work has clearly involved a re-skilling as new technologies and attendant occupational positions have appeared in both public and private organisations.

In some ways, it might even be worth considering whether leisure itself has been subjected to similar processes of de-skilling and re-skilling. As leisure becomes more incorporated within private capital increasingly people experience the skills it involves – such as playing a particular game – by proxy through the TV, for example. Yet, the new technologies associated with leisure – especially computer-based ones – do require the development of new skills to handle the **software**, to 'surf' on the internet, and so on.

software

Computer programmes, manuals, instructions, and other materials that can exist in written form and be used on computer systems.

What is clear is that what was once the most important source of personal identity – the work one does – seems, in this regard, to be declining in significance or at least is being paralleled by the personal identities that are constructed through our self-conscious consumer culture.

Summary of the Chapter

- Industrialisation saw the separation of (paid) work in the formal labour market from non-work. Women's domestic labour is extensive but materially unrewarded.

- Gender division in the labour market reflects and helps reproduce gender divisions in the household.
- Labour process theorists such as Braverman, adopting a neo-Marxist approach to the labour market, argue that there is a general deskilling of work across all occupational groups.
- Against this, more recent analyses suggest that while some deskilling has occurred, there is also evidence for a re-skilling of workers to meet the demands for flexible labour.
- The meaning of work and work satisfaction has to be understood in terms of the technology sector and the advent of new production regimes such as JIT.
- Orientations to work cannot be identified simply through looking at the experience of work itself, but are shown to reflect a number of other factors outside of work.
- Gender, age and ethnicity shape the opportunities for work and the reward it brings.
- There are three main approaches to the relationship between work and leisure: Marxist, feminist and postmodern.
- Leisure and the consumption of leisure goods – especially via the media – provide important sources of social and personal identity, and for many are in fact more important than work itself.

References

Ang, I. (1985) *Watching Dallas – Soap Opera and the Melodramatic Imagination*, London, Macmillan.

Ang, I. (1991) *Desperately Seeking the Audience*, London, Routledge.

Bell, D. (1973) *The Coming of Post-Industrial Society*, London, Heinemann.

Blauner, R. (1964) *Alienation and Freedom*, Chicago, University of Chicago Press.

Bottrup, P. and B. Clematide (1992) *After Taylor and Braverman*, FAST Monitor, CEC, Brussels.

Braverman, H. (1974) *Labour and Monopoly Capital*, New York, Monthly Review Press.

Buckingham, D. (1987) *Public Secrets – EastEnders and Its Audience*, London, British Film Institute.

CEC, Commission of the European Communities (1994) *Human Resources in Europe*, FAST Programme, Brussels.

Clarke, J. and C. Critcher (1985) *The Devil Makes Work: Leisure in Capitalist Britain*, London, Macmillan.

Crompton, R. and K. Sanderson (1990) *Gendered Jobs and Social Change*, London, Unwin Hyman.

Crouch, D. (1994) *The Allotment: Its Landscape and Culture*, Nottingham, Mushroom Press.

Deem, R. (1986) *All Work and No Play*, Milton Keynes, Open University Press.

Devine, F. (1992) *Affluent Workers Revisited: Privatism and the Working Class*, Edinburgh, Edinburgh University Press.

Edwards, R. (1979) *Contested Terrain*, London, Heinemann.

Featherstone, M. (1991) *Consumer Culture and Postmodernism*, London, Sage.

Finlay, W. (1988) *Work on the Waterfront*, Philadelphia, Temple University Press.

Fiske, J. (1992) *Understanding Popular Culture*, London, Routledge.

Friedman, A. L. (1977) *Industry and Labour*, London, Macmillan.

Frissen, V. (1992) 'Trapped in electronic cages', *Media, Culture and Society*, vol. 14, pp. 31–49.

Gallie, D. (1991) 'Patterns of skill change', *Work, Employment and Society*, vol. 5, pp. 319–51.

Glyptis, S. (1989) *Leisure and Unemployment*, Milton Keynes, Open University Press.

Goldthorpe, J. H. *et al.* (1968) *The Affluent Work: Industrial Attitudes and Behaviour*, Cambridge, Cambridge University Press.

Goodwin, A. (1994) 'Ideology and diversity in American television', in J. Mitchell and D. Maidment, *The United States in the Twentieth Century: Culture*, Milton Keynes, Open University Press.

Green, F. and D. Ashton (1992) 'Skill shortage and skill deficiency', *Work, Employment and Society*, vol. 6, no. 2, pp. 287–301.

Grieco, M. (1987) *Keeping it in the Family*, London, Tavistock.

Grint, K. (1991) *The Sociology of Work*, Cambridge, Polity Press.

Hall, S. (1993) 'The television discourse – encoding and decoding', in A. Gray and J. McGuigan (eds), *Studying Culture*, London, Edward Arnold.

Handy, C. (1985) *The Future of Work*, Oxford, Blackwell.

Hartley, J. (1987) 'Invisible fictions: television audiences', *Textual Practice*, vol. 1, no. 2, pp. 121–38.

Hobson, D. (1982) *Crossroads: The Drama of a Soap Opera*, London, Methuen.

Hout, M. J. (1984) 'Status, autonomy and training in occupational mobility', *American Journal of Sociology*, vol. 89, pp. 1379–409.

Jenkins, A. (1994) 'Just-in-time regimes and reductionism', *Sociology*, vol. 28, pp. 21–30.

Kaufman, D. and B. L. Richardson (1982) *Achievement and Women*, New York, Free Press.

Marx, K. (1954) *Capital*, vol. 1, Harmondsworth, Penguin.

McGoldrick, M. and E. Carter (1982) 'The family life cycle', in F. Walsh (ed.), *Normal Family Processes*, New York, Guildford Press.

McGuigan, J. (1992) *Cultural Populism*, London, Routledge.

McRae, S. (1994) 'Labour supply after childbirth', *Sociology*, vol. 28, no. 1, pp. 99–122.

Miller, M. (1989) 'Prime time: deride and conquer', in T. Gitlin (ed.), *Watching Television*, New York, Pantheon.

Morley, D. (1992) *Television Audiences and Cultural Studies*, London, Routledge.

Murdock, G. (1989) 'Redrawing the map of the communications industries: concentration and ownership in the era of privatisation', in M. Ferguson, *Public Communication: The New Imperatives*, London, Sage.

Oakley, A. (1974) *The Sociology of Housework*, Oxford, Blackwell.

Packer, K. (1996) 'The context dependent nature of gendering of technical work: a case study of work in a scientific laboratory', *Work, Employment and Society*, vol. 10, no. 1.

Piore, M. J. (1979) *Birds of Passage: Migrant Labour and Industrial Societies*, Cambridge, Cambridge University Press.

Rojeck, C. (1995) *Decentring Leisure: Rethinking Leisure Theory*, London, Sage.

Roos, P. A. (1983) 'Marriage and women's occupational attainment in cross-cultural perspective', *American Sociological Review*, vol. 48, pp. 852–64.

Scase, R. (1992) *Class*, Milton Keynes, Open University Press.

Schwartz Cowan, R. (1983) *More Work for Mother*, New York, Basic Books.

Shutt, J. and R. Whittington (1987) 'Fragmentation strategies and the rise of small unit cases from the North West', *Regional Studies*, vol. 21, pp. 13–23.

Smythe, D. (1987) 'Communications; blindspots of Western Marxism', *Canadian Journal of Political and Social Theory*, vol. 1, no. 3, pp. 1–27.

Spenner, K. I. (1990) 'Skill: meaning, methods and measures', *Work and Occupations*, vol. 17, pp. 399–421.

Taylor, F. W. (1911) *Principles of Scientific Management*, New York, Harper & Row.

Turner, G. (1990) *British Cultural Studies*, London, Routledge.

Webster, F. and K. Robins (1993) 'I'll be watching you', *Sociology*, vol. 27, no. 2, pp. 243–52.

Williams, R. (1980) *Problems in Materialism and Culture*, London, New Left Books.

Willis, P. (1990) 'Symbolic work at play in everyday cultures of the young', in P. Willis *et al.* (eds), *Common Culture*, Milton Keynes, Open University Press.

Wholey, D. R. (1990) 'The effects of formal and informal training on tenure and mobility in manufacturing firms', *Sociological Quarterly*, vol. 31, pp. 37–57.

13 Health, Illness and Medicine

Aims of the Chapter

This chapter introduces the reader to the main sociological approaches to health, illness and medicine. The intention is to show how the distribution, experience, definition and treatment of illness cannot simply be understood, as most people think, in physical or biological terms. Health, illness and their medical management are part of wider cultural systems and as such are closely associated with processes of social control, by both professions and the state. The sociology of medicine has strong links here to recent analyses in the sociology of the body.

Introduction: The Social Basis of Health, Illness and Medicine

To say that health and illness have a 'social' basis may seem at first sight just another example of sociological arrogance claiming for 'the social' more than can be sensibly and credibly accepted. Health and illness are, surely, simply *bio-logical* descriptions of the state of our bodies. When we're ill, we're ill. A more refined version of this commonsense view underlies the long-standing **biomedical model** of disease, which is, in broad terms, based on the following assumptions:

biomedical model
A model of disease and illness which regards it as the consequence of certain malfunctions of the human body.

- Disease is an organic condition: non-organic factors associated with the human mind are considered unimportant or even ignored altogether in the search for biological causes for pathological symptoms.
- Disease is a *temporary* organic state which can be eradicated – cured – by medical intervention.
- Disease is something experienced by the sick *individual* who is then the object of treatment.
- Disease is treated after symptoms appear; the application of medicine is a *reactive* healing process.
- Disease is treated in a *medical environment* – a surgery or a hospital – away from the site where the symptoms first appeared.

Clearly, this model (admittedly simplified here) has dominated in medical practice because it is seen to 'work': it is based on a technically very powerful science which has made a massive contribution in some key areas of health and well-being in society (through vaccination, for example). The anatomical and neurophysicological structures of the body we now take for granted, and we await the new genetic mapping of the body through the Human Genome Project. The search for the fundamental – i.e. genetic – basis of human pathology is now on,

medical gaze
A concept employed by Foucault to denote the power of modern medicine to define the human body.

whether the target is cancer, AIDS, or Alzheimer's disease. Not surprisingly, this ever closer and more sophisticated inspection of the body – or, as Foucault (1973) would say, the '**medical gaze**' – has brought considerable power and prestige to the medical profession as well as a large and profitable market to corporations, such as major pharmaceutical companies like Glaxo-Wellcome, Zeneca or Merck. The biomedical model also underlies what is regarded as the 'official' definition of health and disease, that definition adopted by state and international authorities. National government and international agencies, such as the World Health Organisation (WHO), often proclaim their long-term goal to be the eradication of modern diseases defined in these terms, such as in 'the fight against cancer'. Sometimes, these are successful, as in the virtual global elimination of smallpox. The rational application of medical science is one of the hallmarks of modernity inasmuch as it has depended on the development over the past two centuries of a powerful, experimentally-based medical analysis of the structure and function of the body and those things likely to attack or weaken it. Through this scientific approach, medicine has very effectively displaced the myths and superstitions of folk or lay medicine. Modernity is about 'expertise' not tradition, about critical inspection not folk beliefs, about control through scientific and technical regulation of the body not customs and mistaken notions of healing.

This development of a 'rational medicine' has also reduced the reliance on patients' own accounts of their illness (Stacey, 1989), and, unlike the situation in the eighteenth and nineteenth centuries, medics rarely rely on the external expression or demeanour of the patient for diagnosis. Instead, clinical instruments – from the stethoscope to NMR (nuclear magnetic resonance imaging) – are used to uncover the deepseated nature of a disease. This *distancing from the patient* is part of the rationality of medical practice as well as an important device for cultivating a mystique of professional expertise. It also means that through patients' records, X-rays, scans, and now chromosomal profiles, cases can be handled by teams of doctors many of whom may not actually *meet* the patient in the flesh. Beck (1992) points out, though, that this growth in the capacity to diagnose illnesses has not necessarily been accompanied by ' the presence or even the prospect of any effective measures to treat them'. Distinguishing between acute (short-term) and chronic (long-term) illnesses, he points out that 'at the start of this century, 40 out of 100 patients died of acute illnesses. In 1980 these constituted only 1% of the causes of mortality. The proportion of those who die of chronic illnesses, on the other hand, rose in the same period from 46 to over 80%. ... A cure in the original sense of medicine becomes more and more the exception. ... Yet this is not the expression solely of a failure. Because of its *successes* medicine also discharges people into illness, which it is able to diagnose with its high technology' (Beck, 1992, pp. 204–5). Moreover, the growing *technical sophistication* of medicine tends to expose patients to an array of equipment and therapeutic techniques which have to be used to justify their expense while, as Richman (1987) notes, 'the criteria of referral are being continuously being adjusted to keep specialists in work'.

Yet the power and status of the profession and the health industry should not deflect us from asking about the social basis of health and illness: in fact, the position of medical professionals is itself a result of socially insitutionalised powers to define and shape the experience of being 'ill' and what treatment is required. Moreover, the more reflective doctor – or health rep – will acknowledge that their definitions of health and illness are not always shared by their 'customers' and that they have to be secured through education, socialisation and expensive advertising. Symptoms that, according to the biomedical model, should force us to go to the doctor or take a pill are not necessarily seen as signs of illness by people. Among a household of smokers, for example, the morning 'smoker's cough' is unlikely to be seen as abnormal or a sign of ill-health: indeed it is often calmed by a good pull on the first cigarette of the day. Among most white Western tourists a suntan evokes health and good looks rather than the prelude to wrinkled skin or, worse, skin cancer. Among the Madi of Uganda, illness is often associated with failure to deal properly with interpersonal relations, such that social or moral – rather than biomedical – repair is needed (Allen, 1992). Or again, *alternative* or *'complementary'* remedies to ill-health often begin from a completely different, typically **holistic**, approach to understanding the cause of illness and its remedy. Studies in the US have shown how patients present themselves to 'the medical gaze' much more rarely than medics might predict or like: Banks *et al.* (1975) provided data that record the relatively infrequent rate at which people visited a doctor across a range of illnesses, as Table 13.1 shows.

holistic
An approach that focuses on the whole rather than on specific parts or aspects.

Table 13.1 *Ratio of symptom episodes to consultations*

Headache	184:1
Backache	52:1
Emotional problem	46:1
Abdominal pain	28:1
Sore throat	18:1
Pain in chest	14:1

Source: Banks *et al*. (1975).

In short, the perception of health and illness – and how to secure the one and avoid the other – is culturally variable, highly context-specific, dynamic and subject to change. Crucially, there is no clear-cut relationship between the existence of physical or emotional feelings and the judgement that these indicate illness (that they are 'symptoms'), and thereby a decision to consult a doctor and become a patient.

Sociologists, anthropologists and historians have described the social basis of health and illness through a wide range of studies including ethnographies of specific communities and analyses of debates over 'health care', the performance of 'the sick role', the construction of 'mental illness' as a disease, the wider creation of medical belief systems, and the relationship between them and power and social control.

The *sociology of health and illness* is concerned with the social origins of and influences on disease rather than with an exploration of its organic manifestation in particular individual bodies. The *sociology of medicine* is concerned to explore the social, historical and cultural reasons for the rise to dominance of medicine – and especially the bio-medical model of the medical profession – in the definition, and treatment of illness. Clearly these two are closely related concerns since the way in which professional (or orthodox) medicine defines and manages illness is inextricably bound up with and reflects wider social dynamics shaping the perception and experience of disease itself.

Theoretical Approaches

The sociology of health and illness has been informed by five distinct theoretical traditions:

Parsonsian functionalism has looked most closely at the role the sick person plays in society: here the focus is on how being ill must take a specific form in human societies in order that the social system's stability and cohesion can be maintained.

Symbolic interactionism has been concerned with examining the interaction between the different role-players in the health and illness 'drama': here the focus is on how illness and the subjective experience of 'being sick' is constructed through the doctor–patient exchange. The argument here is that illness is a social accomplishment between actors rather than merely a matter of physiological malfunction.

Marxist theory has been concerned with the relationship between health and illness and capitalist social organisation; how is the definition and treatment of health and illness crucially influenced by the nature of economic activity in a capitalist society?

Feminist theory has explored the gendered nature of the definition of illness and treatment of patients; here the concern is with the degree to which medical treatment involves male control over women – of both their bodies and their identities.

discourse
A body of ideas, concepts and beliefs which become established as knowledge or as an accepted world-view. These ideas become a powerful framework for understanding and action in social life. For example, Foucault studied the discourse of madness, highlighting its changes over the centuries and its interplay with other discourses such as religious and medical discourses, and illustrated how these shifts affect how madness is perceived and reacted to by others.

Foucauldian theory has described the emergence of a dominant medical **discourse** which has constructed definitions of normality (health) and deviance (sickness). This discourse provides subjects in modern societies with the vocabulary through which their medical needs and remedies are defined. The source and beneficiary of this discourse, for Foucault, is the medical profession itself: it is not the greater 'truth' of the biomedical model which gives the profession power but medics' monopoly over the terms on which medical discourse is constructed in the first place. In addition, Foucault argues that medical discourse plays an important role in the management of individual bodies (what he calls 'anatamo-politics') and bodies *en masse* ('bio-politics'): in this sense, medicine is never merely about medicine as conventionally understood but also about wider structures of power and control.

We can now sketch out the main points of contrast between these theories.

Parsonsian functionalism and 'the sick role'

Although Parsons was interested in a variety of issues concerned with the management of illness, it is for his emphasis on the social importance of the sick role that he is usually remembered. Parsons stresses that there is a significant issue of motivation involved in being sick and getting better; in effect, people have to decide that are sick and that they need treatment. Since being sick means 'choosing' to withdraw from normal patterns of social behaviour, it amounts to a form of deviance; as such, the functioning of the social system depends on the management and control of the sick. The role of medicine is, therefore, the regulation and control of those who have decided they are sick so that they can be restored to health to ensure that they return to the performance of normal tasks and the renewed meeting of normal social obligations and responsibilities. In short, the sick role requires a commitment on the part of those feeling unwell to try to return to normality as soon as possible. Four features define the sick role:

- sick people are legitimately exempted from normal social responsibilities, such as those associated with work and the family;

- sick people cannot make themselves better but need professional help;
- sick people are obliged to want to get better: being sick can only be tolerated if there is a desire to return to health;
- sick people are therefore expected to seek professional treatment.

Doctors too must play their part in the remedying process: in return for the trust placed in them, doctors are obliged to act in the best interests of patients, applying their skill and expertise and guided by professional codes of conduct. Conformity to such norms accords the doctor very unusual rights – the right of authority over the patient's health, rights of examination of the body and information about the patient's personal details.

epidemiology
The study of the patterns of disease.

There have been a number of criticisms directed against Parsons' account. First, the model assumes recovery is always possible: in the twentieth century, however, as we have already mentioned, the growth has been in chronic rather than acute conditions. Second, a number of researchers have pointed out that the arrival at the doctor's surgery is often the last stage in the construction and confirmation of sickness: for example, Scambler (1991) found that a majority of patients consult widely with lay (non-medical) contacts before deciding to vist the doctor. Thus it is perfectly possible to be a sick person without becoming a patient. For this reason, **epidemiological** statistics about the distribution of illnesses, which derive from doctor–patient consultations, should be treated with great caution. The sociological question here is what are the reasons why some kinds of sick people and their sickness remain under-reported, or are dealt with primarily within the lay arena, while others do not. Third, Parsons mistakenly assumes that patients will be knowledgeable and sensitive about their condition in order to know that they should consult a doctor but naive and compliant once inside the surgery. In return doctors are expected to treat patients equally, or universalistically, according to the same criteria. Against this assumption, research shows how doctors' perceptions of the class, age, gender and ethnicity of patients can have important consequences for the kind of treatment provided. For instance, greater consultation time and more explanation of their illness are given to higher social classes than to lower; there is a tendency to treat female patients' problems as related to 'typical' feminine neuroses and complaints while treating similar problems experienced by male patients as work-related, stress products (MacIntyre and Oldham, 1977); patients arriving at emergency US centres, suspected of being DOA (dead on arrival), are treated in very different ways, according to moral, not medical, judgements made about their character – alcoholics, for example, being treated much less sympathetically than those arriving in a sober condition (Sudnow, 1967). In similar vein, medics in British casualty wards have a private argot for classifying newly arrived patients, including the engagingly named variety of 'T. F. Bundy' ('Totally fucked, but unfortunately not dead yet'). These are just a few examples of the variation in practice among doctors.

Despite these criticisms, the notion of the sick role did open up the possibility of exploring the construction and career or 'occupation' (Pollock, 1988; Herzlich, 1973) of being ill. Many patients cope with illness by defining it as a 'job' to be successfully managed and completed by dint of hard work, co-operation with others (medics and kin) and the sharing of information about the state of the illness. Pollock shows how those suffering from chronic forms of mental illness – such as schizophrenia – find this illness-as-a-job option closed to them since they are seen by others as having no control over their illness: the notion of positive coping is seen as socially non-credible. This example tells us much about the *interactive* nature of illness and the social accounting processes surrounding it. It is this which encouraged other sociologists to look more closely at the *interaction* between doctor and patient, to see how this might explain these and other observations. Here, then, we shift our focus towards the symbolic interactionist school.

Symbolic interactionism and the social construction of illness

Interactionism argues that identity is a matter of self-image created through interaction with others, and learning to become a social being effectively means learning how to achieve control over this process – learning how to manage the impressions of others by manipulating their judgements of us (see Chapters 4 and 18).

This creative capacity is evident when we play the role of 'patient' in our encounters with health care practitioners, in the same way that these practitioners cannot help but attempt to create impressions of themselves for us. Given this interpretive element to their social encounter, doctor–patient interactions cannot be presumed to follow the pre-ordained role-playing path laid out by Parsons: instead we should expect, and indeed find, considerable variation in interactive play.

Byrne and Long (1976) construct, for example, a continuum of interaction from exclusively patient-centred communication at one extreme to exclusively doctor-centred communication at the other. Most studies show that the power element in doctor–patient relations has a significant effect, with doctor-centred interaction being by far the most common. Stewart and Roter (1989) have constructed a similar classification, contrasting situations where the patient dominates, as a 'consumer' of medicine (especially apparent in private, market-based health care), to those where the doctor dominates, reflecting a strong 'paternalism' over subordinate clients. Morgan (1985) points out that the sort of relationship characterising encounters between practitioners and patients can move between these different types during the different stages of an illness; as she says, 'at an acute stage of illness it may be necessary or desirable for the doctor to be dominant, whereas at later stages it may be beneficial for patients to be more actively involved and to engage in an adult–adult relationship rather than the adult–child relationship which involves a paternalistic approach'.

The power element in doctor–patient relations becomes particularly significant when a patient is obliged to enter hospital. Following the classic analysis of institutionalisation by Erving Goffman, interactionist research into the nature of hospital life often focuses on the ways in which the hospital regime is designed to restrict the opportunity of patients to fashion their own identities. Hospital life mirrors life in other '**total institutions**' (places where, for a period of time, the whole of an inmate's life is lived out within its confines) such as prisons, mental hospitals, convents, etc. In the hospital, patients' power to control their behaviour is reduced as much as possible, a process that starts as soon as they are admitted.

total institutions
Employed by Goffman, it refers to all forms of diverse institutions, such as prisons and mental hospitals, that assume total control over their inmates.

Most patients are compliant, but some do resist and attempt to control the situation and maintain their sense of personal autonomy and identity by, for example, refusing to comply with ward rules and regulations as rigidly as staff might wish them to. They then become 'difficult patients'. This shows the potential for conflict between practitioners and patients. Conflict emerges too because of the power of others to impose their definition of the meaning of 'being ill' on the patient. That is, there is clearly a **labelling** component in the definition of illness, whether through medical diagnosis or through the way a sick person's friends, relations and others treat him or her. Thus, for others, a cancer patient can be labelled a cancer patient above all else in the eyes of those who know about the illness. However hard the sufferer may try to persuade others that he or she is still a friend, or a lover, or a mother, who also happens to have cancer, interactionist analysis draws attention to the often overwhelming influence of the stigmatic label in the eyes of interpreters. Indeed, such an illness – as in the case of other forms of labelled deviance – can be interpreted as a sign of personal weakness or culpability (Sontag 1979). Rosenhan *et al.* (1973)

labelling theory
From Becker, the process where socially defined identities are imposed or adopted, especially the deviant label. Such labels may have consequences that trap the individual into that identity (*see* stigmatise).

Source: Viv Quinlan

have shown how difficult it is to control the imposition of labelling for those defined as being 'mentally ill'. Horwitz (1977) has also shown that the greater the social gap in terms of class and status between the labeller and the labelled, the more difficult it is for the latter to resist the imposition of the illness stigma. Lemert (1974) has shown how the imposition of stigmatic labels – especially that of being 'mentally ill' – is a serious assault on one's sense of self, since the 'ill' person is effectively being told that their (mental) capacities for self-knowledge are damaged and that their feelings about themselves are probably delusory. The end result is a social construction of mental illnesses – such as paranoia – in which the patient, whether mentally ill or not, finds it impossible not to believe in the reality of the illness. It is at this stage – of self-realisation – that the labellers, especially the medical staff, start to feel hopeful about eventual recovery!

Labelling can work in other ways too. There are circumstances in which despite being physically very fit, some people find that preconceived notions about them simply discount the way they really are. This is a common experience for the aged, as the cartoon above suggests.

This discussion shows how the interactionist approach focuses on the importance of *power* relations in the construction and management of health and illness. It draws our attention to the unequal distribution of resources available to health practitioners and patients, whether in home visits, in the surgery, at the outpatient clinic, or on hospital wards. However, interactionism's weakness is that it offers neither a theory of power nor a theory of the patterns of inequality in which it is interested. In the end, then, it tends to explain power and inequality as somehow functions of the relative strengths of the *personalities* of the parties to the medical encounter. We have to look to the other approaches mentioned earlier to provide a theoretical explanation of such inequality.

Marxist theory

As we have seen in previous chapters, Marxist theory is centrally concerned with the way in which the dominant economic structure of a society determines structures of inequality and power, as well as shaping the social relations upon which major social institutions are built. Medicine is a major social institution, and thereby, within a capitalist society, must be seen to be shaped by capitalist interests. A Marxist account of capitalist medicine has been developed by a number of sociologists and health policy analysts, notably Navarro, Professor of Health Policy at Johns Hopkins University in Baltimore.

According to Navarro (1986), there are four features which define medicine as capitalist, or, as he puts it, which point to 'the invasion of the house of medicine by capital': each of these mirrors similar developments throughout capitalist society, shaping the pattern of work, the structure of authority, and the nature of social class relations. The four are:

- medicine changes from being an individualised craft form of skill to a 'corporate type of medicine';
- medicine becomes increasingly specialised and hierarchical;
- a growth in the wage-labour force within medicine (including, most importantly, employees in the pharmaceutical and related industrial sectors);
- the '**proletarianisation**' of medical practitioners whose professional status is gradually undermined as they become subject to the control of administrative and managerial staffs overseeing health care provision.

proletarianisation
A process whereby some parts of the middle class become absorbed into the working class.

These four processes mean that medicine enters into the market as a commodity, to be bought and sold as any other product. It becomes increasingly profitable for two of the dominant interests within capitalism – the finance sector, through insurance premiums; and the corporate sector; especially through drugs and medical instruments sales. Power to direct and exploit the medical system is accrued by large corporations enjoying monopolistic control over market sectors, again a process characteristic of (late) capitalism as a whole: as Navarro (1986) says, 'monopoly capital invades, directs and dominates either directly (via the private sector) or indirectly (via the state) all areas of economic and social life' (p. 243). This last point illustrates the Marxists' claim that simply because medicine is organised via the state as a 'nationalised' system of health care (as in the UK), this does not mean it is thereby free of capitalist influence. Instead, it has to be seen as part of the medical–industrial–state complex which promotes close relations between large firms and state agencies that buy their drugs and other equipment, subsidise their research through university labs to which they have access, and maintain a large hospital infrastructure which requires their goods: much of the same has happened in the defence sector.

Apart from the provision and sale of medicine, Marxist analysis also claims that the sort of health problems that people experience are closely tied to the unhealthy and stressed work environment that most find themselves in. Rather than seeing health problems as a result of individual frailty or weakness, they must be explained in terms of the unequal social structure and class disadvantage reproduced within capitalism. Patterns of mortality and ill-health (morbidity) are closely related to occupational contexts, especially those of the industrial working class. For example, industrial carcinogens (from working with asbestos, heavy metals, chemicals, etc.) are responsible for over 10 per cent of all male cancers. While 'accidents' at work may be regarded as a result of human error, research has also shown how they reflect pressures on workers to complete tasks in risk-laden environments at speed (Wright, 1994; Tombs, 1990). Legislation to control hazardous workplaces has been introduced over the years in Britain and elsewhere of course and this has had an ameliorative effect in bringing down the rate of death, injury and illness of workers. However, in Britain, the legislation is only effective if policed properly: considerable under-policing of sweat-shop, casualised workplaces is apparent. Moreover, the Health and Safety Executive annual reports show that it has become increasingly difficult to reduce levels of injury below a certain threshold, suggesting that it is at these statistical levels that we can see the structural – and not 'accidental' – character of occupational injury and mortality.

Navarro argues that medicine – as capitalism more generally – is in a state of 'crisis' inasmuch as its inexorable growth is merely matched by an increasing inability to meet society's needs: despite more and more money being spent on health care more and more people experience the system as ineffective. The state's response to this is to disarm any potential attack on the 'medical–industrial–state' complex by declaring more strongly than ever that health problems are problems for the individual, and that any difficulties in coping with them are not the fault of the system itself but the individual. The individual must be 'taught' to become a more discerning 'consumer' of medicine, to take out more extensive (and expensive) private medical insurance, while the state itself reduces its own burdensome costs of medical provision. This latter strategy can cause problems for the 'medical–industrial complex' since a reduced state budget can hit the secure drugs markets enjoyed by the pharmaceutical industry. Again, according to the Marxist view, this is to be expected in medicine as elsewhere since in late capitalism there is never a complete coincidence of interests between powerful corporations and the state, especially at a national level (as we saw in Chapter 3). The danger here for the state is that larger multinational corporations will seek new secure markets and cheaper labour supplies overseas, so reducing the overall contribution they make to a country's GNP. We shall return to this global dimension later in the chapter.

Criticisms of the Marxist view of medicine have tended to focus more on its adequacy rather than questioning its basic insight of locating medicine firmly within capitalism. That is, while it is appropriate to locate medicine and medical practice in the context of the capitalist system, a greater sensitivity to the dynamics of the medical process, the experience of illness and being a patient, needs to be developed. In addition, as Turner (1987) has argued, the Marxist **political economy** of health needs to address how the current *diversity* of capitalist societies relates to medicine, health and illness. As he notes, 'there are major differences between the USA, the UK and Sweden, despite the fact that all three societies are quite distinctively capitalist' (p. 194). The welfare state, within which medicine plays such a key role, operates on a very different basis in each of these (and other) countries. Moreover, Marxists have tended to underplay the genuinely progressive features of the health sector in contemporary capitalism, arguing that they are merely 'ameliorative' rather than solving people's health problems. Navarro makes a gesture in this direction when he acknowledges that medical practitioners do play a 'useful' role in delivering health care, but says too that their primary purpose is to regulate the working classes and 'popular masses'. Finally, the Marxist account can be criticised for failing to give enough attention to the *gendering* of health and medicine, that process which has subordinated women to a dominant professional and **patriarchal** medical control whatever their social class background. This leads us to consider the feminist sociological approach.

political economy
An approach that embraces the concepts of social class, the value and division of labour, and moral sentiments.

patriarchal
A system that perpetuates the dominance of senior men over women and junior men (*see* patriarchy).

Feminist accounts

Feminist analysis of inequality in general has focused on the construction and maintenance of female subordination. It is not surprising that medicine and the debate over health and illness has been of central importance to this analysis precisely because it concerns the body, the site more than any other where gendered interaction takes place. It is not surprising too that feminists have focused much of their attention on birth and maternity since it is here that the potential for, and practice of, patriarchy is said to be most acute where the links between sexuality and reproduction are biologically and socially intertwined. As Turner (1987) notes, the regulation of women's bodies through controlling their sexual expression and reproductive capacity is now secured through medicine whereas in the past religion played this role (see Chapter 15). For women, a healthy body has been tied to a healthy sexuality which has as its priority reproduction within the confines of a lawful marriage.

medicalisation

A process of increased medical intervention and control into areas that hitherto would have been outside the medical domain.

Much of the feminist critique therefore has concentrated on the male-dominated medical profession and the way that it has over the past century **medicalised** events and processes natural to women, including menstruation, pregnancy and childbirth. Medical intervention in these areas – in the past handled by women themselves in conjunction with family and female friends – derived originally from a desire by the newly emerging medical profession to create and capture as much of a medical market as it could. There was little of real benefit in having a medic in attendance at birth; indeed some evidence shows that physicians had little idea about the birth process itself and that medical intervention often endangered both mother and child.

Despite this, motherhood was, by the mid-1950s, a fully medicalised condition (Oakley, 1984). Midwifery had gradually been excluded – in the US by local state legislation – just as had sixteenth- and seventeenth-century female healers been branded as witches. This exclusion of women from positions of control over their bodies, either personally or professionally, has meant that the majority of obstetricians and gynaecologists are men – in the US about 80 per cent, in the UK about 85 per cent. Medical training, textbooks and journals reproduce a patriarchal attitude towards women. And Jordanova (1989) has shown, through her examination of medical journals and magazines, how the classification of illness by gender is commonplace, especially in the adverts they carry: 'Depression, anxiety, sleeplessness and migraine are likely to be associated with women, while disorders that can inhibit full movement and strenuous sporting activities are associated, metaphorically, with masculinity' (p. 144).

The sexual division of labour in medicine reflects the subordination of women. Despite health and related matters being seen to be closely tied to women's caring, nurturing role within patriarchal society, this has not meant that women have a high position in the occupational hierarchy. Thus, while there are many women working in medicine the bulk of them are in the paramedical, nursing jobs with poorer pay and occupational status. Feminists believe that the current gradual increase in the proportion of physicians who are female, while welcome, will be unlikely to bring about any major change, since these women are subject in their medical schools to the same patriarchal attitudes and assumptions that their male colleagues are exposed to.

male-stream
Used to describe institutions or practices that are male dominated.

Feminists argue that only by breaking with the **male-stream** of orthodox medicine can women rediscover control over their bodies. This has inspired the emergence of a feminist health movement led by writers such as Ehrenreich (1979), which challenges the medical establishment and promotes instead a philosophy of self-care and healing by and for women. The explicit recognition here between health, its definition, care and control and, most important, how this relates to the regulation of bodies and sexuality in wider society, is shared too by the last theory we consider here, that of Foucault.

Foucauldian analysis

Foucault insists that in order to understand the role of medicine in society we should see it as part of a wider social requirement for the regulation and surveillance of *bodies* – both in the physical sense of individuals' bodies and in the more abstract sense of bodies of populations. The demand for regulation grows as society becomes more complex – especially as it becomes more urbanised, and so bringing people together in one large mass. Urban spaces have both public and private 'spaces' which dictate the appropriate behaviour for the 'bodies' that occupy them.

Medicine, and especially the medicine of the asylum, the clinic, and the more everyday sense of general public hygiene, has to be understood within this broader context of public control. Foucault argues that medicine plays not merely a clinical but also a *moral* role, especially with regard to 'proper' forms of sexual expression, as he describes in his *History of Sexuality*. This recounts the way in which medicine played an increasingly important role in establishing a regimen of acceptable sexuality. Indeed the concept of 'discipline' is central to Foucault's work, for the emergence of modern 'rational' disciplines – such as economics, urban planning, penology, and notably medicine – were themselves central to the disciplining of people as public and private bodies. In their different ways each of these disciplines legitimated forms of social control and regulation over people: as such they comprised powerful forms of 'social discourse'.

Foucault's concept of discourse is central to his analysis here. As we saw in earlier chapters (especially Chapter 4 and 15), discourses are ways of knowing about, or of representing and so giving some control over, reality and social behaviour. Medical discourse has been – and remains – one of the most powerful of contemporary discourses which defines, organises and controls human bodies from birth to the grave. This discourse appeared during the nineteenth century:

> **A medico-administrative knowledge begins to develop concerning society, its health and sickness, its conditions of life, housing and habits, which serve as the basic core for the 'social economy' and the sociology of the 19th century.**
>
> **[Foucault, 1980, p. 176]**

For Foucault, medical discourse and the medical profession which sustains it have displaced the religious, clergy-based discourses which dominated in previous centuries. Scientific, secular medicine provides a powerful means of social discipline and control. As Turner has suggested:

> **Put simply, the doctor has replaced the priest as the custodian of social values: the panoply of ecclesiastical institutions of regulation (the ritual order of sacraments, the places of vocational training, the hospice for pilgrims, places of worship and sanctuary) have been transferred through the evolution of scientific medicine to a panoptic collection of localised agencies of surveillance and control. Furthermore, the rise of preventive medicine, social medicine and community medicine has extended these agencies of regulation deeper and deeper into social life.**
>
> **[Turner, 1987, pp. 37–8]**

panoptic
Taken from Jeremy Bentham's 'panopticon' – a circular prison with warders' observation area at the centre, enabling the constant monitoring of all prisoners – this term refers to the ability to exercise surveillance over the whole of a population of bodies.

Instead of religious mortification and 'denial' of the body, we now have health régimes, diets and exercise as the modern forms of self- and public-regulation of our bodies.

Foucault's work on medicine opens up new questions for the sociology of health and illness that require us to relate analyses of medicine and the body to long-term historical changes in ways in which regulation over bodies has been secured in society, at both the micro (individual) and macro (population) levels. Medicine cannot be seen, then, as 'merely' an activity associated with clinical healing; the 'medicalisation' of the body – as we shall see below – has to be understood as a process of social control.

Combining perspectives? Turner's contribution

These different sociological perspectives are based on distinct theoretical assumptions about how best to understand health, illness and medicine in society. Parsons' work begins with the proposition that illness and disease create structural and behavioural problems that society needs to resolve through normative, rule-governed role performances. Interactionists in contrast show how both the definitions of illness and the appropriate behaviours surrounding it are more elastic and more precarious precisely because of their being constructed through interaction. Marxists stress the political economy of health, that there is considerable inequality in the way in which health and illness are defined and managed, an inequality that reflects the wider social structures of capitalism. Feminists demand that gender – typically ignored in these other approaches – be incorporated from the start in the analysis of role-relations, the definition of health and illness, and the institutionalised patriarchy that characterises the health care system. Foucauldian analysis ties the issue of medical control to the question of how the individual and the wider collective 'body' is subject to bio-social surveillance and regulation.

Clearly, it is possible to argue that these discrete traditions cannot be merged in some new theoretical model precisely because of their distinct conceptual bases. However, Turner (1987) has made a strong case for regarding these different approaches as reconcilable by suggesting that they can be seen to focus on different aspects of the same phenomena: each can contribute towards sociology's analysis of health, illness and medicine. He begins by distinguishing between three levels of analysis – the 'individual', the 'social' and the 'societal'. At the level of the individual we are interested in the experience of illness and disease: here interactionism plays a valuable role in drawing attention to the perception that people (and patients) have of their illness. Secondly, at the level of the social we concentrate on institutional dynamics (e.g. of hospitals, asylums) and the way in which professionals (medics) define and regulate sickness and disease (whether physical or mental): here Parsonsian and some of the more institutionally-oriented interactionist analysis (such as that of Goffman) would be appropriate. Finally, at the societal level, Turner turns our attention towards wider macro or systemic structures which pattern health care systems: thus, feminist analysis, Marxist political economy and, of course, Foucault's exploration of power and discourse are all of importance. Turner describes his interest in accommodating these different perspectives within one theory as a 'strategy of inclusion': rather than being forced to choose between [these] particular competing paradigms, one could see them as addressing very different issues at rather different levels' (1992, p. 237).

Turner's work has, then, built on these different traditions and can now be regarded as the most developed theoretical approach within contemporary sociology of medicine. His whole strategy relies on tying the sociological analysis of medicine to the sociology of the body. He agrees with Foucault that we can distinguish between the body as an individual entity – as a person – and as a collective entity – as a population. The desires, demands and pathologies of 'the body' at both of these levels are regulated, especially those relating to sexuality. Not surprisingly, Turner has become particularly interested in understanding the 'social' and 'societal' management of the AIDS virus where sexual and biological pathologies are explicitly interlinked. That is, the personal and public 'hygiene' that those in dominant positions demand for regulating and checking AIDS has both a biological and moral form, a corruption of the individual and collective bodies: hence the **homophobia** of the 'gay plague'.

homophobia
Fear of homosexuality and lesbianism.

The Medical Profession and the Power of Orthodox Medicine

All the perspectives outlined above highlight, in their different ways, the power of the established medical profession. How did medicine become so powerful? Here we need to trace the historical emergence of the profession, especially since the late eighteenth century and early nineteenth. Its roots lie in the more general process of '**professionalisation**' which then began for a number of different occupational groups, though at different rates in different fields (Rich, 1974). Professionalisation involves three related processes (Turner, 1987):

professionalisation
The process by which the members of a particular occupation seek to establish a monopoly over its practice. Typically, this is done by limiting entry to those possessing defined qualifications – by claiming that those who lack these qualifications do not possess the requisite expertise.

- the creation and defence of a specialist body of knowledge, typically based on formal university qualifications;
- the establishing of control over a specialised client market and exclusion of competitor groups from that market;
- the establishing of control over professional work practice, responsibilities and obligations while resisting control from managerial or bureaucratic staff.

In short, professions can be regarded as skilled groups enjoying a relatively privileged position in the occupational hierarchy whose members employ an ideology of expertise and client service to legitimate their advantaged position. Professional status can of course only develop where there is sufficient demand for particular skills (Johnston and Robbins, 1975). The demand for the healing powers of medicine has existed no doubt since the origin of society itself. Its particular professionalised form is much more recent. The Western medical profession developed within two distinct contexts during the nineteenth century. In the first, medical research and career opportunities were centred around the university, where the combined role of clinical practitioner/ teacher and researcher was formally established as a salaried occupation, notably in Germany and subsequently in the US. The international reputation of German medicine is indicated by the fact that between the years 1870 and 1914, 15,000 Americans studied medicine in German universities and took the German model back to the US on their return.

The second, very different, context was found in England. Wright (1979) has argued that the English medical system was the product of 'three centuries of dominance by the Royal College of Physicians (RCP)' whose monopolistic practices, legitimated by both royal charter and government legislation, allowed it to control if not eliminate competition from other medical groups, such as the apothecary companies and guilds during the eighteenth century. Wright points out that this dominance of orthodox medicine did not reflect its superior technical or scientific skills and practices compared with other forms of healing, such as astrology. Typically, medics would use bleeding and purging in their treatment, neither of which were likely to have any beneficial effect on the patient. And when more reliable and effective medical techniques did become available, there is evidence that suggests many doctors actually resisted them: scientific medicine might compromise the client-oriented 'bedside-manner' and the patronage this attracted. The most important factor which secured the dominance of medicine was the expansion in the medical market during the nineteenth century and a growing demand for doctors, both via the patronage of rich city-resident clients and also the new urban middle classes keen to secure medical skills not only for their own purposes but also as part of a wider demand for social regulation – for example of urban prostitution and working-class slums – which the medical profession could help deliver.

The growth in the demand for medicine meant that key players such as the RCP sought to consolidate their control, backed by government if possible, over the new health market. The result was the Medical Act of 1858 which established the first national register of recognised practitioners, set the qualifications for registration, restricted thereby the terms of entry to the profession, and confirmed doctors could enjoy a legally sanctioned monopoly to practise. New recruits to the profession were controlled such that though the population of England and Wales grew by 30 per cent between 1861 and 1881, there was only a 5 per cent increase in members of the profession.

There are striking differences between the British and US pattern of medical professionalisation. One result of this is the relative absence of general practitioners and a preponderance of specialist medics in the US: indeed this feature is symptomatic of major historical and cultural differences between the US and UK medical professions.

The two professional systems began to diverge as early as the turn of the century, so we cannot see their distinctions merely deriving from market medicine in the US and nationalised health care here. Instead, it was more to do with the structure and character of the professions and the distinct 'medical markets' within which they operated. In the British case, medical practice could be traced back to the sixteenth-century guilds of physicians, surgeons and apothecaries who provided care for the embryonic middle classes (merchants, other professions, early civil service, etc.), and the much fewer in number of elite practitioners attached to the Royal Colleges (of Surgeons/Physicians) whose members catered on the one hand to the upper classes and, on the other, acted as the principal medical officers to the charitable hospitals catering to the very poor. Subsequent developments during the latter part of the nineteenth century tended to confirm this split between the specialised elite of hospital-based medics and the larger number of general practitioners; the position of this latter group was secured through the 1911 national health insurance act which guaranteed for them a market among the poorer social groups to supplement their increasing middle-class market in the cities. The welfare state provided further support for this model of a health care system based on a two-dimensional specialist and general practice professional structure.

As a result, in Britain today, the GP controls access of patients to primary health care while specialist consultants control hospital provision. Once seen by a specialist the patient is referred back to his or her GP for any next steps – whether to end treatment then or be referred to another specialist, and so on. The professional structure is therefore based on this division between GPs' control over primary health care and specialists' control over secondary health care.

In contrast, in the USA the class basis to the profession evident in England was almost completely absent: there were not the social groups, such as the guilds, the Royal Colleges, the centres of elite patronage, which could act as a framework that would determine subsequent structures. As Rosemary Stevens (1980, p. 110) notes, 'American medicine was a profession without institutions', in the sense that it had to build its institutional base from scratch. As such it tended to do so on the basis of new social institutions, primarily universities, medical colleges, new technologies and the like, and so cultivated a strong predisposition towards a competitive – *specialist-based* – occupational structure. The technical culture of nineteenth-century and early-twentieth-century US medicine was in stark contrast to that prevailing in the UK at the same time. In Britain there was a hostility to new techniques – such as anaesthesia – which were seen, paradoxically perhaps, to 'deskill' the professional skills of surgeons practised in the art of rapid and therefore tolerably painful surgery. In the US, on the contrary, the social context of medical practice encouraged competing specialists to look to new treatments, techniques and therapies, not least to demonstrate specialist skills in a situation where the number of doctors providing care was much greater proportionately than in the UK. Indeed, as we have noted, in the UK the medical schools deliberately restricted the growth of licensed practitioners during the nineteenth and twentieth centuries in order to ensure professional control of medicine, something which the wider and more open medical market of the US never allowed. In addition, the specialist competitive dynamic encouraged much greater emphasis on a research-oriented tradition in the US than in the UK, and this has remained broadly true ever since. Commenting on this difference in the earlier part of this century, the American physician Flexner (1910) observed that research and clinical standards were poor in the UK while the guild-based professional structure was 'admirably calculated to protect honour and dignity, to conserve ceremony, and to transmit tradition'.

The upshot of these differences is that the private specialist medical professional began to dominate in the US, and that as such, medical care was seen to be directly related to what the patient could afford to pay. Higher-quality, more specialised, care attracted higher fees, which in turn encouraged further investment in more specialised, technically-costly medicine – a technical rather than patrician-based medical control over health care.

Whatever the specific historical variation in the professionalisation of medicine, the power of the profession to control its occupational position and reward in the labour market has been carefully documented, especially by sociologists such as Freidson(1988) and Johnson(1972), both of whom seek to lift the lid on client-oriented professional ethics which proclaim service to patients but which are in fact more occupational ideologies that enable the professions to secure considerable autonomy and distance from clients. As Johnson says:

> **The professional rhetoric relating to community service and altruism may be in many cases a significant factor in moulding the practices of individual professionals, but it also clearly functions as a legitimation of professional privilege.**
>
> **[Johnson, 1972, p. 25]**

The power of the profession can be understood through the notion of the *medicalisation* of lay forms of coping with illness and natural body processes such as ageing and pregnancy previously handled within the community. Medicalisation can take three forms:

The first is *the incorporation and redefinition* of lay approaches towards illness and body processes such that they now fall under the 'medical gaze', defined thereby as a form of illness open to medical intervention. For example, mental illness was medicalised in this sense in the late eighteenth century. Deviant or unusual mental states which had been defined in communities as signs of witchcraft or possession (divine as well as evil) were gradually redefined as psychiatric conditions. Religion gradually ceded territory to the newly established psychiatric profession. By the late nineteenth century those who intervened on behalf of a wretched defendant were much less likely to offer to 'save the soul' of 'the sinner' than to rescue the miscreant via mental rehabilitation. Ageing is another area where medicalisation has occurred. The aged tend to be homogenised as a group by the biomedical model of declining health. Unlike other areas of medical discourse, the ageing of the body is seen as incurable. As such, ageing does not fit the conventional biomedical 'curative' discourse. However, the pressure to medicalise ageing is increasing as the community and family structures are no longer in place to take on the responsibility of the aged whose number is growing rapidly: for example, in 1994 in the UK over nine million were aged 65 or over.

Box 13.1: The medicalisation of pregnancy

Common medical procedures associated with pregnancy:

- Regular antenatal checkups
- Iron and vitamin supplements
- Vaginal examinations in pregnancy
- Ultrasound monitoring of pregnancy
- Hospital birth
- Enemas or suppositories in the first stage of labour
- Shaving of the pubic hair in labour

Artificial rupture of the membranes
Pharmacological induction of labour
Vaginal examinations in labour
Bladder catheterisation in labour
Mechanical monitoring of the foetal heart
Mechanical monitoring of contractions
A glucose or saline drip in labour
Epidural analgesia in labour
Pethidine (meperidine) or other pain-killing/tranquillising injections in labour
Birth in horizontal or semi-horizontal position
Episiotomy
Forceps or vacuum extraction of the baby
Cutting the umbilical cord immediately after birth
Accelerated delivery of the placenta by injection of ergometrine and/or oxytocin and pulling on the cord

Source: Anne Oakley, *Becoming a Mother*, 1979, pp. 17–18.

The claimed *efficacy of scientific medicine* is the second powerful element of medicalisation. Better drugs, surgical techniques, therapies, anti-viral and antibiotic agents are all proof of the scientific progress of medical research and clinical practice. While the evidence here is clearly very persuasive, some have stressed the need for caution when evaluating the impact of medicine. Cochrane (1972) once director of the UK Medical Research Council's Epidemiology Unit, produced a powerful critique of the effectiveness of medical treatments precisely because of poor monitoring of these techniques through failing to conduct rigorous comparisons of one technique against any other. When this is done, quite unexpected results appear: 'Possibly the most striking result is [the trial] in Bristol in which hospital treatment (including a variable time in a coronary care unit) was compared with treatment at home for acute ischaemic heart disease. The results do not suggest that there is any medical gain in admission to hospital with coronary care units compared with treatment at home' (p. 74). Moreover, the benefit of 'scientific medicine' is open to challenge by the incidence of so-called **iatrogenic** illness, that is, doctor-induced illness and disability. Illich (1976) has commented that 'the pain, dysfunction, disability and anguish resulting from technical medical intervention now rival the morbidity due to traffic and industrial accidents and even war-related activities, and make the impact of medicine one of the most rapidly spreading epidemics of our time' (p. 24). Illich's strong attack on medicine might seem at first sight perhaps over-stated, but looked at in the light of the damage done to people through drugs' side-effects

iatrogenic
Illness or disability caused by medical treatment.

(such as thalidomide), dangerous contraceptive techniques devised for women, and general malpractice, it is a more credible set of claims. In large, impersonalised hospital systems, however, the personal responsibility of physicians is less clear. Malpractice and negligence may be redefined as merely technical breakdowns in the system rather than the result of ethically questionable treatment by practitioners.

The *marginalisation of alternative medical therapies* is a third aspect of medicalisation. Despite the strength of orthodoxy, popular, lay medical treatment is an important dimension of all health care systems. It is important to recognise that the entrenchment of orthodoxy associated with the formal health care sector does not encompass the whole of what Kleineman (1973) calls the cultural health system. The relationship between orthodoxy and alternative medicine in terms of patient involvement varies: those who suffer illness may always resort to alternative medicine and avoid medics, while many take up alternative medicine because of the perceived failings of orthodoxy.

Over the past twenty years there has been a steady growth in both patient visits to, and practitioners of, 'alternative medicine', which provides a range of treatments such as

- acupuncture
- chiropracture
- osteopathy
- homeopathy
- herbalism
- reflexology
- shiatsu
- Alexander technique

These differ in the extent to which they claim to offer alternative health care or merely a form of treatment complementary to orthodoxy.

Saks (1992) estimates that in the UK there are about 11,000 therapists in alternative medical associations with another 17,000 non-registered practitioners. Popular support for complementary medicine has led to political support within parliament forcing the government to appoint junior ministers with responsibility for alternative medicine. Despite this, alternative medicine (AM) has yet to establish itself as an alternative health care movement: in part this is because of splits among AM practitioners not only in terms of what strategy to adopt professionally but also how to delimit and describe their medicine. Saks notes that there are 'eighty-eight organisations in Britain covering seventeen or more alternative therapies' (p. 16).

Despite this, there has clearly been a steady growth in patient numbers using AM. Stanway (1982) argues there are five main reasons for this:

- people believe orthodox medicine is failing in certain fields – e.g. cancer
- people are afraid of Western medical treatment's iatrogenic effects – e.g. of operations, drugs (thalidomide, cortisone, etc. – see also Illich, 1976).
- some have religious/philosophical reservations about what is being offered by orthodoxy
- some want to protest about what is available via orthodoxy
- some want to experiment with new medicine.

In broader terms, Coward (1989) has argued that the interest in AM is linked with a 'new philosophy of the body, health and nature'. AM conveys ' a new consciousness of the value of involving the individual in her and his well-being and a new sense of being natural'. In this way, AM is part of a wider shift towards a *naturalistic* approach which contrasts lay vs. expert, natural vs. synthetic, organic vs. chemical, and holistic vs. mechanistic. In an even wider cultural context this relates to the green movement and the *natural system* notions within contemporary ecology. If it is 'natural' it must be good: homeopathy makes much of this claim in its treatment.

The challenge posed by AM is mainly restricted to an attack on the philosophy of orthodoxy rather than on its professional base: while patients may vote with their feet in increasing numbers and seek treatment from AM practitioners, the institutional entrenchment of orthodox medics is unlikely to be dismantled. One reason why this is so is that orthodoxy may simply incorporate AM into its practice and turn a threat from competitors into an advantage for themselves. This is especially true in Western Europe where medics have the right to use whatever medical technique they regard as valuable in treating patients – whether prescription medicine, physiotherapy, acupuncture, or endoscopy, etc. In fact the response of orthodoxy towards its control over and marginalisation of AM has varied depending on circumstances.

Box 13.2: Forms of control by orthodoxy over competitors

- Incorporate on own terms competing ideas and skills
  e.g. mesmerism -> neurhypnology (hypnosis)
- Competitors practise in subordinate position in law
  e.g. radiography (when first developed in 1920s)
- Reject competitors completely
  e.g. chiropracture
- Competitor accepts dominance of medical profession
  e.g. osteopathy

There are a number of dilemmas faced by AM practitioners when orthodoxy shows a preparedness to incorporate aspects of their traditional medicine. Incorporation usually means:

- There is a wider acceptance of AM by the public and the possibility of referral by GPs, but this also poses a threat to the medical beliefs and therapies on which AM is based: thus they lose their 'alternative' identity (the very claim that makes them so attractive).
- AM practitioners welcome their access to a new medical 'market' but find they have to develop a recipe knowledge of orthodox medical terms to reassure new patients.
- Recognition provides formal state blessing but on terms which require practitioners to police their AM members.
- New research support may appear but the development of the therapy is likely to be orchestrated by orthodox researchers rather than by AM practitioners themselves.

The challenge of AM will depend as much on patient disaffection with orthodoxy as it will on the capacity of AM lobbies to establish themselves in the medical system.

In terms of one of the key themes of this book, one might wonder whether the AM movement, in its challenging of rational scientific medicine is, thereby, a *postmodern* critique of established medicine. Inasmuch as it poses a wide range of alternative therapies and distances itself from anything that smacks of the authoritarianism of a professional elite, AM is in some sense another illustration of the deconstruction of traditional forms of social authority (the medical profession) and conventional expertise (medical knowledge). Its popularity today might be said to reflect a wider desire to challenge powerful modernist practices and certainties.

To the extent that AM achieves these goals – and its victories have been small and relatively insignificant so far – it might be seen as yet another indication of the onset of a form of postmodernism. However, another view might be to say that while AM challenges orthodox medicine, the sort of knowledge it offers as an alternative is far removed from the unstable, shaky and ephemeral world beloved of the postmodernist. For AM promotes an image of 'natural', holistic medicine which is grounded in a set of strong, overarching principles about nature and our place in it, much like some of the fundamentalist beliefs of left-wing environmentalism. Furthermore, to secure whatever small foothold they have in the health care system, many AM groups have adopted strategies which remind us more of the early attempts by Western medicine to establish their modernist credentials and respectability.

So, much of the advance that groups have made has, as we might expect given our earlier argument, depended on professionalising themselves rather than on demonstrating the efficacy of a radically distinct AM. We have seen, for example, the appearance of registering organisations which can control membership and prevent anyone practising: thus in the UK there is the Council for Complementary and Alternative Medicine which sets standards of AM care that mimics the General Medical Council. Despite this, there is clearly little evidence here of AM posing a major threat to professional entrenchment. If it continues to grow, it is likely that it will do so *through medical practitioners themselves* adopting it as a useful, cheap and patient-centred form of health care. Whatever the form of medicine delivered, there is likely to remain, however, a chronic inequality across different sectors of the population with regard to the general standards of health that they enjoy. It is to this issue that we now turn.

Health Inequalities

In Bethnal Green in 1839 the average age of death was as follows:

Gentlemen and persons engaged in professions and their families	45 years
Tradesmen and their families	26 years
Mechanics, servants and labourers and their families	16 years

[Chadwick, 1842] ”

Although the general standards of health have improved dramatically since Chadwick reported the massive inequalities of early-nineteenth-century London, the prevalence of chronic sickness still varies according to social class, as Table 13.2 shows, which, to point up the contrast, compares professional with unskilled, male and female, young and old.

The figures in the table indicate the continued inequalities in both morbidity and mortality across social classes. Such differences were

Table 13.2 *Chronic sickness rates by social class, UK 1994 (%)*

Socio-economic group	*Male 0–15 yrs*	*Male 65 and over*	*Female 0–15 yrs*	*Female 65 and over*
Professional	16	57	11	53
Unskilled	28	68	8	65

Source: *Social Trends* (Office of Population Censuses and Surveys, 1994, p. 86).

explored in detail in the UK by Townsend and Davidson (1982) who argue that the most important factors affecting health were income, occupation, education, housing and lifestyle. They examined four types of explanation that have been used to account for the statistical data. These are as follows:

(a) *Health inequality as an artefact*: Here the claim is made that health differences are a statistical fiction, artificially created through the way the data themselves are not only gathered but analysed through epidemiological techniques. There is said to be no real causal relationship between class position and the quality of an individual's health.

(b) *Health inequality as a process of social selection*: Here there is an acceptance that health and class inequality *are* related but that the independent variable is health itself. Good health, it is argued, produces upward social mobility while bad health produces downward mobility. Health, then, is seen here as a determinant of class position.

(c) *Health inequality as material deprivation*: Against the second view, this position argues that poverty is directly related to ill-health. The most recent major survey of poverty in the UK (Townsend, 1979) found that 7 per cent of households – 3.3 million people – received an income lower than the Supplementary Benefit level, while 24 per cent of households – almost 12 million people – were on the margins of poverty. Since Townsend's study was published, the figures have remained steady or worsened, especially for single pensioners and single-parent families with children, whose chance of being in poverty has increased by 60 per cent. While these two groups reflect changing demographic patterns in society, the majority of those who are poor are

Source: *Private Eye*

'Have you tried drink?'

so because they can no longer secure work which will provide adequate wages. Millar (1993) relates this to high levels of unemployment, a growth in low-paid work and a considerable increase in part-time, casualised labour.

The evidence suggests a direct relationship between these groups – from elderly pensioners to those in low-paid jobs – and high levels of illness and disease. One measure of this is the very strong relationship between levels of the prescription of medicines and poorer, inner-city areas. Poor nutrition, lack of proper hygienic facilities, exhaustion through long working hours (especially on night shifts) and the general struggle to 'make ends meet' make for poor health chances, especially for the very young and very old.

(d) *Health inequality as cultural deprivation*: Here, in very different terms, it is argued that poor health is more to do with cultural practices and belief than disadvantages in material circumstances. The focus here is on the relative cultural competencies of social classes to use knowledge about health and the health services. Smoking is one practice which might be used to illustrate the point. Why do people smoke despite the evidence of its damaging effects? Why does the incidence of smoking increase among lower social classes such that more working class die from smoking-related lung cancer than any other social group?

cultural deprivation

In the sociology of health and illness, an approach which focuses on factors such as smoking, alcohol consumption and eating habits claiming that life-style choices determine ill-health. It offers an explanation of increased incidences of ill-health in working-class people by directly relating it to life-style factors.

It is argued here that certain social groups experience a form of **cultural deprivation** throughout their lives, within their families and from the medical profession itself in terms of knowing how best to manage their health needs. In addition, members of ethnic minorities or from among the working class may be less likely to regard their illnesses as either appropriate or worthy for a doctor's attention. Finally, it is conceivable that smoking for the working classes – and increasingly for women – acts as a sort of defensive totem which creates a feeling of defiance: a vehicle to assert their identity and personal control in social situations. Tobacco companies, of course, rely on just this sort of association being made with their cigarettes – whether it be the new, assertive women, the 'westernising' East European (smoking 'West' cigarettes) or the Third World entrepreneur stocking the latest line in T-shirts promoting US-based Camel Filter cigarettes. Smoking is clearly a social statement that brings pleasure as well as a chesty cough and, perhaps, lung cancer.

These different interpretations of raw health figures have been subject to sociological and medical debate for many years, and in broad terms the last two – the material and cultural accounts – are typically favoured as explanations of the patterns of morbidity and mortality.

The issues they raise are not simply the concern of academics or members of the medical profession: there is a strong government interest in using certain interpretations to support particular health policies. A particularly attractive line for the government to adopt in a period of reduced state expenditure is that health should be seen as a matter of personal responsibility, a view not far from some of the ideas underlying the 'cultural deprivation' approach. More health services and insurance companies in many advanced countries are penalising smokers because of this. This is given greater momentum by the growing importance of health economics as an expert discipline – a highly modernist approach to the rational rationing of health care – which provides 'scientific' grounds on which one can decide who should and who should not receive medical attention (Ashmore *et al.*, 1989). The ultimate decision will be taken by the managers and professionals within state and private health care. In the UK it is those working in the National Health Service (NHS) who have this responsibility. This takes us to a point where we can consider the NHS in Britain today.

The NHS in the Health Care System Today

The health care system in the UK today is one which relies on medical professionals through a national state-sponsored 'health

Source: *Private Eye*

'First the good news. His temperature has gone down.'

service'. The main social actors involved here, then, are the various 'professions', their 'consumers' (primarily their patients), and the state, which both sustains the basic funding of the system while subjecting it to continual monitoring and evaluation.

Clearly, we have to see the NHS, established in July 1948, as a state-sponsored *medicalised* health care system inasmuch as the professional sector of expert medicine is the principal provider of health care (notwithstanding the high levels of self-healing that prevail). The founding assumption of the NHS is that expert, scientific medicine is good in and of itself, has collective approval, and means that primary care should be given through doctors in general and hospital practice. This is a set of assumptions found in most industrialised countries, though less true of developing countries.

As the NHS has traditionally provided *free* access to health care, so it has tended to be the primary vehicle through which consumers seek medical help and treatment; in fee-paying systems, consumers are found to 'shop around' more for treatments, and as a result the medical market is both more competitive and more litigious.

Box 13.3: Characterising the US health care system

'*Third world medicine at super-power prices*': in such terms did Gavin Esler, the BBC's Chief US Political Correspondent describe the state of health care in the United States. A similar view of a system that mixes deprivation with excess is shared by many commentators on the US: you can get very expensive treatment for rare life-threatening diseases or the most technically demanding operations but you cannot find mass vaccination programmes that provide cheap preventative medicine at $3 a shot. The US spends more than any other country on its health care – about 14 per cent of GDP, more than twice that spent in the UK, with a massive absolute sum approaching $550 billion. Yet over 30 million (out of 250 million) US citizens have no health care provision whatsoever – public or private. That so massive an expenditure still fails to provide basic health for millions poses a growing social and political problem for the US government. It is a problem that will increase, since it has been estimated that at current rates of growth health will absorb 25 per cent of the federal budget by 1998. The policy problem is to reduce the bill while improving the provision of health care. The political problem is that to achieve this will require something of a state-led attack on the most powerful institutions benefiting from welfare: the medical and legal professions, the insurance sector and the pharmaceutical industry.

The latter, for example, is being challenged to reduce its drugs prices because of making excess profits, while insurance companies are under attack from firms whose requirement to provide private sickness benefits and perks for employees has either forced up prices to compensate or eroded corporate profits. The spiralling costs to firms has made many move to a form of self-insurance of their workers' health needs to control health costs more effectively by removing the third party – the insurance company – from the scene. It is evident then that major economic interests – not always convergent with each other – are tied into and depend on the health care system in the US. It should also be evident that although private market relations shape much of the pattern of provision this does not mean that the system 'works' more effectively than one based on collective public provision.

The NHS has a sort of 'protected species' status among the panoply of national British institutions, and any perceived attempt by government to threaten its existence is regarded as tantamount to political suicide. In part this is no doubt because of its free-at-the-point-of-access character: no one wants to pay for treatment. But it is also probably because of a well-rooted belief in health care being 'safer' because of being collaborative as part of a non-commercialised – and so more transparent, accountable, and reliable – 'service'. While this belief no doubt rests on over-sentimentalised attachment to something that has never lived up to this image, it has nevertheless been a powerful myth which both professionals and consumers have helped reproduce over the years.

Yet today it is under something of an attack, albeit hidden in alternative rhetorics of efficiency and patient choice. At present there are a number of crucial changes in the operation of the NHS which will, if given more momentum, probably alter its essential character. These are as follows:

- *community care*: while this is supposed to be a progressive policy promoting de-institutionalisation, in practice it has meant a shift from care *in* the community to care *by* the community.
- *marketisation*: the promotion of patient choice and the creation of fund-holding doctors
- *privatisation*: of services within hospitals (and medicine – e.g. this is proposed for the public health laboratory service)
- *resource costs*: a stress on new managerialism and health economics; an increase in health charges (e.g. prescription charges/dental care); the appearance of self-governing trust hospitals
- *ideology*: the shift from 'health' as *public* health related to social/environmental factors to health as private, with the individual responsible for her/his own well-being.

Together these developments are likely to mean a qualitative change in the NHS, and one which is not necessarily fully coherent: e.g. community care in reality seems to work against 'patient choice' by denying any real alternative to domiciliary burdensome care. Moreover, it is apparent that 'health care' needs are being increasingly redefined to more restricted boundaries, while 'social needs' – such as 'respite care' and 'community carers' – are seen as the responsibility of social services or the family or both. But note that there is a form of **de-medicalisation** of health care happening here – especially for the elderly – as social services take on more responsibility for the sick. And note, too, that the definition and satisfaction of health 'needs' is always as much a political as it is a medical matter: who decides what needs are, how they should be met, and at what level, are questions that are the subject of major political debate, especially when the health care system is ostensibly based on an equitable distribution of its resources provided free of charge.

de-medicalisation
The process whereby orthodox medicine begins to lose its ability to define and regulate areas of human life (*see* medicalisation).

Today the British government has sought to introduce greater 'consumer choice' into the NHS. The notion here is to reduce the power of the professional providers, rather than necessarily give much greater power to the actual customers, the patients. The rhetoric declares a move away from a profession-led towards a consumer-led health care system, but the reality is that government is seeking primarily to reduce its own support role in the provision of services. Community care has to be read in this way, for example, as much as it does in terms of empowering local carers to take control of their ill-health.

Whatever the outcome of this debate, there is a sense that the NHS is under threat through creeping **marketisation** and **privatisation.** We have to put this into context, however; that is, there has always been an element of private care within the NHS just as before its establishment. It is unlikely that patients' charters will generate a new accountability and efficiency from medics. In fact it might raise expectations which actually exacerbate the difficulties of proving health care and raising levels of welfare in the country.

marketisation
An economic concept to describe the process of exchange and distribution of services and goods carried out by private individuals or corporate bodies, based on the dictates of supply and demand.

The problem of the level of the state's support for national medical provision is one which is widely shared in advanced industrial capitalist states. Solutions to the problem involve a mix of increased **managerialism**, an emphasis on health care via the market, and, despite a growth in the bureaucracy overseeing medicine, a tendency towards relying on 'carers' in the community – a responsibility that falls most heavily on women.

privatisation
The process of transfer of state assets from public to private ownership.

managerialism
A process of increased managerial control.

Globalisation of Health, Illness and Medicine

In Chapter 3 we saw how the contemporary world could be regarded as a global system, shaped by major cultural and economic players, notably Sklair's transnational classes. It should not come as a surprise therefore to find that patterns of morbidity and mortality also have globalised dimensions. So, the more the world economy becomes integrated in terms of production and consumption, the more the international division of labour produces similar structures of class inequality; and the more the culture of the West (notably in its 'Americanised' form) predominates the more we should expect to see similar patterns to health and illness, similar patterns of good and poor nutrition, similar patterns of more or less access to health care – but now on a *global* level.

Turner (1987) shows how there is a convergence towards similar patterns of morbidity and mortality throughout the globe, with cancer, strokes and heart disease predominant whatever national context one surveys. Similarly, there is a globalisation of common institutional forms of medicine that respond to the demand for health care, broadly speaking – highly bureaucratic 'rational' systems of medical delivery that go beyond national boundaries. Finally, as a feature of modernity common to all industrialised states we can see that medicine plays an important scientifically and professionally grounded role as regulator of both individual and collective 'bodies' in all societies.

The globalisation of common forms of medical practice and associated technologies – such as scanning devices, the paraphernalia of intensive-care units, and so on – reflects an international professional network of medics who share similar practitioner requirements and standards. It also reflects the way modernity encourages a *standardisation of technologies* and instruments (not only in medicine but elsewhere), as major suppliers of equipment, drugs or other medical facilities are under pressure to adopt the same sort of technical innovations to remain competitive while having to conform to quality standards set by international regulatory agencies. As the major drugs companies merge to become truly global firms – such as SmithKline Beecham or Glaxo-Wellcome – the drugs they develop are geared towards global markets. The recent GATT (General Agreement on Tariffs and Trade) agreement encourages this further by securing the proprietary rights of drugs companies in a much wider range of countries in both the northern and southern hemispheres, so securing and stabilising world markets for them.

In addition, the communication and information technologies that are crucial to the globalisation process play a growing role in medical science and medical practice. Within medical research, international access to computerised databases is of growing importance both to keep up with new developments and to exchange information quickly in standardised formats – crucial, for example, to the current Human Genome Project. From a practitioner perspective, the digitisation of patient records and medical results allows doctors to discuss cases over the Internet without meeting the patient. Not only does this tend to encourage a greater standardisation of symptomatology and diagnosis internationally, it also opens up intriguing questions about doctor–patient relations and the continuing relevance of the notion of 'the bed-side manner'!

At the same time, globalising processes encourage – as we saw in Chapter 3 – resistance at the local level to the tendencies towards convergence. For example, transnational pharmaceutical companies find their global dominance checked by smaller competitor drugs companies in southern hemisphere states as well as by states in the north keen to cut back on their local health prescription bill. Moreover, indigenous or traditional forms of medicine in Africa, Asia and **Pacific Rim** countries are still very strong and often practised alongside 'modern' medicine: indeed, until recently in China, this was actively advocated by the government. Even in Western societies, not only do alternative forms of medicine prevail but so do popular, lay remedies for coping with illness – such as 'feed a cold and starve a fever' – or prescriptions for remaining healthy, such as 'don't go out with your hair wet'. It is doubtful that either of these are global injunctions!

Pacific Rim
Those south-east Asian countries with fast developing economies that border the Pacific Ocean, such as Taiwan, Hong Kong, Malaysia and South Korea.

Conclusion

This chapter has explored the theoretical and empirical basis on which the contemporary sociology of health, illness and medicine is built. It should be clear that medicine plays more than a role as healer of sickness, as is commonly thought. It shapes the definition of both health and illness; it is reproduced by one of the most powerful occupational professions who help recreate its discursive power; it is closely tied to major economic and political interests; and finally, its curative and healing powers can often be less than its modernist self-image would like to portray. Sociologically, therefore, the social basis of health and illness should now be evident, both at the **micro** and **macro** levels of analysis.

micro-level
A level of sociological analysis concerned with face-to-face social encounters or small scale interaction between groups.

macro-level
A level of sociological analysis which focuses either on large collectivities and institutions or social systems and social structures (*see* structures).

Summary of the Chapter

- Sociology challenges the biomedical model of health and illness by demonstrating the social bases that both have.
- The development of rational, scientific medicine is associated with the growth of professional medical expertise and state-sponsored institutions of health care: both exemplify the impact of modernity on the health care system.
- There are five main theoretical approaches towards health, illness and medicine: functionalist, interactionist, Marxist, feminist and Foucauldian.
- Turner (1992) has developed a valuable model which tries to integrate these different perspectives, through arguing the need to distinguish between analysis at the level of 'the individual', 'the social' and 'the societal'.
- The medical profession has established itself as the principal authority in the 'medical market', though there are differences – between the UK and US for example – in the way this power is expressed and in its historical origins.
- Alternative medicine challenges orthodoxy but cannot be seen as a postmodern critique.
- Health inequalities reflect wider social divisions, though there are different possible interpretations of health statistics.
- The NHS in Britain, as similar state-sponsored health care elsewhere, is experiencing fundamental change though its full privatisation seems unlikely.
- Health has its global dimensions not only in terms of patterns on morbidity and mortality but also in terms of the convergence of forms of treatment, drug and equipment markets and use. Localised resistance to these convergent processes is also apparent.

References

Allen, T. (1992) 'Upheaval, affliction and health', in H. Bernstein *et al.* (eds), *Rural Livelihoods*, Milton Keynes, Open University Press.

Ashmore, M. *et al.* (1989) *Health and Efficiency: A Sociology of Health Economics*, Milton Keynes, Open University Press.

Banks, M. *et al.* (1975) 'Factors influencing demand for primary medical care', *Journal of Epidemiology*, vol. 4, pp. 189–95.

Beck, U. (1992) *Risk Society*, London, Sage.

Byrne, A. S. and B. E. L. Long (1976) *Doctors Talking to Patients*, London, HMSO.

Chadwick, E. (1842) *General Report on the Sanitary Conditions of the Labouring Classes of Great Britain*, Edinburgh.

Cochrane, A. (1971) *Effectiveness and Efficiency: Random Reflections on the Health Service*, London, Nuffield Provincial Hospitals Trust.

Coward, R. (1989) *The Whole Truth: The Myth of Alternative Medicine*, London, Faber.

Ehrenreich, B. (1979) *For Her Own Good*, London, Pluto Press.

Flexner, A. (1910) *Report on Medical Education in the United States and Canada*, Boston, no publisher cited.

Foucault, M. (1977) *The Birth of the Clinic*, London, Tavistock.

Foucault, M. (1977) *The History of Sexuality: Volume 1, An Introduction*, London, Allen Lane.

Foucault, M. (1980) *Power/Knowledge, Selected Interviews and Other Writings 1972–1977*, Brighton, Harvester Press.

Freidson, E. (1988) *Profession of Medicine*, 2nd edn, Chicago, Chicago University Press.

Herzlich, C. (1973) *Health and Illness: A Social Psychological Analysis*, London, Academic Press.

Horwitz, A. (1977) 'The pathways into psychiatric treatment', *Journal of Health and Social Behaviour*, vol. 18, pp. 169–78.

Illich, I. (1976) *Medical Nemesis*, New York, Pantheon.

Johnson, T. (1972) *Professions and Power*, London, Macmillan.

Johnston, R. and D. Robbins (1975) 'The development of specialities in industrialised science', *Sociological Review*, vol. 25, pp. 87–108.

Jordanova, L. (1989) *Sexual Visions: Images of Gender in Science and Medicine Between the Eighteenth and Twentieth Centuries*, London, Harvester Wheatsheaf.

Kleineman, A. (1973) 'Towards a comparative study of medical systems', *Science, Medicine and Man*, vol. 1, pp. 55–65.

Lemert, E. (1974) *Human Deviance and Social Control*, Englewood Cliffs, N.J., Prentice-Hall.

MacIntyre, S. and D. Oldham (1977) 'Coping with migraine', in A. Davies and G. Horobin (eds), *Medical Encounters*, London, Croom Helm.

Millar, J. (1993) 'The continuing trend in rising poverty', in A. Sinfield (ed.), *Poverty, Inequality and Justice*, Edinburgh, Edinburgh University Press.

Morgan, M. (1985) *Sociological Approaches to Health and Medicine*, London, Routledge.

Navarro, V. (1986) *Crisis, Health and Medicine*, London, Tavistock Publications.

Oakley, A. (1979) *From Here to Maternity: Becoming a Mother*, Oxford, Martin Robertson.

Oakley, A. (1984) *The Captured Womb: A History of Pregnant Women*, Oxford, Blackwell.

Office of Population Censuses and Surveys (1994) *Social Trends*, London, HMSO.

Pollock, K. (1988) 'On the nature of social stress: production of a modern mythology', *Social Science and Medicine*, vol. 26, pp. 381–92.

Rich, D. (1974) 'Private government and professional science', in A. Teich (ed.), *Scientists and Public Affairs*, London, MIT Press.

Richman, J. (1987) *Medicine and Health*, London, Routledge.

Rosenhan, D. *et al.* (1973) 'On being sane in insane places', *Science*, vol. 179, pp. 260–68.

Saks, M. (1992) *Alternative Medicine*, Oxford, Clarendon Press.

Scambler, G. (1991) *Sociology as Applied to Medicine*, 3rd edn. London, Balliere Tindall.

Sontag, S. (1979) *Illness as Metaphor*, New York, Random House.

Stacey, M. (1989) *Sociology of Health and Healing*, London, Unwin Hyman.

Stanway, A. (1982) *Alternative Medicine*, Harmondsworth, Penguin.

Stevens, R. (1980) 'The future of the medical profession', in E. Ginsberg (ed.), *From Physician Shortage to Patient Shortage: The Uncertain Future of Medical Practice*, Boulder, Col., Westview Press.

Stewart, M. and D. Roter (1989) *Communicating With Medical Patients*, London, Sage.

Sudnow, D. (1967) *Passing On: The Social Organisation of Dying*, Englewood Cliffs, N. J., Prentice-Hall.

Tombs, S. (1990) 'Industrial injuries in British manufacturing industry', *Sociological Review*, May, pp. 324–43.

Townsend, P. (1979) *Poverty in the United Kingdom*, Harmondsworth, Penguin.

Townsend, P. and N. Davidson (1982) *Inequalities in Health*, Harmondsworth, Penguin.

Turner, B. (1987) *Medical Power and Social Knowledge*, London, Sage.

Turner, B. (1992) *Regulating Bodies: Essays in Medical Sociology*, London, Routledge.

Wright, C. (1994) 'A fallible safety system: institutionalised irrationality in the offshore oil and gas industry', *Sociological Review*, vol. 42, no. 1, pp. 79–103.

Wright, P. (1979) 'A study in the legitimisation of knowledge: the 'success' of medicine and the 'failure' of astrology', in R. Wallis (ed.), *On the Margins of Science*, Sociological Review Monograph, 27, University of Keele Press.

14 Understanding Crime

Aims of the Chapter

This chapter examines the diversity of sociological explanations of crime by comparing them along a number of different dimensions. While highlighting key differences between these approaches, we try to show how they have shared a common commitment to the 'modernist project' – that is, to a belief in the possibility and legitimacy of constructing a valid explanation of the phenomenon of crime and, hence, of developing strategies for doing something about it. Maintaining one of our central themes of the book, the debates about modernity and postmodernity, we also introduce the reader to the postmodernist critique of criminology.

Introduction

In the 1990s, perhaps never as vividly before, crime stands at the centre of public consciousness and contemporary political debate. The mass media serve up a regular diet of stories of rising crime, vulnerable victims and uncaring offenders. The public persistently voice their fears and anxieties about crime in opinion surveys, in official government studies and local area studies, prioritising their concern with the issue alongside such fundamentals as the state of the economy and the threat of unemployment and redundancy. Political parties vie with each other to establish their standing and credentials on the issue of 'law and order'. The success of the police in dealing with the crime problem in general and with particular varieties of criminals and criminal activity comes under ever more focused scrutiny, and the effectiveness and rigour of the criminal justice and penal systems generate apparently never-ending controversy.

Crime, then, clearly constitutes a major realm of societal concern, a spectre which looms ever larger in the preoccupations of the state and its agencies and in the lives and perceptions of ordinary people. It is important to keep that spectre in proportion, especially when we bear in mind international comparisons – for instance, the 'crime problem' in Britain pales into relative insignificance when placed alongside that of America, where there are more than 20,000 murders per year compared with Britain's 700–800. However, it remains the case that Britain and many other societies have witnessed substantial increases in the levels of recorded crime in recent decades: in England and Wales, for example, recorded crime has *tripled* in the past 20 years, from approximately 1.67 million in 1971 to 5.6 million in 1992 (see Table 14.1)

Table 14.1 *Recorded crime in England and Wales (indictable/notifiable offences)*

1971	1.666 million
1973	1.658 million
1981	2.964 million
1985	3.612 million
1991	5.276 million
1992	5.592 million
1993	5.526 million

Although those data allow us to draw no *simple* or perfectly precise conclusions about changes in actual criminal behaviour, since the ratio of unrecorded to recorded crimes may have varied at different times, we can nevertheless fairly confidently accept that there have been real, if not precisely measurable, increases in criminal activity in Western Europe and North America and in many societies elsewhere.

But, of course, as numerous Self-Report studies and national and local Victim surveys over the years have confirmed, far more crime occurs than official data indicate. For example, the various British Crime Surveys (1982, 1984, 1988, 1992) estimated that for every recorded crime there were three or four other unrecorded offences, though even this

'Solicitors can make a lot of money. Yes, if I were you I'd mug a solicitor.'

Source: A.-J. Doran (ed.) (1990) *The Punch Cartoon Album*, London, Grafton Books.

figure varies considerably according to offence. Thus, while more than 1 in 2 burglaries went unrecorded, 4 out of 5 woundings and attempted or successful robberies, and 9 out of 10 acts of vandalism and theft failed to find their way into official figures.

Modernist Criminology

Anxieties regarding crime, while perhaps now more intense, are not peculiar to contemporary times. Indeed, preceding generations stretching well back into the nineteenth century have been preoccupied with the problem of crime and the 'criminal classes', and academic analyses of crime have a similarly long pedigree. However, in Western Europe and North America in the nineteenth century and for much of the twentieth, attempts to understand and explain crime were for a long time dominated by academic approaches other than sociological ones – most notably, by biological and psychological explanations. It was not really until the 1950s that a serious sociological challenge to those individualistic explanations became firmly established.

But despite their frequently apparent incompatibilities and mutual exclusiveness in detailed content, these non-sociological and sociological approaches have shared a more fundamental common ground – that is, a commitment to the *modernist project* to which we refer throughout the book. Modernity involves a distinctive position regarding the nature of knowledge and the part it can and should play in the lives of human beings and human societies. Modernists are committed to the idea that it is possible to attain rational, verifiable, cumulative knowledge of society, to construct from that theories through which social phenomena can be represented and explained, and that competing theories or narratives can be evaluated by an appeal to logic and the testing of their claims – that is, a particular theory or narrative can be 'right'. Thus, modernism holds the promise that it can reveal the 'truth' about human behaviour. Moreover, modernism involves belief in the idea of *progress through knowledge* – that the accumulation of knowledge can be acted upon to emancipate human beings, to enrich their lives, improve society and humanity generally, and achieve progress and better futures.

In the study of crime, this has meant a belief, embraced with varying degrees of enthusiasm and conviction, in the possibility of establishing verifiable knowledge about crime, criminals and criminality which will provide a rational basis for intervening in and controlling crime through strategies of prevention or reduction and/or methods of punishment, deterrence, or rehabilitation. As Heidensohn (1989) says:

> **Sociologists have played major parts directly and indirectly in strategies linked to altering levels of criminality. It is, after all, inherent in the nature of the sociological approach, deriving as the discipline does from intellectual reactions to and theories of social change, that its practitioners believe that states can be altered, institutions restructured and communities be redeveloped.**
>
> **[Heidensohn, 1989, p. 181]**

We can highlight some of these sociological approaches (and hence their modernist orientation and credentials) by examining them along four axes, which, while they are neither necessarily exhaustive nor immune to alternative construction, provide useful bases for substantive comparison and contrast:

- Firstly, we can locate them in their *theoretical/political contexts* by identifying their specific academic theoretical origins and pedigree – that is, where they come from and where they stand theoretically – and by examining the socio-political circumstances of their emergence. While it would be too simplistic to see theories simply and solely as 'children of their times', they are clearly not unconnected with prevailing socio-political climates.
- Secondly, we can attempt to distil their *central concerns* – that is, what they see as being the most important things on which the study of crime should focus, what criminology should be 'about'.
- Thirdly, within those broad concerns, we can highlight their *substantive themes* – that is, the key distinguishing ideas which characterise their approaches and explanations.
- Fourthly, we can attempt to show that in criminological theorising, as much if not more so than in other areas of the study of social behaviour, there are and have been important connections made, sometimes explicit and sometimes implicit, between *explanations* of social phenomena and *policy solutions* offered – that is, particular approaches to crime contain within them (often unstated) assumptions about what can and should be done about crime.

Delinquent Subculture Theories

The challenge to individualistic non-sociological explanations of crime was provided by *Delinquent Subculture* theories, which came to fruition in America in the late 1950s and early 1960s, most notably in the work of Albert Cohen (1955) and Richard Cloward and Lloyd Ohlin

(1960). These theories, although differing from the non-sociological approaches in the key variables which they identified as crucial in explaining crime, still rested firmly, like them, within a *positivist* theoretical tradition. Positivism, as we have suggested elsewhere, operates with a conception of the social world as an objective entity which can be directly observed and studied as if it is a series of objects with regular features like those in the natural world. Human behaviour is assumed to be subject to the same principles of cause and effect that typify the behaviour of physical objects: human beings react to social forces 'external' to them, constraining them to behave in certain ways. Thus, explanation of social behaviour centres around the search for the social causes assumed to determine that behaviour.

Within that tradition, Delinquent Subculture theories had little problem in identifying and conceptualising an unproblematic reality for their subject-matter. 'Crime' and 'criminals' were social phenomena subject to relations of cause and effect, 'out there' waiting to be examined and explained: criminals and delinquents were social actors whose behaviour was determined and who were different from non-criminals, and hence the theorists accepted the legitimacy of seeking the *causes* of these differences.

The political credentials of the approach were essentially those of a '*liberal*' positivism, in that its exponents were critical of the prevailing social order in their explanations of crime. But, as we shall see shortly, their critique was essentially a mild one which identified malfunctions in the social order but saw these malfunctions as rectifiable, as capable of being remedied without the necessity for the wholesale restructuring of society. There was, in this view, a social order which was relatively viable if somewhat flawed, and such a view chimed well with the era of post-war liberal optimism about the possibilities of social engineering by means of programmes of social reform, social welfare and education, and with the gradual but increasing recognition (particularly in the USA) of the value of the social sciences and their potential capacity for practical use and problem-solving.

When we turn our attention to the second axis of our analysis, the central concerns of Delinquent Subculture theories, we can see how their acceptance of a given, relatively non-problematic social reality shaped those concerns. It led them to accept and embrace the *official* picture of crime depicted in government statistics of recorded crime as the reality to be studied, and hence to accept and advocate the need to explain the distinctive social pattern of crime and delinquency – that crime was a particularly *male, adolescent, working-class, urban phenomenon*. For Delinquent

Subculture theorists, these were the 'social facts' of crime, and their positivist orientation led them to conclude that these social facts must have social causes, that social structural arrangements were the key crime-producing agents. Their central concern, then, was to identify the social causes of criminality and to seek them in social environments and social experiences.

While it may well be easy, from the vantage point of the 1990s, to see little remarkable in that, it did represent an important systematic step away from a conception of criminality as being a property of individuals towards a view of crime and delinquency as rooted in social systems and therefore as explicable in terms of such social systems. Hence, when we consider the substantive themes of Delinquent Subculture theories, we see immediately that, instead of the causal factors of crime and delinquency lying within individuals who are somehow individually 'abnormal' or 'different' in their biological or psychological make-up, criminals and delinquents are depicted as 'normal' social actors whose motivations are shaped by their (unfavourable) social circumstances and experiences. More specifically, crime and delinquency are to be seen as resulting from the way society works – or, more accurately, from the way it does not work perfectly.

Many Delinquent Subculture theorists took their general inspiration for explaining crime and delinquency from Robert Merton's (1949) reworking of Durkheim's (1952) notion of '**anomie**'. For Durkheim (1952), anomie implied a situation where social conditions produced a *de-regulation* of social life, so that prevailing norms and standards no longer held sway – that is, a condition of normlessness prevailed. For Merton, too, anomie involved a disjunction or breakdown in social arrangements, and more specifically a lack of balance or symmetry between elements of a society's culture and its social structure.

anomie

For Durkheim, a social condition where the norms guiding conduct break down, leaving individuals without social restraint or guidance (*see* norms).

Building on Merton's ideas, Delinquent Subculture theorists argued that crime and delinquency are a product of an imbalance in society's culturally prescribed goals and its opportunity structures. Ideologies of achieving success permeate Western liberal democratic societies, with status and material reward presented as the attainable outcome for anyone if hard work and effort are expended in the process. Thus, the 'good life' is accessible to even those from the most humble backgrounds if they put their backs into it.

But, according to Delinquent Subculture theorists, for some social groups – notably young working-class males – there is a chasm between their lived experiences and the 'American Dream' to which they are exhorted to aspire by the state, the education system, the mass media and other institutions. That is, there is a gap between the culturally prescribed success goals and the structured availability of legitimate opportunities for achieving them which generates a sense of frustration and strain. Working-class male youths have been bombarded with images of success and exhortations to 'make it', and they have come to share that common value commitment to the virtues of high aspirations and ambition. But cold reality reveals that they simply have less access to and are unable to take advantage of the legitimate opportunity structures, largely as a consequence of the family socialisation they have received leaving them ill-prepared for succeeding in the middle-class environment of the school and college.

The result, according to Delinquent Subculture theorists, is that young working-class males must find a way to come to terms with this, and they do so by forming *delinquent subcultures* which provide a collective solution to the problems of status frustration and thwarted aspirations by way of alternative criteria of status and success. As Cloward and Ohlin (1960) put it:

> **Delinquents have withdrawn their support from established norms and have invested officially forbidden norms of conduct with a claim to legitimacy in the light of their special situation.**
>
> **[Cloward and Ohlin, 1960, pp. 19–20]**

Members of such subcultures reject, then, conventional values: they may not be able to succeed in the middle-class standards and values of school and college, but they *are* good at what the delinquent subculture values – they can excel at fighting, doing 'dares', flouting the rules and causing trouble at school, vandalism, petty thieving and the like. In doing so, they gain status and esteem from their peers and, moreover, they are able to give a contemptuous two-fingered salute to respectable society and its values and standards. Embracing the delinquent subculture allows 'the explicit and wholesale repudiation of middle-class standards and the adoption of their very antithesis' (Cohen, 1955, p. 130).

When we consider the fourth axis of our analysis, that of the link between explanation and policy solutions, the liberal pedigree of Delinquent Subculture theories is clearly apparent in their belief that the social structural defects generating the frustration and strain experienced by young working-class males are eradicable through partial social repair work. Tinkering with social arrangements by way of ameliorative social reforms designed to re-socialise or rehabilitate alienated youth and allow them to compete successfully was seen as both legitimate and possible. If the problem was inequality of opportunity and the consequent formation of groups committed to delinquent values, then the solution was to alleviate the disjunction or gap between aspirations and achievement by expanding opportunities. This was to be effected by giving disadvantaged and alienated working-class youths chances to succeed through better educational opportunities, social work and welfare strategies, and social enrichment programmes to combat the value-systems encouraging delinquency. Such solutions found their practical expression in government initiatives in America in the early 1960s with the 'Mobilisation for Youth' Project and the 'War on Poverty' Project of the Kennedy and Johnson administrations respectively.

Box 14.1: Delinquent subculture

[I]t may confidently be said that the working class boy ... is more likely than his middle class peers to find himself at the bottom of the status hierarchy whenever he moves in a middle class world, whether it be of adults or of children. To the degree to which he values middle class status, either because he values the good opinion of middle class persons or because he has to some extent internalised middle class standards himself, he faces a problem of adjustment and is in the market for a solution ...

The delinquent subculture offers him status as against other children of whatever social level, but it offers him this status in the eyes of his fellow delinquents only ... He can perfect his solution only by rejecting as status sources those who reject him. This, too, may require a certain measure of reaction-formation, going beyond indifference to active hostility and contempt for all those who do not share his subculture ...

... The problems of adjustment to which the delinquent subculture is a response are determined, in part, by those very values which respectable society holds most sacred. The same value system, impinging upon children differently equipped to meet it, is instrumental in generating both delinquency and respectability.

[Cohen, 1955, pp. 119, 136–7]

Labelling Theory

symbolic interactionism

A theoretical approach which focuses on the role of symbols and language in human interaction.

What came to be known as *Labelling Theory* in the late 1960s was an apparently different kettle of fish altogether from Delinquent Subculture theories, with a very different theoretical/political context. The theoretical underpinnings of this approach derive from the development in the 1960s of a greater interest in social action theory and **symbolic interactionist** approaches – notably in the work of writers such as George Herbert Mead (1934) and Charles Cooley (1909) – and it emerged as part of the interpretivist critique of positivist and structural sociology.

Whereas positivist sociology started from a view of social reality as being something absolute and directly and uncomplicatedly observable 'out there', **labelling theory** took as its point of departure an *anti-positivist* **relativism**, in which social reality is not straightforward, pre-given and absolute but is essentially socially constructed, problematic and open to interpretation. Once again, it is illuminating to recognise the socio-political context of its development and hence the basis of its attraction to many theorists. The 1960s was an era of increasing challenges to authority and to official views of the world, in the form of political protest, youth subcultures, and alternative life-styles and value-systems. Thus, the anti-Vietnam war movement, hippies, radical students and others were unwilling to sit back and accept 'official' pronouncements and interpretations of the world as unquestionable and absolute: they were merely one version of social reality (albeit a powerful one) which could be tested and contested.

labelling
From Becker, the process where socially defined identities are imposed or adopted, especially the deviant label. Such labels may have consequences that trap the individual into that identity (*see* stigmatise).

relativism
An approach which denies the existence of absolute truth, but maintains that beliefs, values and theories are relative to time and place. Accordingly, traditions and ways of life can only be judged in the context of the age or society that has produced them.

In their approach to crime and deviance, Labelling theorists such as Howard Becker (1963) and Edwin Lemert (1961) reflected that relativist stance in their central concerns. Their major aim was to counteract what they saw as the deterministic assumptions of traditional positivist accounts of crime, and they rejected both the legitimacy and practical utility of any simple search for the 'causes' of crime as a false and foolish enterprise. Their position was *anti-etiological* that is, it sought to relocate the central focus of the study of crime away from causal motivational questions ('what makes them do it?') to questions of definition ('which behaviour and whose behaviour gets defined/labelled as crime and why?') and to analysis of the processes and consequences of interaction and reaction among the key social actors involved. An examination of Labelling theory's substantive themes will elaborate those central concerns.

In any examination of these themes, one key notion stands out – that is, that the labelling of individuals as 'criminals' is essentially a selective and not a universal or uniform process. We all commit crimes at some time or other, but not all of us are caught. Moreover, even among those who are caught, not all become labelled as criminal – their behaviour may be ignored, or excused or be subject to a caution by the police. Thus, a distinction between 'criminals' and 'non-criminals' (the basic starting point for positivist approaches) is essentially fortuitous and highly problematic, and hence a quest for some magical differentiating features between them is equally spurious. So, how *does* labelling happen? How does the behaviour of *some* people come to be officially designated as 'criminal'?

The Labelling theorists' answer is that labels 'emerge' from processes of interaction and reaction between those committing offences and a range of other people involved – victims, witnesses, police officers, social workers, judges and lawmakers. Subtle (and not so subtle) exchanges and perceptions are at work in shaping the outcome of frequently problematic 'deviance situations', in influencing whether suspected offenders find themselves on the receiving end of the label of 'criminal': suspects showing lack of respect to police officers; articulate, assertive and socially influential victims; police officers' and judges' images of 'typical offenders'; and so on.

Box 14.2: Labelling

Social groups create deviance by making the rules whose infraction constitutes deviance, and by applying those rules to particular people and labelling them as outsiders. From this point of view, deviance is not a quality of the act the person commits, but rather a consequence of the application by others of rules and sanctions to an 'offender'. The deviant is one to whom that label has successfully been applied; deviant behaviour is behaviour that people so label.

[Becker, 1963, pp. 8–9]

This emphasis on processes of social interaction inevitably means, for Labelling theorists, that at least as much attention must be paid to the views and activities of those conferring criminal labels as to those on whom they are conferred. Hence, understanding crime involves studying the police, the courts, and other agencies of social control as well as studying offenders, particularly since Labelling theorists stress the *importance of power* in both the *enforcement* and the *construction* of laws. Those with power benefit from it and those without it are disadvantaged in both respects. Law enforcement by the police and courts is a selective process in which certain social groups are more vulnerable to arrest, prosecution, and punishment. They tend to be those of lower social class, non-white ethnic background, and the young – groups with less power and fewer social resources to resist labelling processes. Moreover, our attention should also be directed to the process of how legal rules defining crime come about and to the fundamental definers of crime – that is, to those involved in the making of laws. For Labelling theorists, laws reflect the interests, moral concerns and ideological assumptions of those in positions of power in society.

Source:
I. Hislop (ed.) (1991) *30 Years of Private Eye Cartoons*, London, Private Eye/Corgi.

Their interactionist inclinations and their desire to develop more 'appreciative' accounts of criminals and deviants also led them to focus more fully on what happens to labelled individuals. In their view, the process of social control through the application of criminal labels brings with it only adverse consequences, both for the recipients and for society. Being labelled a criminal and dealt with as such damages both social identity and self-image – it places individuals outside conventional society, seriously restricts their chances of a normal life, and undermines their self-esteem. The result, according to Labelling theorists, is the likelihood of further involvement in criminal activities and subcultures and conformity to the negative label which has been applied: that is, strategies of social control generate processes of **deviance amplification** and the realisation of a **self-fulfilling prophecy**.

deviance amplification

A spiralling sequence of interaction between deviants and those reacting to their behaviour (most typically agents of control such as the police) which generates further deviance, which generates further punitive response and so on.

self-fulfilling prophecy

A situation where social actors, constructing their self-images from the reactions of powerful and persuasive others, come to act out or live up to labels applied, or characteristics attributed, to them, thus confirming the original evaluation.

stigmatisation

A process or experience in which some form of social behaviour or attribute is subject to social disapproval and becomes discredited, resulting in a spoiled identity in the eyes of others and possible exclusion from normal social interaction.

Understanding the connection between explanation and *policy prescription* in Labelling theory follows directly and unambiguously from this. Put baldly, negative labels are the problem; they are more trouble than they are worth, both for those on the receiving end and for society and its social agencies charged with the responsibility for affixing them and for administering the punishments and sanctions associated with them. So, the solution is to do something about negative labelling processes, to eliminate or significantly reduce the **stigmatising** effects of criminal labels.

One logical strategy is to get rid of such labels altogether – that is, to *de-criminalise* certain offences. Thus, for example, in the sphere of drug-taking, advocates of Labelling theory argued that those using (soft) drugs do no one any harm and that their criminalisation, prosecution and labelling is essentially counter-productive because it only forces offenders to commit other offences in order to pay fines, buy more drugs, and so on. Similarly, it was argued, the criminalisation of prostitution generates damaging spin-offs from the provision of a service whose illegality and prosecution encourages problems of kerb-crawling, exploitative pimping, etc.

Advocates of de-criminalisation clearly face the problem of how far such a policy can go – for example, is it possible or appropriate to apply it to robbery, interpersonal violence? Hence, some supporters of Labelling theory, still mindful of the stigmatising effects of labels, advocated reducing rather than eliminating the stigma of labelling people as criminal by means of the less drastic step of *de-escalating punishments* administered to convicted offenders. Typical strategies proposed include developing alternatives to continuous imprisonment (which cuts offenders off from 'normal' socially integrating contacts with family, employment and friends) such as community service, weekend prisons, and so on.

While Labelling theory's emphasis on the problematic nature of social reality and on the socially constructed dimensions of crime and deviance impacted powerfully and influentially on the agenda of criminology, its more micro-sociological inclination and its underdeveloped analyses of structures were seen by some to limit its explanatory potential.

Marxist Criminology

The accusation of incompleteness in Labelling theory's structural analysis was highlighted most distinctly by the development of a Marxist criminology in the 1970s as represented in the work of Frank Pearce (1976), William Chambliss (1976) and Richard Quinney (1980), among others. As we have suggested elsewhere, Marxist approaches employ a *structural-conflict model* of society and social relations, assigning central importance to economic arrangements and seeing societies as typically characterised by divisions of interest and class conflict: as we shall see, Marxist criminologists shared this same broad theoretical orientation. Once again, a distinctive theoretical-political context is evident here, in that the late 1960s and early 1970s saw a resurgence of interest in Marxist theorising becoming increasingly visible and influential in a number of realms of sociology. Moreover, that interest in Marx's ideas reflected the social, economic and political ferments of the time. It was an era which saw the erosion of consensus politics, in which new and often radical social and political movements were more prominent; in which strong trade unions were increasingly pressing for and defending workers' rights in a climate of intensified industrial conflict and militancy; in which Western capitalist economies were coming under increasing pressure and experiencing declining economic growth and problems of competitiveness; and in which the less acceptable face of capitalism – of class division, inequality and poverty, Third World exploitation and imperialism – was being ever more exposed to critical scrutiny.

The central concerns of Marxist criminology reflected much of that, with a stress on the recognition of fundamental social and class divisions and the rejection of the myth of a basically sound society built around value-consensus. These theorists were concerned above all to develop a *materialist* analysis, a *political economy* of crime – that is, one which took as its point of departure and central structural framework the *economic base* of society and which located crime within the systems and social relations of capitalist economic production. Moreover, they sought to rectify one (as they saw it) glaring omission in traditional positivist criminology: namely, that it had somehow managed to produce an analysis of law-breaking – the violation of the state's legal rules – without having recourse to a *theory of the state* and the *legal system*. For the Marxists, then, there are inevitable *political* dimensions to crime which necessitate a central place in any explanatory framework for the role of the state and the legal system. Thus, the study of crime cannot be merely a matter of the uncritical analysis of behaviour which violates 'given' legal norms, since that fails to recognise those political dimensions and perpetuates pluralist myths of impartial law and a simple 'arbiter' role for the state.

Examination of the substantive themes of this approach reveals that their materialist standpoint identifies an integral connection between crime and capitalism. For them, high levels of crime in capitalist societies are simply unsurprising, because capitalism is a *crime-creating system* by virtue of the motivations which it encourages in people and the class relations and inequalities which characterise it. It promotes and prioritises self-interest, personal gain, and the accumulation of wealth and material possessions as supreme virtues and goals. It persuades (through a culture of advertising and media fiction) that life is incomplete without expensive clothes, the latest model of stylish fast car, high-tech leisure items or washing machines, and in doing so it motivates individuals to accumulate by both legal and illegal means. People act upon these exhortations with the resources and options at their disposal: upper-class businessmen have more legal means to realise their material aims and desires (though, Marxists argue, they frequently do use illegal ones), while working-class people have fewer options available to them, of which crime is one. So, if some of them resort more to the latter than to the former, this is because they are at the sharp end of the unequal distribution of resources which typifies capitalist social and economic arrangements. Taylor *et al.* (1975) say:

> **"Property crime is better understood as a *normal* and conscious attempt to amass property than as the product of *faulty* socialisation or inaccurate and spurious labelling. Both working class and upper class crime ... are *real* features of a society involved in a struggle for property, wealth, and self-aggrandisement ... A society which is predicated on unequal right to the accumulation of property *gives rise* to the legal and illegal desire to accumulate property as rapidly as possible."**
>
> [TAYLOR *et al.*, 1975, p. 34]

But, in any case, there is a distorted image in the official picture of 'crime' and the 'typical criminal' resulting from the fact that laws are not neutral – they do not embody a widespread public value consensus and they do not work impartially and for the benefit of everyone. While occasionally instituted against powerful groups, they essentially reflect *partisan class interests*: they are instruments predominantly benefiting and securing the interests of a dominant class and largely working against subordinate groups. The designation of certain kinds of behaviour as 'criminal' is the outcome of this dominant class successfully enshrining *their* definitions of 'crime' in legal statutes, in definitions which simultaneously legitimise the status quo, proscribe and criminalise activities which threaten the reproduction of capitalism, and conceal its inequalities.

Box 14.3: Crime and capitalism

An understanding of crime … begins with an analysis of the political economy of capitalism … Those who own and control the means of production, the capitalist class, attempt to secure the existing order through various forms of domination, especially crime control by the capitalist state. Those who do not own and control the means of production, especially the working class, accommodate and resist the capitalist domination in various ways. Crime is related to this process …

… [W]hen work is thwarted as a life-giving activity, the way is open for activity that is detrimental to self and others. At the same time, some of the behaviours that follow from alienated work are an attempt to set things right again. Some behaviour is a conscious rebellion against exploitation and inhumane conditions. And there is the responsive activity which, in a reproduction of capitalism, is pursued for economic survival or gain. Activity of a criminal nature becomes a rational and likely possibility under the conditions of capitalism. All of this is to say that crime – including both crime control and criminality – is a *by-product* of the political economy of capitalism.

[Quinney, 1980, pp. 66–7, 100–1]

Thus, for Marxist criminologists, laws protect capitalist property predominantly: they are disproportionately directed against and concentrate on shoplifting, burglary, car theft, vandalism and so on, and not on City swindles, business crime, tax evasion, and industrial pollution by multinational companies. Large corporations and business leaders are sufficiently powerful to be able to avoid criminal labels being attached to their activities, though the limited prosecutions of the extensive corporate and white-collar crime which do exist serve the important *symbolic* purpose of sustaining an illusion that the law is non-partisan. A second illusion is also created by this selective construction and enforcement of the law: working-class 'street' crime, and not upper-class 'suite' crime, becomes epitomised as 'the crime problem', both officially and in the minds of working-class people themselves.

When addressing the question of what to do about crime, the Marxist policy solution is simple yet monumental: if capitalism creates crime, if

Source: A.-J. Doran (ed.) (1990) *The Punch Cartoon Album*, London, Grafton Books.

'Fetch me the law for the rich, will you?'

capitalism is 'the problem', then the solution is clear – get rid of capitalism in a root-and-branch restructuring of society through qualitative, wholesale social, economic and political change. Anything stopping short of that is simply insufficient and is merely irrelevant tinkering with (and, indeed, collusion with) an essentially irredeemable system. Piecemeal social reforms are inadequate cosmetic elements because they do not confront the real basis of crime, a capitalist social, economic and political structure. Hence, for example, reforms to the penal system may make life marginally more comfortable for prison inmates, but they do little or nothing to alter the fundamental inequalities of capitalism and its criminal justice system. What is required is the restructuring of society to transform it from capitalism to socialism.

Left Realism

One reaction to both Marxist approaches and to Right Realism (which we shall examine shortly) which has figured prominently, particularly in British criminology since the mid-1980s, has been that of those theorists such as Jock Young, John Lea and Roger Matthews who call themselves *Left Realists* (1984, 1986, 1992). These Left Realists provide an analysis of crime which starts from a *structural* theoretical position: that is, they maintain that it is important to locate the roots of crime in fundamental social and economic relationships, but they accord structural factors a somewhat more diluted importance in the causation of crime. The *political context* of the emergence of this Left Realism was one of the ascendancy of the New Right, to which we have referred earlier in Chapter 10. Those on the Left politically and intellectually were on the defensive and in retreat, political parties wedded to **neo-liberal** economic and political philosophies won a series of election victories in Britain, America and elsewhere, and the communist regimes of Eastern Europe and even of the Soviet Union itself, supposedly founded on Marxist ideas and principles, became progressively unstable and ultimately collapsed.

neo-liberalism

A form of right wing philosophy associated with Thatcherism and laissez-faire liberalism (*see* Thatcherism *and* laissez-faire liberalism).

The Left Realists chose their title deliberately in order to distinguish themselves and their central concerns from those of their Marxist predecessors. The latter, in their view, had over-simplified the criminological agenda into one in which a big, bad capitalism and its biased, dominant class-orientated legal and criminal justice system exploited the working class generally and disproportionately labelled as criminal those sections of it which committed offences in order to survive or to challenge the system. The Left Realists aimed to correct what they regarded as the 'left idealism' of that approach, because it ran the risk, among others, of simply wishing away or underestimating how much of a problem crime actually is. Substantial real increases in crime have occurred, according to Left Realists, and hence, they have constantly sought to re-emphasise the reality of the 'crime problem', the rational basis for people's fear of crime, and hence the real need to attempt to do something about it: in other words, they have stressed the need to take seriously both the problem of crime and the problem of crime control.

For Left Realists, a full understanding of crime will only come through a consideration of all of the components of what they call the 'square' of crime – the state, society or the public at large, offenders, and victims – and the interplay between them. For example, the relations between the state and the public will importantly shape policing priorities, the degree of public co-operation and therefore police effectiveness. Similarly, the relations between the state and offenders, in the form of penal policies, will influence rates of recidivism.

In their substantive themes, Left Realists suggested that the Marxist/radical position seemed to neglect one important but inescapable fact: that is, that victimisation is unevenly distributed within the population and, even more crucially, that crime is a real problem for the *working class*, because they are its principal victims. So, instead of seeing crime predominantly as a problem for, or a response to, or even a challenge to a capitalist system, we should recognise that its most distinctive feature is that it is concentrated in the inner cities, on housing estates, where it is committed *by* working-class people *on* other working-class people – that is, most crime is *intra-class* action. Left Realists acknowledge that the official picture of crime does not tell the complete story: they recognise the under-representation of white-collar and corporate crime in official data and that the police and the criminal justice system may well discriminate against certain categories of offender at certain times. But they reject the idea that the 'crime problem' is simply a socially constructed entity fashioned by official bias. So, for instance, although police and judicial practices and prejudices may exaggerate the involvement of black youth in crime, they insist that the higher levels of officially recorded black crime are a reality which is not merely the product of racist law enforcement, prosecution and sentencing.

But what causes crime? As we suggested earlier, Left Realists share with their Marxist counterparts an emphasis on *structural inequality* as a key component of crime causation, but they seek to avoid the dangers of a narrowly materialist or economic reductionist theorising. For them, crime is importantly but not simply related to structural inequality: there is no one-to-one correlation between poverty, material deprivation, unemployment and the like and involvement in criminality – if that were so, far more working-class and black people would be engaged in crime. Rather than seeing offending in simple deterministic terms, we need to consider the subjective understandings and choices of those involved in crime.

Left Realists echo the themes of Delinquent Subculture theories by arguing that crime is produced by *relative deprivation* and *marginalisation* – that is, it is committed predominantly by those who find themselves on the edge of society, who have a sense of being worse off than others and who feel that such a situation is fundamentally unjust. While such sentiments are clearly likely to be experienced more keenly and more frequently by working-class and black people, they are not exclusive to those social groups. Hence, a sense of relative deprivation may exist throughout the social structure (albeit unevenly distributed), thus motivating criminal behaviour even among the better-off, and such motivations may be intensified by changing economic circumstances and by shifts in prevailing political ideology which centralise and prioritise individualism, competitiveness and a 'me-first' culture.

However, they do see some groups as particularly and increasingly vulnerable to relative deprivation and marginalisation in recent decades –

most notably, young people from working class and ethnic minority communities in the inner cities. Such groups, they argue, feel a diffuse sense of exclusion, resentment and grievance at opportunities denied them to achieve expectations and satisfy societally defined needs. Black Afro-Caribbean youth are especially susceptible: they are predominantly working class and they have the additional disadvantage of being on the receiving end of racial discrimination and prejudice, with the result that they enjoy less success in education and in the competition for good jobs, and they suffer higher levels of unemployment. The result, according to Left Realists, is a sense of alienation and marginalisation and the greater likelihood of involvement in both petty and serious crime.

When we consider the links between explanation and policy solutions advocated by Left Realists, they espouse a rather different attitude from that of Marxist criminologists, whom they frequently characterise as offering only 'utopian' solutions (for example, getting rid of capitalism) and as being unwilling to involve themselves in policy debates about crime and in the advocacy of practical solutions for dealing with crime. Left Realists argue that a failure to do so runs the risk of leaving a vacuum in the policy debates on crime and allows others of less acceptable political persuasions to dominate the policy agenda. Hence, they argue for the practical possibility, social desirability and political necessity of devising ways of doing something about crime, and for the legitimacy of aiming for modest, marginal improvements in dealing with it.

For them, dealing with the crime problem requires multiple, multi-level strategies. At the 'macro' level, the pursuit of social justice is essential, requiring the State to improve material rewards, employment opportunities and housing and community facilities by fundamental shifts in government economic and educational policies. At the 'intermediate' level, it requires more enlightened penal policies which reduce the prison population and replace sentences of imprisonment, where appropriate, with non-custodial alternatives. It also requires more democratically controlled and accountable police forces sensitive to the communities in which they work: that clearly necessitates the police rethinking and, where necessary, amending their methods of operation and patrol methods and their styles of interaction with sections of the public (for example, with black youth). Such changes, Left Realists argue, will forge greater public trust and co-operation and enhance the possibility of both clearing up and preventing crime. And at 'street' level, it requires environmental and design changes which reduce opportunities for crime, such as better street lighting and changes in phone-box design to make them more vandal-proof.

Box 14.4: Left and right realism

Left realism then is the opposite of right realism. Whereas realists of the right prioritise order over justice, left realists prioritise social justice as a way of achieving a fair and orderly society. Whereas right realists descend to genetic and individualist theories to blame the 'underclass', left realists point to the social injustice which marginalises considerable sections of the population and engenders crime ...

Right realism is a new right philosohy: left realism stems from the current debates in democratic socialism. Thus it argues that only socialist intervention will fundamentally reduce the causes of crime, rooted as they are in social inequality, that only the universalistic provision of crime prevention will guard the poor against crime, that only a genuinely democratic control of the police force will ensure that community safety is achieved.

Thus on the one hand, left realism takes an oppositional political and theoretical stance from that adopted by the realists of the right; while on the other, it consciously avoids collapsing into the romanticism and idealism which has been evident in much of the radical and critical criminological literature of the 1970s.

[Matthews and Young, 1992, p. 6]

Right Realism

A common feature of all the approaches we have considered so far is that, despite their many differences, they are all committed to the notion of and the legitimacy of a sociological explanation of crime. What came to be known as *Right Realism* or New Right criminology, represented most notably in the work of James Wilson (1975) and Ernst van den Haag (1975), departed significantly from that pattern. It emerged initially in the 1970s and was developed further in the 1980s, in large part, as we shall see, as an explicit and vehement critique of liberal sociological theorising about crime.

While they frequently expressed a lack of interest in and a hostility towards attempts to develop theories of crime, distinct theoretical assumptions are evident in Right Realist approaches, most notably focused around notions of an essential human nature, combined with voluntaristic conceptions of human action and versions of control theory. These approaches developed and flourished in a distinctive political context – namely, the era of the '*New Right*' or neo-liberal political and economic philosophies of Reaganism and Thatcherism in the USA and Britain, with their emphases on a limited role for state intervention in economic affairs and in social and welfare provision, the reduction of dependence on the 'Nanny State', and the need for greater recognition of individual responsibility and 'standing on one's own feet'.

The central concerns of Right Realists stem from their impatience with and disdain for sociological criminology and basically centre upon the desire to shift the balance away from (in their view) over-sophisticated and essentially unproductive theoretical excursion and on to the practical business of containment and control, of devising realistic and workable strategies for dealing with street crime and those who perpetrate it. While they are not excessively optimistic about the prospect of achieving extensive prevention and control of crime, they do maintain that its impact can be limited by appropriate strategies of *deterrence.* At the same time, however, this does not mean an unambiguously greater responsibility on the part of the state in dealing with the crime problem. As we shall see shortly, Right Realists were also anxious to shift the balance of responsibility for confronting the crime problem away from solely state intervention towards a partnership between state and citizens.

When we examine the substantive themes of Right Realist analysis, their grave misgivings about sociological approaches and their antagonism to the idea of crime as a product of social circumstances stand out clearly. Indeed, they poured scorn on such theorising, arguing that it had been a massively wasteful and damaging enterprise, taking the study of crime off in directions which were both unproductive theoretically and undesirable practically. Liberal and other sociological criminology had focused its attention on issues of opportunity, deprivation, poverty and so on: for Right Realists, even if it were to be established that links between crime and such social variables existed, they are variables which are difficult if not impossible for the state to attempt to manipulate: and, moreover, they are ones in which the state has no business in intervening – it is not the job of the state to attempt to change social conditions. But in any case, they maintained, we should be deeply sceptical about those explanations, since the social factors they identified as associated with crime were simply unproven in their causal effect. In fact, the Right Realists insisted, Western capitalist societies had seen unprecedented improvements in material prosperity and opportunity for more and more people while at the same time experiencing ever-increasing levels of criminal activity. Thus, the period of the extension of welfare services, of poverty reduction policies, education reforms and the like, far from ushering in reductions in crime, had formed the backdrop to large increases in crime and had actually contributed significantly to those increases by weakening people's sense of individual responsibility, breeding a culture of 'state dependency' and undermining the bonds holding society and communities together.

This indictment of sociological criminology and welfarism links closely with Right Realists' conception of human nature and their ideas on conditioning to account for rising levels of crime. They have a fairly unflattering view of human nature: for them, human beings are motivated by self-interest and self-seeking, and high levels of crime are a product of ineffective and inadequate constraints or controls on our naturally anti-social inclinations and desires. A culture of permissiveness and indulgent self-expression has been allowed to develop, fostered by over-liberal parenting and by educators and social workers who have failed to take responsibility for inculcating a proper morality and the virtues of self-restraint and self-control. The result, according to Right Realists, has been a spiralling in the volume of 'street crime' – in petty theft, vandalism and criminal damage, in car theft, in physical assaults, burglaries, robberies and the like. Such activities are doubly damaging, in their view: as well as being intrinsically harmful and inconveniencing in themselves, they are also primarily responsible for undermining social order in communities and causing the collapse of a sense of community. For that reason, such crimes constitute the key problem to be attacked in the fight against crime.

When we turn our attention to the issue of the Right Realists' policy solutions for crime, their prescriptions contrast distinctively with the sociological approaches we have already considered. Given their ideas about human nature and motivations for criminality, they are under no illusions as to the magnitude of the task of confronting the crime problem: they accept that there is only the limited possibility of doing much about it. However, their policy solutions follow inexorably from their central premises – that is, we need to design policies for dealing with crime in the context of our understanding of human nature, and it is necessary to attack those dimensions of the crime problem which can be more easily and deliberately altered by practical strategies of deterrence.

If people are primarily motivated to crime by their self-seeking and self-interested natures, then two fundamental strategies are necessary. One is to deter them from crime by increasing the risks associated with it in such a way that the costs of offending outweigh the benefits, and the other is to decrease the opportunities for offending. Hence, severe punishments in the form of longer custodial sentences, in uncomfortable and demanding prison regimes, are required, with very heavy sentences to isolate and 'incapacitate' recidivists and dangerous individuals. However, while severity of punishment is important, it is not in itself sufficient. It is also necessary to increase the certainty of detection and punishment by more extensive policing.

But, again, this is not simply a matter of more police officers but of *how* they are to be allowed to carry out their policing tasks in the specific process of law enforcement and the more general process of order maintenance. Indeed, many Right Realists prioritise the need to maintain order because of what they see as a vicious circle, in which street crime leads to disorder and decay in communities, which in turn leads to more street crime. Hence, they regard it as vital for the police to be given sufficient powers and freedom both to enforce the law when it is being broken *and* to control the streets by dealing with or pre-empting even trivial instances of unruly behaviour (such as rowdiness, drinking, begging) regardless of whether they are illegal or whether a crime has been committed. If some 'rough justice' is occasionally meted out in such situations, this is an unfortunate but justifiable by-product of the necessity to maintain order on the streets, restore and maintain public confidence, and preserve the community.

Right Realists insist, however, that the burden of responsibility for crime control and order maintenance also lies in the hands of members of the community as well as the police. '*Active citizens*' must also do their bit by disciplining and morally educating their children (preferably by reverting to 'traditional' methods in home and school); by working collectively in the community against crime and disorder (through, for example, Neighbourhood Watch schemes); and by diligently protecting their own property (with better domestic security devices and systems).

Feminist Criminology

All the approaches we have examined so far (with the partial exception of Left Realism) focused their attention, implicitly if not explicitly, on *males* and *male crime* and/or did not make any great attempt to incorporate female offenders into their analyses of crime in any sustained fashion. What we can refer to loosely as *Feminist criminology* has developed in the last two decades to seek to rectify that omission. That title, though, is something of a misnomer, because there is no single feminist perspective prevailing within it, no single alternative theory of crime, no unanimous view on the problem of dealing with crime.

What *is* common to these feminist criminologists, however, in terms of their theoretical-political orientation, is that they are part of the more general critique of *sexist* and *masculinist* theorising in sociology and other social sciences. Though by no means unique, then, to the field of criminology, those accusations were driven home powerfully there: that is, that the study of crime has been persistently characterised by theories which purported to be general and comprehensive explanations of behaviour – in this case, criminal behaviour – but which in reality were talking only about males and male crime.

The political context of this critique, of course, was constituted by the growth in the 1970s and 1980s of feminist ideas and feminist movements, whose common ground was the core notion that women, both historically and contemporarily, have been and continue to be *subordinated* on the basis of their sex, and that action directed towards the elimination of that subordination is an urgent priority.

The central concerns of this Feminist criminology, represented in the work of Carol Smart (1976), Ann Campbell (1981) and Frances Heidensohn (1985) among others, centred on broadening the scope of the criminological agenda in a number of ways. They aimed to expose the absence of women and girls from mainstream (or, as it was sometimes dubbed 'malestream') criminology both as offenders and victims. In doing so, they also sought to develop and establish fully sociological analyses of female crime and delinquency and at the same time to sweep away the persistent tendency of those who did discuss female crime to do so within highly *individualistic* frameworks which represented women in crude stereotypes and perpetuated sexist images and ideologies. Furthermore, they sought to highlight similar and what they saw as related sexism in the treatment of women in the criminal justice system and penal policy. Finally, they stressed that 'bringing women into' criminology also required greater attention to be paid to them as victims and to the processes and consequences of victimisation.

self-report studies
Used in the context of crime research, they normally involve questioning people, by means of questionnaires or interviews, about criminal acts they have committed, whether or not these have been detected. The aim of such studies is to amplify the picture of recorded crime by official criminal statistics.

In their substantive themes, the Feminists' major complaint against much sociological and non-sociological work was that debates on crime had been conducted as if women were non-existent, so that theories of criminality had been developed predominantly from studying males. They acknowledged that female offending is less frequent (and generally less serious) than that of males: official data, for instance, reveal lower recorded crime rates for women and girls, with a ratio of around four male cautions or convictions to every one for females, though data from some **Self-report studies** have suggested a lower male/female ratio of offending than that. But Feminist critics argued that none of this could justify the marginal attention frequently accorded to female offending and the equally frequent exclusion of women and girls from criminological theorising. For them, any adequate theory of crime has to be able to take account of and incorporate both men's and women's criminal behaviour.

Moreover, they also drew attention to the fact that when female crime *was* considered in any detail by mainstream criminology, both conforming and non-conforming women were represented in a highly *stereotypical* and sexist fashion. At the core of much of that theorising was a crude '**biologism**', with explanations of both female conformity and criminality resting on highly dubious biologically-based conceptions of women's special or unique 'nature' and/or their individual pathology. Hence, the conforming woman – the 'normal' woman – was by nature passive, virtuous, domestically inclined and respectful of authority, while the non-conforming woman's criminality was determined by some kind of biological or physiological abnormality or biologically-founded psychological/emotional disturbance of a hormonal, chromosomal, or psycho-sexual kind. Thus, while male crime and delinquency were cast in contexts of blocked opportunity structures and peer group solidarity, or of selective labelling processes, or even of capitalism's crime-generating structures, such social and economic influences remained resolutely absent from explanations of female criminality for a long time.

biologism
A form of biological determinism that claims human behaviour is determined on the basis of biological or genetic characteristics (*see* biological determinism).

However, for Feminist criminologists, it could not simply be a matter of amending or 'converting' existing theories to take account of women: those theories were already fundamentally flawed and partial, since they were a *criminology of men* pursuing 'an exclusive interest in male criminality in a comfortable world of academic machismo' (Heidensohn, 1985, p. 143). A fully social theory of crime had to be capable of reflecting men's and women's experiences and behaviour and of highlighting those factors operating similarly on men and women and those operating differently. Thus, if crime is to be explained as being a product of particular social environments and if males are more frequently involved in crime than females, then it is necessary to identify which social environmental factors exert a more powerful influence on males and to explain why that is so. Or, as Heidensohn and others have argued, we may need to give as much if not more attention to female conformity than to female non-conformity if we are to understand and explain female criminality. Either way, explanations offered have to be able to account for both male and female behaviour and therefore to offer an adequate analysis of crime, sex and gender.

As well as pinpointing the sexism of much criminological theorising, Feminist criminologists also sought to broaden the study of female crime by examining the working of the *criminal justice* and *penal systems*. In their view, men dominate and control women through a variety of mechanisms, agencies and institutions, and the criminal justice and penal systems are no exceptions. Their analyses exposed widespread evidence of sexist ideologies and concomitant discriminatory practices in judicial and penal policy towards women offenders. They pointed to the ways in which traditional gender role expectations and perceptions of female offenders as biologically or psychologically abnormal have persisted in the disposition decisions and subsequent treatment accorded to them. Thus, being judged a 'good mother' can have a significant influence on court decision-making and sentencing; women offenders are more likely to be viewed as 'disturbed' and in need of 'medical' treatment than men; and girls are frequently penalised for behaviour condoned if not encouraged in boys (for example, sexual activity or running away from home) and are more likely to be institutionalised for it.

Feminist criminologists were also significantly instrumental and influential in extending the criminological agenda from the narrower mainstream emphasis on offender-orientated studies to embrace a more focused analysis of *victims* of crime, particularly the analysis of female victimisation, and more particularly still in the realms of domestic violence and sexual offences. They pointed the way to the current recognition that women experience far greater levels of victimisation than were previously acknowledged, and that the incidence of sexual offences against women is far higher than both officially recorded data and even national crime surveys (such as the British Crime Surveys) suggest. They were furthermore prominently responsible for highlighting women's fear of crime and the accompanying constraints on life-styles and life-choices which that generates (for example, going out alone or travelling on public transport at night).

When we turn to the fourth dimension of our analysis, that of policy solutions to crime, consideration of the Feminist position is somewhat less straightforward than with the previous approaches we have examined, partly because, as we suggested earlier, there is no single alternative theory of crime, and also because the Feminist agenda for criminology is rather more diverse. However, some insights into policy prescriptions can be gleaned from their approach.

Firstly, insofar as crime is predominantly a male activity, many Feminists stress that the 'problem' may therefore be essentially one of (aggressive) masculinity, and that no significant inroads into or solutions to crime will be made unless something can be done about that. While many radical feminists stress the irredeemability of men, even the more optimistic regard a process of the wholesale reconstruction or re-casting of the attitudes, values and behaviour patterns of the male of the species as an unlikely prospect, to say the least. Failing that, many Feminists advocate the need for male crimes against women to be taken more seriously by the criminal justice system and to be punished appropriately. That clearly also implies the need for greater attention to be paid to the needs of female (and other) victims of crime and for policy changes in procedures adopted towards them (for example, the handling of victims of rape and sexual assault).

medicalisation
A process of increased medical intervention and control into areas that hitherto would have been outside the medical domain.

Feminist policy solutions in relation to female crime tend to focus on strategies for improving the treatment of female offenders. Thus, rejecting the idea that women criminals are somehow particularly 'abnormal' necessitates abandoning, firstly, the tendency towards the '**medicalisation**' of women's crime in the judicial and penal systems, and, secondly, questioning programmes which assume that turning them into good mothers and home-makers will deflect them away from crime and on to their 'true' path. Finally, many feminist criminologists, recognising, as we suggested earlier, that the legal system is often fundamentally sexist, advocate rectifying *gender biases* in the construction of laws and their enforcement – for example, in prostitution, where women arrested for soliciting are criminalised and are much more likely to be prosecuted than their male clients (who may be persistent nuisances as kerb-crawlers) or their male pimps (who may be exploiting them financially, coercing them, or threatening or perpetrating violence against them).

Modernist Criminology and the Postmodernist Critique

We suggested at the beginning of the chapter that competing approaches to crime have been characterised by and large by their commitment to the modernist project. As we have seen, positivist criminology, both sociological and non-sociological, has been enthusiastically engaged in what David Matza (1964) called 'the search for differentiation' and what David Garland (1994) has more recently designated 'the Lombrosian project ... that tradition of inquiry, begun by Lombroso, which aims to differentiate the criminal individual from the non-criminal' (p. 18). While Labelling theory, Marxist criminology and Left Realism rejected such processes of differentiation as simplistic and misleading, they too were still wedded to the modernist principle of a privileged master-narrative of crime, a verifiable 'knowledge' of crime that is superior and more 'truthful' than other knowledges or accounts, and to the notion of the legitimate applicability of that knowledge to the business of doing something about crime. That is, they maintained that knowledge about crime can be deployed to make progress with the crime problem. Right Realists, too, despite their protestations about and supposed disdain for theorising about crime, do embrace distinct theoretical positions which underpin and inform their prescriptions for dealing with crime, and the feminist critique, while strongly critical of the partial and frequently sexist character of 'malestream' criminology, nevertheless advocates and envisages the construction of a (gender-adequate) theory of crime.

It is interesting, then, that debates within feminism and feminist criminology have been in part responsible for the (beginnings of a) *post-modernist critique* of criminology, initially and notably advanced by Carol Smart (1990) and others. Postmodernists, as we have suggested elsewhere in the book, challenge and reject modernist conceptions of the social world, of knowledge about it, and of the pursuit of progress and better futures. They reject the possibility of large-scale theoretical interpretations of universal application offering unified representations of the world – '**meta-narratives**' or 'totalising discourses', as they call them. Such overarching, unifying grand narratives and claims to truth are no longer credible: there is no social totality and therefore there is no possibility of a totalising social theory in the postmodern world, which is distinctively diverse, fragmented and indeterminate. Rather, there are multiple claims to truth – a 'plurality of discourses' – competing with each other but having no absolute basis for claiming privileged access to truth. Moreover, if there is no basis for such meta-narratives, then they cannot provide guides for human conduct, and the idea of progress and improving the human condition – the canon of the modernist project – goes out of the window.

meta-narrative

Sometimes referred to as 'grand narrative', it is the name given to an all-encompassing theory of human life, especially a vision of social progress.

Smart (1990) argues that criminology is distinctly vulnerable to the postmodernist critique because 'both traditional and realist criminological thinking are especially wedded to the positivist paradigm of modernism' (p. 77). That is, they embrace a belief in establishing verifiable knowledge or truth about crime and its causes and in constructing explanations which will provide a basis for solutions and/or strategies of intervention. But, according to her, criminology commits the modernist errors of **essentialism** and **totalism**. It attributes some essential unity and totality to its objects of study ('crime' and criminals') and assumes that definitive statements in the form of a general theory of crime can be made about them and solutions applied to them. But they share no 'unity' other than merely happening to involve infringements of the

essentialism/ totalism

An approach which assumes some universal essence, homogeneity and unity in the phenomena under study. Such approaches to gender, for example, identify traits and behaviour common to all men and women.

law. Thus, rejecting 'crime' and 'criminals' as essentialist concepts means, for the postmodernist, that any notion of criminology as a unified discipline or discourse is undermined because the central objects of study are dissolved, and particular categories of crime (such as theft, murder, rape and so on) disappear or become disconnected. The deconstruction of crime means the deconstruction of criminality. Smart (1990) says:

> **The whole *raison d'etre* of criminology is that it addresses crime. It categorises a vast range of activities and treats them as if they were all subject to the same laws ... The thing that criminology cannot do is to deconstruct crime. It cannot locate rape or child abuse in the domain of sexuality or theft in the domain of economic activity or drug use in the domain of health. To do so would be to abandon criminology to sociology; but more importantly it would involve abandoning the idea of a unified problem which requires a unified response – at least at the theoretical level ... The core enterprise of criminology is profoundly problematic.**
>
> **[Smart, 1990, p. 77]** ”

Conclusion

This chapter has identified the study of crime as being firmly embedded in the 'modernist project' and has attempted to show how a number of approaches within this tradition, while frequently differing significantly in their focus and emphases, share the common ground of offering and believing in the legitimacy of a *definitive narrative* on crime and an accompanying programme of *social interventions* for dealing with it. But the apparent insolubility of the crime problem may well have shaken faith in the effectiveness of any of those narratives to tell the crime 'story' and, indeed, in the legitimacy and validity itself of attempts to do so.

Thus, for some, interest in 'explanations' of crime has given way to a concern with a more amorphous multiplicity of crime 'issues' such as the fear of crime, victims of crime, or media representations of crime, all of which are stimulating and fruitful concerns in themselves. Such trends towards a process of fragmentation of the criminological project may, for some, confirm the kind of postmodernist critique to which we have just referred.

But those criminologists sceptical about the postmodernist critique continue to argue for the reality of crime for actors on the ground which has consequences for them as victims, members of communities, suspects, offenders, or whatever, and for the quality of their lives and their sense of security and safety. The impact of crime on those living in inner-city communities, for instance, is all too real, whether it results in loss of or damage to their property, personal injury, a climate of fear, or feelings of unease about the policing of their communities. Furthermore, the consequences of sentences for those convicted of crime – for the juvenile offender sent to a youth custody institution, for the street prostitute imprisoned for non-payment of fines, and so on – are as real as ever, both during their incarceration and upon release.

Summary of the Chapter

- Crime as a social problem has been and remains a major focus of public, political and academic concern.
- Explanations of crime can be usefully compared in terms of their theoretical and political contexts, their central concerns, their substantive themes and their policy prescriptions.
- Delinquent Subculture theories attributed crime to a lack of opportunities available to young working-class males.
- Labelling theorists stressed the negative consequences of selective labelling processes which tend to push labelled offenders into criminal careers.
- Marxist criminologists identified the capitalist system as crime-producing and as the prime obstacle to solving the crime problem.
- Left Realists have emphasised the need to take crime control seriously and to see relative deprivation and marginalisation as central elements in crime causation.
- Right Realists have denied the utility of sociological theorising about crime and have stressed the need for policies based on an understanding of human nature which deter people from committing crimes.
- Feminists have criticised much criminological theorising as being over-concerned with males and as neglecting women both as offenders and victims.
- Postmodernist critics have questioned the viability of criminology's traditional 'modernist' orientation based on a commitment to applying reliable knowledge and theorising to construct solutions to the crime problem.

References

Becker, H. (1963) *Outsiders: Studies in the Sociology of Deviance*, Glencoe, Illinois, Free Press.

Campbell, A. (1981) *Girl Delinquents*, Oxford, Blackwell.

Chambliss, W. (1976) 'The State and the Criminal Law', in W. Chambliss and M. Mankoff, *Whose Law? Whose Order?*, New York, Wiley.

Cloward, R. and L. Ohlin (1960) *Delinquency and Opportunity*, New York, Collier Macmillan.

Cohen, A. (1955) *Delinquent Boys*, Chicago, Free Press.

Cooley, C. (1909) *Social Organisation*, New York, Scribner.

Durkheim, E. (1952) *Suicide*, London, Routledge & Kegan Paul.

Garland, D. (1994) 'Of Crimes and Criminals', in M. Maguire *et al.* (eds) *The Oxford Handbook of Criminology*, Oxford, Clarendon Press.

Heidensohn, F. (1985) *Women and Crime*, London, Macmillan.

Heidensohn, F. (1989) *Crime and Society*, London, Macmillan.

Lea, J. and J. Young (1984) *What Is To Be Done About Law and Order?*, London, Penguin.

Lemert, E. (1961) *Social Pathology*, New York, McGraw-Hill.

Matthews, J. and J. Young (eds), (1992) *Issues in Realist Criminology*, London, Sage.

Matza, D. (1964) *Delinquency and Drift*, New York, Wiley.

Mead, G. H. (1934) *Mind, Self and Society*, Chicago, Chicago University Press.

Merton, R. (1949) *Social Theory and Social Structure*, Glencoe, Illinois, Free Press.

Pearce, F. (1976) *Crimes of the Powerful: Marxism, Crime and Deviance*, London, Pluto Press.

Quinney, R. (1980) *Class, State and Crime*, London, Longman.

Smart, C. (1976) *Women, Crime and Criminology*, London, Routledge.

Smart, C. (1990) 'Feminist Approaches to Criminology, or Post-Modern Woman Meets Atavistic Man', in L. Gelsthorpe and A. Morris (eds), *Feminist Perspectives in Criminology*, Milton Keynes, Open University Press.

Taylor, I. *et al.* (1975), 'Critical Criminology in Britain: Review and Prospects', in I. Taylor *et al.* (eds), *Critical Criminology*, London, Routledge & Kegan Paul.

Van Den Haag, E. (1975) *Punishing Criminals*, New York, Simon & Schuster.

Wilson, J. (1975) *Thinking About Crime*, New York, Basic Books.

Young, J. (1986) 'The Failure of Criminology: The Need for Radical Realism', in R. Matthews and J. Young (eds), *Confronting Crime*, London, Sage.

Young, J. (1992), 'Ten Points of Realism', in J. Young and R. Matthews (eds), *Rethinking Criminology: The Realist Debate*, London, Sage.

15 Theorising Modern Family Life

Aims of the Chapter

This chapter attempts to identify the agencies at work in modern society which promote nuclear family living. Different perspectives on the virtues of this form of family are examined and the assumptions about individual freedom and obligation underpinning these are explored. Recent evidence about an increase in diversity in family living offers an opportunity for alternative theories of modern family life to be articulated, and these are the subject of the chapter's concluding section.

Source: Private Eye.

'Don't worry, the wife won't be back from her macramé, or origami, or whatever the hell she's studying these days.'

Introduction

Nuclear family life is something that most of us living in modern industrial societies take for granted as 'normal'. Although other forms of family – such as **extended families**, **single-parent families** and **reconstituted families**, for instance – are far from uncommon in contemporary Britain, most of us still operate with the expectation that

nuclear family
The conventional household unit in modern society, composed of a man and woman in a stable marital relationship, with their dependent children.

extended family
A household unit where more than one generation of husbands and wives reside with their offspring.

single-parent family
A household unit where only one parent, usually the mother, resides with, and takes responsibility for parenting, her children.

reconstituted family
Family units comprising step-parents as a consequence of divorce or remarriage.

people today usually live in nuclear families. Yet it is a form of family living which is culturally and historically specific. Historical and cross-cultural evidence testifies that in other times and places family lives look very different; indeed, some of these are so different from what we are used to that to use the word 'family' to describe them almost renders the term meaningless. In fact, anthropologists, whose interest is in making sense of the enormous cultural variations apparent in different kinds of societies in the world today, usually talk about '**kinship groups**' rather than 'families'. This is because about the only thing they all have in common is that they are made up of people who are related by blood or marriage – that is, that such people are each other's *kin*.

kinship groups
An anthropological term referring to groups who are related by marriage or blood.

Before the rise of industrial capitalism in Europe, the nuclear family did not occupy the privileged position it tends to be accorded today. Among property-owning groups, there was concern about inheritance and transmission of property and privileges, and about the social standing of their 'house', and for all classes, the family unit was an important economic unit, involved in the production of goods and services upon which survival depended. But the nuclear family was closely embedded in the community, and not regarded as a special sphere set apart from the rest of the society.

In *Centuries of Childhood* (1973), Ariès points out that from the fifteenth to the seventeenth centuries the family did not occupy a special place in people's hearts and minds. People married and had children, but, as in other non-industrial contexts, marriage tended to be seen as an alliance, important for the connections it established with others, but hardly the central relationship in people's lives. Marriage did not have the religious connotations it later acquired; as Ariès (1973, p. 345) puts it, 'sexual union, when blessed by marriage, ceased to be a sin, but that was all'. Nor were children creatures around whom their parents' lives revolved. In many European countries it was common practice to send one's children away, at the age of 7 or so, to be 'apprenticed' – that is, to live for up to seven years in another house, where they would be expected to perform menial chores, to be instructed in manners and morals, and perhaps to learn the trade of members of the household. This was regarded as a more suitable preparation for adult life than a coddled existence in the bosom of one's own family. Thus child-rearing was not the prerogative of the child's biological parents and nor were families withdrawn from the wider community.

Ariès argues that the integration of the family into community life was reflected in housing, particularly that of comfortably-off citizens in the town. Daily life centred on a series of social and business encounters, so that business life, social life and family life overlapped. Houses sheltered a shifting population of servants, apprentices, friends, employees, clergy and clerks, as well as the parents and children themselves; rooms were used interchangeably for eating, sleeping, entertaining and arranging business deals. Many people slept together in one room – parents, children, servants and friends alike. The home was definitely not, as we think of it now, a private place reserved for family and intimate friends; nor did the 'family' have the character of a private and privileged unit devoted to the working through of the **conjugal relationship** and the rearing of one's own children.

conjugal relationship
The relationship between husband and wife in marriage.

We can summarise this by saying that nuclear families in European history were less *privatised* – less detached from the wider society – than those of today. Since home and workplace were so often identical before industrialisation, child-rearing groups overlapped with productive groups. Children grew up and worked and played alongside a range of kinfolk, acquaintances and friends; socialisation was a natural by-product of community life, rather than a specialised activity taking place in isolation from activities in the public sphere.

In pre-industrial Europe, then, family life was significantly different from the sort we are used to. If we now turn to look at anthropological evidence from tribal societies, we can see even greater differences.

Probably the most common kinship arrangement in tribal societies is a system of **unilineal descent**, in which descent groups consist not (as in the case of families in our society) of people related by both blood and marriage, but blood relations only. Where descent follows *patrilineal* rules, membership of a descent group is acquired through the male line only. People become members of their father's descent group; such groups consist of generations of brothers and sisters, along with the children of the brothers. (The children of the sisters belong not to their mothers', but to their fathers' descent groups.) In the case of *matrilineal* groupings, descent group membership is acquired through the female line. Here people become members of their mothers' descent group; matrilineal groups consist of generations of brothers and sisters, along with the children of the sisters. The crucial point is that in matrilineal or patrilineal descent systems people related by marriage are not considered as kin in the way in which people who are related by blood are. In contrast with our own society, the major kinship groupings are constructed by excluding marriage altogether.

unilineal descent
An anthropological term used to describe a line of descent of people related by blood acquired through either the male line (patriliny) or the female line (matriliny).

It is usually the case, even in societies with unilineal descent, that the reproductive and child-rearing unit takes a form more similar to the kinds of families with which we are most familiar. Although descent groups consist only of the mother and her kin, or the father and his kin, people usually live, nevertheless, in domestic units based on a conjugal tie – as husbands and wives and children. Where residence follows *virilocal* rules, brothers remain in the descent group home and bring their wives to live with them; the sisters of the descent group eventually leave to marry men living in other descent group homes with *their* brothers. In the case of *uxorilocal* residence, sisters remain at home and import men from other descent groups as husbands, while their brothers leave to marry elsewhere. Residence arrangements such as these enable sexual partners to be in regular contact, while meeting the common cultural requirement that men and women must look *outside* certain categories of kin for their sexual partners. Where unilineal descent prevails, marriage between members of the same descent group is usually forbidden. Marriage outside the descent group has the additional advantage of enabling descent groups to establish alliances between their own and other such groups.

So although in unilineal descent systems kinship groups are made up of individuals drawn from only one side of the biological parent relationship, it is almost always the case that people live together as husband and wife in residence units in which some kind of conjugal tie features strongly, thus bearing a much closer resemblance to our own kind of family than the structure of descent groups would suggest.

Box 15. 1: Family ideologies

Ideas about procreation in matrilineal and patrilineal societies often clearly reflect and support a separation of biological and social parenthood. In many matrilineal societies physiological paternity is either devalued or its role denied altogether. Among the Trobriand Islanders, for example, the biological father is considered to have no part in creating the child; he serves simply to 'open the way' for its eventual birth. The reverse ideology sometimes operates in patrilineal societies, with *women* considered to have no part in creating their own children. This is characteristic of the Tikopia of Polynesia, where the woman is just the 'shelter house' of the child. The Kachin of Burma extend such ideas into the arena of intrafamilial sexual activity; perfectly consistently, Kachin do not classify intercourse with one's mother as incest (she is not your mother after all) but adultery. (Many would argue that beliefs popular in our society about 'maternal instinct' constitute a similar ideological mechanism designed to justify *our* child-rearing arrangements, reliant as they are on women subordinating all other activity to the mother–child bond.)

However, even in uxorilocal and virilocal domestic units in unilineal societies where husbands or wives have got a residential foothold in the descent group, there are still significant differences between those child-rearing arrangements and those of the nuclear family. For one thing, they are often much larger units that our nuclear families, so that although a child's biological parents take most responsibility for its rearing, some aspects of social parenthood are attended to by other people. The fact of common residence encourages kin other than the biological parents to take a more active interest in child-rearing. Furthermore, it must be remembered that in unilineal societies only one of the biological parents belongs to the same descent group as their children; other members of that descent group may claim the right to a greater involvement with the children than the parent who is an 'outsider'.

In contrast to our own society, then, where it is expected that families will be formed on a marital tie, in unilineal societies the marital bond is not the basis for the establishment of descent groups or even residence groups: it is a mechanism by such a group otherwise defined reproduces itself. As Fox puts it:

> **The conjugal tie is variable. There are other ways of dealing with the problems of survival than by the institutionalisation of the conjugal tie, and when we see it firmly institutionalised we should ask why this is so rather than take it for granted.**
>
> [Fox, 1967, p. 40]

There are in all known societies social units concerned with childbearing, with sexual activity and with the daily activities of eating and sleeping; but these social arrangements differ from one society to the next – in terms of the composition of the largest cohesive groups, the composition of the domestic group, the links with the rest of the society, the authority patterns and division of labour within the 'family' – and these differences may often be dramatic.

> **The family, particularly the nuclear family, can be seen, through comparative analysis, as just one very specific means of organising the relationships between parents and children, males and females. It is not, as has so often been claimed, some kind of 'natural', instinctive and 'sacred' unit.**
>
> [Edholm, 1982, p. 177].

If this is so, then we need to explain why nuclear family living became the norm in industrial capitalist societies. The most popular explanation of this phenomenon in family sociology after the Second World War was the structural-functionalist theory of American Talcott Parsons. Cheal (1991) calls this sort of approach 'standard American sociology', because its 'domination of the American discipline in a formative period of growth meant that it had deep and lasting effects ... The influence of standard American sociology also extended far outside the US, since its rise coincided with the high point of American prestige in the period immediately after the Second World War' (pp. 3–4).

Box 15.2: Functionalism and the family

Functionalism maintains that the persistence of any social institution is explained in terms of the benefits it provides for both individuals and the society in which they live. Functionalists thus believe families perform vital functions for their members, and for society. Any society depends upon its major institutions, like the family, performing their functions properly; furthermore, when a society's structure changes through time, its key institutions will evolve and become reshaped, so as to ensure that the society's needs continue to be met. Functionalist theorists of the family have thus been most interested in the 'fit' between the family and society and have argued that the reason why modern industrial societies are characterised by *nuclear* family life is that it is this form of family that best satisfies the particular needs of an industrial economy.

Talcott Parsons

The theory most often associated with the question of the fit between industrial society and nuclear family systems is that of Parsons. His argument – that a nuclear family system is uniquely well adapted to the needs of an industrial society – has two prongs. First, he suggests that the economic differentiation which is so characteristic of industrial societies (the multiplicity of different occupations, with different incomes and life-styles attached) is incompatible with the maintenance of extended families but ideally served by the nuclear family. If the family is restricted to the small nuclear group with a single primary breadwinner who is also head of the family, Parsons argues, potential conflicts between members of an extended family working in different jobs are avoided – conflicts, for example, over where the family should live, or arising from a disparity in the incomes and life-styles associated with the occupations. Here Parsons is suggesting that only a nuclear family system eliminates economic differentiation within the family and thus prevents the competitive elements of industrial wage-labour from undermining family solidarity; at the same time, the nuclear family is a small enough unit to be geographically and economically mobile, as an industrial economy demands.

The second part of his argument concerns the need to resolve a conflict between the values which underpin economic and 'public' activities in industrial societies and those which characterise family relationships. According to Parsons, families must inevitably be characterised by values such as *ascription* (an emphasis upon who people are) and *particularism* (priority for special relationships); for example, it is expected that parents should love and care for *their* offspring above all others, regardless of how 'successful' or 'attractive' these children are by public standards. However, Parsons argues, these same values are unacceptable and harmful in the public sphere; for example, in economic life, hiring, firing and promotion are supposed to take place according to individual merit only. In other words, for Parsons, the efficient operation of the public sphere depends upon constant application of the values of *achievement* and *universalism* – the opposite of those which characterise kinship relations.

public sphere
Based on notions of a public/private dichotomy, refers to the arena outside the home and family, and the kinds of activities associated with paid work.

domestic sphere
Sometimes referred to as the private sphere, based on notions of a public/private dichotomy. It refers to the arena of activity associated with the household and family life.

instrumental
In relation to the family, the term Parsons uses to describe the husband's role of making material provision for his family.

expressive
In relation to the family, the term Parsons uses to describe the wife's role of providing for the emotional needs for her family.

Disruption would occur if kin obligations and occupational obligations overlapped – for example, where one member of the family was a supervisor and another a labourer in the same firm. Such conflicts are avoided, Parsons argues, by (i) segregating the nuclear family from other kin, and (ii) segregating the nuclear family from the **public sphere** (except for the father being the principal breadwinner). Intrusion of family values into work is thus avoided, and work values do not disrupt the solidarity of the family; people do not have constantly to choose between loyalty to kin and the impersonal standards demanded by their occupational roles.

Parsons argues that the nuclear family performs two main functions for its members – the socialisation of children and the 'personality stabilisation' (or 'tension management') of adults. Resources are provided by the husband/father, while the wife/mother runs the **domestic sphere**, caring for the emotional needs of family members. Parsons described this male function as '**instrumental**' and the female as '**expressive**'; this gendered division is based upon a presumption about women's 'natural' abilities: 'The particular tasks assigned to the sexes are, in Parsons' opinion, due to the primacy of the relationship between a small child and its mother. The special nature of that relationship, he claimed, is a consequence of the unique capacities of women for bearing and nursing children' (Cheal , 1991, p. 6).

Clearly this is both a *modernist* theory – it specifies how family life should be lived – and it is a theory at the heart of which is an *idealised* model of family life. We all know that families don't always conform to this model and, of course, Parsons did too. Wives get battered, marriages break down, single-parenting is becoming more and more common, children are unhappy, mistreated and abused, and so on. But Parsons is quintessentially a modernist; he is concerned to specify, through his theorising, the sort of family it is worth aiming at because of its potential benefits for individuals and for society. So what happens when particular families fall short of the ideal, and what should we do to prevent such family 'problems' breaking out? It is hardly surprising that nuclear family supporters in the Parsonsian mould are enthusiastic about outside intervention, both to prop up ailing families and to prevent others going the same way, since this is what the project of modernity is about; the application of theoretical knowledge to achieve improvement in people's lives.

In order to make sense of the kinds of institutional interventions that have become part of modern family life, it will be helpful to turn to the work of French historian and philosopher Michel Foucault and his characterisation of modern society.

Michel Foucault: Discourses and Social Life

According to Foucault, human societies are best understood as places in which *discourses* – forms of knowledge which work like languages – promote certain kinds of people and behaviour and in which regulatory apparatuses develop to police and discipline their members to conform to these prescriptions. For Foucault, the most important discourses in modern societies which do this are those concerned with constituting and regulating the *body* in prescriptive ways.

This *materialist* focus has two main features: first, an historical examination of the kinds of discourse that have emerged in modern times to control the individual body – discourses whose domain is that of *anatomo-politics* – and second, discourses which exercise power over bodies in aggregate, as a mass occupying physical and social space – discourses concerned with the *bio-politics* of a population.

Foucault's perspective on social life is fundamentally concerned with *power*. Prevailing forms of knowledge exercise power over us because they provide us with the language we are obliged to use in order to think about the world, and thereby 'know' about it; discourses constitute us because we have to use their vocabularies in order to make sense of events and phenomena.

> **For Foucault we know or see what our language permits, because we can never apprehend or know 'reality' outside of language. Nothing occurs outside the language ... Different societies and different historical periods have different (languages) and therefore different realities.**
>
> [Turner, 1987, pp. 10–11).

These discourses constitute identity and they construct behaviour; that is, they define who we become as persons/subjects (we are 'subjected' to the power of these prescriptions), and we live our lives in the ways we do because our actions have been 'subjected' to their determining influence. Power is not exercised by discourses suppressing, denying, or preventing ways of living, then: it is not a matter of 'Thou shalt not' but 'Thou shalt'. Disciplinary devices (or 'apparatuses') promote these discourses, and the extent of a discourse's capacity to constitute identity and construct behaviour is a reflection of the regulatory power of these devices. Finally, the outcome, in terms of identities – who we are – and behaviour – what we do – confers power upon particular groups in society, because their interests are unequally served by these discursively created consequences.

We can look at the development and characteristics of modern family life under these three headings. The questions are:

- What are the forms of knowledge which constitute family identities and construct family behaviour?
- What are the disciplinary devices used to promote these discourses?
- Who gains from their influence/power in society?

To answer these questions about any time in a society's history, we have to identify the definitions of the 'normal' family that prevail, how these versions of normality are enforced and who the beneficiaries of these discourses about 'normal' family workings are. In Britain since the Second World War, two discourses have emerged in order to promote nuclear family life which merit particular examination. The *'medicalisation of family life'* summarises ways in which the family has been subject to intervention and constitution by medicine and medical practitioners, while *'family policy'* refers to the state-instituted practices various governments have employed to construct family life in ways of which they have approved. To understand their contemporary significance, we first need some historical background.

Pre-Modern Family Life and Religious Discourses

Historically, *religious* discourses have played a significant role in constituting family members and constructing particular forms of behaviour in families, and the importance of religion on family life has been particularly apparent in discourses concerning female sexuality.

An example of the role of religion in this respect was the 'witchcraft craze' in Medieval Europe. According to Turner, this was primarily a device to regulate the behaviour of women and the attack on women as witches was principally 'a critique of their sexuality'.

> **Women were closely associated with witchcraft, because it was argued that they were particularly susceptible to the sexual advances of the devil ... Women were seen to be irrational, emotional and lacking in self-restraint; they were especially vulnerable to satanic temptation.**
>
> **[Turner, 1987, p. 86]**

Turner argues that later attempts to regulate female sexuality by means of religious discourse have, in the case of Western Europe, to be understood in the context of historically long-term concerns about the problems of managing the control of private property and of ensuring its continuity through time.

Thus, for the land-owning aristocracy, the point of marriage was to produce a male heir to the property of the household. Since both life expectancy and childbirth were uncertain affairs, women had to be more or less continuously pregnant during their marriage to guarantee a living male heir when he became needed. Furthermore, this heir had to be legitimate, to avoid controversies over inheritance. This legitimacy could only be ensured by heads of households marrying virgins and by ensuring the chastity of their wives for the duration of the marriage. Equally, daughters had to be similarly sexually pure so that they could be eligible for marriage to other property-holding families. Such marriages were solely motivated by the need to produce children then, with none of the elements of eroticism and sexual compatibility we demand from our unions today.

In early Europe, these interests were reflected in the character of marriages; they were private, arranged, contracts which could be easily dissolved in the event of their child-production function being compromised by the woman's infertility or infidelity. With the entry of the

Church into marriage control, different definitions of the nature of these religion-sponsored unions emerged. Life-long marriages were now demanded, but with a continued concern to regulate sexuality, and particularly the sexuality of women.

> **Since the Church regarded marriage as a necessary evil against fornication, the Church argued that married couples should not enjoy their sexual relationship, but regard it merely as a system of reproduction. The Church also established a rigid set of conventions regarding sexual positions, homosexuality, perversions and various forms of deviance. Women came to be seen increasingly as a major threat to the stability of these social relations of marriage, since the Church regarded the woman as the weaker partner. It was assumed that the woman would be more susceptible to temptation and deviance. The Church therefore provided a powerful ideology for controlling women through such institutions (regulatory apparatuses) as the confession.**
>
> **[Turner, 1987, p. 96 (our parentheses)]**

As Foucault suggests, we have to understand such discourses as principally concerned with the management of the body: 'Because the government of the body is in fact the management of sexuality, the issue of regulation is in practice the regulation of the sexuality of women' (Turner, 1987, p. 98). Furthermore both bio-politics and anatomo-politics are being exercised here: such discourses were designed to manage both bodies en masse – in order to control population growth – and individual bodies – by controlling individuals' sexual desires.

Though such a requirement became even more important with the emergence of modern, urban, society, the secularisation of such societies involved a transfer of discursive power. While body management remained the priority of nineteenth-century societies, with the need for the control of female sexuality therefore remaining crucial, a change in the discursive basis for the discipline of women took place. Now *medical* discourse took over, becoming the principal modern medium designed to define women as potentially sexually subversive and therefore in need of regulation. Rather than sanctity and purity being the antidotes to sexual deviance, it now became a matter of ensuring women's 'health'; controlling and disciplining her base and dangerous natural propensities became a matter of medical intervention to sustain her, and protect society, against the dangers of an outbreak of sexual 'illness'.

Modern Family Life and Medical Discourses

Foucault claims the nineteenth-century notion of the 'hysterical woman' is testimony to the emerging dominance of medical discourse at that time:

> **The hysterical woman, rather like the 19th century masturbating child and sexual pervert, was a product of the all-pervasive ideology of sex which came to cultural predominance in the 19th century. For Foucault, the discourse of sexuality produced the hysterical woman as the object of a detailed medical discourse and a medical practice.**
>
> [TURNER, 1987, pp. 88–9]

Supposedly originating in female physiology (the term 'hysteria' is derived from the Greed word 'hystera' or uterus), the condition gave rise to weeping, screaming, fainting, an arched rigid body, temper loss, etc. According to nineteenth-century medicine, this illness was provoked by a lack of family membership, and thus typically suffered by young single women, divorced women, widows, or women who pursued careers instead of experiencing normal sexual fulfilment in stable marriages. (It was those kinds of women who were most vulnerable to witchcraft accusations in previous times.) The implication of this illness was that women could only be healthy if they lived normal family lives – being sexually connected to a man in a marriage whose aim was child-production. A similar 'illness', nymphomania, befell women who pursued sexual satisfaction outside marriage. Such a discursive construction thus acted as a promoter of family life; to avoid the danger of ill-health, it was argued that women should pursue sexuality only in order to achieve pregnancy inside marriage and should not delay this goal by, for example, pursuing educational qualifications or by establishing a career prior to motherhood. In this way, a particular way of life was defined as normal and alternatives as deviant; medical discourse provided the vocabulary for, and medical practitioners acted as the regulators of, these definitions while the principal beneficiaries of their enforcement were men.

Twentieth century changes in the position of women, achieved through an increase in employment opportunities, a growth in the availability of education, and particularly, the spread of contraception, enabling women to have a greater degree of control over their fertility, have altered this picture somewhat. Despite such changes, however, medical discourse still constructs family life and, in particular, promotes a definition of 'womanhood' which has strong echoes of the past. As we have said, the power of all discourses lies in the definitions they promote; they do not simply intervene into an already existing reality but they *construct* this reality – things become what the discourse defines them as being. So an interest in medical intervention in family life is important not just because it is concerned with *returning* a family to a state of health, but because by doing so, it *defines* a family's health – it defines what families are, or should be. This is why families need *professional* intervention. Because of their monopoly over medical knowledge, it is the experts' view that counts, not the patients'. Two good examples of such contemporary medical family regulation are the *'medicalisation of motherhood'* and *'family therapy'* – what Morgan (1985)calls the *'medicalisation of marriage'*.

Reproductive technologies and the medicalisation of motherhood

According to Stanworth (1987) contemporary technological interventions into the process of human biological reproduction are of four kinds. The first concerns contraception – fertility control. The second concerns the management of labour and childbirth, and the explosion of technical intervention made possible because of the hospitalisation of the process. Third, intervention has become routine in the ante-natal period, designed to monitor the progress of the foetus. Finally, and most controversially, have been technologies designed to rectify infertility and to promote pregnancy.

At first glance, such a proliferation of technological advancements would seem to be of considerable benefit to women, allowing them for the first time a real chance to influence and control their biology. But as Stanworth points out, the interventions enabled by such technological developments have had the opposite effect, by placing the management of motherhood securely in the hands of the professionals, the great majority of whom are men. As she puts it:

> **new technologies help to establish that gynaecologists and obstetricians 'know more' about pregnancy and about women's bodies than women do themselves. When the majority of the profession is male, it is perhaps not surprising that medical practitioners have been attracted to techniques that enable them to brush aside a woman's own felt experience of menstruation, pregnancy and birth.**
>
> **[Stanworth, 1987, p. 13]**

In Foucauldian terms, then, the emergence of such a medical discourse defining 'healthy'/'normal' reproduction not only dictates this procedure for women by constructing motherhood in particular ways but does so in ways that benefit the (predominantly male) medical profession. This construction of biological motherhood goes hand in hand with a view of 'normal' women as 'mothers', for the provision of fertility control techniques in particular reflects a powerful discourse concerning the 'normal family'. While all women are assumed to instinctively desire motherhood – a 'woman' equals a 'mother' in this discourse as it has traditionally always done in **naturalistic** family theory – nevertheless, from this viewpoint, healthy mothering has to take place within a normal family context: in effect, married women *must* be mothers while unmarried women must *not*. So, although married women who deny their 'maternal instincts' are defined as selfish, deviant or plainly unwell, the medical promotion of healthy motherhood is selective:

naturalistic
Pertaining to nature. For example, a naturalistic theory is one that explains human behaviour in terms of natural instincts and drives.

The idea of maternal instinct is sometimes used to override women's expressed wishes with regard to childbearing – discouraging young married women from sterilisation or abortion, for example – while denying single women the chance to have a child. In other words, a belief in maternal instinct coexists with obstacles to autonomous motherhood – obstacles, that is, to motherhood for women who are not in a stable relationship to a man. According to ideologies of motherhood, all women *want* children; but single women, lesbian women (and disabled women) are often expected to forgo mothering 'in the interests of the child'.

[Stanworth, 1987, p. 15]

By such means, the 'liberating 'potential of reproductive technologies only serves to reinforce a particular view of family life as 'normal' and a particular view of a 'normal' woman as a married mother:

On the one hand, [reproductive technologies] have offered women a greater technical possibility to decide if, when and under what conditions to have children; on the other, the domination of so much reproductive technology by the medical profession and by the State has enabled others to have an even greater capacity to exert control over women's lives.

[Stanworth, 1987, p. 4]

Indeed, one powerful critique of reproductive technology concentrates on the power that the possibilities of such medical manipulation confers on men. Whereas religious discourses focused on regulating female sexuality as the key to social order – constructing virginal and chaste women in order that they could be eligible wives, and then constructing the virtuous wife/mother as fertile and faithful – medical control of fertility has, according to this critique, become an essential *modern* device whereby women today can continue to be regulated by men.

From this point of view, then, contemporary medical discourse and intervention operates in the same kind of discursive and regulatory ways as older family discourses did, and, once again, in the interests of the same beneficiaries.

Family therapy and the medicalisation of marriage

Given the definitions of normality and deviance that successive family discourses have promoted, it is unsurprising that twentieth-century medical discourse has attempted to manufacture marriage in a similar fashion. Though the language has changed – we are now dealing with health and sickness rather than virtue and sinfulness – the aims of the promotion have not. The discursive injunction is still to be happily married and to receive emotional fulfilment from within family life; however, today, failure to secure these benefits is evidence of pathology which requires medical intervention to restore health. The medicalisation of marriage thus uses medical discourse to define marital normality and deviance; the best-known version of such an approach is *Family Therapy*.

Thus, for example, intervention into the sexual relationship of an adult couple presumes a definition of 'normal sexuality' which is thereby reinforced by the intervention: this almost always means promoting genital contact between heterosexuals leading to orgasm. An inability to achieve orgasm is normally defined as a 'dysfunction'. Another example which makes the same point is that of 'premature' ejaculation as 'sexual dysfunction'. Defining this as a 'problem' springs from a normative ideal that sex should be equally pleasurable to both participants; such an ideal, however, is culturally and historically specific. Indeed, the whole basis of such a discourse rests upon an essentially modernist assumption that marital sexual relations are, in principle, capable of being improved with the assistance of knowledgeable experts. Furthermore, underpinning this assumption is another, that there are objective standards by which the performance of particular individuals can be judged. Notions such as 'sexual adequacy' and 'reproductive competence' abound in family therapy discourse and thereby reinforce Foucault's insistence that we should understand the power of discursive definitions as *promoting and prescribing* the lives and identities of human beings. The more family members feel the need to aspire to, and achieve, discursively prescribed levels of competence as sexual partners and as mothers and fathers, the more powerful the discourse that defines these levels becomes, the more powerful the devices that promote the discourse become, and the more powerful those who benefit from its promotion become.

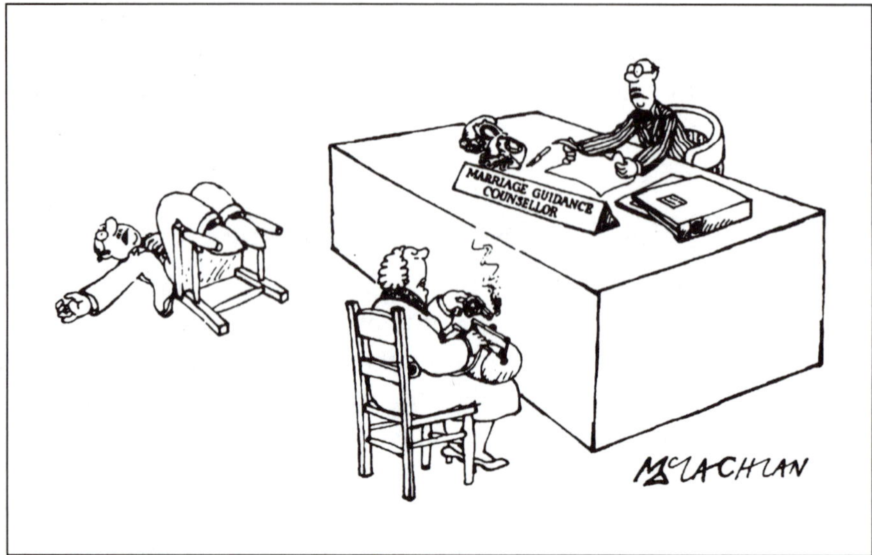

Source: *Private Eye*

'Well, we haven't made a very good start have we, Mrs Turnstone?'

The State and Family Life: The Politics of Family Policy

A significant element in the history of the British family in the second half of this century involves discursive endeavours by the state to promote the nuclear family as characterised by Parsons. Though Parsons expected that people's lives would conform to the pattern he describes because of the needs of the system, historical analysis testifies that in a number of areas the script he wrote has not been acted out by his family actors and that state intervention has increasingly been necessary to prop up the nuclear family. The activities of the state in areas such as family life, health care, education and so on are summarised by the name the '**Welfare State**'. That is, this term is applied to those areas of social life in which governments take some degree of responsibility for the well-being of their citizens. In Britain, the use of the Welfare State has been the major form of intervention and regulation in family life (in the USA, family therapy has been an equally important discursive device whereby the nuclear family has been sustained.) How has this been done?

Welfare State
A system of government where the state assumes responsibility for providing a wide range of welfare benefits for its citizens.

Since the Second World War, 'propping up the nuclear family' by state-sponsored regulation via welfare policies has taken two distinct forms, representing two very different political philosophies. Between 1945 and 1979 a consensus generally prevailed among Conservative and Labour administrations about the necessity for state intervention in family life in order to achieve as much equality of provision as possible for members of families living in unequal material and social circumstances. This is known as '*Welfarism*'. After 1979, however, the state attempted to support the nuclear family for very different political purposes. Instead of sponsoring it to effectively target the needy, Thatcherite promotion of the nuclear family was motivated by a desire to promote and reward individualism, self-help, enterprise and initiative and thereby to reduce the State's involvement in people's lives. This is known as '*New Right*' thinking.

1945–1979 Welfarism

Although a radical left-wing Labour government came to power in 1945 – the prime minister was Clement Attlee – successive Conservative and Labour governments in the 1950s, 1960s and 1970s (under the respective leaderships of Churchill, Eden, Macmillan, Home, Wilson, Heath and Callaghan) all practised policies which could broadly be described as 'centrist' or 'middle-of-the-road'. Eschewing radicalism of either the Right or Left, these governments pursued essentially similar political agendas, with Welfarism at or near the top of them for most of the time. The aim was to use Welfare State provision to promote and practice *benevolence* – intervening in people's lives to promote a more equal distribution of life-chances among a population inevitably made up of unequally advantaged groups. Between 1945 and 1979, Welfarism was a taken-for-granted political orthodoxy; the consensus which prevailed during that time is best indicated by the use of Welfarism, by successive British governments, both Conservative and Labour, to minimise social inequalities and to assist the most deprived groups in society. Welfarism is thus based on the view that impoverishment and disadvantage is not a matter of individual failure but a socially constructed condition characteristic of a stratified society and which needs social intervention to ameliorate it. The use of Welfarism to prop up the nuclear family life, it was believed, would be the most effective way to reach those most in need of support.

1979–1990 anti-welfarism: the New Right

However, after Margaret Thatcher's radical Conservative reign began in 1979, a different orthodoxy, echoing nineteenth-century liberal thinking, was re-born. The use of the Welfare State to promote Welfarism now began to be seen as a costly, unnecessary and morally repugnant political instrument which financially cripples the successful (the able) in order to feather-bed the lives of the disadvantaged (the less able) members of society. For Thatcherites, *individuals* are responsible for their successes or failures, and it is no business of government to intervene in order to minimise those inequalities of reward which are justly visited on citizens by virtue of their abilities and their endeavours. Human beings are unequally talented and the success of a modern economy depends upon the blessed and the industrious inheriting their just desserts. Since Welfare State spending depends on taxation and since taxation is the government-sponsored theft of individuals' private property, Thatcherism attempted to 'roll back its frontiers' and reduce its impact on people's lives.

Paradoxically, however, though Welfarism – the 1945–79 instrument used to sponsor the nuclear family – now became the enemy, for the New Right, this didn't mean also viewing nuclear family living with equal disfavour. For, from this perspective, the nuclear family is still an essential political instrument since it is regarded as the most effective means of pursuing anti-Welfarist, radical conservative, ends. The radical Right insist on prioritising individualism, dismantling the '**nanny state**' and the 'dependency culture' and 'freeing' individuals to take responsibility for their own lives, and the lives of those for whom they have a moral duty to care – children, the non-hospitalised sick and infirm, and the elderly. For such right-wing thinkers, then, since the modern goals of freedom and progress ride on the back of *de*-regulation by government, by reducing intervention by the state into people's lives, and allowing them both to choose how to live and to take responsibility for these choices by supporting themselves and their dependants, the family remains of crucial political importance. Such a philosophy is neatly summarised by Thatcher's now-infamous assertion that 'There is no such thing as society. There are only individuals, and their families.'

'nanny state'
A pejorative term used to describe the Welfare State, which implies that the Welfare system is over-protective and does not encourage individual responsibility.

Thus, though the aims of these two political discourses – 1945–79 Welfarism and 1979–90 anti-Welfarism – were very different, both were nevertheless committed to the Parsonian nuclear family model as one of the most effective instruments to serve their respective political purposes. Furthermore, both targeted precisely the same features of nuclear family life as in need of their sponsorship above all else; despite their contrasting aims, both discourses in regulatory practice attempted to reproduce exactly the same kinds of family members and the same kinds of family lives. Underpinning both kinds of policy-making about the family is the distinction between Parsons' expressive and instrumental, sometimes called the private and the public; this distinction assumes that whereas male family members learn to perform their social, breadwinning functions, for women, it is their natural destiny to be responsible for the private, domestic, familial aspects of human life. As Helen Crowley puts it:

In the process of slow but profound change traced by the emergence of the modern social formation out of the pre-industrial, agrarian society it replaced, the lines of demarcation between the work undertaken by women and the work undertaken by men were drawn and re-drawn, and gradually emerged in a division of the social world into public and private spheres, with women's work being firmly positioned in the latter. One of the dominant explanations for the positioning of women in the private sphere of the family and men in the public sphere of work and polity was, and remains, that women are 'naturally' suited to mothering and caring.

[Crowley, 1992, p. 70]

The dominance of such *naturalistic* assumptions in both Welfarist and New Right discourses is clearly illustrated in examples of family policies from both eras – post-war *'pro-natalism'* and 1980s government policies designed to *promote 'Care in the Community'*.

Pro-natalism

pro-natalism
The view that everything should be done to encourage wives to have children.

Pro-natalism emerged as a significant discourse in the 1930s, when it began to be feared that the birth rate had gone into terminal decline. Though in the event these concerns proved to be unfounded, they gave rise to a concerted effort to promote child production, especially in the 1940s and 1950s, with profound consequences for the lives of women.

The language of pro-natalism included unquestioned linkages between concepts of 'woman' and 'mother', and between 'maternity' and the 'family'. In the immediate post-war period the importance of locating maternity within a stable family environment was strengthened by popular psychological writings about the positive consequences of 'attachment' and the negative consequences of 'separation' between mother and child. New anxieties about 'maternal deprivation', which drew upon psychoanalytical research, reinforced beliefs about the proper location of women as mothers within the family – and not working for wages outside the home.

[Cheal, 1991, p. 58]

Much of the theoretical backing for this idea came from the work of John Bowlby (1965, 1971,1975) who produced a number of well-known studies on how human beings form attachments, and how they experience grief and loss. Bowlby suggested that human beings have from infancy a predisposition to form a deep and overwhelmingly important attachment to one person – and that person will probably be the mother. Disruption of the relationship with the mother in childhood by, for example, prolonged separation, will produce anxiety in the child and effects similar to grief for the loss of a loved one. This experience may colour the child's later emotional make-up, and may interfere with his or her ability to form emotionally stable relationships. Thus, '**maternal deprivation**' in childhood is believed to have effects which are severe and lasting.

maternal deprivation
The psychological damage supposedly experienced by a child as a result of being separated from its mother.

Bowlby's work was a significant force in pro-natalism, whose welfarist support came in the form of family planning and family allowance policies. The effect of this discourse was a pronounced tendency – still very much apparent today – for mothers to be castigated for working in paid employment, or even for taking an occasional evening out. As Elizabeth Wilson (1977) argues, this definition of femininity as indivisible from motherhood was 'central to the purposes of welfarism' and discloses 'a unique demonstration of how the State can prescribe what woman's consciousness should be' – an excellent example of what Foucault has to say about the constituting role of discourse. As Crowley puts it:

> **The Welfare State, in other words, was structuring not just the conditions of motherhood but women's identity as mothers. Motherhood was defined as a labour of love, private and unpaid, although socially supported and recognised.**
>
> **[Crowley, 1992, p. 77]**

Care in the community

Since 1979, the same kind of naturalistic assumptions have underpinned the construction of discourses aimed to use the nuclear family to implement New Right policies designed to cope with a sharp increase in the number of dependent elderly people. In essence, the assumption that expressive, caring capacities are unique to women has informed attitudes towards dependency at the latter stages of life as well as the beginning ones, for '**care in the community**' in effect normally means 'caring by women'. Thus, the evidence points to a life-cycle of dependence being experienced by women, with the private, domestic sphere being constructed and utilised by geriatric policy for community care purposes as well as child-care purposes, on the naturalistic grounds that women's 'natural' abilities should be commandeered not just to perform the 'maternal function' but to provide care for the elderly who need it too. The implications of such a discourse are clearly illustrated

care in the community
A range of informal and professional care of the elderly, disabled and sick undertaken in the community, rather than in hospital or institutional settings, typically by female relatives.

by the fact that it wasn't until the late 1980s, when an appeal to the European Court of Justice succeeded, that the British government was forced to allow a non-waged woman caring for an elderly dependent relative to receive an 'attendance allowance' – the sum paid to a non-related community carer for doing the same work.

For both Welfarism and anti-Welfarism, then, the nuclear family has been of fundamental political significance: for Welfarists it can help administer social justice, while for the New Right it enables the Welfare State to be rolled back.

Problematising the Nuclear Family: Sociological Responses to Welfarism

In the same way as New Right thinking is clearly revealed by its attitude to the Welfare State, so post-war contributions to family sociology can also usefully be considered as responses to Welfarist discourses. Two distinct kinds of responses are apparent, one arguing for more Welfarist support and the other totally opposed to this. We can call the first response pro-Welfarism or *Social Conservatism* and the second anti-Welfarism or *Individual Liberationism.*

Social Conservatism draws allegiance from the large centre of the political spectrum, including centre-left Conservatives and centre-right Labour and Liberal-Democrat supporters. Social Conservatism considers the nuclear family to be an inherently weak unit and criticises Welfarist policies for not going anything like far enough in supporting it. Supporters of this position point to a number of different kinds of problems nuclear family members have faced in trying to live this kind of life and to the strategies they themselves have been forced to employ in the absence of the kinds of Welfarist support they have actually needed. The argument is that nuclear family life is so difficult to live without proper support that the evidence now abundantly available of rapid family change in recent years – for example, in the form of sharp increases in the numbers of divorces, single-parent families and working mothers – should be perfectly easy to understand: they represent a failure of Welfarism to do its job properly.

Individual Liberationism rejects Welfarism, though from a range of viewpoints and for very different reasons. Since the 1960s, a variety of sociological critics of Welfarism, for whom modern progress should be about extending individual liberty, have attacked the nature of this sort of state involvement in post-war family life. Marxists and Feminists (and sometimes writers who are both Marxist and Feminist) as well as writers on sexual liberation have argued that the policy of promoting the ideal of the nuclear family as the source of social justice and social cohesion fails to recognise the truth that this kind of family is in fact a site of disadvantage, subordination and oppression for its members, particularly women. For such theorists, nuclear family life subjugates its members, and Welfarism is thus an instrument of their subordination.

Here, then, is a nice irony: theorists from both the liberationist Left and the radical Right, though holding each other's views in contempt, are nonetheless united in defining Welfarism as the source of individual unfreedom. Indeed, here is a version of modernity very different from that held by Parsons and his political supporters. Instead of seeing progress exemplified by the nuclear family contributing to social cohesion by promoting social justice, these political opponents agree on a version of modernity which sees progress as the enablement of *individual* freedom and self-fulfilment, above all else. The relationships between these perspectives on welfarism and the nuclear family are summarised in Figure 15.1.

	Pro-Welfarism	**Anti-Welfarism**
Pro-nuclear family	Social Conservatism	New Right
Anti-nuclear family		Individual Liberationism

Figure 15.1 Perspectives on welfarism and the nuclear family

Social Conservatism: Pro-Welfarism in Sociology

Box 15.3: The Parental Deficit

'Underlying many of today's concerns is a sense that the quality of parenting has fallen. Millions have left to work outside the home, to be replaced by inadequate, poorly paid and insecure childcare workers. This isn't the fault of the women's movement. All women did was demand what men had long taken for granted, and few expected that women's emancipation would produce a society suffering from an acute parenting deficit, in which all adults would act like men who in the past were inattentive to children.

So tackling the parenting deficit does not mean a return to having women at home and men working outside the household. But those concerned with the quality of parenting cannot be oblivious to the rising divorce rate. While it is true that some single parents do as good a job or better than two parents, it is not the case across the board. American studies show that children from broken homes are more likely to have intellectual (learning) and social (behavioural) problems than children from intact families. They also have worse criminal records. Critics say that this is because single parents have a lower income, which is partly true. But even this is also in part caused by divorce. It simply costs more to run two households than one.

Above all, bringing up a child is a labour-intensive mission. There are never enough hands and voices to do what needs to be done. Africans say that it takes a whole village to raise a child. In the past, the extended family helped the two-parent family: today, when both parents work outside the household, they have a hard time finding enough time and energy for their children. A single parent is more likely to be beleaguered.

To make families stronger, we need to teach interpersonal skills in schools. Findings show that stable couples fight about as often as unstable couples, but they fight better. One can teach people to attack the issue and not the person, to set aside a cooling-off period before issues are tackled, and not to bring up everything that ever happened before at each opportunity.

We also need more marriage preparation sessions. In the US, churches and synagogues provide sessions so that prospective marriage partners can discuss basic issues – such as how family finances will be handled, whether or not to have children, and what to do if one partner gets a job in another city. Family counselling and mandatory delays for those who have elected to divorce also help. What matters even more than these arrangements is the change in culture they signify: marriage is not passé and family is important – for the sake of the children and the society that must live with the consequences when children are not brought up right.

It is always better to provide people with positive messages and incentives than to coerce them. Firstly, if simply punished, they will often not comply. (Penalties on welfare mothers in the US have little influence on how many children they have and how they are treated. There is very little a welfare mother can do to make a teenager attend school, or to stop him dealing drugs.)

Second, the penalties fall on innocent children when benefits are cut. Last but not least, it is easy to tell when penalties on parents on benefits really aim at changing their behaviour, and when they are aimed at saving money for the state: if the goal is behaviour modification, the income penalties generated should be dedicated to providing incentives for those who 'behave'. When this is opposed, the champions of welfare penalties reveal what is uppermost in their mind.

communitarianism
Echoing Durkheimian thinking, a 1990s' political philosophy stressing the importance of community and shared values for social order and stability.

For **communitarians** who want to shift the balance back from the radical individualism of the eighties towards the needs of the community, the priority is to work both on the side of culture and on the economy. The communitarian agenda calls for a change in values and for new measures to provide jobs and encourage flexible working. It seeks to motivate people to do their duty and favours penalties only as a last resort. Above all, it recognises that nothing is more important for society than that parents should be urged, and enabled, to be good parents.'

Source: Amitai Etzioni, *The Guardian*.

As we have already emphasised, the naturalistic assumptions underpinning Welfarism are particularly apparent in its attitude to mothering. In effect, the reasoning is that so long as a bride can walk up the aisle and say 'I do' – so long as a woman can get married – and so long as she is physically capable of biological reproduction, then she should be left to get on with the job. The desire to be a wife and the ability to reproduce are sufficient guarantees that she will be an effective mother, for her 'natural' abilities to ensure care for her offspring will then step in and take over; so long as she is given welfare support in the form of child allowance and a few post-natal visits from a Health Visitor then all will be well. The husband/father will provide the material support and the wife/mother can rely on her natural talents, springing from maternal 'instinct', to do the rest.

Those proposing a great extension in Welfarism argue that such assumptions seem incredibly optimistic and naive when viewed in the light of the realities of modern nuclear family life. The reasoning is as follows:

The domestic division of labour

The labour involved in child care, especially in the child's early years, is relentless. Unless a safety-net, in the form of an extended family, neighbours, or close-knit community, is there – which, according to the Parsonsian model, will increasingly be absent in modern societies – the wife/mother has to perform a 24-hour, incredibly burdensome task, virtually alone. But surely husbands help out?

Since the war, confident assertions have been made that modern nuclear family life would have as one of its principal features a growing equality in the relative contributions to the running of the home by the

domestic division of labour
The division of labour and the allocation of tasks between men and women in the household.

husband and wife – an arrangement known as the '**domestic division of labour**'. For example, the media has been proclaiming the imminent arrival of the '**new man**' for a number of years now, while the best known sociological account putting such a case is that of Young and Willmott (1973). They predicted the widespread establishment of a '**symmetrical family**', in which, although the husband and wife still carry out some specific tasks alone, a rigid division of labour has nonetheless broken down, with the husband contributing much more equally to domestic work than he had previously done.

However, later research has painted a different picture (see Chapter 8). As Bradley points out, even when married women enter paid employment, they still shoulder most of the burden of domestic labour:

new man
A recently developed concept used to describe the emergence of a new kind of man, who supports gender equality by being more involved in child care and willing to perform domestic tasks. His existence is much disputed.

> **Anne Oakley's pioneering study (1974) suggested that house work was a major constraint on women's opportunities and that increased participation by husbands was, in the main, only 'help' with a limited range of tasks. Since Oakley carried out her research there has been a rise in male unemployment and a continued upward trend in married women's employment, but recent surveys indicate that changes to the domestic division of labour have been slight. For example, the Women and Employment Survey (WRES) findings on housework and childcare showed that women in the mid-1980s were still doing the bulk of the work ... men help selectively but prefer washing up and taking children to the park to ironing the shirts and changing dirty nappies.**
>
> [BRADLEY, 1992, p. 30]

Mothering

symmetrical family
Developed by Young and Willmott to describe a more equal domestic division of labour between men and women. It suggests that although men and women may well perform different kinds of tasks, the workload in the household is becoming more shared.

The mother performs childcare tasks without any guidance about how to do it. The assumption is that natural instincts are enough, coupled, maybe, with an education gleaned from her own mother's performance. Welfarism in the form of Social Services intervention only happens after disaster has struck; taking children 'into care' is in essence a case of shutting the stable door after the horse has bolted. Compare this with the hoops through which *non*-biological parents – foster parents or adoptive parents – have to jump before being granted a child to care for, and the constant surveillance which the state then imposes on them during the child's development. It is not as if this is an area where discourses are unavailable; child psychology, for example, is a flourishing educational industry which informs the judgements of the professional overseers of adoptive/foster parenting – but such knowledge is never made available as a matter of course to prospective natural parents. The sales of books by such as Benjamin Spock and Penelope Leach over the last few decades heavily underline the need for this kind of support Welfarism has failed to give natural mothers – for fear of interfering with her 'rights'. The rights of children to receive informed care are thereby neglected.

Marriage and divorce

Nuclear family childcare is performed, uniquely among the world's kinship systems, by two adults alone, and primarily by the mother. The norm is that the presence of these adults in the child's life is enabled by marriage, which, in modern cultures, is supposed to be founded on romantic love. A high rate of marital breakdown, the death of these romances, is an inevitable consequence of building relationships on such an unstable and fragile basis. If it was this relationship alone that was involved in such marital failures then it would simply be a matter for the adult partners to cope with. But the nuclear family model is founded on the notion that these two adults, who want each other for potentially transitory romantic reasons, nonetheless can, alone, provide a stable and enduring caring environment for their children. Here is a basic contradiction in nuclear family life. When adult romantic love dies, we make legal provision for separation, which is right and proper. Yet child-rearing depends on such adult relationships *surviving*. We cannot have it both ways: in nuclear family societies, the rights of individuals to seek personal fulfilment in loving relationships too often contradicts the rights of children to have both their parents around.

Divorce statistics and single-parent statistics tell us part of the story about marital breakdown. The 1990 figures reveal that in Britain over one-third of all marriages end in divorce and 20 per cent of children experience the divorce of their parents by the time they reach the age of 16. 'It is anticipated that this trend will grow and that by the turn of the century only 50% of children will experience [a] "conventional family life".' (Crowley, 1992, p. 82). One in seven families are single-parent families. But these statistics do not tell us about the number of marriages which have broken down but not broken up. We just do not know the numbers of couples who 'stay together for the sake of the children'.

In such circumstances, truly efficient Welfarism would make at least material provision for the single parent. However, the 1993 case of a single mother imprisoned for leaving her three-year-old child alone in order to go out to work because her wage was too low for her to afford the childcare she would have had to purchase privately, is a poignant illustration of the lot faced by large numbers of single mothers. Most single parents are single mothers; nearly two-thirds of single parents live below the poverty line and most rely on social security benefits as their principal means of support.

Working mothers

Material disadvantage is not just a problem for single parents however. The figures of working mothers, most of whom *have* to work to supplement their husband's income, paint an equally vivid picture of the problems faced by large numbers of nuclear families in modern Britain. Lister (1984) estimated that the number of families living in poverty would increase by a third if the wife did not work. In 1990, both husband and wife were employed in over a half of all married couples with children. Henwood *et al.* (1987) stated that 'a breadwinning husband with a non-working wife at home with two dependent children accounts for a mere 8% of all working men'. It could be argued that such a picture illustrates again the failure of Welfarism to properly address the material needs of nuclear families and of working-class families in particular.

Care in the community

Welfarism has also signally failed the old and the infirm. Since the war there has been a burgeoning of residential care, both state-sponsored and private, in response to the growing numbers of elderly people in need of care. But, as we have already discussed, in recent years, as part of the Conservative 'Care in the Community' policies, there has been an increasing reliance on the family to undertake the care of dependent relatives. Since, in practice, 'caring in the community' really means caring by women, the figures demonstrate a naturalistic exploitation of supposed womanly qualities, but a woeful lack of Welfarist support for these carers. The General Household Survey of Carers (Green, 1988) revealed six million adults caring for dependent relatives. Women form the majority of these carers with about half delivering more than 50 hours of care a week:

> **The over-65 age group has practically doubled since 1951, and in 1987 was over 11 million. The care of the elderly involves an immense amount of work for women and for many, these additional demands on their labour prove impossible ... If a growing number of women, for whatever reason, prove unable or unwilling to provide unwaged labour in the care of the elderly population, the economic consequences for State expenditure would be enormous. A recent Equal Opportunities Commission survey (1989) estimated that women's private care of vulnerable adults would cost approximately £24 billion per year if provided in the public sector and out of public funds.**
>
> [Crowley, 1992, p. 84]

So, although women spend less time caring for children and more time in waged (most of it part-time) work, 'the time spent caring for the elderly and infirm has increased, and will continue to do so. Thus the burden of care has shifted and women's waged labour continues to be influenced by the demands of their unwaged labour' (Crowley, 1992, p. 84).

The Individual Liberationist Critique of Social Conservatism

Box 15.4: Happy families: a game of charades

'On one thing most politicians and social theorists agree – family breakdown is A Bad Thing and Something Must Be Done. The right call for a return to lifelong fetters in divorce law, the left for counselling and mediation. Some look westwards for their social inspiration and call for birth outside wedlock (among the poor and genetically challenged) to be punished by a variety of Dickensian measures, mothers locked up in barracks, their offspring in orphanages.

... Marriage rates are at their lowest since records began 150 years ago. One in three births occurs outside marriage. One in four new marriages will end in divorce. One in five families with dependent children is headed by a lone parent. Social mayhem, push the moral panic button, crank up your instant indignators, ... and blame it all on the 1960s.

Let me say it out loud – the permissive society is the civilised society ... These figures represent the fruits of freedom. Current social problems make us forget history all too easily. A brutal past is blotted out in nostalgia for the golden days of the family when Darby and Joan hobbled contentedly into the sunset, never a cross word between them.

Oral historians ... have been collecting old people's stories about their own lives – love, sex, marriage, childbirth and parenthood. And it does not look rosy at all. Old people talk of a lifetime of despair, harnessed to the wrong partner. Social stigma, poverty and the divorce laws shackled people together in silent misery, or worse.

A brief fling in pre-contraceptive days could destroy a girl. Some were locked up in mental institutions by their caring, sharing old-world families. Many left their babies ... in ... orphanages, where they promptly saved money by dying. More often, the shame of pregnancy forced the pair into marriage with a partner they hardly knew; parish records show how many babies always were conceived before marriage. This is something 'communities' do.

Everything looked good on the outside, and it was never the business of the state to inquire what went on behind family doors. But was it socially 'better'? There is no Fall. Antediluvian solutions don't work, and you can't unwind the myriad changes in economy and society that have taken place in the 20th century. There is no quantifier for collective happiness. All I know is which society I would rather live and bring up my children in ...

The word Family is a dangerous political talisman. Family, community, nation ... A whiff of something faintly suspicious can be caught, from time to time, wafting from Tony Blair's camp. According to Amitai Etzioni, the guru of communitarianism, "the United Kingdom has not yet reached the levels of moral anarchy we witness in the United States, but the trends are clear. Increases in rates of violent crime, illegitimacy, drug abuse, children who kill and show no remorse and political corruption are all significant symptoms."

Etzioni talks of "grave social ill health" and the cracking of moral and social foundations. If the family is the building block of a stable society, the implication is that if we put it back together again, with everyone behind the right front doors, all will be well. There is a curious mismatch between the real world of our friends, relations, colleagues, soap operas on television, the gossip we read and indulge in – in short, the life we live – and the words of concern about the family that trip so readily off the tongues of policy makers. Have they no daughters, step-daughters, sisters, lovers, ex-wives? Is there no divorce all around them, too? Some may even have sons who are having affairs with older women. Public morality has always been a code for the morals of the poor. In other words, it isn't about morality at all, but about money, and how to pay for the poor.

Three times more children are poor than in 1979. Thirty-two percent of children now live in families with less than half average income, and that is due in part to divorces and single parenthood. Society is still modelled on a system where the man works and the woman minds. When the man departs, the woman is largely helpless, since women still earn only 75% of men's wages. The huge growth in working women is mainly in part-time jobs as second earners. Few can earn enough to become breadwinners. The single mother problem is really a problem of inequality between women and men ...

The idea of a tax incentive to marriage recently excited the Archbishop of York. The inadvertent effects of tax policies made without due regard to social impact are legion. But to swing it the other way would now be to penalise single parents, who struggle most. A bribe to couples might make more co-habiters bother to get the bit of paper, but would it induce them to stay together if the relationship fails?

That's just the trouble. Policy makers are clutching at levers in disused signal boxes: nothing much happens when you pull them. The sad history of the Child Support Agency is a good case. By punitive seizure of funds from fathers, it was supposed to make men think again before abandoning their families. It was severe enough to have an effect, but it didn't send men scuttling home. They simply rebelled, with the full support of most of the newspapers who lead the pack in social moralising.'

Source: Polly Toynbee, *The Independent*, 22 February 1995.

Individual liberationist anti-welfarism (1): Marxism and the nuclear family

For Marxists, capitalist society is best understood as being based on a particular kind of economy – a class-based way of producing goods. This is described by Marxists as a '**mode of production**' in which a '**dominant class**' of capital-owners exploit the '**labour power**' of a '**subordinate class**' of commodity producers, giving them wages in return for their labour of much less value than the market value of the goods they produce by working.

mode of production
A Marxist concept which refers to the structured relationship between the means of production (raw materials, land, labour and tools), and the relations of production (the ways humans are involved in production).

dominant class
A Marxist term which refers to the property owning class who, by virtue of their ownership of the means of production, possess political power.

labour power
In Marxist theory a commodity to be bought and sold; this term refers to the workers' ability to produce goods.

subordinate class
A Marxist term for the working class who are exploited by the dominant class (*see* dominant class).

Typical Marxist analyses of social life in modern industrial capitalist societies seek to demonstrate that the ways people live will always have benefits for capitalism as a particular form of *economic* activity, however remote from economic life these may appear to be. Thus, Marxists are interested in identifying both those features of nuclear family living which have direct pay-offs for capitalist commodity production *and* the kinds of methods used to encourage people to live in this economically beneficial way. These methods include encouraging people to want to live this sort of family life but also include arranging things so that they have little or no choice. Ideas which people learn through socialisation in capitalist society which persuade them that this is the right way to live or which seek to hide from their gaze the realities of the exploitation capitalism is based on are called '*ideologies*' by Marxists. So Marxist analyses of modern family life seek to reveal not only the ways in which the kinds of lives lived by nuclear family members benefit capitalism but also that the kinds of ideas they have – the ways in which they are encouraged to think about their world – do so too. In sociological jargon, this is described as being interested in revealing both the *structural* features of the nuclear family and its *ideological* supports. What is it about contemporary nuclear family life that Marxists could use to demonstrate their case? The following arguments have been made:

- Capitalist commodity producers are exploited labourers. Encouraging them to value family life above all else diverts their attention away from the realities of their work experiences.

- Women are encouraged to want to be wives and mothers – to believe that this is a nature-directed destiny. Marxists – and Marxist-Feminists – say that such ideological coercion produces enormous benefits for capitalism, and at no cost. The domestic labour performed by wives and mothers is unpaid. If commodity producers had to purchase domestic services, their employers would have to pay far higher wages to cover these costs. Furthermore, child-rearing is, from a capitalist's point of view, the reproduction of new generations of commodity producers, free.

reserve army of labour

Used to describe how women are brought into the work place in times of labour shortage, and then, when they are no longer needed, are encouraged, by prevailing ideologies, to return to the home (*see* ideology).

- Women constitute a '**reserve army of labour**', available to be temporarily used as commodity producers in times of crisis, until such time as they are no longer needed, when naturalism can be reinvoked to encourage them to return to the domestic sphere.

- Because a wife is deemed to be economically dependent on her husband, when she does enter the waged labour market she can be treated far worse than a male labourer has to be. She can be – and usually is – paid less than a man, denied access to the better-paid jobs, consigned to part-time, casual or seasonal work and denied entitlements such as sick pay, holiday pay, proper pension rights, access to incremental rewards, or a proper career structure; she can be denied maternity leave, denied the chance of a job at all because of her child-producing potential, and so on. (Indeed, on 15 September 1993, an RAF servicewoman who was discharged because she became pregnant was awarded £20,000 compensation. At the time of writing, 400 similar cases concerning RAF personnel are pending, which it is estimated could eventually cost the RAF up to £100 million.)

- Some Marxists have argued that children and the elderly are similarly disadvantaged. Entering and leaving the labour market can be manipulated for these categories of people and disguised as humanitarianism and benevolence. Thus, it could be said that childhood is socially constructed to deny young people the chance to earn a wage until reaching a particular age and then typified as being in the child's interest. Furthermore, being forced to remain the responsibility of their parents for a long period encourages in children the internalisation of values beneficial to employers, such as the acceptance of authority and of the normalcy of gendered life chances. Similarly, older people are forced to leave paid employme at a certain age and this is justified by the exercise of ideologies regarding ageing and dependency. In both these ways, the unemployment rate is manipulated and reserve armies of labour similar to that made up by women are made available in case of emergencies.

Individual liberationist anti-welfarism (2): radical feminism and the nuclear family

It is the gender prescriptions inherent in naturalistic family discourse that radical feminists have attacked. For them, Welfarism, however well-meaning, because it is aimed at propping up a particular version of family life, is in effect an instrument of women's subordination. For radical feminism, the nuclear family is a prime site in which women are exploited in modern society; activities and ideas designed to reproduce and strengthen such a family form are therefore by definition social and cultural weapons by which women are oppressed.

For radical feminists, the shackling of women in such a way is part of a general system of oppression they call *Patriarchy*, which means 'Rule by Men'. Pointing out that the Marxist-feminist interest in social relations and ideologies in capitalist societies as the source of female subordination ignores the ubiquity of the oppression experienced by women in non-capitalist societies too, radical feminists seek to identify a much more general source. For many of them, the culprit is family life based on heterosexual partnerships, and for this sort of feminism the nuclear family is the repository of patriarchy in modern societies. Though acknowledging the importance in the construction of patriarchy of the discourses which discipline family life in the ways we've already described, some radical feminists have, in recent years, focused more on intra-familial male–female relationships as its root cause. Arguing that the '**personal is the political**', a strong version of radical feminism focuses on sexuality and violence in male-female relationships as both the engine, and a mirror, of patriarchy.

personal is the political
Adopted originally by Radical feminists to draw attention to issues of sexuality and violence in interpersonal male–female relationships.

compulsory heterosexuality
Associated with Adrienne Rich, this concept implies that heterosexuality is not so much the natural form of sexual preference but is imposed upon individuals by social constraints.

For example, Adrienne Rich speaks of the '**compulsory heterosexuality**' underpinning male–female relationships in nuclear families and, in the same way as other writers on sexual freedom have done, problematises the naturalistic discourse which normalises heterosexuality. Why should penetrative sex, which involves the male exploiting the body of women, be deemed to be 'natural' while other forms of sexuality are not? With Masters and Johnson having disposed of the vaginal orgasm as a physiological myth, radical feminists argue that the discourse promoting penetrative sex as 'normal' is thereby exposed as a patriarchal device. Indeed, heterosexual relations are, for many radical feminists, essentially *power* relations, as the kind of language they employ indicates: typically, they see the women's body being 'colonised' and 'occupied' by the man for his pleasure, with such an appropriation symbolising the subjugation of the women's life, mind and identity which constitutes patriarchy. Indeed, the symbolic violence which such radical feminists see perpetrated on women by men in their sexual relations for them leads directly to the actual physical and mental violence often used by men against their wives in modern nuclear families.

separatism
A position put forward by some radical feminists as a solution to patriarchy. Based on the notion that the sexual act embodies patriarchal exploitation of women, it proposes that women should live separate lives from men (*see* patriarchy).

It is from this critique that the solution to patriarchy favoured by some radical feminists springs. Called '**separatism**', the injunction is for women to live lives – even lesbian ones – separately from men, since only by doing so can they be liberated from the patriarchal construction of heterosexual, penetrative, sex as normal.

Individual liberationist anti-welfarism (3): sexual liberationism

Writers on sexual liberty have argued that the naturalism inherent in Welfarism's view of normal family life is not restricted to the activity of mothering or caring for the elderly, since it also informs the view that a 'normal' sexual relationship can only be monogamous and heterosexual. Such a discourse, it is argued, not only ignores the diversity of sexual practices equally validly engaged in by humans. More sinister is its castigation of such practices as deviant – as abnormal or perverse, thereby denying alternative sexual lifestyles and their practitioners the legitimacy that modern thinking should afford them. In effect, the argument is that the promotion of monogamous heterosexuality as 'normal' within 'normal' families marginalises and stigmatises practitioners of other forms of sexuality such as homosexuals and lesbians, masturbators, the sexually active (at least if they are female), and sadomasochists, rubber or bondage enthusiasts, for example. The language employed in such a sexuality discourse powerfully evokes the normalising consequences of its promulgation: 'queers', 'poofs' and 'dykes'; 'wankers' and 'tossers'; 'sluts' and 'tarts'; 'perverts' and fetishists – nobody describes enthusiastic monogamous heterosexuality as perversion or fetishism! All these bodily practices are condemned as abnormal by the dominance of a discourse whose project is to promote a particular form of sexuality in a particular form of family. The liberationist argument is that while love and affection may be a precondition for individual happiness, there is no reason to suppose that it can only be experienced by adults involved in stable, monogamous, heterosexual unions.

Box 15.5: The Social Conservative critique of individual liberationism

'Slowly, the ratchet of hard facts is yanking debate about the family painfully in the right direction … accumulated evidence shows children whose parents separate run greater risks of educational, health and behaviour problems than those whose families remain intact …

[However], anyone who has pointed this out during the last few years has had to run a gauntlet of abuse from people claiming – falsely – that the facts are otherwise. Since those people form the vocal majority in the social sciences and the media, the pressures on those who have tried to tell the truth are formidable and deeply unpleasant. They have been treated as intellectual and political pariahs.

When the sociologist A. H. Halsey stood up and said it in 1991, he was denounced as senile and, far worse, right-wing. His ethical socialist colleague, Norman Dennis, battled away to reveal how research on the family was misrepresented by cowardly and self-serving intellectuals. Many who go in for this misrepresentation are divorced themselves, or have bust up other people's marriages, or are currently cheating on their spouses. Policy discussions on the family are thus almost inevitably the continuation of personal predicaments through other means. Now, however, the sheer weight of the evidence is forcing the debate into the realm of reality. But the resistance is still massive …

The death of the traditional family is said to be much exaggerated. But nobody is saying it is dead. The alarm is over [the 30 per cent of families with young children, not headed by both natural parents] and the personal and social damage that follows from that. Thirty per cent means a lot of children. And the further alarm is over the fact that the trend is growing, not to mention the exponential growth of the problem. Children from fractured families are more likely to grow up unable to form permanent relationships and produce in turn children whose emotional stability is yet weaker still. It is the Self-Serving Intellectuals whose position on this point is illogical. They shout that society can't turn the clock back, that the changes in family structure are irrevocable (and a good thing too! they roar) that everyone is now into individual lifestyle choices. They dance on the grave of the nuclear family. Now, however, they claim that same, hated nuclear family is still the model for the over-whelming majority of the population, and so there's no reason for alarm! The facts are rather that those minority lifestyle choices are growing as fast as they are because these SSIs have campaigned to turn them into the norm. The custodians of popular culture connive at promoting the impression that everyone is into serial relationships. And it is obviously vital to that campaign to play down or deny any evidence that such behaviour produces harmful consequences …

Some children who are raped by their fathers grow up to be stable, well-adjusted adults. Why some children survive circumstances that pulverise others remains a mystery. That hardly means we should be indifferent to the destructive effects of rape on children. So it should follow with family breakdown. Unpredictability of outcomes is a straw argument clutched by people who are desperate to deny that presumption of harm resulting from family breakdown.

Another straw is that the real killer for children is marital conflict, rather than separated parents. Well, of course such conflict is destructive. But it is pretty obvious that parental conflict is likely to increase around *and after* separation, when one of the main areas of contention is – double horror – the children themselves ... the family debate [is characterised] as polarising between those who pin various social ills on the decline of the nuclear family and those who see economic insecurities as the enemy of family stability ... [This] omits the crucial point that the latter group largely endorses the decline of the traditional family. They insist that any problems associated with new family structures can be overcome.

To think otherwise would be to acknowledge the dreadful truth, that adults now require children to pay a terrible price for their own gratification. Facing up the that would mean our society would again actively promote marriage as a social good, thus changing the cultural climate.'

Source: Melanie Phillips, *The Observer*, 26 February 1995.

The New Right Critique of Individual Liberationism

Clearly Individual Liberationist arguments are also anathema to New Right thinking, and in recent years, despite many of the protagonists on both sides being committed to a version of modernity which sees progress as a matter of individual emancipation, a violent debate has been conducted, which because of the genuine philosophical and moral detestation involved, has been, and still is, largely a dialogue of the deaf. Thus, the New Right has proclaimed itself vehemently opposed to crucial items on individual liberationism's family agenda such as:

- the right to easily dissolve an unhappy marriage
- the right of single parents – and particularly mothers who want to work – to be adequately supported by the state

- the right of a woman to terminate a pregnancy
- the right to pursue sexual satisfaction in other than monogamous, heterosexual ways
- the right of women not to want to be mothers
- the right of family members not to care for elderly relatives, and
- the concomitant right of the needy old to be fully supported by the state.

Thus, though New Right views represent an ideological position profoundly committed to promoting the nuclear family against the satanic anti-Welfarist liberationist views of some wicked sociologists, they nonetheless involve the claim that true freedom for family members involves reducing Welfarism as much as possible. So they earnestly support the traditional family with all its features but not only deny the *necessity* for Welfarism but propose it is positively destructive in that it involves the legislation and regulation of what individuals should decide on and arrange for themselves.

Three points need to be made however. First, despite the 'freedom for the individual' version of modernity reflected in New Right discourse, it appears that freedom for individual women to do other than perform family functions is a freedom too far, even for radical libertarians. Second, from a Foucauldian point of view, New Right thinking, though designed to liberate individuals and enable them to be free to choose, in fact merely constitutes a new form of regulation, prescription and control; here is a discourse which uses the withdrawal of state facilities as the disciplinary device designed to ensure we feel we must live in nuclear families and feel we must fend for ourselves. Finally, we should note the important link with *economic* laissez-faire individualistic thinking here. 'Fending for ourselves' not only means taking moral and social responsibility for our kin. It also, and usually explicitly, insists on the virtue of using privately financed welfare provision in order to help us meet these obligations. Though acknowledging that in modern societies the capacity to support family members adequately may sometimes require resources other than those generated by women fulfilling their unique expressive, biologically endowed, caring family destinies, New Right thinking still insists that true freedom for the individual means being able to *choose* who to spend your money on and being able to *choose* how much to spend. Taxation denies individuals these freedoms. The fact that material inequalities between the better-off and the badly-off are thus not only reproduced but widened by low taxation policies is not, however, unfair. As we said earlier, this perspective insists that people are rich or poor because of their abilities, not because of factors outside their control ('There is no such thing as society ...')

Taxation penalises the able by forcing them to bail out the less able; to be truly free means being free to fail as well as succeed. Therefore, only the expansion of *private* welfare facilities, which we can choose to buy or not to buy, can thus ensure that justice is done – that we get what our efforts in life deserve.

Difference and Diversity in Modern Family Life

Theorists of modernity may disagree about the meaning of progress and about the route humans should take to move nearer to their respective utopias but they do not disagree about the possibility of such progress – so long as we organise ourselves in the way they tell us. Thus, Parsons, Social Conservatives, the New Right, and Individual Liberationists all provide us with a *meta-theory* of the family; despite their great differences, they each propose a grand, all-embracing solution to the problems posed by family life in modern society.

However, other theorists of the modern family do not claim to have such a set of universally applicable theoretical solutions to these problems. In effect, they demand that we stop thinking of contemporary family life as susceptible to generalised answers, asking instead that we realise that humans today necessarily differ in the construction of their identities as men, women and children, husbands and wives, mothers and fathers, grandmothers and grandfathers. For them, the only thing we should realise is that there is no one right answer to the problem of living a human life and that the pursuit of such a modernist holy grail – looking for the key to unlock the door leading to human happiness – is pointless. For them we should instead acknowledge the *pluralism* and *diversity* inherent in the contemporary human condition and abandon ideas that one single narrative or story can outline for us the lines we should learn to fulfil our potential and to live secure and contented lives.

The problem for modernist family theorists is that the recent research evidence does seem to support this pluralist view, contradicting the idea that monolithic, unitary prescriptions are worth pursuing. People in modern societies today seem to be living very different kinds of family lives from each other – and the differences seem to be getting bigger and bigger. As Boh (1989) puts it, writing about Europe, the only 'uniform trend in the overall development of family patterns [is] … the trend towards a recognition of diversity'. Summarising American research, Cheal says

> There is evidence (in the United States) of a growing percentage of teenage births occurring to unmarried women (Furstenberg *et al.*, 1987), and more generally of increased cohabitation before or independent of marriage (Trost, 1977; Cotton *et al.*, 1983) and of 'commuter marriages' between partners who live in different cities (Gross 1980; Gerstel and Gross, 1984). Increased divorce rates and single parenthood by choice indicate that the marriage bond is less binding, and perhaps less important, than it once was (Renvoize, 1985; Ahrono and Rodgers, 1987). This would also be confirmed by the way in which never-married and voluntarily childless life-styles have come to be recognised as viable forms of social life, that are not necessarily devoid of family ties (Veevers 1980; K. Allen, 1989). It also appears that when husbands and wives both earn large incomes they may decide not to pool them (Hertz, 1986).
>
> [CHEAL, 1991, pp. 123–4]

In Britain, Rapoport, Fogarty and Rapoport (1982) concluded that:

> Families in Britain today are in a transition from coping in a society in which there was a single overriding norm of what family life should be like to a society in which a plurality of norms are recognised as legitimate and, indeed, desirable.
>
> [RAPOPORT, FOGARTY and RAPOPORT, 1982, p. 476]

According to Henwood *et al.* (1987), as we mentioned earlier, 'a bread-winning husband and a non-working wife at home with two dependent children accounts for a mere 8% of all working men'. As Crowley puts it, today 'The "normative family" is a statistical minority' (1992, p. 80).

Life-cycle or life-course?

life-cycle
A developmental model which outlines the social changes encountered as a person passes through childhood, adolescence, mid-life, old age and death. In the context of the family the life-cycle includes courtship, marriage, child rearing, children leaving home, etc. (*see* life-course).

Such claims about the difference and diversity in contemporary family living have led to a demand that the traditional concept of the '**life-cycle**' of families be replaced with that of the **life-course** of the individual. Life-cycle theory rests upon the belief that 'normal' families go through 'normal' stages of birth, growth and decline. Marriage conceives the family, the arrival of children develops and expands it, their departure contracts it, and it ends with the death of one of the married partners. At each stage in the cycle specific problems emerge which need managing – sometimes described as the 'developmental tasks' in the normal life-cycle. Progress and fulfilment for the family – for both its members and for the society of which it is a part – depend upon

life-course
This approach dwells on the diversity of experiences and difference in the courses of people's lives. It claims that contemporary experience is more diverse and less predictable than traditional concepts of the life-cycle suggest (*see* life-cycle).

each of these tasks being successfully completed. Essentially modernist in approach, and echoing the medicalist assumptions of family therapy, the argument is that social scientific knowledge should be utilised to assist families to cope with the different demands that the life-cycle places on them: family therapists sometimes claim, for example, that family 'stress' is greater during the transition from one stage in the cycle to another and that it is at these times that the intervention of specialist knowledge can be most helpful. The analogy with medicalist assumptions about normal individual growth and development and with the notion that 'stress' resulting in 'dysfunctional' behaviour is often rooted in the transition from one role to another brought about by ageing is clear: functionalist theorising about adolescent behaviour or of responses to retirement offer obvious examples of this similarity.

Life-course studies reject the assumptions of normality and development of life-cycle theory, arguing that the contemporary diversity and difference in people's lives have detonated any validity such an approach may once have had. The argument is that life-cycle thinking can only work where male and female family lives are predictable; the evidence from contemporary life of the growth in delayed marriages, female wage-labour, single parenthood, marital and occupational instability, the large variety of educational and occupational opportunities available throughout life, the dissolution of traditional distinctions between people of different ages, and so on, demands we conceptualise family lives in ways which are much more compatible with such diversity and difference. Thus, life-course thinking 'recommends that we adopt the individual rather than the family as the basic unit of analysis ... the focus ... is on the individual's passage through a sequence of social situations, and on how each individual is affected by the passages of others' (Cheal, 1991, p. 139).

Theorising difference in family life

How should we theorise these facts of difference and diversity in contemporary family living? Two options present themselves: *action theory* and *post-modernist theory*. Action theory, anti-deterministically, explains contemporary pluralism as reflecting the capacity of actors, or subjects, to choose and negotiate alternative life-styles in the light of their perceptions of their circumstances and as their structural conditions allow. In contrast, postmodernism explains pluralism as a consequence of the fact that social worlds today are made up of complexes of competing and contradictory discourses, which act upon humans in different historical, social and cultural circumstances, thereby constituting them and constructing their identities in different ways. That is, action theory focuses on human *agency* to explain pluralism and difference in modern social life; postmodernists use *post-structural* theory to explain it, as the consequence of a new complexity in discourse-directed social existences.

Human agency and the family

Janet Finch (1987) insists on the relevance of action theory to family sociology, arguing that the study of family obligations is 'part of the central task of understanding ... the puzzle of human agency' in contemporary societies:

> **On the one hand, family obligations can be seen as part of normative rules which operate within a particular society, and which simply get applied in appropriate situations. On the other hand, they can be seen as agreements which operate between specific individuals and are arrived at through a process of negotiation ... using the concept of 'negotiation' very much in an interactionist sense ... a full understanding of what family obligations mean and how they operate almost certainly contain elements of both.**
>
> [Finch, 1987, pp. 155–6]

To illustrate her argument, Finch asks us to consider the position of a family of siblings who know their ageing parents will eventually need

Source: *Private Eye*

'Oh, look mother, it's Mabel's special – alphabet noodle soup'

some sort of care. British family norms specify an obligation on children to care for dependent relatives if it becomes necessary. However, Finch argues that theorising on the basis of such norms alone cannot tell us the whole story: probably without realising they are doing it, children in such a position will negotiate among themselves the manner in which such an obligation is to be fulfilled. As she puts it:

> **it is unlikely ... that the three siblings will wait until the time comes when their parents actually need care, then open up round-the-table talks to decide precisely how each will fulfil his or her responsibilities. Probably such overt negotiations will never be necessary, because over a period of time – probably covering many years – it will gradually become 'obvious' to all concerned that when the time comes, one particular sibling (almost certainly a daughter) will actually be the one to provide daily care, another will perhaps provide some financial support, and the third will take the parents for a month in the summer. In this instance, concrete obligations between specified individuals have been arrived at in some way through a process of negotiation, but these negotiations themselves are shaped by the general normative prescriptions about children taking responsibility for their elderly parent. I see it as a central tack of any empirical work in this field to explore the relationship between moral norms and negotiation of obligations, and to understand the processes through which such arrangements ... become 'obvious'.**
>
> **[Finch, 1987, pp. 156–7]**

interpretive
Having an interest in the meanings underpinning social action. Synonymous with social action theory (*see* social action).

structuration theory
The emergence and transformation of structural patterning in social life. For Giddens, the theory that links structure and agency as simultaneous dimensions of social life (*see* structure *and* agency).

Finch thus argues that an **interpretive** element must always be added to the normative analysis of family life, and on these grounds rejects the exclusively systemic orientation of life-cycle theorising, and, by implication, of monolithic modernist approaches to family life. For neither in the case of the individual nor the family, she says, is it satisfactory to use an approach which sees life progressing through predictable stages. Instead, because individual and family biographies are constructed through *time*, we have to recognise the need to build in 'an understanding of the social, political and economic contexts in which obligations are negotiated, honoured and abandoned' (p. 168). Finch thus endorses Abrams's view that sociological analysis must recognise that 'history and society are made by constant and more or less purposeful human action and that individual action, however purposeful, is made by history and society' (Abrams, 1982, p. xiii).

Such a dual interest is given more systematic theoretical endorsement by the **structuration theory** of Tony Giddens (see Chapter 18). Giddens attempts a synthesis of structural and action approaches. Human actors, he says, should be seen as '**knowledgeable agents**' who construct their own theories of their circumstances which then motivate them to act in particular ways. However, not only do the structural conditions of their existence exercise real constraint and impose limitations, but such structural features are indissolubly bound up with such actions, being either reproduced, or transformed, by these actions. That is, structures cannot be created independently of actions while actions can never take place except within structural circumstances. From this point of view, families and family obligations are real objective features in a world of real normative and material factors; however, not only do the interpretive capacities of actors inform their negotiation of their lives within these factual circumstances, but by so doing, they thereby either reproduce these external features or transform them. Among action theorists, only ethnomethodologists, for whom social occasions are sites in which human actors make unique, context-bound efforts to make these occasions work, would deny the interplay between structure and action in family life. As a result, all ethnomethodological work, whether about family life or anything else, is only concerned with revealing the contingent and epistemologically relative methods members of social occasions use to establish order in them.

knowledgeable agents
Employed by Giddens, a description of the capacity human actors have to reflexively construct theories of their own circumstances and form courses of action (*see* reflexivity).

Relativism also underpins the *post-structuralist* theory on which *post-modern* approaches to contemporary family diversity rest; but here the relativism involved is not *subject*-centred, but *discourse*-centred. To put this another way, while postmodern writers argue for a view of social life which results in difference, following Foucault, they say that the selection of different ways of living is not a choice freely made by the subject; instead, it is a *discursively* directed route.

relativism
An approach which denies the existence of absolute truth, but maintains that beliefs, values and theories are relative to time and place. Accordingly, traditions and ways of life can only be judged in the context of the age or society that has produced them.

Postmodern theorising and the family

Here we have an anti-agency sociology of the kind favoured by traditional structural theorising. However, it is *post*-structural in that the view of a monolithic structure of forces generating social life is abandoned in favour of an emphasis on the variety of constituting discourses. As in the case of language, where we are obliged to learn already-existing ways of describing the world in order to identify it for ourselves at all, so in the case of discourse-centred reality, different ways of knowing about the world exercise similar compulsion over us. But difference and diversity is inevitable since reality is revealed to subjects via discourses in competing and contradictory ways; though sometimes the dominance of a discourse makes a particular way of knowing about the world *appear* to be objectively true – and, by obvious implication, alternatives false – this is only because of the greater power of such a discourse, not its nearer approximation to 'the' truth.

The result is an epistemology completely embracing relativism. All forms of knowing about the world are as likely to be true as any other – no priority can be given to one over another. As subjects, we are inevitably in the thrall of the discourses we encounter and though these provide us with our versions of reality, such accounts (though they don't seem so to us) are entirely contingent and relative: humans always see their worlds selectively, partially, discursively. Our 'chosen' ways of living can be traced to forces outside ourselves, but, as human beings too, sociologists have no way of judging the truth about such forces, since their sociological knowledge is discursively constructed too. No subject – sociologist or not – can know except via discourse.

In this way, post-structuralism provides an epistemological foundation for postmodernism. The modernist project must be abandoned in favour of a recognition of the pluralism and difference inherent in the constitution of human identities and in the construction of human knowledge. Thus postmodern theorising 'indicates a move away from universalism towards the tolerance of local knowledge (Lyotard, 1984) and the need to admit the "other" as co-equal speaker in human dialogues' (Featherstone and Hepworth, 1989, p. 145).

In this emphasis, post-structuralism and post-modernity have detonated the presumptions of objective virtue characteristic of modernist forms of theorising of whatever kind; we must be tolerant of the accounts of the world provided by others and we must acknowledge the relativity – and fortuity – of our own.

Difference and diversity is the only certain characteristic of human living. Thus, modern family life is inevitably a world of contrasts and even opposition: no one form of sexuality, or of partnership, or of marriage, or of child-rearing, or of growing older, can be judged to be superior to any other – at least, not by another human being, whose judgements are themselves directed by discourse.

Does this solve the matter then? Is it a case of 'anything goes' – we do our own thing and let others do theirs? But both practical and moral difficulties arise from such a position. What if others doing their own thing prevents us from doing ours? Do we let them? *Can* we let them? Surely humans can only live their lives by acting on their judgements, morals and values? Should we not fight for our versions of the decent life, even if we recognise the relativity of their foundations? In effect, do we encourage tolerance against dogmatism or should we respect conviction and commitment against indifference? What do you think? Are *you* modern or postmodern? (See Chapters 16 and 19 for further discussions of these issues.)

Summary of the Chapter

- Forms of the family vary enormously, both historically and cross-culturally.
- Functionalist theories of the modern family argue that the nuclear family best meets the needs of an industrial economy.
- Using the ideas of Michel Foucault, it becomes possible to identify modern discourses which have promoted nuclear family life and fostered the importance of nuclear family identities.
- Two principal discursive agencies designed to do this have been medicine and post-Second World War state-sponsored family policies.
- Both Social Conservative and New Right political philosophies have, for different reasons, emphasised the importance of the nuclear family in modern societies.
- Individual Liberationist objections to the nuclear family, and to the discourses which promote this family form, focus on the lack of individual freedom and empowerment experienced by nuclear family members.
- Recent evidence shows a rapid increase in the diversity of family living.
- Two theoretical explanations of this differentiation offer themselves: action theory and postmodernism.

References

Abrams, P. (1982) *Historical Sociology*, London, Open Books.

Ahrono, C. and R. Rodgers (1987) *Divorced Families*, London, W. W. Norton.

Allen, K. (1989) *Single Women/Family Ties*, Newbury Park, Sage.

Ariès, P. (1973) *Centuries of Childhood*, Harmondsworth, Penguin.

Boh, K. (1989) *Changing Patterns of European Family Life*, London, Routledge.

Bowlby, J. (1965) *Child Care and the Growth of Love*, Harmondsworth, Penguin.

Bowlby, J. (1971) *Attachment and Loss, vol. I*, Harmondsworth, Penguin.

Bowlby, J. (1975) *Attachment and Loss, vol. II*, Harmondsworth, Penguin.

Bradley, H. (1992) 'Changing social divisions: class, gender and race', in R. Bocock and K. Thompson (eds), *Social and Cultural Forms of Modernity*, Oxford, Polity Press.

Cheal, D. (1991) *Family and the State of Theory*, Hemel Hempstead, Harvester Wheatsheaf.

Cotton, S. *et al.* (1983) 'Living together', in A. Burns *et al.* (eds), *The Family in the Modern World*, London, Allen & Unwin.

Crowley, H. (1992) Women and the Domestic Sphere in R. Bocock and K. Thompson (eds), *Social and Cultural Forms of Modernity*, Oxford, Polity Press.

Edholm, F. (1982) 'The unnatural family', in E. Whitelegg *et al.* (eds), *The Changing Experience of Women*, Oxford, Martin Robertson.

Etzioni, A. (1995) 'The parental deficit', *The Guardian*.

Featherstone, M. and M. Hepworth (1989) 'Ageing and old age: reflections on the postmodern life course', in B. Bytheway *et al.* (eds), *Becoming and Being Old*, London, Sage.

Finch, J. (1987) 'Family obligations and the life course', in A. Bryman *et al.* (eds), *Rethinking the Life Cycle*, London, Macmillan.

Fox, R. (1967) *Kinship and Marriage*, Harmondsworth, Penguin.

Furstenburg, F. *et al.* (1987) *Adolescent Mothers in Late Life*, Cambridge, Cambridge University Press.

Gerstel, N. and H. Gross (1984) *Commuter Marriage*, London, Guildford Press.

Green, H. (1988) *Informal Carers* (*General Household Survey 1985*, Supplement) London, HMSO.

Gross, H. (1980) 'Dual-career couples who live apart' *Journal of Marriage and the Family*, 42.

Henwood, M. *et al.* (1987) *Inside the Family: Changing Roles of Women and Men*, London, Family Policy Study Centre.

Hertz, R. (1986) *More Equal than Others*, Berkeley, Calif., University of California Press.

Lyotard, J.-F. (1984) *The Postmodern Condition*, Manchester, Manchester University Press.

Lister, R. (1984) 'There is an alternative', in A. Walker and C. Walker (eds), *The Growing Divide*, London, CPAG.

Morgan, D. H. J. (1985) *The Family, Politics and Social Theory*, London, Routledge & Kegan Paul.

Oakley, A. (1974) *The Sociology of Housework*, London, Martin Robertson.

Phillips, M. (1995) *The Observer*, 26 February.

Rapoport, R. N., M. Fogarty and R. Rapoport (1982) *Families in Britain*, London, Routledge & Kegan Paul.

Renvoize, J. (1985) *Going Solo*, London, Routledge & Kegan Paul.

Stanworth, M. (1987) *Reproductive Technologies*, Oxford, Polity Press.

Toynbee, P. (1995) 'Happy families: a game of charades', *The Independent*, 22 February.

Trost, J. (1977) 'The family life cycle: a problematic concept', in J. Cuisenier (ed.), *The Family Life Cycle in European Societies*, The Hague, Mouton.

Turner, B. (1987) *Medical Power and Social Knowledge*, London, Sage.

Veevers, J. (1980) *Childless by Choice*, Toronto, Butterworth.

Wilson, E. (1977) *Women and the Welfare State*, London, Tavistock.

Young, M. and P. Wilmott (1973) *The Symmetrical Family*, London, Routledge & Kegan Paul.

16 Knowledge, Belief and Religion

Aims of the Chapter

This chapter examines one of the major debates concerning the emergence of modern social life: does the rise of rationalism, represented by scientific thinking and practices, mean that modern human beings have access to a form of cognition, and consequently, a kind of knowledge, which is markedly superior to any other kind?

Or should science be seen as just one more human endeavour, whose knowledge-claims are no better and no worse than other kinds, whether these others coexist with science in modern societies or whether they are found in times and places different from our own?

This debate is sometimes described as being about the existence of a Big Ditch or Great Divide between forms of knowledge; we can summarise it as being between supporters of Rationalism and supporters of Relativism.

Introduction

It is only human to want to acquire knowledge we can be sure of. However, it is also only human to have wishes and desires, hopes and dreams. How then can humans discover the truth about their world? Is it possible for us to find out the way things really are or will our feelings about the way we'd *like* things to be always get in the way? Is it possible for humans to describe the world as it would describe itself if it could? According to its supporters, it is only by using *scientific* thinking and practices that humans can reveal the truth about the world. While there always have been, and always will be, any number of alternative accounts of how and why the world is as it is, such as religious or magical explanations, for example, its advocates insist that only by using science can humans prove the truth of their knowledge-claims. According to this viewpoint, the emergence of science as a way of thinking and acting represented the great leap forward for humankind. The realisation that it is possible for humans to think *rationally* and therefore act scientifically was, according to this account, the defining moment in the history of human thought. The name given to this historical moment is the '**Enlightenment**' and, for those who argue for the unique and superior qualities of scientific thinking and practices over all others, it was the Enlightenment that allowed humans, for the first time, to really know the nature of things. In fact, for rationalists, it was during the Enlightenment that humans crossed the 'Great Divide', from ignorance, guesswork and faith, to certainty and truth.

the Enlightenment
An eighteenth century philosophical movement based on notions of progress through the application of reason and rationality. Enlightenment philosophers foresaw a world free from religious dogma, within human control, and leading ultimately to emancipation for all humankind.

Source: *Private Eye*

'Well I don't call it heaven when we're not allowed to sniff each other's bottoms'

Great Divide Thinking

A good example of Great Divide thinking is found in the work of the philosopher and anthropologist Ernest Gellner. Gellner wishes to distinguish between:

- *a non-rational* knowledge/explanatory system, such as a religion, which 'believes in a unique truth and which believes itself to be in possession of it' (1992, p. vii);
- *relativism*, which denies the existence of a unique, objective truth, arguing that all beliefs and knowledge-claims have equal validity;
- *rationalism*, which
  (a) believes in the existence of an objective truth, but does not think that humans can ever acquire this knowledge for certain;
  (b) claims it is superior to any other form of knowledge, not because it argues for the supremacy of any particular set of ideas, but because of the uniquely effective *method* of producing knowledge it uses.

This is how Gellner characterises relativism, which, for him, totally fails to portray adequately knowledge in the modern world, on this side of the Great Divide:

Relativism ... postulates a symmetrical world. Culture A has its own vision of itself and of culture B, and, likewise, B has its own vision of itself and of A. The same goes for the entire range of cultures. A must not sit in judgement on B nor vice versa, nor must B see A in terms of itself ...

Often members of both A and B are likely to be somewhat ethnocentric, given to thinking that their own concepts capture the world as it really is, and that the Other should see himself and everything else in their own terms, and is being silly if he fails to do so ...

(For relativism) The truth is that all cultures are equal, and no single one of them has the right to judge and interpret the others in its own terms ... above all ... it must not claim that the world is correctly described in its own terms.

[Gellner, 1992, pp. 56–7]

According to Gellner, this description bears no relation to the actual state of knowledge in modern societies:

The world we actually inhabit is totally different. Some two millennia and a half ago, it did perhaps more or less resemble the world the relativist likes to paint ... there was a multiplicity of communities, each with its own rites and legends. It would have been truly absurd to try to elevate one of them above the others, and, still more, to claim that the truth about any one of them was only to be had in the terminology of another.

[Gellner, 1992, p. 57]

Then the world became transformed. The Great Divide occurred, when rationalism, a secular, non-religious, non-magical way of thinking, emerged, producing knowledge we now know as *natural science*. Scientific ideas and practices are unique:

- The knowledge science produces applies to any cultural setting;
- When this knowledge has been applied to achieve particular ends, it has totally transformed human existence;
- Scientific knowledge is indifferent to culture and morals. Indeed, it often confounds our most deeply held desires and hopes, giving us an account of reality which resolutely and persistently fails to comfort or to console, or to reassure us that things really are the way we would like them to be. In this it is in direct contrast to previous forms of learning.

Scientific knowledge is cumulative, growing 'faster and faster ... it does not endlessly retrace its steps or fragment arbitrarily or go round in circles as had been the general fate of previous essays at theorising about the world' (Gellner, 1992, p. 59). This is because scientists, whatever their disagreements about the meaning of particular results, nevertheless agree about how to produce knowledge, about how to go about replacing existing ideas with better ones.

Unlike relativism, then, rationalism holds 'all men and minds but *not* all cultures and systems of meaning, to be equal' (Gellner, 1992, p. 37). Every human mind is capable of discovering the truth, but only by employing the correct method to do so. Rationalism argues that, in effect, 'there are an awful lot of meanings and opinions about, that they cannot all be right, and that we'd better find, and justify, a yardstick which will sort the sheep from the goats' (Gellner, 1992, p. 38). The Great Divide opened up when this method was devised. How does it work? What is unique about scientific knowledge production?

What is Science?

positivism

A doctrine which claims that social life should be understood and analysed in the same way that scientists study the 'natural world'. Underpinning this philosophy is the notion that phenomena exist in causal relationships and these can be empirically observed, tested and measured.

Scientific activity operates with specific assumptions, usually associated with the term **positivism**, which can be summarised as follows. Things – phenomena which have an existence identifiable by human senses – are in an endless chain of causation. Anything which the human senses can identify is as it is because it has been caused by some other thing which our senses also allow us to recognise. Sometimes science deals with abstract phenomena too. Concepts (ideas) like volume, pressure, temperature, etc. are highly significant aspects of the reality dealt with by science. However, scientists always try to give such concepts physical indicators identifiable by senses; thus a thermometer renders temperature visible, a barometer does the same for pressure and so on. This is called *operationalising* concepts. To be sure of a cause-and-effect relationship between things, we have to be able to demonstrate its existence to other humans. Scientists insist that we can be certain of the causes of things – to be able to claim we have knowledge which other humans cannot dispute – only if we can *prove* their existence. Such proof can only be acquired by producing empirical evidence – evidence which the human senses can recognise. That is, scientific knowledge is solely based on *facts* – demonstrable evidence of the nature of things. How can science guarantee the exclusive factual basis of its knowledge-claims?

Science doesn't make facts – its aim is to reveal their existence. That is, facts are *objective* – they exist, whether we like it or not. Though we may not like the fact that grass is green, or that a full bladder requires emptying, or that smoking is likely to cause lung cancer, they are nonetheless natural and biological features of our existence that we can do nothing about. Of course, humans are not only able to recognise facts but are capable of being *subjective* too – of having opinions and exercising judgements about such facts. However, positivism demands that this human ability to have a viewpoint – to value something or not, to have feelings about how things ought to be – must be ignored by scientists when seeking to produce knowledge based on empirical evidence. For us to be able to rely on scientific evidence – to trust its account of reality – we must be sure that whatever scientists may personally think about the way things are, they nonetheless describe the facts they uncover *objectively*, ignoring any feelings, favourable or unfavourable, they may have about this state of affairs.

Karl Popper (1902–1994) was one of the most famous philosophers of science. According to Popper, only one kind of methodological procedure can ensure such an objective, value-free, disclosure of the facts of reality. He called this the *Hypothetico–deductive* method. This involves breaking the world down into the particular individual cause-and-effect relationships which it is believed together make it up and trying to produce empirical evidence of the existence of each relationship in isolation from all the others. This aspect of science is sometimes described as the '*atomisation*' of reality, since it involves breaking the whole up into its constituent parts. Scientists use the term *hypothesis* to describe a particular cause-and-effect relationship believed to be a part of reality but as yet uninvestigated. In the natural sciences, hypothesis-testing usually involves the physical isolation in a *laboratory* of the phenomena believed to be in a causal relationship. Laboratory research takes the form of an *experiment*, which involves measuring, or *quantifying*, the extent to which something – the *independent variable* in the experiment – causes something else – the *dependent* variable.

According to Popper, however, there is logically no way we can ever be sure that things will always remain the way the facts suggest they are at the time we uncover them. As he says in a famous example, just because we have always seen white swans coming round a river bend, this doesn't prove that a black swan won't appear next time we look. This human inability to be sure of the future means that our knowledge, even if exclusively factually-based, can only be seen as provisional. Because of this, Popper insists that experiments must take a definite form. Instead of endlessly repeating particular experiments which have produced positive results in the belief that the more times a relationship is demonstrated the nearer certainty we are, the scientist should always try to disprove an hypothesis. Though Popper acknowledges that this goes against a natural human desire to be convinced our inspired ideas are correct and to seek proof, not disproof, of their validity, proper science must involve a ceaseless attempt to court failure – to constantly find new ways of trying to *falsify* a belief about the world. Confirmation of the existence of an hypothesised relationship proves nothing for certain; we are only certain about the status of an hypothesis which has been falsified. (As Einstein said, 'While thousands of scientists can't prove me right, it only takes one to prove me wrong.') For Popper, then, the only way science can justify its claim to be superior to other forms of knowledge is to rely on this unique form of *cognition*; in order to justify the rationalist claim that it is only science that allows humans to know things for certain, it is this method of producing knowledge that matters.

Popper acknowledges that in the realms of non-scientific thinking and knowing, such as religions and magic, humans are typically so enthusiastic and reassured by these explanations of reality that they fall over backwards to avoid putting them to any real, genuine test: 'Popper is of course fully aware that man is, cognitively speaking, addicted to cowardice. Men and societies do put forward theories about the world, but they generally fortify and insure them for all they are worth' (Gellner, 1974, p. 171).

epistemology
A philosophical concept meaning the theory of knowledge, which underpins methodology. For example, the type of methodology employed in a piece of social research will be determined by epistemological assumptions.

Popper acknowledges that some, if not most, scientists are guilty of the same conservatism and lack of courage. (The work of Thomas Kuhn (see pp. 565–6, later in the chapter) is an exploration of this tendency in science.) However, he is not describing what actually happens in science but what should happen; and though evidence of timidity and wishful thinking is apparent in much scientific work, nevertheless, according to Popper, there are élite scientists who do exhibit courage in their thinking, whose **epistemology** and methodology does match the ethic he extols. For rationalists, where science *is* practised properly, where scientists do invite the spectre of failure, this makes it the ultimate form of cognition and knowledge production to which human beings should aspire and which distinguishes it from all other forms. This is why science represents such a leap forward:

> **Its success is due not to the fact that it is more certain ... but, on the contrary, that it is less certain, that it accepts and rejoices in uncertainty, seeks it out, and possesses devices, such as accurate and unambiguous formulation, which increase the exposure to risk.**
>
> **[Gellner, 1974, p. 171]**

So it is the shift from beliefs based on faith and commitment to beliefs based on criticism which produced the Great Divide. The origins of two elements in this new way of thinking in particular need explaining, since it is a form of belief where the believer is committed most of all to a never-ending effort to undermine his/her beliefs – to prove them false; where 'truth' is always provisional – where what is true is only true because it has, up until now, resisted the attempts of its adherents to show themselves misguided; it is a truth which for the moment has not yet been falsified.

These elements make science, unlike religion and magic, a form of knowledge production which is *never-ending* as well as *cumulative*. However,

> **This rational or orderly world, in which alone falsification or criticism works, only emerges at some point ... it is not something inherent in any and all worlds. We had to acquire such a world, to achieve the kind of thought which 'makes' such a world. It was not our birthright, it was not given to us on a plate.**
>
> [GELLNER, 1974, p. 177]

How did it emerge?

Weber and the Rise of Rationalism

Max Weber is the thinker most closely associated with the study of the rise and characteristics of rationalism. For Weber, the question is why particular human beings, at a particular time in history, and in a particular place, began to act in a rational way.

Box 16.1: Religion, capitalism and rationalisation

'Much of Weber's historical, comparative work is focused on the influence of religious beliefs on action. It is in this tradition that he sets out his account of the factors that encouraged the emergence of capitalism in those countries where it took root. This form of modern society, he argues, represents the institutionalisation of *rational* action above all else; whereas in other times and places other forms of action have prevailed, it is only in modern industrial capitalist societies that it has become routine for actors to act due to reasons of *efficiency* and *calculability*, rather than because of emotional or traditional reasons, or because of a single-minded dedication to an overriding goal. For Weber, modernity is best understood as the triumph of this way of thinking, this way of looking at the world, and this way of acting (though the last thing he wants to do is to join in the celebration). Modern capitalism is the end result of a *rationalisation process*, rooted in the historical influence of specific intellectual traditions.

The emergence of this way of living and acting is, for Weber, "the central problem in a universal history of civilisation"; his investigation into this history is guided by the question of why it was, in non-Western countries, that "neither scientific not artistic nor political nor economic development followed the path of rationalisation which is unique to the West".

In Weber's account, ... the role of religious leaders in promoting differing kinds of ideas and orientations in different societies is crucial. For example, the Buddhist monk withdrew from all worldly activity in order to achieve a spiritual elevation, while the Confucian Mandarin engaged in administration on the basis of highly traditionalistic and non-scientific literary knowledge. Only in the West did a cultural orientation emerge which favoured rationalisation.

The part of Weber's argument which has become most famous concerns the role of Puritan Protestantism, and particularly Calvinism, in this process. In *The Protestant Ethic and the Spirit of Capitalism* (1977) Weber outlines the affinity he sees between the kind of lives Calvinists were encouraged to lead by their religion, and the kind of behaviour and attitudes necessary for capitalism to work effectively. Weber stresses how, unlike in most religions, Calvinists are encouraged to concentrate on worldly work as the most virtuous activity and, at the same time, are exhorted to live ascetic – frugal, thrifty and austere – lives. Weber argues that this emphasis on the importance of industriousness and hard work, coupled with a demand for an ascetic lifestyle, is unique to Puritan religions, and that this combination of religious prescriptions gives capitalism the chance to take root. Calvinists believe they cannot prove to themselves and others that they have been called by God to salvation, as a predestined member of his Elect, unless they are successful and productive in their life's work; their belief is that the Lord will only let the worthy prosper. Their lives therefore become a dedication to efficiency and rationality, in order to maximise their productivity. But the symbols of their achievement, material riches accumulated through constant, ever-more-efficient labour, cannot be consumed in any profligate, ostentatious or self-indulgent fashion, since this would contradict the other Calvinist virtue of asceticism. Thus, although wealth accumulation is the symbol of virtuous and efficient hard work for Calvinists, the consumption of the fruits of this labour is denied the believer because of the need to live an ascetic life.

Here is the affinity with capitalism. Unlike other forms of economy, for capitalism to work, capital has to be accumulated; not to be consumed, but to be reinvested in the pursuit of ever-more-efficient, and profitable, techniques of production. The need is for the constant pursuit of rational means of production, by ploughing back the fruits of labour. The more wealth is made, and the more successful the capitalist enterprise is, the more resources are available to improve the efficiency of production. Work is therefore an end in itself; profit to be reinvested is virtuous, and brings its own reward.

Weber's account is clear. Only Puritanism expects of its followers a way of thinking and a way of living which matches the peculiar demands made on capitalist producers. Without a population dedicated to worldly work for its own sake, prepared to eschew as sinful any signs of extravagance, capitalism could not have got off the ground. The creation of such a world thus represents the perfect example of the Weberian view of the role of beliefs and action in social change; for Weber, capitalism is the child of a particular way of thinking and acting, not a mode of production spawned by economic forces. But, also for Weber, this child should have been strangled at birth, because it has grown into a monster. ...

For Weber, the pursuit of technical efficiency, whatever the (non-material) cost, is inevitable and irreversible in modern industrial capitalism, and while in bureaucratic administration it reaches its zenith, it also represents humanity's nadir. Weber tells us that the rise of this form of society means it is now wholly illusory to hope to build the sort of Utopia which the birth of modernity promised for so many thinkers. A world dominated by rationality – a world where efficiency, calculability and predictability are the dominant goals – means a world bereft of meaning, or of mystery, or of a concern with spiritual fulfilment. Weber tells us instead to resign ourselves to the 'iron cage of bureaucracy' and the 'polar night of icy darkness' which modernity has created. For Weber, the triumph of capitalism as a form of life signals the end of the line for progress; the train bearing the hopes for humanity's spiritual welfare has run into the buffers of terminal rationality.'

Source: Pip Jones, *Studying Society*, 1993, pp. 72–3.

Science, Rationalism and Disenchantment

While exhorting us to appreciate the uniqueness and cognitive power of post-Enlightenment thinking – we must recognise the chasm between science and non-science – rationalists are usually only too aware of the drawbacks of living life on this side of the Great Divide. There are two big ones:

- There is the loss of what Weber calls enchantment – a loss of mystery, imagination and of faith in the unknown. It is a world in which objectivity triumphs over subjectivity. Things are what they are, not as we would wish them to be; science reveals an icy, cold, inhospitable world, where we have no choice about the way things are. For Weber, then, a rational world, however efficient and ordered, is a *disenchanted* world for its inhabitants. So, although human and therefore as likely to be as disenchanted as anyone else, scientists are nevertheless required to be prepared to be alarmed, aghast or even repelled by the results of their work, and yet to continue to do it. Truth is a matter for assessment by employing one yardstick only – the facts. Other criteria, more human, more personal, almost certainly more comforting, fulfilling and rewarding, are irrelevant: 'Truth is *not* beauty; nor virtue, nor utility, nor the advancement of any political cause.' (Gellner, 1979, p. 144).

- Furthermore, although, like everyone else, scientists would like to know how to live, they cannot expect the knowledge they produce to help them: science should not be seen to provide a 'charter for social arrangements' (Gellner, 1974, p. 184). Not only are our feelings, judgements, values, hopes, aspirations and fears irrelevant for the rational investigation of the world, but scientific evidence about this world cannot guide us or instruct us about how we should organise ourselves. Cognitive truths are not moral truths; knowing what is cannot help us decide how individual human lives should be lived or how human societies should be organised.

Other knowledge-systems, though unable to explain accurately and, therefore, direct the attempt to control reality as science can, at least make humans feel at home in the world. Indeed, as we shall see in the next section, for many thinkers this is precisely the advantage of these systems. Whether religious, magical or whatever, such systems furnish their believers with comfort and succour; the stories they typically tell are of a universe to which humans naturally belong and in which they have a particular – usually elevated – place. Such belief-systems both explain the world and tell humans how they should live their lives; they provide both *explanatory* accounts and *morally prescriptive* ones.

However, with the rise of science, we leap the Great Divide – we now know the falsehoods contained in these other accounts. Uniquely, then, it is post-Enlightenment, *modern* humans who can know real truth – but only at a huge cost; for, also uniquely, it is we moderns who are denied any moral guidance by our knowledge. This is the double-edged sword of rationality; it arms us with the means to know what really is but provides us with no prescriptions about how we should live or how we should organise ourselves. Despite famous attempts to do so, such as the French Revolution, the construction of Nazi Germany and of Communism, scientific knowledge can never be employed to construct Utopia and such projects are doomed to failure; science, though born of specific religious influences, is no secular religion. It merely presents us with cold reality in a hard-nosed way:

> **it desecularizes, disestablishes, disenchants everything substantive: no privileged facts, occasions, individuals, institutions or associations. In other words, no miracles, no divine interventions ... no saviours, no sacred churches or sacramental communities.**
>
> [GELLNER, 1992, p. 81]

Perspectives on Scientific and Non-Scientific Knowledge

Symbolic anthropology and phenomenology

For some writers on the sociology of knowledge, it is the inability of science to offer psychological and emotional comfort that explains the presence and influence of *non*-scientific knowledge in human lives, even in a rational world. From this point of view, the important thing about beliefs is not what they are but the fact that they are there for people to believe in them: it is the reassurance their existence provides that matters.

phenomenology
In sociology, a focus (from Schutz) on the taken for granted knowledge that social actors share and which underpins everyday life. It is part of the idealist tradition which focuses on consciousness and meaning, not structural social phenomena.

ontological security
A stable mental state derived from a sense of continuity and order in events.

Associated with symbolic anthropology and some versions of **phenomenology**, this is a perspective which argues that since all humans require reassurance that the world is a safe and ordered place – that they have what Giddens calls a desire for '**ontological security**' – all societies will have forms of knowledge which perform this hermeneutic/psychological task. Furthermore, unlike *secularisation theories* (see p. 541 and pp. 546–53) it is a perspective which does not characterise the development of modern societies as a process in which non-scientific knowledge becomes less and less important. Since, as rationalists themselves recognise, scientific knowledge manifestly fails to satisfy the human need for ontological security, we should expect other forms of knowledge, other systems of meaning, which do perform this task, to be as influential in rational, scientific cultures as anthropology shows us they are in pre-modern ones. Here, then, is a sociology of knowledge which, unlike the believers themselves, cares little about the content, truth or efficacy of systems of knowledge, concentrating instead on the benefits they provide for those who do the believing.

Functionalism

Functionalist perspectives also eschew an interest in the content of beliefs in favour of examining their effects, but, unlike symbolic anthropology and phenomenology, point to the benefits for *social* organisation of non-science which scientific knowledge fails to deliver. Belief-systems are seen as encouraging social order and social stability in the worlds in which they are found in ways which rationally-based knowledge cannot. From this point of view, it is the benefits for *society* that explains the existence of non-rational accounts of reality. Since modern societies require the provision of such benefits as much as pre-modern ones, these theorists, like the anthropologists and phenomenologists who point to the psychological benefits of non-rational accounts of things, also tell us to be unsurprised when we moderns find science and non-science co-existing in our world, since they are different kinds of knowledge, performing different functions.

In effect then, these two kinds of perspective, both interested in the *effects* of systems of knowledge rather than on the content of their ideas, argue that though science *is* able to tell us how things actually are, it isn't able to make us feel better or make our social worlds nicer places in which to live. Since non-scientific stories are able to do this (albeit at the cost of telling the truth) they can, and do, co-exist with science. However, the problem is that believers in such stories *do* think they tell the truth.

Rationalism

It is on these grounds that rationalist writers object to these two approaches, arguing that they fail to explain why believers in a system of non-scientific knowledge *do* think it tells the truth and that its ideas *are* right, even though science shows these to be wrong. This position insists that we have to explain forms of knowledge from the point of view of those who believe in them, and not in terms of any beneficial psychological or societal effects an outside observer may see them as producing. The argument here is that people do not believe in God or practise magic or think witches cause misfortune because they think by doing so they will be providing themselves with psychological reassurance, or in order to achieve greater cohesion for the social groups to which they belong. They do so because they think such beliefs are correct – that they tell them the truth about the way the world is. For scholars in this intellectualist, rationalist tradition then, the problem of non-scientific knowledge is why people believe in falsehoods.

evolutionism
A doctrine based on the notion that historical, biological and social changes are subject to a process of development and progressive unfolding (*see* Darwinism).

Nineteenth-century rationalist writers, reflecting the **evolutionist** spirit of their times, tended to explain the lack of rationality and the dominance of false beliefs in pre-modern worlds in terms of the deficient mental equipment of their inhabitants. Such peoples were seen as possessing a pre-logical, or non-rational, mentality. Twentieth-century rationalist thinking has generally rejected such a view, subscribing à la Gellner to the Great Divide position that pre-modern people do not possess inferior minds, but that they lack the social and cultural conditions needed to promote rationalism. From this perspective the history of modern societies is depicted as the inexorable rise of scientific knowledge and the equally inexorable decline in the significance of non-rational beliefs. Some of these beliefs – magic, witchcraft – have disappeared as part of this process, while others – religious ones – have become marginalised in one way or another. It is this perspective that has spawned *secularisation* theories of various kinds. For some in this tradition, secularisation is primarily a matter of progress, for others it is substantially a process of disenchantment, while for others it is neither – merely the substitution of one form of knowledge by another.

Relativism

Our final perspective on knowledge takes a different tack, questioning the basic claim of rationalism/Great Divide thinking that science can itself give us truth. It is this sort of approach that leads to *Relativism*. Here, the argument is that a close inspection of scientific thinking and practices reveals that they are much more like those found in non-scientific systems than rationalists claim. As a result, like the other opponents of rationalism, relativists argue that there is no reason to suppose that science will dispatch non-science off the face of the modern world. However, relativists do not argue this case because of the beneficial effects of non-scientific accounts, but because they claim that science in fact cannot perform the task it sets out to do – to give us objective truth. Taking on rationalism on its own ground, here is also a focus on scientific method – on how scientific knowledge is produced. Though the critiques vary in character, they all in the end argue that since scientists are social beings too, they can never hope to suspend this socialness when they are doing science. From this viewpoint, scientific activity is so suffused by social and cultural influences brought to the process by the scientists engaged in it that though there may *be* a true story about reality to be told, humans, scientists or not, can never hope to tell it. It is this relativist position, that human stories are of equal validity and that the pursuit of objective truth is a doomed project, that leads to the critique of the Enlightenment/modernist/rationalist enterprise known as **postmodernism**.

postmodernism
Often perceived as a cultural and aesthetic phenomenon associated with contemporary literature and the arts, it often combines apparently opposed elements to subvert meaning and fragment totality. It is characterised by a pastiche of cultural styles and elements, but implies a deeper scepticism about order and progress. Instead diversity and fragmentation are celebrated.

The characteristics of these four perspectives on knowledge, and their relationships with each other, are summarised below in Figure 16.1.

	Science	Non-science	Conclusions
Symbolic Anthropology Phenomenology	True	Beneficial for the believer	Co-existence of science and non-science
Functionalism	True	Beneficial for society	Co-existence of science and non-science
Rationalism	True	False	Secularisation in modern societies
Relativism	Flawed	Flawed	Postmodernism

Figure 16.1 Perspectives on knowledge

Source: *Private Eye*

'Two hundred billion people up here and I'm supposed to remember the usual?'

The Consequences of Modernity: Rationalist Perspectives on Knowledge and Belief

Post-Enlightenment thinkers have used evidence from belief-systems in pre-modern worlds to highlight the gulf between the two sides of the Great Divide. Equipped with the only method which can allow humans to know how things really are, such rationalist thinking has had two aims. The first is to work out why pre-modern humans have failed to develop this sort of knowledge for themselves and, furthermore, why they are happy to continue to believe in ideas which are untrue. Such an approach is particularly interested in technical and instrumental knowledge in such worlds – knowledge, such as magic and witchcraft, applied to achieve specific goals. Since this (incorrect) knowledge cannot work, the question is, why do people continue to use it, even after it has failed them, as it always must?

The second aim is to show how such incorrect knowledge is bound to lose significance in proportion to the increase in true – scientific – knowledge. According to this position, the *secularisation* of knowledge will inevitably be a principal feature of modern societies, leading to the marginalisation, or even the total elimination, of different kinds of unfounded, false beliefs.

Nineteenth-Century Evolutionist Anthropology

Evidence about the existence of non-scientific knowledge-systems in pre-modern worlds increased steadily in nineteenth-century modernity, mainly as a result of the **colonial penetration** of such societies. However, the systematic anthropological study of **pre-modernity** didn't become established until after the First World War, when the work of such as Bronislaw Malinowski and E.E. Evans-Pritchard became extremely influential (see pp. 554–6). Nineteenth-century examinations of pre-modern thought were generally undertaken by 'armchair anthropologists', who never went near the cultures they wrote about.

colonial penetration
see colonialism.

pre-modernity
Refers to traditional societies prior to the onset of modernity (*see* modernity).

Strongly influenced by **Darwinism**, such accounts were based upon the assumption that human societies evolved through different stages and that pre-modern thought and social organisation represent the lower rungs on the ladder of human development. Armed with this evolutionary perspective, writers such as Sir James Frazer and Sir Edward Tylor explained the existence and persistence of pre-modern systems of knowledge such as religion, magic, witchcraft and superstition in terms of the mental equipment of their believers. Unable to reason rationally, possessed of a 'pre-logical mentality' (Lévy-Bruhl), the reason for the emergence and continued use of such knowledge lies in the intellectual immaturity of pre-modern people. According to Tylor, we can see such immaturity at work when pre-moderns are obliged to judge the technical effectiveness of such knowledge – in their attitudes towards, for example, the success or failure of magic or ritual.

Darwinism
A theory of evolution by Darwin which proposes that species survive and evolve by a process of natural selection, resulting in the survival of the fittest.

According to Tylor, there are four reasons for the persistence of magic:

- Some of the results aimed at by magic *do* occur, though for other reasons. For example, magic is often associated with common-sense behaviour; again, the instruments used in a magical rite, although believed to have a magical effect, can in fact have a practical use. For example, Evans-Pritchard describes the Zande method of catching termites, which involves holding a piece of magic bark and blowing smoke into the termite mound. Because the termites emerge after the smoke and the bark have been used, the magical efficacy of *both* is confirmed.
- Failure can be attributed to error in the prescriptions or proscriptions which accompany the magical rite – to mischanted spells, broken taboos and so on.
- Failure can be attributed to counter-magic by other magicians.
- Positive cases count considerably more than negative ones; rather like astrology in modern societies, 1 success out of 10 can be quite enough to prove the worth of the system.

Box 16.2: Evolutionary explanations of pre-modern knowledge

'Tylor ... coined the term "animism" which was, he argued, the earliest and most fundamental form of religion from which all others have evolved and he defined religion ... as "belief in spiritual beings". The earliest conception of spiritual beings, he thought, was the animistic one of indwelling souls. Reality could be controlled and manipulated by controlling and affecting these spiritual entities. Animism was the theoretical aspect of the first belief system while magic was its practical technology.

Tylor ... speculated that the source of such notions lay in the experience of dreams and visions ... it was the human capacity for and tendency to generalise that led to the attribution of souls to all things, or, in other words, to animism ...

Since the spiritual beings with which early humans populated the world derived from a human model, Tylor reasoned that they would be attributed with human characteristics such as intention, purpose, will, and so on. But certain of them, those governing major aspects of nature, were believed to be vastly superior to humans and much more powerful and therefore able to control their fate. They had to be propitiated, persuaded, cajoled in much the same way that other human beings are treated – by appeal, entreaty, giving gifts, the religious counterparts of which are prayer and sacrifice.

Tylor distinguished between religion and magic which he saw as based not upon the belief in spiritual beings but in impersonal powers and forces.

Magic operates, he argued, on the principle of likeness and association. Things which resemble one another, in magical thought, are believed to be causally connected with one another. By operating upon or using something in certain ways the magician thinks it is possible to affect those things it resembles. Magic is, therefore, rather like science but based upon false reasoning …

Frazer, like Tylor, characterised magical beliefs and practices as being a kind of primitive science and technology … Also, like Tylor, he thought that magical thought involved association of ideas in which certain types of perceived connection or association were taken to indicate real causal connections between things.

Frazer distinguished between two kinds of magic, homeopathic or imitative, and contagious. In the former because two things are perceived to be similar, it is concluded that they must be connected such that, for example, what is done to one will take effect upon the other. Thus if a wax effigy of someone is made and a pin is thrust through it, then harm will be caused to the individual it resembles. Contagious magic is based upon the belief that if two things have been in intimate contact then action performed upon one will affect the other. For example, the hair or nail clippings of someone could be used to harm them by burning them whilst casting the appropriate spell.

Since such techniques do not actually produce the desired effects, Frazer went on to argue, in the course of time resort was made to other beliefs and practices, namely those of religion. Religion is based upon the analogy of human conduct … The manipulative techniques of magic give way to supplication and propitiation of spirits. By a process of projection the faculties and powers of human beings are attributed to postulated supernatural beings who can be induced to aid humans in their purposes by various means.

Finally, as more and more is discovered of the real nature of the material world, religion itself begins to decline and to be replaced by solid scientific knowledge … The prevalence of magic diminished during the surge of religious thought … [although] it is not entirely extinguished, vestiges remaining even in the scientific age. Religion lives on until eventually it will fade away as we find we have no further use for it.'

Source: Malcolm B. Hamilton, *The Sociology of Religion: Theoretical and Comparative Perspectives* (1995) pp. 24–6.

Theories of Secularisation in Modern Societies

There are echoes of this approach in the work of various twentieth-century secularisation theorists, for whom modernity is also about the replacement of pre-modern forms of knowledge by science. However, secularisation theorising is different from evolutionist anthropology in two ways: first, non-science is not predicted to die out completely, but instead to progressively lose its former significance – to become increasingly marginalised. Second, secularisation is not defined as the outcome of an evolution of the capacity for reason among humans, but as the result of the emergence, in ways explained by Weber, of a form of knowledge which is uniquely successful, both because its claims are demonstrably true and because, when applied, it actually works. Different secularisation theorists emphasise the element of progress involved in the development of scientific knowledge to different degrees.

Ernest Gellner

As we have already seen (pp. 537–9), Gellner acknowledges that of course there are drawbacks to living in a world whose principal form of knowledge is confined to facts we can do nothing about and which provides us with no guidelines about how to live and how to organise ourselves. In this we are manifestly worse off than pre-modern people, whose knowledge, while incorrect and technically worthless, at least does provide such prescriptions for living. However, Gellner insists that these psychological and social disadvantages are far outweighed by the enormous technological advances modern societies have experienced as a result of the application of scientific knowledge.

Unlike the evolutionists, Gellner does not claim that non-scientific knowledge is in the process of dying out in modern society. For example, he knows perfectly well that religions in various shapes and sizes continue to attract adherents. He also acknowledges that other modern forms of belief and meaning, such as those provided by art, music, literature, popular culture (a specifically modern phenomenon), 'dropping-out', drug-taking, political protest and so on, are important for many people. But he is contemptuous of a relativist interpretation of this state of affairs – that in modernity scientific knowledge is just one among many accounts of existence all of which have equal validity. This is because, for Gellner, such alternatives to science are profoundly insignificant when it comes to the crunch; we have to remember that

existentialism

A philosophy which emphasises free will and the individual's responsibility for his or her own actions.

such non-scientific accounts are technically impotent – only science can *do* things and improve our physical and material circumstances. In effect, he says, we can only afford to be preoccupied with **existential** questions about meaning, life, death and eternity – 'Who am I?' 'Where am I going?' 'What's it all about?' – because we can take for granted the kind of world that science has constructed for us. It is this that makes Gellner a secularisation theorist. He sees the modern preoccupation with 'meaning and being' as a self-indulgence only made possible because scientific knowledge has enabled our world to advance so rapidly and so far. Unlike those in pre-modern worlds today, whose overriding, and desperate, priority is to get hold of scientific knowledge to begin to develop as we have, we can afford to sit back in the luxury of our well-appointed world and concentrate on navel-gazing. However, when things really matter, we know on which side our bread is buttered.

Box 16.3 Ironic cultures and the meaning industry

'Modern societies are not systematically and consistently secularised; luxuriant, self-indulgent, cosy or ecstatic faiths are present in a thousand forms, new, old or revivalist. It would be most rash to say that they are on the decline …

It is, I suppose, conceivable that the whole Disenchantment thesis was profoundly mistaken, and that, on the contrary, the total indiscipline, the uncritical self-indulgence, the luxuriant slush of Californian-style religion-and-protest are a real foretaste of the future … But … it … remains true that all this is froth rather than substance …

Why is it ultimately superficial? Society continues to be based on a productive, administrative, and order-enforcing technology which is scientific, which transcends cultural boundaries … The new pseudo-cultures continue to rely on this technology for a standard of living to which its members are accustomed and which they are certainly not seriously prepared to forego … It is precisely because the basic and assured standard of living is so fabulously high that so many can "opt out" and sacrifice some marginal benefits … Such conspicuous abstention from these marginal extras is one thing, and a genuine return to the squalor of pre-industrial poverty would be quite another. There is no sign whatever that anyone is genuinely willing to opt for the latter; and that whole populations should *choose* such a course is unthinkable.

And as it continues to live by and rely on powerful, manipulatively effective, scientific knowledge, society also habitually turns to it in real need, in any field in which this type of knowledge is genuinely established … It is only in the residual sphere, where nothing very serious is at stake, that the scientific vision has become optional …

... It is for this reason that the Weberian disenchantment thesis is in partial error. What is true is that modern cognition does bureaucratise nature, and must necessarily do so; but, serious cognition need not pervade all aspects of daily life ...

This, then, is a very important general trait of modern societies; the emergence of what may be called ironic cultures. The irony ... resides in the fact that the whole organisation of such cultures, the way in which they are implemented and enforced in life, the limits within which they are enforced, work in a manner which tacitly presupposes and admits that they are not to be taken seriously, as knowledge ... Real knowledge is to be found elsewhere; and it does have the cold forms which ... Weber discerned and anticipated. But more colourful, human, cosier worlds and thought-styles are at the same time available to envelop our daily life, and they have reached their quiet accommodation ... with the island of truth. The world in which we think is not the same as the one in which we live ... The colder the one, the more fanciful the other, perhaps ...

... The scientific vision, for instance, does not dictate any sartorial or gastronomic style ... But we must wear and eat *something* ...

... A culture, a sartorial, gastronomic, moral style and tradition is indeed adopted and imposed, by the normal methods of shared expectation, education, social pressure and so forth ... But (it) is no longer continuous with, possessing the same status as, the best cognitive and productive equipment of the society. On the contrary, there is a deep fissure between the two. In a traditional society, the rationale of dietary regulation, say, may well come from exactly the same source as the premises governing fundamental therapeutic, political or productive activities, and hence can have similar status. This is no longer so, and cannot be so. When serious issues are at stake – such as the production of wealth, or the maintenance of health – we want and expect real knowledge. But when choosing our menu or our rituals, we turn to culture and religion. In these frills of life, we ... must use *some* culture or other, and select it in *some* other way. (We must, because our truth no longer generates or selects its own). But all this is not serious ... Culture remains rich and human and is even, in various ways, more luxuriant than it used to be; but it is no longer all of a piece with the serious and effective convictions of a society. These, at any rate, tend to be as ... Weber claimed they must be ...

... In this limited sphere of "culture", relativism is indeed valid. In the sphere of serious conviction, on the other hand, relativism is not an option open to us *at all*.

Source: Ernest Gellner, *Legitimation of Belief* (1974) pp. 191–207.

Bryan Wilson

Wilson is a writer on secularisation who is not so sanguine about the nature of living in a society dominated by scientific knowledge. His work is in the tradition of Weber, who as we have already seen, sees modern societies as places in which rationality – a concern with identifying cause and working out technical efficiency, with *how* things work and with calculating how they can be made to work more effectively rather than *why* they are as they are – comes to dominate life and thought. For Weber, such worlds are disenchanted: existential questions about the mysteries of human existence, concerning issues of meaning and identity, become less and less significant in lives preoccupied with the kinds of concern exemplified and promoted by scientific activity.

Though Wilson, like Weber, is only too aware of the consequences for life in modernity, and of the compensations which a continued role for non-rational meaning-systems would bring, insists that the evidence shows that such systems – and religious ones in particular – have suffered an irreversible decline. He has engaged in a long debate with those who dispute his secularisation thesis – for whom religious beliefs and practices in modern societies remain significant. These critics of secularisation theorising adopt a variety of positions: some argue that traditional religions, like Church-centred ones, have merely become displaced in importance by a proliferation of non-traditional ones, like cults and sects of various kinds; some that religion has become an individual, rather than a collective, organised, affair; some that functional alternatives to traditional religion – such as nationalism and patriotism – have emerged to promote social solidarity and so on (see pp. 559–62). Wilson, however, while acknowledging the presence of a large variety of non-scientific forms of meaning and knowledge in modern societies, argues that this in fact is actually evidence of the decline of religion: the increase in the number and diversity of such systems is evidence of the modern marginalisation of religion – its removal from the central structural location it used to occupy in pre-modernity. As Hamilton puts it:

> **“The situation where one can choose between one religious interpretation and another, where rival interpretations and organisations compete in the ‘market place’ of religions, as Berger puts it, is likely to result in a devaluation or loss of authority for the religious view generally. The pluralistic situation where one can choose one’s religion is also a situation where one can choose no religion at all.”**
>
> [HAMILTON, 1995, pp. 172–3]

Box 16.4: The characteristics of a secular society

According to Wilson, secularisation in modernity involves the following features:

- the sequestration by political powers of the property and facilities of religious agencies;
- the shift from religious to secular control of the various erstwhile activities and functions of religion;
- the decline in the proportion of their time, energy and resources which men devote to super-empirical concerns;
- the decay of religious institutions;
- the supplanting, in matters of behaviour, of religious precepts by demands which accord with strictly technical criteria;
- the gradual replacement of a specifically religious consciousness (which might range from a dependence on charms, rites, spells or prayers) to a broadly spiritually-inspired ethical concern;
- the abandonment of mystical, poetic and artistic interpretations of nature and society in favour of matter-of-fact description and, with it, the rigorous separation of evaluative and emotive dispositions from cognitive and positivistic orientations.

Source: Wilson, *Religion in Sociological Perspective* (1982) p. 189.

Wilson has an alarming vision of the potential consequences of secularisation:

post-structuralism
A modern development in French theory following from linguistics structuralism, which goes further by treating social life as a 'text' which may be analysed without reference to any author (or creative subject/actor) (*see* texts *and* deconstruction).

At present, in the West, the remnants of religion are, if receding, as yet still in evidence, but generally it may be said that western culture lives off the borrowed capital of its religious past. It is by no means clear what sort of society is coming into being as religious values wane. The consequences, not only for the arts and high culture, but also, and perhaps more importantly, for the standards of civic order, social responsibility, and individual integrity, may be such that the future of western civilisation itself may be thrown into jeopardy.

[Wilson, 1982, p. 88]

Michel Foucault

As we have seen elsewhere (see especially Chapters 4 and 15), Foucault is a **post-structuralist** who sees forms of knowledge – **discourses** – that work like languages as the only reason that human existence is possible at all. Languages/discourses define reality for us; in

discourse
A body of ideas, concepts and beliefs which become established as knowledge or as an accepted world-view. These ideas become a powerful framework for understanding and action in social life. For example, Foucault studied the discourse of madness, highlighting its changes over the centuries and its interplay with other discourses such as religious and medical discourses, and illustrated how these shifts affect how madness is perceived and reacted to by others.

order to think at all, we are obliged to do so by using these definitions; the knowledge we have about the world is provided for us by the languages and discourses we encounter in the time and places in which we live out our lives. Thus, who we are – what we know to be true and what we think – is discursively constructed; our knowledge and thoughts – our *identities* – are fashioned by definitions of reality outside our control. In post-structuralist jargon, we are *constituted* by discourses.

Foucault defines history as the rise and fall of discourses. Social change is about changes in prevailing forms of knowledge; the job of the historian is to chart these changes and identify the reasons for the substitution of one by another. Unlike rationalists, however, Foucault sees no element of progress in this process; the replacement of one way of knowing reality is not a victory for truth but simply the result of politics – the exercise of *power*. He thus has a similarly relativistic view of knowledge to that held by Kuhn about scientific knowledge (see pp. 565–7). For Kuhn, scientific knowledge is relative to particular paradigms, while for Foucault, human knowledge in different cultures and times in history is relative to discourses. For both, the production of knowledge is a political process – the outcome of the exercise of *power*.

The question of power is at the heart of Foucauldian thinking:

- Power is exercised by discourses over subjects (people) because in order to think at all – to 'be' – they have to do so in the terms provided by a discourse: they are subjected to the power of the discourse
- Power is exercised in order for particular discourses to come to prevail – they are promoted and sustained in power by **discursive practices** (disciplinary or regulatory apparatuses, as Foucault calls these)
- Power is exercised because of the dominance of particular forms of knowledge – different groups benefit unequally as a result of the power of a particular discourse.

discursive practices
Related to Foucault's conception of power/knowledge, refers to a system of regulatory or disciplinary devices which reflects and promotes discourse (*see* discourse).

These features are central to Foucault's account of the rise of modern society: for him modernity is principally about the emergence of new forms of discourse – defined knowledge. What is particularly apparent in modernity, says Foucault, is the rise of discourses concerned with the control and regulation of the body:

If Foucault's epistemological work represents analyses of knowledge/power, his historical inquiries centre on the body/society. The object of these investigations is the emergence of ... practices by which the body is organised and controlled within social space.

[TURNER, 1991, p. 130)

According to Foucault, the rise of such body-centred discourses involves a process of secularisation. Pre-modern forms of knowing are dominated by religion: things are defined as good or evil, virtuous or sinful, and social life is structured around these concepts. With the emergence of modern, urban society, scientific definitions of reality take over, with *medical* science a crucial element in this new form of knowledge: modern life becomes increasingly subject to medical control – the **clinical gaze** as Foucault calls it (see Chapter 13).

the clinical gaze
see medical gaze.

Thus, scientific psychiatry is employed to control vagrant, unemployed bodies, and 'madness' becomes defined as 'illness' for the first time. The asylum or mental hospital emerges as the place for the mentally ill to be confined and regulated. Even more important, clinical medicine rises to prominence along with the hospital, where sick bodies can be subject exclusively to the clinical gaze. Furthermore, in late modernity, we have seen the penetration of medicine into other aspects of life: 'community medicine' and 'health education' are aspects of this process as are the modern notions of 'normal' and 'healthy' sexuality as primarily a matter of medical definition.

The rise to power of science and of medicine in particular, coincides with a progressive loss in the power of religious forms of knowledge. For example, normality and deviance are now more a matter of health and illness rather than good or evil, and the doctor/physician takes over from the priest the role of defining, promoting and treating deviance.

Bryan Turner

materialist
For Turner, following Foucault, a focus on the body as an object of analysis.

feudalism
A social and political power structure prevalent in parts of Europe during the twelfth and thirteenth centuries, where power was fragmented and overlapping among authorities including church, monarchy and local lords.

Turner offers a **materialist** theory of religion and secularisation, very much in the tradition of Foucault. Though also interested in the effects of religious beliefs rather than their content, he is dismissive of both Durkheimian functionalist 'social cement' thinking and the phenomenological, subjectivist interest in religion as the allocation of meaning to existence (see pp. 556–9). He argues that we must see the role of religion and its decline in modernity as closely linked to the two main material aspects of human existence – the production of goods and the management of the body. His interest is in pointing up the pre-modern role of religion in controlling the sexuality of the body for the benefit of the economy, and in charting the decline in significance of religion when it no longer becomes economically necessary for this.

Though Turner sees strong links between religion and the economy, he is no Marxist. For Marxists, religion is a significant feature of class societies, especially **feudal** ones. As a form of knowledge which usually encourages

superstructure
A Marxist term, which refers to social forms other than the economy, e.g. politics and culture, that are determined by the economic base (*see* economic base).

ideology
A perception of reality or way of thinking. Its usage is associated with Marx, where the term implies a mistaken sense of reality or false consciousness (*see* false consciousness).

a belief in individual freedom via salvation in an after-life, it has to be seen as an important element in the **superstructure** – an **ideological** device encouraging members of an exploited class to acquiesce in their subordination in this world in favour of the expectation of liberation in the next. It functions, as Marx put it, as an 'opiate of the people'.

For Turner, in contrast, it is religion's influence on sexuality that is its *raison d'être,* and the decline of religion in modern societies can be traced to its loss of economic importance. Like Wilson, Turner insists that the modern growth in the number of small, marginalised religious organisations and the individuation of religious belief is in fact incontrovertible evidence of its loss of *structural* significance and the secularisation of such worlds.

Box 16.5: Property, sexuality and secularisation

According to Turner, 'religion has the function of controlling the sexuality of the body, in order to secure the regular transmission of property via the family … In feudalism, religious control of sexuality, especially the sexuality of wives and sons, was crucial to the control of private feudal rights to land; the confessional, penance and other sacraments were important in the social control of women and the production of legitimate offspring. In competitive capitalism, religious control of sexuality was again important in the distribution of property, where the capitalist family was the primary source of further investment for accumulation …

In late capitalism, where there is a degree of separation of ownership and control, the importance of the family for economic accumulation declines and there is less emphasis on the importance of legitimacy and monogamy … there is no longer an economic requirement for sexual restraint among property-owners since the public corporation rather than the family firm dominates the economy. There is, however, still the need for the regulation of urban populations in time and space, in order to achieve public order and to secure taxation.

Traditional religious controls over the body are now transferred to public disciplines which are exercised within the school, factory, prison and other "total institutions" … Religion may continue within the private sphere of the body of an individual, but the public sphere of the body of populations is now subordinated, not to the conscience collective (Durkheim), the sacred canopy (Berger) or the Civil religion (modern functionalists) but to secular disciplines, economic constraint and physical coercion.'

Source: Turner, *Religion and Social Theory* (1992) p. 9.

Anti-Secularisation Perspectives

The co-existence of science and non-science in pre-modernity

When anthropologists began to leave their armchairs to study contemporary pre-modern societies for themselves, the 'pre-logical' assumptions of the nineteenth-century evolutionists were soon found wanting. The first-hand experience of knowledge and belief in such worlds found no evidence of intellectual deficiencies among their inhabitants; in particular, it was very soon apparent that these people used both science *and* non-science to make sense of, and attempt to control, their worlds.

Malinowski was the first anthropologist to undertake a long-term study of such a people – the Trobriand Islanders, who live on islands situated off the south-east tip of New Guinea. Malinowski demolished evolutionist assumptions by demonstrating that the Trobrianders use empirically-based knowledge where appropriate and only turn to other forms, such as magic and ritual, where their scientific ideas cannot work. Thus, the Trobrianders know perfectly well the difference between watering crops and entreating them; they know when, how and why crops should be planted and cared for in order to achieve a successful harvest. They only use magic and ritual to affect events over which they have no empirical control – to prevent storms, drought, insect infestation, and so on. In Malinowski's most famous example of this, he showed

Source: *Times Higher Educational Supplement,* 3 November 1995 (cartoon by Felix Bennett)

how attempts to fish successfully are based on different kinds of knowledge, depending on the circumstances. When fishing in lagoons, the Trobrianders use their empirically-based knowledge of the effects of poison to secure their catch; it is only when fishing in the open sea, where poisoning is very unlikely to work, that spells, entreaties and rites are used.

Evans-Pritchard (1937) also produced a famous account of the collaboration of scientific and non-scientific knowledge in a pre-modern society. The Azande, of the Nile/Congo basin, explain misfortune by means of witchcraft beliefs. Witchcraft – called 'mangu' – is believed to be a physical phenomenon which enters the body of an unsuspecting person and causes them to harm others, their victims usually being those living in close proximity to them. To explain a misfortune, such as damage to property, an accident, illness or whatever, an Azande assumes this is the result of witchcraft. Though knowing *how* things happen – how canoes are damaged by hippos, or fragile items like pots shattered by a fall, or stomach illnesses by food poisoning – the question the Azande turns to witchcraft belief to answer is: 'Why should this misfortune happen to *me*? Why do things happen to *particular* people and not others?' While we can only answer such questions with reference to concepts like luck, fate, or chance, the Azande, because of their knowledge of witchcraft, not only have an explanation for misfortune (like us) but the means of doing something about it (unlike us).

In the event of misfortune the Azande will hypothesise who might be the harbourer of the mangu and take steps to confirm, or falsify, these suspicions. This is done by consulting an oracle. The most effective Azande oracle is 'benge', or poison-oracle, controlled by a witch-doctor. The poison is asked whether the suspected person is indeed the witch; the oracle replies by killing or not killing a young chick to whom the poison is administered by the witch-doctor. If the questioner asks the poison to kill the chick if the suspicion is correct, the death of the chick is the proof needed. If the chick does not die, another suspect has to be thought of. The interrogation of the oracle continues until the witch is identified. Upon being informed of the results, the witch will normally apologise profusely and ritually spit out water to expel the mangu. This is enough to explain a misfortune such as an accident. In the case of illness, the ritual is supposed to restore health. Since most ill people get better anyway, the system is seen to have worked. In the case of persistent illness, either the witch is believed to have been insincere in his or her attempts to expel the mangu, or it is assumed that a new witch has become contaminated. Investigations and ritual expulsions of the witchcraft continue until the sick person recovers. In the case of a fatal illness, a witch-doctor is employed to identify the witch who has caused the death. The next Azande in the locality to die is believed to be that witch, killed by the witch-doctor's magic.

As we shall see later (pp. 563–5), some writers argue that there are strong parallels between the logic of Azande thinking about witchcraft and that apparent in scientific activity, notwithstanding the claims of rationalism, since both are designed to maintain confidence in the system for the benefit of those who depend on them for their knowledge.

These famous accounts of the use of both scientific and non-scientific knowledge to explain and manage events still leave an important question unanswered, however. Is it the case that the Trobrianders and the Azande themselves make a distinction between scientific and non-scientific beliefs and practices, or is it only apparent to us? Do they know one works and the other doesn't, or not? If they don't recognise the difference, why not? If they do know, why do they continue to use beliefs and techniques which don't work? While evolutionism provided answers in terms of inferior capacities to reason, as Tylor tried to do when showing the logic of a form of thinking which avoids revealing the technical deficiencies in such systems, twentieth-century anthropology has typically done so by concentrating on the *non-instrumental benefits* of technically impotent actions and beliefs, arguing that such an approach explains non-science in modernity too.

The argument here is that people continue to use beliefs and practices which cannot be shown to be correct not because of a failure to recognise that they do not work, but because they do work, albeit not technically; they work either by providing psychological and emotional benefits for the believer or by performing important integrative functions for the culture in which they exist (or both). As we said earlier, the first sort of explanation, focusing on the benefits for the individual, is associated with symbolic anthropology and phenomenology; the second – focusing on the societal functions of beliefs – is that of functionalism. These explanations both develop into universalistic accounts, arguing that we should expect to find both scientific *and* non-scientific knowledge co-existing in *all* societies, however modern, or scientifically developed, they are.

Religion Is What Religion Does: (1) Knowledge and the Search for Meaning

The role of knowledge identified in this tradition is that of providing the individual with Giddens's ontological security – a sense that the world is a meaningful, ordered and coherent place. *Symbolic anthropologists* focus principally on the construction of meaning in pre-modern worlds: *phenomenologists* look at the search for meaning as a universal human project.

Symbolic anthropology

Human existence always throws up apparently inexplicable threats to ontological security, such as suffering and misery, calamities and disasters, the inhuman actions of some of our fellow beings, and so on. From this perspective, non-scientific knowledge and beliefs are necessary to help us make sense of such apparently senseless features of our lives. According to this view, they do so in two ways: they give us explanations which help us cope and they also offer us ways of behaving which allow us to represent and express our desire for meaning and order in our worlds. Thus, symbolic anthropology argues that *ritual*, for example, should be seen as a kind of language, allowing those who engage in it to *symbolise* their feelings about the world – it enables them to articulate, through action, the way they'd like the world to be. Therefore, even if a rite seems to be aimed at a particular goal, and even if its participants describe this as its purpose, we should be prepared to look for its real significance elsewhere. That is, rituals 'work' in the same way that any language works – as a means of expression.

> **the whole procedure, or rite, has an essentially expressive aspect, whether or not it is thought to be effective instrumentally as well. In every rite something is being said as well as done. The man who consults a rain-maker, and the rain-maker who carries out a rain-making ceremony, are stating something; they are asserting symbolically the importance they attach to rain and their earnest desire that it should fall when it is required ...**
>
> **... once the essentially expressive, symbolic character of ritual ... has been understood, it becomes easier to answer the question, often asked: how is it that so many people continue to believe in and practise magic, without either noticing its ineffectiveness or attempting to test it empirically as they test their practical techniques? It is simply that there would be no point in doing so, for if and insofar as the rite is expressive ... it would be inappropriate, even meaningless, to put them to the kinds of tests which might disprove them.**
>
> **[Beattie, 1964, pp. 203–4]**

It might also be counter-productive, as we hinted earlier in our comment on Azande attitudes to their witchcraft rituals. If you carry out a ritual to achieve a specific goal but which is also symbolically important and you are particularly rigorous or persistent in judging its instrumental effectiveness and find it wanting, you could be cutting off your nose to spite your face. In effect, you would be in danger of denying yourself the chance to say what you feel; according to symbolic anthropology, the need for humans to have available a coherent means of expressing sentiments which are dear to them is often far more important than the need for empirical proof of technical effectiveness. Indeed, as we shall examine in more detail shortly (see the discussion on Polanyi, pp. 563–5), some commentators on science argue that this goes a long way to explaining the similar disinclination on the part of scientists to subject their knowledge-claims to real, formidable testing; after all, scientists have hopes too – particularly that their ideas are correct and that the world can be rendered a little more meaningful by their actions.

Clearly, religious beliefs and rituals are particularly useful for generating meaning and reassurance, since, according to most definitions, it is religious rituals that are *meant* to be exclusively symbolic, and recognised by believers as such, differing from magic in that they rarely aim at any practical, instrumental end as well.

Phenomenology

Phenomenology is a form of sociology whose principal interest is in the ubiquitous human activity of attaching meaning to reality; inherent in human existence is the necessity to make sense of experience, for without the capacity to do so, human life would not be possible (see Chapter 18, pp. 628–9). It is this theoretical preoccupation that has led some phenomenologists to take a special interest in religion.

As with the case of the functionalist approach to religion, which we will look at next, the definitions used make religion *universal*. If religious ideas and practices are defined in terms of their effects, whenever these effects exist, so must religion. For functionalists, religion performs an **integrative** function in society. Since, according to functionalism, the survival of any social collectivity depends upon it being integrated, then religion must be universal. Similarly, if being human is defined as being bound to attach meaning to reality, and if religion is defined as this activity, then, by definition, being human means being religious – a human being *must* be a religious being.

social integration
The unification of diverse groups of people in a community.

The idea that there is an inherent religiosity in being human underpins the work of Peter Berger, whose *The Social Reality of Religion* (1973), dominated the sociology of religion in the 1970s. His argument is that knowledge and religion are inextricably linked. In order for a human to know the world requires interpretation – the allocation of meaning. This is done symbolically – mainly through language, though other forms of representing meaning are obviously also important. The creation of such a symbolic world is, according to Berger, what being religious is, whether it takes a culturally conventional form or not; to use Berger's phrase, being religious involves the construction of a *'sacred canopy'*, under which humans can shelter and live out their lives, confident in the knowledge, *which they have created for themselves*, that the world is a meaningful and intelligible place. Thomas Luckmann, Berger's erstwhile collaborator, develops this argument. He characterises the evidence cited by secularisation theorists, of a modern decline in established, structurally central, religious belief and practice, as simply evidence of a decline in one form of religion in such societies. All that has happened in modernity, says Luckmann, is that new forms of religion have emerged, less to do with the collective membership of religious groups and organisations than with an exclusively individual search for meaning. According to Luckmann, much more typical of being religious in the modern world is the search for one's self – the construction of a meaningful *identity*. As he puts it: 'The social structure is secularised – but the myth of secularisation fails to account for the fact that the individual is not secularised' (Luckmann, 1983, p. 132).

However, as we shall now see, such an emphasis on religion in modernity as an essentially individual affair cannot be further away from the functionalist explanation of the phenomenon.

Religion Is What Religion Does: (2) Religion, Integration and Solidarity – the Functionalist Perspective

The functionalist approach to non-scientific knowledge is closely bound up with the Durkheimian tradition in sociology (see Chapters 4 and 17). As in the case of symbolic anthropology and phenomenology, for whom, as we have just discussed, the explanation for the existence and persistence of such forms of knowledge lies in terms of their beneficial effects for the individual believer, the functionalist approach also focuses on the effects of such systems. It usually concentrates on religious beliefs and practices, defining religion as any institutionalised form of thinking and acting which functions to integrate, or achieve social solidarity in, the social collectivity in which it is found. Since, according to functionalist theory, the continued existence of any collectivity depends upon its integration/solidarity, then religion must be a universal phenomenon. From such an **inclusivist** point of view, two related aspects of religion, which other, **exclusivist**, definitions consider crucial, are relatively unimportant: the content of the beliefs themselves, and the meanings which the beliefs and practices have for the individual believers. According to functionalism, however different the particular beliefs and practices of particular religions are, and however different from each other the believers in different religions think themselves to be, their existence and essential character can be explained in the same way – with reference to the integrative functions they perform for the social worlds in which they are found.

inclusivist
A definition of religion that includes systems of beliefs and practices which, however different in content, nevertheless produce similar effects.

exclusivist
A definition of religion that excludes any system of beliefs and practices which do not conform to very specific criteria.

Durkheim (1976), in *The Elementary Forms of Religious Life*, based his theory on his analysis of *totemism* among the Arunta. When they were first visited by two explorers, Spencer and Gillen, the Arunta, an indigenous people in Australia, divided themselves into two groups – bands and clans. The band was the small group of Arunta who lived together while the clan was a much larger group, including kin from different bands, who believed themselves to be related. Since bands had to be nomadic to survive, the likelihood of any routine contact between clan members was very remote. However, on rare occasions, clan-wide association did take place, in order to hold a ceremony at the centre of which was the clan emblem – its totem. The totem of an Arunta clan was an object in natural life – a plant, animal or bird, for example. The aim of the ceremony so far as the Arunta were concerned was to ensure the totem thrived and multiplied. Apart from being the ceremonial centre of attention at a gathering of the clan, Arunta clan members treated their totem as a special object, demanding respect and awe if they came upon it during their day-to-day lives. According to Durkheim, for Arunta clan members, their totem was a *sacred* object – special, set apart and different from all other – *profane* – things.

Durkheim argues that totemism was indispensable for the survival of the Arunta. Since day-to-day life was lived out in the band, unless some means was present of reminding Arunta of their membership of the wider society, their sense of themselves would be restricted to their band membership. This would endanger solidarity: members of different bands would feel no allegiance to one another, and there would be no sense in which the Arunta could be described as – or recognised by themselves to be – an integrated unit. For Durkheim, these two conditions cannot be separated: each is dependent on the other. The existence of the sacred object – the totem – provided the motive for clan-wide association, and encountering it and treating it as set apart from other (profane) things during everyday life served as a reminder of their clan's existence for its members. In effect, says Durkheim, it was only the existence of a symbol of the clan that made its continued existence possible.

According to Durkheimian functionalists, the same features are found in all religions, and religions are found wherever there are social groups. There will be objects believed to be sacred – emblems which symbolise the collectivity of members – and there will be occasions when the members together celebrate – worship – the existence of the symbols. This twin combination of symbols and collective action serves to integrate the group by promoting in its members a recognition of the group's existence and of their membership of it. This focus on the importance of a shared recognition of a common identity – a sense of shared belonging – for social solidarity is quintessential Durkheim. Theoretically, Durkheim argues that the sharing of common sentiments – a **conscience collective** as he called it – is the basis for social life itself. By defining religious beliefs and practices as the source of such sentiments, he is defining religion as a precondition for social survival. The fate of the group and the fate of its members are bound up with each other: on the one hand its members depend on the group to survive, and on the other, the group's survival depends on its members recognising their membership – and it is religion which ensures a happy ending. Religious symbols represent the group and the worship of these symbols by the group reproduces its existence. Thus it is no surprise to find that for Durkheim, religious worship of the sacred is in fact a celebration of the group itself.

conscience collective
Coined by Durkheim, a pre-requisite for social integration, referring to the shared beliefs and values of a collectivity. Such collectively held ideas promote both a sense of belonging for the individual and the continuity of the group (*see* social integration).

This definition of religion is inclusivist because it allows for all sorts of collective commitment and activity to be subsumed under the heading of religion – on the grounds that religion is what religion does. Writers in this tradition have thus seen religiosity in such apparently disparate sources of collective identity as membership of nations, political movements and even sports clubs and associations. It is a tendency clearly apparent in the claim, by Robert Bellah, that a '**civil religion**' performs the required functions in present-day America:

civil religion
Associated with non-supernatural religious objects whose existence promotes solidarity for the group and a sense of belonging for the individual.

Bellah finds evidence for the existence of civil religion in such events as Presidential Inaugurations. Inaugural addresses tend to be couched in a religious idiom, referring to God in general terms and to the travails of America as a modern Israel led out of Egypt. This stylised rhetoric is taken as indicating a real commitment on the part of participants to symbols and values which unify and integrate the

community and provide sacred legitimation for its affairs. Other more frequent ceremonials such as Thanksgiving Day and Memorial Day are similarly held to integrate families into the civil religion, or to unify the community around its values. ”

[Wallis, 1983, p. 44]

Scientists Are Human Too: Demystifying Scientific Rationality and Objectivity

Interpretive sociologists base their ideas on the *lack* of similarity between nature and society; unlike natural phenomena, humans make sense of their world and act in the light of these interpretations. Post-structuralists, too, see human lives as the product of allocating meaning, though differing crucially from interpretivism by seeing the *content* of thought and interpretation as itself the outcome of the influence of language. Either way, these are sociologies which draw a fundamental distinction between the natural world and the social world. Since humanly constructed accounts of reality are inevitably the products of meaning, most of what is critical to human existence – the use of consciousness – cannot be explained by using the methods of the natural sciences.

This raises an important question which we touched on at the beginning of the chapter. Since scientists are human too, if these sociologies are correct, the most important factor in their lives must also be the use of their minds to make sense of the world. Furthermore, these meaningful accounts, like all human accounts, cannot be seen as *objectively* true, but only true so far as the owner of the mind is concerned. Human theories or accounts of anything, that is, can only ever be *relative* – to particular occasions of social interaction, or to the cultures or languages which underpin their creation. If this is so, how can it not also be true of the accounts of the natural world produced by humans we call scientists? To put the question differently, how can human scientists produce objective, value-free accounts of nature if these accounts are inevitably the products of the use of their minds? How can human scientists somehow suspend their socialness and remove themselves from the influence of those social and cultural factors which make thought and social life possible? How can scientists produce knowledge which is uncontaminated by the effects of social interaction, language or culture?

For many sociologists of science, the answer to these questions is that they cannot – science is a social product, like any other humanly created knowledge. If this position is correct, then it is obviously devastating for the post-Enlightenment claim at the heart of Great Divide thinking – that humans *are* capable of producing objectively true knowledge and that it is science that enables them to do so. As we said earlier in the chapter, it is this position – that scientific knowledge amounts to just one more account of the world, no nearer the truth about the way things are than any other humanly constructed account – that is known as Relativism. How does this sort of sociological analysis of scientific activity lead to Relativism?

Wishful Thinking: Non-Rational Thinking in Science and Magic

Evans-Pritchard recognised that Zande beliefs about witchcraft did not form a perfectly consistent body of ideas. However, inconsistencies do not undermine the Zande faith in witchcraft because the analytical questions bringing them into relief are never considered by the Zande. Such questions would presuppose assumptions and a perspective that is no part of what Evans-Pritchard (1937, p. 338) calls the 'idiom of their beliefs': 'They reason excellently in the idiom of their beliefs, but they cannot reason outside, or against, their beliefs because they have no other idiom in which to express their thoughts.' Thus, for example, the Azande would laugh at a European who asked whether poison would kill the chicken without any accompanying address. As Evans-Pritchard (1937, p. 315) says, 'If the fowl died they would simply say that it was not good 'benge'. The very fact of the fowl dying proves to them its badness.' Any such 'test', then, would actually reinforce rather than undermine the Zande belief-system. Within its terms, the Zande reason logically and coherently. If an oracle contradicted itself it would simply be said to have been addressed or prepared improperly, once again reaffirming the basic assumptions of the belief-system. These assumptions are used to account for the world, and to establish the point at which reasoning and further questions come to an end.

Evans-Pritchard's sympathetic treatment of the Zande culture led to much philosophical debate about the logical form of magic compared with that of science. Polanyi, for example, believes that it is possible to identify an idiom of belief operating at the heart of all scientific knowledge, albeit in a covert form. Implicit beliefs and assumptions have been screened from our eyes by the ideology of '**objectivism**' in modern science, an ideology that insists that scientific truth is a matter of objectivity and

objectivism
A doctrine which purports that scientific truth is a matter of factual evidence, not belief (*see* objectivity).

not faith. This assumes that scientific theories are built on the observation of empirical 'facts' and the systematic consideration of evidence. Peering behind this curtain of 'objectivism', Polanyi (1958) brings to light a number of features common to both witchcraft and science.

There are, he says, three features working together to ensure that any belief-system is sustained as right and proper (for those who profess it) despite 'evidence' challenging its validity: their combination guarantees that questions, problems or issues not covered by the belief-system's assumptions will be 'unhesitatingly ignored'. First, Polanyi points to the 'circularity' of the ideas that constitute any belief-system: each idea in the system is explained through reference to another idea, the validity of which is never doubted. This other idea, however, only makes sense itself through reference to the original idea. All languages as **symbolic systems** embody this circular aspect. Thus, for example, a dictionary presupposes a literary circularity of meaning and legitimation; the definition of a word may itself be explained in terms of the original word – 'marriage' may give 'wedlock' which in turn is defined as 'a state of marriage'. This circularity promotes the stability of a system of ideas and beliefs: if one belief is doubted, it is justified through reference in terms of the original belief. Hence, as Polanyi (1958, p. 289) says, 'So long as each doubt is defeated in its turn, its effect is to strengthen the fundamental convictions against which it was raised.'

symbolic systems
Systems, such as languages, of connected elements, each one representing or symbolising an aspect of reality.

Second, Polanyi, rather as Tylor did (see pp. 544–5), suggests that all belief-systems hold in reserve a supply of 'subsidiary explanations for difficult situations'. For the Azande, for example, failure of the oracle could be accounted for in terms of incorrect use of the device; similarly in science, certain events or phenomena not conforming to expectation may be explained away in terms of some auxiliary hypothesis. Thus conflicting evidence is often discussed in science as 'anomalous findings', quirks of investigation that can be ignored. In physics and chemistry many experiments are designed to show constant relations between two phenomena, which can then be plotted as a straight-line graph. Sometimes, one point on the graph is consistently out of line with the rest: students may be told to ignore this apparent anomaly, which is frequently dismissed as the result of incorrect method at some point in the experiment, an explanation which an Azande student would find most appropriate!

Third, belief-systems reject alternative views of the world by refusing to grant any legitimacy to the assumptions on which rival conceptions depend. This may mean that new ideas challenging orthodox knowledge-claims are suppressed from their first appearance, and those making them denied any respectability within the community of 'experts'.

According to Polanyi, then, these three features explain how, in practice, contradictory evidence or inconsistent findings do not normally lead to the overthrow of a set of ideas, be it Zande magic or European science. Such evidence can be explained away, denied any validity and meaning, or simply ignored. Hence all systems of knowledge rest on basic premises which are sustained by virtue of actors' *commitment* to them as 'true': ideas are reaffirmed as much by faith and trust as they are by any 'methodologically correct' procedures: 'believing is seeing, as much as seeing is believing'.

Polanyi's commentary forces us to reconsider the way in which scientific knowledge-claims are certified as correct by scientists. Most important, we are required to abandon the customary view that regards science as an activity which, by unbiased, neutral observation, accumulates evidence from which the universal laws of nature are derived. It would seem, then, that an intrinsic feature of scientists' work is their selective inattention to evidence or knowledge-claims which do not conform to their picture of reality.

Science as a Social Product

paradigm
This term refers to the set of questions, practices and institutional arrangements which characterise scientific activity for a particular historical period. For Kuhn, paradigms produce forms of scientific knowledge which appear to be objective, but which in reality reflect very specific sets of interests.

Recent contributions to the area known as 'the sociology of science' have extensively documented the way in which the production and acceptance of scientific ideas depend on social and cultural factors. The growth of this area of sociological research was partly due to the influential work of Thomas Kuhn (1970). Kuhn (1972, p. 82) identified what he called 'the dogmatism of mature science', which he defines as 'a deep commitment to a particular way of viewing the world and of practising science in it'. As a scientific field such as physics becomes more mature or developed, as the number of practitioners increases, as education courses are established and textbooks produced, so those working and training within it adopt a common ideological commitment to what it is 'to be a physicist and study physics'. This dogmatic commitment provides the scientist with 'the rules of the game', what is to be treated as a scientific puzzle and how it is to be solved. These rules constitute what Kuhn calls 'the **paradigm**' of a scientific field or speciality:

> **Their paradigm tells [scientists] about the sort of entities with which the universe is populated and about the way the members of that population behave; in addition, it informs them of the questions that may legitimately be asked about nature and of the techniques that can properly be used in the search for answers to them.**
>
> [KUHN, 1972, p. 93]

Kuhn's notion of paradigmatic science, can, then, be set against the misleading notion that scientists test their theories by collecting observable 'facts' which exist 'out there' in nature, awaiting observation and classification. Instead, scientists 'go out' armed with their respective paradigms seeking evidence, dealing with problems, that *confirm* it. As Kuhn argues, 'the challenge is not to uncover the unknown, but to obtain the known'. This clearly parallels Polanyi's concept of the 'circularity' of belief-systems, in as much as it suggests how scientific research operates in terms of a relatively closed system of ideas that are self-confirming. If counter-evidence to the paradigm does appear, it is typically ignored as an anomaly, and, says Kuhn, for good reason. An anomalous finding or unexpected discovery is, by definition, potentially subversive: it threatens to change the 'rules of the game' by which the paradigm works. Hence, the paradigm is a source of resistance to innovation in science. This is, of course, in direct contrast to Popper's claim about the courage and lack of conservatism characteristic of real science. But if one stopped here, major innovations in science that have occurred – such as the shift from Newtonian to Einsteinian physics – would remain inexplicable. Kuhn explains that innovation takes place when anomalous findings become 'particularly stubborn or striking' such that they force scientists 'to raise questions about accepted beliefs and procedures'. When the paradigm consistently fails to deal with an increasing number of anomalous results, the scientific field experiences a period of major intellectual and social crisis, overcome by the formulation of a new paradigm.

Box 16.6: Scientific thinking and scientific practice

Kuhn's analysis of the paradigmatic nature of science extends the general ideas raised by Polanyi. Polanyi was concerned to show how the *conceptual logic* of science is very similar in form to that sustaining the Zande belief-system; Kuhn indicates the way in which aspects of the *social institution* of science – textbooks, curricula, research communities – continuously sustain the conceptual commitments of its practitioners, guiding their activities, interpretations and accounts of the natural world, and reinforcing the stability of their scientific belief-system.

A commitment to a particular scientific interpretation of the world is therefore an ever-present resource that scientists use to justify their knowledge-claims, and encourages resistance to new ideas or 'deviant' interpretations. A considerable body of literature in the sociology of science examines the way in which non-orthodox knowledge-claims are received and evaluated by orthodox science (see, for example, Wallis, 1979). Case studies – for example, on parapsychology (Collins and Pinch, 1979), on acupuncture (Webster, 1979) – show how 'fringe' groups that threaten the conceptual and social status quo of science have been dismissed, but not on the basis of open-minded impartial scientific theorising and experiment. Instead, many scientists have simply asserted from the outset that the existence of the kind of phenomena proposed is inconsistent with known reality, and therefore any findings, however carefully presented, must be the result of fraud or experimental error, and thus need not be taken seriously. Hence, as Mulkay comments on parapsychology:

> **For the critics of parapsychology, the central assumption that paranormal phenomena do not exist was never in question. Rather it pervaded and gave meaning to the whole armoury of formal arguments which they employed. It ensured that, for these critics, every item of evidence and every claim of reasoning provided further grounds for rejection of the deviant views.**
>
> [Mulkay, 1979, p. 91]

This once again draws our attention to the circulatory and self-confirming nature of orthodox science as an idiom of belief: as Polanyi argues, the stability of a belief system is apparent by 'the way it denies to any rival conception the ground in which it might take root'.

Interpretive sociology discloses another source of social and cultural contamination in scientific activity. As usual for this kind of sociology, the focus is on the dynamics of local, small-scale interaction. The argument is that face-to-face interaction among scientists – in the laboratory, for example – is a matter of negotiated collaboration between the particular individuals involved, however routine the scientific work may appear to be. For **ethnomethodology** in particular, this has profound consequences for the nature of the knowledge produced. When individual scientists work together on any specific occasion, this is a unique social event, with the outcome of the interaction inevitably being context-bound and contingent, or, as Ethnomethodology calls it, *indexical*. The knowledge produced can only be understood by an examination of the interpretive methods used by the particular participants involved (the members) to arrive at an agreement about the occasion – to decide, together, 'What does this mean?' or 'What's going on here?' Like all social occasions, then, it is the work put in by those party to it to arrive at an interpretation of its meaning that matters: the result of the work, the 'knowledge' produced, cannot be objective since it is the end-product of wholly subjective, interpretive, effort. It is inevitably relative

ethnomethodology
Associated with the work of Harold Garfinkel, it is an approach used to study the methods people deploy in their everyday lives to make sense of social life and enable meaningful exchange with one another.

knowledge, then – relative to the occasion and to the sense-making efforts of the particular scientists involved. Only by the **ethnographic** study of particular scientific occasions can the process of producing this inherently subjective knowledge be understood (see Chapter 5).

ethnography
A research technique based on direct observation of the activity of members of a particular social group or given culture.

Post-structural sociology also points to the impossibility of scientific knowledge being uncontaminated by human interpretation. Here however, the interpretation is not the result of subjects creatively collaborating to produce an agreed account, but the result of the impact of discourse – the meanings imposed on the subjects by the languages they are obliged to use to think, and attach meaning, at all. While humans of course *experience* reality for themselves, they can only *know* what this reality means if they are provided with pegs to hang the experience on. It is languages – systems of symbols representing meanings – that provide these pegs. Whatever form these symbols take – sciences use mathematical, statistical and chemical ones, for example – what they mean is not the decision of the subject who uses them. Furthermore, this means others may take them to mean something different. Just as the novelist is not in charge of the meanings conveyed by the language he or she uses to write – the novelist is not the author of the language – nor is the scientist the creator of scientific knowledge. As with all forms of human production, then, what these accounts mean is relative to the languages used. To understand their meaning, all one can do is to **deconstruct** the text which represents these meanings. Thus, scientific knowledge is as far from an objective account of things as is the artist's painting or the novelist's story.

deconstruct
To break down texts in order to grasp their implicit meaning by exposing their underlying and hidden assumptions (see texts).

Relativism

The rationalist/Great Divide claim is that science is unique among systems of knowledge because of the particular method of producing knowledge it employs. Since it is only this method that can eliminate subjective influences, only scientific knowledge is objective and, therefore, true. However, as we have just seen, a great deal of the sociology of science claims to have demonstrated that social and cultural influences are bound to be involved in the human practice of science, so that the knowledge produced by science is bound to be contaminated. If you like, this means not so much that all human accounts of reality are equally true, but that all such accounts are going to be equally flawed. As we have seen, it is this position that is known as Relativism.

Relativism involves the claim that all systems of meaning, or all accounts of reality, produced by humans are equal. In addition, it argues that because the criteria by which the truth or falsehood of an account is judged are themselves provided by a system of knowledge, there is no way truth or falsehood can be objectively identified by human beings, since they are inevitably implicated in a particular system or systems. Thus, for their believers, Religions A, B and C are true, for their users the ideas underpinning magical systems X, Y and Z are true, while for those who believe in it, producers and users, scientific knowledge is true. Furthermore, since Religions A, B and C, magical systems X, Y and Z and science all use different criteria by which to identify truth or falsehood, knowing the truth for sure is not possible for human beings, since they cannot 'know' except via particular systems.

This sort of argument has led to a number of relativistic propositions about the nature of humanly produced knowledge:

- Scientific knowledge is not powerful because it is true; it only seems to be true because it is so powerful. It is therefore *politics* that matters in the establishment of this – or any – particular account of reality as influential: it is not the proximity to truth that explains the dominance of a system of knowledge in any time or place but the methods which its exponents and supporters use to promote it.

- Since the exercise of power in any realm of human activity means that there must be losers as well as winners, the dominance of one form of knowledge implies the marginalisation and subordination of others. Though justified in the name of Truth, such domination should be recognised for what it is – the imposition of one way of making sense of the world at the expense of others. It is, in effect, the epistemological equivalent of **colonialism** or **imperialism** – the use of political power to oppress the weak. Relativists have sometimes explicitly drawn the parallel.

colonialism
The establishment of rule by Western nations over distant territories and peoples (*see* imperialism).

imperialism
Common form of Western imperial rule in the late nineteenth early twentieth centuries. Characterised by the extension of the power of the state through the acquisition, normally by force, of distant territories (*see* colonialism).

Modernity involved the pursuit of objective truth. Once armed with this truth, modernisers saw it as their duty to become missionaries – to oppose falsehoods. Thus, the standard-believers of science have marched against other forms of knowledge, crusaders on behalf of freedom from ignorance. According to relativism, to understand the meaning of this missionary project, we must remember that political colonialism – for example by European states over the last few centuries – has almost always been justified in precisely these terms: premodern cultures could only progress through the influence of modernising forces. Because relativism believes it has demonstrated the impossibility of achieving objective truth in any sphere of human thinking, such claims to altruism, whether concerning knowledge or political and economic development, are exposed for what they are. Rationalism and colonialism are revealed as cultural and political oppression cloaked in missionary garb, as élitist and racist attempts to subordinate or eradicate other belief-systems and cultural traditions.

■ Relativism thus provides the epistemological foundation for *Postmodernism*. The inability of humans to produce true accounts of reality means that the project of modernity initiated by the Enlightenment – to employ Rationalism to discover the way things really are – has to be abandoned. We have to accept that we can never suspend our humanity and socialness and produce a '**meta-narrative**' which gets at The Truth. We have to accept that we live in a *postmodern* world, where different human ways of creating knowledge and making sense of existence deserve equal respect and tolerance.

meta-narrative
Sometimes referred to as 'grand narrative', it is the name given to an all-encompassing theory of human life, especially a vision of social progress.

■ Unlike rationalists, we should not assert the epistemological supremacy of our dominant form of knowledge over others, but accept the ever-presence and legitimacy of 'Other' ways of knowing and living. Though these may well seem odd, bizarre, or even repellent from our point of view, because they have as much meaning and virtue for their adherents as ours do for us, they therefore have as much right as ours to an untroubled existence. In the words of Francois Lyotard, we should 'let a thousand flowers bloom', or as Paul Rabinow puts it:

Epistemology must be seen as an historical event ... one amongst others, articulated in ... seventeenth century Europe ... We do not need ... a new epistemology ... we should be attentive to our historical practice of projecting our cultural practice onto the other ... We need to anthropologise the West: show how exotic its constitution of reality has been.

[Rabinow, 1986, p. 000]

Responses to Relativism

Relativism argues that humans are principally cultural creations and that what we think is true and what we think is right is a product of the different times and places in which we live out our lives. This leads to the sort of anti-**provincialist**, anti-**ethnocentric** position, of Clifford Geertz (1984) which implies both *moral* relativism and *cognitive* relativism – that both moral systems (judgements about good and bad) *and* forms of knowledge are equally valid.

provincialist, ethnocentric
Inability to understand the validity or integrity of cultures other than one's own.

Objections to cognitive relativism

Like Gellner (see pp. 537–9), some rationalists insist that while it may not be possible to identify a *morality* as objectively correct, it is certainly possible to identify a form of *cognition* which is, and that scientific knowledge is the product of that form of cognition. The proof of the pudding, they argue, lies in the fact that it is this form of cognition that has enabled the application of the knowledge it produces to have achieved such prodigious success in transforming lives in the developed world. For relativists to minimise such stupendous advances is absurd, they say, especially since this also ignores the almost universal efforts of non-advanced societies to get hold of this knowledge in order to achieve similar progress for themselves.

Objections to moral relativism

Others see major difficulties with moral relativism. If this position is sustainable, and there are no standards which are objectively good, then no human being has the moral justification to deny others the right to live their lives in whatever way they see fit. This can be seen as a laudable endorsement of the importance of tolerance in human life. However, its critics argue that there are disturbing implications in such a position.

Does it mean that we have to tolerate any of the ideas or behaviour of others, however repellent they may seem to us? For example, does it mean we should accept racism, sexism or religious intolerance in others in our own culture? Does it mean we should have accepted the right of Hitler to exterminate the Jews or of Stalin or Pol Pot to annihilate millions in order to achieve their political ends? Furthermore, does it mean that we have to accept the cultural and historical relativity of our*selves*? Are we entirely at the mercy of social and cultural sources of identity, so that who we are and what we think as right or wrong, good or evil, is entirely fortuitous? Does it mean that since we could, given social and cultural circumstances, literally be *any*body, with *any* beliefs, we should not take our principles too seriously?

To avoid such problems, many thinkers are led to a sort of Human Rights position – to insist that there must be limits to tolerance and that a civilised existence depends upon the identification of correct, universally applicable values. The search for such universal standards of behaviour – the presence of ways of thinking and living which all humans should subscribe to, irrespective of historical or cultural circumstances – is apparent in the work of such as Midgely and Spiro (see Geertz, 1984).

The idea that certain emotions and feelings are a universal aspect of being human also seems to be, at least implicitly, present in the work of some of the most resolute of contemporary advocates of rationalism and science. The recent claims and predictions of natural scientists such as Richard Dawkins and Francis Crick can be seen as part of an extreme rationalist project to deny any significant role for social and cultural influences in the formation of human personality and identity. For example, Crick has recently claimed that:

> **Free will is located in or near the anterior cingulate sulcus ... In practice, things are likely to be more complicated. Other areas in the front of the brain may also be involved.**
>
> **[Crick, 1994, p. 268]**

Crick summarises his position as follows:

> **The Astonishing Hypothesis is that 'You', your joys and sorrows, your memories and your ambitions, your sense of personal identity and free will, are in fact no more than the behaviour of a vast assembly of nerve cells and their associated molecules. As Lewis Carrol's Alice might have phrased it: 'You're nothing but a pack of neurons.'**
>
> **[Crick, 1994, p. 3]**

The implication of this sort of argument is that human biology will be found to be the source of universals in human emotions as well as differences; it is in this tradition that claims for the genetic basis of criminality have recently resurfaced.

nihilism
A philosophy that rejects the notion that any moral position is worth holding.

reductionism
An outlook which explains phenomena in terms of a simple causal determining factor (*see* determinism).

For many sociologists, the real danger of relativism is that it leads to **nihilism** – the total rejection of all moral principles – and therefore that the sort of rationalist **reductionism** peddled by Crick and his cronies will come to fill the void. It is because of this they insist that sociology must remain committed to the original modernist project – the quest for true knowledge *and* the pursuit of human liberation and fulfilment through the reconstruction of society. This ultimately leads to the question 'what is sociology for?' and it is to this question that we now turn in our final chapters.

Summary of the Chapter

- Great Divide thinking argues that the rise of rationalism, enabling the rapid growth in scientific knowledge, was the real motor behind modernity.
- Weber was concerned to emphasise the disenchantment of a world pervaded by rationalism.
- Symbolic anthropology and phenomenology argue that non-rational beliefs will always be important, even in a scientific, modern society, because of the feeling of security they generate for individuals.

- Functionalist writers on religion argue that systems of religious beliefs will be found in all societies, even modern ones, because of the integrative functions these perform.
- Rationalist writers disagree with both these viewpoints, claiming modern societies have become secularised.
- Sociologists of science have attempted to disclose the inability of human scientists to provide a truly objective account of the world.
- This has led to relativism – the claim that scientific accounts are no nearer objective truth than non-rational ones.
- Such a relativist position can be seen to lead to post-modern accounts of human knowledge with all the problems this entails.

References

Beattie, J. (1964) *Other Cultures*, London, Cohen & West.

Berger, P. (1973) *The Social Reality of Religion*, Harmondsworth, Penguin.

Collins, H. and T. Pinch (1979) 'The construction of the paranormal', in R. Wallis (ed.), *On the Margins of Science*, Sociological Review Monograph No. 37, Keele, Keele University Press.

Crick, F. (1994) *The Astonishing Hypothesis: The Scientific Search for the Soul*, London, Touchstone.

Durkheim, E. (1976) *The Elementary Forms of Religious Life*, London, Allen & Unwin.

Evans-Pritchard, E. E. (1937) *Witchcraft, Oracles and Magic Among the Azande*, Oxford, Clarendon Press.

Geertz, C. (1984) 'Anti anti relativism', *American Anthropologist*, pp. 263–78.

Gellner, E. (1974) *Legitimation of Belief*, Cambridge, Cambridge University Press.

Gellner, E. (1979) *Spectacles and Predicaments*, Cambridge, Cambridge University Press.

Gellner, E. (1992) *Postmodernism, Reason and Religion*, London, Routledge.

Hamilton, M. (1995) *The Sociology of Religion: Theoretical and Comparative Perspectives*, London, Routledge.

Jones, P. (1993) *Studying Society*, London, Harper Collins.

Kuhn, T. (1970) *The Structure of Scientific Revolutions*, Chicago, University of Chicago Press.

Kuhn, T. (1972) 'Scientific paradigms', in B. Barnes (ed.), *Sociology of Science*, Harmondsworth, Penguin.

Luckman, T. (1983) *Life-World and Social Realities*, London, Heinemann Educational Books.

Mulkay, M. (1979) *Science and the Sociology of Knowledge*, London, Allen & Unwin.

Polanyi, M. (1958) *Personal Knowledge*, Chicago, University of Chicago Press.

Rabinow, P. (1986) in J. Clifford and G. E. Marcus (eds), *Writing Culture: The Poetics and Politics of Ethnography*, Berkeley, CA, University of California Press.

Turner, B. (1991) *Religion and Social Theory*, London, Sage.

Wallis, R. (ed.) (1979) *On the Margins of Science*, Sociological Review Monograph No. 37, Keele, Keele University Press.

Wallis, R. (1983) an entry in M. Mann (ed.) *The Macmillan Student Encyclopaedia of Sociology*, London, Macmillan.

Weber, M. (1977) *The Protestant Ethic and The Spirit of Capitalism*, London, Allen & Unwin.

Webster, A. (1979) 'Scientific controversy and socio-cognitive metonymy', in R. Wallis (ed.) *On the Margins of Science*, Sociological Review Monograph No. 37, Keele, Keele University Press.

Wilson, B. (1982) *Religion in Sociological Perspective*, Oxford, Oxford University Press.

PART 4

Theorising Contemporary Society

17 Sociologists, Modernity and Progress

Aims of this Chapter

We open this chapter by recapping some of the main features of modernity in order to understand how key founding sociologists shaped theories in response to this new society. Focusing throughout on social structure, the chapter asks how far sociologists have been able to sustain a belief in social progress backed by scientific knowledge. We see how deep-seated doubts about the consequences of modernity in the twentieth century replaced earlier optimism. Finally we discuss current theories which claim that sociology must once again come to terms with a profound transition to a new society: that is, the emergence of postmodernity.

Introduction

The roots of sociology are entangled with the structure of a new form of society in the early nineteenth century. This new social world (which we now look back on as '**modernity**') gave birth to a new area of knowledge – the systematic study of society that we call sociology. From the start, this new social science was part of a great optimistic project. It was believed that human beings could know their world accurately, and thus control and shape their world. At this time it was assumed that humans should control and shape nature; it was a radical innovation to proclaim that we could understand and reshape the social world in the same way.

modernity
A term designed to encapsulate the distinctiveness, complexity and dynamism of social processes unleashed during the eighteenth and nineteenth centuries, which mark a distinct break from traditional ways of living.

Sociology began as part of this great project to achieve *progress through reason* – that is, to gain knowledge and use it to speed on the natural progress towards a better social world. With access to *truth* we can promote *progress,* which leads to the *good society*. Knowledge gives humans the power to shake off the past and shape their destiny – and sociology brings this power into the social world. One side of the early vision of sociology did embody all this: hope of progress, faith in our knowledge and sheer thrill at the open potential of a rapidly changing society that has shaken off its past. As Marx and Engels expressed it in the *Communist Manifesto* of 1848:

“

All fixed, fast-frozen relations, with their train of ancient and venerable prejudices and opinions, are swept away, all new-formed ones become antiquated before they can ossify. All that is solid melts into air, all that is holy is profaned, and men at last are forced to face ... the real conditions of their lives and their relations with their fellow men.

[Marx and Engels]

But this was not the only side of the sociological vision. For while celebrating the new, early sociologists also asked what was *lost* in this transformation, this transition to modernity. Just how good was this future we were rushing towards? Sociologists always had grave doubts about the shape of modernity as it actually emerged. This ambivalence is expressed by Marshall Berman in a passage that is itself a modern classic:

> **There is a mode of vital experience – experience of space and time, of the self and other, of life's possibilities and perils – that is shared by men and women all over the world today. I will call this body of experience 'modernity'. To be modern is to find ourselves in an environment that promises us adventure, power, joy, growth, transformation of ourselves and the world – and at the same time, that threatens to destroy everything we have, everything we know, everything we are. Modern environments and experiences cut across all boundaries of geography and ethnicity, of class and nationality, of religion and ideology: in this sense, modernity can be said to unite all mankind. But it is a paradoxical unity, a unity of disunity: it pours us all into a maelstrom of perpetual disintegration and renewal, of struggle and contradiction, of ambiguity and anguish. To be modern is to be part of a universe in which, as Marx said, 'all that is solid melts into air'.**
>
> **[Berman, 1983, p. 15]**

From the roots of modern sociology at the end of the eighteenth century, many key theorists have felt this ambivalent response to social change. The disorder brought about by rapid social and political change led sociologists to propose solutions which attempted to recreate social order and integration in some progressive way. No major sociologist tried to turn the clock back to a rigid, ranked, static society. The question was how to simultaneously promote social progress and social unity at the same time. Different theorists with differing political and philosophical colours gave us dramatically different answers, as we shall see. Even so, for nearly two centuries these were sociology's goals: the desire was to move through all this change and transformation toward a new stability, where human needs would be fulfilled. Sociologists as different as Durkheim and Marx each wished to resolve social disorder into a higher, better form of society.

Things changed from the turn of the twentieth century, as the hopes and catastrophes of our age took us from revolution to genocide, from scientific triumph to nuclear nightmare. Modernity began to seem less liberating and more like a deadly trap. Science and technology brought us deeper fears as well as grander powers. The dream that sociological knowledge could help us quickly progress to a good, harmonious society came to seem more and more hollow. Our faith in progress – the belief that we had the power to build our own future and make our own history – came to seem shallow. The challenge of today is whether we can find a way to reclaim our optimism about human powers and potential. Can we ever again believe in progress through reason?

The Promise of Modernity

The fundamental promise of modernity is that human beings – potentially *all* human beings – can be in command of their own future and free to shape it for the better. Two things are fundamental for this: we must firstly be unshackled from the past and we must secondly gain real, effective powers and abilities. Old static restraints must be swept aside whether these are aged social institutions, established power structures, or overbearing moral rules. There is almost a denial of history – modernity must start afresh without being shaped by the past. But this revolution in ideas, beliefs and authority will mean nothing if we cannot create new forms of organisation and production which expand human capacities – society must allow people to achieve more, produce more, and change the world faster than ever. For these reasons it is often said that sociology, like modernity in general, finds its roots in revolutionary transformations which break with the past. These revolutions transformed knowledge and belief as well as social institutions; they also had great consequences for individual identity. None of these 'revolutions' happened overnight and they did not occur simultaneously. The rise of modernity took centuries – but the pace of change accelerated so that compressed periods bring more and faster transformation as we get closer to the present social order. In earlier chapters, especially Chapter 2, 'Living in Modernity', we emphasised the scale and scope of the changes which together have made up modernity as a form of society; these are summarised for convenience in Table 17.1. Most of this chapter will deal with the ways in which sociologists have responded to this transition, especially in their analysis of social structure and social problems. Later in this chapter we turn to some current theories which claim that another great transformation is taking place which is transforming society beyond modernity into something new: **postmodernity**.

postmodernity
For its supporters, the further transformation in social, cultural, economic and political arrangements which takes a society beyond modernity.

The promise of modernity: knowledge and belief

Imagine a society where our view of the world is given to us by dominant social institutions. Certain values and beliefs (usually religious

Table 17.1 *Key dimensions of modernity*

Institutions	Belief-systems	Self and identity
Increased complexity Differentiation into specialised, interdependent institutions	Erosion of tradition and supersition	Social positions achieved not ascribed
	Static, rigid moral rules discredited	Flexible roles and fast-changing social expectations
Rationalisation of institutions	Secularisation Decline of Church Authority;	Increased self-consciousness and reflexivity
Economy	Separation of Church and State	
Religion and values	Rise of non-religious morality, e.g. rule of law	
State and law	Minority faith in sects and cults; fundamentalist revivals	Capacity to 'remake' our selves and our social identity, e.g. through youth cultures
Bureaucracy	A crisis of faith among the majority?	
Dynamic expansion of capitalism	Dominance of materialistic and individualistic values in capitalism	
New classes and social mobility		Powerful influences seek to shape our identity and influence our self-image, e.g. commercial advertising
Urbanism Decline of community, social control and binding social ties?		

ones) hold sway and are backed up by authority (such as the Church) and, if necessary, force. These values are embodied in strong moral rules, backed by the law, which demand conformity and punish disobedience. Alternative beliefs are a sign of barbarism (outside the society) or heresy (within). Either way, they are not to be tolerated, and if there is a consensus it is one backed by authority and force. In such a world the individual is subordinate to this collective moral order, embodied in powerful institutions. Freedom of thought, doubt and scepticism are threatening. The individual is much less important than the whole.

However much this is a simple stereotype it conveys an image of the medieval state of mind that lurks in the background behind modern sociology. The notion of progress sees a long development out of the darkness of forced collective belief and conformity. Instead we move to free-thinking individuals and questioning, rational thought. The

the Renaissance
'The rebirth' of art, science and creativity which originated in the fourteenth century and brought widespread renewal in European culture.

rationality
A concept of reason as the process of rational thought, based upon clear, objective ideas, which can be clearly demonstrated and understood by other intelligent human beings.

positivism
A doctrine which claims that social life should be understood and analysed in the same way that scientists study the 'natural world'. Underpinning this philosophy is the notion that phenomena exist in causal relationships and these can be empirically observed, tested and measured.

Renaissance brought humanism and creativity to the fore with a growing spirit of rational enquiry. The Protestant Reformation rebelled against a form of Church which placed a hierarchy between God and the individual, and instead extolled individual critical thought as well as individual faith. Here was fertile ground for the growth of critical scientific enquiry; the **rational** thought of Descartes and Newton underpinning the challenge to religion embodied in science, rationalism and Enlightenment in the eighteenth century. **Positivism**, with its total optimism about progress through scientific knowledge (without any residue of religion) follows triumphantly in the nineteenth century. As a consequence, sociologists usually assumed that modernity will normally bring **secularisation** in belief. That is, we all seek rational worldly explanations and lose faith in God. We also reject the moral authority of religions over our conduct and rigorously exclude religious influence) from powerful institutions. All of these assumptions look more questionable today. Is modernity necessarily secular?

A proportion of people in modern Western societies have felt dissatisfaction with the lack of spirit and religious meaning in the contemporary world. A dominant culture of rationalism and materialism has left many people longing for something more. Some find this in established churches, while a minority are attracted to fundamentalist movements, to sects, or even to cults. Elsewhere in the world, a transition to modernity has not necessarily displaced religion. Indeed, religion can form a means of cultural resistance to outside influence from more powerful nations.

The promise of modernity: social institutions

secularisation
The process whereby religious beliefs, practices and institutions lose their significance in society.

If rapid changes in beliefs and values often seemed both threatening and liberating the same is certainly true of social institutions. In the period 1780–1830 there were revolutions in social life which shaped the core concerns of sociology. In politics, the American and French Revolutions threw off established power and privilege and proclaimed the message that social structures could be ripped up and redesigned by human will and collective endeavour – history was in human hands. Accumulated power and authority could be challenged; traditions were not sacred; new values could be created. Out of this creative maelstrom of political change came a range of ideas, containing great tensions but still setting the terms for our thinking: human rights; freedoms of thought, expression and worship; democracy instead of authority based on tradition; individual citizenship; class interests and group conflict.

Just as political ideas were transformed, state institutions (all the arms of government) greatly gained in power. The capacity to control and administer society hugely increased (e.g. Napoleon's state reforms in France). Bureaucratic administrative and tax-gathering extended the state's hold over the rest of the society, whilst at the same time it forced the state to depend more on laws and rules, and less on the will of the ruler. At the same time as individuals and classes fought for more power, state institutions gained much more capacity to control society.

In the economy the pace of change greatly increased. Capitalism is a restlessly dynamic economic system, seeking new sources of profit in trade and commerce and not hesitating to transform social life in the process. European capitalism had been developing new economic groups and expanding across the globe for centuries. But the late eighteenth century saw capitalism grow fast into a fully-developed system of commercial agriculture and industrial production. The industrial revolution transformed society's productive potential – never before could so much wealth be created so fast. It was a huge expansion of human powers. But equally, of course, the sense of loss was immense. Old forms of skill and craft and the ways of life that went with them were swept aside. The new order was massively dynamic and frighteningly insecure for the capitalist, while it was hideously repressive for the new urban worker. Sociologists reflected all these mixed results in their prescriptions for a better industrial society – ranging from Marx's revolutionary call for destroying capitalism to Durkheim's call for reform and regulation. Urbanisation itself was seen as grossly disruptive of established social life – former moral codes and social controls did not apply or could not be enforced. The city might liberate and open up possibilities (for Marx it was an escape from 'the idiocy of rural life') but for others urbanisation was a terrifying threat to **social integration** and order.

social integration
The unification of diverse groups of people in a community.

At a more or general level, many sociologists have emphasised the increased specialisation in modern social institutions. More areas of social life are dealt with by formal bureaucratic agencies such as schools, welfare services, etc. while others such as the family or churches have a much more limited function. Modern societies are more complex and more internally differentiated. But they are more interdependent as a result – the complex social system depends upon the different parts working together. Early sociologists set themselves the task of showing how this new, more complex society could be made stable, integrated and just.

The promise of modernity: self and identity

Modernity has not only promised to expand our practical powers and change knowledge and belief. The optimistic vision of progress also sees a liberation for the individual in terms of social position, personal potential and autonomy. This becomes possible because the society is fluid and dynamic. Social positions are not ascribed by birth and family – instead they are achieved through work and education. Instead of slotting into one of a narrow range of roles, there is a diverse **division of labour**. There are supposed to be few formal barriers to prevent matching talent to social position – though of course all sociologists stress the inequalities of opportunity which exist in practice.

division of labour
Specialisation of tasks in ways that may involve exclusion from some opportunities. Hence, closure of labour opportunities exists in employment or by gender.

Despite that, the faster society changes the more it is possible to find new social identities and question old roles and rules. In that sense the unstable fluidity of social life gives people the chance to be **individualistic** and assert their own identity. Modern Western political ideas greatly reinforce this, with a stress on the legal and political rights of the individual, and the idea of democracy as above all representing individual citizens. Legal and politically, modern society treats us as individuals and we fervently believe in our own individuality.

individualism
Doctrines or ways of thinking that focus on the autonomous individual, rather than on the attributes of the group.

Group membership and conformity has not generally been a dominant priority within modern Western European societies. Going together with this strong sense of individuality is a heightened self-consciousness – a looking-at-ourselves to ask who we are. We know we can change. We feel we can construct our social identity and present it to others as Goffman and other theorists of social action have emphasised. At the same time we know that influential voices in society – from psychoanalysts to Slim-Plan consultants – try to tell us how we should feel and what our real needs are. Our self-identity is one of the battlegrounds of contemporary society. As we shall see, not all sociologists feel that we really have progressed towards liberation.

Today it is much less fashionable to voice optimism about progress in modern society and about the benefits of science. At one level Westerners do believe in some vague sense of progress – technology and knowledge systems get more sophisticated, goods are produced more cheaply, bombs give more bang for the buck – but to what extent are Westerners confident that their social and moral life is improving, or that the planet itself can cope with all their economic and military impositions?

Certainly nearly all the founding sociologists had severe doubts about the health or justice of the social system of their time. Each of them sought change, whether gradual reform or grand revolution, to put society to rights. They did not share all our concerns (such as the environment) but we still share the concerns they did express. We have simply gained more worries to add to theirs.

Positivism and Progress

If any founding sociologists were real believers in progress through knowledge then Henri Saint-Simon and Auguste Comte must be counted among them. Saint-Simon was the great proponent of industrial society as the fullest expression of human powers. His backers were liberal industrialists and bankers who celebrated the power of the new, and wanted barriers to economic progress swept away. Although Saint-Simon provided some of our concepts of class, his vision was not one of conflict between capitalists and workers. They should be united as industrial classes against old privilege and traditional ideas – the only problem about progress is that it should come faster.

Box 17.1: Auguste Comte (1798–1857)

Born:	Montpellier, France, 1798.
Education:	Ecole Polytechnique, Paris, 1814.
Career:	Taught privately. Assisted H. Saint-Simon, 1817–24.
Main works:	*Course in Positive Philosophy*, 1842.
	System of Positive Polity, 1851–4.

Comte worked with Saint-Simon as a young man, sharing his optimism about economic progress, but he added his own positivist vision. For Comte, society was nearing the culmination of progress because it was rapidly progressing towards true knowledge – a rational, scientific vision where the knowledge of many disciplines culminated in the most complex of all – sociology, as the 'queen of the sciences'! Instead of the delusions of theological or metaphysical thought, human society now had access to the truth through the methods of positive science.

Although Comte's birth coincided with the height of revolutionary change in French society, his mature work consists of an attempt to recreate order in that society through the application of true knowledge, as produced by science. The fact that Comte coined the label 'sociology' (previously he had dubbed the subject 'social physics') is not the only reason to regard him as the founder of modern sociology: he was also the first prophet of social science modelled on natural science.

Knowledge had to be constructed out of the evidence from the senses, out of empirical data, even if there was a role for theoretical conceptualisation to make sense of this data. Truth, therefore, could never be attained through abstract speculation or pure intellectual philosophising. On the contrary, the laws which governed all events in the world (for all were caused in discoverable regular ways) were available to the rigorous observer. The scientist could then formulate these laws in order to subject them to test and verification (or disproof). All this of course was hardly new – British philosophy had said as much for nearly two centuries – but what *was* radical was the application of the positivist faith in discoverable laws to *social* phenomena. The implications were colossal, for positive sociological knowledge could offer the means for peaceful reconstruction of social order by the elite of enlightened scientists and intellectuals – social change need not depend upon revolutionary violence and the manipulation of the mob. It should be no surprise to find that social change is explained by Comte in **evolutionary** terms, since this implies gradual adaptation rather than transformation.

evolutionary
Pertaining to a process of developmental change through stages, which progressively unfold (*see* evolutionism).

The evolutionary process Comte identifies develops through three stages of thought: theological, metaphysical and positive. This third stage brings the light of reason to the human mind, through the discovered truths of positivist science. It follows that those who know the truth about social life, the sociologists, should control things for the good of all. In particular, they can recreate moral order on a scientific basis through (as Comte argued in the *Positive Polity)* a new secular religion. Positivist knowledge gives scientists the authority and right to overcome conflict and prescribe the conditions for a healthy society.

Emile Durkheim

Box 17.2: Emile Durkheim (1858–1917)

Born:	Lorraine, France, 1858.
Education:	Ecole Normale Superieure, 1879.
Career:	Schoolteacher in philosophy, 1882–87.
	University lecturer, Bordeaux, 1887.
	Taught sociology and education, Sorbonne, Paris, 1902.
	Professor of Education and Sociology, 1913.
Main works:	*The Division of Labour in Society*, 1893.
	Rules of Sociological Method, 1895.
	Suicide, 1897.
	The Elementary Forms of Religious Life, 1912.

Durkheim's Project: social progress through sociological reason

moral consensus
Desire for, and agreement upon, a set of prescribed moral values.

The work of Durkheim is of far more significance for the development of sociology than that of Comte – in fact one of the prime motivations of Durkheim's project was the aim of establishing sociology as a credible and respectable academic discipline within universities. But more than this, Durkheim wished to apply sociological knowledge to social intervention by the state in order to recreate social harmony. In these aims there is clearly a direct continuation of the legacy left by Comte. Durkheim regarded himself as a progressive, pursuing reform guided by positive sociological laws; indeed, he felt that his commitment to reform for the good of society made him a socialist. Paradoxically, however, the goal of his reformism seems close to the traditional conservative aims of **moral consensus** and stable hierarchy. Progress was towards *social order,* rather than towards the emancipation of the individual human being. As Table 17.2 (p. 590) shows, Durkheim's core concerns were with re-establishing *social integration* and *moral order* in the modern industrial world. He saw the science of sociology as providing a sound basis of knowledge to underpin social intervention to bring society forward to new state of harmonious health.

Modernity as a more sophisticated social order

mechanical solidarity
For Durkheim, the form of social cohesion that binds people through conformity to norms, especially in traditional societies (*see* norms).

organic solidarity
For Durkheim, the desirable form of social cohesion in modern society that binds people in societies of greater and specialised complexity.

Durkheim's earliest work was his doctoral thesis *The Division of Labour in Society* (1893), which provides a key to his earliest ideas on the problems of contemporary society and their possible solutions. In content, the book is purely speculative, imposing a grand conception of the evolution of social institutions reminiscent not only of Comte but also of the Enlightenment philosophers Montesquieu and Rousseau. Durkheim's general thesis in *The Division of Labour* (1993) operates with the commonplace distinction (common among evolutionists) between 'traditional' and 'modern' society. The diversity and complexity of human civilisations is supposedly encompassed by this simple distinction, which stresses an evolution away from the **mechanical solidarity** characterising primitive societies, to the sophisticated **organic solidarity** which will provide the basis for a new harmonious integration within industrial society.

Primitive societies, he argues, were 'segmental', in that they were just the aggregation of kin-groups into clans and tribes, where these larger groupings had little real cohesion since each local unit could be self-sufficient as hunters or agriculturalists. Hence, like a worm, the society was divided into similar segments which could survive perfectly well if severed from one another. Even within these 'segments' social cohesion depended upon the power of rigid collective norms governing behaviour in every detail, so that total conformity was enforced; if any transgression did occur then revenge would be the basic social response. The primary source of conformity, however, was the shared consensus of norms and values, the **conscience collective** which was absorbed and reproduced by every member of society. For Durkheim, *mechanical solidarity* was a phrase which conveyed this rigidity and crudity of social form.

conscience collective
Coined by Durkheim, a pre-requisite for social integration, referring to the shared beliefs and values of a collectivity. Such collectively held ideas promote both a sense of belonging for the individual and the continuity of the group (*see* social integration).

In contrast to the ideas of other contemporary writers, Durkheim portrays 'traditional' primitive society not as an ideal, harmonious, integrated unity, but as a collection of fragmentary units embodying repressive conformity. For Durkheim, modern society is not inevitably fragmented by the breakdown of traditional community; instead the evolution of society provides an underlying potential for more stable and sophisticated social cohesion. The key to this potential is social evolution which takes the form of increased social differentiation, whereby society develops specialised institutions which deal with particular distinct areas of social life (e.g. religion, production). Just as the evolution of animals produces more sophisticated specialised organs to perform particular functions for the whole creature, society comes to develop a range of distinct institutions which deal more adequately with particular needs of the social whole. Just like anatomical organs, they are mutually dependent for their survival, and correct functioning depends upon the healthy functioning of each other organ, and the maintenance of correct integration of all the organs. The potential, then, built into modern society is for *organic solidarity*. If the component parts of society can be induced to develop 'a lively sentiment of their mutual dependence' then the conflicts and crises so prevalent can be swept aside. Once again, a new *moral consensus* must be constructed to bring forth order; unlike that in primitive society, however, this moral order is flexible and adaptable to allow it to cope with the diverse social roles and positions in a complex society – the individual has more freedom within the social constraints. A prime task for contemporary sociology is therefore the construction of a new central civic morality which will be disseminated efficiently by a state education system. Durkheim was directly involved in the development of precisely these educational aims and techniques in his academic work and in advice given to the French government.

Because Durkheim conceives of society as primarily a *moral order* constituted by the institutionalised norms and values, the goal of recasting moral values is absolutely central to his sociological project. But new moral values are not enough: social reform also has to have an institutional basis. Durkheim identifies chaotic economic competition as the root of conflict and class struggle; as a result he advocates regulation of the economy and of the worker-employer relationship. He even suggests joint *corporations* or guilds to mediate between worker, industrialist and state. Equally important, he argues, is the abolition of the *forced division of labour,* where inequality of opportunity denies individuals access to positions to suit their talents. Since unequal rewards must be given to different positions, then conflict will be created if individuals do not obtain suitable positions, even though education is designed to instil the idea of circumscribed tasks and limited horizons.

anomie

For Durkheim, a social condition where the norms guiding conduct break down, leaving individuals without social restraint or guidance (*see* norms).

All the other reforms are directed at overcoming the *anomic* division of labour, where economic life is characterised by **anomie** – that is, the lack of regulating norms. As we shall see in Durkheim's explanations of suicide, he regards the lack of sufficient normative regulation as a key cause of social and individual ill-health. Without such norms, humans develop insatiable appetites, limitless desires and general feelings of irritation and dissatisfaction. Modern competitive market society encourages all of this and, despite its claims, condemns people to 'unfreedom'. The 'unfreedom', due to anomie, rests on the conservative assumptions about human nature discussed earlier – humans without normative constraint could only be uncivilised beasts, slaves of their own whims and passions. Individuals must be subordinate to society, they must play their humble part in the functioning of the social organism. The collective consensus may allow them some choice between roles, but once allotted their position they must conform or else become pathological deviants. As Durkheim describes his vision of the correct relation between individuals and society:

> **The individual submits to society and this submission is the condition of his liberation. For man freedom consists in the deliverance from blind, unthinking physical forces; this he achieves by opposing against them the great and intelligent force which is society, under whose protection he shelters.**
>
> **[Durkheim, 1974, p. 72]**

Thus society is outside us and above us; it constrains us and shapes our lives and our physical responses. What is good for social integration is good for the individual. These are Durkheim's core themes and they lead him to his solutions to social problems: these views are summarised in Table 17.2.

Scientific remedies for social problems

This emphasis on externality and constraint links directly to Durkheim's conception of scientific explanation as presented in *The*

Table 17.2 *Durkheim's analysis of problems and solutions in modernity*

Problems in modernity	Causes	Durkheim's solutions
Anomie: lack of moral regulation; limitless ambitions; sense of worthlessness; lack of meaning in life.	Rapid social change. Decline of moral authority (e.g. religion). Increased complexity in social roles and rules. Fragmentation of work.	A new non-religious civic moral order. This is to be promoted through the State, laws and education. Moral unity to be based on a sense of mutual social interdependence.
Lack of social integration. Excessive individualism.	Unfettered market system. Unregulated competition.	Regulation of markets and working conditions.
Class conflict.	Unequal opportunity for natural talents.	Equal opportunity. Abolish inheritance. Fair inequality of reward.

Rules of Sociological Method (1982), an essay which was, as Lukes says, 'at once a treatise in the philosophy of social science, a polemic and a manifesto' (Lukes, 1973, p. 226). The book showed all these qualities, for in it Durkheim developed conceptions of the subject-matter of sociology and of suitable methodology which were dictated by his view of science. Since sociology must be established as a scientific discipline (thus enabling social intervention on the basis of positive knowledge), then the conception of science must *dictate* methods and concepts. The view of science that Durkheim adopted was, of course, a fairly crude positivistic one.

Deriving ideas from his contemporaries and teachers, Durkheim assumes that a particular science can only have the status of being a distinct discipline if it has a separate subject-matter not shared by any other science. At the same time, this subject-matter must be empirically accessible (which is why we must 'treat social facts as things'), and variations in the phenomena must be explained by causes which also lie within the scope of that particular discipline. These (false) assumptions led Durkheim to assert that sociology must become the *science of social facts*. These social facts can only be explained in terms of other social facts so that, for example, variations in suicide rates are social facts which must be explained by characteristics of the social group, such as lack of normative control. The claim that there are social facts, then, is important, for it establishes that there is a distinct level of social phenomena which are not reducible to individual characteristics or intentions – indeed they constrain the individual:

> **A social fact is every way of acting, whether fixed or not, capable of exerting over the individual an external constraint; or which is general over the whole of a given society whilst having an existence of its own, independent of its individual manifestations.**
>
> **[Durkheim, 1982, p. 59]**

Although Durkheim accepted in principle that one could only observe the *effects* of social facts in their concrete manifestations, as in legal codes or in individual acts of suicide, he nevertheless had a marked tendency to **reify** society and speak of social reality as a separate, detached realm from social action. He often referred to social forces such as 'suicidogenic currents' which impose an external causal effect on individual action; this search for external causes is of course part of his general positivistic orientation.

reify
To treat a social phenomenon as if it is an independent thing, with its own qualities.

normlessness
Associated with functionalism, a state of being without the guidance of socially accepted 'correct' or 'proper' forms of behaviour (*see* norms *and* anomie).

egoism
Normally a reference to selfishness, it also refers to a social setting where individual self-interest is the basis of morality.

altruism
The principle of acting without selfish concern, in the interest of others.

functionalism
A theoretical perspective, associated with Durkheim and Parsons, based on an analogy between social systems and organic systems. It claims that the character of a society's various institutions must be understood in terms of the function each performs in enabling the smooth running of society as a whole.

Durkheim's model of scientific sociology is put directly into practice in his study of *Suicide*, (1952), which followed two years after the *Rules*. Firstly, the methods used exemplify the emphasis on social facts, in that constant suicide *rates* are described, which are established empirically and statistically (even if later commentators criticise his dependence on official statistics). Secondly, these rates concern *group* propensities to suicide and do not involve any attention to individual cases. Hence Durkheim can explain these social facts solely by other social facts – the propensity of the social group to **normlessness**, **egoism** or **altruism** that depends upon the organisation and culture of the group as a whole. Durkheim therefore sticks rigidly to his methodological precepts and attempts to exclude psychological and physiological explanations. Most commentators agree that this is productive only to the extent that it discloses the importance of social factors; it is, however, profoundly mistaken and misleading to attempt to divorce sociological explanations from other complementary ones. Suicide is a phenomenon which must be explained by a range of factors which fall within the fields of many disciplines; this in no sense undermines the scientific status of any one of these sciences. Thirdly, the explanations of variations in suicide rates clearly embody the **functionalist** concern for the social cohesion of the collectivity. If egoistic suicide derives from insufficient social integration, altruistic suicide is the result of an excess of it; moral regulation, in contrast, can only be too low (producing anomic suicide), for the 'fatalistic' form of suicide has only a shadowy existence. Thus the two dimensions of the social group that matter are social integration and moral regulation, and the element in society that most strongly influences both is the *moral order* – frequently embodied in religion.

For Durkheim, social life is built out of patterns of behaviour governed by norms and values. Although related to other aspects of society, **culture** remains the key dynamic force shaping individuals and governing human behaviour. Religion is (as Durkheim put it):

> **the most primitive of all social phenomena. It was the source, through successive transformations, of all other manifestations of collective activity: law, morality, art, science, political forms, etc. In the beginning all is religious.**
>
> **[in Lukes, 1973]**

Thus social organisation and cohesion are explained by a shared normative system (usually religious), common throughout the social group. Changes in this structure do not 'reflect' changes elsewhere; instead, they are the prime movers of social adaptation. This view is shared by functionalists and it clearly stands opposed to any form of Marxist **economic determinism**. As such, this approach directs our attention away from economic relationships, political and economic domination, or variations in class structure. The evolution of culture within the integrated organic society is seen as far more illuminating than the study of concrete structures of power, which vary in historical circumstances. Rather than historical analysis, Durkheimian sociology seeks the *universal laws* governing social order and social evolution.

economic determinism

Associated with Marxism, an approach which claims that social life is determined by society's economic base (*see* economic base).

This concern for the universal significance of religion led Durkheim towards his later ideas in *The Elementary Forms of Religious Life* (1915). His views here lie outside our scope, but they lay the foundations for a tradition of speculative anthropology, which attempts to link the basic elements of social structure with the most basic elements in human thought – concepts such as space and time are seen as reflecting the structure of the group (e.g. Lévi-Strauss, 1970). The general notion that shared ideas are a main integrating force in society is reflected in Durkheim's view of religion as the most basic of collective representations; 'Religion is, in a word, the system of symbols by means of which society becomes conscious of itself; it is the way of thinking characteristic of collective existence.' Religion must derive from something 'higher': for Durkheim this must be society. Even though modern society has lost its religious sensibility, Durkheim regarded the construction of a moral consensus to guide and constrain action as a vital necessity. Humans are more civilised to the extent that they can deliberately construct their own moral order and then live by it (see Chapter 16, 'Knowledge, Belief and Religion').

Karl Marx

Box 17.3: Karl Marx (1818–83)

Born: Trier, Rhineland, 1818.
Education: University of Bonn, 1835.
University of Berlin, 1836–41.
Work: Editor, *Rheinische Zeitung*, 1842.
Paris, 1843; Brussels, 1845; Germany 1848; London 1849–83.
Main works: *Poverty of Philosophy*, 1847.
Communist Manifesto, 1848.
The Eighteenth Brumaire of Louis Bonaparte, 1852.
Grundrisse (Outline of a Critique of Political Economy) 1857.
Preface to a Contribution to the Critique of Political Economy, 1859.
Theories of Surplus Value, 1862–3.
Capital, Volumes 1–3, 1863–7.
Critique of the Gotha Programme, 1875.

Roots of Marx's ideas

Marx's ideas have been hugely influential. This is not only because he was the great prophet of the end of capitalism. It is also because Marx forged an original vision by critically drawing upon three diverse intellectual traditions – **German idealist philosophy**, **French socialism** and **British political economy**. Marx's theories responded to the establishment of capitalism in the middle years of the nineteenth century through a critical rejection of all those sources; he rejected Hegel's idealist philosophy in favour of a **materialist** approach to history, and he attempted to put socialism on a scientific basis by specifying the conditions for socialism created by the structural weaknesses built into the capitalist economic system. As a result, his theory is original and wide-ranging, but also a product of a particular period in the history of a particular part of the world.

German idealist philosophy
A philosophical approach based on the metaphysical thesis that the only things that really exist are minds and their contents. It proposes that human progress comes through the advancement of human reason.

French socialism
A political doctrine which emerged during the French Revolution, emphasising social progress led by new industrial classes.

Modernity as the emancipation of human potential

In his earliest writings, Marx displays his philosophical training through abstract criticisms of the philosopher Hegel, whose ideas dominated German intellectual life in the 1840s. For Hegel, the development of human society had to be seen as an uneven and fitful progress towards a state of true, full humanity. The ideal qualities of truth, reason and justice were only imperfectly embodied in the material world at any point in this evolution; but humans gradually recovered knowledge of their true nature through the development of theology and then philosophy. Hegel's system was a culmination of this development of

British political economy
The economic and social analysis of early capitalism by writers such as Adam Smith and David Ricardo.

materialism
In its Marxist usage, an emphasis on economic and political relations.

Reason. As a result, once armed with Hegel's solution, the philosopher could subject the currently existing world to *critique* and discover within it the tendencies moving towards the fulfilment of our true human potential. Philosophy was the means by which humanity might discover its real potential, while the state (as the home of law and justice) was the institution which demonstrated these higher qualities in contrast to mundane '**civil society**'. Thus, despite its potential for being critical of an imperfect present society, Hegel's philosophy instead came to justify the existing Prussian state as the closest embodiment of Reason.

civil society
An imprecise concept which normally refers to social institutions outside the political state.

Radical Young Hegelians – including the young Marx – accepted this role for the philosopher as all-seeing liberator, but wished to criticise the contemporary state. While joining in this, Marx took things much further. Firstly, he drew upon the French socialist ideas which developed out of the French Revolution, going further to suggest that the **proletariat** could be the 'universal class' that would actually bring the philosopher's critique to fruition through revolution. At this stage (1843–4) the role of this class was not derived from real economic analysis, but Marx did make the radical step of rejecting the notion that the state is the embodiment of Spirit or Idea, Hegel's force behind history. Instead, Marx came to see the state as a reflection of class relations in civil society, and he began to see these social relations as shaping human nature. This constitutes a complete rejection of idealism in favour of a *materialistic* explanation of history in terms of humans' practical actions within the constraints of particular social structures.

proletariat
A Marxist term for wage-earners, the propertyless class within capitalism.

However, any imperfection in the structure of these social relations will necessarily create imperfection in people who cannot reach their ultimate human potential. There is no constant 'human nature' but there is a full, ideal human condition which is never reached until social relations are perfected. The faith behind Marx's vision is that society is perfectible by human action, given the historical circumstances which allow the movement to communism. In his mature work, Marx develops economic and political analysis of capitalism in order to provide understanding of the weaknesses in capitalism that will allow it to be superseded by a whole new social order – socialism. Lying behind this, throughout his work, is a vision of what humans could and should be if social conditions would allow. This is expressed in his theory of **alienation**. This is set out schematically, together with Marx's proposed remedy, in Table 17.3.

alienation
Originally utilised by Marx to describe feelings of estrangement experienced by workers under industrial capitalism. Now more generally employed to describe people's feelings of isolation, powerlessness, and self-estrangement.

Alienation: the denial of human creative potential

The basis for this theory is the notion that what singles out humans from other species is the capacity to control nature by creative activity;

Table 17.3 *Marx on capitalist modernity and the socialist solution*

Crisis/Social problem	Cause	Marx's solution
Chronic social conflict. Class struggle.	All social relations in capitalism embody exploitation and domination, reflecting the underlying relations of production.	A new social organisation of production to end capitalist social relations. Social justice is possible with material abundance and an end to exploitation: 'From each according to their ability; to each according to their need.'
Alienation: from work; from the products made in work; from fellow human beings; from the human potential for creative, constructive activity.	Capitalist economic relations: labour is a commodity, bought and sold; the tools and products are owned and controlled by the employer; co-operation is destroyed; workers are prevented from controlling their work and being creative.	Socialist economic relations; work and products no longer to be commodities. An end to the rigid division of labour, especially between mental and physical work. Full development of every person's potential.
System crises of capitalism: collapse of capital accumulation; monopolies replace competition; worker resistance becomes more effective.	Falling rate of profit stops investment and hence growth; large capital displaces small; workers brought together in large workplaces and cities, with common interests as a class.	The proletariat take advantage of economic crises to build class struggle and destroy capitalist economic and social relations by revolution. They then begin to build socialism. For the first time in history, the subordinate majority gain power, so class exploitation and domination must therefore cease.

they can work out a conception of what they wish to create and then put this into practice. Work can therefore be the expression of human intellect and creative capacity, unless it is *alienated,* by being either concerned merely with survival, or organised socially in such a way that work is debased and made into a burden. The conditions for true humanity are therefore the conditions which abolish alienated labour; these must include abundance, abolition of the current division of production into meaningless tasks, and a removal of all economic domination and exploitation. Alienation of labour reaches its worst forms, Marx argued, with industrial capitalism, for here workers are tied to the machine in the performance of a meaningless task, only part of a larger process. They are forced to sell their ability to work (their labour-power) to the employer as a *marketable commodity*. Human creativity is therefore turned into an object, bought for the cheapest price. The product of this labour is owned and sold by the capitalist and so the harder workers labour, the more they are exploited by the capitalist.

Since employers own the factory, the raw materials, the labour power of their workers; and the product, they therefore claim the right to design and control the whole labour process, so that the worker's creativity and intellect are constantly stifled and controlled by others (see also the discussion in Chapter 12, '*Work and Non-Work*'). Quite clearly, in order to overcome these aspects of alienation, the basic economic relations which create it must be abolished – by revolutionary means. The whole structure of society must be transformed:

In a higher phase of communist society, after the enslaving subordination of the individual to the division of labour, and therewith also the antithesis between mental and physical labour, has vanished; after labour has become not only a means of life but life's prime want; after the productive forces have also increased with the all-round development of the individual, and all the springs of co-operative wealth flow more abundantly – only then can ... society inscribe on its banners: From each according to his ability, to each according to his needs!

[Marx, *Critique of the Gotha Programme*, 1875]

Whether communist society really could sustain abundance through high productivity and still abolish alienation is a complex and contentious issue.

Economic exploitation and class conflict

mode of production
A Marxist concept which refers to the structured relationship between the means of production (raw materials, land, labour and tools), and the relations of production (the ways humans are involved in production).

As Europe approached its year of revolutions in 1848, Marx became much more closely involved in practical politics through journalism and the Communist League, and he began to specify his account of social relations in terms of the social organisation of production. Marx came to see the structure of economic relations as the most basic and important element in society as a whole. We saw in the previous section that functionalist social theorists regard economic activity as merely a mundane necessity facilitating the cultural structures which depend upon it; for Marx (and Engels) the reverse is true because the rest of society – more or less directly – reflects these economic relations. The key to understanding a particular society is its predominant **mode**

forces of production
The tools and techniques of production.

relations of production
A Marxist term which refers to class relations that produce an unequal structure of economic benefit and political and ideological power.

of production which consists of the tools and techniques (**forces of production**) and the compatible **relations of production**. The latter constitute *class relations* which in all non-communist societies produce an unequal structure of economic benefit and political and ideological domination. There is no 'common interest' or spontaneous 'consensus' at the level of social integration; fundamental class divisions are one aspect of the inherently unstable system – integration of the mode of production. Conflicts take infinitely varied forms in society (e.g. religious or territorial) but they ultimately concern benefit or loss to different classes, and the conflicts have consequences for social relations and, hence, class structure. In this broad sense, then, Marx and Engels argue that 'the history of all hitherto existing society is the history of class struggles' *(Communist Manifesto,* 1848).

Behind these struggles, however, lie the *structural conditions for conflict,* and these derive from the structural features of the economic base. By 1859, Marx argues that 'The mode of production of material life conditions the social, political and intellectual life in general' *(Preface to a Contribution to the Critique of Political Economy,* 1859). Changes occur when structural strains emerge: 'At a certain stage of their development, the material productive forces of society come into conflict with the existing relations of production.' For example, the development of economic progress during the transition to capitalism in Britain came to be *held back* by feudal economic relations. As a result, Marx claims, these social relations must change: 'Then begins an epoch of social revolution. With the change of the economic foundation the entire immense **superstructure** is more or less rapidly transformed.'

superstructure
A Marxist term, which refers to social forms other than the economy, e.g. politics and culture, that are determined by the economic base (*see* economic base).

economic base
A Marxist term for the economy, which has a determining effect on the superstructure (*see* superstructure).

ideology
A perception of reality or way of thinking. Its usage is associated with Marx, where the term implies a mistaken sense of reality or false consciousness (*see* false consciousness).

The economic conditions for revolution in social institutions can, Marx claims, be known scientifically, but an apparent element of uncertainty is introduced by the fact that 'men become conscious of this conflict and fight it out'. We might thus conclude that this consciousness may vary, and that outcomes will be unpredictable, but Marx squashes such doubts by arguing that the consciousness of those struggling cannot be taken at face-value; they may delude themselves, and 'this consciousness must be explained from the contradictions of material life' – indeed 'mankind only sets itself such tasks as it can solve'. The main thrust of the *Preface* is, then, the emphasis on changes in the **economic base**, and these in turn produce **ideologies** which induce people to fight out social struggles – even if they do not fully understand the real consequences of these struggles. As it stands, this materialist conception of history certainly encourages us to regard the 'evolution' of the economic base as the key to social change – what Engels called 'the law of development of human history' – but we must qualify this in the context of other aspects of Marx's idea.

Firstly, this 'law' is only a general principle and we should not assume that all historical change can be reduced, simply and directly, to economic factors; on the other hand, the economic level is still seen as determinant in the last instance. In his historical essays, Marx showed no neglect of political and ideological factors but constantly related them to class interests and class divisions. However, no systematic theory is ever developed in general terms and so later Marxists have been led to produce widely varying elaborations which have often been mutually incompatible.

Secondly, the relationship between revolution and class struggle is problematic. We are accustomed today to regard revolution as a sudden seizure of political power, after which radical changes are made – and certainly Marx worked hard as a revolutionary for such a goal. However, the 'epoch of social revolution' Marx refers to in the *Preface* must mean the lengthy process of transformation of one mode of production (and related social structure) into another. According to Marxist historians of the transition from feudalism to capitalism in Britain, this took anything up to five hundred years – a very long revolution! Perhaps the answer is that revolutions as political crises are turning points made possible by the gradually emerging economic changes, which create new classes with an interest in breaking out of old institutional constraints – for example the emerging bourgeoisie extending its political and economic freedom in the French Revolution. The revolution that breaks out from capitalism is vitally different because for the first time the subordinate class seizes power instead of a new ruling minority – and so class domination is abolished forever.

This simply raises once again the previous problem concerning ideology and politics, for we need to know not only the material conditions which make possible such change, but also how the working class is to take advantage of its historical opportunity. The material conditions are based in the tendency for capitalism to generate more collectivised and centralised forms of production through monopolies and banks. At the same time, this collectivised system cannot operate for the collective good because it is still tied to the logic of profit and capital accumulation. Eventually, the economy can progress no further until capitalist social relations are swept aside. However, we still need to know whether this consciousness develops inevitably, or whether there are powerful forces resisting the rise of revolutionary political action. Without better accounts of politics and ideology, we are in danger of viewing consciousness as a mere automatic side-effect of material change. The continued survival of capitalism, the collapse of state communism and the defeat of the West European Left have only intensified the pressure on Marxists to give an adequate theoretical answer to these questions. The problem of consciousness remains, however, and Marxists have been bitterly divided over this issue – especially over the role of party leadership as opposed to 'spontaneous' class consciousness. Marx's own writings gave no real answer to this question, but the structure of his mature writings put so much emphasis on economic analysis that they encourage an almost exclusive concentration on the material conditions for change. The crisis and internal strains generated by capitalism create the conditions for the downfall of the system. Almost inevitably, the three volumes of *Capital*, plus *Theories of Surplus Value*, outweigh all other aspects of his theory, despite Marx's original intention to follow *Capital* with studies of landed property, wage labour, the state, international trade and the world market.

In the event, Marx died with only Volume I completed for publication and the broader studies were never begun. More generally, we can also see how the concern for the dynamics and contradictions of capitalism centres our attention on the economy as a separate institutional area of social life. This is possible in capitalism, for here economic activity operates with a logic and dynamic of its own through capital accumulation, expansion and competition. This is much less obviously applicable in pre-capitalist modes of production where economic domination is hard to separate from military, political and ideological relations. When this is the case, it is much harder to see a 'logic of development' for social structure deriving from the economic base. We need a much more complex account of the relations between economic, political and ideological aspects of social life.

We also need to build much clearer theories linking social action to its structural consequences, though Marx did begin to move us toward this. His account of the rise of capitalist class relations did stress the deliberate creation of new economic relations by the capitalist gentry – so we must conclude that the social structure can only control our actions once it is established as a general dominant system with specific dynamics and tendencies. Then the capitalist is constrained almost as much as the proletarian. At the same time, these structural features create the conditions for recapturing human control by those who seek to transform the social structure. Thus there is a complex relation between human action and underlying social structures. For Marx the real causes lie at a level of structural causation which cannot be seen by looking at individual events or experiences. These structures are, however, constantly changing and developing in uneven, contradictory and crisis-ridden ways. They therefore constantly generate new possibilities for historical change and thus for intervention by groups of actors.

Box 17.4: Karl Marx and Max Weber

In contrast to Durkheim's desire for moral unity in modernity, the work of Marx and Weber is united by a determination to specify modernity's historical origins, character and future in terms of material structures, power and conflict. Marx and Weber each recognise that capitalism is only one possible form of modernity, and that the particular economic relationships which give this type of social structure its character are also vital for the understanding of other aspects of society. Marx extended this into a general principle of the primacy of economic relations over other aspects of social structure which was to apply to all unequal societies. Weber bitterly opposed any such general theory of history, and stressed the equal or greater importance of culture and politics. We cannot fully understand the nature of modernity, Weber argues, by analysing capitalism. Despite these disagreements, they share the concern to distinguish *types* of social structure by specifying material structures (economic, ideological and political) and thus avoiding the search for ahistorical sweeping generalisations about the 'universal' features of society, or of 'modern' or 'traditional' societies. This sensitivity to specific historical developments and variations allows both Marx and Weber to have some account (however different) of the role of human actions in shaping history, even if neither approach can be seen as fully adequate. While Marx does offer answers to the theoretical problem of system integration and the structural conditions for change, Weber opposes this account as excessively mechanical. Instead, he regards political, cultural and economic structures as institutional frameworks in which social action takes place; ultimately, for him, historical outcomes are the result of the intentional motivated acts of individuals. As a result, Weber gives less account of the 'internal dynamics' of structures than Marx.

Max Weber

Although Weber died only a few years after Durkheim, he seems much more a figure of the twentieth century than either Durkheim or Marx. This is due to Weber's doubts and fears, and the anxious pessimism which underlies his account of the prospects for modernity. When he tells us that what lies ahead is a 'polar night of icy darkness' we hardly hear the sense of thrilling progress that earlier sociologists felt. Although Weber was committed to the value of knowledge, and although he was certainly committed to values (such as individual liberty) he felt no faith in the future. Modernity is irreversible, and brings material gain and increases in power, but it does not necessarily serve our human needs. A system that expands economic and political power so dramatically may also have the perverse consequence of trapping us more cruelly than ever in a debased and inhuman society. As he puts it in the bleak conclusion to *The Protestant Ethic and the Spirit of Capitalism*:

> **“Specialists without spirit, sensualists without heart; this nullity imagines that it has attained a civilisation never before achieved.”**
>
> **[Weber, 1930, p. 182]**

Box 17.5: Max Weber (1864–1920)

Born:	Erfurt, Thuringia, 1864.
Education:	University of Heidelberg, 1882.
	University of Berlin, 1884–5.
	University of Gottingen, 1885–6.
Career:	Teaches Law, Berlin, 1892. Professor of Political Economy, Freiburg, 1894. Professor of Economics, Heidelberg, 1896.
Main works:	*Methodological Essays*, 1902.
	Protestant Ethic and the Spirit of Capitalism, 1902–4.
	Economy and Society, 1910–14.
	Sociology of Religion, 1916.

Rationalisation and modernity

Max Weber devoted most of his formidable scholarship to placing modern capitalism in its historical context. Born into an academic family he pursued an intellectual career that spanned economic history, law, sociology, and philosophy. Despite psychological illness he achieved a prolific output, but his body of work has often seemed to others to be fragmentary; Weber does not immediately appear to have any central organising theory to guide his work in the way that Marx did. However, certain guiding interests and theoretical perspectives *can* be seen as unifying the diverse themes within his work. His first major concern was with the political paradoxes facing German society at the turn of the century. Weber was acutely aware that although Germany had become a strong capitalist state, the **bourgeoisie** had not succeeded

bourgeoisie

A Marxist term used to describe the property owning capitalist class.

status groups
For Weber, groups who share the same high or low status, in terms of explicit social judgements of honour or prestige (see status).

liberal-democratic
A form of government based on politics by electoral representation, whose citizens have a range of individual rights and freedoms.

bureaucracy
A type of organisation run by officials, and based on a hierarchical structure of authority, best suited for the efficient pursuit of organisational goals.

rationalisation process
For Weber, a process where beliefs, social institutions and individual actors all become more logical and orderly. Sensual, spiritual, traditional and irrational aspects of social life decline.

in securing independent political power. As a result, Germany lacked democratic institutions; instead, traditional **status groups** such as the Prussian Junker aristocracy and their high-born functionaries in the army and state bureaucracies unified and ruled Germany. At the same time, the German working class was the most highly organised in Europe and was nominally Marxist. Weber was deeply committed to the pursuit of a **liberal-democratic** bourgeois regime, but was haunted by the threats from Marxism on the one side and all-powerful **bureaucracy** on the other. As a direct result, he engaged in passionate debate against the theories of Marx (or more precisely, the Marxists) while at the same time accepting that the contemporary world could only be understood by economic and historical analysis. His other connected interest concerned the historical conditions for the rise of modern capitalism and science in the West. He posed the question:

Through what combination of circumstances did it come about that precisely, and only, in the Western world certain cultural phenomena emerged which represents a direction of development of universal significance and validity?

[WEBER, Origins of Industrial Capitalism in Europe, 1920]

For Weber, science and modern capitalism were each part of an even broader cultural development: the **rationalisation process**. Unlike other areas of the globe, Western Europe developed from its Ancient civilisations in ways that gradually removed the influence of magic and superstition and ultimately undermined the basis of spiritual faith. Instead, social institutions and individual action began to show more calculating, instrumental rationality. Law, administration and economic activity became formalised and rationalised, while the connected rise of science undermined the power of religious elites. Only in the West is there true science, and this new situation thereby allows us to look back at history and understand scientifically how we came to this position. The rise of this rational knowledge is, moreover, intimately linked to the rise of rational economic behaviour, institutionalised in the structure of modern capitalism.

For Weber, any pursuit of profit through exchange could be regarded as capitalistic, and so he saw most societies as containing some element of capitalist activity. In the modern West, however, the whole economy comes to be dominated by rational capitalism of a new form. The distinctive feature of this is the 'rational capitalist organisation of (formally) *free labour*'. These 'proletarians' are employed as propertyless wage-earners by an industrial 'bourgeoisie'. This employing class pursues capital accumulation (the continual growth of capital through profits) by using *rational calculation,* which Weber argues is only possible with free wage-labour (as opposed to serfs or slaves). The emergence of this particular form of capitalism is thus 'the central problem in a universal history of civilisation'. It is with this question in mind that Weber embarks upon his vast comparative studies of economic, legal and religious institutions of countries outside the West; he is guided by the question 'Why was it in general that in those countries neither scientific nor artistic nor political nor economic development followed the path of *rationalisation* which is unique to the West?' At the most general level, the explanation Weber provides is in terms of the institutionalised world-views encouraged by other cultural traditions. The rulers and intelligentsia of other cultures are seen as being prevented from pursuing the road of rationalisation by the nature of the doctrines and intellectual orientations which they themselves produced. For example, the Buddhist monk withdrew from all worldly activity in order to achieve a spiritual elevation, while the Confucian Mandarin engaged in administration on the basis of highly traditionalistic and non-scientific literary knowledge. Only in the West did a cultural orientation emerge which favoured rationalisation. At one level, the non-theological philosophical thought of Ancient Greece and Rome bequeathed an intellectual heritage; this could later fuse with the worldly orientation of Judaic-Christian tradition to provide a basis for rationalistic art and science in the Renaissance. Later still, the Reformation sowed the seeds of a Puritan asceticism which, combined with the worldliness of Christianity, produced a transformation in economic behaviour *(The Protestant Ethic and the Spirit of Capitalism).* This came about because, Weber claimed, Puritanism demanded sober worldly activity – doing one's duty in a 'calling'. If this produced riches it was a sign of God's favour and demonstrated good work. However, this worldly wealth was not to be *consumed* (as the wealthy in non-capitalist societies and eras had all done) but instead the wealth must be reinvested to create the basis for further dutiful work. This was demanded, of course, by the ascetic nature of Puritanism – the demand that the godly should reject all earthly pleasures. This combination of asceticism with worldly work was seen by Weber as a unique cultural development, and one which fitted perfectly with capital accumulation: wealth is amassed but it is continually reinvested to accumulate further wealth. No other religious ethic had ever demanded this combination from the whole population of believers (rather than just from religious 'virtuosos'), none had revered worldly work so highly for its own sake. Therefore, Weber argued, the origins of modern rational capitalism must be seen in Western culture and above all in Puritan Protestantism. This is not an appropriate context to judge the historical validity of

Weber's thesis, even though it has stimulated a long and acrimonious debate among historians. We must concentrate on the form of explanation that Weber employs, and in outline this seems to be based on the opinion that general world-views have a crucial effect on the intentional motivated actions of individuals. These world-views derive most usually from the doctrines produced by religious elites who hold positions of intellectual dominance. Although the content of the ideas and the extent to which they are accepted may be influenced by economic or political interests, these cultural ideas must be accepted as independent causal elements in their own right:

> **For those to whom no causal explanation is adequate without an economic (or materialistic as it is unfortunately still called) interpretation, it may be remarked that I consider the influence of economic development on the fate of religious ideas to be very important ... On the other hand, those religious ideas themselves simply cannot be deduced from economic circumstances. They are ... the most powerful plastic elements of national character and contain a law of development and a compelling force entirely their own.**
>
> **[Weber, 1930, p. 277, n. 84]**

instrumental calculation
A process of using the most efficient means to secure a particular goal.

Weber goes on to suggest that the next most important factors are political and not economic; yet even so, he discounted the importance of any political move towards socialism. Even if Germany did move in a socialist direction, Weber argued, the rationalisation process could not be reversed. As a result, humanitarian goals (whether liberal or socialist) were doomed by inexorable and irreversible growth of rational bureaucratic administration. Sober **instrumental calculation** would dominate all social life and the individual would be stifled by the constraints of his role within the 'iron cage of bureaucracy':

> **More and more the material fate of the masses depends upon the steady and correct functioning of the increasingly bureaucratic organisation of private capitalism. The idea of eliminating these organisations becomes more and more utopian.**
>
> **[Weber, 1978, p. 988]**

humanism
A position which stresses the importance of human needs and the human mind above all else, and rejects belief in a supernatural deity. It implies a belief that humans have the potential for goodness.

Utopian doctrines of all kinds were pathetic delusions, for rationalisation creates a world of technical efficiency and undemocratic administration that cannot be transcended; the sociologist must not fall prey to such illusions but instead face bravely the 'polar night of icy darkness' that is humanity's inevitable fate. The development of Western culture leads inevitably to a future which derides the very **humanistic** values which it earlier generated. This dismal account of contemporary problems demonstrates the opposition to Marxist economic determinism in

Weber's perspective, for he is clearly insistent on viewing culture as an independent factor. In consequence, one might think that this places Weber close to Durkheim with his stress on the primacy of cultural phenomena. This view cannot be sustained, for Weber always approaches 'culture' in a grounded, historical way as the ideas institutionalised in society by intellectual elites, and so it remains a materialist account of the role of ideas.

Weber is also very different in regarding social institutions as ultimately reducible to individual acts, although these intentional acts are shaped by this social context. Implicitly the grand historical studies connect with a philosophy of social action which stresses the deliberate intentions and motives of the individual actor (a view we will examine in the next section). As a result, Weber is led away from structural *explanations* in terms of the nature of the social system. Weber only makes reference to social structure and types of social organisation in an *analytical* and descriptive manner – not in terms of structural explanations deriving from an account of the society as *system*. One source of this perspective lies in his approach to history; Weber refers to the 'meaningless infinity of the world-process'. We only see pattern and order in this infinity of unique events by imposing ordering concepts (the **ideal types** – e.g. 'feudalism') and making comparisons. He rejects any notion of universal causal laws governing society, and is therefore certainly not a positivist. However, as a result of his view of history Weber resists making distinctions between different 'types' of society, and certainly does not attempt to offer analysis of the structural dynamics of any type of social structure. He may have described the basic features of capitalism and acknowledged that competition constrains the capitalist, but Weber makes no attempt to analyse the possible sources of crisis and change within capitalism itself. As a result, he displays a curiously fatalistic pessimism about the 'inevitability' of being trapped in materialistic and bureaucratic capitalism. Since capitalism embodies rationality of technical means, it is inescapable. Curiously, progress ends, because Weber fails to acknowledge the potential for change generated by the failings of both capitalism and bureaucracy.

ideal type

For Weber, a model, a set of exaggerated characteristics defining the essence of certain types of behaviour, or institutions observable in the real world. Ideal signifies 'pure' or 'abstract' rather than desirable.

Weber's vision of the possibilities available in modern society was far from optimistic, as Table 17.4 shows. His proposed reforms are modest, and the escapes are purely individualistic. There seems to be no hope of escape from this monolithic, rationalised world of bureaucratic capitalist domination. We can only try to build some countervailing democratic controls whilst retaining some private, personal space to escape the burdens of modernity.

Table 17.4 *Weber's dilemmas in modernity and rationalisation*

Apparent benefits of modernity	Actual negative consequences	Weber's solutions or escapes
Increase in human powers.	Enslavement to new forms of domination.	None.
Choice and control over society and nature.	Impersonal control over individuals. Bureaucratic power.	Control of bureaucracy through parliament. Government by elected elite.
Secularisation. Liberation from forced belief.	Crisis of belief; loss of meaning and ethical rules.	Personal preference for humanistic liberal values. Sects and cults may revive faith.
Rational reason: end of uncritical faith.	Relativity of values; loss of ultimate values; dominance of mundane material goals.	Remain true to one's own individually held values. Pursue scientific knowledge in an ethical manner. Charismatic leaders may inspire new faith in their followers.
Reflexive sense of self; individuality.	Others may be treated as instruments or objects.	Defend individual human creativity.
Rational approach to mind and body.	Loss of sensuality, physicality, physicality, eroticism.	Protect private love/desire.
Dynamic expansionism of capitalism.	Domination by impersonal market forces.	None.

Source: Adapted from essays in Whimster and Lash (1987).

If all this seems desperately depressing, it is important to emphasise some of the assumptions Weber is making which may well be erroneous. Weber seems to envisage an inescapable trend to impersonal bureaucratic forms of power and organisation, with an increasing concentration of control. This view does not take account of the rich variety of organisational forms that may be rational for different purposes. A profitable capitalist film company may operate very differently from a car company; even the car company may innovate in working practices and management structures. The dynamism of capitalism throws up great diversity, and there is no one deterministic model of power or organisation. Capitalism has also continued to expand as a world system, and the way firms divide their operations around the globe leads to complex and apparently fragmented forms of organisation. It is also very one-dimensional to suggest that we all become little more than cogs in the bureaucratic machine. There is much more to identity and self-image than this, and many people experience modernity as giving us more scope and opportunity to choose roles and re-define our social identity. Weber was right to emphasise the power and force of modern institutions, but he may have been much too one-dimensional in his pessimistic view of the future.

A range of recent theories has tried to analyse the dramatic and complex ways in which capitalist modernity is transforming itself today. For some theorists, the changes are so profound that we are moving out of a long phase of modernity into a new stage: postmodernity. Evaluating this claim will occupy the rest of this chapter.

From Modernity to a New Era of Postmodernity?

Towards a postmodern society?

We live in a time of turbulence. A shifting, unstable sense of transformation hangs in the air in contemporary advanced societies; once again, it seems, 'all that is solid melts into air'. It is not just that we approach the end of a supremely eventful century, it is also that the pace of change seems to constantly accelerate. Change that is so fast and so far-reaching must, it seems, take us to a new phase, a new form of society. These are the perceptions behind much current writing on '*postmodernity*' (referring to a new form of social institutions) and '*postmodernism*' (referring to a specific cultural and intellectual movement).

This sense of an overwhelming pace of change is not accompanied by any confident sense of progress. Instead we have lost our bearings, and lost any clear sense of what sort of society we are moving towards. In a way, this is embodied in the labels themselves – 'postmodernity' is something distinct from modernity – but the name does not give any clue to a *new* organising principle to postmodern society – though that, in a sense, is the point. Our world has no coherence, no totality. There is among the qualities associated with it a fragmentation, absence of clear structures, diversity of social institutions and social identities. Postmodernity is contrasted with the apparent clarity of modern society, based on industrial manufacturing, class division, politics linked to economic group interest, as well as on rational science and hierarchical bureaucratic organisation. Postmodern art and culture also celebrates the fragmented, diverse immediacy of contemporary culture where art and architecture show the play of surface appearances and the juxtaposition of disparate stlyles from unconnected times. All this subverts any notion of underlying unity or integrity of form. Playful diversity is celebrated. Instead of heroic struggles for progress, postmodern society has no vision of a better future and no more heroes (whether classes, groups or individuals) to be the agents of change to a better society. Postmodern theorists may celebrate the possibility of carnival – pleasures and creativity combined in frenetic information-based social experiences – but this denies faith in reason and rational knowledge as a key to understanding and bettering social life.

There is an underlying tension between different perspectives, however. For many who promote postmodernism (e.g. the French theorist Baudrillard 1988, 1989), our social world is primarily a cultural phenomenon of signs and discourses which refer to each other in a bewildering excess of information and image. In this sense we no longer inhabit the 'modern' world of solid social institutions and material social relations. We exist socially in and through images and signs which are hugely numerous and diverse.

For other theorists (e.g. Harvey, 1989 or Jameson, 1984), this cultural phenomenon of postmodern*ism* reflects and expresses a period of turbulence in economic and political relations. The world is in transition, and thus it is not surprising if a sense of rootless fragmentation in social life and values becomes widespread. The various writers agree that this is a cultural phenomenon (postmodernism) which is significant but they offer a materialist explanation of it (e.g. Jameson, 1984, pp. 56–7).

For these writers, postmodern culture is a by-product of a new phase of capitalism. At the very moment when capitalist predominance in the world is most assured and powerful, we see a range of theories that reject the 'totalising' models of class analysis, economic power and mode of production. Jameson and Harvey argue that we should not be misled by capitalism's move into a new phase. Even if advertising, image and consumption are the core dynamic of capitalism now, this does not change its nature as the material structure underpinning cultural change.

Postmodernism and contemporary culture

In the centre of Cambridge, at the heart of those quaint streets where tourists often purchase heritage goods and Scottish woollens, McDonald's have opened a new and successful hamburger outlet. Customers entering the stone facade first find themselves in a modern-tabled eating area with mock seventeenth-century plasterwork, imitating the famous Pepys Library. A visual surprise follows as they go to order, walking into a fibreglass Roman Coliseum to fetch their American meal. Fun and superficial, this pastiche of different styles is jumbled together with the highly controlled, labour-intensive processing of factory food that is the super-commercial hallmark of McDonald's. There is no unity of design, and form does not seem to follow function – unless we say that the real product is the experience of consuming, which is at least as important as the standardised meal itself.

While no one claims this restaurant to be a gem of post-modern architecture, it does demonstrate some of the fundamental characteristics implied by Venturi when he advocated *Learning from Las Vegas* (Venturi *et al.* 1977) to his fellow architects. This postmodern approach is playful, full of self-parody and denying seriousness of purpose. It reacts against the overbearing purity of form of the anonymous modernist glass tower block, which is devoid of all decoration or personality, whose simplicity of design gives no clue to function beyond a joyless rationality – seemingly a symbol of the faceless bureaucracy within. Instead, postmodernism celebrates ornament, surface detail, and either parodies old styles or mixes disparate ones together. There is no claim to a unique artistic 'aura' of originality, tied to the integrity of the artist. Authenticity is nothing to be valued. Instead artists, architects and designers can celebrate a throw-away commercialism that allows no one style or design principle to dominate. In film and the novel there is a rejection of straightforward narrative or character development in favour of unsettling jumps and discontinuities, or unexplained and bizarre juxtapositions. Structure and unity count for little; instead there is a sense of dynamic instability.

This is art for a society of consumers where images and signs form the substance of reality. Our perception of fragmentation in contemporary society is expressed through all this, emphasising 'our inability to experience the world as a coherent and harmonious whole' (Callinicos, 1989, p.17). As Eagleton puts it:

> **There is, perhaps, a degree of consensus that the typical post-modernist artefact is playful, self-ironizing and even schizoid; and that it reacts to the austere autonomy of high modernism by impudently embracing the language of commerce and the commodity. Its stance towards cultural tradition is one of irreverent pastiche, and its contrived depthlessness undermines all metaphysical solemnities.** ”
>
> **[EAGLETON, cited in Harvey, 1989, pp. 7–8]**

meta-narrative
Sometimes referred to as 'grand narrative', it is the name given to an all encompassing theory of human life, especially a vision of social progress.

Underpinning this approach is a deep reluctance to accept any all-embracing 'totalising' explanation (or '**meta-narrative**') of how society

authoritarianism
The imposition of power in ways that subordinates cannot control or resist; the celebration of a strong authority.

develops, or what we should believe. For the postmodernist, these 'great stories' are delusions that lead directly to **authoritarianism**, as these doctrines are imposed by those who claim to have the unifying key. Instead, postmodernists celebrate diversity and difference since this can reinforce dislocation to offer an open, unpredictable future.

Behind their rejection of any big political theories of progress (such as Marxism) there is also a rejection of any grand philosophy of knowledge. Claims to certainty and truth are brought into question by a wide range of modern philosophers, but postmodernism goes further to regard all truth-claims as competing narratives – or rival stories. Postmodernists equally distrust claims to political salvation and to scientific certainty. This profound change in ideas is shown schematically in Table 17.5.

Table 17.5 *Culture and knowledge: from modernism to postmodernism?*

C17	*C18*
Foundations of Rational Science: Descartes, Bacon, Newton.	Enlightenment: Rationalism, science and faith in reason. Political revolutions; faith in human rights and powers.
Early C19	***Late C19–Early C20***
Against urban, industrial modernity: Romanticism. Faith in progress through science: Positivism.	Doubt and fear concerning the consequences of modernity: Nietzsche, Weber.
Early C20	***Late C20: Postmodernism?***
Simple models of truth and reality are questioned. Relativity in Science: Einstein, Planck. High Modernism in Art and Literature: individual, original art of serious purpose. Joyce, Proust, Braque, Picasso, Surrealism, avant-garde.	Fragmentation, cultural diversity, plurality of identities. Post-structuralism in cultural theory. Mass reproduction of images. Super-abundance of signs. Distinction between 'high art' and commercial culture weakens. Postmodern art as playful, eclectic, ironic, superficial.

Postmodernity: a new phase of capitalism?

Capitalism has had no serious rival as an economic system since the collapse of state socialism in 1989. That is not to say that no alternative might ever be proposed, nor that capitalism is the best imaginable form of economy. It is simply a description of the contemporary world where capitalist corporations constantly increase their global reach and ensure that more and more of the world's life activity involves commodities, bought and sold for a price.

It is in this context of unparalleled capitalist dominance that we see a huge range of social theories informing us that class is dead and that culture and consumption are predominant in shaping our lives – not work (Gorz, 1982). If this seems paradoxical, then one answer lies in the idea that capitalism has entered a new phase, where the economic structures and mode of profit-making are very different. A number of phrases are used by different theorists to capture this idea: 'post-Fordism' (e.g. Lipietz, 1987), 'disorganized capitalism' (Lash and Urry, 1987); 'flexible accumulation' (Harvey, 1989). No one is quite certain what to call it, but there is a widespread sense of a new economic phase being born.

At the heart of these models is an emphasis on the ways in which capitalism simultaneously becomes more global and more divided and separated geographically. In the older industrial nations the extent of manufacturing, manual worker employment and hence working-class politics, all decline. Production shifts to newly-industrialised countries and old industrial centres decline, while the service sector expands.

These points are developed systematically in the Fordism/post-Fordism model that derives from regulation theory – a current branch of Marxist political economy (Lipietz, 1987).The contrast between these two different capitalist 'regimes' is summarised in Table 17.6. In this view, a certain way of organising profitable production, a 'Regime of Accumulation', must be underpinned by a 'Mode of Regulation' – that is, a set of social and political arrangements which support and reproduce this way of organising production.

Fordism characterises the period of economic boom which lasted three decades after 1945. Western societies mostly had state policies to promote welfare and full employment, and workers were tied to the system through this as well as by rising standards of living. Workers were able to buy the standardised goods they mass-produced, and they could afford to pay the taxes to provide welfare through the state. All this binds the majority of people into a shared economic and political order, and few are marginalised.

Table 17.6 *Fordism and post-Fordism*

(a) Fordism

Regime of accumulation	Mode of regulation		Culture and world-view
Mass production Standardised products Rigid bureaucracy Routinised work High productivity and wage growth Strong, large trade unions Wages bargained collectively	State manages the economy for growth and full employment Universal welfare provision Redistribution of incomes Strong interest groups influence policy and bargain with government	Class is the central social and political identity Work identity is more important than consumer identity Collectivist class interests oppose groups with individualist values in shaping politics.	Modernist culture Belief in social and technical progress Emphasis on social justice as well as profitable production

(b) Post-Fordism

Regime of accumulation	Mode of regulation		Culture and world-view
Flexible specialisation: - in *production*; global manufacturing - in *products*; designer goods for market niches; - in *workers*; polarisation into core and secondary labour forces - in *organisation*; devolution; delayering; horizontal structures	Private welfare for core workers, basic state provision for the rest Resistance to planning or state coordination Fragmentation of group interests	Diverse social identities and interests Self-expression through consumption and lifestyle Non-class issues and identities are focus for political action New social movements	Postmodern culture Commercial and artistic cultures overlap Mass-produced images more significant than individual art Image and surface appearance more important than structure

Post-Fordism contrasts dramatically with this. Now products are more diverse, and workers are much more divided by skill, reward, security and geographical location. Manufacturing is divided into simple and complex operations, with a global division of tasks across huge distances. A core of workers benefits very well from rewards for their flexible skills, while many others (perhaps in other countries) are made 'flexible' through low wages, unemployment and low-skill work. Social groups become divided from one another, and social differences widen between the affluent groups and the dispossessed minority. In the affluent countries there is much less shared commitment to paying taxes for universal state welfare – instead, unequal private and state welfare divides people further and right-wing governments appeal to individualism.

It is difficult for anyone in society to understand and picture this new emerging economic system. Although this new capitalism is linked as a system by dispersed and complex connections on a global scale, it gives the appearance of being fragmented and 'disorganised'. Particular social groups in particular places, who are on the receiving end of this new impersonal global system, find it very difficult to visualise it – let alone know whom to fight or protest about when their plant is closed or their jobs become redundant. No one can hit back at their local top-hatted capitalist any more. Since it is so hard to understand the complex, diversified linkages of capitalism beyond one's own community or society, it is hard for people to have clear models of social class or opposed interests – whom do you fight, and where? So class politics within the 'core' industrial countries becomes more fragmented and disunited, and it may seem that new forms of politics emerge which are not purely economic in focus. Feminist and green politics are obvious examples.

These interlocking features of the new economic and political structures are summarised in Table 17.7, which gives some guide to the timing and development of these changes.

The political consequences of globalisation and the end of Soviet power were explored in Chapter 10 on 'Power, Politics and The State'. Few writers on contemporary global politics would wish to be associated with the ideas of postmodernism – culture and signs seem less immediate than the brute reality of civil wars and ageing nuclear arsenals. However, many current developments might be seen to lend weight to the notion of postmodernity. The upsurge of nationalist struggles and the fragmentation into small nation-states occurs simultaneously with all the forces for economic and cultural linkage. It is hard to maintain the modernist notion of natural political progress towards secular,

Table 17.7 *From economic modernity to postmodernity?*

Britain: C17–C18	*1780–1830*
Capitalism dominant in agriculture, finance and trade.	Industrial Revolution. Urbanism. Modern class identities and organisations develop.
Late C19	*C20*
Faster global communication by sea and telegraph. Monopoly capitalism. Imperialism.	Air travel and radio shrink distance. Mass production and consumption. Consumer society and welfare state.
Late C20: Postmodernity?	
Instant electronic communication and mass air travel shrink time and space dramatically. Information revolution. Globalisation of manufacturing and finance. Growth of new service industries. Advertising/marketing: 'buying the image'. World markets, products designed for localised consumers.	Global political linkage: transnational institutions, e.g. EC, UN, IMF. Local political fragmentation: nationalism and regionalism. Beyond the superpowers: collapse of communism, triumph of capitalism. Fragmentation of class politics. Rise of new social movements. New sources of political identity.

constitutional and perhaps democratic states. We see the rise of emotive nationalism using potent symbols and new associations between religion and politics from Muslim fundamentalism to born-again Christian pressure-groups in the USA. For the moment, at least, it seems to be a world that has lost belief in utopias.

Conclusion: Sociologists and Progress

Sociology is a discipline that must constantly renew itself if it is to understand the fast-changing societies it serves. Sociologists have always been concerned to analyse their immediate time and place, even though this carries serious dangers of misrepresenting social change when one does not have the benefit of hindsight. Because societies constantly change, it is self-evident that sociological accounts must change too; sociology must offer descriptive and analytical accounts of social trends. However, there is a problem with this. At what point do we decide that our established frameworks and concepts are no longer productive? When do we conclude that established theories hinder us rather than help us to understand the changes in society?

Increasingly, sociologists are sceptical about the value of the classic frameworks and concepts derived from studies of modernity. This scepticism has two main dimensions:

- rejection of the priorities of classic theories on the grounds that many important issues in social life are neglected;
- claims that we are moving to a qualitatively new form of society known, for the want of a better name, as postmodernity.

Important social movements in contemporary society have had a powerful impact on social theories. Feminism, environmentalism, and anti-nuclear peace movements have challenged previous priorities. Many sociologists today argue strongly that classic social theories focused on production, class and economic inequality and seriously neglected such issues as warfare and nationalism, the impact of technology and social divisions of race and gender. As we have seen in many of the preceding chapters, much recent structural sociology has worked to redress this imbalance so as to offer a less narrowly-focused analysis of power, conflict and inequality. (Other theorists, as we see in the next chapter, extended the sociology of action and meaning in very diverse directions.) The preoccupations of the present day were not always shared by the founding sociologists, but modernity embodied then, as now, patriarchy, environmental domination, militarism and diverse forms of social division. The puzzle is why sociology neglected them for so long.

The critique which sees a newly emerging postmodern society is of a different order. Instead of pointing to neglected issues, this approach demands the recasting of sociological frameworks and concepts to make them appropriate for a new social world. Social theorists are very divided on the merits of this claim. Bauman, for example, declares that postmodernity has its own distinct features rather than being a faulty or transitory version of modernity: 'a theory of postmodernity therefore cannot be a modified theory of modernity ... it needs its own vocabulary' (Bauman, 1992, p. 188). This contrasts sharply with the approach of Giddens (1990a) who argues that 'high' or 'radicalised' modernity is a more accurate descriptive label than postmodernity. His aim, then, is the extension and renewal of modernism's theoretical legacy, not its wholesale rejection.

Giddens, moreover, has a wider aspiration for renewal in social theory. He emphasises the way in which sociology contributes to social change by providing part of the knowledge that members of society use in adapting and transforming their social context. Contemporary modernity has a greater capacity for this self-monitoring, Giddens argues, and so sociology more than ever has a part to play in changing the social world. While we can no longer believe in any models of guaranteed progress, we can envisage better societies and use sociological knowledge to help create them. In this sense, the postmodern world will be one where people in society have overcome some of the limits and problems of modernity by pursuing visions of a better world – 'practical utopias' in Giddens's phrase (Giddens, 1990b).

The following, final, chapter focuses on this issue. Can sociological knowledge be coolly detached, or is it necessarily involved in a critique of existing society and the progressive pursuit of a better future?

Summary of the Chapter

- The founding sociologists all saw profound transformations in the shift to modernity, but they differed greatly in their views on the potential and the pitfalls of this new society.
- Among those committed to social progress, some were reformist (e.g. Durkheim) while others sought radical change (e.g. Marx). In either case, there was an optimistic belief that modernity could be changed into the good society.
- The pessimistic fears concerning the consequences of modernity expressed by Weber, for example, have important resonance today.
- The accelerating pace of change in contemporary society leads many theorists to claim that we are witnessing a profound transformation to a new form of social structure – often labelled postmodernity.
- Although most theorists acknowledge that this postmodern society still has capitalism as its mainspring, the scale of change in culture, identity, work and organisations is seen to be so great that 'classic' social theories rooted in modernity can no longer be useful.
- This has led to a widespread search for ways to renew sociological theories and concepts.
- Most modern sociologists have abandoned any notion of guaranteed social progress towards a predictable future. However, this need not prevent us from using sociological knowledge as we work to fulfil our visions of a possible better society.

References

Baudrillard, J. (1988) *Selected Writings*, Cambridge, Polity Press.

Baudrillard, J. (1989) *America*, London, Verso.

Bauman, Z. (1992) *Intimations of Postmodernity*, London, Routledge.

Berman, M. (1983) *All That is Solid Melts into Air*, London, Verso.

Callinicos, A. (1989) *Against Postmodernism*, Cambridge, Polity Press.

Durkheim, E. (1915) *The Elementary Forms of Religious Life*, London, George Allen & Unwin.

Durkheim, E. (1933) *The Division of Labour in Society*, London, Collier-Macmillan.

Durkheim, E. (1952) *Suicide*, London, Routledge, & Kegan Paul.

Durkheim, E. (1974) *Sociology and Philosophy*, New York, Free Press.

Giddens, A. (1990a) *The Consequences of Modernity*, Cambridge, Polity Press.

Giddens, A. (1990b) 'Modernity and Utopia' *New Statesman*, November 2 pp. 20–22.

Gorz, A. (1982) *Farewell to the Working Class*, London, Pluto.

Harvey, D. (1989) *The Condition of Postmodernity*, London, Blackwell.

Jameson, F. (1984) 'Postmodernism, or the cultural logic of late capitalism', *New Left Review*, No. 146.

Lash, S. and Urry, J. (1987) *The End of Organised Capitalism*, Cambridge, Polity Press.

Levi-Strauss, C. (1970) *The Raw and the Cooked*, London, Cape.

Lipietz, A. (1987) *Mirages and Miracles*, London, Verso.

Lukes, S. (1973) *Emile Durkheim*, London, Allen Lane.

Marx, K. (1859) *Preface to a Contribution to a Critique of Political Economy* in Marx, K. and F. Engels 1968.

Marx, K. (1875) *Critique of the Gotha Programme* in Marx, K. and F. Engels (1968).

Marx, K. and Engels, F. (1848) *The Communist Manifesto* in Marx, K. and F. Engels (1968).

Marx, K. and Engels, F. (1968) *Selected Works in One Volume*, London, Lawrence and Wishart.

Runciman, W. G. ed. (1978) *Weber Selections*, Cambridge, Cambridge University Press.

Smart, B. (1993) *Postmodernity*, London, Routledge.

Venturi, R. *et al.* (1977) *Learning from Las Vegas*, Cambridge, MIT Press.

Weber, M. (1930) *The Protestant Ethic and the Spirit of Capitalism*, London, George Allen & Unwin.

Weber, M. (1978) *Economy and Society*, Berkeley, University of California Press.

Whimster, S. and Lash, S. eds (1987) *Max Weber, Rationality and Modernity*, London, Allen & Unwin.

18 Making Social Life: Theories of Action and Meaning

Aims of the Chapter

Theories which account for the Making of Social Life in terms of action, language and meaning are the focus of this chapter. In the first part, we examine a range of theories which centre on active, creative social action. Although we begin by looking at theories where actors are shaped by society, the emphasis in the action theories discussed is on the creative construction of social life by actors in settings. In the second part of the chapter the emphasis shifts to theories which seek the key to social life in the nature of language and discourse. We argue that these theories are capable of providing critical accounts of discourses in society even though post-structuralist theories seem to abandon the search for knowledge for a postmodern vision of endlessly diverse interpretations. Finally, we see how some recent theories of the self and identity re-assert the idea of creative social actors.

Introduction

As human beings we make and remake society through our own actions, but we do not do so in circumstances of our own choosing. This statement (paraphrased from Marx) expresses one of sociology's most fundamental puzzles. Can we portray the nature of social life in a way that reflects not only human creativity, but also the power of society to shape our actions?

Any sociologist must give some account of the relationship between individuals and the wider society, but this does not mean that there is any general agreement on how to portray it. In the first part of this chapter we shall focus mainly on theories of action and meaning *in relation to the creative actor*. These can generally be regarded as **humanistic** action theories, concerned to affirm the creativity of actors. Even so, we shall see that there are great differences among the various concepts of social action, and a variety of views on the way society and social action relate. One way to think of this is to imagine a continuum between those that see society as largely shaping action, and those who regard small-scale action as the true source of social life.

humanism
A position which stresses the importance of human needs and the human mind above all else, and rejects belief in a supernatural deity. It implies a belief that humans have the potential for goodness.

By contrast, in the second part of the chapter the nature of social processes will be approached in ways which focus much less on actors and their behaviour in small settings. Instead we see various different approaches, all of which see language as the key to understanding the nature of social life. Even so, there are great differences among these approaches, as we shall see.

Actors and Their Meanings: Varieties of Action Theory

unintended consequences
Repercussions or outcomes which result from actions initiated for other purposes. This is thought to be a key dimension of social activity, though these social effects cannot be explained by actors' intentions.

As we saw in Chapter 17, structural sociology has tended to emphasise how society pre-exists the individual. Predetermined social roles and powerful belief-systems socialise the actor into conformity to an existing culture which is stronger and longer-lasting than any individual. By contrast, theories emphasising social action remind us that social life cannot continue at all without being creatively remade by people acting and interacting. One dispute concerns how far this small-scale action reproduces the wider social setting, rather than transforming it. Central to this are the consequences of action – whatever the meanings and intentions actors may hold, the consequences of their actions may escape actors' control or understanding. Social action theorists who focus on the immediate social setting may have little interest in this, but theorists of structure will see **unintended consequences** as a key dimension of the reproduction of society.

Table 18.1 *Actors, meanings and society*

Example of action theory	*Nature of meanings*	*Form of action studied*
Weber on religion and action Parsons' theory of action	Meanings derived from established culture/values/ belief systems in the society or social group.	Goals and rational motives for intended actions deriving from belief-systems.
Symbolic Interactionism	Meanings and identity are constructed through social interaction, or imposed through powerful shared symbols and labels.	Face-to-face interaction. Processes of labelling and the negotiation of social identity.
Weber's Verstehen	Intentions held by an actor in relation to a separate act; Goals for rational action.	Individual acts; understand the motive of the actor and the beliefs available to the actor.
Phenomenology	Meanings are a common stock, used in a common-sense way to construct actions. They are taken-for-granted definitions of reality: 'common sense'.	Meanings must be interpreted on their own terms, and seen as real to the actors, and true in their setting.
Ethnomethodology	Meanings are accounts of everyday life by which actors make sense of their setting and achieve order within it.	Context-specific speech and behaviour. Routine social practices which sustain order and meaning in social settings.

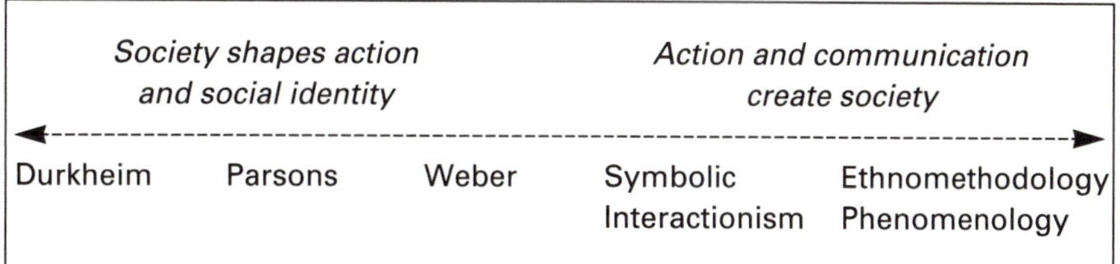

Figure 18.1 Society and social action

There is little real agreement among different social action theories concerning the relationship between action and society. The more radical accounts (like ethnomethodology) deny the existence of wider structures at all – except as convenient fictions which help us to act in routine ways without bringing every situation into doubt. Others (like Mead) see the acting self as a social product, uniquely individual perhaps, but only existing through socialisation into the socially available roles and symbols that make action possible. So even such basic terms as 'social action' and 'meanings' are used in diverse ways by different theories. Table 18.1 shows some of the diversity. In this chapter we shall compare and contrast these differing accounts of action and discuss whether we can distil from them a viable theory of action.

Action and meaning as a social product

As we saw in Chapter 1, few sociologists would claim that a person's behaviour is a simple direct effect of mechanical causes, whether from inside (instincts, genetics, etc.) or from outside (environment, social climate, etc.). On the other hand, many sociologists have been committed to explaining the way people behave in terms of external circumstances and influences from society. We cannot act just as we please because there are always social constraints and limited possibilities. Equally, we cannot have total free will because individuals are made into social actors by growing up in society. The question is how far we as social actors are able to re-make social situations and re-form our own social identity.

mechanistic
A form of behaviour that is determined by either external forces or internal constraints (*see* biological determinism *and* social structure).

The work of Parsons illustrates this issue. In his early work (Parsons, 1939) he argues strongly against **mechanistic** models of human behaviour. Instead, human actors do act creatively, because they try to achieve particular goals, and in doing so make choices about action. However, these choices about what goals to pursue, and what actions to use, are decisively influenced by the wider social context of norms and values in the society. Social values favour some goals (e.g. material success) and social norms favour some ways of achieving them (e.g. not favouring organised crime or bribery). Indeed, if there is a strong, effective socialisation process then society shapes what the individual believes and decides. All this is very reminiscent of Durkheim's claim that our freedom rests in being liberated from our blind, pre-social drives – by conforming to society we become civilised, and therefore genuinely free. The 'problem of order' – why doesn't society collapse into warring individuals? – is solved by shared values, norms and socialisation. However we should not exaggerate the influence of this **functionalist** 'consensus' model. Max Weber's work was also extremely influential on 'macro' or structural accounts of values and social action; indeed, Weber's study *The Protestant Ethic and the Spirit of Capitalism* was translated into English by Parsons. Here we see a much more grounded and historical account of the power of ideas in shaping social action.

functionalism
A theoretical perspective, associated with Durkheim and Parsons, based on an analogy between social systems and organic systems. It claims that the character of a society's various institutions must be understood in terms of the function each performs in enabling the smooth running of society as a whole.

A key part of the argument in *The Protestant Ethic* is that a change in a belief system (the rise of puritan Protestantism) led to changes in the world-view held by groups of people. This in turn led them to act in ways which were guided by new goals and by new (puritan) norms. So people began to behave differently in practical ways, becoming rational, calculating and self-denying, and imbued with the work ethic. Now Weber certainly offered more complexity than this. He saw an affinity between the economic interests of certain groups and their religious need to make sense of their lives in congenial ways (their 'ideal interests'). The new beliefs made sense of their economic lives and legitimated them, but the new ideas also pushed them towards new ways of acting and thinking. In this way, an external change in belief-systems will have a direct effect on the values, goals and actions of the individual, so long as those beliefs are adopted and accepted by the actors. In so far as the actor lives in a society imbued with a certain culture and world-view, then these will usually underpin the individual goals and actions. It may be sensible to see Parsons' early work as (amongst other things) an amalgam of the theories of Weber and Durkheim.

In these ways, structural sociology has given an account of action, but from a 'macroscopic' point of view, stressing the impact of the society or the wider belief-system on the actor. We shall see shortly that Weber also deals with individual action, but not in a way that comes to terms with interaction, innovation and small-scale settings. These are explored in an independent American tradition of theory (which Parsons neglected): *symbolic interactionism*. There is a profound contrast between the American and German traditions of action theory, especially if we leave aside the influence of Simmel (Frisby, 1992). The American tradition, rooted in Chicago, started from a humanistic focus on the creative,

symbolic interactionism
A theoretical approach which focuses on the role of symbols and language in human interaction.

pragmatism
A philosophy of US origin which treats values and knowledge as means to practical human ends. Concepts and values are regarded as true for so long as they prove useful. Knowledge and social life itself are therefore fluid, changing, human creations.

positivism
A doctrine which claims that social life should be understood and analysed in the same way that scientists study the 'natural world'. Underpinning this philosophy is the notion that phenomena exist in causal relationships and these can be empirically observed, tested and measured.

conscious actor. Deterministic, mechanical explanations of behaviour (e.g. through inborn female instincts) were rejected. Instead, actors possessed creative selves which initiated conduct. These creative actors did not act in isolation, however; interaction and the practical negotiation of conduct was central to the constant renewal and adaptation of social life. **Symbolic interactionism** grew as a practical approach based on field-work, with an apparently simple philosophical underpinning. Their philosophy of **pragmatism** saw the same source for both social life and social science knowledge: creative human interaction. Social actors define situations and how to act; and when this action includes creatively seeking knowledge, then practical human debate actively considers concepts and evidence before agreeing, for practical purposes, that certain ideas should be regarded as knowledge. (This seemingly simplistic philosophy has become extremely influential in recent years; philosophers now emphasise that knowledge is a collective human product, with no timeless status as truth.)

In contrast, the German tradition was much more abstractly philosophical, drawing on traditions deeply opposed to **positivist** models of knowledge – especially in social science. One tradition was the neo-Kantian approach, which strongly influenced Weber; it stressed the gulf between the natural world and the human world. In social science, meanings and acts needed to be understood by insight and understanding – not through empirical causal facts. An alternative tradition was Idealism, stressing that knowledge and truth were to be discovered in thought itself: that is, within the mind of the thinker, not through reference to an objective outside reality. The **phenomenological** approach grew directly from this idealist root, stressing a view of the social world which saw it as purely consisting of human taken-for-granted meanings.

Symbolic interactionism

phenomenology
In sociology, a focus (from Schutz) on the taken for granted knowledge that social actors share and which underpins everyday life. It is part of the idealist tradition which focuses on consciousness and meaning, not structural social phenomena.

The American social action tradition emerged early this century, particularly in Chicago. It is distinctive for its stress on face-to-face interaction in small-scale social settings, as well as for its concern with social identity and the 'public face' that we present to others. At the heart of this lies the notion of a creative, consciously-acting *self* – even though the self is itself a social product developed in a social setting through learning and socialisation. The symbolic interactionist (SI) approach has emphasised, indeed celebrated, diversity and difference in social life. This gives the tradition a liberal, humanistic character which refuses to judge or condemn and instead seeks to understand social life

ethnography
A research technique based on direct observation of the activity of members of a particular social group or given culture.

on its own terms, through direct contact 'in the field'. This has affinities with **ethnographic** studies of different ways of living, whether done by anthropologists or socially aware journalists. Today symbolic interactionism has come to emphasise the diversity of social roles and subcultures and the way that social rules and social identities are constructed by actors through their interaction. For example, Plummer has traced how people establish their homosexual self-identity (1975) while Becker emphasised the importance of powerful labels imposing deviant identities (1963).

definition of the situation
Associated with symbolic interactionism to describe an actor's interpretation of an occasion (*see* symbolic interactionism).

looking-glass self
Coined by Cooley to convey how individuals perceive their identity through the responses of others (*see* symbolic interactionism).

'I' and the 'me'
Terms used by Mead to refer to the impulses for social action: 'I' and the socially constructed self ('me') (*see* symbolic interactionism).

significant other
A particular individual whose views, opinions and reactions contribute to, and influence, the conception we have of ourselves.

generalised other
Expectations of conduct general in a social group; 'what is expected of you'.

The first roots of symbolic interactionism lie in a reaction against mechanistic or biological accounts of behaviour based on instinct. Central to this was the humanistic idea of the self-conscious acting individual, actively choosing actions. This self was not, however, a pre-formed inbuilt characteristic. Instead we had to learn our selfhood, our identity, through the responses of others. This is captured in Cooley's notion of the 'looking-glass self' (Cooley, 1964). Once we possess this conscious self, we create actions in ways that are not just simple reactions to stimuli. As Thomas (1909) insisted, we actually respond to our interpretation or **definition of the situation**: in so far we define a situation as real, it is real in its consequences. So a creating, choosing self intervenes between social influences and social actions. However this is not a purely individualistic perspective. These writers also stressed the way in which we draw upon shared symbols which attach meaning and social significance to objects or actions (Is this object a dining-table or is it an altar? The answer rests in meaning and symbol, not carpentry).

Individuals monitor their own behaviour by conscious thought, and this thought can only operate through symbols learnt in a social context largely through language. Through shared language we gain access to shared meanings and social expectations. We come to know 'who we are' and 'what we should do' through the responses of others to our actions – which we have to interpret using our social knowledge of meanings. These general notions develop in sophistication from Cooley's '**looking-glass self**' to Mead's conceptions of the **'I' and the 'me'**, but they all begin from face-to-face interaction. While Cooley's work mainly portrayed society as an interlocking network of small groups, Mead did come to acknowledge more general roles and patterns in society. Mead also stressed how our self has to develop in a social context through learning and socialisation. He describes how the development of personality moves beyond a stage where the child responds to the demands of a '**significant other**' (e.g. the mother) until the adult knows the demands of the '**generalised other**' in the roles he or she plays. At the same time, this world of roles remains flexible because actors can always try to renegotiate the nature of the roles through interaction. In these ways, the self is a social construction, but society is constantly remade by the actions of these social selves.

Society, then, comes to be seen as interlocking interactions between individuals based on actors' perceptions and expectations of each other. The content of action depends on the way actors come to define the appropriate patterns of action in the situation: to repeat our earlier reference to Thomas (1909), situations defined as real are real in their consequences. In other words, the nature of the social world ultimately depends on the shared definitions of roles and identities constructed through interaction. Both self and society remain essentially fluid and adaptable:

> **"The individual is continually adjusting himself in advance to the situation to which he belongs and reacting back upon it. The self is not something that exists first and then enters into a relationship with others, but is, so to speak, an eddy in the social current and so still a part of the current."**
>
> [MEAD, 1934, p. 182]

qualitative
Information that is not easily quantified.

The real strength of the symbolic interactionist approach lies not so much in its theoretical foundations as in the practical **qualitative research** that the approach has generated. Writers such as Hughes (1958), Becker (1963) and Goffman (1959, 1967) have all pioneered qualitative research methods that aim to 'get in where the action is' and 'tell it like it is'. In other words, we should try to understand the world as seen by our subjects – be they homosexuals, mental hospital patients or 'trainee' marihuana users. The task is to see how *they* make sense of the world and cope with others with different expectations or who have power over them (Goffman, 1974); researchers therefore must use sensitive empathy and participant observation.

total institutions
Employed by Goffman, it refers to all forms of diverse institutions, such as prisons and mental hospitals, that assume total control over their inmates.

mortification of the self
Rituals of entry, especially in total institutions, which debase the old identity in order to impose a new institutional identity (see total institutions).

Indeed, Goffman's accounts illustrate some of SI's key characteristics. Goffman (1961) shows how a *similarity of form* can be found in settings with quite different content: **total institutions** as diverse as monasteries or prisons may insist on a '**mortification of the self**' which strips away one's old identity through taking away clothes, cutting hair, and renaming or numbering; a new institutionally-defined identity is then imposed. Implicit in such an account is the importance of individual identity, and the powerful ways in which this may be distorted; equally implicit is the commitment valuing individual autonomy and authenticity. This liberal, humanistic sentiment is at the heart of SI (in stark contrast to some later postmodernist approaches). Similarly, Goffman emphasises how apparently irrational behaviour (such as the hoarding of useless objects by patients in mental hospitals) can be revealed as having a sensible logic – once it is understood on its own terms, in the context of that social setting. This approach generously assumes that actors' behaviour has its own rationality, and it follows that we have a duty to understand and accept social action on its own terms. Interactionists have often seen themselves as subverting orthodox judgements about what is acceptable or reasonable behaviour: tolerance of diversity is their goal.

Very frequently, the concept of a 'career' guides SI accounts of the way a new social identity (as pot-smoker, physician, etc.) is negotiated. This will involve learning appropriate behaviour, applying initiative, or possibly resisting unwelcome labels being imposed by others. For example, a teenager caught stealing might try to resist the label of 'criminal'. However, undergoing the process of conviction and sentencing to a penal institution may impose such a social identity in the eyes of others. This **labelling** (and its consequences for employment), together with the skills learnt inside, may help produce an acceptance of the criminal self-identity by the person himself; this would be a completed 'deviant career' (see Chapter 14). Generally, these qualitative methods are closely associated with sympathy for the underdog and SI often appears as a manual for individual resistance to pressures from powerful social institutions, and a defence of the dignity and rationality of the individual actor.

labelling theory

From Becker, the process where socially defined identities are imposed or adopted, especially the deviant label. Such labels may have consequences that trap the individual into that identity (*see* stigmatise).

For all the attractiveness and plausibility of this account of social life, certain problems remain. The first and most obvious is that social structures are neglected. Social institutions may be acknowledged as a backdrop to interaction but social systems and their related structures of economic and political power have only the most shadowy existence. Certainly, the claim that social life consists *solely* of actors' definitions is not sustainable. The consequences of inequality (for example) remain real, whether or not the actors define them as real, and the consequences of actions in a complex social structure may be outside the control or knowledge of any actors. In order to understand such consequences we need an account of the structure (cf. Plummer, 1979). However, it is unfair to direct these criticisms only at SI, for they may apply with even more force to other action perspectives. We can also question the adequacy of their notions of self and action since it might be argued that SI overemphasises the degree of conscious monitoring of action and manipulation of situations. Social life seems like a very consciously played game, and perhaps more scope should be allowed for unconscious drives and for social action which is less consciously 'controlled'. A quite different criticism has been levelled at SI's liberal tolerance of deviant diversity. This seems humanistic when SI champions gay people or those with a social stigma. But can tolerance be extended to the rapist or the drug-baron? Is any way of life really as good as any another? This liberal perspective can too easily slip into always justifying action on its own terms, without concern for the wider consequences or effects on others. These issues about the relativity and diversity of social life have become central debates. Chapters 15 ('Theorising Modern Family Life') and 16 ('Knowledge, Belief and Religion') explore some of these implications.

Weber's theory of social action

In turning away from symbolic interactionism, we return to the German tradition. Weber's work spans both structural and action sociology. He attempted to reconcile large-scale historical comparative studies with a methodology which began from the individual social act. Weber argued that historical trends and social institutions can ultimately be reduced to unique individual actions; but at the same time, actions have characteristic motives and goals which derive from the broader cultural context. For example, the instrumental, calculating rationality of Western individuals derives from a much broader trend of historical development. While Weber tries to bridge structure and action in these ways, he does not succeed in unifying them. Weber also tries (probably unsuccessfully) to reconcile scientific sociology with the special methodology needed for understanding social action. He attempts this through the method of **verstehen** (interpretative understanding) – a process where the sociologist attempts to gain access to the meaning of action for the actor.

verstehen

A German term usually translated as 'understanding'. Employed by Weber to define his approach to the study of social life, namely the interpretative understanding of human agents and the meaning they themselves attach to their actions.

This meaning of the act for the actor is seen by Weber as the *motive* present in their mind, and this motive is the 'cause' of the act. As we mentioned in Chapter 4, Weber distinguishes four types of motive:

- traditional conformity to habit,
- emotional behaviour,
- rational behaviour oriented to an ultimate value (such as salvation),
- rational behaviour oriented to a mundane goal (such as earning a living).

Scientific explanation involves using *verstehen* to understand the correct motive. We do this partly by locating the act in its context – we know that a woodcutter chops wood for rational reasons connected with pay. Generally, though, Weber's whole emphasis is on explaining actions by informed guesses about the actor's reasons for acting. This definition of action is inadequate since it remains excessively individualistic, apparently failing to locate thought and action in any real social context.

In practice, as in his study of *The Protestant Ethic and the Spirit of Capitalism*, Weber did relate motives and meanings to much larger world-views and belief-systems beyond the actor. Weber clearly does pay enormous attention to the context for action given by belief systems and historical social structures, but the connection between these and action is never explained adequately. This is very unfortunate, because critics of Weber's methodology – above all the phenomenologist Schutz – have radicalised action theory while at the same time abandoning Weber's historical and structural concern for the origin and significance of beliefs and meanings.

Phenomenological sociology

Alfred Schutz, an Austrian philosopher and banker, is best known for *The Phenomenology of the Social World* (Schutz, 1976), a work in which he used the philosophies of Husserl and Bergson to criticise Weber's methodology and construct a radical account of the nature of social action. In Schutz's view, Weber's theory of action was too individualistic. Schutz emphasised that we can only act by drawing upon a shared set of social concepts, symbols and meanings. Schutz argued that Weber's account of the relation between actions and reasons or motives was too mechanical.

We saw above that symbolic interactionists show how actors share definitions of situations and roles, and show how symbolic communication through language is fundamental. However, symbolic interactionists see these things as built up out of interaction in a creative manner, whereas Schutz's emphasis is quite different.

life-world
From Schutz, the world of shared social meanings in which actors live and interact.

common-sense knowledge
From Schutz, the practical social knowledge that we take for granted as the basis for everyday actions.

Instead, Schutz argues that the '**life-world**' is a precarious set of shared meanings available to the whole social group. It is a shared stock of **common-sense knowledge**, of taken-for-granted assumptions about society, other actors, and the world. In this sense, the reality of social life is only created by these shared arbitrary assumptions and conceptions – social order only lasts so long as we collectively believe in it. However, the precarious fragility of this shared 'definition of reality' is not recognised by actors in normal circumstances, because we adopt the '*natural attitude*' – that is, we see the world as solid, inflexible and constraining, even though it is really only a product of our shared ideas. It is only by a 'painful effort' that the phenomenologist can suspend this common-sense knowledge to see the real nature of social life. For Schutz, the basic structure of the social world therefore rests solely upon 'acts of establishing or interpreting meaning'. Phenomenologists therefore claim that conventional positivistic sociology is suffering from the same commonsensical self-delusions as any ordinary member of society – because positivism assumes that there really is a constraining world of social facts 'out there'.

In contrast to Weber's view of action, Schutz rejects the idea that single acts have particular motives. Instead, actors engage in a constant flow of action which takes place through a continuous use of *'recipe-knowledge'*: practical knowledge of how-things-are-done. We do not constantly reflect on future acts and clarify a goal (though we do have long-term projects): we just use our common sense and get on with doing things. Only sometimes do we look back at an 'act' and give an account of our motives. In the course of our action we employ assumptions about society and how it works, and we use *verstehen* in a crude way to predict the action of others. This last point is a major innovation compared to Weber, and perhaps also SI. According to phenomenology we are *all* amateur sociologists if we are successful social actors. This raises profound questions about the relationship between common sense and sociology.

Equally important is the fact that phenomenologists insist we should understand the socially given meaning of an act in its context. This *socially given meaning* (e.g. of a gesture at an auction) is quite separate from any motive the actor might hold. All actors take part in a social collectivity which primarily consists of a shared universe of meanings.

Ethnomethodology

Ethnomethodology grows directly from Schutz's phenomenological work, but it brings less concern for pure philosophy and more commitment to practical grounded research. The general aim is to demonstrate the truth of phenomenological arguments by practical experiments. Although only prominent since the mid-1960s, ethnomethodology has its roots in America through a fusion of action research and phenomenology. Harold Garfinkel is the founding figure and he coined the name. He intended this name to express a particular aim: the ethnographic description and analysis of the methods used by actors to sustain social life. In other words, ethnomethodologists work to show by practical studies that the social world is produced and reproduced by the practical actions of actors, on the basis of taken-for-granted assumptions – just as Schutz described.

Garfinkel (1967) developed ethnomethodology as a new answer to the 'problem of order'. Functionalism had previously solved this by emphasising 'moral order'. Garfinkel rejected Parsons' solution; instead he wished to search for the processes which allow 'orderliness' to emerge out of the flux of everyday life. For Garfinkel, only this will capture the real nature of social life. The task of ethnomethodology is therefore to expose the mundane everyday processes of social life as skilful accomplishments of the actors: even in a routine conversation, we use knowledge, skills and taken-for-granted assumptions. The point is that we are, as lay actors, unaware of all this. Only a painful effort, a disruption, or an incomprehensible response from another will make us aware of just how much we are taking for granted. So when Garfinkel sent his students home to behave like boarders – polite, well-behaved and respectful – their families responded with incomprehension or even hostility. As in his other experiments, Garfinkel is arranging for '**background expectancies**' to be violated so that the social setting ceases to make sense to the actors. Thus ethnomethodologists seek appropriate methods to turn Schutz's 'natural attitude' into a researchable phenomenon, exposing the organised artful practices of everyday life. In this way, because mundane interaction is treated as 'anthropologically strange', grounded observation and ethnographic description become the appropriate methods.

background expectancies
Coined by Garfinkel to describe the taken for granted assumptions and expectations about human behaviour in a given context.

For many sociologists, these ethnomethodological insights are illuminating, if limited; they should simply be added to the range of sociological perspectives (Goldthorpe, 1973). This view has been unacceptable to ethnomethodologists because they have claimed to displace conventional sociology altogether. For a time, ethnomethodologists claimed that the processes they expose tell us the whole story concerning social reality. For them, the typologies and structural concepts of conventional sociology are not only illusory: when they portray social processes as solid and constraining, they merely reproduce the natural attitude of the lay actor. Ethnomethodology dissolves away the patterns and regularities which are the focus of mainstream sociology; for there are no social phenomena which are not open to transformation in the flux of everyday life. What is more, social action and understanding only really operates, they claim, in the particular social situation, since meanings are '**indexical**' or tied to the immediate context. This applies equally to the actor using understanding, and to the social scientist who seeks to understand. Consequently, it is not at all clear that any account can make any definitive claim to truth or certainty: knowledge seems to be made relative and even arbitrary, unless we can find a way to justify our particular interpretations.

indexical
From ethnomethodology, the claim that meanings can only be gained in the context of their social setting (*see* ethnomethodology).

> In short, ethnomethodology does not think of itself as telling either the whole or a part of the story, but of trying to examine the ways in which *any* story might be told, with the ways in which stories are projected and interpreted as intelligible, coherent, plausible, demonstrably correct and so forth.
>
> [Sharrock and Anderson, 1986, p. 104]

In other words, we cannot choose between stories, but we can show how stories come to be constructed and believed. Is this enough to satisfy those who want sociology to tell us something of substance about the world?

Summary: creative social action

As we have traced the development of social action theories, it is apparent that there is quite a variety of ways in which the creative actor (or *subject*) is conceived. Equally, there is an increasing sense as we follow the theories that the social world is an arbitrary and relative construction.

Action theories give varying accounts of the ways in which social actors make social life, and how the actor has the ability to be creative and competent in doing so. We saw that Weber noted the human potential for *goal-directed rational action*, even if much of the time we acted out of habitual, traditional or emotional motives. We also saw how wider belief-systems in society may shape the goals of the individual and govern action through rules and norms. In modern society, Weber tells us, actors are forced to be increasingly rational in their pursuit of increasingly mundane and worldly goals. In contrast, the symbolic interactionist's actor is a creative, reflexive self. Although socialisation shapes our social identity and develops our capacity to play roles and interact with others, once we are mature we can re-cast our identity and negotiate how to behave in social settings. Goffman and the labelling theorists showed how this could be a matter of power and resistance – for example over the imposition of a 'deviant' label. But behind this lies the faith that there is a potentially autonomous actor with an integrity and a will that is under threat. Symbolic interactionism is thus an intensely humanistic, **subject-centred** perspective.

subject-centred
An approach to social analysis which centres on the active, creative human subject.

Phenomenology and ethnomethodology place more emphasis on the tacit skills and knowledge and social skills which actors use without fully realising it. On this view, we creatively re-make society, but by drawing on taken-for-granted recipe knowledge and sustaining routines which preserve the illusion of a stable, solid social reality. In

reflexive
Normally employed to indicate a process of self-reflection, which may modify beliefs and action (*see* reflexivity).

discourse
A body of ideas, concepts and beliefs which become established as knowledge or as an accepted world-view. These ideas become a powerful framework for understanding and action in social life. For example, Foucault studied the discourse of madness, highlighting its changes over the centuries and its interplay with other discourses such as religious and medical discourses, and illustrated how these shifts affect how madness is perceived and reacted to by others.

this sense, actors are not fully self-aware, **reflexive** subjects. However, there is an underlying assumption that we are all competent social actors, unknowingly deploying great social skills. The formation or development of these skilled actors is not explored: it is the processes of acting that count.

Language, Discourse and Social Life

Recent theories have provided new twists to these themes about social reality and the subject. Over a long period, a range of theories have emphasised the centrality of language in social life. In very diverse ways, theorists as far apart as Winch, Lévi-Strauss and Habermas have been influenced by philosphical moves to stress language as the key to social existence. Partly growing out of opposition to action theories, postmodernist theories add an intense scepticism about the idea of creative autonomy for human subjects. Instead of the humanistic focus of action theories, postmodernist theories trace the ways in which particular **discourses** develop which *define* and *constitute* knowledge, social reality, and the nature of the subject.

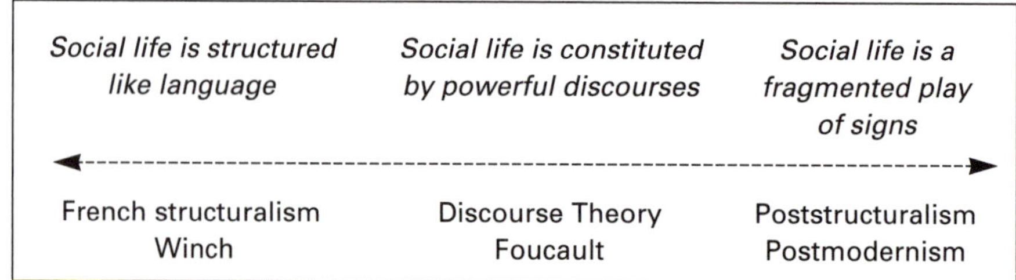

Figure 18.2 Society, language and meaning

Language and social life: structuralism and post-structuralism

French ***linguistic structuralism*** was one of the most influential theories of the 1960s, ranging from anthropology (Lévi-Strauss) to psychoanalysis (Lacan). The root of this approach was Saussure's new science of linguistics, developed in the first part of this century. Saussure was interested in how language worked as a system. What made language work was its internal structure, the relationship and differences between its component parts. We should not be concerned with the unique content of particular pieces of speech or text, or focus on the origins of the language used. Instead, what matters is similarity of form and structure. There is much emphasis on binary distinctions (hot/cold, raw/cooked) and on underlying similarities of logic behind apparently different phenomena (e.g. Levi-Strauss's studies of primitive myths). If Lacan could argue that the unconscious mind was structured like a language, the same idea could be applied to social life more generally. We should be concerned with uncovering structural form, not with human actions and motives.

Within sociology, the dry formalism of this approach limited its influence. Perhaps the most influential theory for a time in the 1970s was Althusser's highly structuralist version of Marxism, which strongly resisted humanistic notions of creative struggle in favour of a Marxist science which revealed the underlying complex structural determinants of social change. Althusser's 'hyper structuralism' produced strong critical reactions (Thompson, 1978). Among more recent French writers such as Derrida (1978), Lyotard (1984), and Baudrillard (1988), there has been a post-structuralist movement which is an important part of postmodernism.

Post-structuralism strongly shifts the emphasis away from the actor who has motives and exercises will. Active speech is not the important side of language. Instead, for Derrida, 'there is nothing outside the text'. In other words, meanings always escape the intentions of their author (the actor); meanings are always interpreted by others in various ways. In this sense our focus must always be on the *process* of interpretation – meaning and content are destabilised. As Bauman explains:

> **The central message of Derrida is that interpretation is but an extension of the text, that it 'grows into' the text from which it wishes to set itself apart, and thus the text expands while it is being interpreted, which precluded the possibility of the text ever being exhausted in interpretation. Derrida's philosophy asserts the inescapability of multiple meaning and the endlessness of the interpretative process.**
>
> **[Bauman, 1992, p. 131]**

Inevitably, this relativises knowledge – we have an endless succession of interpretations, and 'truth' is forever *deferred*. Consequently there can be no notion of progress through knowledge. We have no certainty; interpretations endlessly shift, analysis **deconstructs** apparent meaning and order. What is more, language is not grounded in any external 'real' point of reference. Language always refers to language, discourses refer to discourses (e.g. advertisement images which relate to other images, not to anything real about products).

deconstruct

To break down texts in order to grasp their implicit meaning by exposing their underlying form and hidden assumptions (*see* texts).

Fundamental to all approaches rooted in structural linguistics is the idea that we inhabit a world of signs – we do not relate to objects

signifier
From linguistics, associated with structuralism meaning words or signs which represent the concept of an object.

directly, but instead we know the world through **signifiers**, words which represent the concept of the object. Sometimes this has been employed to give a critical account of the ways in which signs can be exploited to bring particular associations to our mind (e.g. the work of Roland Barthes).

In the post-structuralist view, however, there is a lack of any critical account of signs. Instead, we have to accept that we live within a multitude of signs and messages, none of which has any special priority. We are set adrift in an endless play of signs referring to other signs, and texts interpreting other texts (Callinicos, 1989, p.44). This is profoundly unsettling to anyone who clings to more old-fashioned notions of truth and knowledge. It is equally disturbing to those who (like Callinicos) want social knowledge to be committed to radical change in society. Postmodernism (including post-structuralism) seems instead to celebrate the fluidity and flux of endlessly proliferating signs and endlessly deferred knowledge. We can be playful and frivolous, celebrating diversity and subverting the idea of order. In the previous chapter we set some of the broad features of postmodernism – in the next chapter we will explore the implications for sociology as a critical discipline.

Language and social life: ordinary language, rules and discourse

Winch and Rules An influential early discussion of language and social life was published by Peter Winch (Winch, 1958). He challenged functionalist and positivist ideas by reviving Weber's action theory (described earlier in this chapter), and drawing on the philosophy of ordinary language of Wittgenstein, Austin and others. Winch made a number of claims about the nature of social life which strongly challenged prevailing notions of social science.

He started from the assumption that social reality consists *solely* of shared meanings: 'Social relations are expressions of ideas about reality.' He went on to claim (1958, p. 123) that sets of ideas are always related logically, so that sets of social relations ('forms of life') had an internal logic. In other words, a certain way of life was always logical and consistent on its own terms. It was pointless to bring any analysis or judgement from outside. Different forms of life had to be accepted on their own terms. It was a mistake to look for external causes or explanations of this way of life – people just lived that way because they shared meanings and rules which were conventional among themselves. Thus, each form of life is a game with its own rules. If you do not follow the rules, you are not playing that game – picking up the ball and running for the goal line in the soccer World Cup Final is not only 'against the rules', it also undermines the whole activity. Thus, for Winch, behaviour which is not rule-governed is literally meaningless.

There are many difficulties with Winch's account and they have been much debated: Can 'forms of life' really be sealed off from one another so completely? How can we step into another form of life and understand it? Is it adequate to see society as *purely* composed of shared conventions? Is all our behaviour rule-governed, and why should we assume that rules are logical and coherent? There are many more questions raised by Winch's highly relativist position, and by his trenchant rejection of anything 'real' in society beyond shared rules. But these questions can be asked of many of the theories we are discussing, and here the issues are exposed in a very stark form.

Discourse Theory More recent theorists have referred to discourses rather than 'forms of life' but the basic propositions (and the roots in Wittgenstein) are very similar. The fundamental starting point is the proposition that humans can only know the world, and act on it, by means of language. There is no room for direct experience or empirical sense data – our experiences are all mediated by language. Laclau and Mouffe (1987) provide a clear example of this approach. While not denying that physical objects exist outside us, they argue that they only exist *for us* in terms of some concept or discursive framework: 'In our interchange with the world objects are never given to us as mere existential entities; they are always given to us within discursive articulations' (p. 85). Thus a discursive activity like building a wall involves both language (asking for some more mortar) and non-linguistic acts (laying the brick); but the combination is what makes up the discourse of wall-building. This discourse, say Laclau and Mouffe, is a human construct: 'natural facts are also discursive facts'.

These formulations are clearly very similar to Winch's. The world only exists for us in and through the meanings we share – and this claim is very widespread in modern social theory. It implies that social life can be disconnected from any causes or consequences outside discourses or meanings.

This anti-realist assumption is not beyond challenge, however. What if one brick fell down and hit the discourse theorist on the head? Would her experience be mediated by arbitrary language? Would the consequences for her skull be determined by her framework of meanings? If not, are there any social phenomena which would have a similar, direct, unmediated impact on us – poverty, for example? This question exposes the fundamental split between realist approaches and the wide-ranging tide toward discourse theory, post-structuralism and postmodernism. That is not to argue, of course, that discourses are unimportant. Much of what is interesting in social life relates to competing discourses – whether these are warring political ideologies, or differing prescriptions for moral conduct. Stuart Hall, for example, has written very influential accounts of New Right discourse, especially as it crystallised into 'Thatcherism' in Britain. But as Hall emphasises (1988, p. 10), 'I do not believe that ... ideologies are logically consistent or homogeneous; just as I do not believe that the subjects of ideology are unified and integral "selves".' Hall rejects the postmodern notion of an unstructured and open diversity of discourses. Instead he argues that:

> **All discourse has 'conditions of existence' which, although they cannot fix or guarantee particular outcomes, set limits or constraints on the process of articulation itself. Historical formations, which consist of previous but powerfully forged articulations, may not be guaranteed forever in place by some abstract historical law, but they *are* deeply resistant to change and do establish lines of tendency and boundaries which give to the fields of politics and ideology the 'open structure' of a formation and not simply the slide into an infinite and never-ending plurality.**
>
> [HALL, 1988, p. 10]

This is a very interesting corrective to post modernism, which leaves us with no means to understand where social life is leading, or what is possible within existing social arrangements. For the moment, though, we have no developed theory of the conditions of existence which constrain discourses. Perhaps social theory has come closest to this through the work of Foucault. As he wrote in 'What is an Author?', we should turn to

> **the historical analysis of discourse. Perhaps it is time to study discourses not only in terms of their expressive value or formal transformations, but according to their modes of existence.**
>
> [FOUCAULT, in RABINOW, 1984, p. 117]

archaeology of knowledge
From Foucault, to describe his excavation of past discourses in an archaeological fashion, in order to trace their emergence (*see* discourse).

genealogy of power/knowledge
From Foucault, the tracing of powerful claims to knowledge and their application by techniques of power, e.g. madness treated in asylums.

In pursuing this aim, Foucault's work attempts to go beyond humanistic action theories (such as phenomenology) and beyond structuralist theories (such as Marxism). His work is opposed to structural explanations, but also sceptical of any notion of free, creative social action by autonomous subjects. In a particular sense, his work is historical, for it tries to trace aspects of modernity first through an '**archaeology of knowledge**' (as in *The Birth of the Clinic: an archaeology of medical perception*) and later through a **'genealogy' of power/knowledge** (as in *Discipline and Punish*). But this is an approach which rejects any sequential narrative of events or any overarching explanations. He tries to trace the cumulative development of powerful discourses (such as psychiatry) and their associated techniques of power (such as the asylum). These discourses are bodies of ideas, concepts and theories which define the phenomenon they describe (possession by spirits, or in a different discourse, schizophrenia) and make it exist for people in a certain form: that is, it *constitutes* social reality. For example, today we 'know' that witchcraft does not exist, but schizophrenia does (see Chapter 16, 'Knowledge, Belief and Religion', for further discussion). Thus Foucault extends further the notion that social reality is arbitrary and relative. Again, social reality is built from meanings, but these are now analysed as historically developing discourses. It follows from this view of social life that there can be *no theoretical key to underlying order or progress*. This implication was not really thought through in the social action theories we examined earlier; in Foucault, as in other postmodern theories, this is proclaimed as a major argument. They proclaim it in deliberate opposition to theories which hope to explain social change structurally and set the terms for progress to a better future.

For Foucault, then, our identity as subjects – who we are and what we are capable of – has been constructed or constituted through particular discourses. For example, in the modern West people 'know' that women are independent, rational actors, capable of making choices which overcome the dictates of instincts, hormones or emotions. Hence women are eligible to exercise full legal and political rights as individual citizens; females are not simply extensions of their more rational fathers or husbands. Now, however obvious all that may seem, this conception of women is recent and even now precariously established. The discourses of individualism, citizenship, and rational conduct were for a long time applied only to men. It took struggles to *constitute* women as *really possessing* these qualities in the eyes of society. Feminists had to get existing powerful discourses applied to them (e.g. citizenship) as well as trying to initiate their own new discourse (or discourses) of feminism.

Hence discourses may consist principally of meanings and language, but that does not diminish their power. Discourses have a general power if we take them for granted and live within their bounds. From a Foucauldian viewpoint, if we conceive of ourselves and our social world in terms of a particular discourse, then that *is* who we are and how we live. However, Foucault is acutely aware that discourses link to power in another way: they are a terrain for struggle and domination as discourses are established and resisted. The genealogy of a particular discourse (e.g. penal policy) traces this process.

To summarise, Foucault's work aims to provide an 'archaeology' of the human sciences, tracing their development as distinct discourses about madness, the body or about criminality, as well as aiming to trace the genealogy of establishing power/knowledge through institutional practices, such as the design of prisons or the treatment of madness in asylums. Changing discourses define and constitute human qualities in different ways in different eras (e.g. concepts of 'rehabilitating' criminals, or notions of sexuality since Freud). This may also be enacted or enforced through techniques of power/knowledge – the practical implementation of a powerful discourse. This in turn leads subjects (i.e. conscious individuals) to define themselves and their nature in particular ways. Hence we are constituted as humans through particular discourses and practices: our own subjectivity (our identity and will to act) is relative and constructed.

Rediscovering the self

As we have seen through the second part of this chapter, recent social theories have launched a sustained assault on the humanistic idea of a willed, creative, choosing actor. The focus has shifted to understanding social life in terms of constructed meanings, forms of life and discourses. Instead of human individuals being the originators of social life, their own nature and powers are defined discursively in society. As Foucault claimed, the very notion of the originating actor (or 'subject') is a historically-specific construction:

> **How, under what conditions, and in what forms can something like a subject appear in the order of discourse? What place can it occupy in each type of discourse, what functions can it assume, and by obeying what rules? In short, it is a matter of depriving the subject ... of its role as originator, and of analysing the subject as a variable and complex function of discourse.**
>
> **[in Rabinow, 1984, p. 118]**

However, this formulation raises as many questions as it solves. If we really are constituted by discourse, then do we actually acquire the characteristics of willed subjects, once that discourse is established? Or, to put it another way, has modernity and its discourses transformed the powers of individual human beings? Foucault's wry, subversive scepticism never allowed him to acknowledge this possibility. Instead, in his latest writings, Foucault re-emphasised the constructed nature of identity – but this time as an aesthetic self-stylisation:

> **We have hardly any remnant of the idea in society, that the principal work of art which one has to take care of, the main area to which one must apply aesthetic values, is oneself, one's life, one's existence.**
>
> **[in Rabinow, 1984, p. 362]**

This seems a narcissistic way to reintroduce the capacity of individuals to reshape themselves and negotiate identity. Foucault again seems to have a yearning for some departed self-autonomy which discipline and rationality have suppressed in modernity.

This contrasts sharply with the new notion of self-identity in the recent work of Giddens (1991), and with the new emphasis on life-histories and autobiography in sociological research. As Erben puts it:

> **There are very few sociologists of even the most insistent Foucauldian tendencies who would accept that personal experience is merely a bit of cosmic twitching circuitry in the neurones of the discourses which compose us ... Many sociologists would argue, however, that the cultural is a highly complex domain and that the individual is constituted in the very formation of the ego at the social level.**
>
> [Erben, 1993, p. 23]

For Giddens (1991), human powers have been enhanced in modernity even if many dilemmas remain. Human beings do act on the basis of knowledge to reflect on their conduct and their society – and this need not be limited to small-scale social settings. Modern societies continually accumulate information and use it to influence the social world as well as the natural world. The increased openness of roles and identities in late modernity allows greater scope for renegotiating social relations. Giddens emphasises the flexibility with which we redefine familial roles after divorce, as well as the increasingly voluntary nature of family roles – as divorce exemplifies.

ontological security
A stable mental state derived from a sense of continuity and order in events.

Of course, much of this can equally be expressed in negative terms, as in Lasch's *Culture of Narcissism* (1980). Here narcissism refers to self-obsession, not self-love. If our identity and our appearance are supposedly under our own control, then we must also anxiously accept responsibility. Hence, a neurotic obsession with beauty, fitness and health may overtake us, with damaging effects. Giddens acknowledges some of this anxiety as he emphasises our need for **ontological security**. In other words, we need to protect ourselves from fears of our own vulnerability and distance ourselves from threats – whether from disease, death, or uncontrolled emotional violence. In the absence of established meaning-systems (such as religion) to provide security, we face 'the looming threat of personal meaninglessness' (Giddens, 1991, p. 201). Modernity destroys security at the same time as enhancing our powers. Despite knowledge, we face uncertainty in a fragmented world that is extremely difficult to understand. Despite our own space to change our lives, powerful forces relentlessly commercialise our world and build anonymous empires of influence that may leave us feeling powerless, or inadequate. Despite all this though, Giddens appears to have faith in the human capacity to learn and reflect, to resist, and to modify our conduct. We have the power to re-make ourselves and rebuild our social world.

On that note of hope, tinged with doubt, we turn to the final chapter which explores these themes.

Summary of the Chapter

- We can distinguish theories focused on creative social action from those which begin from theories of language and meaning. Within each category there are diverse accounts of how social life is made in social processes.
- A number of more humanistic perspectives put their emphasis on the creative human actor who negotiates situations and identities in face-to-face settings.
- These approaches (e.g. symbolic interactionism) tend to assume that actions 'make sense' if understood on their terms in the context of the particular setting; consequently these theories tend to advocate social tolerance of diverse norms and identities.
- Phenomenology and ethnomethodology place rather less stress on conscious motives and reflection by the actor. Instead an essentially changing and precarious social world is maintained unwittingly through our shared meanings and our practical social skills.
- Theories which stress language have much less focus on actors and their motives or skills. Instead, the general nature of social life is understood through theories of linguistic structure, rules of language use, or by analysing discourses which exist beyond the individual actor.
- There is a distinction between accounts of discourses which depict their history and their power (e.g. Foucault) and the post-structuralist accounts (e.g. Derrida) which suggest an endless succession of interpretations and re-interpretations.
- The stance of post-structuralism and postmodernism which denies the active, creative human subject has been rejected by many recent theories which re-examine the consequences of contemporary society for the self and identity.

References

Baudrillard, J. (1988) *Selected Writings*, Cambridge, Polity Press.

Baudrillard, J. (1989) *America*, London, Verso.

Bauman, Z. (1992) *Intimations of Postmodernity*, London, Routledge.

Becker, H. (1963) *Outsiders*, New York, Free Press.

Callinicos, A. (1989) *Against Postmodernism*, Cambridge, Polity Press.

Derrida, J. (1978) *Writing and Difference*, London, Routledge.

Erben, M. (1993) 'The problem of other lives: social perspectives on written biography', *Sociology*, vol. 27, no. 1.

Foucault, M. (1979) *Discipline and Punish*, Harmondsworth, Penguin.

Foucault, M. (1986) *The Birth of the Clinic*, London, Routledge.

Frisby, D. (1992) *Simmel and Since: essays on Georg Simmel's Social Theory*, London, Routledge.

Garfinkel, H. (1967) *Studies in Ethnomethodology*, Cambridge, Polity Press.

Giddens, A. (1991) *Modernity and Self-Identity*, Cambridge, Polity Press.

Goffman, E. (1959) *The Presentation of Self in Everyday Life*, Garden City, Doubleday.

Goffman, E. (1961) *Asylums*, Garden City, Doubleday.

Goffman, E. (1967) *Interaction Ritual*, Garden City, Doubleday.

Goffman, E. (1974) *Frame Analysis*, Harmondsworth, Penguin.

Goldthorpe, J. (1973) 'A Revolution in Sociology?' *Sociology*, vol. 7, no. 3.

Hall, S. (1988) *The Hard Road to Renewal*, London, Verso.

Hughes, E. C. (1958) *Men and Their Work*, New York, Free Press.

Laclau, E. and C. Mouffe (1987) 'Post-Marxism Without Apologies', *New Left Review*, no. 166

Lasch, C, (1980) *The Culture of Narcissism*, London, Abacus.

Lyotard, J.-F. (1984) *The Postmodern Condition*, Manchester, Manchester University Press.

Mead, G. H. (1934) *Mind, Self and Society*, Chicago, Chicago University Press.

Parsons, T. (1939) *The Structure of Social Action*, New York, Free Press.

Plummer, K. (1975) *Sexual Stigma: an Interactionist Account*, London, Routledge.

Plummer, K. (1979) in D. Downes and P. Rock (eds) *Deviant Interpretations*, London, Martin Robertson.

Rabinow, P. (ed)(1984) *The Foucault Reader*, Harmondsworth, Penguin.

Schutz, A. (1976) *The Phenomenology of the Social World*, London, Heinemann.

Sharrock, W. and B. Anderson (1986) *The Ethnomethodologists*, London, Tavistock.

Smart, B. (1993) *Postmodernity*, London, Routledge.

Thompson, E. P. (1978) *The Poverty of Theory*, London, Merlin.

Winch, P. (1958) *The Idea of a Social Science*, London, Routledge.

19 Making Our Futures: Sociological Knowledge and Social Change

Aims of the Chapter

In this final chapter we argue that there is still a vital role for sociology to play in helping people to shape their own lives and build their own diverse futures. Despite all the doubts about the modernist project of progress through reason, sociology can still claim to offer vital insights to people in society about the possibilities and limits that face them.

Introduction

Sociology has simultaneously turned two faces to the world – a face of hope and a face of doubt. Some sociologists have had faith in the future, in progress, and for them sociology's rational understanding of social life is empowering – it allows us to use this knowledge to change our own world. In Chapter 17 we saw how optimistic social theorists from Comte to Marx to Durkheim shared this vision, however much else divided them. Other sociologists committed to hope have pinned their faith on the creative powers of human agents (or actors, or subjects, as they are also called). In the preceding chapter we saw how the symbolic interactionist and phenomenological traditions have emphasised a view of social life as an actively created construction – whether or not we realise what we are creating. There is a potential for optimism here, if nothing else because social life has open-ended possibilities – it can be endlessly re-made through action.

When we turn to sociology's doubting face, we must not jump to the conclusion that a critical, doubting approach pushes optimistic hope aside. On the contrary, doubt about the present can be the basis of a burning commitment to make the future better. Marx's critique of capitalism, and Durkheim's critique of egoistic, unregulated society, were each founded on a powerful belief that human action, enlightened by their social and political analysis, could overcome the faults of the present social world.

At the heart of sociology's commitment to critique lie two fundamental convictions:

- the knowledge that society need not necessarily be the way it is at present;
- the hope that some future form of society can, and will, be better than what we have now.

As Jeffrey Alexander recently expressed it:

Despite the fact that we have no idea what our historical possibilities will be, every theory of social change must theorise not only the past but the present and future as well. We can do so only in a non-rational way, in relation not only to what we know but to what we believe, hope and fear. Every historical period needs a narrative that defines its past in terms of the present, and suggests a future that is fundamentally different, and typically 'even better' than contemporary time.

[Alexander, 1995, pp. 66–7]

In other words, even though sociologists have always wanted to explain why society has its current form, we have nearly always believed that this form is temporary and open to change. The way things currently are is never natural, normal, or inevitable, and the future promises something better.

Doubt, today, runs deeper. Already by the end of the nineteenth century, writers such as Weber and before him the philosopher Nietzsche were questioning Western society's claims to progress, knowledge and superior civilisation. Today, **postmodernist** theories take these doubts even further, regarding issues of truth and value as essentially relative and even arbitrary. When doubt extends this far, it extinguishes critique, for dreams of progress or a better future lose all resonance when there is no criterion for what might actually be better, and hence human struggles for change appear pointless. This degree of **relativism** is more at home with wry detachment than committed struggle: it is a recipe for disengagement from the troubles of the world. So can such a sceptical position be justified? One example of a theorist who rejected active commitment to Marxist critique in favour of postmodern doubt is the French writer Lyotard. In his influential book *The PostModern Condition* (1984) he rejected the authoritarian stance of the Soviet Union, which culminated in the suppression of popular reform in Hungary (1956), Czechoslovakia (1968) and Poland (1980). For Lyotard, and for others such as Foucault, these events demonstrate the authoritarian potential in Marxism's grand theory of historical progress (Smart, 1993, pp. 35–9). By claiming that they possess the key to social progress through their knowledge, social scientists or the politicians guided by them inflict their doctrines upon people from above. Lyotard thus rejects not just Marxism but any '**meta-narrative**' or 'great story' of progress. More generally this leads to 'a deep suspicion of Hegel, Marx and any form of universal philosophy' (Sarap, 1988, p. 132). We have no grounds for criticising the present by comparison to the image of a future that we wish to impose.

postmodernist theory

see postmodernism.

relativism

An approach which denies the existence of absolute truth, but maintains that beliefs, values and theories are relative to time and place. Accordingly, traditions and ways of life can only be judged in the context of the age or society that has produced them.

meta-narrative

Sometimes referred to as 'grand narrative', it is the name given to an all encompassing theory of human life, especially a vision of social progress.

authoritarianism
The imposition of power in ways that subordinates cannot control or resist; the celebration of a strong authority.

As a critique of **authoritarianism**, this has its attractions. But Lyotard's position leaves us without any grounds to offer a critique of what currently exists. As with Winch and Discourse Theory, discussed in Chapter 18, social life comes to be viewed as wholly relative forms of life or language games. Observers have to accept forms of life however arbitrarily people live. Similarly, we saw how phenomenological sociology refuses to correct or criticise the ways of life it observes – we must maintain a detached 'ethnomethodological indifference'. From these perspectives, the sociologist can never aspire to be more than the wry, detached commentator who does not engage with the lives and futures of the people who are studied.

post-structuralism
A modern development in French theory following from linguistics structuralism, which goes further by treating social life as a 'text' which may be analysed without reference to any author (or creative subject/actor) (*see* texts *and* deconstruction).

This detachment goes even further if, like the **post-structuralists**, we reject the humanistic vision of phenomenology. We saw in Chapter 18 how post-structuralists like Derrida or Foucault refuse to see human agents as actively, creatively, constructing their society. If, like Foucault, we subvert the idea of self-consciously creative social actors then there are further problems for a critical sociology: we cannot know if anyone might listen to our findings and act upon them. If everything is destabilised and made relative, why try to analyse society at all? Baudrillard, it seems, came to the conclusion that there was indeed no point:

For Baudrillard the disorder of things modern, associated with the emergence of postmodern conditions, renders sociology redundant. Within the force-field constituted by the media and the masses the social dissolves and, supposedly, along with it sociology.

[Smart, 1993, p. 55]

Is Sociology Any Use?: A Practical Example

Before we turn to criticisms of these post-modernist ideas, let us turn to something less abstract and more optimistic. Here we take a recent situation – the nuclear tests run by France in the Pacific during 1995 despite world-wide protest. By looking at this case, it may be easier to think about the ways in which sociology might find a more constructive relationship with people in society, helping them to understand and criticise the social situations that constrain them.

Despite the smoke, the view from the offices of Hiti Tau, an umbrella group for Tahitian environment, development, women, youth and cultural organisations, is quite clear.

Fires burn, the shops are looted or boarded up, there are explosions

every few minutes, but for the first time anyone can remember, says one youth worker, 'there is harmony in Tahitian society'.

Everyone here is united against France and the nuclear testing. The anger is enormous. 'What makes it worse is that even with all these voices, local government didn't listen,' says Vaihere Bordes, who runs a women's group. The fight against testing and the call for independence cannot be separated, she says. 'Our call for social justice and an end to environmental destruction are one and the same. France has said for years that if we allow the bombs then we can have work. It's political colonisation, but it's worse; it's colonialism of the mind. We have not been allowed self-determination, to decide anything for ourselves.

Someone else wants to decide our environment, how we should live and think. They give us money. 'Here's money,' they say, 'now be quiet.' But the young people don't care anything for this.'

Her nephew is at the airport and has been involved in the rioting. Like 25 per cent of Tahiti's young, he is unemployed. He tells her: 'You have demonstrated peacefully for months about this and no one has paid any attention. This is the only way.'

'I did not want to see violence. The French pushed the button, and now the Tahitians are pushing the button,' says Roti Make, a social worker who has protested for two months about the tests. 'The French have treated us as rubbish, as rats, and now you see what happens.'

'Violence is not the Polynesian way,' says Roland Oldham, a union organiser. He is not surprised by the virulence of the protests, only the violence. 'We tried to get our voices heard, pacifically, but local government and the French state have shown nothing but arrogance. They took no notice of local people. We have been treated as if we didn't exist.'

He sees the rise of the rubbish society everywhere. This week is a perfect example of what happens when people are first divorced from the culture, and then governments do not listen to people. 'It is an uprising against remoteness, an explosion of localism. The development model imposed by the French is being questioned as never before.'

'Minds have changed,' says Bordes. 'If you go back just 30 years our parents didn't realise what nuclear power meant. In 1966 we didn't have radio, TV or an airport. Now we're in contact with the world, and we see the catastrophe.'

That's the problem, says Oldham. He is 43, just old enough to remember the easy-going post-war Polynesia. He links the violence with Tahiti's entry into the global economy at the expense of the informal, local one; the introduction of wage labour, the alienation of ordinary Tahitians from communal use of land and other resources.

Local political structures, he says, have been undermined. 'Land everywhere no longer belongs to Polynesians. Once Polynesians were separated from their land, it was the beginning of the end of their culture. Here we are now between two worlds. We are really mixed up.'

Most people at the Hiti Tau centre appreciate that Greenpeace and global environmental issues have provided Tahitians with the trigger for local political action. They are wary. 'Greenpeace came with their own agenda,' says one local environmentalist. 'They were not particularly interested in us. But they have provided the catalyst.'

'The nuclear issue,'says Oldham, 'is the ultimate symbol of dangerous, remote authority. One defining moment in Polynesia was when the nuclear industry came 29 years ago. It was the beginning of complete colonial dependence. With it came the big money. Until then we had really only been farmers. Then people left the islands to work in the industry for three times the salary.'

The message was money rather than people. It was important: 'From then on we were in two worlds and we really began to lose our values and solidarity. More and more we find our society is losing its roots. The arrival of the nuclear industry was fundamental to the changes in society.'

'The French used the argument of economics, money, jobs and employment. We didn't know what it meant,' says an environmental activist. 'Now we think how can you accept it when your health and environment will be destroyed? How can you propose that? It's a crime.'

Oldham says: 'The cold war is over. Times have changed. We question the West's notion of progress. We see half the world starving; the rich getting richer and environmental destruction everywhere worsening. Maybe it's time to look at the wisdom that doesn't come from the West, but from people who have been living in an ecological way for centuries. There are still places where life is not based on money, but on nature. Perhaps we should look there.' ”

[Vidal, 1995]

In this article, we hear reported the voices of people who feel that critique and hope really do mean something. Vaihere Bordes speaks of social justice, and condemns 'colonialism of the mind'; she wishes to fight for 'self-determination'. We also see a sociologically informed analysis by Roland Oldham clearly articulating the changed social and economic relations which underpin current discontents. The critical discourses of anti-colonialism and environmentalism are fused together in a way that is connected to Tahiti's social and political circumstances. The Western environmentalist agenda of Greenpeace was used and transformed by local concerns.

In the words reported from Tahiti we can see sociological analysis being used as a resource by people themselves as they wish to criticise their society and make it better. But the form this social critique takes, and the goals it aids, are intertwined with other things. Other discourses fuse together with the social analysis, such as romantic views of a lost past. But this does not mean that their account of Tahitian society is arbitrary and relative. It is an interpretation of specific social circumstances for specific goals. It is a discourse well worth saying and contains within it truth-claims which cannot be dismissed.

Against Postmodernist Doubts

The sweeping claims of writers like Lyotard and Baudrillard have not gone unchallenged. Critics fall into two broad camps: those who reject the whole notion of postmodernity together with postmodern philosophy (e.g. Habermas, 1981), and those who accept the widespread phenomenon of social change, but propose a renewal of social theory to allow a sociology of postmodernity (Bauman, 1992), or of '**late modernity**' (Giddens, 1990); Gregor McLennan (1992) has provided a detailed account of these critical debates.

late modernity

A term which implies change within modernity, characterised by increased reflexivity and globalisation, but without a qualitative shift to postmodernity. Similar phrases are high modernity and radicalised modernity (*see* reflexivity *and* globalisation).

One basic objection is that postmodernism does itself offer an account of social development when it constructs a notion of the transition from modernity to postmodernity. What is more, the notion of a clear, coherent postmodern account of contemporary society is rather contradictory, since fragmentary incoherence and uncertainty are the hallmarks of the viewpoint in Lyotard, Baudrillard and, to a lesser extent, Foucault (Giddens, 1990). At the same time, the fact that postmodernists continue to write books shows that intellectuals will always offer claims to knowledge, however much these are acknowledged to be partial and provisional. Denying the quest for knowledge is self-defeating.

Additionally, many writers reject the way in which postmodernists take the Enlightenment dream of 'progress through scientific reason' as the whole picture of modernity. Callinicos (1989) and many others emphasise how there were much more radical and questioning elements within modernism itself – for example, the innovative artists and writers of the early twentieth century, such as Picasso or James Joyce. They went far beyond descriptive realism or simple narrative stories to explore and experiment with the structure of their own craft – whether two-dimensional painting or language in the novel. This was a deeper, more serious questioning of reality than the postmodernists' superficial playfulness (see Table 17.5 in Chapter 17).

Finally, as we saw in Chapter 18, it is extremely difficult and unconvincing for postmodern theory to deny that human beings are creative agents who play some active part in shaping their social settings. Most sociologists are seeking ways to renew our conception of human agency, not reject it (e.g. Bauman, 1992, pp. 192–4; Giddens, 1991).

Reflexive Sociology: Renewing the Sociological Project

Anthony Giddens, in *The Consequences of Modernity*, declares that:

> **The practical impact of social sciences is both profound and inescapable. Modern societies, together with the organisations that compose and straddle them, are like learning machines, imbibing information in order to regularise their mastery of themselves ... Only societies reflexively capable of modifying their institutions in the face of accelerated social change will be able to confront the future with any confidence. Sociology is the prime medium of such reflexivity.**
>
> [Giddens, 1990, p. 21]

This concept of a reflexive sociology is nothing new but it can give us a key to understand the place of sociological understanding today. It is worth analysing some things that are *not* said in the above passage. Giddens is not suggesting that because social scientists know best, they can direct social development from above. The people who take action for social change are not social scientists, but members of society with varying amounts of power. Social science knowledge is a resource which can be drawn upon in the process of social change. It is also important to see that human beings constantly act upon their society and change it to some extent. It is not just programmes of reform or revolution that use social science knowledge. All of us need frameworks to interpret our world and act upon it; social science is one important source (amongst others) for these frameworks' guiding action. This means that sociology does not provide a critique of society on behalf of people, dictating their future. If sociological knowledge is used as a resource by people shaping their own lives, then Lyotard's condemnation of authoritarian 'meta-narratives' need not apply.

Even so, there is inevitably a critical dimension if sociology is not merely defending the way things are, but instead offering people understanding of their social position. Alvin Gouldner emphasised all this in 1971 with *The Coming Crisis of Western Sociology*. We may say that his crisis certainly arrived and persisted, and the solution he offered then – a liberating, reflexive sociology – is extremely relevant today.

recursiveness of social knowledge
Employed by Giddens, the notion that social science informs actors in society who may then act to change their society, which requires renewed social analysis and so on. Sociology and social change are linked by internal feedback.

Since 1971, however, social theorists have become cautious about making claims for our knowledge which imply finality or authority. Instead, there is a widespread sense of what Giddens calls the **'recursiveness' of social knowledge**. That is, sociologists' knowledge can never be wholly neutral and detached because, in whatever form, it is used by people to interpret and reshape the very society that the sociologists have studied. So the study needs to be renewed, and that new knowledge feeds back into social life ... and so on. This endless, looping process of interaction between sociology and social life has important consequences. For one thing, sociologists need never be out of work, for our knowledge of a particular society can only be provisional and temporary. As Bauman expressed in an interview:

> **I am rather inclined to see sociology today as an eddy on a fast-moving river, an eddy which retains its shape but which changes its content all the time ... sociology is a constant interpretation of, or commentary on, experience ... and this commentary is sent back into the society itself.**
>
> [Bauman, 1992, p. 213]

Once again, though, Bauman wishes sociologists to be critical without being prescriptive. He says that our questioning investigations:

> **revitalise the existing interpretations of reality ... The one right it [sociology] claims to itself is the right to expose the conceit and arrogance, the unwarranted claims to exclusivity of others' interpretations, but without substituting itself in their place.**
>
> [Bauman, 1992, p. 214]

So it seems that we can subvert any claim that society 'has to be this way' but we must stop short of prescribing what it should become. Making the future is for the members of society to do.

Limits and Possibilities

Nearly a century ago, in his lectures on 'Science as a Vocation' and 'Politics as a Vocation' (1970), Weber argued that sociology could not tell members of society what values to hold, but it could demonstrate the possibilities and constraints facing them within their social structure. This is an aspiration worth remembering. There is a serious danger that we lose this goal as a result of the relativising perspectives of postmodernism and those based on language philosophy.

Although sociology is abandoning any pretence of predicting the future, we need not regard change in society as wholly arbitrary. As Hall (1988, p. 10) asked of discourse theory, what *conditions of existence* can we analyse for certain developments? Which outcomes are much less possible than others? If, as well, we acknowledge that human acts produce *unintended consequences* in society, then sociology must consider how to explain these in terms which do not only refer to small-scale action. Giddens noted that although societies used knowledge to learn to adapt, this can never give full control because of the perversity of unintended consequences, and the unpredictability of social change (1990, p. 21).

However, this role for sociology in explaining social outcomes begs many questions about the nature of social structural explanations. Theorists have attempted to bridge the gulf between social action and social structure (especially Giddens, with his theory of **structuration**, 1984), but there is far from full agreement on whether such a unified account of social life is achievable.

structuration theory
The emergence and transformation of structural patterning in social life. For Giddens, the theory that links structure and agency as simultaneous dimensions of social life (*see* structure *and* agency).

At the very least, sociology must study society to analyse 'the sum total of resources for all possible action' which are available to actors as the 'inventory of ends and the pool of means' (Bauman, 1992, p. 191). But this is a minimal aspiration. If we regard the consequences of agency as patterned and non-random, then we will wish to analyse more than the resources available to actors. Going on to analyse unintended outcomes of action raises once again debates about social structural explanation.

Thinking back to our earlier discussion of the Tahitians' protests over nuclear tests, we can recall how informed actors in Tahiti used sociological frameworks and explanations to understand their own situation and act upon it. Social science did not define their interests or their reality for them, but it provided a resource for understanding. However, simply possessing this understanding does not in itself give those Tahitian people the power to control the things they condemn. This imposition of Western modernity could not be undone, the past could not be recovered. But despite the heavy limits and frightening constraints imposed by their social circumstances, Tahitians' future will still be shaped in part by their own actions. Once some future outcome has appeared, resulting from the complex combination of their actions, the constraints of the social situation, and the responses from outside Tahiti, then maybe Tahitians will turn again to sociology to help them make sense of their new situation and act upon it. Thus social life and reflexive sociology can come together in the ceaseless, complex struggle to make our own futures. In this struggle we as social scientists are participants – 'perhaps better informed and more systematic' – in this 'never-ending, self-reflexive process of re-interpretation' (Bauman, 1992, p. 204). We may not be prophets, we are not able to predict or prescribe how people should live, but we can provide a form of ever-changing knowledge that exposes the constraints and possibilities in social life, so helping people to shape their own diverse futures.

Summary of the Chapter

- Sociological knowledge will always have an impact on the societies we study. People in society will inevitably use this knowledge, directly or indirectly, to change the way they live.
- This means that sociology must continually renew its knowledge as society changes; it also means that sociology cannot claim any simple, neutral detachment from the societies it studies.
- Sociology inevitably demonstrates that society need not necessarily remain the way it currently is; there is thus a potential for critique in the very nature of the discipline.
- However this does not mean that sociologists should prescribe how people should live, or how to change their social world. Social and political values are diverse, and sociology cannot dictate them.
- Consequently, sociological knowledge can be a vital resource available for different groups to pursue the varying social and political values to which they are committed. Sociology can help diverse groups to struggle towards diverse futures.

References

Alexander, J. (1995) 'Modern, Anti, Post, Neo' *New Left Review*, no. 210.

Bauman, Z. (1992) *Intimations of Postmodernity*, London, Routledge.

Callinicos, A. (1989) *Against Postmodernism*, Cambridge, Polity Press.

Giddens, A. (1984) *The Constitution of Society*, Cambridge, Polity Press.

Giddens, A. (1990) *The Consequences of Modernity*, Cambridge, Polity Press.

Gouldner, A. (1971) *The Coming Crisis of Western Sociology*, London, Heinemann.

Habermas, J. (1981) 'Modernity versus Postmodernity', *New German Critique*, no. 22.

Hall, S. (1988) *The Hard Road to Renewal*, London, Verso.

Lyotard, J.-F. (1984) *The Postmodern Condition*, Manchester, Manchester University Press.

McLennan, G. (1992) 'The Enlightenment Project Revisited' in S. Hall, D. Held and T. McGrew (eds) *Modernity and its Futures*, Cambridge, Polity Press.

Sarap, M. (1988) *An Introductory Guide to Post-structuralism and Postmodernism*, Brighton, Harvester Wheatsheaf.

Smart, B. (1993) *Postmodernity*, London, Routledge.

Vidal, J. (1995) 'Rats of the rubbish society fight back', *The Guardian*, 9 September, p. 23.

Weber, M. (1970) 'Politics as a Vocation' and 'Science as a Vocation' in H. H. Gerth and C. W. Mills (eds) *From Max Weber*, London, Routledge, & Kegan Paul.

Glossary

agency

Purposeful action. This term implies that actors have the freedom to create, change and influence events.

alienation

Originally utilised by Marx to describe feelings of estrangement experienced by workers under industrial capitalism. Now more generally employed to describe people's feelings of isolation, powerlessness, and self-estrangement.

altruism

The principle of acting without selfish concern, in the interest of others.

anomie

For Durkheim, a social condition where the norms guiding conduct break down, leaving individuals without social restraint or guidance (*see* norms).

anti-school culture

A way of behaving which is dedicated to subverting school rules, typically exhibited by those pupils who see themselves as educational failures.

archaeology of knowledge

From Foucault, to describe his excavation of past discourses in an archaeological fashion, in order to trace their emergence (*see* discourse).

ascriptive characteristics

Traits or characteristics that are inherited (e.g age, colour, sex, height), rather than being the result of personal achievement.

authoritarian populism

A term used by Hall to describe Thatcherism's mixture of free market economics, conservative moral values, and its appeal to individualistic and authoritarian elements in popular 'common-sense' values (*see* Thatcherism).

authoritarianism

The imposition of power in ways that subordinates cannot control or resist; the celebration of a strong authority.

autonomous motherhood

Single parents who, either by choice or circumstance, have taken on independent responsibility for caring for their children.

background expectancies

Coined by Garfinkel to describe the taken for granted assumptions and expectations about human behaviour in a given context.

base/infrastructure

A Marxist term for the economy (*see* economic base *and* superstructure).

berdache

A practice among the native people of North America to allocate male gender roles on the basis of cultural preference rather than on the assumption of a biological predisposition (*see* gender).

biological determinism

A simple causal, reductionist approach that explains human behaviour in terms of biological or genetic characteristics.

biologism

A form of biological determinism that claims human behaviour is determined on the basis of biological or genetic characteristics (*see* biological determinism).

biomedical model

A model of disease and illness which regards it as the consequence of certain malfunctions of the human body.

black economy

A form of unofficial economic activity; for example, work carried out for payment in kind or for unrecorded payments for tax avoidance purposes.

blue-collar worker

A term used to describe manual workers.

bourgeoisie

A Marxist term used to describe the property-owning capitalist class.

British political economy

The economic and social analysis of early capitalism by writers such as Adam Smith and David Ricardo.

bureaucracy

A type of organisation run by officials, and based on a hierarchical structure of authority, best suited for the efficient pursuit of organisational goals.

capitalism

An economic system in which the means of production are privately owned and organised to accumulate profits within a market framework, in which labour is provided by waged workers.

care in the community

A range of informal and professional care of the elderly, disabled and sick undertaken in the community, rather than in institutional settings, typically by female relatives.

caste system

A system of social division and stratification, influenced by Hinduism on the Indian subcontinent, in which an individual's social position is fixed at birth.

cathexis

Originally employed by Freud to describe a psychic charge or the formation of an emotional attraction towards another person. More generally associated with the social and psychological patterning of desire and the construction of emotionally charged relationships.

causal relationship

A relationship where one phenomenon has a direct effect on another.

civil religion

Associated with non-supernatural religious objects whose existence promotes solidarity for the group and a sense of belonging for the individual.

civil society

An imprecise concept which normally refers to social institutions outside the political state.

class

A term widely used in sociology to differentiate the population on grounds of economic considerations, such as inequality in terms of wealth or income.

class consciousness

Though originally a Marxist term used to describe a situation when the proletariat becomes aware of its subjugated position in relation to the bourgeoisie, it now encompasses a broader definition which includes any collective sense of identity among members of a social class.

class decomposition

The breaking down of traditional class structures and identity.

class reproduction

The process by which class inequalities reproduce themselves.

the clinical gaze

see medical gaze.

closed-ended question

The most commonly used form of question asked in questionnaires, the answers to which fall within a predicted range and thus can be pre-coded (*see* open-ended question).

colonial penetration

see colonialism.

colonialism

The establishment of rule by Western nations over distant territories and peoples (*see* imperialism).

common-sense knowledge

From Schutz, the practical social knowledge that we take for granted as the basis for everyday actions.

communitarianism

Echoing Durkheimian thinking, a 1990s' political philosophy stressing the importance of community and shared values for social order and stability.

compensatory education

An approach introduced in the 1960s and

1970s to inner city schools with high proportions of working class children, or children from ethnic communities. It involved an allocation of extra resources and special facilities aimed at counteracting what was perceived to be educational disadvantage as a result of cultural differences.

compulsory heterosexuality

Associated with Adrienne Rich, this concept implies that heterosexuality is not so much the natural form of sexual preference but is imposed upon individuals by social constraints.

conflict perspective

A theoretical approach, such as Marxism, focusing on the notion that society is based on an unequal distribution of advantage and is characterised by a conflict of interests between the advantaged and the disadvantaged.

conjugal relationship

The relationship between husband and wife in marriage.

conscience collective

Coined by Durkheim, a pre-requisite for social integration, referring to the shared beliefs and values of a collectivity. Such collectively held ideas promote both a sense of belonging for the individual and the continuity of the group (*see* social integration).

consumerism

A culture centred on the promotion, sale and acquisition of consumer goods.

consumption sector cleavage

A social division based on people's relationship to consumption and their location within the private or public sectors of production and consumption.

content analysis

The analysis of the content of communication; usually refers to documentary or visual material.

corporatism

A way of linking organised interests, especially economic ones, to the State, where the corporate 'partners' contribute to shaping and sometimes implementing policy.

cultural advantage

Life-styles, religious beliefs, values, or other practices which give people a greater chance of obtaining economic success or social status.

cultural capital

Refers to the extent to which individuals have absorbed the dominant culture. Associated with Pierre Bourdieu, who claimed that the greater degree of cultural capital individuals possessed (the more absorbed they were in the dominant culture), the more successful they would be in the educational system.

cultural deprivation

In the sociology of health and illness, an approach which focuses on factors such as smoking, alcohol consumption and eating habits, claiming that life-style choices determine ill-health. It offers an explanation of increased incidences of ill-health in working-class people by directly relating it to life-style factors.

cultural imperialism

The aggressive promotion of Western culture, based on the assumption that its value system is superior and preferable to those of non-Western cultures.

cultural relativism

An approach that denies that any one way of living is superior to others: all cultures are equal.

Darwinism

A theory of evolution by Darwin which proposes that species survive and evolve by a process of natural selection, resulting in the survival of the fittest.

de-industrialisation

A concept used to describe economic changes due to the decline of industrial manufacturing and the increase of output and employment growth in the service sector of the economy.

de-medicalisation

The process whereby orthodox medicine begins to lose its ability to define and regulate areas of human life (*see* medicalisation).

deconstruct

To break down texts in order to grasp their implicit meaning by exposing their underlying and hidden assumptions (*see* texts).

definition of the situation

Associated with symbolic interactionism to describe an actor's interpretation of an occasion (*see* symbolic interactionism).

demographic age profile

The size and structure of the population based on age.

dependency theory

A theory most commonly associated with the work of Andre Gunder Frank. It challenges modernisation theory by arguing that underdevelopment is not an early stage in a country's evolutionary process, but a condition resulting from its exploitation by modern first world countries and regions (*see* underdevelopment *and* First World).

dependent variable

A technical term used in empirical research to denote a phenomenon that is caused by or explained by something else (*see* independent variable).

deskilling

Developed by Braverman to describe what he believed to be strategies of employers to reduce the skills required of their labour force, which often occurs alongside the introduction of new technological processes into the work place.

determinism

A simple causal, reductionist explanation (*see* biological determinism).

deviance amplification

A spiralling sequence of interaction between deviants and those reacting to their behaviour (most typically agents of control such as the police) which generates further deviance, which generates further punitive response and so on.

diaspora

Migration or dispersal of people or communities. Originally associated with the Jewish experience, this now more generally refers to the ways in which ethnic groups, although dispersed throughout the world, nevertheless share elements of a common culture or heritage.

discourse

A body of ideas, concepts and beliefs which become established as knowledge or as an accepted world-view. These ideas become a powerful framework for understanding and action in social life. For example, Foucault studied the discourse of madness, highlighting its changes over the centuries and its interplay with other discourses such as religious and medical discourses, and illustrated how these shifts affect how madness is perceived and reacted to by others.

discursive practices

Related to Foucault's conception of power/knowledge, refers to a system of regulatory or disciplinary devices which reflects and promotes discourse (*see* discourse).

division of labour

Specialisation of tasks in ways that may involve exclusion from some opportunities. Hence, closure of labour opportunities exist in employment or by gender.

domestic division of labour

The division of labour and the allocation of tasks between men and women in the household.

domestic sphere

Sometimes referred to as the private sphere, based on notions of a public/private dichotomy. It refers to the arena of activity associated with the household and family life.

dominant class

A Marxist term which refers to the property owning class who, by virtue of their ownership of the means of production, possess political power.

double burden

A term used to refer to the double oppression of sexism and racism experienced by black women.

double standard of sexual morality

The assumption that promiscuous or sexually assertive behaviours are to be expected or admired in men, but that the same forms of behaviour are deviant and innapropriate in women. For example, there is no male equivalent of the term 'slag'.

downsizing

Management jargon for reducing job numbers.

dual sector model

A model of work which suggests there are both primary and secondary labour markets (*see* polarisation of the labour market).

economic base

A Marxist term for the economy, which has a determining effect on the superstructure (*see* superstructure).

economic determinism

Associated with Marxism, an approach which claims that social life is determined by society's economic base (*see* economic base).

economic power

A measurement of the ability to control events by virtue of material advantage (*see* material advantage).

egoism

Normally a reference to selfishness, it also refers to a social setting where individual self-interest is the basis of morality.

embourgeoisement thesis

An explanation for declining working-class solidarity which claims that, through increasing affluence, the working class tend to adopt middle class values, and thus become absorbed into the middle class.

the Enlightenment

An eighteenth century philosophical movement based on notions of progress through the application of reason and rationality. Enlightenment philosophers foresaw a world free from religious dogma, within human control, and leading ultimately to emancipation for all humankind.

enterprise culture

An environment which acclaims and rewards those who take initiative by setting up businesses and creating wealth.

entrepreneurial

Activity in business or economic development based on the promotion of new innovative ideas and decision making.

epidemiology

The study of the patterns of disease.

epistemology

A philosophical concept meaning the theory of knowledge, which underpins methodology. For example, the type of methodology employed in a piece of social research will be determined by epistemological assumptions.

essentialism, totalism

An approach which assumes some universal essence, homogeneity and unity in the phenomena under study. Such approaches to gender, for example, identify traits and behaviour common to all men and women.

ethnic absolutism

An understanding of ethnic divisions which views them as fixed and absolute, resting on unchanging cultural traditions.

ethnicity

To be distinguished from 'race', which emphasises biological differences based on skin colour, ethnicity denotes a sense of belonging to a particular community whose members share common cultural traditions.

ethnocentric

A description of the inability to understand the validity or integrity of cultures other than one's own.

ethnography

A research technique based on direct observation of the activity of members of a particular social group or given culture.

ethnomethodology

Associated with the work of Harold Garfinkel, it is an approach used to study the methods people deploy in their everyday lives to make sense of social life and enable meaningful exchange with one another.

eugenics

A nineteenth and early twentieth century scientific and political movement directed towards the genetic improvement of the human species.

evolutionary

Pertaining to a process of developmental change through stages which progressively unfold (*see* evolutionism).

evolutionism

A doctrine based on the notion that historical, biological and social changes are subject to a process of development and progressive unfolding (*see* Darwinism).

exclusivist

A definition of religion that excludes any system of beliefs and practices which do not conform to very specific criteria.

existentialism

A philosophy which emphasises free will and the individual's responsibility for his or her own actions.

expressive

In relation to the family, the term Parsons uses to describe the wife's role of providing for the emotional needs of her family.

extended family

A household unit where more than one generation of husbands and wives reside with their offspring.

false consciousness

Ways of thinking about the world or apprehending reality that are defective and which obscure the truth. Associated, though not exclusively, with Marx.

Fascism

An authoritarian and undemocratic system of government in the twentieth century, characterised by extreme nationalism, militarism, anti-communism and restrictions on individual freedom. The will of the people was held to be embodied in the leader (e.g. Mussolini in Italy).

female infanticide

The murder of female babies and infants.

femininities

Various socially constructed collections of assumptions, expectations and ways of behaving that serve as standards for female behaviour.

feminisation of poverty

A pattern of increasing concentration of poverty among the female population.

feudalism

A social and political power structure prevalent in parts of Europe during the twelfth and thirteenth centuries, where power was fragmented and overlapping among authorities including church, monarchy and local lords.

finance fraction

That part of capital, for example banking, concerned solely with financial activities rather than production.

First World

Modern industrial capitalist societies, such as those of Europe, North America and Japan.

forces of production

The tools and techniques of production.

Fordism

A form of industrial economy based on mass production and mass marketing prevalent in the post-war period. These techniques and processes were pioneered by Henry Ford in the manufacture and sale of Ford motor cars.

free market

A form of trade or business environment free from outside interference or restrictions.

French socialism

A political doctrine which emerged during the French Revolution, emphasising social progress led by new industrial classes.

functionalism

A theoretical perspective, associated with Durkheim and Parsons, based on an analogy between social systems and organic systems. It claims that the character of a society's various institutions must be understood in terms of the function each performs in enabling the smooth running of society as a whole.

gender

Distinct from 'sex', this concept often refers to the socially constructed categories of masculine and feminine that are differently defined in various cultures. Many contemporary theorists use a broader definition to refer to the variable sets of beliefs and practices about male and female (or other genders) that not only feed into individual identities, but are fundamental to social institutions and symbolic systems.

gendered division of labour

The division of work roles and tasks into those performed by men and those performed by women.

gendering

The process by which division occurs according to gender. For example, the gendering of the labour market refers to the labour division where women are concentrated in certain job areas, usually low paid, part-time, often casual ones and men are concentrated in others.

genealogy of power/knowledge

From Foucault, the tracing of powerful claims to knowledge and their application by techniques of power, e.g. madness treated in asylums.

generalised other

Expectations of conduct general in a social group; 'what is expected of you'.

German idealist philosophy

A philosophical approach based on the metaphysical thesis that the only things that really exist are minds and their contents. It proposes that human progress comes through the advancement of human reason.

glass ceiling

A metaphorical concept used to explain how women are prevented from attaining top (managerial and professional) jobs.

globalisation

The process whereby political, social, economic and cultural relations increasingly take on a global scale, and which has profound consequences for individuals' local experiences and everyday lives.

the Great Transformation

The name given by Karl Polanyi to the historical moment, characterised by massive social, political, technological, economic and intellectual change, which marks the onset of modernity (*see* modernity).

growth rates

Levels of economic expansion.

habitus

Pierre Bourdieu's term for the everyday habitual practices and assumptions of a particular social environment. People are at once the product of, and the creators of, their habitus.

hegemony

Commonly used to describe the domination of one class, nation, or group of people over others. It was extended by Gramsci to denote a more general and intellectual dominance, especially when hegemonic ideas influence people's political and cultural perceptions.

holistic

An approach that focuses on the whole rather than on specific parts or aspects.

homophobia

Fear of homosexuality and lesbianism.

horizontal gender segregation

The separation of men and women into qualitatively different types of jobs.

humanism

A position which stresses the importance of human needs and the human mind above all else, and rejects belief in a supernatural deity. It implies a belief that humans have the potential for goodness.

hypothesis

A set of ideas or a speculative theory about a given state of affairs that is proposed for empirical testing.

'I' and the 'me'

Terms used by Mead to refer to the impulses for social action: 'I' and the socially constructed self ('me') (*see* symbolic interactionism).

iatrogenic

Illness or disability caused by medical treatment.

ideal type

For Weber, a model, a set of exaggerated characteristics defining the essence of certain types of behaviour or institutions observable in the real world. 'Ideal' signifies 'pure' or 'abstract' rather than desirable.

identity politics

A form of political agenda based around issues of shared experiences and forms of self-expression (*see* personal is the political).

ideology

A perception of reality or way of thinking. Its usage is associated with Marx, where the term implies a mistaken sense of reality or false consciousness (*see* false consciousness).

immigrant–host model

An approach to racial inequality in Britain in the post-war period which saw assimilation as the solution to racial disadvantage, based on the view that the problems experienced by immigrants arose from their situation as new arrivals.

imperialism

Common form of Western imperial rule in the late nineteenth and early twentieth centuries. Characterised by the extension of the power of the state through the acquisition, normally by force, of distant territories (*see* colonialism).

inclusivist

A definition of religion that includes systems of beliefs and practices which, however different in content, nevertheless produce similar effects.

independent variable

A technical term used in empirical research to denote a phenomenon whose existence causes or explains the presence of another variable (*see* dependent variable).

indexical

From ethnomethodology, the claim that meanings can only be gained in the context of their social setting (*see* ethnomethodology).

individualism

Doctrines or ways of thinking that focus on the autonomous individual, rather than on the attributes of the group.

informal economy

Includes unwaged work such as housework or labour-sharing between households.

information technology

Computerised, electronic, technology related to the gathering, recording and communicating of information.

institutional

Social practices that are regularly and continuously repeated, legitimised and maintained by social norms (*see* norms).

institutional racism

A theory of racism which draws attention to the ways institutions reproduce racial disadvantage.

instrumental (1)

An approach which involves the adoption of a strategy best suited to the attainment of a particular goal, as opposed to following a course of action for its own sake.

instrumental (2)

In relation to the family, the term Parsons uses to describe the husband's role of making material provision for his family.

instrumental calculation

A process of using the most efficient means to secure a particular goal.

instrumentalism

An approach by workers to work which seeks to derive satisfaction not so much in the task or job itself, but from benefits such as good rates of pay or secure employment.

intelligence quotient (IQ)

A measurement of intelligence based on the ratio of a person's mental age (as measured by IQ tests) to his or her actual age.

intergenerational mobility

The movement of individuals, between different generations, from one social position within the hierarchy to another. Usually refers to positions of broad occupation or social class.

interpretive

Having an interest in the meanings underpinning social action. Synonymous with social action theory (*see* social action).

intragenerational mobility

The movement of individuals, within one generation, from one social position within the hierarchy to another. Usually refers to positions of broad occupation or social class.

jobless growth

Economic growth which fails to produce rising levels of employment.

just-in-time production

A finely balanced and controlled manufacturing production system designed to produce goods to meet demand as and when required.

kinship groups

An anthropological term referring to groups who are related by marriage or blood.

knowledgeable agents

Employed by Giddens, a description of the capacity human actors have to reflexively construct theories of their own circumstances and form courses of action (*see* reflexivity).

labelling

From Becker, the process where socially defined identities are imposed or adopted, especially the deviant label. Such labels may have consequences that trap the individual into that identity (*see* stigmatise).

labour market

The supply and availability of people who are willing and able to work.

labour power

In Marxist theory a commodity to be bought and sold; this term refers to the workers' ability to produce goods.

laissez-faire liberalism

A political and economic approach based on a general principle of non-interference by government and freedom for markets and property owners.

late modernity

A term which implies change within modernity, characterised by increased reflexivity and globalisation, but without a qualitative shift to postmodernity. Similar terms are high modernity and radicalised modernity (*see* reflexivity *and* globalisation).

lean production

A highly competitive, streamlined, flexible manufacturing process which operates with a minimum of excess or waste (*see* just-in-time production).

liberal-democratic

A form of government based on politics by electoral representation, whose citizens have a range of individual rights and freedoms.

life-course

This approach dwells on the diversity of experiences and difference in the courses of people's lives. It claims that contemporary experience is more diverse and less predictable than traditional concepts of the life-cycle suggest (*see* life-cycle).

life-cycle

A developmental model which outlines the social changes encountered as a person passes through the stages of childhood, adolescence, mid-life, old age and death. In the context of the family, the life-cycle is a process which includes courtship, marriage, child rearing, children leaving home, etc. (*see* life-course).

life-cycle of earnings

The pattern of earnings over the length of an employee's working life.

life-world

From Schutz, the world of shared social meanings in which actors live and interact.

looking-glass self

Coined by Cooley to convey how individuals perceive their identity through the responses of others (*see* symbolic interactionism).

macro-level

A level of sociological analysis which focuses either on large collectivities and institutions or social systems and social structures (*see* structures).

male-stream

Used to describe institutions or practices that are male dominated.

managerialism

A process of increased managerial control.

market capacity

The level of reward secured by individuals from the sale of their skills in the labour market.

market position/situation

A term relating to the skills one has to sell in the labour market relative to others.

marketisation

An economic concept to describe the increased emphasis on the process of exchange and distribution of services and goods carried out by private individuals or corporate bodies, based on the dictates of supply and demand.

masculinities

Various socially constructed collections of assumptions, expectations and ways of behaving that serve as standards for forms of male behaviour.

material advantage

The possession of money and other material goods which offer people a greater chance of success in life than they would otherwise have.

materialism (1)

In its Marxist usage, an emphasis on economic and political relations.

materialism (2)

For Turner, following Foucault, a focus on the body as an object of analysis.

maternal deprivation

The psychological damage supposedly experienced by a child as a result of being separated from its mother.

means of production

A Marxist concept which refers to the raw materials, land, labour and tools required for the production of goods.

mechanical solidarity

For Durkheim, the form of social cohesion that binds people through conformity to norms, especially in traditional societies (*see* norms).

mechanistic

A form of behaviour that is determined by either external forces or internal constraints (*see* biological determinism *and* social structure).

medical gaze

A concept employed by Foucault to denote the power of modern medicine to define the human body.

medicalisation

A process of increased medical intervention and control in areas that hitherto would have been outside the medical domain.

meritocracy

A democratic system based on the allocation of position or occupation according to merit.

meta-narrative

Sometimes referred to as 'grand narrative', it is the name given to an all-encompassing theory of human life, especially a vision of social progress.

micro-economy

The productive activities of any small area located within a wider, macro-economy.

micro-level

A level of sociological analysis concerned with face-to-face social encounters or small scale interaction between groups.

mode of production

A Marxist concept which refers to the structured relationship between the means of production (raw materials, land, labour and tools) and the relations of production (the ways humans are involved in production).

modernity

A term designed to encapsulate the distinctiveness, complexity and dynamism of social processes unleashed during the eighteenth and nineteenth centuries, which mark a distinct break from traditional ways of living.

moral consensus

Desire for, and agreement upon, a set of prescribed moral values.

mortification of the self

Rituals of entry, especially in total institutions, which debase the old identity in order to impose a new institutional identity (*see* total institutions).

multi-culturalism

An approach which acknowledges and accommodates a variety of different cultural practices and traditions.

Muslim fundamentalism

A contentious, often pejorative, term used to describe a political and religious movement which adopts a fundamental interpretation of Islamic religious law.

'nanny state'

A pejorative term used to describe the welfare state, which implies that the welfare system is over-protective and does not encourage individual responsibility.

nation-state

A form of political authority unique to modernity comprising of various institutions such as the legislature, judiciary, police, armed forces, and central and local administration. It claims a monopoly of power and legitimacy within a bounded territory.

National Curriculum

A standardised educational course of study taught in British State schools as specified by the Department for Education.

naturalistic

Pertaining to nature. For example, a naturalistic theory is one that explains human behaviour in terms of natural instincts and drives.

neo-liberal

A form of right-wing philosophy associated with Thatcherism and laissez-faire liberalism (*see* Thatcherism *and* laissez-faire liberalism).

neo-Marxism

Contemporary schools of thought based on a development of Marxist philosophy.

neo-Weberian

A theoretical approach based on a revision of Weber's work.

new man

A recently developed concept used to describe the emergence of a new kind of man, who supports gender equality by being more involved in child care and willing to perform domestic tasks. His existence is much disputed.

new racism

Forms of racism which are based on ideas of cultural difference rather than claims to biological superiority.

New Right

A strand of right-wing Conservatism, which is primarily concerned with the non-interference of the state into economic and business affairs and the realm of individual autonomy. Although the state is seen as coercive in limiting individual freedom, a strong element of moral conservatism often exists in New Right thinking.

nihilism

A philosophy that rejects the notion that any moral position is worth holding.

normative

An approach which sees social behaviour as the result of conformity to norms (*see* norms).

normlessness

Associated with functionalism, a state of being without the guidance of socially accepted 'correct' or 'proper' forms of behaviour (*see* norms *and* anomie).

norms

Socially accepted 'correct' or 'proper' forms of behaviour. Norms either prescribe given types of behaviour or forbid them.

nuclear family

The conventional household unit in modern society, composed of a man and woman in a stable marital relationship, with their dependent children.

objective

Factual.

objectivism

A doctrine which purports that scientific truth is a matter of factual evidence, not belief (*see* objectivity).

objectivity

An approach to knowledge acquisition that claims to be unbiased, impersonal and free from prejudice. Commonly associated with positivism (*see* positivism).

ontological security

A stable mental state derived from a sense of continuity and order in events.

open-ended question

A type of question used in questionnaires to elicit narrative information from the respondent, the answer to which cannot be pre-coded.

organic solidarity

For Durkheim, the desirable form of social cohesion in modern society that binds people in societies of greater and specialised complexity.

outsourcing

The process of subcontracting work, i.e. securing certain research and development needs from external contractors that were previously met inside the firm.

Pacific Rim

Those south-east Asian countries with fast developing economies that border the Pacific Ocean, such as Taiwan, Hong Kong, Malaysia and South Korea.

panoptic

Taken from Jeremy Bentham's 'panopticon' – a circular prison with warders' observation area at the centre, enabling the constant monitoring of all prisoners – this term refers to the ability to exercise surveillance over the whole of a population of bodies.

paradigm

This term refers to the set of questions, practices and institutional arrangements which characterise scientific activity for a particular historical period. For Kuhn, paradigms produce forms of scientific knowledge which appear to be objective, but which in reality reflect very specific sets of interests.

participant observation

A research method based on observation of a group where the researcher takes part in the group or community being studied (*see* ethnography).

patriarchal

A system that perpetuates the dominance of senior men over women and junior men (*see* patriarchy).

patriarchy

Traditionally means 'rule of the father' and used to describe a type of household organisation in which the older man dominates the whole household. It is now more generally used to describe the dominance of men over women.

pedagogy

The science and principles of teaching.

personal is the political

Adopted originally by Radical feminists to draw attention to issues of sexuality and violence in interpersonal male–female relationships.

phenomenology

In sociology, a focus (from Schutz) on the taken for granted knowledge that social actors share and which underpins everyday life. It is part of the idealist tradition which focuses on consciousness and meaning, not structural social phenomena.

polarisation of the labour market

A labour market divided between jobs which are well paid and secure and those which are not.

political consciousness

Awareness of politics or political ideas.

political economy

An approach that embraces the concepts of social class, the value and division of labour, and moral sentiments.

polyarchy

A pluralistic view of the distribution of power which rejects the notion of class division. It sees power emerging through the interplay of various social groups with multiple cross-cutting political interests.

positivism

A doctrine which claims that social life should be understood and analysed in the same way that scientists study the 'natural world'. Underpinning this philosophy is the notion that phenomena exist in causal relationships and these can be empirically observed, tested and measured.

post-Fordism

Computer controlled and sophisticated production systems which emerged during the 1970s. Their key emphasis is on flexibility and the production of specialised, tailored goods to meet the demands of a competitive world economy.

post-industrial society

A society where industrial manufacturing declines as a rapid growth in service and information sectors occurs.

post-socialist states

The former Soviet states of central and Eastern European countries who, since the 1980s, have abandoned or adapted socialist practices and principles in favour of capitalist ones.

post-structuralism

A modern development in French theory following from linguistics structuralism, which goes further by treating social life as a 'text' which may be analysed without reference to any author (or creative subject/actor) (*see* texts *and* deconstruction).

postmodernism

Often perceived as a cultural and aesthetic phenomenon associated with contemporary literature and the arts, it often combines apparently opposed elements to subvert meaning and fragment totality. It is characterised by a pastiche of cultural styles and elements, but implies a deeper scepticism about order and progress. Instead diversity and fragmentation are celebrated.

postmodernity

For its supporters, the further transformation in social, cultural, economic and political arrangements which takes a society beyond modernity.

power bloc

An alignment of social groups, generally under the dominance of one of them, which is able to monopolise the levels of political power in a society over a sustained period.

pragmatism

A philosophy of US origin which treats values and knowledge as means to practical human ends. Concepts and values are regarded as true for so long as they prove useful. Knowledge and social life itself are therefore fluid, changing, human creations.

pre-modernity

Refers to traditional societies prior to the onset of modernity (*see* modernity).

privatisation

The process of transfer of state assets from public to private ownership.

privatism

A concept used to describe a focus centred on the home and family life.

pro-natalism

The view that everything should be done to encourage wives to have children.

productive wealth

Wealth which generates additional income, such as capital invested in property or stocks and shares.

professionalisation

The process by which the members of a particular occupation seek to establish a monopoly over its practice. Typically, this is done by limiting entry to those possessing defined qualifications – by claiming that those who lack these qualifications do not possess the requisite expertise.

project of modernity

A belief in the possibilities opened up by modernity, which involves a commitment to social progress through a rational and reasoned engagement with the world (*see* modernity).

proletarianisation

A process whereby some parts of the middle class become absorbed into the working class.

proletariat

A Marxist term for wage-earners, the propertyless class within capitalism.

provincialist

see ethnocentric.

psychoanalytic

Pertaining to the unconscious processes of the mind. A psychoanalytic approach would attempt to explain human behaviour by uncovering some of these processes.

public sphere

Based on notions of a public/private dichotomy, refers to the arena outside the home and family, and the kinds of activities associated with paid work.

qualitative

Information that is not easily quantified.

QUANGOS – Quasi Non-Governmental Organisations

Nominally independent bodies whose members are funded and appointed by central government to supervise or develop activity in areas of public interest.

quantitative

Used to describe a form of data or data analysis that is based on precise measurement.

race

A contentious concept within sociology, typically associated with a group connected by common origin, typically associated with skin colour.

rationalisation process

For Weber, a process where beliefs, social institutions and individual actors all become more logical and orderly. Sensual, spiritual, traditional and irrational aspects of social life decline.

rationality

A preoccupation with calculating the most efficient means to achieve one's goals.

reconstituted family

Family units comprising step-parents as a consequence of divorce or remarriage.

recursiveness of social knowledge

Employed by Giddens, the notion that social science informs actors in society who may then act to change their society, which requires renewed social analysis and so on. Sociology and social change are linked by internal feedback.

reductionism

An outlook which explains phenomena in terms of a simple causal determining factor (*see* determinism).

reflexive

Normally employed to indicate a process of self-reflection, which may modify beliefs and action (*see* reflexivity).

reflexivity

A process of examining, questioning and monitoring the behaviour of the self and others promoted by the social conditions and experiences of late modernity.

reify

To treat a social phenomenon as if it is an independent thing, with its own qualities.

relations of production

A Marxist term which refers to class relations that produce an unequal structure of economic benefit and political and ideological power.

relative autonomy

Where a link exists between two institutions, for example the State and the economy, but where each institution has a degree of independence in causing outcomes.

relative deprivation

Developed by Townsend in the late 1970s to conceptualise the condition of deprivation in terms of living standards when compared to the vast majority of the population.

relativism

An approach which denies the existence of absolute truth, but maintains that beliefs, values and theories are relative to time and place. Accordingly, traditions and ways of life can only be judged in the context of the age or society that has produced them.

the Renaissance

'The rebirth' of art, science and creativity which originated in fourteenth century and brought widespread renewal in European culture.

reserve army of labour

Used to describe how women are brought into the work place in times of labour shortage, and then, when they are no longer needed, are encouraged by prevailing ideologies, to return to the home (*see* ideology).

restricted code of speech

A form of speech which relies on terse exposition and sometimes slang to communicate, as opposed to elaborated forms of speech.

risk

A term encapsulating the distinctiveness of people's experiences of danger in late modernity. Increasingly, the threats we face are of global proportion and are side-effects of social development. Awareness of risk can undermine our confidence in abstract systems of knowledge, expertise and social organisation (*see* late modernity, trust *and* reflexivity).

sampling frame

Used in sociological research, it is an accurate list of the subjects of a total population, for example an electoral roll. Research subjects are subsequently selected from such a list.

secondary data

Data, normally in the form of official statistics or documentary sources, that have not been generated by the researcher.

secular

Not concerned with religion.

secularisation

The process whereby religious beliefs, practices and institutions lose their significance in society.

segmentation

The restructuring of social class boundaries associated with the polarisation and fragmentation of occupational groups.

self-fulfilling prophecy

A situation where social actors, constructing their self-images from the reactions of powerful and persuasive others, come to act out or live up to labels applied, or characteristics attributed, to them, thus confirming the original evaluation.

self-report studies

Used in the context of crime research, they normally involve questioning people, by means of questionnaires or interviews, about criminal acts they have committed, whether or not these have been detected. The aim of such studies is to amplify the picture of recorded crime by official criminal statistics.

separatism

A position put forward by some radical feminists as a solution to patriarchy. Based on the notion that the sexual act embodies patriarchal exploitation of women, it proposes that women should live separate lives from men (*see* patriarchy).

sex

The division of human beings into male and female on the basis of chromosomal and reproductive differences; it has been defined as a biological category, in contrast to the social category of gender (*see* gender).

sexual script

Culturally defined set of guidelines prescribing appropriate forms of sexual behaviour and ways of managing sexual encounters.

significant other

A particular individual whose views, opinions and reactions contribute to and influence the conception we have of ourselves.

signifier

From linguistics, associated with structuralism, meaning words or signs which represent the concept of an object.

single-parent family

A household unit where only one parent, usually the mother, resides with, and takes responsibility for parenting, her children.

social action

A perspective that usually concentrates on the micro-level of social life, in order to show how human interpretation, arising out of the interaction with others, gives rise to social action.

social chapter

A set of EU guidelines and recommendations which offers protection, such as a minimum wage guarantee, to workers.

social closure

Employed by Weber to describe the efforts made by social groups to deny entry and therefore benefit to those outside the group in order to maximise their own advantage.

social construction

The process whereby 'natural', instinctive, forms of behaviour become mediated by social processes. Sociologists would argue that most forms of human behaviour are socially constructed.

social framing

To place within a particular bounded social context.

social integration

The unification of diverse groups of people in a community.

social mobility

The movement of individuals, within a stratified society, from one position within the social hierarchy to another. Usually refers to positions of broad occupation or social class.

social reproduction

The concept that over time groups of people, notably social classes, reproduce their social structures and patterns.

social stratification

The division of a population into unequal layers or strata based on income, wealth, gender, ethnicity, power, status, age, religion or some other characteristic.

socialisation

An on-going process whereby individuals learn to conform to society's prevailing norms and values (*see* norms *and* values).

socialism

An economic theory or system in which the means of production, distribution and exchange are owned collectively, usually through the state.

software

Computer programmes, manuals, instructions, and other materials that can exist in written form and be used on computer systems.

status

Associated with Weber, it denotes the relative prestige of a person's social standing.

status groups

For Weber, groups who share the same high or low status, in terms of explicit social judgements of honour or prestige (*see* status).

stigmatisation

A process or experience in which some form of social behaviour or attribute is subject to social disapproval and becomes discredited, resulting in a spoiled identity in the eyes of others and possible exclusion from normal social interaction.

streams

Within a school, the division of cohorts into separate classes that are ranked according to perceived ability, e.g. lower stream, upper stream.

structural

Pertaining to the organisation and form of society or institutions.

structural unemployment

Chronic, long-term unemployment due to changes in the structure of the economy.

structuration theory

The emergence and transformation of structural patterning in social life. For Giddens, the theory that links structure and agency as simultaneous dimensions of social life (*see* structure *and* agency).

structures

Refers generally to constructed frameworks and patterns of organisation which, in some way, constrain or direct human behaviour.

sub-proletariat

Used by some neo-Marxists to describe a socio-economic group that is a sub-division of the area lower than working class (*see also* underclass).

subculture

The set of values, behaviour and attitudes of a particular group of people who are distinct from, but related to, the dominant culture in society.

subject-centred

An approach to social analysis which centres on the active, creative human subject.

subordinate class

A Marxist term for the working class who are exploited by the dominant class (*see* dominant class).

superstructure

A Marxist term, which refers to social forms other than the economy, e.g. politics and culture, that are determined by the economic base (*see* economic base).

surplus value

A term coined by Marx to describe the difference between the value of the labour and the value of the product of that labour.

symbolic annihilation

A term used to signify how, as a result of under-representation in the media, women have been dismissed and ignored in the public domain.

symbolic interactionism

A theoretical approach which focuses on the role of symbols and language in human interaction.

symbolic systems

Systems, such as languages, of connected elements, each one representing or symbolising an aspect of reality.

symbolic world

The world of thought; a conception of reality based upon mental perceptions.

symmetrical family

Developed by Young and Willmott to describe a more equal domestic division of labour between men and women. It suggests that although men and women may well perform different kinds of tasks, the work load in the household is becoming more shared.

technophilic

An aptitude for, and willingness to engage with, technology.

techonophobic

Fear of, and reluctance to engage with, technology.

texts

Any form of symbolic representation of meanings which take on a physical form, e.g. writing, film.

Thatcherism

A system of political principles, beliefs, policies and practices, based on notions of economic individualism and the free market, expounded by Margaret Thatcher and her Conservative governments between 1979 and 1990 (*see* free market *and* New Right).

Third World

Developing countries not aligned politically with the large power blocs.

total institutions

Employed by Goffman, it refers to all forms of diverse institutions, such as prisons and mental hospitals, that assume total control over their inmates.

transnational corporations (TNCs)

Large corporations, emanating principally from the US, Japan and Europe, whose activities are aimed at global markets.

transsexuals

People whose gender identity is at odds with the gender indicated by their body and who take steps to change their body to match their perceived identity.

trust

Modern life requires people to rely on large-scale, abstract systems of knowledge, expertise and social organisation beyond their full understanding or control (*see* risk *and* reflexivity).

underclass

A concept used to describe a group at the bottom of the social hierarchy who are economically, politically and socially marginalised from the rest of society.

underdevelopment

A term coined by Andre Gunder Frank to describe the economic and social conditions of those Third World countries whose markets, labour and resources have been exploited by the development of Western capitalism (*see* dependency theory *and* Third World).

underlying structures

Associated with realism, this concept refers to organisational features of society which, though not observable, nevertheless affect human behaviour.

unilineal descent

An anthropological term used to describe a line of descent of people related by blood, acquired through either the male line (patriliny) or the female line (matriliny).

unintended consequences

Repercussions or outcomes which result from actions initiated for other purposes. This is thought to be a key dimension of social activity, though these social effects cannot be explained by actors' intentions.

values

Associated with Parsons, whose concept of shared values refers to a consensus of morals, principles and standards of behaviour.

verstehen

A German term usually translated as 'understanding'. Employed by Weber to define his approach to the study of social life, namely the interpretative understanding of human agents and the meaning they themselves attach to their actions.

vertical gender segregation

The separation of men and women within the same occupation, where women are concentrated at the lower levels of the occupational hierarchy.

welfare state

A system of government where the state assumes responsibility for providing a wide range of welfare benefits for its citizens.

white-collar worker

Non-manual employees, such as office or administration staff.

worker resistance

Strategies employed by workers to subvert the labour process.

Name Index

Subject Index